JAMES J. JENKINS and DONALD G. PATERSON

UNIVERSITY OF MINNESOTA

Editors

STUDIES IN

Individual Differences

THE SEARCH FOR INTELLIGENCE

NEW YORK

APPLETON-CENTURY-CROFTS, INC.

PRINTED IN THE UNITED STATES OF AMERICA

PREFACE

This book of readings is designed to meet what we feel is a critical need in contemporary courses in tests and measurements and differential psychology. The two editors have taught one or another of these courses more than one hundred times. We hold that at least three requisite things— good psychological judgment, an elusive quality called perspective, and a grasp of the strategies of psychological measurement—are fostered most rapidly when students encounter original research papers in their historical sequence. It is difficult for the student, presented with a concise textbook summary of today's knowledge, to imagine the long, hard struggle which produced that knowledge. Equipped with a textbook alone, he is in position to see only dimly, if at all, the initial inspirations, false starts, first approximations, and attained half-truths. Certainly this is poor preparation for a student who, in embarking on new studies of his own, is bound to encounter difficulties seldom mentioned in his text.

In searching for a topic to serve as a model problem in measurement we quickly settled on intelligence. The tools for measuring intelligence were neither easy to develop nor were they what the "good" psychologists had prescribed. The early work proved discouraging or misleading. The whole field was, and still is, fraught with controversy, both within psychology and between that science and the lay population. However, over-riding all other considerations, the issues are of vital importance in a host of practical situations; few persons remain untouched by what the psychologist does in this domain. The search for intelligence was, then, *par excellence* the kind of model problem we wanted to illustrate in a book of readings.

In selecting this one topic it is obvious that we have no intention of supplanting current textbooks, which, in fact, we believe are of very high quality. However, these textbooks by their very nature cannot give the student the kind of understanding of the work and the workers that we are striving for here. It is our conviction that this book will supplement the standard texts in a valuable way for students with inquiring minds and an intellectual curiosity about the origins of the evidence upon which our present knowledge of intelligence rests.

What were its origins? One of our students a few years ago made an abstract of what Plato had to say in *The Republic* about the abilities essential for a member of the warrior class in his perfect city-state. Putting it

v

in modern terms, he developed an "Athenian General Classification Test." But though Plato was deeply concerned with the social and ethical importance of individual (or at least class) differences, we can hardly consider him seriously as an ancestor of modern science in this field. Three things were necessary before such a science could emerge. The requirements were (1) a breaking down of the fixed belief that the "mind" was beyond measurement, followed by the development of methods of measurement; (2) a concern with individuals, as distinct from the search for "general laws"; and (3) the invention of statistical tools for describing, relating, and interpreting measurements, once they were obtained.

The first requirement was met when the new science, psychology, was developed in Germany largely through the combined contributions of physiologists, physicists, and philosophers. These innovators boldly broke through the barriers separating mental from physical to establish psychophysics, or the science of the relation of mental processes to physical events.

The second requirement, perhaps always met in some degree, was furthered by the birth of political and social philosophies which respected the individual for what he was rather than for his class, his wealth, or his beliefs. The work of the French psychopathologists proved that here was a fruitful scientific field. But most important of all was the dramatic emphasis that Darwin put on individual variability as the key to survival and the evolution of species.

The third requirement was met by statisticians devising formulas to serve various purposes, as diverse as computing gambling odds or describing the biological characteristics of census populations. These mathematicians devised statistical methods of dealing both with populations (distributions) of data in place of single measures and with the relations between sets of distributions—methods which proved to be an enormous contribution to all the social sciences.

Each of these lines of influence converged on one exceptionally gifted Englishman, Sir Francis Galton, and it is with his work that the science of individual differences may be said to truly begin. A selection from his first book, appropriately, has been chosen to open these readings.

Despite our efforts to include examples of most of the important methodologies, our sampling of modern statistical methods is weak, unavoidably so, we believe, in a book that preserves a reasonable size. We do claim, however, that the interplay between problems and methodologies is adequately and tellingly demonstrated. Most of the "hot" issues, such as racial and national differences, have been touched on at least once. In the preparation of this book we have considered hundreds of other studies, but in the end we have been forced to settle on this set, discarding many papers of equal value. Overall, we do not claim that these are the best, and certainly not the only, readings that might have been included. We do feel, however, that those we have selected are valuable, thought-provoking, and representative of the chief contributions to the field.

Attention is directed to the omission of what might be called the "blinder" of the blind alleys in the search for intelligence. Peak and Boring, for example, tried out Army Alpha on five graduate students and found a high correlation between Alpha score and reaction time, but their claims were discredited by the work of Farnsworth, Seashore, and Tinker. Travis reported a startling correlation of about +.80 between score on the Otis Higher Examination and speed of neural impulse as measured by the knee jerk, a finding soon retracted by Travis himself. A high correlation (+.80) was claimed by Hinton of Northwestern University to exist between basal metabolic rate and IQ; this, too, has remained unconfirmed by other researchers. Careful study of the readings by Wissler and Paterson in this book will dispose one to be skeptical when other startlingly close relationships between mental and physical traits are reported. But it remains possible to keep one's skepticism harnessed to empirical open-mindedness.

There is a very good reason for studying historical contributions in any field of knowledge. As Boring put it: "One finds that he needs to know about the past; not in order to predict the future, but in order to understand the present."[1] In this same paper Boring pointed out that since 1894 psychology has listed a total of more than 300,000 articles in its published semiofficial bibliographies. Any real punctilious scholar, in order to master what is known on any topic or subtopic, must comb the literature (*and read it!*). The purpose of this injunction is to warn the student that this book of readings, comprehensive though it may seem to be, can only hit some high spots. A thorough knowledge of any specific topic is truly hard to come by.

In the same Phi Beta Kappa address, Boring elaborated on the role of the *Zeitgeist* in discovery. What he was talking about is the importance of the general intellectual, social, and economic trends of a particular time in facilitating discovery and invention. The *Zeitgeist* is, metaphorically speaking, the climate of the times—a whole complex of variables; its influence is beautifully illustrated in relation to the search for intelligence by the swing of the pendulum from a predominant emphasis on heredity as an explanation of differences in intelligence up to the mid 1920s, over to an emphasis on environment thereafter. In recent years there has been something of a swing back to *genes*. Thus we have the continuing nature-nurture controversy. A part of this oscillation results from the biases and prejudices of men of science who, although quietly sure that they are completely objective and disposed to discover things as they are, are unknowingly caught up in the cross-currents of national and international tensions.

The perceptive student will recognize the role of the Zeitgeist in those readings which deal with racial and national differences. Here an open

---

[1] E. G. Boring. Science and the Meaning of Its History. *The Phi Beta Kappa Key Reporter*, 1959, *24* (No. 2, July), 2-3.

mind is required, for these are emotionally explosive and controversial topics. It is wholesome for students to discover that there can be no simple pat answer to some problems and that further work—indeed much, much more work—will be required to reach even a tentatively defensible conclusion.

Ninety per cent of the work involved in preparing this book was done by Jenkins. Paterson, however, is happy to take his full share of responsibility for the product. In conclusion, we are grateful to Drs. R. M. Elliott and K. MacCorquodale, editors of the Century Psychology Series, and to the late president of Appleton-Century-Crofts, Dana H. Ferrin, for encouraging us to undertake this task. Acknowledgment to the publishers of each paper, and to the authors whenever possible, is made in footnotes throughout the book.

J. J. J.

D. G. P.

CONTENTS

Contents

STUDIES IN INDIVIDUAL DIFFERENCES

This chapter illustrates many of Galton's characteristics: his beautiful style, his concern with variation and its quantification, and his basic premise that mental traits are largely inherited. The "classification" here proposed was, of course, the forerunner of the "standard score" so essential in mental measurement today.

Classification of Men According to Their Natural Gifts*

FRANCIS GALTON

1869

I have no patience with the hypothesis occasionally expressed, and often implied, especially in tales written to teach children to be good, that babies are born pretty much alike, and that the sole agencies in creating differences between boy and boy, and man and man, are steady application and moral effort. It is in the most unqualified manner that I object to pretensions of natural equality. The experiences of the nursery, the school, the University, and of professional careers, are a chain of proofs to the contrary. I acknowledge freely the great power of education and social influences in developing the active powers of the mind, just as I acknowledge the effect of use in developing the muscles of a blacksmith's arm, and no further. Let the blacksmith labour as he will, he will find there are certain feats beyond his power that are well within the strength of a man of herculean make, even although the latter may have led a sedentary life. Some years ago, the Highlanders held a grand gathering in Holland Park, where they challenged all England to compete with them in their games of strength. The challenge was accepted, and the well-trained men of the hills were beaten in the foot-race by a youth who was stated to be a pure Cockney, the clerk of a London banker.

Everybody who has trained himself to physical exercises discovers the extent of his muscular powers to a nicety. When he begins to walk, to row, to use the dumb bells, or to run, he finds to his great delight that his thews strengthen, and his endurance of fatigue increases day after day. So long as he is a novice, he perhaps flatters himself there is hardly an assignable limit to the education of his muscles; but the daily gain is soon discovered to diminish, and at last it vanishes altogether. His maximum performance becomes a rigidly determinate quantity. He learns to an inch, how high or how far he can jump, when he has attained the highest state of training.

* This is the third chapter of the book *Hereditary Genius: An Inquiry into its Laws and Consequences*. The text is taken from the edition published by D. Appleton & Co. in 1870. The book has recently been reprinted (New York, Horizon Press, 1952).

He learns to half a pound, the force he can exert on the dynamometer, by compressing it. He can strike a blow against the machine used to measure impact, and drive its index to a certain graduation, but no further. So it is in running, in rowing, in walking, and in every other form of physical exertion. There is a definite limit to the muscular powers of every man, which he cannot by any education or exertion overpass.

This is precisely analogous to the experience that every student has had of the working of his mental powers. The eager boy, when he first goes to school and confronts intellectual difficulties, is astonished at his progress. He glories in his newly-developed mental grip and growing capacity for application, and, it may be, fondly believes it to be within his reach to become one of the heroes who have left their mark upon the history of the world. The years go by; he competes in the examinations of school and college, over and over again with his fellows, and soon finds his place among them. He knows he can beat such and such of his competitors; that there are some with whom he runs on equal terms, and others whose intellectual feats he cannot even approach. Probably his vanity still continues to tempt him, by whispering in a new strain. It tells him that classics, mathematics, and other subjects taught in universities, are mere scholastic specialties, and no test of the more valuable intellectual powers. It reminds him of numerous instances of persons who had been unsuccessful in the competitions of youth, but who had shown powers in after-life that made them the foremost men of their age. Accordingly, with newly furbished hopes, and with all the ambition of twenty-two years of age, he leaves his University and enters a larger field of competition. The same kind of experience awaits him here that he has already gone through. Opportunities occur—they occur to every man—and he finds himself incapable of grasping them. He tries, and is tried in many things. In a few years more, unless he is incurably blinded by self-conceit, he learns precisely of what performances he is capable, and what other enterprises lie beyond his compass. When he reaches mature life, he is confident only within certain limits, and knows, or ought to know, himself just as he is probably judged of by the world, with all his unmistakable weakness and all his undeniable strength. He is no longer tormented into hopeless efforts by the fallacious promptings of overweening vanity, but he limits his under-takings to matters below the level of his reach, and finds true moral repose in an honest conviction that he is engaged in as much good work as his nature has rendered him capable of performing.

There can hardly be a surer evidence of the enormous difference between the intellectual capacity of men, than the prodigious differences in the numbers of marks obtained by those who gain mathematical honours at Cambridge. I therefore crave permission to speak at some length upon this subject, although the details are dry and of little general interest. There are between 400 and 450 students who take their degrees in each year, and of these, about 100 succeed in gaining honours in mathematics, and are ranged by the examiners in strict order of merit. About the first forty of those who take mathematical honours are distinguished by the title of wranglers, and it is a decidedly creditable thing to be even a low wrangler; it will secure a fellowship in a small college. It must be carefully borne in mind that the distinction of being the first in this list of honours, or what is called the senior wrangler of the year, means a vast deal more than being the foremost mathematician of 400 or 450 men taken at hap-hazard. No doubt the large bulk of Cambridge men are taken almost at hap-hazard. A boy is intended by his parents for some profession; if that profession be either the Church or the Bar, it used to be almost requisite, and it is still important, that he should be sent to Cambridge or Oxford. These youths may justly be considered as having been taken at hap-hazard. But there are many others who have fairly won their way to the Universities, and are therefore selected from an enormous area. Fully one-half of the wranglers have been boys of note at their respective schools, and, conversely, almost all boys of note at schools find their way to the Universities. Hence it is that among their comparatively small number of students, the Universities include the highest youthful scholastic ability of all England. The senior wrangler, in each successive year, is the chief of these as regards mathematics, and this, the highest distinction, is, or was, continually won by youths who had no mathematical training of importance before they went to Cambridge. All their instruction had been received during the three years of their residence at the University. Now, I do not say anything here about the merits or demerits of Cambridge mathematical studies having been directed along a too narrow groove, or about the presumed disadvantages of ranging candidates in strict order of merit, instead of grouping them, as at Oxford, in classes, where their names appear alphabetically arranged. All I am concerned with here are the results; and these are most appropriate to my argument. The youths start on their three years' race as fairly as possible. They are then stimulated to run by the most powerful inducements, namely, those of competition, of honour, and of future wealth (for a good fellowship is wealth); and at the end of the three years they are examined most rigorously according to a system that they all understand and are equally well prepared for. The examination lasts five and a half hours a day for eight days. All the answers are carefully marked by the examiners, who add up the marks at the end and range the candidates in strict order of merit. The fairness and thoroughness of Cambridge examinations have never had a breath of suspicion cast upon them.

Unfortunately for my purposes, the marks are not published. They are not even assigned on a uniform system, since each examiner is permitted to employ his own scale of marks; but whatever scale he uses, the results as to proportional merit are the same. I am indebted to a Cambridge examiner for a copy of his marks in respect to two examinations, in which the scales of marks were so alike as to make it easy, by a slight proportional adjustment, to compare the two together. This was, to a certain degree, a confidential communication, so that it would be improper for me to publish anything that would identify the years to which these marks refer. I simply give them as groups of figures, sufficient to show the enormous differences of merit. The lowest man in the list of honours gains less than

TABLE I

Scale of Merit Among the Men who Obtain Mathematical Honours at Cambridge

The results of two years are thrown into a single table.
The total number of marks obtainable in each year was 17,000.

Number of marks obtained by candidates	Number of candidates in the two years, taken together, who obtained those marks
Under 500	24[1]
500 to 1,000	74
1,000 to 1,500	38
1,500 to 2,000	21
2,000 to 2,500	11
2,500 to 3,000	8
3,000 to 3,500	11
3,500 to 4,000	5
4,000 to 4,500	2
4,500 to 5,000	1
5,000 to 5,500	3
5,500 to 6,000	1
6,000 to 6,500	0
6,500 to 7,000	0
7,000 to 7,500	0
7,500 to 8,000	1
	200

[1] I have included in this table only the first 100 men in each year. The omitted residue is too small to be important. I have omitted it lest, if the precise numbers of honour men were stated, those numbers would have served to identify the years. For reasons already given, I desire to afford no data to serve that purpose.

300 marks, the lowest wrangler gains about 1,500 marks; and the senior wrangler, in one of the lists now before me, gained more than 7,500 marks. Consequently, the lowest wrangler has more than five times the merit of the lowest junior optime, and less than one-fifth the merit of the senior wrangler.

The precise number of marks obtained by the senior wrangler in the more remarkable of these two years was 7,634; by the second wrangler in the same year, 4,123; and by the lowest man in the list of honours, only

237. Consequently, the senior wrangler obtained nearly twice as many marks as the second wrangler, and more than thirty-two times as many as the lowest man. I have received from another examiner the marks of a year in which the senior wrangler was conspicuously eminent. He obtained 9,422 marks, whilst the second in the same year—whose merits were by no means inferior to those of second wranglers in general—obtained only 5,642. The man at the bottom of the same honour list had only 309 marks, or one-thirtieth the number of the senior wrangler. I have some particulars of a fourth very remarkable year, in which the senior wrangler obtained no less than ten times as many marks as the second wrangler, in the "problem paper." Now, I have discussed with practised examiners the question of how far the numbers of marks may be considered as proportionate to the mathematical power of the candidate, and am assured they are strictly proportionate as regards the lower places, but do not afford full justice to the highest. In other words, the senior wranglers above mentioned had more than thirty, or thirty-two times the ability of the lowest men on the lists of honours. They would be able to grapple with problems more than thirty-two times as difficult; or when dealing with subjects of the same difficulty, but intelligible to all, would comprehend them more rapidly in perhaps the square root of that proportion. It is reasonable to expect that marks would do some injustice to the very best men, because a very large part of the time of the examination is taken up by the mechanical labour of writing. Whenever the thought of the candidate outruns his pen, he gains no advantage from his excess of promptitude in conception. I should, however, mention that some of the ablest men have shown their superiority by comparatively little writing. They find their way at once to the root of the difficulty in the problems that are set, and, with a few clean, apposite, powerful strokes, succeed in proving they can overthrow it, and then they go on to another question. Every word they write tells. Thus, the late Mr. H. Leslie Ellis, who was a brilliant senior wrangler in 1840, and whose name is familiar to many generations of Cambridge men as a prodigy of universal genius, did not even remain during the full period in the examination room: his health was weak, and he had to husband his strength.

The mathematical powers of the last man on the list of honours, which are so low when compared with those of a senior wrangler, are mediocre, or even above mediocrity, when compared with the gifts of Englishmen generally. Though the examination places 100 honour men above him, it puts no less than 300 "poll men" below him. Even if we go so far as to allow that 200 out of the 300 refuse to work hard enough to get honours, there will remain 100 who, even if they worked hard, could not get them. Every tutor knows how difficult it is to drive abstract conceptions, even of the simplest kind, into the brains of most people—how feeble and hesitating is their mental grasp—how easily their brains are mazed—how incapable they are of precision and soundness of knowledge. It often occurs to persons familiar with some scientific subject to hear men and women of mediocre gifts relate to one another what they have picked up about it from some lecture—say at the Royal Institution, where they have sat for an hour listening with delighted attention to an admirably lucid account, illustrated by experiments of the most perfect and beautiful character, in all of which they expressed themselves intensely gratified and highly instructed. It is positively painful to hear what they say. Their recollections seem to be a mere chaos of mist and misapprehension, to which some sort of shape and organization has been given by the action of their own pure fancy, altogether alien to what the lecturer intended to convey. The average mental grasp even of what is called a well-educated audience, will be found to be ludicrously small when rigorously tested.

In stating the differences between man and man, let it not be supposed for a moment that mathematicians are necessarily one-sided in their natural gifts. There are numerous instances of the reverse, of whom the following will be found, as instances of hereditary genius, in the appendix to my chapter on "Science." I would especially name Leibnitz, as being universally gifted; but Ampere, Arago, Condorcet, and D'Alembert, were all of them very far more than mere mathematicians. Nay, since the range of examination at Cambridge is so extended as to include other subjects besides mathematics, the differences of ability between the highest and lowest of the successful candidates, is yet more glaring than what I have already described. We still find, on the one hand, mediocre men, whose whole energies are absorbed in getting their 237 marks for mathematics; and, on the other hand, some few senior wranglers who are at the same time high classical scholars and much more besides. Cambridge has afforded such instances. Its lists of classical honours are comparatively of recent date, but other evidence is obtainable from earlier times of their occurrence. Thus, Dr. George Butler, the Head Master of Harrow for very many years, including the period when Byron was a schoolboy, (father of the present Head Master, and of other sons, two of whom are also head masters of great public schools,) must have obtained that classical office on account of his eminent classical ability; but Dr. Butler was also senior wrangler in 1794, the year when Lord Chancellor Lyndhurst was second. Both Dr. Kaye, the late Bishop of Lincoln, and Sir E. Alderson, the late judge, were the senior wranglers and the first classical prizemen of their respective years. Since 1824, when the classical tripos was first established, the late Mr. Goulburn (brother of Dr. Goulburn, Dean of Norwich, and son of the well-known Serjeant Goulburn) was second wrangler in 1835, and senior classic of the same year. But in more recent times, the necessary labour of preparation, in order to acquire the highest mathematical places, has become so enormous that there has been a wider differentiation of studies. There is no longer time for a man to acquire the necessary knowledge to succeed to the first place in more than one subject. There are, therefore, no instances of a man being absolutely first in both examinations, but a few can be found of high eminence in both classics and mathematics, as a reference to the list published in the "Cambridge Calendar" will show. The best of these more recent degrees appears to be that of Dr. Barry, late Principal of Cheltenham, and now Principal of King's College, London (the son of the eminent architect, Sir Charles Barry, and brother of Mr. Edward Barry, who succeeded his father as architect). He was fourth wrangler and seventh classic of his year.

In whatever way we may test ability, we arrive at equally enormous intellectual differences. Lord Macaulay (see under "Literature" for his remarkable kinships) had one of the most tenacious of memories. He was able to recall many pages of hundreds of volumes by various authors, which he had acquired by simply reading them over. An average man could not certainly carry in his memory one thirty-second—ay, or one hundredth—part as much as Lord Macaulay. The father of Seneca had one of the greatest memories on record in ancient times (see under "Literature" for his kinships). Porson, the Greek scholar, was remarkable for this gift, and, I may add, the "Porson memory" was hereditary in that family. In statesmanship, generalship, literature, science, poetry, art, just the same enormous differences are found between man and man; and numerous instances recorded in this book, will show in how small degree, eminence, either in these or any other class of intellectual powers, can be considered as due to purely special powers. They are rather to be considered in those instances as the result of concentrated efforts, made by men who are widely gifted. People lay too much stress on apparent specialties, thinking overrashly that, because a man is devoted to some particular pursuit, he could not possibly have succeeded in anything else. They might just as well say that, because a youth had fallen desperately in love with a brunette, he could not possibly have fallen in love with a blonde. He may or may not have more natural liking for the former type of beauty than the latter, but it is as probable as not that the affair was mainly or wholly due to a general amorousness of disposition. It is just the same with special pursuits. A gifted man is often capricious and fickle before he selects his occupation, but when it has been chosen, he devotes himself to it with a truly passionate ardour. After a man of genius has selected his hobby, and so adapted himself to it as to seem unfitted for any other occupation in life, and to be possessed of but one special aptitude, I often notice, with admiration, how well he bears himself when circumstances suddenly thrust him into a strange position. He will display an insight into new conditions, and a power of dealing with them, with which even his most intimate friends were unprepared to accredit him. Many a presumptuous fool has mistaken indifference and neglect for incapacity; and in trying to throw a man of genius on ground where he was unprepared for attack, has himself received a most severe and unexpected fall. I am sure that no one who has had the privilege of mixing in the society of the abler men of any great capital, or who is acquainted with the biographies of the heroes of history, can doubt the existence of grand human animals, of natures pre-eminently noble, of individuals born to be kings of men. I have been conscious of no slight misgiving that I was committing a kind of sacrilege whenever, in the preparation of materials for this book, I had occasion to take the measurement of modern intellects vastly superior to my own, or to criticize the genius of the most magnificent historical specimens of our race. It was a process that constantly recalled to me a once familiar sentiment in bygone days of African travel, when I used to take altitudes of the huge cliffs that domineered above me as I travelled along their bases, or to map the mountainous landmarks of unvisited tribes, that loomed in faint grandeur beyond my actual horizon.

I have not cared to occupy myself much with people whose gifts are below the average, but they would be an interesting study. The number of idiots and imbeciles among the twenty million inhabitants of England and Wales is approximately estimated at 50,000, or as 1 in 400. Dr. Seguin, a great French authority on these matters, states that more than thirty per cent of idiots and imbeciles, put under suitable instruction, have been taught to conform to social and moral law, and rendered capable of order, of good feeling, and of working like the third of an average man. He says that more than forty per cent have become capable of the ordinary transactions of life, under friendly control; of understanding moral and social abstractions, and of working like two-thirds of a man. And, lastly, that from twenty-five to thirty per cent come nearer and nearer to the standard of manhood, till some of them will defy the scrutiny of good judges, when compared with ordinary young men and women. In the order next above idiots and imbeciles are a large number of milder cases scattered among private families and kept out of sight, the existence of whom is, however, well known to relatives and friends; they are too silly to take a part in general society, but are easily amused with some trivial, harmless occupation. Then comes a class of whom the Lord Dundreary of the famous play may be considered a representative; and so, proceeding through successive grades, we gradually ascend to mediocrity. I know two good instances of hereditary silliness short of imbecility, and have reason to believe I could easily obtain a large number of similar facts.

To conclude, the range of mental power between—I will not say the highest Caucasian and the lowest savage—but between the greatest and least of English intellects, is enormous. There is a continuity of natural ability reaching from one knows not what height, and descending to one can hardly say what depth. I propose in this chapter to range men according to their natural abilities, putting them into classes separated by equal degrees of merit, and to show the relative number of individuals included in the several classes. Perhaps some persons might be inclined to make an offhand guess that the number of men included in the several classes would be pretty equal. If he thinks so, I can assure him he is most egregiously mistaken.

The method I shall employ for discovering all this, is an application of the very curious theoretical law of "deviation from an average." First, I will explain the law, and then I will show that the production of natural intellectual gifts comes justly within its scope.

The law is an exceedingly general one. M. Quetelet, the Astronomer-Royal of Belgium, and the greatest authority on vital and social statistics, has largely used it in his inquiries. He has also constructed numerical tables, by which the necessary calculations can be easily made, whenever it is desired to have recourse to the law. Those who wish to learn more than I have space to relate, should consult his work, which is a very readable octavo volume, and deserves to be far better known to statisticians than it appears to be. Its title is *Letters on Probabilities,* translated by Downes, Layton and Co. London: 1849.

So much has been published in recent years about statistical deductions, that I am sure the reader will be prepared to assent freely to the following hypothetical case:—Suppose a large island inhabited by a single race, who intermarried freely, and who had lived for many generations under constant conditions; then the average height of the male adults of that population would undoubtedly be the same year after year. Also—still arguing from the experience of modern statistics, which are found to give constant results in far less carefully-guarded examples—we should undoubtedly find, year after year, the same proportion maintained between the number of men of different heights. I mean, if the average stature was found to be sixty-six inches, and if it was also found in any one year that 100 per million exceeded seventy-eight inches, the same proportion of 100 per million would be closely maintained in all other years. An equal constancy of proportion would be maintained between any other limits of height we pleased to specify, as between seventy-one and seventy-two inches; between seventy-two and seventy-three inches; and so on. Statistical experiences are so invariably confimatory of what I have stated would probably be the case, as to make it unnecessary to describe analogous instances. Now, at this point, the law of deviation from an average steps in. It shows that the number per million whose heights range between seventy-one and seventy-two inches (or between any other limits we please to name) can be predicted from the previous datum of the average, and of any one other fact, such as that of 100 per million exceeding seventy-eight inches.

The diagram on Figure 1 will make this more intelligible. Suppose a million of the men to stand in turns, with their backs against a vertical board of sufficient height, and their heights to be dotted off upon it. The board would then present the appearance shown in the diagram. The line of average height is that which divides the dots into two equal parts, and stands, in the case we have assumed, at the height of sixty-six inches. The dots will be found to be ranged so symmetrically on either side of the line of average, that the lower half of the diagram will be almost a precise reflection of the upper. Next, let a hundred dots be counted from above downwards, and let a line be drawn below them. According to the con-

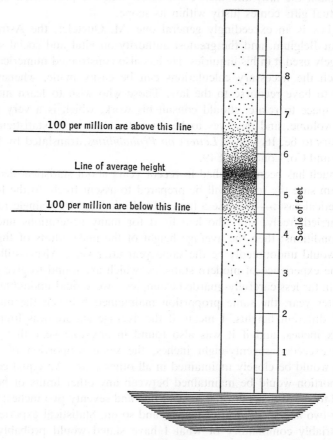

100 per million are above this line

Line of average height

100 per million are below this line

Scale of feet

Figure 1

ditions, this line will stand at the height of seventy-eight inches. Using the data afforded by these two lines, it is possible, by the help of the law of deviation from an average, to reproduce, with extraordinary closeness, the entire system of dots on the board.

M. Quetelet gives tables in which the uppermost line, instead of cutting off 100 in a million, cuts off only one in a million. He divides the intervals between that line and the line of average, into eighty equal divisions, and gives the number of dots that fall within each of those divisions. It is easy, by the help of his tables, to calculate what would occur under any other system of classification we pleased to adopt.

This law of deviation from an average is perfectly general in its application. Thus, if the marks had been made by bullets fired at a horizontal line stretched in front of the target, they would have been distributed according to the same law. Wherever there is a large number of similar events, each due to the resultant influences of the same variable conditions, two effects will follow. First, the average value of those events will be constant; and, secondly, the deviations of the several events from the average, will be governed by this law (which is, in principle, the same as that which governs runs of luck at a gaming-table).

The nature of the conditions affecting the several events must, I say, be the same. It clearly would not be proper to combine the heights of men belonging to two dissimilar races, in the expectation that the compound results would be governed by the same constants. A union of two dissimilar systems of dots would produce the same kind of confusion as if half the bullets fired at a target had been directed to one mark, and the other half to another mark. Nay, an examination of the dots would show to a person, ignorant of what had occurred, that such had been the case, and it would be possible, by aid of the law, to disentangle two or any moderate number of superimposed series of marks. The law may, therefore, be used as a most trustworthy criterion, whether or no the events of which an average has been taken are due to the same or to dissimilar classes of conditions.

I selected the hypothetical case of a race of men living on an island and freely intermarrying, to ensure the conditions under which they were all supposed to live, being uniform in character. It will now be my aim to show there is sufficient uniformity in the inhabitants of the British Isles to bring them fairly within the grasp of this law.

For this purpose, I first call attention to an example given in Quetelet's book. It is of the measurements of the circumferences of the chests of a large number of Scotch soldiers. The Scotch are by no means a strictly uniform race, nor are they exposed to identical conditions. They are a mixture of Celts, Danes, Anglo-Saxons, and others, in various proportions, the Highlanders being almost purely Celts. On the other hand, these races, though diverse in origin, are not very dissimilar in character. Consequently, it will be found that their deviations from the average, follow theoretical computations with remarkable accuracy. The instance is as follows. M. Quetelet obtained his facts from the thirteenth volume of the *Edinburgh Medical Journal,* where the measurements are given in respect to 5,738 soldiers, the results being grouped in order of magnitude, proceeding by differences of one inch. Professor Quetelet compares these results with those that his tables give, and here is the result. The marvellous accordance between fact and theory must strike the most unpractised eye. I should say that, for the sake of convenience, both the measurements and calculations have been reduced to per thousandths:—

TABLE II

Measures of the chest in inches	Number of men per 1,000, by experience	Number of men per 1,000, by calculation	Measures of the chest in inches	Number of men per 1,000, by experience	Number of men per 1,000, by calculation
33	5	7	41	1,628	1,675
34	31	29	42	1,148	1,096
35	141	110	43	645	560
36	322	323	44	160	221
37	732	732	45	87	69
38	1,305	1,333	46	38	16
39	1,867	1,838	47	7	3
40	1,882	1,987	48	2	1

I will now take a case where there is a greater dissimilarity in the elements of which the average has been taken. It is the height of 100,000 French conscripts. There is fully as much variety in the French as in the English, for it is not very many generations since France was divided into completely independent kingdoms. Among its peculiar races are those of Normandy, Brittany, Alsatia, Provence, Bearne, Auvergne—each with their special characteristics; yet the following table shows a most striking agreement between the results of experience compared with those derived by calculation, from a purely theoretical hypothesis.

TABLE III

Height of men	Number of men Measured	Number of men Calculated
Under 61.8	28,620	26,345
61.8 to 62.9	11,580	13,182
62.9 to 63.9	13,990	14,502
63.9 to 65.0	14,410	13,982
65.0 to 66.1	11,410	11,803
66.1 to 67.1	8,780	8,725
67.1 to 68.2	5,530	5,527
68.2 to 69.3	3,190	3,187
Above 69.3	2,490	2,645

The greatest differences are in the lowest ranks. They include the men who were rejected from being too short for the army. M. Quetelet boldly ascribes these differences to the effect of fraudulent returns. It certainly seems that men have been improperly taken out of the second rank and put into the first, in order to exempt them from service. Be this as it may, the coincidence of fact with theory is in this instance also, quite close enough to serve my purpose.

I argue from the results obtained from Frenchmen and from Scotchmen, that, if we had measurements of the adult males in the British Isles, we should find those measurements to range in close accordance with the law of deviation from an average, although our population is as much mingled as I described that of Scotland to have been, and although Ireland is mainly peopled with Celts. Now, if this be the case with stature, then it will be true as regards every other physical feature—as circumference of head, size of brain, weight of grey matter, number of braind fibres, &c.; and thence, by a step on which no physiologist will hesitate, as regards mental capacity.

This is what I am driving at—that analogy clearly shows there must be a fairly constant average mental capacity in the inhabitants of the British Isles, and that the deviations from that average—upwards towards genius, and downwards towards stupidity—must follow the law that governs deviations from all true averages.

I have, however, done somewhat more than rely on analogy. I have tried the results of those examinations in which the candidates had been derived from the same classes. Most persons have noticed the lists of successful competitors for various public appointments that are published from time to time in the newspapers, with the marks gained by each candidate attached to his name. These lists contain far too few names to fall into such beautiful accordance with theory, as was the case with Scotch soldiers. There are rarely more than 100 names in any one of these examinations, while the chests of no less than 5,700 Scotchmen were measured. I cannot justly combine the marks of several independent examinations into one fagot, for I understand that different examiners are apt to have different figures of merit; so I have analysed each examination separately. I give a calculation I made on the examination last before me; it will do as well as any other. It was for admission into the Royal Military College at Sandhurst, December 1868. The marks obtained were clustered most thickly about 3,000. so I take that number as representing the average ability of the candidates. From this datum, and from the fact that no candidate obtained more than 6,500 marks, I computed the column B in the following table, by the help of Quetelet's numbers. It will be seen that column B accords with column A quite as closely as the small number of persons examined could have led us to expect.

The symmetry of the descending branch has been rudely spoilt by the conditions stated at the foot of column A. There is, therefore, little room for doubt, if everybody in England had to work up some subject and then to pass before examiners who employed similar figures of merit, that their marks would be found to range, according to the law of deviation from an average, just as rigorously as the heights of French conscripts, or the circumferences of the chests of Scotch soldiers.

TABLE IV

Number of marks obtained by the candidates	Number of candidates who obtained those marks	
	A According to fact	B According to theory
6,500 and above	0⎤	0⎤
5,800 to 6,500	1	1
5,100 to 5,800	3	5
4,400 to 5,100	6⎬ 73	8⎬ 72
3,700 to 4,400	11	13
3,000 to 3,700	22	16
2,300 to 3,000	22	16
1,600 to 2,300	8⎦	13⎦
1,100 to 1,600	Either did not ven-	8⎤
400 to 1,100	ture to complete, or	5⎬
below 400	were plucked.	1⎦

The number of grades into which we may divide ability is purely a matter of option. We may consult our convenience by sorting Englishmen into a few large classes, or into many small ones. I will select a system of classification that shall be easily comparable with the numbers of eminent men, as determined in the previous chapter. We have seen that 250 men per million become eminent; accordingly, I have so contrived the classes in the following table that the two highest, F and G, together with X (which includes all cases beyond G, and which are unclassed), shall amount to about that number—namely, to 248 per million.

It will, I trust, be clearly understood that the numbers of men in the several classes in my table depend on no uncertain hypothesis. They are determined by the assured law of deviations from an average. It is an absolute fact that if we pick out of each million the one man who is naturally the ablest, and also the one man who is the most stupid, and divide the remaining 999,998 men into fourteen classes, the average ability in each being separated from that of its neighbours by equal grades, then the numbers in each of those classes will, on the average of many millions, be as is stated in the table. The table may be applied to special, just as truly as to general ability. It would be true for every examination that brought out natural gifts, whether held in painting, in music, or in statesmanship. The proportions between the different classes would be identical in all these cases, although the classes would be made up of different individuals, according as the examination differed in its purport.

TABLE V

Classification of Men According to Their Natural Gifts

Grades of natural ability, separated by equal intervals		Numbers of men comprised in the several grades of natural ability, whether in respect to their general powers, or to special aptitudes	
Below average	Above, average	Proportionate, viz. one in	In each million of the same age
a	A	4	256,791
b	B	6	162,279
c	C	16	63,563
d	D	64	15,696
e	E	413	2,423
f	F	4,300	233
g	G	79,000	14
x	X		
all grades below g	all grades above G	1,000,000	1

On either side of average 500,000
Total, both sides 1,000,000

It will be seen that more than half of each million is contained in the two mediocre classes a and A; the four mediocre classes a, b, A, B, contain more than four-fifths, and the six mediocre classes more than nineteen-twentieths of the entire population. Thus, the rarity of commanding ability, and the vast abundance of mediocrity, is no accident, but follows of necessity, from the very nature of these things.

The meaning of the word "mediocrity" admits of little doubt. It defines the standard of intellectual power found in most provincial gatherings, because the attractions of a more stirring life in the metropolis and elsewhere, are apt to draw away the abler classes of men, and the silly and the imbecile do not take a part in the gatherings. Hence, the residuum that forms the bulk of the general society of small provincial places, is commonly very pure in its mediocrity.

The class C possesses abilities a trifle higher than those commonly possessed by the foreman of an ordinary jury. D includes the mass of men who obtain the ordinary prizes of life. E is a stage higher. Then we reach F, the lowest of those yet superior classes of intellect, with which this volume is chiefly concerned.

On descending the scale, we find by the time we have reached f, that we are already among the idiots and imbeciles. We have seen that there are 400 idiots and imbeciles, to every million of persons living in this country; but that 30 per cent. of their number, appear to be light cases, to whom the name of idiot is inappropriate. There will remain 280 true idiots and imbeciles, to every million of our population. This ratio coincides very closely with the requirements of class f. No doubt a certain proportion of them are idiotic owing to some fortuitous cause, which may interfere with the working of a naturally good brain, much as a bit of dirt may cause a first-rate chronometer to keep worse time than an ordinary watch. But I presume, from the usual smallness of head and absence of disease among these persons, that the proportion of accidental idiots cannot be very large.

Hence we arrive at the undeniable, but unexpected conclusion, that eminently gifted men are raised as much above mediocrity as idiots are depressed below it; a fact that is calculated to considerably enlarge our ideas of the enormous differences of intellectual gifts between man and man.

I presume the class F of dogs, and others of the more intelligent sort of animals, is nearly commensurate with the f of the human race, in respect to memory and powers of reason. Certainly the class G of such animals is far superior to the g of humankind.

Galton's discovery of a single index expressing the degree of relationship between two variables offered a solution to a problem which had long vexed scientists. The technique which he developed was polished and expanded by Karl Pearson into an extraordinarily useful tool, not only for psychology but for the social and biological sciences in general. The reader should notice that the general solution of the correlation problem depends on "standard scores" for the variables involved. Here one can see further ramifications of Galton's earlier work represented in the first paper.

Co-relations and their Measurement, Chiefly from Anthropometric Data*

FRANCIS GALTON

1888

"Co-relation or correlation of structure" is a phrase much used in biology, and not least in that branch of it which refers to heredity, and the idea is even more frequently present than the phrase; but I am not aware of any previous attempt to define it clearly, to trace its mode of action in detail, or to show how to measure its degree.

Two variable organs are said to be co-related when the variation of the one is accompanied on the average by more or less variation of the other, and in the same direction. Thus the length of the arm is said to be co-related with that of the leg, because a person with a long arm has usually a long leg, and conversely. If the co-relation be close, then a person with a very long arm would usually have a very long leg; if it be moderately close, then the length of his leg would usually be only long, not very long; and if there were no co-relation at all then the length of his leg would on the average be mediocre. It is easy to see that co-relation must be the consequence of the variations of the two organs being partly due to common causes. If they were wholly due to common causes, the co-relation would be perfect, as is approximately the case with the symmetrically disposed parts of the body. If they were in no respect due to common causes, the co-relation would be nil. Between these two extremes are an endless number of intermediate cases, and it will be shown how the closeness of co-relation in any particular case admits of being expressed by a simple number.

To avoid the possibility of misconception, it is well to point out that the subject in hand has nothing whatever to do with the average propor-

* *Proceedings* of the Royal Society of London, XLV (1888), pp. 135-145.

tions between the various limbs, in different races, which have been often discussed from early times up to the present day, both by artists and by anthropologists. The fact that the average ratio between the stature and the cubit is as 100 to 37, or thereabouts, does not give the slightest information about the nearness with which they vary together. It would be an altogether erroneous inference to suppose their average proportion to be maintained so that when the cubit was, say, one-twentieth longer than the average cubit, the stature might be expected to be one-twentieth greater than the average stature, and conversely. Such a supposition is easily shown to be contradicted both by fact and theory.

The relation between the cubit and the stature will be shown to be such that for every inch, centimetre, or other unit of absolute length that the cubit deviates from the mean length of cubits, the stature will on the average deviate from the mean length of statures to the amount of 2.5 units, and in the same direction. Conversely, for each unit of deviation of stature, the average deviation of the cubit will be 0.26 unit. These relations are not numerically reciprocal, but the exactness of the co-relation becomes established when we have transmuted the inches or other measurement of the cubit and of the stature into units dependent on their respective scales of variability. We thus cause a long cubit and an equally long stature, as compared to the general run of cubits and statures, to be designated by an identical scale-value. The particular unit that I shall employ is the value of the probable error of any single measure in its own group. In that of the cubit, the probable error is 0.56 inch = 1.42 cm.; in the stature it is 1.75 inch = 4.44 cm. Therefore the measured lengths of the cubit in inches will be transmuted into terms of a new scale, in which each unit = 0.56 inch, and the measured lengths of the stature will be transmuted into terms of another new scale in which each unit is 1.75 inch. After this has been done, we shall find the deviation of the cubit as compared to the mean of the corresponding deviations of the stature, to be as 1 to 0.8. Conversely, the deviation of the stature as compared to the mean of the corresponding deviations of the cubit will also be as 1 to 0.8. Thus the existence of the co-relation is established, and its measure is found to be 0.8.

Now as to the evidence of all this. The data were obtained at my anthropometric laboratory at South Kensington. They are of 350 males of 21 years and upwards, but as a large proportion of them were students, and barely 21 years of age, they were not wholly fullgrown; but neither that fact nor the small number of observations is prejudicial to the conclusions that will be reached. They were measured in various ways, partly for the purpose of this inquiry. It will be sufficient to give some of them as examples. The exact number of 350 is not preserved throughout, as injury to some limb or other reduced the available number by 1, 2, or 3 in different cases. After marshalling the measures of each limb in the order of their magnitudes, I noted the measures in each series that occupied respectively the positions of the first, second, and third quarterly divisions. Calling these measures in any one series, Q_1, M, and Q_3, I take M, which is the median or middlemost value, as that whence the deviations are to be measured, and ½ $(Q_3 - Q_1) = Q$, as the probable error of any single measure in the series. This is practically the same as saying that one-half of the deviations fall within the distance to ± Q from the mean value, because the series run with fair symmetry. In this way I obtained the following value of M and Q, in which the second decimal must be taken as only roughly approximate. The M and Q of any particular series may be identified by a suffix, thus M_c, Q_c might stand for those of the cubit, and M_s, Q_s for those of the stature.

TABLE I

	M.		Q.	
	Inch	*Centim.*	*Inch*	*Centim.*
Head length	7.62	19.35	0.19	0.48
Head breadth	6.00	15.24	0.18	0.46
Stature	67.20	170.69	1.75	4.44
Left middle finger	4.54	11.53	0.15	0.38
Left cubit	18.05	45.70	0.56	1.42
Height of right knee	20.50	52.00	0.80	2.03

NOTE.—The head length is its maximum length measured from the notch between and just below the eyebrows. The cubit is measured with the hand prone and without taking off the coat; it is the distance between the elbow of the bent left arm and the tip of the middle finger. The height of the knee is taken sitting when the knee is bent at right angles, less the measured thickness of the heel of the boot.

Tables were then constructed, each referring to a different pair of the above elements, like Tables II and III, which will suffice as examples of the whole of them. It will be understood that the Q value is a universal unit applicable to the most varied measurements, such as breathing capacity, strength, memory, keenness of eyesight, and enables them to be compared together on equal terms notwithstanding their intrinsic diversity. It does not only refer to measures of length, though partly for the sake of compactness, it is only those of length that will be here given as examples. It is unnecessary to extend the limits of Table II, as it includes every line and column in my MS. table that contains not less than twenty entries. None of the entries lying within the flanking lines and columns of Table II were used.

The measures were made and recorded to the nearest tenth of an inch. The heading of 70 inches of stature includes all records between 69.5 and 70.4 inches; that of 69 includes all between 68.5 and 69.4, and so on.

The values derived from Table II, and from other similar tables, are entered in Table III, where they occupy all the columns up to the last three, the first of which is headed "smoothed." These smoothed values were obtained by plotting the observed values, after transmuting them as above described into their respective Q units, upon a diagram such as is shown in the figure. The deviations of the "subject" are measured parallel to the axis of y in the figure, and those of the mean of the corresponding values of the "relative" are measured parallel to the axis of x. When the stature is taken as the subject, the median positions of the corresponding cubits, which are given in the successive lines of Table III, are marked with small circles. When the cubit is the subject, the mean positions of the correspond-

TABLE II

Stature in inches	Length of left cubit in inches, 348 adult males								Total cases
	Under 16.5	16.5 and under 17.0	17.0 and under 17.5	17.5 and under 18.0	18.0 and under 18.5	18.5 and under 19.0	19.0 and under 19.5	19.5 and above	
71 and above ..	—	—	—	1	3	4	15	7	30
70	—	—	—	1	5	13	11	—	30
69	—	1	1	2	25	15	6	—	50
68	—	1	3	7	14	7	4	2	48
67	—	1	7	15	28	8	2	—	61
66	—	1	7	18	15	6	—	—	48
65	—	4	10	12	8	2	—	—	36
64	—	5	11	2	3	—	—	—	21
Below 64	9	12	10	3	1	—	—	—	34
	9	25	49	61	102	55	38	9	348

ing statures are marked with crosses. The firm line in the figure is drawn to represent the general run of the small circles and crosses. It is here seen to be a straight line, and it was similarly found to be straight in every other figure drawn from the different pairs of co-related variables that I have as yet tried. But the inclination of the line to the vertical differs considerably in different cases. In the present one the inclination is such that a deviation of 1 on the part of the subject, whether it be stature or cubit, is accompanied by a mean deviation on the part of the relative, whether it be cubit or stature, of 0.8. This decimal fraction is consequently transmuted into inches. If the stature be taken as the subject, then Q_s is associated with $Q_c \times 0.8$; that is, a deviation of 1.75 inches in the one with 0.56 × 0.8 of the other. This is the same as 1 inch of stature being associated with a mean length of cubit equal to 0.26 inch. Conversely, if the cubit be taken as the subject, then Q_c is associated with $Q_s \times 0.8$; that is, a deviation of

TABLE III

Stature M_s = 67.2 inches; Q_s = 1.75 inch. Left Cubit M_c = 18.05 inches; Q_c = 0.56 inch.

No. of cases	Stature	Deviation from M_s reckoned in		Mean of corresponding left cubits	Deviation from M_c reckoned in			Smoothed values multiplied by Q_c	Added to M_c
		Inches	Units of Q_s		Inches	Units of Q_c observed	smoothed		
	inches			inches					
30	70.0	+2.8	+1.60	18.8	+0.8	+1.42	+1.30	+0.73	18.8
50	69.0	+1.8	+1.03	18.3	+0.3	+0.53	+0.84	+0.47	18.5
38	68.0	+0.8	+0.46	18.2	+0.2	+0.36	+0.38	+0.21	18.3
61	67.0	−0.2	−0.11	18.1	+0.1	+0.18	−0.08	−0.04	18.0
48	66.0	−1.2	−0.69	17.8	−0.2	−0.36	−0.54	−0.30	17.8
36	65.0	−2.2	−1.25	17.7	−0.3	−0.53	−1.00	−0.56	17.5
21	64.0	−3.2	−1.83	17.2	−0.8	−1.46	−1.46	−0.80	17.2

No. of cases	Left cubit	Deviation from M_c reckoned in		Mean of corresponding statures	Deviation from M_s reckoned in			Smoothed values multiplied by Q_s	Added to M_s
		Inches	Units of Q_c		Inches	Units of Q_s observed	smoothed		
	inches			inches					
38	19.25	+1.20	+2.14	70.3	+3.1	+1.8	+1.70	+3.0	70.2
55	18.75	+0.70	+1.25	68.7	+1.5	+0.9	+1.00	+1.8	69.0
102	18.25	+0.20	+0.36	67.4	+0.2	+0.1	+0.28	+0.5	67.7
61	17.75	−0.30	−0.53	66.3	−0.9	−0.5	−0.43	−0.8	66.4
49	17.25	−0.80	−1.42	65.0	−2.2	−1.3	−1.15	−2.0	65.2
25	16.75	−1.30	−2.31	63.7	−3.5	−2.0	−1.85	−3.2	64.0

0.56 inch in the one with 1.75 × 0.8 of the other. This is the same as 1 inch of cubit being associated with a mean length of 2.5 inches of stature. If centimetre be read for inch the same holds true.

Six other tables are now given in a summary form, to show how well calculation on the above principles agrees with observation.

From Table IV the deductions given in Table V can be made; but they may be made directly from tables of the form of Table III, whence Table IV was itself derived.

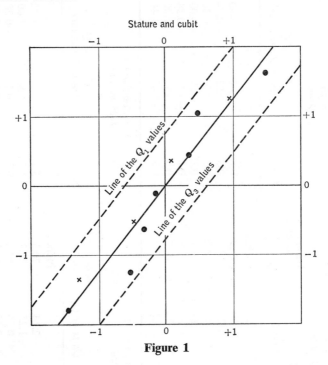

Figure 1

When the deviations of the subject and those of the mean of the relatives are severally measured in units of their own Q, there is always a regression in the value of the latter. This is precisely analogous to what was observed in kinship, as I showed in my paper read before this Society on "Hereditary Stature" (*Roy. Soc. Proc.*, XL, (1886), 42). The statures of kinsmen are co-related variables; thus, the stature of the father is correlated to that of the adult son, and the stature of the adult son to that of the father; the stature of the uncle to that of the adult nephew, and the stature of the adult nephew to that of the uncle, and so on; but the index of co-relation, which is what I there called "regression," is different in the different cases. In dealing with kinships there is usually no need to reduce the measures to units of Q, because the Q values are alike in all the kinsmen, being of the same value as that of the population at large. It however happened that the very first case that I analysed was different in this respect. It was the reciprocal relation between the statures of what I called the "mid-parent" and the son. The mid-parent is an ideal progenitor, whose stature is the average of that of the father on the one hand and of that of the mother on the other, after her stature has been transmuted into its male equivalent by the multiplication of the factor of 1.08. The Q of the mid-parental statures was found to be 1.2, that of the population dealt with was 1.7. Again, the mean deviation measured in inches of the statures of the sons was found to be two-thirds of the deviation of the mid-parents, while the mean deviation in inches of the mid-parent was one-third of the deviation of the sons. Here the regression, when calculated in Q units, is in the first case from $\frac{1}{1.2}$ to $\frac{2}{3} \times 1.7 = 1$ to 0.47, and in the second case from $\frac{1}{1.7}$ to $\frac{1}{3} \times \frac{1}{1.2} = 1$ to 0.44, which is practically the same.

The rationale of all this will be found discussed in the paper on "Hereditary Stature," to which reference has already been made, and in the appendix to it by Mr. J. D. Hamilton Dickson. The entries in any table, such as Table II, may be looked upon as the values of the vertical ordinates to a surface of frequency, whose mathematical properties were discussed in the above-mentioned appendix, therefore I need not repeat them here. But there is always room for legitimate doubt whether conclusions based on the strict properties of the ideal law of error would be sufficiently correct to be serviceable in actual cases of co-relation between variables that conform only approximately to that law. It is therefore exceedingly desirable to put the theoretical conclusions to frequent test, as has been done with these anthropometric data. The result is that anthropologists may now have much less hesitation than before, in availing themselves of the properties of the law of frequency of error.

I have given in Table V a column headed $\sqrt{(1 - r^2)} = f$. The meaning of f is explained in the paper on "Hereditary Stature." It is the Q value of the distribution of any system of x values, as x_1, x_2, x_3, &c., round the mean of all of them, which we may call X. The knowledge of f enables dotted lines to be drawn, as in the figure above, parallel to the line of M values, between which one half of the x observations, for each value of y, will be included. This value of f has much anthropological interest of its own, especially in connexion with M. Bertillon's system of anthropometric identification, to which I will not call attention now.

It is not necessary to extend the list of examples to show how to measure the degree in which one variable may be co-related with the combined effect of n other variables, whether these be themselves co-related or not. To do so, we begin by reducing each measure into others, each having the Q of its own system for a unit. We thus obtain a set of values that can be treated exactly in the same way as the measures of a single variable were treated in Tables II and onwards. Neither is it necessary to give examples

TABLE IV

No. of cases	Length of head	Mean of corresponding statures		No. of cases	Height	Mean of corresponding lengths of head	
		Observed	Calculated			Observed	Calculated
32	7.90	68.5	68.1	26	70.5	7.72	7.75
41	7.80	67.2	67.8	30	69.5	7.70	7.72
46	7.70	67.6	67.5	50	68.5	7.65	7.68
52	7.60	66.7	67.2	49	67.5	7.65	7.64
58	7.50	66.8	66.8	56	66.5	7.57	7.60
34	7.40	66.0	66.5	43	65.5	7.57	7.56
26	7.30	66.7	66.2	31	64.5	7.54	7.53

No. of cases	Height	Mean of corresponding length of left middle finger		No. of cases	Length of left middle finger	Mean of corresponding statures	
		Observed	Calculated			Observed	Calculated
30	70.5	4.71	4.74	23	4.80	70.2	69.4
50	69.5	4.55	4.68	49	4.70	68.1	68.5
37	68.5	4.57	4.62	62	4.60	68.0	67.7
62	67.5	4.58	4.56	63	4.50	67.3	66.9
48	66.5	4.50	4.50	57	4.40	66.0	66.1
37	65.5	4.47	4.44	35	4.30	65.7	65.3
20	64.5	4.33	4.38				

No. of cases	Left middle finger	Mean of corresponding lengths of left cubit		No. of cases	Length of left cubit	Mean of corresponding length of left middle finger	
		Observed	Calculated			Observed	Calculated
23	4.80	18.97	18.80	29	19.00	4.76	4.75
50	4.70	18.55	18.49	32	18.70	4.64	4.69
62	4.60	18.24	18.18	48	18.40	4.60	4.62
62	4.50	18.00	17.87	70	18.10	4.56	4.55
57	4.40	17.72	17.55	37	17.80	4.49	4.48
34	4.30	17.27	17.24	31	17.50	4.40	4.41
				28	17.20	4.37	4.34
				24	16.90	4.32	4.28

TABLE IV (Continued)

No. of cases	Length of head	Mean of corresponding breadths of head		No. of cases	Breadth of head	Mean of corresponding lengths of head	
		Observed	Calculated			Observed	Calculated
32	7.90	6.14	6.12	27	6.30	7.72	7.79
41	7.80	6.05	6.08	36	6.20	7.72	7.70
46	7.70	6.14	6.04	53	6.10	7.65	7.65
52	7.60	5.98	6.00	58	6.00	7.68	7.60
58	7.50	5.98	5.96	56	5.90	7.50	7.55
34	7.40	5.96	5.91	37	5.80	7.55	7.50
26	7.30	5.85	5.87	30	5.70	7.45	7.46

No. of cases	Stature	Mean of corresponding heights of knee		No. of cases	Height of knee	Mean of corresponding statures	
		Observed	Calculated			Observed	Calculated
30	70.0	21.7	21.7	23	22.2	70.5	70.6
50	69.0	21.1	21.3	32	21.7	69.8	69.6
38	68.0	20.7	20.9	50	21.2	68.7	68.6
61	67.0	20.5	20.5	68	20.7	67.3	67.7
49	66.0	20.2	20.1	74	20.2	66.2	66.7
36	65.0	19.7	19.7	41	19.7	65.5	65.7
				26	19.2	64.3	64.7

No. of cases	Left cubit	Mean of corresponding heights of knee		No. of cases	Height of knee	Mean of corresponding left cubit	
		Observed	Calculated			Observed	Calculated
29	19.0	21.5	21.6	23	22.25	18.98	18.97
32	18.7	21.4	21.2	30	21.75	18.68	18.70
48	18.4	20.8	20.9	52	21.25	18.38	18.44
70	18.1	20.7	20.6	69	20.75	18.15	18.17
37	17.8	20.4	20.2	70	20.25	17.75	17.90
31	17.5	20.0	19.9	41	19.75	17.55	17.63
28	17.2	19.8	19.6	27	19.25	17.02	17.36
23	16.9	19.3	19.2				

of a method by which the degree may be measured, in which the variables in a series each member of which is the summed effect of n variables, may be modified by their partial co-relation. After transmuting the separate measures as above, and then summing them, we should find the probable error of any one of them to be $\sqrt{n}$ if the variables were perfectly independent, and n if they were rigidly and perfectly co-related. The observed value would be always somewhere intermediate between these extremes, and would give the information that is wanted.

TABLE V

Subject	Relative	r.	In units of Q $\sqrt{(1-r^2)}$ $=f$	In units of ordinary measure As 1 to	f
Stature	Cubit	0.8	0.60	0.26	0.45
Cubit	Stature			2.5	1.4
Stature	Head length	0.35	0.93	0.38	1.63
Head length	Stature			3.2	0.17
Stature	Middle finger	0.7	0.72	0.06	0.10
Middle finger	Stature			8.2	1.26
Middle finger	Cubit	0.85	0.61	3.13	0.34
Cubit	Middle finger			0.21	0.09
Head length	Head breadth......	0.45	0.89	0.43	0.16
Head breadth......	Head length			0.48	0.17
Stature	Height of knee	0.9	0.44	0.41	0.35
Height of knee	Stature			1.20	0.77
Cubit	Height of knee	0.8	0.60	1.14	0.64
Height of knee	Cubit			0.56	0.45

To conclude, the prominent characteristics of any two co-related variables, so far at least as I have as yet tested them, are four in number. It is supposed that their respective measures have been first transmuted into others of which the unit is in each case equal to the probable error of a single measure in its own series. Let y = the deviation of the subject, which ever of the two variables may be taken in that capacity; and let x_1, x_2, x_3, &c., be the corresponding deviations of the relative, and let the mean of these be X. Then we find: (1) that y = rX for all values of y; (2) that r is the same, whichever of the two variables is taken for the subject; (3) that r is always less than 1; (4) that r measures the closeness of co-relation.

Surveying the progress of psychology in the United States, Jastrow sees a trend toward functionalism as a resultant of the "new pivotal force," the concept of evolution. Of particular interest to us (and the only portion of his address reprinted here) are his remarks concerning the investigations of intelligence. Although research in this field had in the main proved fruitless, Jastrow defended it against the traditional experimentalists. He argues for a kind of "construct validity," drawing criteria from several sources, and is remarkably sensitive to coming needs: units of measurement, correlations, norms, and so on. Notice, however, that he reflects the expectation of most of his colleagues that the answers will be found in the measurement of the elementary processes to be discovered by finer analysis.

Some Currents and Undercurrents in Psychology*

JOSEPH JASTROW

1901

In surveying the addresses of my several predecessors in this office, I am pleased to find that the precedents which they have set for the tenor and purpose of the presidential address to this Association are sufficiently diverse to enable me with propriety to follow my personal inclinations on the present occasion. Though various in trend and content, the several addresses embody two tendencies: the one accepts the obligation of presenting, in some comprehensive outlook, the status of a general problem, or of a sphere of psychological influence, or a portrayal of the bearings and relations that may most wisely pertain between different divisions or aspects of psychology, or between it and other departments of learning with which it has natural affiliations; the other utilizes this occasion for the presentation of a more specific theme representing the outcome of the reflection and investigation of the specialist. My topic introduces both types of considerations. I fear, however, that my representation will not be presidential in character, but rather that of a secretary who reports, with what skill he can command, the contributions of others, and describes, albeit with personal comment and as he sees it, the status of affairs within his chosen province.

*   *   *

Holding in mind the functional aspects of psychological processes, I shall next call attention to the threefold manner of approach to many of

* President's Address, American Psychological Association, *The Psychological Review*, 8 (1901), 1-26. Reprinted by permission of the American Psychological Association.

the significant problems of psychology—a contribution in my judgment that represents one of the most interesting and valuable deposits which the waves of recent investigation have washed upon our shores. This trinity may be spoken of as the genetic or comparative, the normal, and the decadent or abnormal phases of mental phenomena. I shall select for illustration of these phases the study of intelligence. Useful and legitimate criteria of intelligence are derivable from each of these phases, and each completes and corroborates the others.

A conception of intelligence, to be adequate, must be founded upon the recognition of the comparative status of the reactions, simple and complex, which in their composite extent are properly brought within the connotation of this term. The exact fixation of the boundaries of intelligence, both above and below, need not detain us; the middle ground is well enough indicated by the ordinary psychological usage of the term, while the method of more precisely determining the scope and criteria of intelligence may in some measure find illustration as we proceed. Intelligence must first be realized as an advantage-gaining factor in the evolutionary struggle; that struggle is not merely, and indeed in all the stages that here come into consideration, not mainly a conflict of tooth and nail, a contest of strength of claw and fleetness of foot, but a war of wits, an encounter of skill and cunning, a measure of strategy and foresight. The reaction of bodily structure and psychological utilization of structure forms one of the most interesting phases of the study of intelligence. In this field lies the problem of instinct versus intelligence, with all its many ramifications; it is this that gives zest to the study of animal life, from the painstaking account of the courtship of a spider or the experiments upon the visual powers and the memory of an ant, to the dramatic and idealized narratives of Kipling's jungle, and Seton-Thomson's forest and prairie. In brief, an adequate conception of intelligence is not derivable from the contemplation of human activities; its validity must be further justified by its consistent applicability to the phenomena of animal intelligence.

Nor is this the only application of the genetic or comparative point of view; two other developments are of equal theoretic importance, though each of the three differs widely from the others in the actual conditions of its applicability. The genetic growth of the individual in the unfoldment of infancy and childhood and youth and maturity offers another and an indispensable aspect of the study of mental endowment. The same is true of the growth of the race from savagery to civilization. Whatever criteria a scientific investigation shall decide as the proper criteria of intelligence must with due modifications and allowances find corroboration when applied to these three genetic series. It is the growing recognition of this requisite that I look upon as a significant current in modern psychology.

Let me point out, also, that not only does this comparative aspect furnish a widening outlook over the range of mental processes, but that a truer insight into the nature of human activities is as likely to be the outcome of investigation in this field as of the direct study of the data of human psychology. This mutual illumination and suggestiveness of animal and human psychology contributes at once to the charm and the profit of this mode of approach. As a concrete instance I may cite Lloyd Morgan's exposition of the focal and marginal elements in perception. That lucid and acute analysis was the result of a study in regard to the differentiation of human and animal mentality; it leads Professor Morgan to regard the perception of relations (thus necessitating the serial focal apprehension of marginal details) as the essential criterion of and prerequisite to rationality. It may indeed be said that the valuable contributions which Lloyd Morgan has made to our conception of psychological functions, and also to their analysis and their internal economy, are the result of his exceptionally able utilization of the comparative point of view, in the manner which is here emphasized.

The study of intelligence with reference to its status and the method of testing it in the normal individual is, to my thinking, one of the lines of investigation most deserving of increased attention, and one which I had in mind when deploring that in some directions progress had not been so definite nor so satisfactory as was to have been expected and as remains desirable. The functional endowment of the average man is a worthy object of the psychologist's devoted attention. It may contribute little or nothing to an analysis of mental processes, but it stimulates that branch of psychological investigation because its more detailed progress depends upon such analysis.

We cannot test a process properly and discriminatingly until we have analyzed and discovered its relation to other processes, with some of which it usually combines to make a functional unit. One of the chief difficulties in the designing and execution of such tests is the ambiguity attaching to them by reason of an insufficient analysis of the mental attitude and of the processes contributing to the result. If consequences were always preceded by the same antecedents, if recognizable objective results were the infallible indices of determinate subjective processes, the path of the psychological investigator would be, not indeed strewn with roses, but certainly less beset by thorns. In the study of mental functions, important and trivial, nothing should be kept more constantly in mind than the truly complex and intricate logical relation that pertains between process and result.

I am pleased to have occasion to cite once more Professor Morgan's researches for their excellent illustration of the essential connection and organic unity of human and animal psychology. Lloyd Morgan emphasizes the dangers of disregarding processes and accepting results—ends accomplished—as criteria of the status of mental actions. The example of Tony the dog and his learning to carry a stick in his mouth in passing through an open place in the rail fence has come to be quite familiar. The passer-by, who happens to see the dog take the stick up properly by one end and draw it through after him, remarks: "Clever dog that, sir; he knows where the hitch do lie." But the experimenter, who has recorded the stages of trial and error, of haphazard holding and tugging at the stick in all possible directions, has a different and a more accurate conception of the dog's mental processes, which are seemingly indicated by the result accomplished. *Ab uno disce omnes.* Let no one look upon the study of mental functions and the determination of mental standards as a matter of technique and a facility in the use of apparatus, or as a process unrelated to a painstaking, analytical investigation.

An adequate set of tests of normal functional efficiency, that shall receive a considerable authoritative sanction, is a great desideratum for present-day needs, and an end by no means beyond the goal of properly directed endeavor. Its starting point is a correct analysis of the most distinctive modes of exercise of the several elementary components of our mental functions; the next step is the devising of tests that shall most simply, naturally and definitely measure the functional efficiency of a selected factor or process; this accomplished, the way is prepared for the extensive utilization of such standards or norms of efficiency, by (*a*) their correlation with one another, (*b*) by a comparison with similar results obtained upon children at different stages of their development, thereby gaining an insight into the order and nature of genetic unfoldment, (*c*) by a comparison with irregular, undeveloped, defective and decadent forms of such processes, as they occur in connection with individual variations, with the consequences of mental stimulation, or in disease.

This programme, which could readily be expanded, is even in outline a most extensive one—rich in detail, fertile in mutual suggestiveness of its parts, possibly momentous in its practical consequences. The conclusion is obvious that for a host of comparative purposes the determination of norms or standards of functional mental efficiency is indispensable. That such determination involves conventions and artificialities is true and proper and inevitable. But neither is a foot, nor a meter, nor a candle-power, nor a horse-power, nor a volt, nor an ohm a natural and predestined *ding-an-sich.* Yet the arbitrary and conventional character of these units does not interfere with their utility.

I am not advocating a ready-made mental yardstick which shall show in what measure all men are not equal, and how each may discover the thumb-marks of his individual success or failure. All this has been attempted before, and with necessarily futile results. The problem is recognized to be one of a general statistical nature, freighted doubtless with practical consequences, but the application of which must always be uncertain and dependent for its success upon judgment and insight. There is no serious danger of being misunderstood in this respect.

Some other forms of objection, however, to what I have advanced I must not seem to disregard. Having these in mind, I can only say that I cannot bring myself into an attitude of sympathy with those who, on grounds possibly legitimate in themselves, but not pertinent to the functional aspect of mental processes, question the possibility or the utility of mental measurements. A searching critique of the fundamenta of such measurements, of the assumptions which they involve, is helpful; it clears the atmosphere and brings out the perspective of things with sharpness and precision; it distinguishes between the true goal of such investigation and unattainable ideals; it points out sources of error and prevents misconception. Such criticism is wholesome and pertinent; but a transcendental skepticism in regard to the possibility of such measurements itself transcends its proper sphere when it impugns the value of the scientific study of mental functions by quantitative methods.

I have equally little sympathy with those who admit the possibility and even the utility of such investigation, but question its psychological character. They speak of it, and somewhat disparagingly, as mental anthropometry, and thus in a measure restrict psychology to that which yields definite and, if possible, original analytical results. In part the difference between this attitude and the one I am advocating is one of terminology, and thus unimportant; in another aspect it is a difference in the interpretation of the scope of psychology—a subject certainly capable of supporting differences of view. I prefer to cast my lot with the wider conception of its scope, and mainly for the reason that the relations between mental problems are so intricate and manifold that one can never anticipate from what sources further illumination may come. Call it mental anthropometry if you will, but do not disregard the valuable contributions to other divisions of psychology and to the general conception of this science, which such investigation has the possibility and, in my opinion, the probability of contributing.

The study of the normal efficiency of that composite group of processes which contribute to our common humanity has, I confidently believe, an important and a practical future. Its progress is dependent upon careful analysis, upon systematic investigation, upon the coöperative and the coordinate labors of many, upon interpretative skill and psychological insight. An auspicious start has been made; the day of the production of works and fruit cannot be far off.

This monograph was important in both methodology and content. It introduced the correlational technique into the mental measurement field and it provided a large-scale test of the utility of laboratory measures as indices of intelligence. James McKeen Cattell had proposed some years before that psychologists standardize their procedure and agree on what to measure and how to measure it. In illustrating and implementing this program, he was responsible for the compilation of the data Wissler set out to analyze. The results of the analysis show clearly that standardization would have been sterile and misleading. At this point certainly Jastrow's optimism in the preceding paper seems ill-founded.

The Correlation of Mental and Physical Tests*

CLARK WISSLER

1901

INTRODUCTION

This research is occasioned by the fact that psychologists and students of education have proposed certain tests, put them to trial and recorded their results, hoping thereby to find a means by which the fundamental elements of general and specific ability could be isolated and valued. In this they have not been without precedent, since upon the same assumption fitness for the civil and military service, for academic degrees and honors, for professional and technical licenses, etc., is usually determined by arbitrary tests and estimated by numerical averages in grade books. Our work is primarily with the grade book of the psychologist. It is of both theoretical and practical importance to know what relations exist between the results of his tests and those of others. The contention that all tests are arbitrary and futile has no weight in this connection so long as people go on using them. Educational, professional, physical and psychological tests are with us and bid fair to remain, at least until something better is found. Thus the times demand that the results obtained by the various tests be made an object of study. The most obvious line of approach in this problem is through correlation. If a test is general, then its results should correlate with many other special tests, and, in turn, if there is an integral relation between general and special ability, the results of the latter should correlate with the former. Should two tests show no correlation whatever, we can do no more than regard them as defining two entirely independent forms of activity. To determine the relative value of tests with respect to their

* *Psychological Review Monograph Supplement* 3, No. 6 (1901), p. 62. Reprinted by permission of the American Psychological Association.

general or specific significance, we must find some way of estimating the degree of correlation in terms of variability.

To the reader is due some explanation as to the methods of treating data. It is not proper to demonstrate these methods here, because they are not the objects of investigation, but, while they are treated at length in the appropriate literature, the mode of presentation is beyond the comprehension of all save the expert or those few who can afford to spend their time working up to them. So it seems necessary to give a few words to the methods employed.

The first thing to learn is that when mathematical formulas are resorted to it is only for purposes of convenient and exact statement. Long ago astronomers and engineers discovered that errors of observation are distributed in a certain orderly manner and are consequently susceptible to mathematical statement. By proper treatment they are able to estimate the precision of measurements, determine the number of observations necessary to a given standard of precision, etc. It was soon discovered that biological variation followed similar laws and that such variation could be measured accurately, thus enabling us to determine differences of race, type, species, etc. When psychologists took up their side of the question as to the precision of observations they soon discovered that all human performances, when objectified in units of space, time, etc., seem to follow certain laws of variability, and that these laws are in turn similar to those already worked out. In other words, variability is no longer a barrier to the study of human activity, because we can measure that variability. In more recent times it has been found possible to deal with variability in such a way that the functional and structural relations between phenomena can be accurately estimated, or, in technical terms, a method of correlation has been developed. As may be inferred, these methods are based upon empirical study, they have been attested by use and are the work of some of the best mathematicians and scientists of the past and present centuries. The reader who doubts their validity must look to the authors themselves.

*   *   *

It remains for the writer to define his relation to this research. The tests were devised and conducted by Professor J. McKeen Cattell and his associates, but for the methods of compilation, together with all conclusions and opinions respecting the results and the validity of the various tests, the writer is responsible. The conception of the problem and the accumulation of material must be credited to the former, while the latter has only undertaken the compilation of results.

THE TESTS EMPLOYED

These tests are made yearly upon sixty to seventy freshmen of Columbia College and repeated with those who remain to the end of the senior year.

The tests now made in the psychological laboratory are as follows: length and breadth of head, strength of hands, fatigue, eyesight, color vision, hearing, perception of pitch, perception of weight, sensation areas, sensitiveness to pain, perception of size, color preference, reaction time, rate of perception, naming colors, rate of movement, accuracy of movement, perception of time, association, imagery, memory (auditory, visual, logical and retrospective). Records of stature, weight, etc., together with data concerning parentage, personal habits and health, are a part of the gymnasium tests required of all students in Columbia College.

*   *   *

Perception of Size.—This test is made first, in order that retrospective memory may be tested at the end of the series. A sheet of paper bearing a 5 cm. line is placed before the student and a blank sheet of the same size on the right. Without moving them or altering much his point of view he is required to draw a line as nearly as possible the length of the standard. This done he is requested to bisect the line drawn and from the middle draw a perpendicular as long as the whole line and then bisect the right-hand angle. The student is required to do this quickly.

Size of Head.—In measuring the head the maximum length and breadth are taken with calipers. For length the directions to observers are, to place one point of the calipers on the most prominent point of the forehead, between the eyebrows. If in this region very prominent bony ridges are felt, take a second measurement from a point just above the ridges and note both. Bring the other point of the calipers down to the posterior part of the head and move it along the middle line until the greatest length of head is found. For breadth of head take the maximum above the ears wherever found. Hold the calipers horizontally and perfectly symmetrically. Make two measurements of each diameter independently and record the results in mm. in the order in which they were made. Repeat until the average variation of the accordant measurements is about 1 mm. Leave a record of all measurements made.

Strength of Hand.—This test is made with the oval dynamometer. The student is shown how to hold the instrument and makes the test standing. He is not to see the dial or the record while making the test. The order is right-hand, left, right, left—four trials in all.

Fatigue.—The test is made with Cattell's ergometer. The pressure is applied by the ends of the index finger and thumb and the tension of the spring registered on a counter dial. The right hand is used and one trial of 50 efforts in a rhythm of about one a second is taken as the result. The observer records the reading for each ten efforts.

Eyesight.—These tests are made with Galton's instrument which gives the distance in cm. at which diamond numerals can be read by each eye singly. The right eye is tested first, beginning at a distance of 44 cm. From this the student proceeds until a card is reached where he can read at least eight out of ten numerals. The test is made in ordinary daylight.

Color Vision.—The subject is required to select the green shades from the woolen skeins supplied by the Cambridge Scientific Instrument Company in accordance with Mr. Galton's instructions.

Hearing.—The test is made in a quiet room with the ticking of a stopwatch as the standard. 5 m. and above is taken as the normal distance and under 1 m. as abnormal.

Perception of Pitch.—The test is made with a monochord tuned so that F below middle C is given when the bridge is at 75 cm. The directions for making the test are as follows: "Give tone F twice at an interval of about two seconds to the student, whose back is turned. Then shift the bridge to about 50 and let the student find the tone. He must be warned against humming the tune and must probably be taught in advance how to use the monochord. Record the position of the bridge and then give the original tone twice and shift the bridge to the place where it was left by the student in his first trial, telling him that it is put back to this place. Let him now find the tone and record the position. Ask the student whether he plays a musical instrument or sings and record his answers."

Perception of Weight or Force of Movement.—In this test the lift is vertical and the dynamometer gives a pressure of 1 kg. to 10 cm. A mechanical stop is provided at a pressure of 1 kg. to give the student his standard. In making the test he is told to lift the handle to the stop three times and then make ten attempts to lift it to the same height after the operator has removed the stop. Each lift is to be made in about 2 sec., with equal pauses between. A graphic record of the lifts is taken on a kymograph and filed with the other data.

Sensation Areas.—The points of the æsthesiometer are 2 cm. apart and the instrument is applied longitudinally to the back of the left hand, between the bones of the second and third fingers. Five tests are made, the student being touched with one or two points in the order, two, two, one, one, two, and being required to decide in each case whether he was touched with one or with two points.

Sensitiveness to Pain.—This is determined for the ball of the thumb of the right and left hands. An algometer is used in which the surface applied is of rubber, 1 cm. in diameter and rounded at the corners. The instrument is applied with gradually increasing pressure by the observer and the student is told to say as soon as the pressure becomes disagreeable. If he shows signs of discomfort the pressure is stopped. Two tests are made on each hand in alternation, beginning with the right hand.

Color Preference.—Rectangles (5x3 cm.) of red, orange, yellow, green, blue, violet and white are shown in an irregular group on a black ground and the student asked to specify his likes and dislikes.

Reaction-time.—The reaction-time for sound is taken five times in succession with the Hipp chronoscope. After the reactions the student is asked whether he attended to the sound, to the hand or to both.

Rate of Perception.—A blank is provided containing 500 11-point capital letters, of which 100 are A's. Each of the other letters occurs 16 times and the whole series is arranged in an order drawn by lot. The student is required to mark as quickly as possible all the A's, the observer taking the time with a stop-watch. The blank is kept as a part of the student's test record and shows the accuracy of the performance as well as its quickness.

Naming Colors.—One hundred 1 cm. squares of colored paper (red, orange, yellow, green, blue, violet, pink, gray and black) arranged in chance order on a white ground are to be named as quickly as possible. The observer takes the time with a watch and notes the errors. This is really a test in rate of reading or naming familiar things. Care is taken to see that all students have a ready name for each color on the card before taking the test.

Rate of Movement.—A blank ruled into one hundred 1-cm. squares into each of which the student must put a dot, completing the task as quickly as possible, constitutes this test. The observer records the time with a watch and preserves the record.

Accuracy of Movement.—Here a blank with 100 dots arranged in the form of a 10-cm. square is provided, the student being required to strike at each dot in succession, the aim being to hit them as nearly as he can and as quickly as possible. The time is taken by the observer and the blank preserved for the computation of accuracy.

Rhythm and Perception of Time.—The present test is of the ability to follow a given rhythm. The student makes with a telegraph key taps in the rhythm of sounds which occur one per second. He is told to continue tapping fifty times at the same rate after the sounder is stopped, which is after ten beats. The standard is given by a telegraph sounder operated by a clock. The student's tapping is recorded on a kymograph with a clock line in parallel.

Association.—A blank is provided containing the following words in bold-faced type: house, tree, child, time, art, London, Napoleon, red, enough. The observer explains the test to the student, and, when everything is ready, the blank is handed to the latter, who writes after each word as quickly as possible what it suggests to him, preferably a single word. The observer takes the time and files the blank.

Imagery.—The student answers the following questions:

Think of your breakfast table as you sat down to it this morning; call up the appearance of the table, the dishes and food on it, the persons present, etc. Then write answers to the following questions:
1. Are the outlines of the objects distinct and sharp?
2. Are the colors bright and natural?

3. Where does the image seem to be situated? In the head? Before the eyes? At a distance?

4. How does the size of the image compare with the actual size of the scene?

---

1. Can you call to mind better the face or the voice of a friend?

2. When "violin" is suggested, do you first think of the appearance of the instrument or the sounds made when it is played?

3. (*a*) Can you call to mind natural scenery so that it gives you pleasure? (*b*) Music? (*c*) The taste of fruit?

4. Have you ever mistaken an hallucination for a perception, *e.g.,* apparently heard a voice or seen a figure when none was present? If you answer "yes," describe the appearance on the back of this sheet.

Memory.—Four different tests are made in the order given here. The observer instructs the student as to what is expected of him in each case.

1. Auditory.—Each series of numerals in the following is read at a rate of about 2 per second, after which the student writes it from memory:

4	8	3	7	1	9	6	2
7	5	9	2	8	6	4	1
3	7	5	2	9	6	4	8

2. Visual.—Corresponding numerals are shown at the same rate.

3	9	5	2	6	8	1	4
8	5	2	7	4	6	3	1
5	1	6	2	7	3	4	8

3. Logical.—The following passage containing 100 words is read to the student, who then writes as much of it as he can. He is directed to give the words wherever possible, but attempt to give the thought completely.

Tests such as we are now making are of value both for the advancement of science and for the information of the student who is tested. It is of importance for science to learn how people differ and on what factors these differences depend. If we can disentangle the complex influences of heredity and environment we may be able to apply our knowledge to guide human development. Then it is well for each of us to know in what way he differs from others. We may thus in some cases correct defects and develop aptitudes which we might otherwise neglect.

4. Retrospective.—At the beginning of the test a 5-cm. line was shown the student in the size test. At the end of the hour he is reminded of the line and requested to draw it from memory. This was devised as a test of memory for a thing which one had no special object in remembering.

*   *   *

THE CORRELATION OF RESULTS

The most important consideration in a series of tests is their correlation. It is desirable to know to what extent ability in one case assures us of ability in another. This is the real question in all tests. But before going into the subject proper some attention must be given to method. Let us take for example the stature and weight of students, as a case in which we should expect some correlation. In Table I. the cases are grouped in differences of 5 kg. and 5 cm. and so arranged that the weight of any group can be com-

TABLE I

Stature in cm	Weight in kg								Total
	45–50	51–55	56–60	61–65	66–70	71–75	76–80	81–85	
155–160	1	1		1					3
161–165	1	2	7	1	2				13
166–170	1	5	7	10	3				26
171–175		2	9	11	8	2	1		33
176–180			4	11	6	3	2	2	28
181–185			1	3	3	4	2	3	16
186–190								1	1
Total.	3	10	28	37	22 ·	9	5	6	120
Av. Stature.	162.5	166.5	169.8	172.8	173.6	178.6	178.5	181.6	172.5

pared with its stature. The average stature of all is 172.5 cm., weight 63.4 kg. At the foot of each column is the average stature for the corresponding weight. Here we see that those of average weight are also of average stature and that weight increases with stature. Had there been no relation between weight and stature, the averages for the columns would have been approximately the same.

These relations may be presented in graphic form as in Fig. 1. Let AB represent the place of average statures, if there were no correlation; CD their place in perfect correlation; the point of intersection, the place of the group having both average stature and average weight; then plotting the actual averages gives the line EF.

In estimating the degree of correlation it is customary to proceed by the formula

$$r = \frac{\Sigma xy}{n\mu_1\mu_2},$$

in which x and y represent the variations of an individual from the respective averages of the two distributions to be correlated, μ_1 and μ_2 the mean square deviations of the distributions and r the coefficient of correlation.

When r equals unity correlation is perfect, when equal to zero the correlation is that of chance. Applying this formula to the data for stature and weight (Table I.) we find $r = 0.66$. This coefficient expresses the relation between the averages for the successive columns, or arrays, in the table or the place of EF in Fig. 1. The probable variation of an array may be found from $p\sqrt{1 - r^2}$. Since $r = 0.66$, this expression becomes $0.75\ p$; calculating p for all statures in the table gives 4.6 cm., from which it follows that the probable variation for an array should be 3.3 cm. Calculating the actual

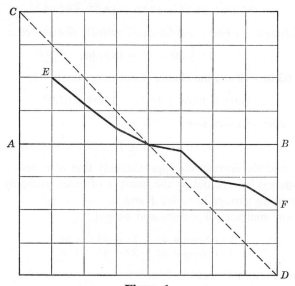

Figure 1

variation in statures for weights of 56–60, 61–65 and 66–70 we obtain 3.5, 3.7 and 3.8. The significance of $r = 0.66$ is now apparent; if we select students according to weight, their statures will fall within approximately ¾ the limits for students selected at random. In the same way it may be shown that a coefficient of $0.43 = 0.90\ p$; $0.66 = 0.75\ p$; $0.87 = 0.50\ p$; $0.97 = 0.25\ p$; etc., from which the significance of the various coefficients in the following pages may be estimated.

Since the coefficients of correlation depend upon the mean square deviations, their own probable errors can only be estimated in the same terms. According to the method employed, it appears that for the following data differences greater than 0.10 have considerable certainty.

In order to save time the writer used another form of this method which may be illustrated by an actual case. In reaction the cases may be divided roughly into four groups as

(1) $68 + 70 + 55 + 63 = 256$

and in the A test

(2) $57 + 80 + 66 + 53 = 256.$

Now, if a mere chance relation held between these tests, the 68 cases in reaction should be distributed in series 2 as

$$\frac{57}{256} + \frac{80}{256} + \frac{66}{256} + \frac{53}{256} \text{ of } 68$$

or

$$15.14 + 21.24 + 17.50 + 14.07 = 67.95.$$

Counting through, we find these 68 cases actually distributed as

$$15 + 20 + 15 + 18 = 68.$$

Taking the 63 in series 1, the chance occurrence should be

$$14.02 + 19.68 + 16.24 + 13.04 = 62.98.$$

The actual order of cases was

$$12 + 21 + 18 + 12 = 63.$$

Thus we find the correlation approximately that of chance. The method can be shortened by calculating the number of cases probably agreeing in the corresponding groups in series 1 and 2.

In the same manner for stature and weight,

(1) Stature $42 + 33 + 45 = 120$
(2) Weight $41 + 37 + 42 = 120.$

The 42 short men in 1 occur in 2 as

$$25 + 12 + 5 = 42.$$

By chance they should be

$$14.4 + 12.9 + 14.7 = 42.0.$$

The tall men occur

$$5 + 14 + 26 = 45.$$

By chance,

$$15.3 + 13.8 + 15.7 = 44.8.$$

Thus we find evidences of correlation in this case.

In a series of tests like the following, where there are over six hundred possible correlations to consider, a shorter method still will be useful. Correlation may be detected by simply taking account of the distribution of cases. Returning to Table I. we find in regard to stature about the same number above as below the average group. Arranging the 42 short men, the 45 tall and the 33 average men according to weight, we find them distributed as follows:

Short men,	3 ...	8 ...	14 ...	12 ...	5 ...	0 ...	0 ...	0	42
Tall men,	0 ...	0 ...	5 ...	14 ...	9 ...	7 ...	4 ...	6	45
Av. men,	0 ...	2 ...	9 ...	11 ...	8 ...	2 ...	1 ...	0	33
Total,	3 ...	10 ...	28 ...	37 ...	22 ...	9 ...	5 ...	6	120

That tall men are heavier than short men is now evident. In practice we need but find the distribution of cases with high and low values, say above $+ p$ and below $- p$. A judicious use of this method makes a rough-and-ready estimate of the degree of correlation possible in any case.

The data discussed in the following pages were first arranged according to this last method; then the actual distributions were compared with the theoretical chance distributions: finally all the important tests and all giving any evidence of correlation were treated by the Pearson formula and the coefficients taken as the basis of discussion. Thus the treatment has been sufficiently thorough to give a reliable conclusion as to the general degree of correlation between such tests as are considered.

Results

[The detailed discussion of results must be omitted but Wissler's summary table is sufficient to impress the reader with the generally negative aspect of his findings.]

*   *   *

By way of a general summary all the coefficients of correlation as calculated by the Pearson formula are here enumerated:

QUICKNESS AND ACCURACY

	Cases	r
Reaction and marking out A's,	252	− 0.05
Reaction and naming the colors,	118	+ 0.15
Reaction and association time,	153	+ 0.08
Reaction and movement time,	90	+ 0.14
Naming the colors and marking out A's,	159	+ 0.21
Naming the colors and movement time,	97	+ 0.19
Drawing and bisecting a line,	123	+ 0.38
Accuracy and speed in marking out A's,	252	− 0.28

MEMORY

Auditory and visual—correctly written,	144	+ 0.29
Auditory and visual—correctly placed,	144	+ 0.39
Logical and auditory—correctly written,	94	+ 0.05
Logical and auditory—correctly placed,	94	+ 0.04
Logical and retrospective,	91	− 0.07
Force of movement and drawing line,	123	− 0.08

Logical memory and naming the colors,	93	+ 0.03
Logical memory and reaction time,	96	+ 0.12
Auditory memory and reaction time,	112	+ 0.17
Visual memory and reaction time,	104	+ 0.06
Pitch memory and reaction time,	100	+ 0.01

PHYSICAL TESTS

Strength of hand and class standing,	204	− 0.08
Fatigue and class standing,	132	+ 0.23
Fatigue and strength,	140	− 0.34
Length of head and logical memory,	99	+ 0.21
Breadth of head and logical memory,	99	− 0.05

CLASS STANDING

Class standing and reaction time,	227	− 0.02
Class standing and marking out A's,	242	− 0.09
Class standing and association time,	160	+ 0.08
Class standing and naming the colors,	112	+ 0.02
Class standing and logical memory,	86	+ 0.19
Class standing and auditory memory,	121	+ 0.16
Class standing and gymnasium,	119	+ 0.53
Latin and mathematics,	228	+ 0.58
Latin and rhetoric,	223	+ 0.55
Latin and French,	130	+ 0.60
Latin and German,	129	+ 0.61
Latin and Greek,	121	+ 0.75
Rhetoric and French,	122	+ 0.30
Rhetoric and German,	132	+ 0.61
Rhetoric and mathematics,	222	+ 0.51
German and mathematics,	115	+ 0.52
Mathematics and logical memory,	90	+ 0.11
Latin and logical memory,	90	+ 0.22

The general conclusions are:

1. That the laboratory mental tests show little intercorrelation in the case of college students.

2. That the physical tests show a general tendency to correlate among themselves but only to a very slight degree with the mental tests.

3. That the markings of students in college classes correlate with themselves to a considerable degree but not with the tests made in the laboratory.

*   *   *

DISCUSSION OF RESULTS

In summing up the foregoing it appears that all the tests in this series have little interdependence. The idea of correlation implies some structural or functional relation. It is generally assumed that such relation in mental phenomena is functional rather than structural, and the conception of the analysis of mental processes and the search for the fundamental elements of the same imply a close correlation between simple processes. The direction of thought is that such ideas as quickness, accuracy, regularity, etc., represent some fundamental attribute of the individual that characterizes all his acts, and hence, tests giving results in the same category must correlate. On the other hand, when it is said that correlation does not exist, it is understood that the relations are those of chance. In other words, in a given number of tests we can approximate the number of individuals quick, medium and slow in all, as well as the number for any combination of positions in the various distributions. Since this conforms to the general result of the mental tests of this series we must look for the practical value of such tests in an extended series; the superior individuals in all-around quickness, for example, are those few who happen to be quick in the majority of such tests. Thus it becomes evident that the outcome of this research raises questions which throw us back into one of the great problems of psychology, viz., What constitutes mental ability? The significance of this question becomes apparent when we consider its relation to educational practice alone. It is plain that if we accept the conclusions of this research as final, an individual must be regarded as the algebraic sum of a vast array of small abilities of almost equal probability, the resulting combination conforming to the laws of chance.

* * *

In general, so far as the writer can see, the results of other investigators agree with his own. Correlations have been found to correspond in degree, in so far as it is possible to estimate them from the data given, when calculated for students of approximately the same advancement as college freshmen, but in no case is there reason to believe that decisive correlations have been found for mental tests.

We come now to the apparent contradiction between the results of this research and the experience of life. It is often claimed that quickness, for example, will show itself in all our acts, and that therefore there must be a correlation in tests of quickness. Experience is able to produce cases of all-around quickness, dexterity or mental ability, and these are set up as proofs of functional relations. But this comes from a misconception. A chance correlation does not mean that no one will manifest such efficiency, but that the number of such individuals is governed by accident. That is to say, given a number of directions of activity, the number of individuals excelling in all can be closely approximated according to the laws of chance. In this instance one exception does not break the rule. Some authors have made this very error in estimating correlations for their data. The trouble is that experience keeps no record of numbers but deals in isolated cases. It is only by such methods as have been employed in this research that any idea of the relative number of cases can be obtained. And lastly, the claim that such tests have nothing in common with the tasks of life is really not an

In this monumental paper Spearman, running far ahead of the field, laid the basis for the correlational study of mental traits. Drawing attention to sources of error in interpreting correlations, he pointed up the need for information concerning the reliability of mental measurements at a time when most psychologists were but dimly aware of the existence of such a statistical technique. Although some of the procedures are now "old-fashioned," you will find a careful study of this article rewarding.

The Proof and Measurement of Association Between Two Things*

C. SPEARMAN

1904

INTRODUCTORY

All knowledge—beyond that of bare isolated occurrence—deals with uniformities. Of the latter, some few have a claim to be considered absolute, such as mathematical implications and mechanical laws. But the vast majority are only *partial;* medicine does not teach that smallpox is inevitably escaped by vaccination, but that it is so generally; biology has not shown that all animals require organic food, but that nearly all do so; in daily life, a dark sky is no proof that it will rain, but merely a warning; even in morality, the sole categorical imperative alleged by Kant was the sinfulness of telling a lie, and few thinkers since have admitted so much as this to be valid universally. In psychology, more perhaps than in any other science, it is hard to find absolutely inflexible coincidences; occasionally, indeed, there appear uniformities sufficiently regular to be practically treated as laws, but infinitely the greater part of the observations hitherto recorded concern only more or less pronounced *tendencies* of one event or attribute to accompany another.

Under these circumstances, one might well have expected that the evidential evaluation and precise mensuration of tendencies had long been the subject of exhaustive investigation and now formed one of the earliest sections in a beginner's psychological course. Instead, we find only a general naïve ignorance that there is anything about it requiring to be learnt. One after another, laborious series of experiments are executed and published with the purpose of demonstrating some connection between two events, wherein the otherwise learned psychologist reveals that his art of

* Adapted from *The American Journal of Psychology,* 15 (1904), pp. 72-101. Reprinted by permission of the publisher.

proving and measuring correspondence has not advanced beyond that of lay persons. The consequence has been that the significance of the experiments is not at all rightly understood, nor have any definite facts been elicited that may be either confirmed or refuted.

The present article is a commencement at attempting to remedy this deficiency of scientific correlation. With this view, it will be strictly confined to the needs of practical workers, and all theoretical mathematical demonstrations will be omitted. . . .

At the same time, and for the same reason, the meaning and working of the various formulæ have been explained sufficiently, it is hoped, to render them readily usable even by those whose knowledge of mathematics is elementary. The fundamental procedure is accompanied by simple imaginary examples, while the more advanced parts are illustrated by cases that have actually occurred in my personal experience. . . .

In conclusion, the general value of the methodics recommended is emphasized by a brief criticism of the best correlational work hitherto made public, and also the important question is discussed as to the number of "cases" required for an experimental series.

PART I

Elementary Correlation and "Accidental Deviation"

Requirements of a Good Method of Correlation.

(a) Quantitative expression.

The most fundamental requisite is to be able to measure our observed correspondence by a plain numerical symbol. There is no reason whatever to be satisfied either with vague generalities such as "large," "medium," "small," or, on the other hand, with complicated tables and compilations.

The first person to see the possibility of this immense advance seems to have been Galton, who, in 1886, writes: "the length of the arm is said to be correlated with that of the leg, because a person with a long arm has usually a long leg and conversely." He then proceeds to devise the required symbol in such a way that it conveniently ranges from 1, for perfect correspondence, to 0 for entire independence, and on again to −1 for perfect correspondence inversely. By this means, correlations became comparable with other ones found either in different objects or by different observers; they were at last capable of leading to further conclusions, speculative and practical; in a word, they now assumed a scientific character.

Mathematically, it is clear that innumerable other systems of values are equally conceivable, similarly ranging from 1 to 0. One such, for instance, has been worked out and extensively used by myself. It therefore becomes necessary to discuss their relative merits.

(b) The significance of the quantity.

Galton's particular system is defined and most advantageously distinguished from all the others by the important property, that if any number of arms, for instance, be collected which are all any amount, $x\sigma_a$, above the mean, then the corresponding legs will average $rx\sigma_1$ above the mean (with a middle or "quartile" deviation of $\sigma_1 \sqrt{1 - r^2}$); where $\sigma_a =$ the quartile variation of the arms, $\sigma_1 =$ that of the legs, and r is the measure of the correlation.

But another—theoretically far more valuable—property may conceivably attach to one among the possible systems of values expressing the correlation; that is, that a measure might be afforded of the *hidden underlying cause of the variations*. Suppose, for example, that A and B both derive their money from variable dividends and each gets $1/x^{th}$ of his total from some source common to both of them. Then evidently their respective incomes will have a certain tendency to rise and fall simultaneously; this correspondence will in any of the possible systems of values always be some function $1/x$, but in only one of them will it actually be itself $= 1/x$; in such a favored case, if A and B get, say, 20% of their respective incomes from the common source, the correlation between these two incomes will also show itself as 0.20; and conversely, if A's income happens to be found correlated with that of B by 0.20, then there is a likelihood that 0.20 of A's income coincides with 0.20 of B, leaving to either 0.80 disposable independently. The observed correlation thus becomes the direct expression of the relative amount of underlying influences tending for and against the correspondence.

In the above imagined instance, this desirable expressiveness belongs to the same above system of values proposed by Galton (and elaborated by Pearson). But this instance is exceptional and fundamentally different from the normal type. Evidently, A and B need not necessarily derive exactly the same proportion of their incomes from the common source; A might get his 0.20 while B got some totally different share; in which case, it will be found that the correlation is always the geometrical mean between the two shares. Let B be induced to put *all* his income into the common fund, then A need only put in $0.20^2 = 0.04$, to maintain the same correlation as before; since the geometrical mean between 0.04 and 1 is equal to 0.20.

Now, in psychological, as in most other actual correspondences, A and B are not to be regarded as in the fixed bisection of our first case, but rather as in the labile inter-accommodation of our second case. Hence A, in order to be correlated with B by $1/x$, must be considered to have only devoted $1/x^2$ (instead of $1/x$) of his arrangement to this purpose, and therefore to still have for further arrangements $1 - 1/x^2$, which will enable an independent correlation to arise of $\sqrt{1 - 1/x^2}$. In short, not Galton's measure of correlation, but the *square thereof,* indicates the relative influence of the factors in A tending towards any observed correspondence as compared with the remaining components of A tending in other directions.

(c) Accuracy.

From this plurality of possible systems of values for the measure of the correlation must be carefully distinguished the variety of ways of calculating any one of them. These latter, again, have various advantages and disadvantages, of which the principal is their respective degrees of liability to "accidental deviation."

For, though the correlation between two series of data is an absolute mathematical fact, yet its whole real value lies in our being able to assume a likelihood of further cases taking a similar direction; we want to consider our results as a truly representative *sample*. Any one at all accustomed to original investigation must be aware how frequently phenomena will group themselves in such a manner as to convincingly suggest the existence of some law—when still more prolonged experiment reveals that the observed uniformity was due to pure hazard and has no tendency whatever to further repeat itself.

Luckily, this one great source of fallacy can be adequately eliminated, owing to the fact that such accidental deviations are different in every individual case (hence are often called the "variable errors") and occur quite impartially in every direction according to the known laws of probability. The consequence is that they eventually more or less completely *compensate one another,* and thus finally present an approximately true result. Such elimination, however, must always remain theoretically incomplete, since no amount of chance coincidence is absolutely impossible; but beyond certain limits it becomes so extremely unlikely that for practical purposes we can afford to neglect it. When a person loses 14 times running at pitch-and-toss, he can reckon that such a series would not occur by mere accident once in 9,999 times, and consequently he will feel justified in attributing the coincidence to some constant disturbing influence. Similarly, to estimate the evidential value of any other observed uniformity, we only require to know how nearly the odds against chance coincidence have approached to some such standard maximum as 9,999 to 1. But, as any standard must always be more or less arbitrary—some thinking it too lenient and others unnecessarily severe—it is usual to employ a formula giving not the maximum but the middle deviation or "probable error." We may then easily find the probability of mere hazard from the following comparative table:

If the observed correlation divided by the probable error be =	1	2	3	4	5	6
then the frequency of occurrence by mere hazard =	$\frac{1}{2}$	$\frac{1}{6}$	$\frac{1}{23}$	$\frac{1}{143}$	$\frac{1}{1250}$	$\frac{1}{19000}$

Now, the smallness of this probable error depends principally upon the number of cases observed, but also largely upon the mathematical method of correlation. Though a faultiness in the latter respect can theoretically be made good by increasing the range of the observations, yet such increase is not always possible, and, besides, has other grave disadvantages which will be discussed later on. Other things being equal, therefore, *the best method is that one which gives the least probable error*. For the benefit of the reader, this probable error should always be plainly stated; nothing more is required than a rough approximation; for while it is highly important to distinguish between a deduction worth, say, 0.9999 of perfect certainty and one worth only 0.75, it would be a mere splitting of straws to care whether a particular experiment works out to a validity of 0.84 or to one of 0.85.

(d) Ease of application.

The most accurate ways of calculation are generally somewhat difficult and slow to apply; often, too, there occur circumstances under which they cannot be used at all. Hence, in addition to a standard method, which must be used for finally establishing the principal results, there is urgent need, also, of *auxiliary methods* capable of being employed under the most varied conditions and with the utmost facility.

But here a word of warning appears not out of place. For such auxiliary methods are very numerous and their results, owing to accidents, will diverge to some extent from one another; so that the unwary, "self-suggested" experimenter may often be led unconsciously—but none the less unfairly— to pick out the one most favorable for his particular point, and thereby confer upon his work an unequivocality to which it is by no means entitled. Any departures from the recognized standard methods are only legitimate, either when absolutely necessary, or for mere preliminary work, or for indicating comparatively unimportant relations.

* * *

[The remainder of this part of the article is taken up with formulas and explanations of product-moment correlation, rank correlation, "cross-multiples," and several auxiliary methods. In Part II Spearman turns to considerations important in the use and interpretation of correlation methods in psychological research.]

PART II

Correction of "Systematic Deviations"

Systematic Deviations Generally.

In the first part, we have seen that any correlational experiments, however extensive, can only be regarded as a "sample" out of the immense reality, and will consequently present a certain amount of accidental deviation from the real general tendency; we have further seen that this accidental deviation is measurable by the "probable error," whose determination, therefore, becomes an indispensable requisite to all serious research.

But now we are in danger of falling from Scylla into Charybdis. For after laboriously compiling sufficient cases and conscientiously determining the probable error, there exists a very human tendency to cease from labor and inwardly rejoice at having thus risen from common fallacious argument to the serene certainty of mathematics. But whether or not such complacency may be justifiable in pure statistical inquiry, it is at any rate altogether premature in the kind of research that we are at present contemplating; we are not dealing with statistics, but with a line of work so fundamentally different, that it may be aptly distinguished by the term of "statisticoids." Here the accidental deviation is not the sole one, nor even the most momentous; there are many other enemies who are unmoved by the most formidable array of figures. These consist in such deviations as, instead of merely being balanced imperfectly, lie wholly on the one side or the other. As in ordinary measurements, so too in correlation, we may speak, not only of "accidental," "variable," or "compensating" inaccuracies, but also of "systematic," "constant," or "non-compensating" ones.

These systematic deviations are of very varied nature, the most insidious being, as usual, *self-suggestion*. To take, for instance, one of our recent examples, suppose that we have applied the Griessbach test to a number of children before and after their lessons, and have found the desired correlation between fatigue and cutaneous insensitivity, it still remains exceedingly difficult to convince ourselves that we executed our tests entirely without favor or affection; for it is almost impossible to determine a series of sensory thresholds without some general tendency, either to bring them towards the desired shape, or else—endeavoring to escape such bias—to force them in the opposite direction. To convince others of our impartiality may be harder still. Even this sort of deviation is to be remedied by our proposed exact method of procedure, for by it we obtain perfectly definite results which any impartial experimenters may positively corroborate or refute.

"Attenuation" by Errors.

It will be obvious that a correlation does not simply depend on the amount of concording factors in the two compared series, but solely on the proportion between these concording elements on the one hand and the discording ones on the other. In our example, it did not matter whether A and B each had one pound or a thousand pounds in the common funds, but only whether the amount was a small or large fraction of their whole incomes. If the discordance, $1 - x$, be nil, then the concordance, x, is thereby perfect, that is, $= 1$; and if the influence of the discordant elements be sufficiently increased, then any concordance will eventually become infinitely small.

To consider a still more concrete example, suppose three balls to be rolled along a well-kept lawn; then the various distances they go will be almost perfectly correlated to the various forces with which they were impelled. But let these balls be cast with the same inequalities of force down a rough mountain side; then the respective distances eventually attained will have but faint correspondence to the respective original momenta.

Thus it will be clear that here the accidental deviations have a new consequence simultaneous with, but quite distinct from, that discussed in the last chapter. For there, they impartially augmented and diminished the correlation, tending in a prolonged series to always more and more perfectly counterbalance one another; and in ordinary measurements, this is their sole result. But here in correlations, they also have this new effect which is always in the direction of "attenuating" the apparent correspondence and whose amount, depending solely on the size of the middle error, cannot be in the least eliminated by any prolongation of the series. The deviation has thus become general or "systematic."

Now, suppose that we wish to ascertain the correspondence between a series of values, p, and another series, q. By practical observation we evidently do not obtain the true objective values, p and q, but only approximations which we will call p′ and q′. Obviously, p′ is less closely connected with q′, than is p with q, for the first pair only correspond at all by the intermediation of the second pair; the real correspondence between p and q, shortly r_{pq} has been "attenuated" into $r_{p'q'}$.

To ascertain the amount of this attenuation, and thereby discover the true correlation, it appears *necessary to make two or more independent series of observations of both p and q.* Then,

$$ r_{pq} = \frac{r_{p'q'}}{\sqrt{r_{p'p'} \cdot r_{q'q'}}} $$

where $r_{p'q'}$ = the mean of the correlations between each series of values obtained for p with each series obtained for q.

$r_{p'p'}$ = the average correlation between one and another of these several independently obtained series of values for p.

$r_{q'q'}$ = the same as regards q.

and r_{pq} = the required real correlation between the true objective values of p and q.

Thus, if for each characteristic two such independent series of observations be made, say $p_1 \ p_2 \ q_1$ and q_2, then the true

$$ r_{pq} = \frac{r_{p_1q_1} + r_{p_1q_2} + r_{p_2q_1} + r_{p_2q_2}}{4 \sqrt{(r_{p_1p_2} \times r_{q_1q_2})}} $$

Should circumstances happen to render, say, p_1, much more accurate than p_2, then the correlations involving p_1 will be considerably greater than those involving p_2. In such case, the numerator of the above fraction must be formed by the geometrical instead of by the arithmetical mean; hereby the accidental errors of the respective observations cease to eliminate one another and therefore double their final influence; they also introduce an undue diminution of the fraction.*

In some exceptional and principally very theoretical cases, it may happen that either of the actual measurements, say p'_1 is connected with q' (or q) quite independently of p or any other link common to p'_2. Then, the correlation $r_{p'q'}$ will be to that extent increased without any proportional increase in $r_{p'p''}$; hence our above formula will fallaciously present too large a value.

A greater practical difficulty is that of obtaining two series sufficiently independent of one another. For many errors are likely to repeat themselves; even two separate observers are generally, to some extent, warped by the same influences; we are all imposed on by, not only the "Idola Specus," but also the "Idola Tribus" and the "Idola Fori." In such case, the above formula is still valid, only its correction does not go quite far enough,—a fallacy at any rate on the right side.

An actual instance will best show the urgent necessity of correcting this attenuation. In a correlation between two events, say P and Q, I obtained three independent observations both of P and of Q. The average correlation for those of P with those for Q was 0.38 ($= r_{p'q'}$); the average correlation of those for P with one another was 0.58 ($= r_{p'p'}$); the same for Q was 0.22 ($= r_{q'q'}$). Therefore, the correspondence between the real events, P and Q, comes by reckoning to $\dfrac{0.38}{\sqrt{0.58 \times 0.22}} =$ approximately 1; so that the correspondence, instead of being merely 0.38, appeared to be absolute and complete.

Attenuation by errors can also be corrected in another manner, which has the great advantage of an independent empirical basis, and therefore of not being subject to either of the two above mentioned fallacies besetting the other method. Hence, when the results coincide both ways, the fallacies in question may thereby be considered as disproved, for it is very unlikely that they should both be present and in such proportions as to exactly cancel one another. In this method, instead of directly employing the values p_1 p_2 p_3, etc., we amalgamate them into a single list; by this means we clearly eliminate *some portion* of the individual observational errors, and

* By an inversion of the above formula, the correlation between two series of observations will be found a useful measure of the accuracy of the observations.

thereby we cause any really existing correspondence to reveal itself in greater completeness. Now, this increase in correlation from this partial elimination of errors will furnish a measure of the increase to be expected from an *entire* elimination of errors. Assuming the mean error to be inversely proportional both to this increase in the correlation and to the square root of the number of lists amalgamated, the relation will be:

$$ r_{pq} = \frac{\sqrt[4]{mn} \cdot r_{p''q''} - r_{p'q'}}{\sqrt[4]{m\,n} - 1} $$

where m and n = the number of independent gradings for p and q respectively,

$r_{p'q'}$ = the mean correlation between the various gradings for p and those for q,

and $r_{p''q''}$ = the correlation of the amalgamated series for p with the amalgamated series for q.

In the above quoted instance, the three observations for series P were amalgamated into a single list, and similarly those for series Q. Upon this being done, the two amalgamated lists now presented a correlation with one another of no less than 0.66 ($= r_{p''q''}$). Thus by this mode of reckoning, the real correspondence became

$$ = \frac{\sqrt[4]{3 \times 3} \times 0.66 - 0.38}{\sqrt[4]{3 \times 3} - 1} = \text{once more approximately 1,} $$

so that this way also the correspondence advanced from 0.38 to absolute completeness.

If more than two independent series of observations are available, we may acquire additional evidence by trying the effect of *partial* amalgamation. Instead of throwing all our obtained values together, we may form a set of smaller combinations for each of the two compared characteristics, and then see the mean correlation between one set and the other. In our above instance instead of summarily considering $p'_1 p'_2 p'_3$, we can have $p'_1 p'_2$, $p'_1 p'_3$, and $p'_2 p'_3$, and find out their mean correlation with similar values for q. This works out actually to 0.55. Hence

$$ r_{pq} = \frac{\sqrt[4]{2 \times 2} \times 0.55 - 0.38}{\sqrt{2 \times 2} - 1} = \text{approximately 1.} $$

Thus, again, by this third way, where both terms are the mean of 9 observed correlational values, the correspondence once more rises from the apparent 0.38 to the real 1.*

---

* The exactness of the coincidence between the two methods of correction is in the above instance neither greater nor less than generally occurs in practice. It was

Limits of Associative Problems.

We have seen that "the length of the arm is said to be correlated with that of the leg, because a person with a long arm has usually a long leg and conversely;" also that this correlation is defined mathematically by any constant which determines the function of any definite size of arm to the mean of the sizes of the corresponding legs. These terms, taken literally, are very wide reaching and express what we will call the "universal" correlation between the two organs.

But evidently not the most painstaking investigation can possibly secure any adequately representative sample for such universal correlations, even in the simple case of arms and legs. To begin with, they would have to be equally derived from every stage of growth, including all the prenatal period; since this is the most influential of all causes of variation in size. In the next place, they would have to come from every historical epoch, containing their fair proportion of big Cro-Magnons, little Furfoozers, etc. Further, they must impartially include every living race, from the great Patagonians to the diminutive M'Kabbas; also every social class, from the tall aristocrats to the under-sized slummers.

Practically, then, the universal correlation, even if desirable, is quite inaccessible. We are forced to successively introduce a large number of restrictions: the sample is confined to adults, to moderns, to some particular country, etc., etc. In a word, we are obliged to deal with a *special* correlation.

When we proceed to more narrowly consider these restrictions, it soon becomes clear that they are far from being really detrimental. For every serious investigation will be found to be directed, however vaguely and unconsciously, by some hypothesis as to the causes both of the correspondence and of the digression therefrom. This hypothesis will determine a particular system of restrictions, such as to set the correspondence in the most significant relief.

But from these restrictions will at the same time proceed several kinds of grave errors. In the first place, since the restrictions are not explicitly recognized, they often are not carried out in a manner scientifically profitable; then, the result, however true, may nevertheless be trivial and unsuggestive. For instance, a series of experiments was recently executed by one of our best known psychologists and ended—to his apparent satisfaction—in showing that some children's school-order was largely correlated with their height, weight, and strength. As, however, no steps had been taken to exclude the variations due to difference of age, the only reasonable conclusion seemed to be that as children grow older they both get bigger

---

singled out, in order to show that the formulæ still hold perfectly good even for such an enormous rise as from 0.38 to 1. The possibility of such a rise is due to the unusual conditions of the experiment in question, whereby the three observations of the same objective series presented the extraordinarily small inter-correlation of 0.22.

and go up in the school! Such explanation turned out in fact to probably be the true and sufficient one.

The next fault to be feared is equivocality. For even if the controlling under-thought be good, yet its indistinctness in the mind of the experimenter causes the restriction to be carried out so unsystematically, that the results inevitably become ambiguous and fruitless.

The last is that, even with the clearest purpose, this specialization of the correlation is an exceedingly difficult matter to execute successfully. Only by a profound knowledge of the many factors involved, can we at all adequately exclude those irrelevant to our main intention.

Now, all such elements in a correlation as are foreign to the investigator's explicit or implicit purpose will, like the attenuating errors, constitute impurities in it and will quantitatively falsify its apparent amount. This will chiefly happen in two ways.

"Constriction" and "Dilation."

Any correlation of either of the considered characteristics will have been admitted irrelevantly, if it has supervened irrespectively of the original definition of the correspondence to be investigated. The variations are thereby illegitimately constrained to follow some irrelevant direction so that (as in the case of Attenuation) they no longer possess full amplitude of possible correlation in the investigated direction; the maximum instead of being 1 will be only a fraction, and all the lesser degrees of correspondence will be similarly affected; such a falsification may be called "constriction." Much more rarely, the converse or "dilation" will occur, by correlations being irrelevantly excluded. The disturbance is measurable by the following relation:

$$r_{pq} = \frac{r'_{pq}}{\sqrt{1 - r^2_{pv}}}$$

where r'_{pq} = the apparent correlation of p and q, the two variables to be compared,

r_{pv} = the correlation of one of the above variables with a third and irrelevantly admitted variable v.

and r_{pq} = the real correlation between p and q, after compensating for the illegitimate influence of v.

Should any further irrelevant correlation, say r_{pw}, be admitted, then

$$r_{pq} = \frac{r'_{pq}}{\sqrt{1 - r^2_{pv} - r^2_{pw}}}$$

In the reverse case of "dilation,"

$$r_{pq} = r'_{pqd} \cdot \sqrt{1-r^2_{pv} - r^2_{pw}}$$

These formulæ will be easily seen to be at once derivable from the relations stated earlier. Small, irrelevant variations evidently do not affect the result in any sensible degree, while large ones are capable of revolutionizing it.

The following is an actual illustration of this construction. I was investigating the correspondence between on the one hand intelligence at school lessons and on the other the faculty of discriminating musical pitch. The correlation proved to be 0.49. But, upon inquiry, it turned out that more than half of the children took lessons in music and therefore enjoyed artificial training as regards pitch; here, then, was a powerful cause of variation additional and quite irrelevant to the research, which dealt with the correspondence between the two natural faculties. When this disturbant had once been detected, there was no difficulty in eliminating its influence by the above formula; the correspondence between pitch discrimination and music lessons was measured at 0.61; so that the true required correlation became

$$\frac{0.49}{\sqrt{1-0.61^2}} = 0.62.$$

In this particular case, the more desirable course was open of eliminating the constriction, *practically,* by confining the experiment to those children who were learning music and therefore were on a sufficient equality as regards the training. The correlation then gained in this purely empirical way exactly coincided with the former result, being again 0.62.

"Distortion."

Whereas Attenuation and Constriction have wholly tended to reduce the apparent correlation, and Dilation to enlarge it, we now come to a third kind of impurity that may equally well reduce or enlarge. Its effect is thus analogous to the first consequence of accidental errors discussed in the first part of this article, but, unlike the latter, this Distortion does not in the least tend to eliminate itself in the longest series of observations.

Distortion occurs whenever the two series to be compared together both correspond to any appreciable degree with the *same* third irrelevant variant. In this case, the relation is given by

$$r_{pq} = \frac{r^1_{pq} - r_{pv} \cdot r_{qv}}{\sqrt{(1-r^2_{pv})(1-r^2_{qv})}}$$

where r^1_{pq} = the apparent correlation between p and q, the two characteristics to be compared,

r_{pv} and r_{qv} = the correlations of p and q with some third and perturbing variable v,

and r_{pq} = the required real correlation between p and q, after compensating for the illegitimate influence of v.

Should the common correspondence with v have been irrelevantly excluded instead of admitted, the relation becomes

$$r_{pq} = r^1_{pq} \cdot \sqrt{(1-r^2_{pv})\ (1-r^2_{qv})} + r_{pv} \cdot r_{qv}$$

In the course of the same investigation above alluded to, but in another school, the correlation between school intelligence and discrimination of pitch turned out to be -0.25, so that apparently not the cleverer but the stupider children could discriminate best! But now it was observed that a superiority in discrimination had been shown by the older children, amounting to a correlation of 0.55; while, for a then unknown reason, the schoolmaster's estimate of intelligence had shown a very marked (though unconscious) partiality for the younger ones, amounting to a correlation of 0.65. Hence, the true correlation reckoned out to

$$\frac{-0.25 - 0.55 \times (-0.65)}{\sqrt{(1-0.55^2)\ (1-[-0.65]^2)}}$$

$= +0.17$. This latter low but direct correlation was—under the particular circumstances of the experiment—unquestionably about correct; so that the one originally observed of $= -0.25$ would have been entirely misleading.

* * *

Number of Cases Desirable for an Experiment.

This leads us to the important question, as to how many cases it is advisable to collect for a single series of experiments. In actual practice, the greatest diversity has been apparent in this respect; many have thought to sufficiently establish important correlations with less than ten experimental subjects, while others have thought it necessary to gather together at least over a thousand.

Now, a series of experiments is a very limited extract, whose disposition is, nevertheless, to be accepted as a fair sample of the whole immense remainder. Other things equal, then, the larger the sample, the greater its evidential value and the less chance of a mere occasional coincidence being mistaken for the permanent universal tendency.

This danger of accidental deviation has been discussed in the first part and there shown to be strictly measurable by the "probable error." We there saw, also, that this danger can never be entirely eliminiated by *any sample however large,* so that it is necessary to accept some standard less rigorous than absolute certainty as sufficient for all practical purposes;

usually, the danger of mere chance coincidence is considered to be inappreciable when a correlation is observed as much as five times greater than the probable error, seeing that mere chance would not produce this once in a thousand times. Hence, evidently, the accidental deviation depends, not only on the number of cases, but also on the largeness of the really existing correspondence; the more perfect the latter, the fewer the cases that will be required to demonstrate it conclusively; and this tendency is augmented by the fact that the probable error, besides varying inversely with "n," does so to a further extent with "r." It was shown in the same part that the size of the probable error also varies according to the method of calculation—and to such an extent that twenty cases treated in one of the ways described furnish as much certitude as 180 in another more usual way. If the common trifold classification be adopted, an even greater number is required to effect the same purpose; and if the correlation be not calculated quantitatively at all, but instead be presented in the customary fashion to the reader's general impression, then no number of cases whatever appear sufficient to give reasonable guarantee of proof.

While thus the number of subjects is not by any means the sole factor in diminishing even the accidental deviation *it has no effect whatever upon the far more formidable systematic deviation,* except that it indirectly leads to an enormous augmentation thereof. When we are taking great pains to be able to show upon paper an imposing number of cases and a diminutive probable error, we are in the selfsame process most likely introducing a systematic deviation twenty times greater.

From all this, we may gather that the number of cases should be determined by the simple principle, that the measurements to be aggregated together should have their error brought to the *same general order of magnitude.* An astronomical chronometer, with spring-detent escapement, is not the best travelling clock; nor is there any real advantage in graving upon a milestone (as has actually been done by an infatuated mathematician!) the distance to the nearest village in metres to three decimal places. Now, the present stage of Correlational Psychology is one of pioneering; and, instead of a few unwieldy experiments, we require a large number of small ones carefully carried out under varied and well considered conditions. At the same time, however, the probable error must be kept down to limits at any rate small enough for the particular object of investigation to be proved. For such a purpose a probable error may at present be admitted without much hesitation up to about 0.05; so that, by adopting the method of calculation recommended, two to three dozen subjects should be sufficient for most purposes. The precision can always be augmented subsequently, by carrying out similar experiments under similar conditions and then taking averages. Only after a long preliminary exploration of this rougher sort, shall we be in a position to effectually utilize experiments designed and executed from the very beginning on a vast scale.

In the history of psychology this famous paper marks an important milestone as the original work from which factor analysis was to develop. It provoked a storm of controversy from the experimentalists on the one hand and the measurement researchers on the other; it set the stage for the long debate which was to follow over "general" versus "specific" traits.

"General Intelligence," Objectively Determined and Measured*

C. SPEARMAN

1904

CHAPTER I: INTRODUCTORY

Signs of Weakness in Experimental Psychology

To-day, it is difficult to realize that only as recently as 1879 Wundt first obtained from the authorities of Leipsic University one little room for the then novel purpose of a "psychological laboratory."

In twenty-four years, not only has this modest beginning expanded into a suite of apartments admirably equipped with elaborate apparatus and thronged with students from the most distant quarters of the globe, but all over Germany and in almost every other civilized country have sprung up a host of similar institutions, each endeavoring to outbid the rest in perfection. The brief space of time has sufficed for Experimental Psychology to become a firmly established science, everywhere drawing to itself the most vigorous energies and keenest intellects.

But in spite of such a brilliant career, strangely enough this new branch of investigation still meets with resolute, widespread, and even increasing opposition.

And, indeed, when we without bias consider the whole actual fruit so far gathered from this science—which at the outset seemed to promise an almost unlimited harvest—we can scarcely avoid a feeling of great disappointment. Take for an example Education. This is the line of practical inquiry that more than all others has absorbed the energy and talent of the younger workers and that appears to offer a peculiarly favorable field for such methods. Yet at this moment, notwithstanding all the laborious experiments and profuse literature on the subject, few competent and unprejudiced judges will venture to assert that much unequivocal information of capital

* Adapted from *The American Journal of Psychology*, 15 (1904), pp. 201-292. Reprinted by permission of the publisher.

importance has hitherto thus come to light. Nor have the results been more tangible in Psychiatry or in any other department of applied psychology.

Those, then, who have the highest opinion concerning the potentialities of this new science, will feel most bound to critically examine it for any points of structural incompleteness.

The Cause of this Weakness

Most of those hostile to Experimental Psychology are in the habit of reproaching its methods with insignificance, and even with triviality. They regard it as an infatuation to pass life in measuring the exact average time required to press a button or in ascertaining the precise distance apart where two simultaneous pinpricks cannot any more be distinguished from one another; they protest that such means can never shed any real light upon the human soul, unlock the eternal antinomy of Free Will, or reveal the inward nature of Time and Space.

Such blame, however, would appear ill founded—at any rate, in principle. This same apparent triviality lies at the base of every successful science. The three laws of Newton on first inspection are by no means remarkably significant; yet by a large number of instructed persons they have been found implicitly to contain the supreme key to every event on the earth below and in the heavens above. When starting any new branch of mathematics, again, most people have had occasion to be astonished at the curious suddenness with which the seemingly shallow beginnings have shelved down into drowning deep water. The general fact is that our limited intellects can only hope to deal with the infinite complexity of Nature after analyzing it down into its bare unæsthetic elements.

On the other hand, it must frankly be admitted that such a procedure is, after all, only indirect; that it does not immediately handle the things which really interest us, but other things which are believed to accurately enough betoken the former; that the results arrived at concerning the simpler terms are therefore always worthless, except in proportion as their elements have been proved beyond dispute to be identical with those of the more complex terms. Now, even in physical sciences this proof is not such an infallible operation that we can afford to neglect the possibility of lurking errors which may vitiate all our conclusions; and in psychical research such dangers are enormously magnified. When we pass an electric current through water until it vaporizes away into bubbles of hydrogen and oxygen, we can with reasonable precautions be tolerably certain that we have still got in our jars almost the whole of the same material substance, only reduced to simpler forms. But when we assert that the decision of Regulus to vote against making peace with Carthage was no more than a conglomeration of visual, auditory, and tactual sensations in various stages of intensity and association, then there is an undeniable risk that some precious psychical elements may have slipped through our fingers.

On this vital matter, it must reluctantly be confessed that most of Wundt's disciples have failed to carry forward the work in at all the positive spirit of their master. For while the simpler psychoses of the Laboratory have been investigated with great zeal and success, their identification with the more complex psychoses of Life has still continued to be almost exclusively ascertained by the older method of introspection. This pouring of new wine into old bottles has not been to the benefit of either, but rather has created a yawning gulf between the Science and the Reality. The results of all good experimental work will live, but as yet most of them are like hieroglyphics awaiting their deciphering Rosetta stone.

The "Identities" of Science

Here, we naturally arrive at the important question as to what actually constitutes "identity" for scientific purposes.

As regards the material atoms of the physical sciences, this relation is of two orders. There is the Identity in the looser use of the word, which really means no more than uniformity of potential function, or the fact of having like reactions under like conditions; this alone constitutes the proper topic of the science. And then there is the true Identity involved in the metaphysical idea of persistence of substance, which in science is only a convenient working hypothesis to aid in establishing uniformities of the former order.

For psychology, also, the identification is of two orders. First, there is once more Uniformity of Function, and again this appears to be the proper topic of the positive science. But the second order is quite disparate from anything in physics, being that of inward resemblance as ascertained by introspection: such a "Conceptual Uniformity," though in metaphysics perhaps of primary importance, in psychology is but an indispensable substructure—and one of lamentable fallibility. It cannot even be forthwith assumed necessarily to imply complete Functional Uniformity; and it is peculiarly insusceptible of scientific precision, propositions scarcely ever admitting of either decisive confirmation or refutation.

Now, it is one of the great merits of experimental psychology to have largely introduced the direct investigation of these Functional Uniformities, which have the infinite advantage of being eventually susceptible of conclusive proof, and on being securely established are in their turn capable of throwing back a valuable corrective light upon the Conceptual ones also. So far, however, this matter of research seems to have been almost entirely confined to such correspondences as are approximately complete (these, indeed, being the only ones attainable without a new development of methodics). But the vast majority of the functional relations are not thus complete; they are more or less thwarted by other factors; they outwardly present themselves only in the form of stronger or weaker *tendencies*. And precisely of this incomplete nature are most of the Functional Uniformities which connect the psychics of the Laboratory with those of real Life.

Scope of the Present Experiments

The present article, therefore, advocates a "Correlational Psychology," for the purpose of positively determining all psychical tendencies, and in particular those which connect together the so-called "mental tests" with psychical activities of greater generality and interest. These will usually belong to that important class of tendencies produced by community of organism, whereby sufficiently similar acts are almost always performed by any one person in much the same manner; if, for example, he once proves good at discriminating two musical tones, he may be expected to manifest this talent on any subsequent occasion, and even in another portion of the scale.

For finding out the classes and limits of these individual functions, modern psychology seems to have mainly contented itself with borrowing statements from the discredited "faculties" of the older school, and then correcting and expanding such data by inward illumination. The following work is an attempt at the more fatiguing procedure of eliciting verifiable facts; the good intention and the difficulty of such an enterprise may, perhaps, be allowed to palliate the shortcomings in its execution. Our particular topic will be that cardinal function which we can provisionally term "General Intelligence;" first, there will be an inquiry into its exact relation to the Sensory Discrimination of which we hear so much in laboratory work; and then—by the aid of information thus coming to light—it is hoped to determine this Intelligence in a definite objective manner, and to discover means of precisely measuring it. Should this ambitious programme be achieved even in small degree, Experimental Psychology would thereby appear to be supplied with the missing link in its theoretical justification, and at the same time to have produced a practical fruit of almost illimitable promise.

CHAPTER II: HISTORICAL AND CRITICAL

History of Previous Researches

[Here Spearman reviews the literature of attempts to measure intelligence, largely through psychophysical tests of discrimination, perception, memory span, tapping speed, reaction time, susceptibility to illusions, and so on. He recognizes the work of Ebbinghaus on completion tests and the suggestions of Binet and Henri as being of an "intermediate character between the elementariness of normal laboratory work and the complexity of practical activities." The work of some thirty-two investigators is summarized, but the findings fail to reveal any clear patterns of relationship.]

*   *   *

Conclusions to be Drawn from these Previous Researches

Thus far, it must be confessed, the outlook is anything but cheerful for our project contemplated at the end of the first part, or, indeed, for Experimental Psychology in general. There is scarcely one positive conclusion concerning the correlation between mental tests and independent practical estimates that has not been with equal force flatly contradicted; and amid this discordance, there is a continually waxing inclination—especially noticeable among the most capable workers and exact results—absolutely to deny any such correlation at all.

Here, then, is a strange enough answer to our question. When Laboratory and Life, the Token and the Betokened, are at last objectively and positively compared as regards one of the most important Functional Uniformities, they would seem to present no correspondence whatever with one another. Either we must conclude that there is no such thing as general intelligence, but only a number of mental activities perfectly independent of one another except for this common word to designate them, or else our scientific "tests" would appear to have been all so unhappily invented as to lie outside the widest limits of those very faculties of which they are supposed to form a concentrated essence.

It is true that Functional Uniformities might conceivably exist of other kinds; but for any such there is even less evidence; nor would they appear at all a priori probable, in view of the complete and surprising absence of that important one constituted by community of organism. Failing all Functional Uniformities, any connection between the experimental procedure and practical intelligence can then be no more than "Conceptual." But this is a position scarcely tenable for those whose chief claim is finally to have escaped from the endless tangle of purely introspective argument; moreover, such an admission would shear every experimental research of almost its whole worth and deprive the systems built thereon of their essential base.

Further, if thus the only correspondences hitherto positively tested, those between intelligence and its variously supposed Quintessences, have totally failed to reveal any real existence, what shall we say of all the other by no means so apparently self-evident correspondences postulated throughout experimental psychology and forming its present backbone? To take one of the most extensive and painstaking of them, Dr. Schuyten, from 1893 to 1897, continuously amassed evidence to prove a close relation of the middle European temperature with the faculty of "voluntary attention" and even more generally with "the intensity of cerebral activity;" he seem to have repeated his observations on about five hundred different days, upon each occasion indefatigably proceeding round Antwerp from one school to another, visiting most of the time as many as eight. Now, his actual test of "voluntary attention" and "cerebral activity" consisted entirely in noting how many children kept their eyes on their lesson books for five consecutive minutes; but, as far as I am aware, there has not yet been any positive proof that this posture sufficiently coincides with all the other activities coming under this general term of "voluntary attention;" and in view of the universal breakdown of evidence for much more plausible correlations, Schuyten's a priori assumption can hardly be admitted as an adequate basis for his wide reaching theoretical and practical conclusions. To try another example, we have seen that a favorite test, successively adopted by Oehrn, Bourdon, and Binet, is that of erasing from a printed page certain given letters of the alphabet; but sceptics are still able to contend that because any person can dash a stroke through a's and i's with unusual speed, he need not therefore be summarily assumed to possess an abnormally large capacity for discrimination generally speaking, say, for telling a fresh from an over-night deer's trail, or distinguishing sound financial investments from un-sound. Precisely similar criticism may be extended to almost the whole mass of laborious attempts to establish practical applications of Experi-mental Psychology, whether for pedagogical, medical, or other purposes.

Nor is the case much otherwise even with those stricter and more theo-retical researchers who are rather inclined to regard as superficial any ex-periments involving large numbers of subjects. For however modest and precise may seem the conduct of their own actual investigation, it nearly always terminates with and justifies itself by a number of sweeping con-clusions; and these latter will be found to essentially imply some assumed general function or process, such as "memory," "association," "attention," "fatigue," "practice," "will," etc., and at the same time that this function is adequately represented by the laboratory test. To take for instance the speed of mental association, there is hardly a psychologist of note who has not at some time or other made wide reaching assertions on this point, often indeed finding herein one of the pillar stones of his philosophy; the more practically minded, as Kraepelin and his school, content themselves with demonstrating the details of its actual conduct, showing us how the rate will rise with practice or on imbibing tea, how it sinks in proportion to fatigue or mental disorder, how under the influence of alcohol it for a brief moment slightly ascends and then becomes permanently and profoundly depressed. But all these conclusions are derived from observation of one or two supposed typical forms of this "association;" while the extensive experiments of Aiken, Thorndike, and Hubbell reveal that every form of association, however closely similar on introspection, must, nevertheless, always be considered separately on its own merits, and that "quickness of association as an ability determining the speed of all one's associations is a myth." The most curious part of the general failure to find any correspond-ence between the psychics of the Laboratory and those of Life is that experimental psychologists on the whole do not seem in any way disturbed by it. But sooner than impute to them—the avowed champions of positive evidence—such a logical crime as to prefer their own a priori convictions to this mass of testifying facts, it is perhaps pardonable to suspect that many of them do not realize the full significance of the situation!

Criticism of Prevalent Working Methods

There is, however, an intermediate way between ignoring all this serious testimony and submissively accepting it; this consists in subjecting it to the most searching criticism of which one is capable. . . . For the present, we must limit ourselves to the following brief exposition of the chief deficiencies appearing especially to characterize the long series of experiments just reviewed.

In the first place, only one out of them all (Wissler at Columbia) attains to the first fundamental requisite of correlation, namely, a *precise quantitative expression*. Many writers, indeed, have been at great trouble and have compiled elaborate numerical tables, even bewilderingly so; but nowhere do we find this mass of data focused to a single exact result. In consequence, not only has comparison always been impossible between one experiment and another, but the experimenters themselves have proved quite unable to correctly estimate even their own results; some have conceived their work to prove that correspondence was absent when it really existed to a very considerable amount; whereas others have held up as a large correlation what in reality is insignificantly small. Later on, we shall come upon examples of both kinds of bias. With this requisite is closely bound up another one no less fundamental, namely, that the ultimate result should not be presented in some form specially devised to demonstrate the compiler's theory, but rather should be a perfectly impartial representation of the *whole* of the relations elicited by the experiments.

Next, with the same exception as before, not one has calculated the "probable error;" hence, they have had no means whatever of judging how much of their results was merely due to *accidental coincidence*. This applies not only to the experiments executed with comparatively few subjects, but even to those upon the most extensive scales recorded. The danger of being misled by combinations due to pure chance does, indeed, depend greatly upon the number of cases observed, but in still larger degree upon the manner in which the data are calculated and presented.

Thirdly, in no case has there been any clear explicit definition of the problem to be resolved. A correspondence is ordinarily expressed in such a general way as neither admits of practical ascertainment nor even possesses any great theoretical significance; for a scientific investigation to be either possible or desirable, we must needs restrict it by a large number of qualifications. Having done so, any influence included (or excluded) in contravention of our definition must be considered as an *irrelevant and falsifying factor*. Now, in many of the experiments that we have been discussing, even in those upon quite a small scale, the authors have tried to kill

as many birds as possible with one stone and have sought after the greatest
—instead of the least—diversity; they have purposely thrown together
subjects of all sorts and ages, and thus have gone out of their way to invite
fallacious elements into their work. But in any case, even with the best of
intentions, these irrelevant factors could not possibly be adequately obviated,
until some method had been discovered for *exactly measuring* them and
their effect upon the correlation; this, to the best of my knowledge, has
never been done. As will presently be seen, the disturbance is frequently
sufficient to so entirely transform the apparent correlation, that the latter
becomes little or no evidence as to the quantity or even direction of the
real correspondence.

Lastly, no investigator seems to have taken into any consideration another very large source of fallacy and one that is inevitably present in every
work, namely, the *errors of observation*. For having executed our experiment and calculated the correlation, we must then remember that the latter
does not represent the mathematical relation between the two sets of real
objects compared, but only between the two sets of measurements which we
have derived from the former by more or less fallible processes. The result
actually obtained in any laboratory test must necessarily have in every case
been perturbed by various contingencies which have nothing to do with
the subject's real general capacity; a simple proof is the fact that the
repetition of an experiment will always produce a value somewhat different
from before. The same is no less true as regards more practical appraise-
ments, for the lad confidently pronounced by his teacher to be "dull" may
eventually turn out to have quite the average share of brains. These un-
avoidable discrepancies have always been ignored, apparently on some
tacit assumption that they will act impartially, half of them tending to
enhance the apparent correlation and half to reduce it; in this way,
it is supposed, the result must in the long run become more and more
nearly true. Such is, however, not at all the case; these errors of observation
do not tend to wholly compensate one another, but only partially so; every
time, they leave a certain balance *against the correlation,* which is in no
way affected by the number of cases assembled, but solely by the size of
the mean error of observation. The amount of consequent falsification is in
physical inquiry often unimportant, but in psychology it is usually large
enough to completely vitiate the conclusion. This falsifying influence has in
many of the above experiments, especially the more extensive ones, occurred
in exaggerated form; for even those experimenters who are most careful in
the ordinary routine of the laboratory have yet allowed themselves to be
seduced by the special difficulties attending this sort of work; urged on the
one hand by the craving after an imposing array of cases—somewhat ad
captandum vulgus—and sternly restricted on the other side by various
personal considerations (such as restiveness and fatiguability of the youthful
subjects, fear of deranging school hours, etc.), they have too often fallen

into almost incredibly hurried and inadequate methods of testing. Here, again, mere goodness of intention will not avail beyond a very limited extent, for the most painstaking work is far from entitling us to assume that the observational fallacy has been reduced to insignificant dimensions; we can have no satisfactory guarantee, until some method has been devised of precisely measuring the disturbance, and this does not seem to have ever been attempted.

The above criticism, of a perfectly general nature, must suffice for the bulk of the researches cited in this chapter; later on will be found a more detailed examination of those three particular ones which have dealt with precisely the same topic as the present article. If here methodological imperfections have admitted of formulation with unusual sharpness, the fact must by no means be taken as an especial condemnation of these and kindred experiments. Certain faults have, indeed, been especially prominent, as, for instance, the large errors of observation; but, on the whole, the majority of them would appear to contain at least as much good solid work as most of those more strictly confined to the laboratory and to a very small number of "trained" subjects; the former have only afforded a firmer foothold for criticism, because they have confined the question to a more simple unequivocal issue—though not yet nearly *enough* so—and because they have assailed their problem in a square positive manner. The final inconclusiveness of all their labor is not so much due to individual shortcomings of the investigators, or even of the whole branch of investigation, as to the general non-existence of any adequate system for proving and measuring associative tendencies.

Under all these circumstances, in spite of the many previous inconclusive and negatory verdicts, the question of correspondence between the Tests of the Laboratory and the Intelligence of Life cannot yet be regarded as definitely closed. The only thing so far demonstrated is that the old means of investigation are entirely inadequate. The present undertaking, therefore, has only ventured once more to approach the problem, because believing to have elaborated a new and reasonably complete methodological procedure, such as appears capable of at last bringing light upon this and innumerable other important regions hitherto inexplorable.

CHAPTER III: PRELIMINARY INVESTIGATION

[At this point Spearman details the methods for obviating the four criticisms above. He introduces the correlation coefficient, estimates of probable error, and formulas for computing reliability, and he urges greater concern with experimental procedures and techniques. He then reviews the literature on factors affecting discrimination of pitch, weight, and shades of gray as a preliminary to his use of these as measurements of individual skills.]

CHAPTER IV: DESCRIPTION OF THE PRESENT EXPERIMENTS

The Choice of Laboratory Psychics

We will now turn to a description of the experiments that form the basis of the present article. Their many deficiencies can scarcely be clearer to any one than to their author; so true is it that we first learn how properly to conduct any experiment—when we have ended it.

As regards the nature of the selected Laboratory Psychics, the guiding principle has been the opposite to that of Binet and Ebbinghaus. The practical advantages proffered by their more complex mental operations have been unreservedly rejected in favor of the theoretical gain promised by utmost simplicity and unequivocality; there has been no search after condensed psychological extracts to be on occasion conveniently substituted for regular examinations; regardless of all useful application, that form of psychical activity has been chosen which introspectively appeared to me as the simplest and yet pre-eminently intellective. This is the act of distinguishing one sensation from another.

With respect to the particular senses preferred, the present experiments have been confined to Hearing, Sight, and Touch. The other five, Taste, Smell, Pain, Heat, and Cold, do not admit of such practicable or satisfactory examination; also, probably on this account, they have as yet been investigated very incompletely, and therefore do not form a good unequivocal foundation for research of more advanced order. Further, in the chosen three we have already the widest range of type: for Touch is the most direct of the senses, the physiological organ being apparently of such a simple structure as to convey the stimulus to the brain in a purely mechanical manner; Sight, on the other hand, offers the most perfect example of peripheral transformation, seeing that our visual presentations are but very remotely derived from the really external ether waves with which they are popularly confused; while Sound gives us a half-way stage between the above extremes.

In all three cases, the test has been of relative, not of so-called "absolute," Discrimination; the trial has not been as to how small an external stimulus can cause a sensation perceptible at all, but as to how great the difference in the external stimuli has to be for the reagent to notice any difference in the sensation; everyone knows the uncertainties attending the former kind of investigation. Similar motives have in Sound made Pitch seem preferable to Intensity; and in Light, Luminosity to Color. It is perhaps less easy to justify Touch being represented by that form of it often termed the "muscular sense," which despite its notoriety and historical importance is now well known to be really most complex and obscure. Among other reasons for this choice, it was desired to see whether any correlation of Discrimination with Intelligence might not reasonably be attributed to adroitness in outward approach to the distinguishment rather than to superiority in the essential act itself; should this be the case, then the correspondence should be much more manifest in an active practical comparison of two weights than in the purely passive acceptance of two tones.

In short, the experiments were so chosen that any conclusions very uniformly attained in these three ways might be provisionally considered to hold good for Sensory Discrimination in general.

[The writer here reports on his selection of instruments for measuring discrimination and describes the testing of five experimental groups. Two of these groups (twenty-four children from a "village school" and thirty-three children from an upper-class preparatory school) are retained for careful analysis; the others are dropped from discussion. Intelligence was estimated by teacher and peer rating in the village school and by examination marks in the preparatory school. Spearman exhibits his methodological virtuosity by correcting and recorrecting his correlation coefficients for such factors as assumed reliability of the discrimination tests, the estimated reliability of ratings, and the effect of age and musical training. His corrected coefficient for the theoretical relationship between general discrimination and general intelligence approximates +1.00, which leads him to argue for the "theoretical unity of the intellective function."

It is clear to us now that such corrections on small samples are likely to be extraordinarily misleading, especially when the reliabilities of the instruments are low, but Spearman's work was a pioneering venture and may be excused on that ground.

Further study of his data in the preparatory school leads him to the famous argument for the "hierarchy of the intelligence."]

The Hierarchy of the Intelligences

The Theorem of Intellective Unity leads us to consider a corollary proceeding from it logically, testing it critically, and at once indicating some of its important practical uses. This corollary may be termed that of the Hierarchy of the Specific Intelligences.

For if we consider the correspondences between the four branches of school study, a very remarkable uniformity may be observed. English and French, for instance, agree with one another in having a higher correlation with Classics than with Mathematics. Quite similarly, French and Mathematics agree in both having a higher correlation with Classics than with English. And the same will be found to be the case when any other pair is compared with the remainder. The whole thus forms a *perfectly constant Hierarchy* in the following order: Classics, French, English, and Mathematics. This unbroken regularity becomes especially astonishing when we regard the minuteness of the variations involved, for the four branches have average correlations of 0.77, 0.72, 0.70, and 0.67 respectively.

When in the same experimental series we turn to the Discrimination of

Pitch, we find its correlations to be of slightly less magnitude (raw) but in precisely the same relative rank, being: 0.66 with Classics, 0.65 with French, 0.54 with English, and 0.45 with Mathematics. Even in the crude correlations furnished by the whole school without excluding the non-musicians, exactly the same order is repeated, though with the general diminution caused by the impurity: Classics 0.60, French 0.56, English 0.45, and Mathematics 0.39.

Just the same principle governs even Musical Talent, a faculty that is usually set up on a pedestal entirely apart. For it is not only correlated with all the other functions, but once again in precisely the same order: with Classics 0.63, with French 0.57, with English 0.51, with Mathematics 0.51, and with Discrimination 0.40. Ability for music corresponds substantially with Discrimination of tones, but nevertheless not so much as it does with algebra, irregular verbs, etc.

The actual degree of uniformity in this Hierarchy can be most conveniently and summarily judged from the following table of correlation; the values given are those actually observed (theoretical correction would modify the relative order, but in no degree affect the amount of Hierarchy or otherwise). Each number shows the correlation between the faculty vertically above and that horizontally to the left; except in the oblique line italicized, the value always becomes smaller as the eye travels either to the right or downwards.

	Classics	French	English	Mathem.	Discrim.	Music
Classics,	*0.87*	0.83	0.78	0.70	0.66	0.63
French,	0.83	*0.84*	0.67	0.67	0.65	0.57
English,	0.78	0.67	*0.89*	0.64	0.54	0.51
Mathem.,	0.70	0.67	0.64	*0.88*	0.45	0.51
Discrim.,	0.66	0.65	0.54	0.45		0.40
Music,	0.63	0.57	0.51	0.51	0.40	

Altogether, we have a uniformity that is very nearly perfect and far surpasses the conceivable limits of chance coincidence. When we consider that the probable error varies between about 0.01 for the ordinary studies to about 0.03 for music, it is only surprising that the deviations are not greater. The general Hierarchy becomes even more striking when compared with the oblique line, which is no measure of the central Function and where consequently the gradation abruptly and entirely vanishes.[1]

----

[1] The only other data of this kind with which I am acquainted are some comparisons made between the different branches of study at the Columbia University. The correlations there obtained, which were throughout somewhat smaller than the above, manifest only a limited concordance with our above principle of Hierarchy. But a university is clearly not the place in which to look for natural correspondence between functions; at that time of life, strong ties of a wholly artificial sort have intervened; each student singles out for himself that particular group of studies tending to his main purpose and devotes to them the most judicious amounts of

The above correlations are raw, and therefore do not tell us either the true rank of the respective activities or the full absolute saturation of each with General Intelligence. For the former purpose we must eliminate the observational errors, and for the latter our result must further be *squared*. Thus we get:

Activity	Correlation with Gen. Intell.	Ratio of the common factor to the specific factor
Classics,	0.99	99 to 1
Common Sense,	0.98	96 4
Pitch Dis.,	0.94	89 11
French,	0.92	84 16
Cleverness,	0.90	81 19
English,	0.90	81 19
Mathematics,	0.86	74 26
Pitch Dis. among the uncultured,	0.72	52 48
Music,	0.70	49 51
Light Dis.,	0.57	32 68
Weight Dis.,	0.44	19 81

It is clear how much the amount of any observable raw correlation depends upon the two very different influences: first, there is the above intellective saturation, or extent to which the considered faculty is functionally identical with General Intelligence; and secondly, there is the accuracy with which we have estimated the faculty. As regards the ordinary school studies, this accuracy is indicated by the oblique italicized line, and therefore appears about equal in all cases (not in the least following the direction of the Hierarchy); but in other cases there is a large divergence on this head, which leads to important practical consequences. Mathematics, for example, has a saturation of 74 and Common Sense has one of about 96; but in actual use the worth of these indications becomes reversed, so that a subjective impression as to a child's "brightness" is a less reliable sign than the latter's rank in the arithmetic class; almost as good as either appears a few minutes' test with a monochord.

In the above Hierarchy one of the most noticeable features is the high position of languages; to myself, at any rate, it was no small surprise to find Classics and even French placed unequivocally above English (note that this term does not refer to any study of the native tongue, but merely to the aggregate of all the lessons conducted therein, such as History, Geography, Dictation, Scripture, and Repetition).

However it may be with these or any other special facts, here would seem to lie the long wanted general rational basis for public examinations. Instead of continuing ineffectively to protest that high marks in Greek

---

relative energy. To determine natural correlations, we must go to where the pupils meet each other in every department on relatively equal terms.

syntax are no test as to the capacity of men to command troops or to administer provinces, we shall at last actually determine the precise accuracy of the various means of measuring General Intelligence, and then we shall in an equally positive objective manner ascertain the exact relative importance of this General Intelligence as compared with the other characteristics desirable for the particular post which the candidate is to assume (such as any required Specific Intelligences, also Instruction, Force of Will, Physical Constitution, Honesty, Zeal, etc.; though some of these factors cannot easily be estimated separately, there is no insuperable obstacle to weighing their *total influence* as compared with General Intelligence). Thus, it is to be hoped, we shall eventually reach our pedagogical conclusions, not by easy subjective theories, nor by the insignificant range of personal experiences, nor yet by some catchpenny exceptional cases, but rather by an adequately representative array of established facts.

* * *

Summary of Conclusions

To conclude, the following is a brief summary of the principal conclusions indicated by the foregoing experiments:

I. The results hitherto obtained in respect of psychic correlation would, if true, be almost fatal to experimental psychology as a profitable branch of science. But none of these results, as at present standing, can be considered to possess any value other than suggestive only; this fact is not so much due to individual shortcomings of the investigators, as to the general non-existence of any adequate system of investigation.

II. On making good this methodological deficiency, there is found to actually occur a correspondence—continually varying in size according to the experimental conditions—between all the forms of Sensory Discrimination and the more complicated Intellectual Activities of practical life.

III. By this same new system of methodics, there is also shown to exist a correspondence between what may provisionally be called "General Discrimination" and "General Intelligence" which works out with great approximation to *one or absoluteness.* Unlike the result quoted in the preceding paragraph, this phenomenon appears independent of the particular experimental circumstances; it has nothing to do with the procedure selected for testing either Discrimination or Intelligence, nor with the true representativeness of the values obtained by these tests, nor even with the homogeneousness of the experimental reagents; if the thesis be correct, its proof should be reproducible in all times, places, and manners—on the sole condition of adequate methodics.

IV. The above and other analogous observed facts indicate *that all branches of intellectual activity have in common one fundamental function (or group of functions), whereas the remaining or specific elements of the activity seem in every case to be wholly different from that in all the others.* The relative influence of the general to the specific function varies in the ten departments here investigated from 15:1 to 1:4.

V. As an important practical consequence of this universal Unity of the Intellectual Function, the various actual forms of mental activity constitute a stably interconnected Hierarchy according to their different degrees of intellective saturation. Hence, the value of any method of examination as to intellectual fitness for any given post is capable of being precisely ascertained, since it depends upon:

(a) the accuracy with which it can be conducted;

(b) the hierarchical intellective rank of the test;

(c) the hierarchical intellective rank of the duties involved in the post.

Methods have been given whereby all these three points can be sufficiently ascertained.

This paper represents one of the first approaches to the nature-nurture issue through the study of correlations involving twins versus sibling pairs. The genetics of twinning were poorly understood and it is likely that Thorndike's sample contained fraternal as well as identical twins. Nevertheless, the early development of the rationale of this investigation is of considerable interest and the summary contains a good deal of wisdom concerning the relative effects of heredity and environment.

Measurement of Twins*

EDWARD L. THORNDIKE

1905

The following is a summary of the results of a study of the comparative importance of original nature and training in the case of fifty pairs of twins.

The Resemblances of Twins and Siblings

From the information at hand, which is not so satisfactory as information I hope to obtain during the next few years, the resemblance of twins in mental traits is roughly twice that of ordinary siblings; according to the actual figures of my measurements of siblings, more than twice. I have reason, however, to believe that the correlation coefficients obtained for siblings are affected by constant errors which make them too low; namely, the selection of mentally alike pairs by the conditions of the methods of obtaining siblings and the absence of suitable data to make sufficient correction for attenuation. Table I gives the facts.

TABLE I
The Resemblances of Twins and Siblings Compared

| | Coefficients of correlation | |
Ability	Twins	Siblings
"A" test	.69	.32
Word test	.71	.29
Opposites test	.90	.30

I use the words "resemblance of" and "likeness of" as synonyms for "coefficients of correlation between." A resemblance of .50 means, a

* The Journal of Philosophy, Psychology and Scientific Method, 2 (1905), pp. 547-553. Reprinted by permission of the Journal of Philosophy, Inc.

Pearson correlation coefficient of .50. I use the terms A test, word test, misspelled word test, opposites test, addition and multiplication to mean the tests, or at times the abilities measured by the tests, to describe which would take too much space. I give for siblings the obtained results. Since the correction for attenuation had to be made in an imperfect form, the true resemblances are probably somewhat higher, but not over .40.

The Resemblances of Young and of Old Twins

The older twins show no closer resemblance than the younger twins, and the chances are surely four to one that with an infinite number of twins tested the 12-14 year olds would not show a resemblance .15 greater than the 9-11 year olds. The facts are given in Table II.

TABLE II
The Resemblances of Young and Old Twins Compared

	In corrected coefficients		In raw coefficients	
	Twins 9–11	Twins 12–14	Twins 9–11	Twins 12–14
(1) "A" test	.66	.73	.58	.67
(2) Word test	.81	.62	.62	.49
(3) Misspelled word test	.76	.74	.76	.74
(4) Addition	.90	.54	.83	.46
(5) Multiplication	.91	.69	.81	.53
(6) Opposites	.96	.88	.79	.78
Marks in (1), (2) and (3) combined			.71	.69
Marks in (4), (5) and (6) combined			.90	.75
Averages	.83	.70	.75	.64

The Resemblances in Traits Little and in Traits Much Subject to Training

The variations in the closeness of resemblance of the twins in the different traits show little, and possibly no, direct correlation with the amount of opportunity for environmental influences. The traits most subject to training (addition and multiplication) do show closer resemblances than the traits moderately subject to training (the "A" test and word test); but on the other hand show less close resemblances than the traits moderately subject to training (the misspelled word test and opposites test). The hypothesis that the true resemblance varies in amount inversely with the amount of opportunity for environmental influence would not be irreconcilable with the facts, and the hypothesis that the differences between the different traits are due to chance (including in that term the variable errors of the measurements and the possibility of the unequal inheritance of different traits) is the most probable of all. The difference between the traits most subject and those least subject to training is no greater than the median difference between any one trait of the six and any other. Surely there is no evidence here of any large contribution from similarity of training to similarity of achievement. The facts are given in Table III.

TABLE III
The Resemblances of Twins in Traits Little and in
Traits Much Subject to Training

	Coefficients of correlation	Averages
(1) "A" test	.69⎫	
(2) Word test	.71⎭	.70
(3) Misspelled word test	.80⎫	
(6) Opposites	.90⎭	.85
(4) Addition	.75⎫	
(5) Multiplication	.84⎭	.795
Marks in (1), (2) and (3) combined	.70 (raw)	
Marks in (4), (5) and (6) combined	.82 (raw)	

The Resemblances in Mental Traits Compared with the Resemblances in Physical Traits

It is highly probable from the facts so far given that the similarity of twins in ancestry and conditions of conception and birth accounts for almost all of their similarity in mental achievement,—that only a small fraction of it can be attributed to similarity in training. On general principles it is also highly probable that similarity of ancestry and conditions of conception will produce equal similarity in original physical nature and in original mental nature. Certain resemblances in original physical nature are in all probability neither increased nor decreased by such similarities and differences of home training as act upon twins and non-related children, respectively, within a group such as ours; e.g., resemblances in cephalic index, ratio of height sitting to total height, eye color and hair color. Other resemblances in original physical nature are increased and decreased slightly and perhaps not at all; e.g., circumference of head, length of head, width of head, length of forearm and length of finger joints.

If then, the resemblances of twins were almost entirely due to original nature, we should expect them to be only slightly in excess of the resemblances in physical traits. The existence of the latter as a fact may properly be taken as a partial verification of the former as a general hypothesis. The evidence of its existence is given in Table IV.

Summary and Criticism

These facts prove that among one hundred twins living and attending school in New York City in 1903-4, the mental resemblances of a twin

TABLE IV

The Resemblances of Twins in Mental and in Physical Traits

In mental traits		In physical traits	
1. "A" test	.69	11. Cephalic index	.76
2. Word test	.71	12. Ht. sitting/ht.	.76
3. Misspelled	.80	13. Height	.78
4. Addition	.75	14. Height sitting	.83
5. Multiplication	.84	15. Circ. of head	.75
6. Opposites	.90	16. Width of head	.86
7. Combined mark in 1–3	.70	17. Arm length	.72
8. Combined mark in 4–6	.82	18. Finger length	.71

7, 8 and 12–15 are raw correlations and the correction of attenuation might raise them by .01 or .02.

Median of 1–6	.78	Average of 11–12	.76 (possibly .77)
		„ 13–18	.77 (possibly .78 or .79)
Average of 1–6	.78	Median of 13–18	.77 (possibly .78 or .79)
		„ 11–18	.76 (possibly .77)
Average of 7–8	.76 (Possibly .80)	Average of 11–18	.76 (possibly .77)

pair are about twice as great as those of a pair of siblings similarly chosen, are as great or nearly as great in the case of the younger as of the older half of the group, are as great or nearly as great in the case of the "A," word, misspelled word and opposites test as in the case of addition and multiplication, and are only slightly, if at all, greater than resemblances in physical traits which could have been caused, in some cases, only by original nature.

The facts are easily, simply and completely explained by one simple hypothesis: namely, that the natures of the germ-cells—the conditions of conception—cause whatever similarities and differences exist in the original natures of men, that these conditions influence body and mind equally, and that in life the differences in modification of body and mind produced by such differences as obtain between the environments of present-day New York City public school children are slight.

Certain other hypotheses seem possible at first sight, but become involved in great difficulties when one tries to explain all the facts by any of them. These difficulties I will point out briefly.

It may be said that all that has been proved of the twins is that they are alike in general mental maturity (i.e., in the points of development which they have reached).

Traits like those tested are of course influenced by maturity directly and indirectly through the relation between maturity and advance in school and the relation between the latter and certain of the traits tested. But maturity is by no means the total cause of efficiency in these traits. Nor is it a cause comparable in amount of influence with individual differences apart from maturity. Nor is there any evidence that there is any greater resemblance of twins in maturity than in other factors, such as eyesight. If maturity were the total cause of efficiency in the six traits measured, these traits should in the same individual show perfect correlation with each other. They do not, nor, indeed enough correlation to assign maturity a very important place as a contributory cause. If resemblance in maturity were the cause of the resemblances found, these should be largest in the traits most subject to maturity. The opposite is the case.

It may be said that all that has been proved of the twins is that the environmental conditions from 9 to 14 years count little; that the similarities in environment in utero and during childhood are left as possible causes of the resemblances found; and that these are the real causes. But that the conditions in utero are the cause of the resemblances of related individuals is disproved by the fact that paternal is as great as maternal resemblance in the case of those traits where parents and offspring have been compared; and that similarities in environment from 0 to 9 years should produce a far greater effect on the children's abilities to add, multiply, mark misspelled words and write opposites than do similarities in environment from 9 to 15 is a notion utterly devoid of probability.

It is equally difficult to accept original nature as a cause of a moderate amount of the resemblance found and to explain the rest as due to training. Suppose, for instance, that some one assumes that the force of the germ-natures,—of the conditions of conception, is sufficient to produce a resemblance of .20 in siblings and .40 in twins in mental traits. He must be then willing to believe that the likeness in training of a twin pair is enough greater than the likeness in training of a sibling pair, two or three years apart in age, to make the .40 rise to .80, whereas the .20 rises only to .40 or less. He must also be willing to believe either that inborn mental make-up is inherited by a totally different law from that regulating inborn physical make-up or else that the similarities in training of twins will raise .40 to .80 in physical traits such as cephalic index, and that the similarities in training of siblings will raise the .20 only to .40 or .50. He must also place the bulk of influence of this training previous to the tenth year and assume that it is of such a generalized sort as would raise the resemblances in marking A's or words containing r and e as much as that in multiplication.

Doubtless we all feel a repugnance to assigning so little efficacy to environmental forces as the facts of this study seem to demand; but common opinion also feels a repugnance to believing that the mental resemblances of twins, however caused, are as great as the physical resemblances. Yet they are. I can not here discuss the general facts and detailed studies which bear upon the question of the amount of influence of such likenesses and differences in environment as existed in the case of these twins.

I shall also spend but little time in comments upon the application of the facts so far presented to theories of education and human action and to the practical problems of social control. The inferences with respect to the enormous importance of original nature in determining the behavior and achievements of any man in comparison with his fellows of the same period of civilization and conditions of life are obvious. All theories of human life must accept as a first principle the fact that human beings at birth differ enormously in mental capacities and that these differences are largely due to similar differences in their ancestry. All attempts to change human nature must accept as their most important condition the limits set by original nature to each individual.

We must be careful, however, not to confuse two totally different things: (1) the power of the environment,—for instance, of schools, laws, books and social ideals,—to produce differences in the relative achievements of men, and (2) the power of the environment to produce differences in absolute achievement. It has been shown that the relative differences in certain mental traits which were found in these one hundred children are due almost entirely to differences in ancestry, not in training; but this does not in the least deny that better methods of training might improve all their achievements fifty per cent, or that the absence of training, say in spelling and arithmetic, might decrease the corresponding achievements to zero. Similarly, the fact that Mr. Rockefeller has amassed one of the great fortunes of the age is undoubtedly due almost exclusively to his original capacity, not to circumstances; but this does not deny that it is almost exclusively circumstances which make the average wealth of men to-day greater than it was a thousand years ago or that future changes in the environment might, without any change in capacity make nine men out of ten the owners of automobiles, race-horses, tall hats and the other blessings of wealth.

The argument has been limited entirely to the causes which make one person differ from another in mental achievements under the same general conditions of life at the beginning of the twentieth century in New York City as pupils in its school system. If the resemblance of twins had been measured in the case of a group made up partly of New York City school children and partly of children of equal capacity brought up in the wilds of Africa, the variability of the group in addition and multiplication would have increased and the correlation coefficients would rise. They would then measure the influence of original nature plus the now much increased influence of the environment.

The relative impotence of such similarities of home training as existed in our fifty pairs of twins to create similarities of achievement does, however, make one suspect that the magnitude of the influence of the training given by schools, periods of civilization and the like has been exaggerated. For other reasons, also, I imagine this to be the case, but to prove or disprove it, one would need data quite different from the records of these hundred twins.

It is, then, folly to conclude that the inheritance of mental capacities from immediate ancestry implies the futility of education and social control in general—the wisdom of fatalism and laissez faire. Such studies as this merely prove the existence of and measure one determinant of human intellect and character and demonstrate that the influences of the environment are differential, the product varying not only in accord with the environmental force itself, but also in accord with the original nature upon which it operates. We may even expect that education will be doubly effective, once society recognizes the advantage from or need of wise investment. . . .

To the real work of man for man,—the increase of achievement through the improvement of the environment,—the influence of heredity offers no barrier. But to the popular demands from education and social reforms it does. For the common man does not much appreciate absolute happiness or absolute betterment. He does not rejoice that he and his children are healthier, happier and more supplied with noble pleasures than were his ancestors of a thousand years ago. His complaint is that he is not so well off as some of those about him; his pride is that he is above the common herd. The common man demands relative superiority,—to be above those of his own time and locality. If his son leads the community, he does not mind his real stupidity; to be the handsomest girl in the county is beauty enough. Social discontent comes from the knowledge or fancy that one is below others in welfare. The effort of children in school, of men in labor and of women in the home is, except as guided by the wise instincts of nature or more rarely by the wisdom of abstract thought, to rise above some one who seems higher. Thus the prizes which most men really seek are, after all, in large measure given or withheld by original nature. In the actual race of life, which is not to get ahead, but to get ahead of somebody, the chief determining factor is heredity.

Without question one of the "giants" of this period was Alfred Binet. Probably no psychological innovation has had more impact on the societies of the Western world than the development of the Binet-Simon scales. In place of Spearman's zeal for methodology, Binet had a driving concern for validity and a consistent orientation toward his problem—the measurement of intelligence. Over the course of many years Binet had tried and discarded a host of techniques, including even phrenology and palmistry, in his never-flagging efforts to develop measures which could meet the needs of the clinic and the school.

Dr. Henry H. Goddard, Director of the Vineland Training School and one of the first American psychologists to realize the importance of the work of Binet and Simon, arranged for the translation of many of the papers dealing with the development of the scales in order to better acquaint psychologists with the instrument and to forestall unwarranted criticism. It is difficult now to imagine the departure from accepted thought that the scales represented and the criticism directed at such testing. Goddard himself, though he had worked successfully with the "1905 tests", could not accept initially the "1908 Scale." He writes in his introduction to the translated papers, "Probably no critic of the scale during the past six years has reacted against it more positively than did I at first reading. It seemed impossible to grade intelligence in that way . . . The article was laid aside for some weeks. One day while using the old tests, whose inadequacy was great, . . . I decided to give it a fair trial . . . Our use of the scale was a surprise and a gratification. It met our needs. A classification of our children based on the Scale agreed with the Institution experience."

Binet's writings on intelligence would fill several books. We have tried to select excerpts which show something of the background from which the tests arose, the materials in the tests, and the development of the scale of intelligence.

The Development of Intelligence in Children*

ALFRED BINET and THEOPHILE SIMON

1905–1908

Upon the Necessity of Establishing a Scientific Diagnosis of Inferior States of Intelligence

L'Année Psychologique, 11 (1905), pp. 163–191.

We here present the first rough sketch of a work which was directly inspired by the desire to serve the interesting cause of the education of subnormals.

* Reprinted from *The Development of Intelligence in Children*, by Alfred Binet and Th. Simon (translated by Elizabeth S. Kite). Publication of the Training School

In October, 1904, the Minister of Public Instruction named a commission which was charged with the study of measures to be taken for insuring the benefits of instruction to defective children. After a number of sittings, this commission regulated all that pertained to the type of establishment to be created, the conditions of admission into the school, the teaching force, and the pedagogical methods to be employed. They decided that no child suspected of retardation should be eliminated from the ordinary school and admitted into a special class, without first being subjected to a pedagogical and medical examination from which it could be certified that because of the state of his intelligence, he was unable to profit, in an average measure, from the instruction given in the ordinary schools.

But how the examination of each child should be made, what methods should be followed, what observations taken, what questions asked, what tests devised, how the child should be compared with normal children, the commission felt under no obligation to decide. It was formed to do a work of administration, not a work of science.

It has seemed to us extremely useful to furnish a guide for future Commissions' examination. Such Commissions should understand from the beginning how to get their bearings. It must be made impossible for those who belong to the Commission to fall into the habit of making haphazard decisions according to impressions which are subjective, and consequently uncontrolled. Such impressions are sometimes good, sometimes bad, and have at all times too much the nature of the arbitrary, of caprice, of indifference. Such a condition is quite unfortunate because the interests of the child demand a more careful method. To be a member of a special class can never be a mark of distinction, and such as do not merit it, must be spared the record. Some errors are excusable in the beginning, but if they become too frequent, they may ruin the reputation of these new institutions. Furthermore, in principle, we are convinced, and we shall not cease to repeat, that the precision and exactness of science should be introduced into our practice whenever possible, and in the great majority of cases it is possible.

The problem which we have to solve presents many difficulties both theoretical and practical. It is a hackneyed remark that the definitions, thus far proposed, for the different states of subnormal intelligence, lack precision. These inferior states are indefinite in number, being composed of a series of degrees which mount from the lowest depths of idiocy, to a condition easily confounded with normal intelligence. Alienists have frequently come to an agreement concerning the terminology to be employed for designating the difference of these degrees; at least, in spite of certain individual divergence of ideas to be found in all questions, there has been an agreement to accept *idiot* as applied to the lowest state, *imbecile* to the inter-

at Vineland, New Jersey, No. 11, 1916. By permission of the estate of Henry H. Goddard and the Vineland Training School.

mediate, and *moron* to the state nearest normality. Still among the numerous alienists, under this common and apparently precise terminology, different ideas are concealed, variable and at the same time confused. The distinction between idiot, imbecile, and moron is not understood in the same way by all practitioners. We have abundant proof of this in the strikingly divergent medical diagnoses made only a few days apart by different alienists upon the same patient.

Dr. Blin, physician of the Vaucluse Asylum, recently drew the attention of his fellow physicians to these regrettable contradictions. He states that the children who are sent to the colony come provided with several dissimilar certificates. "One child, called imbecile in the first certificate, is marked idiot in the second, feeble-minded in the third, and degenerate in the fourth." M. Damaye, former house surgeon of Dr. Blin, adds this observation: "One would have only to look through several folders of records belonging to children of the colony, in order to collect almost the same number of different diagnoses."

We cannot sufficiently deplore the consequence of this state of uncertainty recognized today by all alienists. The simple fact, that specialists do not agree in the use of the technical terms of their science, throws suspicion upon their diagnoses, and prevents all work of comparison.

What importance can be attached to public statistics of different countries concerning the percentage of backward children if the definition for backward children is not the same in all countries? How will it be possible to keep a record of the intelligence of pupils who are treated and instructed in a school, if the terms applied to them, feeble-minded, retarded, imbecile, idiot, vary in meaning according to the doctor who examines them? The absence of a common measure prevents comparison of statistics, and makes one lose all interest in investigations which may have been very laborious. But a still more serious fact is that, because of lack of methods, it is impossible to solve those essential questions concerning the afflicted, whose solution presents the greatest interest; for example, the real results gained by the treatment of inferior states of intelligence by doctor and educator; the educative value of one pedagogical method compared with another; the degree of curability of incomplete idiocy, etc. It is not by means of *a priori* reasonings, of vague considerations, of oratorical displays, that these questions can be solved; but by minute investigation, entering into the details of fact, and considering the effects of the treatment for each particular child. There is but one means of knowing if a child, who has passed six years in a hospital or in a special class, has profited from that stay, and to what degree he has profited; and that is to compare his certificate of entrance with his certificate of dismissal, and by that means ascertain if he shows a special amelioration of his condition beyond that which might be credited simply to the considerations of growth. But experience has shown how imprudent it would be to place confidence in this comparison, when the two certificates come from different doctors, who do not judge in exactly the same way, or who use different words to characterize the mental status of patients.

* * *

Perhaps someone will raise an objection and say this uncertainty, has no special application to diagnosis of the degrees of mental debility; it is also to be found in mental pathology and, in a general way, in the diagnosis of all maladies; it is the result of the empirical nature which is characteristic of clinical studies. It might be added, that, if anyone took the trouble to make a statistical study of the divergence in the diagnosis of different physicians upon the same patient, it would probably be found that the percentage of disagreement is very great in all branches of medicine.

We believe it worth while to examine their objection because it permits us to enter more deeply into the analysis of the question. The disagreements of practitioners might come from three very different classes of causes:

1. Ignorance, that is, the lack of aptitude of certain physicians. This is an individual failure, for which abstract science is not responsible. It is certain that, even when the symptoms of a disease are absolutely clear, such a physician might fail to recognize them through incapacity. There are many accountants who make mistakes in calculation, but these errors do not discredit mathematics. . . .

2. The variable meaning of terms. Since the same expression has a different sense according to the person who uses it, it is possible that the disagreement of diagnosis may be simply a disagreement of words, due to the use of different nomenclature.

3. Lack of precision in the description of the symptoms which reveal or which constitute a certain particular malady; different physicians do not examine the same patient in the same manner and do not give the symptoms the same importance; or, it may be they make no effort to find out the precise symptoms, and no effort to analyze carefully in order to distinguish and interpret them.

Of these three kinds of error, which is the one that actually appears in the diagnosis of inferior states of intelligence? Let us set aside the first. There remain the faults of nomenclature, and the insufficiency of methods of examination.

The general belief seems to be that the confusion arises wholly from an absence of a uniform nomenclature. There is some truth in this opinion. . . . Undoubtedly it would be a good work to bring about a unification of this nomenclature as has been done for the standard of measurements and for electric units. But this reform in itself is not sufficient and we are very sure that they deceive themselves who think that at bottom this is only a question of terminology. It is very much more serious. We find physicians who, though using the same terminology, constantly disagree in their diagnosis of the same child. . . . Each one according to his own fancy, fixes the boundary line separating these states. It is in regard to the facts that the doctors disagree.

In looking closely one can see that the confusion comes principally from a fault in the method of examination. When an alienist finds himself in the presence of a child of inferior intelligence, he does not examine him by bringing out each one of the symptoms which the child manifests and by interpreting all symptoms and classifying them; he contents himself with taking a subjective impression, an impression as a whole, of his subject, and of making his diagnosis by instinct. We do not think that we are going too far in saying that at the present time very few physicians would be able to cite with absolute precision the objective and invariable sign, or signs, by which they distinguish the degrees of inferior mentality.

A study of the historical side of the question shows us very clearly that what is lacking is a *precise basis for differential diagnosis*.

*   *   *

Enumeration of symptoms. Authors incorporate into their definitions a great number of motor troubles and disorders of every sort, belonging to the digestive and secretive apparatus, growth, etc. This enumeration would be in place in a clinical record, where all the observable symptoms of a patient are collected; but it has this disadvantage that it misleads the mind, when one attempts a definition where only the essential should be noted. Thus we see the authors laying great stress upon motility, locomotion, prehension and speech in distinguishing the different degrees of idiocy. We admit, that one frequently observes motor troubles with idiots, and that in a general way, the intensity of these troubles is greater in the most profound cases of idiocy. This is not surprising. From the moment that idiocy is admitted to be the result of a number of very different diseases of the brain, it is logical to infer that the diseases which produce an arrested or perverted development in the intellectual functions should also provoke divers disorders in the sphere of motility; as for instance in the respiratory, circulatory, secretory functions, since all the functions of the living being are directly or indirectly under the influence of the nervous system. But it is no less necessary to establish in the definition of idiocy, a distinction between it and troubles of a different nature. Idiocy, as Esquirol was the first to recognize, consists in a weakness of the intelligence. If the physician gives a child the diagnosis of profound idiocy or of imbecility, it is not because the child does not walk, nor talk, has no control over secretions, is microcephalic, has the ears badly formed, or the palate keeled. The child is judged to be an idiot because he is affected in his intellectual development. This is so strikingly true that if we suppose a case presented to us where speech, locomotion, prehension were all nil, but which gave evidence of an intact intelligence, no one would consider that patient an idiot.

It results from these observations that the directing principle of most classifications does not seem to us correct. The view is lost that here it is a question of inferior states of intelligence, and that it is only by taking into account this inferiority that a classification can be established. In other words *a classification of idiocy is a clinical classification to be made by means of psychology.*

Our conception would be badly understood if it were supposed that we intend to eliminate from the definition of idiocy all the purely somatic disorders so frequently observed in these unhappy cases. On the contrary it is very useful to take note of these symptoms, especially in cases where by their nature or their mechanism they reveal to us a mental weakness or insufficiency. They have less value in themselves than in what they imply. Hence the necessity for their analysis. Take for example a child of five years who does not walk. The retardation in locomotion is not in itself a sign of idiocy, since it might come from a great number of anatomical or pathological causes which are quite independent of the functioning of the intelligence, for example, Little's disease, or infantile paralysis. The motility of the lower members must first be examined to see if it is normal and if the members are strong enough to bear the weight of the child and if that which is lacking is only the psychical factor of locomotion, that is to say the desire, the will to walk and the intelligent coördination of the movements of the two limbs. The same analysis must be made in relation to the inability to retain secretions, and in a general manner to all troubles belonging to the sphere of motility, holding firmly in mind the idea that the physical disorders of idiocy have no value except as signs which reveal the intelligence.

The second criticism to the current classifications, which is more serious than the first, has to do with the gradation of the symptoms. After one has perused the formulas which the alienists employ, he perceives that very little has been learned, because of their extreme vagueness. They are merely differences of more or less which are pointed out, and these differences, which are declared sufficient to establish the degrees, and consequently diagnostic differences, are not defined at all.

We are told for profound idiocy: *"There is here a fugitive attention."* What is that—a fugitive attention? In what does it consist? *"Motility exists but a little."* What does "little" signify? We are assured that imbecility differs from idiocy in this: in idiocy *"there is a gleam of intelligence,"* in imbecility *"the intellectual faculties exist in a very incomplete degree."* We should like to know what difference must be established between "a gleam" of intelligence and "very incomplete degree" of the intellectual faculties. We are again informed that in profound idiocy *"the attention is fugitive,"* while in imbecility, *"the attention is fleeting."* We are unable to grasp the distinctive shade of meaning. We are also ignorant of the value of the following symptoms which are noted in the definition of imbecility, *"defective speech,"* *"limited language."* We admit that we have no idea what precise defect of articulation corresponds to "defective speech." There are people who stammer slightly, and others whose speech is scarcely intelligible. All have defective speech. The same remark is true for "limited language." Very many peasants have a limited language. What extent of vocabulary must one possess in order to have a "limited language?" Again we are told for the diagnosis of imbecility *"Will without energy."* These are still the same kind of expressions so vague that they might be applied even to normals. What shall we say of the formula for "slight imbecility"—with which we shall close. ". . . . *the intellectual faculties . . . are noticeably below the faculties of children of the same age."* "Noticeably" is the word which forms the best résumé of the essential character of these classifications.

* * *

We were therefore right in saying as we did, that it is a fixed basis of differential diagnosis which is lacking with the alienists. The vagueness of their formulas reveals the vagueness of their ideas. They cling to characteristics which are by "more or less," and they permit themselves to be guided by a subjective impression which they do not seem to think necessary to analyze, and which therefore would be impossible to justify. We shall never be able to emphasize sufficiently how far removed from scientific methods are such empirical processes. *Quantitative differences, such as we have noted, are of no value unless they are measured, even if measured but crudely.*

In spite of these objections we willingly recognize that alienists, because of their practice and their medical insight, arrive very quickly at judging and classifying a child. But these judgments and these classifications are made by subjective processes, and no alienist would be able to tell with precision, for example, how many years a certain backward child was behind a normal one of the same age. The distinction between slight mental defect and normality, which is so difficult to trace and yet so interesting, remains therefore completely inaccessible.

Following the symptomatic classifications, we find another type, that of *psychological classifications.*

In these, less attention is paid to somatic symptoms, while the interest is concentrated on the degree of intelligence. The idea is quite recent. . . .

P. Sollier was the first to propose a psychological classification, the first, in reality, who attempted to establish a classification of the degrees of idiocy based on a single psychological characteristic. That characteristic is the state of the attention. The author, having formulated this principle, deduces schematically the following division:

Absolute idiocy, characterized by the absolute and complete absence of attention.
Simple idiocy, in which there is weakness or difficulty of attention.
Imbecility, in which there is instability of attention.

This curious attempt seems to us to be rightly directed because it is essentially psychological. It is by a mental quality alone that Sollier attempts to distinguish idiots. Perhaps, however, he did not himself realize the value of the principle which directed him, because he continued to reproduce the definition of his predecessors according to whom idiocy is "an affection of the brain. . . . characterized by trouble with the intellectual, sensory and motor functions." The expression "motor" which he uses seems to prove that, in his thought, idiocy is not exclusively *a mental infirmity*. As to the intellectual faculty by which Sollier chose to distinguish different kinds of idiots, he has made an unhappy selection. Why should he have chosen attention before memory, or imagination, or comprehension, or judgment? This has very truly the appearance of the *a priori* system. A distinction of this nature ought to be made only from observations taken from life. The intellectual functions which are the first to develop should be sought out, how they arrange themselves, in what order they appear, how they coördinate. This is the true, the only method. To be sure this is laborious enough; very many patients must be examined, and when one is willing to analyze concrete facts, he seldom arrives at conclusions that can be elegantly expressed in so brief a formula. These brief formulas belong to literature. The classification of Sollier is more literary than clinical.

*   *   *

In closing this history we wish to speak of a recent experiment, scarcely a year old, due to the efforts of Dr. Blin and his pupil, Dr. Damaye. It has been explained by Dr. Blin, in a short article upon mental weaknesses. Dr. Damaye has shown in detail in a thesis how the method of examination, conceived by his master, can be applied to patients; this thesis contains an account, unfortunately rather brief, but very interesting, of the attempt to apply it to 250 idiots, imbeciles, and morons of the Vaucluse Colony. We have not therefore to judge of a purely theoretical idea, but of a method which has really been applied.

Before entering on its exposition, let us say that in precision Dr. Blin's study seems to us superior to anything previously accomplished. The criticisms which we shall make will not cause us to forget that we have here a first attempt to apply a scientific method to the diagnosis of mental debility.

The method consists of a pre-arranged list of questions which are given to all in such a way that, if repeated by different persons on the same individual, constantly identical results will be obtained. The examination is composed of a series of twenty topics. A certain number of questions, graded in several of the series according to their difficulty, are prepared upon each of these topics.

*   *   *

There are questions that seem superfluous, or of mere erudition (what is the chief town of such and such a department). In some the form is unfortunate; for example those which can be answered by yes or no, because such replies do not sufficiently prove whether the question has been thoroughly understood. It would be better to turn the question so as to oblige the child to somewhat develop his thought if he has one. But these are trifles. That which appears to us in most need of criticism is the method employed for grading the replies. The marking is from 0 to 5. How is it given? It is given by the total of the replies to a topic, that is to say according to the bearing of at least 4 replies. There is no special mark for each question. The examiner judges and estimates as a whole: estimation is subjectively made.

The first note is of the more or less intelligent appearance of the face. It seems that for the others, what is considered especially is the more or less intelligent nature of the replies. It is again a synthetic impression. It seems to us that such an estimate is rather too arbitrary. By this means, there enters into the examination that variable element which one so justly wishes to eliminate. When a questioner marks 5 for the total of replies, he is not certain but that another examiner would mark 4. M. Blin and M. Damaye could have made some control experiments by asking their colleagues to suggest markings according to the written replies submitted to them.

The same arbitrary spirit is found also in the choice of topics. For each topic the same mark is given, thus making them all of equal rank. One assumes therefore that all the topics present the same amount of difficulty, and that there would be the same reward for a child to answer all the questions about names as to answer all those about religion. Again, in each topic the gradation of difficulty seems to have been made equally arbitrarily; that is to say, it would appear that the author has been guided by his own estimation. Moreover, one has the proof in the fact, that the three series of questions, graded according to their difficulty, (1) for children of 10 years, (2) from 10 to 13 years, and (3) for those above 13 years, are nevertheless answered with the maximum of points by children of from 7 to 8 years. It is the same error that we encounter throughout. Consequently, the whole system constitutes a scale established *a priori*. It is possible, and we very willingly believe that in attempting the application it has been found necessary to mend the system, to correct it in certain points, so that it may harmonize better with practice. But whatever may be the importance of these corrections of detail, they do not in the least take away the schematic character of the plan which seems to us to have sprung fully armed from the brain of a theorist.

Here then is what seems to us the chief defect of this method of examination. Notwithstanding this defect, in practice it must necessarily render a real service, because it creates difficulties which all pupils cannot successfully master, and consequently permits us to make a selection among them. Therefore it is small matter that other tests of intelligence might bring about the same result. Small matter that the themes of others give a result on the whole nearly the same. When one has given examinations he sees that. And the method of M. Blin, fundamentally, is only an examination for scholarship, . . . with this advantage we admit, of being a test, whose questions, fixed in advance, do not suffer from the bad humor or the bad digestion of the examiner.

Consequently there is no room for surprise, if we do not find in this collection of questions, any idea upon the gradation of intelligence. The child who has passed through this rolling mill comes before us with a certain total of marks, 36 for instance, or 70. We understand that 70 is nearer normal than 36 and that is all. We have no precise notion of the mental level of these candidates, no notion of what they can or cannot do. Did the one who obtained 36 have any comprehension of abstract ideas? We do not know, and cannot divine. How much is he behind normal children of the same age? We know this no better.

This brings us very naturally to an exposition of the plan of our work. It will be seen that our directing idea is different from that of M. Blin although our system of measurement, like his, is essentially psychological.

A. BINET AND TH. SIMON.

New Methods for the Diagnosis of the Intellectual Level of Subnormals

L'Année Psychologique, 11 (1905), pp. 191–244

Before explaining these methods let us recall exactly the conditions of the problem which we are attempting to solve. Our purpose is to be able to measure the intellectual capacity of a child who is brought to us in order to know whether he is normal or retarded. We should therefore, study his condition at the time and that only. We have nothing to do either with his past history or with his future; consequently we shall neglect his etiology, and we shall make no attempt to distinguish between acquired and congenital idiocy; for a stronger reason we shall set aside all consideration of pathological anatomy which might explain his intellectual deficiency. So much for his past. As to that which concerns his future, we shall exercise the same abstinence; we do not attempt to establish or prepare a prognosis and we leave unanswered the question of whether this retardation is curable, or even improvable. We shall limit ourselves to ascertaining the truth in regard to his present mental state.

*   *   *

To what method should we have recourse in making our diagnosis of the intellectual level? No one method exists, but there are a number of different ones which should be used cumulatively, because the question is a very difficult one to solve, and demands rather a collaboration of methods. It is important that the practitioner be equipped in such a manner that he shall use, only as accessory, the information given by the parents of the child, so that he may always be able to verify this information, or, when necessary, dispense with it. In actual practice quite the opposite occurs. When the child is taken to the clinic the physician listens a great deal to the parents and questions the child very little, in fact scarcely looks at him, allowing himself to be influenced by a very strong presumption that the child is intellectually inferior. If, by a chance not likely to occur, but which would be most interesting some time to bring about, the physician were submitted to the test of selecting the subnormals from a mixed group of children, he would certainly find himself in the midst of grave difficulties, and would commit many errors especially in cases of slight defect.

The organization of methods is especially important because, as soon as the schools for subnormals are in operation, one must be on his guard against the attitude of the parents. Their sincerity will be worth very little when it is in conflict with their interests. If the parents wish the child to remain in the regular school, they will not be silent concerning his intelligence. "My child understands everything," they will say, and they will be very careful not to give any significant information in regard to him. If, on the contrary, they wish him to be admitted into an institution where gratuitous board and lodging are furnished, they will change completely. They will be capable even of teaching him how to simulate mental debility. One should, therefore, be on his guard against all possible frauds.

In order to recognize the inferior states of intelligence we believe that three different methods should be employed. We have arrived at this synthetic view only after many years of research, but we are now certain that each of these methods renders some service. These methods are:

1. *The medical method,* which aims to appreciate the anatomical, physiological, and pathological signs of inferior intelligence.

2. *The pedagogical method,* which aims to judge of the intelligence according to the sum of acquired knowledge.

3. *The psychological method,* which makes direct observations and measurements of the degree of intelligence.

From what has gone before it is easy to see the value of each of these methods. The medical method is indirect because it conjectures the mental from the physical. The pedagogical method is more direct; but the psychological is the most direct of all because it aims to measure the state of the intelligence as it is at the present moment. It does this by experiments which oblige the subject to make an effort which shows his capability in the way of comprehension, judgment, reasoning, and invention.

The Psychological Method

The fundamental idea of this method is the establishment of what we shall call a measuring scale of intelligence. This scale is composed of a series of tests of increasing difficulty, starting from the lowest intellectual level that can be observed, and ending with that of average normal intelligence. Each group in the series corresponds to a different mental level.

This scale properly speaking does not permit the measure of the intelligence, because intellectual qualities are not superposable, and therefore cannot be measured as linear surfaces are measured, but are on the contrary, a classification, a hierarchy among diverse intelligences; and for the necessities of practice this classification is equivalent to a measure. We shall therefore be able to know, after studying two individuals, if one rises above the other and to how many degrees, if one rises above the average level of other individuals considered as normal, or if he remains below. Understanding the normal progress of intellectual development among normals, we shall be able to determine how many years such an individual is advanced or retarded. In a word we shall be able to determine to what degrees of the scale idiocy, imbecility, and moronity correspond.

The scale that we shall describe is not a theoretical work; it is the result of long investigations, first at the Salpêtrière, and afterwards in the primary schools of Paris, with both normal and subnormal children. These short psychological questions have been given the name of tests. The use of tests is today very common, and there are even contemporary authors who have made a specialty of organizing new tests according to theoretical views, but who have made no effort to patiently try them out in the schools. Theirs is an amusing occupation, comparable to a person's making a colonizing expedition into Algeria, advancing always only upon the map, without taking off his dressing gown. We place but slight confidence in the tests invented by these authors and we have borrowed nothing from them. All the tests which we propose have been repeatedly tried, and have been retained from among many, which after trial have been discarded. We can certify that those which are here presented have proved themselves valuable.

We have aimed to make all our tests simple, rapid, convenient, precise, heterogeneous, holding the subject in continued contact with the experimenter, and bearing principally upon the faculty of judgment. Rapidity is necessary for this sort of examination. It is impossible to prolong it beyond twenty minutes without fatiguing the subject. During this maximum of twenty minutes, it must be turned and turned about in every sense, and at least ten tests must be executed, so that not more than about two minutes can be given to each. In spite of their interest, we were obliged to proscribe long exercises. For example, it would be very instructive to know how a subject learns by heart a series of sentences. We have often tested the advantage of leaving a person by himself with a lesson of prose or verse after having said to him, "Try to learn as much as you can of this in five minutes." Five minutes is too long for our test, because during that time the subject escapes us; it may be that he becomes distracted or thinks of other things; the test loses its clinical character and becomes too scholastic. We have therefore reluctantly been obliged to renounce testing the rapidity and extent of the memory by this method. Several other equivalent examples of elimination could be cited. In order to cover rapidly a wide field of observation, it goes without saying that the tests should be heterogeneous.

Another consideration. Our purpose is to evaluate a level of intelligence. It is understood that we here separate natural intelligence and instruction. It is the intelligence alone that we seek to measure, by disregarding in so far as possible, the degree of instruction which the subject possesses. He should, indeed, be considered by the examiner as a complete ignoramus knowing neither how to read nor write. This necessity forces us to forego a great many exercises having a verbal, literary or scholastic character. These belong to a pedagogical examination. We believe that we have succeeded in completely disregarding the acquired information of the subject. We give him nothing to read, nothing to write, and submit him to no test in which he might succeed by means of rote learning. In fact we do not even notice his inability to read if a case occurs. It is simply the level of his natural intelligence that is taken into account.

But here we must come to an understanding of what meaning to give to that word so vague and so comprehensive, "the intelligence." Nearly all the phenomena with which psychology concerns itself are phenomena of intelligence; sensation, perception, are intellectual manifestations as much as reasoning. Should we therefore bring into our examination the measure of sensation after the manner of the psycho-physicists? Should we put to the test all of his psychological processes? A slight reflection has shown us that this would indeed be wasted time.

It seems to us that in intelligence there is a fundamental faculty, the alteration or the lack of which, is of the utmost importance for practical life. This faculty is judgment, otherwise called good sense, practical sense, initiative, the faculty of adapting one's self to circumstances. To judge well, to comprehend well, to reason well, these are the essential activities of intelligence. A person may be a moron or an imbecile if he is lacking in judgment; but with good judgment he can never be either. Indeed the rest of the intellectual faculties seem of little importance in comparison with judgment. What does it matter, for example, whether the organs of sense function normally? Of what import that certain ones are hyperesthetic, or that others are anesthetic or are weakened? Laura Bridgman, Helen Keller and their fellow-unfortunates were blind as well as deaf, but this did not prevent them from being very intelligent. Certainly this is demonstrative proof that the total or even partial integrity of the senses does not form a mental factor equal to judgment. We may measure the acuteness of the sensibility of subjects; nothing could be easier. But we should do this, not so much to find out the state of their sensibility as to learn the exactitude of their judgment.

The same remark holds good for the study of the memory. At first glance, memory being a psychological phenomenon of capital importance, one would be tempted to give it a very conspicuous part in an examination of intelligence. But memory is distinct from and independent of judgment. One may have good sense and lack memory. The reverse is also common. Just at the present time we are observing a backward girl who is developing before our astonished eyes a memory very much greater than our own. We have measured that memory and we are not deceived regarding it. Nevertheless that girl presents a most beautifully classic type of imbecility.

As a result of all this investigation, in the scale which we present we accord the first place to judgment; that which is of importance to us is not certain errors which the subject commits, but absurd errors, which prove that he lacks judgment. We have even made special provision to encourage people to make absurd replies. In spite of the accuracy of this directing idea, it will be easily understood that it has been impossible to permit of its regulating exclusively our examinations. For example, one can not make tests of judgment on children of less than two years when one begins to watch their first gleams of intelligence. Much is gained when one can discern in them traces of coördination, the first delineation of attention and memory. We shall therefore bring out in our lists some tests of memory; but so far as we are able, we shall give these tests such a turn as to invite the subject to make absurd replies, and thus under cover of a test of memory, we shall have an appreciation of their judgment.

Measuring Scale of Intelligence

General recommendations. The examination should take place in a quiet room, quite isolated, and the child should be called in alone without other children. It is important that when a child sees the experimenter for the first time, he should be reassured by the presence of someone he knows, a relative, an attendant, or a school superintendent. The witness should be instructed to remain passive and mute, and not to intervene in the examination either by word or gesture.

The experimenter should receive each child with a friendly familiarity to dispel the timidity of early years. Greet him the moment he enters, shake hands with him and seat him comfortably. If he is intelligent enough to understand certain words, awaken his curiosity, his pride. If he refuses to reply to a test, pass to the next one, or perhaps offer him a piece of candy; if his silence continues, send him away until another time. These are little incidents that frequently occur in an examination of the mental state, because in its last analysis, an examination of this kind is based upon the good will of the subject.

We here give the technique of each question. It will not suffice simply to read what we have written in order to be able to conduct examinations. A good experimenter can be produced only by example and imitation, and nothing equals the lesson gained from the thing itself. Every person who wishes to familiarize himself with our method of examination should come to our school. Theoretical instruction is valuable only when it merges into practical experience. Having made these reservations, let us point out the principal errors likely to be committed by inexperienced persons. There are two: the first consists in recording the gross results without making psychological observations, without noticing such little facts as permit one to give to the gross results their true value. The second error, equally frequent, is that of making suggestions. An inexperienced examiner has no idea of the influence of words; he talks too much, he aids his subject, he puts him on the track, unconscious of the help he is thus giving. He plays the part of pedagogue, when he should remain psychologist. Thus his examination is vitiated. It is a difficult art to be able to encourage a subject, to hold his attention, to make him do his best without giving aid in any form by an unskillful suggestion.

[Here the writers present the 1905 tests. They describe each test, give a detailed procedure for administration, and add remarks on interpretation of the child's behavior. In brief the tests are as follows:

1. Following a moving object with one's eyes.
2. Grasping a small object which is touched.
3. Grasping a small object which is seen.
4. Recognizing the difference between a square of chocolate and a square of wood.
5. Finding and eating a square of chocolate wrapped in paper.
6. Executing simple commands and imitating simple gestures.
7. Pointing to familiar named objects.
8. Pointing to objects represented in pictures.
9. Naming objects in pictures.
10. Comparing two lines of markedly unequal length.
11. Repeating three spoken digits.
12. Comparing two weights.
13. Susceptibility to suggestion.
14. Defining common words by function.
15. Repeating a sentence of fifteen words.
16. Telling how two common objects are different.
17. Memory for pictures.
18. Drawing a design from memory.
19. Telling how two common objects are alike.
20. Comparing two lines of slightly unequal length.
21. Placing five weights in order.
22. Discovering which of the five weights has been removed.
23. Making rhymes.
24. Sentence completion.
25. Using three words in one sentence.
26. Reply to an abstract question.

27. Reversal of the hands of a clock.
28. Paper cutting.
29. Defining abstract terms].

The Development of Intelligence in the Child

L'Année Psychologique, 14 (1908), pp. 1–90.

"The Measurement of Intelligence" is, perhaps, the most oft repeated expression in psychology during these last few years. Some psychologists affirm that intelligence can be measured; others declare that it is impossible to measure intelligence. But there are still others,* better informed, who ignore these theoretical discussions and apply themselves to the actual solving of the problem. The readers of *L'Année* know that for some time we have been trying approximations, but they were not so well thought out as are those which we now present.

We have constantly kept in mind the point of view of pedagogy, normal as well as pathological. For several years we have tried to gather all the data and material capable of shedding light upon the intellectual and moral character of children. This is by no means the minor part of pedagogy, the least important, nor the least difficult. We set for ourselves the following program: first, to determine the law of the intellectual development of children and to devise a method of measuring their intelligence; and, second, to study the diversity of their intellectual aptitudes.

We hope that we shall be able to keep faithfully to this rather extensive program, and especially that we shall have the time and the strength to realize it, but already we see that the subject is far richer than we at first imagined. Our minds always tend to simplify nature. It had seemed to us sufficient to learn how to measure the child's intelligence. This method of measurement we now set forth, which if not complete is at least established upon correct lines, and already usable. But our experience has taught us that there are other problems equally important connected with this. The child differs from the adult not only in the degree and quantity of his intelligence, but also in its form. What this childish form of intelligence is, we do not yet know. In our actual experiments we have only caught glimpses of it. It certainly demands careful study. . . .

For the moment we must content ourselves with studying what pertains to intellectual development and the processes to be used in measuring it.

* We have sometimes been accused of being opposed with blind infatuation, to all theory and to the *a priori* method. It is an unjust reproach. We admit the use of theory before the experimental researches, in order to prepare them and afterwards to interpret them; what we strongly reject, are theoretical discussions which are either intended to take the place of an exploration of facts or which are established upon obscure, equivocal and legendary facts, such as are gathered from books, for this is what certain people call observing; it is reading. In our opinions, the ideal of the scientific method must be a combination of theory and of experimentation. Such a combination is well defined in the following formula: prolonged meditation upon facts gathered at first hand.

It will be seen that these researches will interest not only the dilettante in psychology but certainly will render great service to psychiatry and to medico-legal surveys.

Let us limit our subject still further. In previous publications we have shown that it is possible to divide the methods of measuring intelligence into three groups: (1) the anatomical method; (2) the pedagogical method; (3) the psychological method (measurement of the uncultured intelligence). . . . Here we shall consider only the psychological measurement of intelligence.

This measurement is taken by means of a series of tests, the gradation of which constitutes what we call a "Measuring Scale of Intelligence." It is important, above all, to set forth these tests with sufficient precision to enable any one to repeat them correctly who will take the trouble to assimilate them.

To avoid making our description a monotonous methodology, we shall describe and discuss many of the replies obtained from children by these tests, and we shall try through all our experiments to let the reader form a picture of the child in the course of its development.

[At this point the writers describe the intellectual development of the child as revealed by the tests, specifying the activities normally developed at each age level. Unfortunately this fascinating description is much too lengthy (52 pages) for inclusion here. Later in the article a list of the tests, classified by age given, presents the skeleton of the discussion.]

General Conditions of the Examination

First the testing should take place in a quiet isolated room. The examiner should be alone with the child and when possible he should have a secretary whose duty is to record verbatim the child's answers. This secretary may be a child of thirteen or fourteen years, provided he is very intelligent and one can supervise his work a little. The subject to be examined should be kindly received; if he seems timid he should be reassured at once, not only by a kind tone but also by giving him first the tests which seem most like play, for example—giving change for 20 sous. Constantly encourage him during the tests in a gentle voice; one should show satisfaction with his answers whatever they may be. One should never criticise nor lose time by attempting to teach him the test; there is a time for everything. The child is here that his mental capacity may be judged, not that he may be instructed. Never help him by a supplementary explanation which may suggest the answer. Often one is tempted to do so, but it is wrong.

Do not become over anxious nor ask the child if he has understood, a useless scruple since the test is such that he ought to understand. Therefore one should adhere rigorously to the formulas of the experiment, without any addition or omission. Encouragement should be in the tone of voice or in meaningless words, which serve only to arouse him. "Come now!

Very good! Hurry a little! Good! Very good! Perfect! Splendid! etc. etc."
If witnesses are inevitable impose upon them a rigorous silence. How
difficult this is to obtain! Every teacher wishes to interfere in the examination, to supplement the explanation of an embarrassed pupil, especially if
he belongs to her class. Have the courage to insist that they keep silent.

Always begin with the tests that fit the child's age. If one gives him
too difficult work at first he is discouraged. If, on the contrary, it is too
easy it arouses his contempt, and he asks himself if he is not being made
fun of, and so makes no effort. We have seen manifestations of this misplaced self-esteem.

On the part of the experimenter, some conditions are necessary. He must
not allow himself to be influenced by information regarding the child
obtained from other sources. He must say to himself that nothing which
he already knows about the child counts at all. He must consider the child
as an X to be solved by this means alone. He must be entirely convinced
that by using this method, he will be able by it alone to obtain a thorough
knowledge of the child without depending on any outside help. But this
self-confidence is liable to many fluctuations. In the beginning everything
seems easy; it is the period of illusions. After a few trials, if one has at
all the critical spirit, errors are seen everywhere, and this leads to discour-
agement. But if one keeps at it faithfully, patiently, confidence will return
little by little; it is no longer the optimism of the beginner, but a confidence
grounded upon deliberate reason and proof; one has a consciousness of
his own power as well as of his limitations.

This period of initiation should last through at least 5 or 6 sessions of
two hours each, and bear upon a total of twenty children. Every experimenter wishing to commence should submit himself to a similar preparation.

Classification of the tests according to age. We here give the series of
tests ranged according to the ages at which the majority of children succeed
in them. This constitutes our measuring scale of intelligence. Those who
adopt our method will very often need to refer to it.

Three years

Show eyes, nose, mouth
Name objects in a picture
Repeat 2 figures
Repeat a sentence of 6 syllables
Give last name

Four years

Give sex
Name key, knife, penny
Repeat 3 figures
Compare 2 lines

Five years

Compare 2 boxes of different weights
Copy a square
Repeat a sentence of 10 syllables
Count 4 sous
Put together two pieces in a "game
  of patience"

Six years

Repeat a sentence of 16 syllables
Compare two figures from an esthetic
  point of view

Define by use only, some simple objects
Execute 3 simultaneous commissions
Give one's age
Distinguish morning and evening

Seven years

Indicate omissions in drawings
Give the number of fingers
Copy a written sentence
Copy a triangle and a diamond
Repeat 5 figures
Describe a picture
Count 13 single sous
Name 4 pieces of money

Eight years

Read selection and retain two memories
Count 9 sous. (3 single and 3 double)
Name four colors
Count backward from 20-0
Compare 2 objects from memory
Write from dictation

Nine years

Give the date complete (day, month, day of the month, year)
Name the days of the week
Give definitions superior to use

Retain 6 memories after reading
Make change, 4 sous from 20 sous
Arrange 5 weights in order

Ten years

Name the months
Name 9 pieces of money
Place 3 words in 2 sentences
Answer 3 comprehension questions
Answer 5 comprehension questions

Eleven Years

Criticize sentences containing absurdities
Place 3 words in 1 sentence
Find more than 60 words in 3 minutes
Give abstract definitions
Place disarranged words in order

Twelve years

Repeat 7 figures
Find 3 rhymes
Repeat a sentence of 26 syllables
Interpret pictures
Problem of facts

Thirteen years

Paper cutting
Reversed triangle
Give differences of meaning

A few words upon the value of this classification. It is not exact for the age of three years, because certain tests placed at the level of that age can be done by much younger children, children of two years for instance. But this does not trouble us, for the measuring scale that we present is designed only for children of school age. Should a child of three years present himself these tests are sufficient to classify him. The only difficulty that could arise would be in classifying a child of two years.

At the other extremity of the scale, there is also a little uncertainty. A pupil who passes all the tests for the thirteenth year may have a mental capacity superior to that age. But how much? Our tests do not show us.

*   *   *

Experimental verifications. All of the authors who have devised methods of measuring intelligence, or the various faculties of intelligence, have yielded more or less to a false tendency, which consists in limiting themselves to *a priori* constructions. The methods of diagnosing inferior states which have heretofore been published are certainly not the result of experimentation; but their authors have made use of experimentation only to give examples and to illustrate the tests. In spite of our aversion to this method, we have shown very often that we naturally were led to treat the present study from a solely theoretical point of view. One must believe that the formulation of rules leads one logically to ignore facts. But one should retrace his steps. We wish to demonstrate the part of experimentation, that is to say, of truth in our work.

First of all, it will be noticed that our tests are well arranged in a real order of increasing difficulty. It is as the result of many trials, that we have established this order; we have by no means imagined that which we present. If we had left the field clear to our conjectures, we should certainly not have admitted that it required the space of time comprised between four and seven years, for a child to learn to repeat 5 figures in place of 3. Likewise we should never have believed that it is only at ten years that the majority of children are able to repeat the names of the months in correct order without forgetting any; or that it is only at ten years that a child recognizes all the pieces of our money.

In order to make perfectly clear the real hierarchy of our tests, we have made a very simple calculation and one easy to explain. We have already said that when a child passed all but one of the tests of a certain age, he has the intellectual level of that age. Let us see if it happens that, according to this rule, a child may lack the level of a given age but at the same time reach that of a higher age. If such a case presented itself, it would be an argument against the hierarchy that we have admitted. Let us suppose that such a case could present itself; the independence of the intellectual faculties is great enough to explain this. But is such a case often presented? Out of 70 children whose replies we have examined from this point of view, the hierarchical depreciation mentioned has not presented itself a single time. Let us conclude that it must therefore be very rare. Let us also conclude that this forms a first experimental confirmation of the order we have established in our tests.

We have a second means of learning if our measuring scale of intelligence is gauged accurately. This means consists in trying out a large number of children of all ages and seeing if on the average they pass the intellectual tests of their age. We have made that experiment at length, in the Primary and Maternal schools for boys in Paris, on children of the age of three, four, five—twelve years or within two months of this age. We have studied 203 children individually, each of whom was examined during a period lasting a half hour at the least. What result may we hope to obtain from this study? And what must we require of this result for it to be a confirmation of our investigation? We ought not to expect that all the children of a given age should be of the same intellectual level. That is very evident. All are not equally intelligent; and if all were able to reply in the same manner to any one test it would simply prove that the test was poorly made, and subject to some error, for example to suggestion. Let us reckon then that in a group of children of the same age some are necessarily behind in intelligence, others in advance, others regular. What we have a right to demand is that there should be a balance between those who are behind and those who are in advance; if we have twice as many behind as we have in advance it would show that our tests are too difficult. But the equalization of those retarded and those in advance can only be made on large groups. What we ought further to demand is that in the comparison of two successive ages, the number retarded from the higher age shall not equal the number of at-age pupils of the lower age. In order to fix our ideas let us imagine some figures; let us compare nine and ten years. If the advanced at nine years number 50, and the at-age 40, and at ten years there are 50 at-age and 40 retarded, it is evident that the results obtained by these two different ages are identical, and that in consequence the children are poorly classified; if they have faculties of a different level, they have been badly graded. It is necessary that the advanced of one year shall not equal in number the at-age pupils of the higher year, and that the at-age of one year shall not equal the number of retarded pupils of the preceding year.

Glance at our results and see if they satisfy these various conditions. At three and four years, we have a considerable number of backward pupils. This is explained by particular conditions. Young children often refuse to answer from ill-will, or from timidity. The latter influence is perhaps the more rare, for timidity is a feeling of social decorum, a trait of intelligent children, and this trait usually develops later than three or four years. But ill-will is frequent. We have seen a child of three years who would not take the pencil offered him; he would not make any movement even of defense when the pencil was put under his nose. As that child walks and talks, we attribute his action to ill-will, for taking the pencil was a more simple act than speech.

Let us remark also that between nine and ten years the differences are not great. Is it because our tests are insufficient? We do not know.

Nevertheless it is true that the backward pupils of ten years are almost equal in number to the regular pupils of nine years, and that the advanced pupils of nine years equal in number the regular pupils of ten. Aside from these remarks it seems to us that our scale follows in a satisfying manner the progress of age, as the following table, which is the result of many experiments, shows very clearly.

So 103 pupils are at-age, have exactly the mental level that we attribute to their age; 44 are advanced; 56 are retarded. We have here a confirmation, which is greater even than we supposed *a priori*. In fact we should not have thought that so large a proportion of children of normal intelligence could exist, that is to say, having the intelligence of their age, and that those advanced or retarded should form such a small minority.

Let us add a detail; we speak of advanced and retarded pupils. But how

TABLE I

**Showing the Number of Pupils Intellectually at Age,
Advanced, and Retarded for the Different Ages
of School Life**

Ages	3	4	5	6	7	8	9	10	11	12	Totals
At age.............	3	9	13	5	7	16	11	14	13	2	103
Advanced by 1 year ...	3	2	6	8	7	5	9	2			42⎫ 44
Advanced by 2 years ..		1				1					2⎭
Retarded by 1 year.....	4	4	4	6	3	1	2	9	5	5	44⎫ 56
Retarded by 2 years....		1		1	1			3	2	4	12⎭

many are there? There are 86 who are irregular by one year; only a very limited number, 14, who are irregular by two years; now this is really very interesting. The insignificance of these deviations proves to us that the degree of the intelligence, estimated according to our procedure, varies less from one subject to another than the volume of the head or even the height.

If it were necessary we could cite other verifications of our scale, which though partial seem no less significant. Often we have asked that the brightest pupil be sent to us and that subject has always brilliantly passed our test. On the contrary almost all the subnormals, that is, pupils having a scholastic retardation of three years, show a serious defect in intelligence. Thus, having recently had to examine 14 subnormal pupils who were three years backward, we found the following intellectual retardation: -2.5, -1, -4, -3.5, -1, -3, -3, -2, -1, -1, -3.5, -5, -3.5, -2.

One notices here a retardation of intelligence which is extremely great, and to which we found nothing analogous among normal pupils. All these facts confirm the preceding; they appear to us less convincing than those which show the correspondence between the age and our tests; but they add to the demonstration, the force of individual observations.

* * *

The Use of the Measuring Scale of Intelligence

Our principal conclusion is that we actually possess an instrument which allows us to measure the intellectual development of young children whose age is included between three and twelve years. This method appears to us practical, convenient and rapid. If one wishes to know summarily whether a child has the intelligence of his age, or if he is advanced or retarded, it suffices to have him take the tests of his age; and the performance of these tests certainly does not require more than thirty minutes which should be interrupted by ten minutes rest if one thinks this necessary for the child.

Furthermore when one wishes to be more precise, or to make a closer approximation, one may make many more tests; if the child is seven years old, he may attempt the tests of eight, nine and ten years for example. One would also be able after an interval of several days to substitute analogous tests.

One question remains to be examined. To what purpose are these studies? In reading the reflections which we have interspersed in the course of our treatise, it will be seen that a profound knowledge of the normal intellectual development of the child would not only be of great interest but useful in formulating a course of instruction really adapted to their aptitudes. We fear that those who have drawn up the programs actually in force, are educated men who in their work have been led more by the fancies of their imaginations than by well-grounded principles. The pedagogical principle which ought to inspire the authors of programs seems to us to be the following: the instruction should always be according to the natural evolution of the child, and not precede it by a year or two. In other words the child should be taught only what he is sufficiently mature to understand; all precocious instruction is lost time, for it is not assimilated. We have cited an example of it in regard to the date, which is taught in the Maternal School, but which is not known and assimilated before the age of nine years. This is only one example, but it is eloquent; it shows the error of what has hitherto been done; it suggests a method which will enable us to improve upon the past,—a method less literary, less rapid, and even extremely laborious, for it demands that one establish by careful investigations the normal evolution of a child's intelligence, in order to make all our programs and methods of instruction conform to that evolution, when it is once known. If by this labor we have succeeded in showing the necessity for a thorough investigation conducted after this plan, our time has not been lost. But we are far from flattering ourselves that we have inaugurated a reform. Reforms in France do not succeed except through politics, and we cannot readily imagine a secretary of state busying himself with a question of this kind. What is taught to children at school! As though legislators could become interested in that!

It now remains to explain the use of our measuring scale which we consider a standard of the child's intelligence. Of what use is a measure of intelligence? Without doubt one could conceive many possible applications of the process, in dreaming of a future where the social sphere would be better organized than ours; where every one would work according to his known aptitudes in such a way that no particle of psychic force should be lost for society. That would be the ideal city. It is indeed far from us. But we have to remain among the sterner and the matter-of-fact realities of life, since we here deal with practical experiments which are the most commonplace realities.

We shall not speak of parents; although a father and mother who raise a child themselves, who watch over him and study him fondly, would have great satisfaction in knowing that the intelligence of a child can be measured, and would willingly make the necessary effort to find out if their own child is intelligent. We think especially of teachers who love their profession, who interest themselves in their pupils, and who understand that the first condition of instructing them well, is to know them. All such teachers seek, more or less successfully, to make an estimate of the intelligence of their pupils; but they have no method, and in the normal schools the courses in psychology are generally so antiquated, that one cannot learn there how to observe mental phenomena. Primary School inspectors have often told us of zealous teachers who have had the ingenious idea of composing psychological portraits of their pupils, and we have looked over these collections of portraits with interest. We have congratulated and encouraged the authors without telling them frankly what we thought, which was that they were working without method, like a very intelligent but unscientific man who would try experiments in bacteriology with unclean tools.

It seems that the simplest process that comes to the mind of an instructor, when he wishes to elucidate intellectual characteristics, would be to interest himself in every one of his pupils and to apply to each one separately all the information he has gleaned here and there. Seeking to make a study, of which he expects an individual application, he confines himself to the individual. That appears very logical, very simple. One proposes to himself a goal and runs thither directly. But in the sciences the straight line is not always the shortest road. Even when one seeks only the individual application, it would be better to make a detour, and go from the individual to the general in order to come back to the individual. This is the precise point that our instructors have not understood, the route that they have not found, or which, after entering, they have not followed, deeming it too long. In consequence their investigations profit them alone; they remain empirical and arbitrary. In any case, we offer them our method which has been built on particular facts generalized, and which in consequence might and should render service to everyone. We are certain in advance that many instructors will desire to make use of it. Some having witnessed our experiments, and being charmed by what they saw, have already commenced its use.

But we are of the opinion that the most valuable use of our scale will not be its application to the normal pupils, but rather to those of inferior grades of intelligence.

It is well known, as we have often affirmed, that the alienists are not agreed on the definitions of the words *idiot, imbecile* and *moron*. There are as many definitions as writers. Moreover the formulae employed and the processes of diagnosis in use, are so vague that the most conscientious author is not sure of remaining constantly consistent with himself. How, for instance, can one make use of formulae of diagnosis, founded on difference of degree, when these differences are not measured? Finally, the most serious criticisms that one can make of the actual medical practice is that if by chance, a child of normal intelligence were presented at a clinic, the alienist would not be able to know that he is dealing with a normal child. He will be unable for a very simple reason; he does not know what is necessary in order for a child to be normal; let us add that everyone is equally ignorant of how an individual intelligence can be studied and measured. This is then a consequence of much weight. The doctor suspects every child who is brought to a mental clinic of being backward, and if, by chance, he is not at all backward, the alienist will not know it; he will not even have the means of finding out.

But one will say: You are making objections built on purely theoretical cases, cases possible, but invented at pleasure to sustain a thesis, cases which in reality have never been presented. You do not know an example of an error so great. It is true, we answer, that a certain number of children who are brought to the asylum either by parents or by officers, are so noticeably deficient that there is no need to be a doctor to recognize that they are not normal. When a boy of seven years does not know how to dress himself, when he does not understand a sentence, when he drivels, he would be recognized as feeble-minded by the first attendant who passed him.

But besides these cases so evidently feeble-minded, one meets others whose deficiency is much less noticeable, and whose diagnosis must be much more delicate.

During the past year one of us examined 25 children who for various reasons had been admitted to Sainte-Anne and later confined at the Bicêtre, at Salpêtrière, or at other places. We applied the procedure of our measuring scale to all these children, and thus proved that *three of them were at-age in intelligence, and two others were a year advanced beyond the average.*

On reflection, these cases should not surprise us; and it is not necessary to be in touch with questions of mental medicine to inveigh against arbitrary segregation. One ought to confine a child of normal intelligence, or even of super-normal, if he has epilepsy, or irresistible impulses which constitute a danger to his neighbors or to himself. But it is none the less true that the doctors who were obliged to diagnose these cases, have had to judge the degree of intelligence of these children; it is very interesting to show the errors of diagnosis which have been committed in this regard. To two of these children who showed normal intelligence we regret to say that the term *mental debility* had been applied without consideration. The third had received the term, truly extraordinary of its kind, of *"enfant idiot."* The child was named T——, aged seven years. A doctor had written concerning him, "Idiotic, with attacks of furious anger. Wishes to bite. Does not know how to read or write." This last is a little too naïve. Since the normal child does not know how to read and write at seven years, to be astonished that T—— who is just seven is still illiterate, is like reproaching a three year old baby for not knowing how to play the piano. Finally, one of these children who was a year in advance, was classed as a moron; and as to the other nothing was said concerning his mentality. Nothing could show more clearly, that with the means which it has at its command, the mental clinic is not in a position to diagnose correctly a child's intelligence.

Let us show in what practical manner one ought to utilize our scale. Two cases are to be distinguished: the backward adult and the backward child. Let us begin with the simpler of these cases which is the first.

We shall use the customary words idiot, imbecile, and moron, giving to them a precise definition and a possible application by means of the tests of our scale. An idiot is a person who cannot communicate with his fellows by means of language; he does not speak and does not understand; he corresponds to the level of normal intelligence between birth and the age of two years. To establish a differential diagnosis between the idiot and the imbecile it suffices to employ the following tests: first, to give verbal orders like touching the nose, mouth, eyes; second, to have him name some easy familiar objects that he can find and point out in a picture. These are our tests for the age of three years; in reality they belong as much to two years as to three.

The border line between imbecility and moronity is not more difficult to establish. An imbecile is a person who is incapable of communicating with his fellows by means of written language; he can neither read, nor understand what he reads, nor write from dictation nor write spontaneously in an intelligible manner. To him may be applied the tests for eight years. As it is possible that one may sometimes have to deal with a person who is illiterate through lack of schooling, one would need to employ many other tests of seven and eight years; the description of pictures, the counting of mixed coins, the comparison of two objects from memory; these supplementary tests define the boundary which separates imbecility and moronity.

There remains a third limit to establish—that which separates moronity from the normal state. This is more complicated; we do not consider it fixed but variable according to circumstances. The most general formula that one can adopt is this: an individual is normal when he is able to conduct himself in life without need of the guardianship of another, and is able to perform work sufficiently remunerative to supply his personal needs, and finally when his intelligence does not exclude him from the social rank of his parents. As a result of this, an attorney's son who is reduced by his intelligence to the condition of a menial employee is a moron; likewise the son of a master mason, who remains a servant at thirty years is a moron; likewise a peasant, normal in ordinary surroundings of the fields, may be considered a moron in the city. In a word, retardation is a term relative to a number of circumstances which must be taken into account in order to judge each particular case. We can make the boundary between moronity and the normal state more definite by considering a special category of subjects. We wish to speak of defective adults whom we have had occasion to observe in the Parisian hospitals who were subjects for custodial care. This forms a special category for many reasons: first on account of nationality and race, it is a question as to whether they are Parisians or persons living in the region of Paris; second, on account of social conditions; all belong to the laboring class. The limit that we place for them would not be correct for any others; we express complete reserve for the application of it which one would wish to make for subjects of different environments.

In making a detailed study of the intellectual faculties of 20 of these inmates, we found that the best endowed did not surpass the normal level of nine or ten years, and in consequence our measuring scale furnished us something by which to raise before them a barrier that they could never pass. There is always a reservation to be made in applying our scale to them, which was prepared exclusively from observations upon young persons. Some of our tests consist of the usual knowledge that children acquire somewhat late. Thus the names of the days, of the months, of colors, of the principal pieces of money, are notions that an ordinary child does not possess before the age of eight, nine or ten. A defective adult even of inferior degree, for example an imbecile of forty, who is in general of the mental level of five years, may often recite without a mistake the names of the days, months, colors, pieces of money, and even the playing cards. From this point of view he is certainly much superior to the child of five years, and the reason is that he has profited by an experience very much longer. Let us then lay aside these practical notions which have no bearing here. There remain six or seven fundamental tests uniquely expressive of the intelligence; these are the tests that may be considered as forming for the laboring class of Paris and its environs the border line between moronity and the normal state. These tests are: first, arrangement of weights; second, answers to questions difficult of comprehension; third, the construction of a sentence containing three given words; fourth, the definition of abstract terms; fifth, the interpretation of pictures; sixth, the making of rhymes. Our subjects in the hospital were able to pass some of these tests but not one could pass all, nor even three of them. Now this is not a special localized success which is important for diagnosing a level of intelligence. All our work has shown that intelligence is measured by a synthesis of results. We hope then that we are not dangerously precise in admitting that the six preceding tests will apprehend all feeble-minded adults; and that one who can pass the majority of them, or at least four, is normal. For us every subject from the laboring class of the region of Paris is normal if he has satisfied the condition of this examination of intelligence; however, the examination shows only that he has intelligence enough to live outside of an institution, and that intelligence may coexist with accentuated instability, or with irresistible impulses, or even with other pathological symptoms grave enough to necessitate his segregation.

The mental level of a backward person having been determined, one may conjecture what advantages can be drawn from the medico-pedagogical treatment of the person, and what progress can be attributed to that treatment. It has sometimes been proposed to treat the drowsy class of subnormals with thyroidine, and those who have recommended this new medication have pronounced its results marvelous. Instead however of allowing one's self to be too optimistic, or of relying upon the statements of hypnotized relatives, it would be much simpler to take a measure of the intelligence before and after treatment. That would be a means for ascertaining once for all what is the value of the famous medico-pedagogical treatment of defectives, so lyrically chanted by certain alienists, and in which the pedagogue sees only certain procedures which are themselves very defective.

Other investigations which are a little different, will be equally aided by the measure of intelligence; thus the cephalometric study of the relation of the mental functions with the cranium development, will gain in value when one knows how to make an accurate measure of intelligence. Autopsies will become more eloquent when the anatomo-pathologic study of the brain will be made clear by a study of the quantitative psychology which will have been made on the living subject. . . .

Let us pass to cases where the backward subject is young and in the course of mental development; the subject to be studied is eight years old.

The problem is complex; one is unwilling to class the child, as if he were an adult, in a special group of defectives, without taking account of his age, and of all which that age permits him to attain. If he is eight years old we have not the right to consider him an imbecile simply because he does not know how to read; a normal child of eight years does not read very well, and one would never have the temptation to class him as an imbecile. To establish the diagnosis of the subnormal child we must take into account two elements; his age and his intellectual level.

But how combine these two elements? We shall not know with certainty until an extensive experience will have taught us what we do not yet know; how do idiots, imbeciles and morons develop; and what prognosis can be made from a certain retarded condition at a certain age? These are investigations of prime importance though hitherto impracticable, since empiricism was the only method, and consequently there was no way of measuring the mental development of the feeble-minded.

The process that we now recommend may be only provisional. We have sought to render it as simple as possible. In examining the table of our experiments upon normal pupils, one will notice that an intellectual retardation of one year is so frequent that it becomes insignificant; one need attach no particular value to it. On the contrary a retardation of two years is rare enough; it is found only in the proportion of 7 to 100. Let us admit that this retardation has in itself a prejudicial significance; let us admit that every time it occurs, the question may be raised as to whether the child is subnormal, and in what category he should be placed. The first determination being made, and its extreme facility is evident, the child is placed in the category to which he belongs by actual development. Thus idiocy corresponds to a development of from 0 to 2 years; imbecility from 2 to 7 years; moronity begins at 8 years.

Whenever one deducts the retardation of a child from his real age he falls into one of these categories. For example the child B——, who is seven years old, and five years behind the normal grade, presenting in consequence the development of a two year old child, is found at the limit between idiocy and imbecility; Br——, who is thirteen years of age and seven years behind has in consequence a development of six years, and is an imbecile who approaches the limit of moronity. Lay——, who is nine years old, is four years behind, and has a five year development; she is plainly in the class of imbecility.

It is understood that these diagnoses apply only to the present moment. One who is imbecile today, may by the progress of age become a moron, or on the contrary remain an imbecile all his life. One knows nothing of that; the prognosis is reserved.

There is a third class of subnormals of which it remains for us to speak; these are the subnormals in the school. They differ from the subnormals in institutions only by a less accentuated state of backwardness or of instability. We could then limit ourselves to saying that the same methods of diagnosis are applicable to them as to the subnormals in institutions, if the necessity of entrusting the selecting of them to persons who are not professional alienists did not oblige us to simplify the procedure they are to make use of in order to recognize them in the crowd of normal school children among whom they are placed. In a recent work we have given a very practical definition of a subnormal, in stating that it is one who is three years behind in his studies without the excuse of having been frequently absent from school.

That formula is usually sufficient to guide the pedagogic diagnosis; but it sometimes happens that one lacks information on the scholarship of a child, especially if he comes from a parochial school, or if he has passed successively through different public schools where he remained only a short time. In this case the examiner must establish the value of his retardation; but one hesitates at the interpretation of this retardation, and questions if it is by fault of scholarship or by fault of intelligence that he has been retarded. The intellectual test allows us to avoid all doubt, and we habitually resort to it when it is the question of a candidate for a special class.

Evidently, let us say it in the most emphatic manner, our test of intelligence will not suffice to know absolutely that a child is subnormal; we have shown above, with an example for the support of the theory, that one may be among the less brilliant in the test of intelligence and yet follow the course of study for his age at school; when one is able to follow the course of study for his age, he is saved from a suspicion of backwardness.

We consider only a situation where there are doubts on the causes of scholastic backwardness; and in such a case, if to a serious retardation of scholarship is added a serious intellectual retardation, there is sufficient reason for sending the pupil to a special class. Thus in a recent study, we have examined some twenty children who had been proposed by their teachers for that class; the information in regard to their scholarship seemed to us vague for the majority of them. Three of the candidates were but one year behind; we sent those to an ordinary school, and sent to the special class only those who were two or more years retarded.

One of these cases, to us a very striking one, was that of little Germaine, a child of eleven years who came from a Paris school. Her parents, having carried their Penates to Levallois-Perret, had sent their child to one of the schools for girls in that city. But the directress refused little Germaine under the pretext that her school was full; in reality because the child was extremely backward. In fact the retardation was at least three years; her reading was hesitating, almost syllabic; faults of orthography spoiled her dictation exercise. She wrote the following phrase under our eyes: The pertly litl grils stude the flwr that the gathrd yesty (which signifies: The pretty little girls studied the flowers that they gathered yesterday). Her number work was equally poor. She was asked, "If I have 19 apples, and eat 6 of them, how many have I left?" The child, reckoning mentally, said "12" which is inexact but reasonable. Trying it on paper, she was lost; she made an addition instead of subtraction and found 25. In other calculations she showed that she had the power to reckon mentally, but not on paper; in the last case she made the addition correctly when she should have subtracted. It is however a frequent, not to say constant rule that those backward in arithmetic do the operations better than the problems, and do more easily operations of addition and multiplication than those of subtraction and division. In short, this child had a retardation of three years; but knowledge of her scholarship was lacking. On the other hand her wide awake and mischievous air, and the vivacity of her speech made a favorable impression upon us. We made the test of intelligence and that showed us that her intelligence was normal; she was backward scarcely a year. This is a characteristic example which shows the use of our measuring scale.

In terminating this account, it will suffice to make a very brief allusion to the appreciation of penal responsibility; there also our scale will render service. The problems of penal responsibility such as are actually placed before the tribunals, are most complex and recently have caused discussions that are highly curious on account of the attention which has been paid to words rather than to things. We have scarcely the space here to make the multiple distinctions which would be necessary in making clear the real situation. It will suffice to remark that in certain cases experts have to give their opinion on the degree of intelligence of an accused person; and that according to their customary point of view which consists in distinguishing health from illness they are preoccupied in learning if the accused should or should not enter the group of feeble-minded. It is strange that so far, no other criterion than a subjective impression can guide them; they weigh each case with their good sense, which presupposes in the first place that this is a possession common to all men, and in the second place that everybody's good sense is equal to every other person's.

We suggest to them that they should use the six differentiating tests that we have described above. By the methodical employment of these tests, they will arrive at precise and controllable conclusions, which at the same time cannot help but enhance in the mind of the judges the value of the medico-legal appraisement of the alienists.

These examples to which we could add many others show that the methods of measuring the individual intelligence have not a speculative interest alone; by the direction, by the organization of all the investigations, psychology has furnished the proof (we do not say for the first time but in a more positive manner than ever before), that it is in a fair way to become a science of great social utility.

ALFRED BINET AND TH. SIMON.

Of the many rejoinders to Spearman's "General Intelligence" article, this one is of particular interest. Thorndike was
the champion par excellence of specific traits and understood
correlational analysis thoroughly. His views were very influential in both educational and psychological circles, doing
much to set the patterns for mental measurement in the United
States.

The Relation of Accuracy in Sensory Discrimination to General Intelligence*

EDWARD L. THORNDIKE

WILFRID LAY

P. R. DEAN

1909

The purpose of this paper is to present certain new data concerning the
relationship mentioned in the title and to show the bearing of these data
upon the conclusion set forth by Spearman in his *General Intelligence
Objectively Determined and Measured* which appeared in this *Journal* in
April, 1904.

THE ORIGINAL MEASURES

The measurements from which conclusions will be drawn were made by
Dr. Lay upon 37 young women students in a normal school and by Mr.
Dean upon 25 high school boys (all in the 3rd year of the high school
course). The 37 young women drew each 90 lines, 30 as nearly as possible
equal to a 100 mm. standard, 30 as nearly as possible equal to a 75 mm.
standard and 30 as nearly as possible equal to a 50 mm. standard. They
also each filled 16 boxes with shot, 8 as nearly as possible equal to a 100 g.
standard and 8 as nearly as possible equal to a 200 g. standard. Each one
rated all the rest in order of merit for general intellect, using each her own
conception of what general intellect was as the basis of grading. Eight of
the professors in the normal school also graded each of them (with a few
exceptions in the case of three of the teachers) in the same way. Their
scholastic records in the normal school were also used as measures. I use
the average deviation from the standard as the measure of inaccuracy in
the case of the tests with lines and weights. Some reasons might be adduced

* *The American Journal of Psychology*, 20, No. 3 (1909), pp. 364-369. Reprinted
by permission of the publisher.

for choosing the variability around the individual's constant error instead, but there are far weightier reasons against doing so.

The 25 boys drew lines similarly except that some drew fewer than the 90 while others drew more; made up weights similarly; were estimated similarly by 6 of their own members and 4 of their teachers.

The lines were drawn and the weights made up under the same conditions for all students within each group. The tests covered several days for each individual, so that spurious correlation from fatigue, temporary illness, etc., was reduced to a small amount. Within each group, differences of age and maturity are for our purpose so slight as to be negligible. The median deviation of the young women in age was only 10 months and that of the boys only about one year.

We have then for the women fairly accurate measures of accuracy of discrimination of these lengths, accuracy of discrimination of these weights, intellect as judged by one's fellow students and intellect as judged by one's teachers. Such measures from two random halves of the scores correlate to .665, .504, .915, .72 and .62 respectively, which means that the measures used from the entire scores for each individual would correlate with other similar sets to about .8, .7, .9½, .9 and .8 respectively.

In the case of the boys the opinions of intellect of fellow pupils and teachers were combined. We have then for the boys fairly accurate measures of discrimination of these lengths, discrimination of these weights, intellect as judged by one's teachers and fellow students, and scholarship. Such measures from two random halves of the scores correlate to .691, .722, .869 and .873 respectively, which means that the measures used would correlate with other similar sets to about .8, .8, .9½ and .9½ respectively. The "raw" correlations from which we have to argue are consequently subject to only very moderate "attenuation" from chance variations in the obtained measures from the true measures for which they stand. The number of cases is sufficient to determine close correlations with a very small margin of probable deviation from the true result. When the relationship is only slight, the reliability of the result is, of course, much less, but is still sufficient to prevent insecurity in any of the general conclusions which are of interest.

THE MEASURES AS SAMPLES OF 'INTELLECT' AND OF 'SENSORY DISCRIMINATION'

Intellect as judged by teachers and intellect as judged by fellow students are much the same thing. The raw correlation in the case of the woman students is .85. This becomes about .95 when allowance is made for the inadequacy of the original measures. The raw correlation in the case of the high school boys is .76. This becomes nearly .9 when the Spearman correction is applied. The women preparing to become teachers naturally weight aspects of intellect more in the fashion of the teachers than do the high school boys. But the congruence of school-boy's and school-teacher's opinion is remarkable.

In the case of the normal school women scholarship is an almost perfect symptom of intellect as they and their teachers judge the latter. The correlation between the combined judgment of fellow pupils and teachers and the scholarship record is .85, which becomes about .95 when allowance is made for the inaccuracies of the latter. And much the same would of necessity hold of the judgment of fellow-pupils alone.

With the high school boys scholarship is by no means a perfect symptom of intellect either as judged by the boys or as judged by their teachers. The correlation is naturally somewhat higher in the latter case, but it is by no means high. These relations are approximately

.6 for scholarship and intellect by the combined judgment,

.6 "   "   "   "   " " teachers' judgment, and

.4 "   "   "   "   " " pupils' judgment.

This difference is, of course, what should be found from accurate measures, since the students in the professional school do devote their intellects to scholarship, and do, so to speak, measure their intellects by it, more than is the case with the high school boys. Scholarship is, with the latter, in large measure a product of interest rather than ability.

From these facts it is evident that in the case of the high school boys the three measures,—teachers' opinions, fellow-students' opinions, and school marks,—are something like a fair sampling of measures of general intellect. In the case of the women students the sampling is much weighted in favor of the scholarly sort of intellect.

The discrimination of lengths and the discrimination of weights are known to be random samples of sensory discriminations for the very good reason that they were picked at random.

THE RELATION OF 'INTELLECT' TO 'SENSORY DISCRIMINATION'

From his measurements Spearman calculates that the factor common to school marks and ratings as to 'common sense' by fellow-students and teachers, correlates perfectly with, and hence is identical with, the factor common to discrimination of pitch, discrimination of light intensities and discrimination of weights, and concludes that there exists "a correspondence between what may provisionally be called 'General Discrimination' and 'General Intelligence' which works out with great approximation to *one* or *absoluteness*."

The measurements obtained in the present investigation do not in the least support this hypothesis. The correlation between whatever is common to (A) drawing 50, 75 and 100 mm. lengths accurately and (B) making weights equal to 100 g. and 200 g. standards and whatever is common to

(C) intellect as judged by fellow-students and (D) intellect as judged by teachers does not come out as 1.00 but as .26 or .15 according as we apply the first or second of Spearman's correction-formulæ. When, in the case of the high school pupils, the two measures of general intellect taken are (C) combined student's and teacher's estimates and (D) school marks, the correlation comes out .29 and .22 by the two methods.

That is, the most probable relation between the factor common to all sensory discriminations and the factor common to intellect judged in these three ways is, from our data, not 1.00, but .23.

It is perhaps best to wait for further and fuller measurements of the relation in question before attempting to explain the difference between this result and Spearman's. But one fact may be noted now. With young children. a test designed to measure sensory discrimination may easily become, to a considerable degree, a measure of ability to understand instructions, that is, of one feature of general intellect.

The variety of measures taken and the elaborate corrections made by Spearman make a detailed comparison step by step of his and the present research difficult and in the end unproductive. The essential differences are (1) that Spearman does not give measures of the reliability of his measures of any species of sense discrimination or of any but a few of his measures of intellect and (2) that his material is complicated by age and sex.

The theoretical importance of Spearman's conclusion lies in the support which it would give, if verified, to the hypothesis that the efficiency of what may be called the general mammalian foundation of the central nervous system is closely correlated with what may be called the specifically human neurone-connections. The present results support the contrary hypothesis, that the efficiency of a man's equipment for the specifically human task of managing ideas is only loosely correlated with the efficiency of the simpler sensori-motor apparatus which he possesses in common with other species.

Spearman's other main conclusion is *"that all branches of intellectual activity have in common one fundamental function (or group of functions), whereas the remaining or specific elements of the activity seem in every case to be wholly different from that in all the others."* This is, of course, contradicted by the correlation of .23 instead of 1.00, and also by the fact that we obtain a much higher correlation between discrimination of lengths and discrimination of weights than between either one of them and general intelligence. From our figures the correlations, if perfect original measures were at hand, would be about .15, .25 and .50 respectively for accuracy in drawing lines with general intelligence, accuracy in making up weights with general intelligence and accuracy in drawing lines with accuracy in making up weights.

I may add that other studies of correlation made by my students and myself are unanimous in contradicting Spearman's ingenious hypothesis of one sole common element as the cause of all positive correlations. We find,

TABLE I

Actually Obtained ("Raw") Correlations: Pearson Coefficients

	I	II
1. Scores from half of the 100, 75 and 50 mm. lines with scores from the other half	.665	.69
2. ,, ,, ,, ,, 100 and 200 gram weights ,, ,, ,, ,, ,,	.505	.72
3. ,, ,, ,, ,, pupils' impressions of intellect ,, ,, ,, ,, ,,		.915
4. ,, ,, ,, ,, teachers' impressions of intellect ,, ,, ,, ,, ,,		.72
5. ,, ,, ,, ,, academic records ,, ,, ,, ,, ,,		.87
6. ,, ,, ,, ,, combined pupils' and teachers' impressions of intellect ,, ,, ,, ,, ,,		.87
7. Scores from all the lines with scores from all the weights	.52	.25
8. ,, ,, ,, ,, ,, ,, ,, ,, pupils' impressions of intellect	.25	
9. ,, ,, ,, ,, ,, ,, ,, ,, teachers' ,, ,, ,,	.12	
10. ,, ,, ,, ,, ,, ,, ,, ,, pupils' and teachers' impressions of intellect combined		.055
12. ,, ,, ,, ,, ,, ,, ,, ,, academic records		−.01
11. Scores from all the weights, with scores from all the lines	.52	.25
13. ,, ,, ,, ,, ,, ,, ,, ,, pupils' impressions of intellect	.235	
14. ,, ,, ,, ,, ,, ,, ,, ,, teachers' ,, ,, ,,	.08	
15. ,, ,, ,, ,, ,, ,, ,, ,, pupils' and teachers' impressions of intellect combined		.205
16. ,, ,, ,, ,, ,, ,, ,, ,, academic records		.21
17. Scores from all the pupils' impressions of intellect with scores from all the teachers' impressions of intellect		.85
18. Scores from all the pupils' and teachers' impressions of intellect with scores from entire academic records		.54
19. Scores from all the lines and weights with scores from all the teachers' and pupils' impressions of intellect combined		.165
20. Scores from all the lines and weights with scores from combination of teachers' impressions, pupils' impressions and academic records		.145

Coefficients Corrected for Chance Variations in the Original Measures by the Spearman Methods of Correction

I. (A) The factor common to accuracy in lines and accuracy in weights with (B) the factor common to pupils' impressions of intellect and teachers' impressions of intellect　.20

(A) As above, with the factor common to the combination of teachers' and pupils' impressions and academic scholarship.　.255

The most probable correlation between "general discrimination" and "general intelligence" is thus .23.

for example, that efficiency in marking A's on a sheet of printed capitals, efficiency in finding circles or hexagons or isosceles triangles on a sheet of printed geometrical forms and efficiency in finding misspelled words are in adults all very closely intercorrelated (to .8 or more), but are by no means so closely correlated to general intellect. In general there is evidence of a complex set of bonds between the psychological equivalents of both what we call the formal side of thought and what we call its content, so that one is almost tempted to replace Spearman's statement by the equally extravagant one that there is *nothing whatever* common to all mental functions, or to any half of them.

The table of correlations is on the facing page. Column I gives the results from the women students; Column II gives the results from the high school boys.

In this paper Woodworth reviews the available evidence on racial differences and sketches the results of his experiments at the World's Fair in St. Louis in 1904. Although the data are subject to grave criticisms, much may be learned from Woodworth's dispassionate consideration of race differences, possible causal factors, and difficulties of investigation.

Racial Differences in Mental Traits*

R. S. WOODWORTH

1910

One of the most agreeable and satisfying experiences afforded by intellectual pursuits comes from the discovery of a clean-cut distinction between things which are superficially much alike. The esthetic value of such distinctions may even outweigh their intellectual value and lead to sharp lines and antitheses where the only difference that exists is one of degree. A favorite opportunity for this form of intellectual exercise and indulgence is afforded by the observation of groups of men. The *type* of man composing each group—that is what we should like to find; and we hear much of the "typical" scientist, the typical business man, the typical Englishman or Frenchman, the typical southerner, the typical Bostonian. The type of any group stands as a sort of ideal within the group, and, more or less caricatured, as the butt of the wit of other groups. There is one peculiar fact about these types: you may have to search long for an individual who can be taken as a fair example. And when you have at last found the typical individual, you may be led to ask by what right he stands as the type of the group, if he is a rarity amidst it.

If we would scientifically determine the facts regarding a group of men, we should, no doubt, proceed to examine all the individuals in the group, or at least a fair and honest representation of them. The first fact that meets us when we proceed in this way is that the individuals differ from each other, so that no one can really be selected as representing the whole number. We do find, indeed, when we measure the stature or any other bodily fact, or when we test any native mental capacity, that the members of a natural group are disposed about an average, many of them lying near the average, and few lying far above or far below it; and we thus have the average as a scientific fact regarding the group. But the average does not generally coincide with the type, as previously conceived, nor do the averages of different groups differ so much as the so-called types differ.

* *Science*, 31 (1910), pp. 171-186. Reprinted by permission of the publisher and the author.

Moreover, the average is itself very inadequate, since it does not indicate the amount of variation that exists within the group—and this is one of the most important facts to be borne in mind in understanding any collection of individuals. It is specially important in comparing different groups of men, since the range of variation within either group is usually much greater than the difference between the averages of the groups. The groups overlap to such an extent that the majority of the individuals composing either group might perfectly well belong to the other.

No doubt statements like this will be readily accepted as far as concerns the different nations belonging to the same race. One could not seriously doubt that the nations of Europe, though they might differ slightly on the average, would so much overlap one another that, except for language and superficial mannerisms, the great majority of the members of one nation might be exchanged with a majority from another nation without altering the characteristics of either. But when we extend our view to all the peoples of the earth, the case would at first appear quite changed. Certainly whites and negroes do not overlap, to any extent, in color of skin, nor negroes and Chinamen in kinkiness of hair, nor Indians and Pygmies in stature. Such specialization of traits is, however, the exception. Whites and negroes, though differing markedly in complexion and hair, overlap very extensively in almost every other trait, as, for example, in stature. Even in brain weight, which would seem a trait of great importance in relation to intelligence and civilization, the overlapping is much more impressive than the difference; since while the brain of negroes averages perhaps two ounces lighter than the brain of Europeans, the range of variation within either race amounts to 25 ounces.

Our inveterate love for types and sharp distinctions is apt to stay with us even after we have become scientific, and vitiate our use of statistics to such an extent that the average becomes a stumbling-block rather than an aid to knowledge. We desire, for example, to compare the brain weights of whites and of negroes. We weigh the brains of a sufficient number of each race—or let us at least assume the number to be sufficient. When our measurements are all obtained and spread before us, they convey to the unaided eye no clear idea of a racial difference, so much do they overlap. If they should become jumbled together, we should never be able to separate the negroes from the whites by aid of brain weight. But now we cast up the average of each group, and find them to differ; and though the difference is small, we straightway seize on it as the important result, and announce that the negro has a smaller brain than the white. We go a step further, and class the white as a large-brained race, the negro as a small-brained. Such transforming of differences of degree into differences of kind, and making antitheses between overlapping groups, partakes not a little of the ludicrous.

We seem to be confronted by a dilemma; for the group as a whole is too unwieldy to grasp, while the average, though convenient, is treacherous.

What we should like is some picture or measure of the *distribution* of a given trait throughout the members of a group; and, fortunately, such measures and pictures can be had. Convenient and compact measures of variability are afforded by the science of statistics, and are of no less importance than the average. But still better, because closer to the actual facts, are graphic or tabular pictures of the distribution of the trait, showing the frequency with which it occurs in each degree. The distribution of a trait is for some purposes more important than the average. Let us suppose, for instance, that two groups were the same in their average mental ability, but that one group showed little variation, all of its members being much alike and of nearly the average intelligence, while the other group showed great variability, ranging between the extremes of idiocy and genius. It is evident that the two groups, though equal on the average, would be very unequal in dealing with a situation which demanded great mental ability. One master mind could supply ideas for the guidance of the group, and his value would far outweigh the load of simpletons which the group must carry.

If groups of men differ in average intelligence, this difference would have an influence on their effectiveness in mental work, and so, no doubt, on their advance in civilization. If groups differ in variability, this would probably have a still greater influence. There is one respect in which groups certainly do differ. They differ in size, and size is an important consideration, even from a purely biological point of view. The more numerous the individuals born into a group, the greater the absolute number of gifted individuals to be expected; and in some respects it is the absolute rather than the relative number of able men that counts. Besides this, the larger the group, the greater the chance of its producing a truly effective genius, just as, in the experiments of Burbank and other breeders, a vast number of plants are grown, in order to increase the chance of sports occurring.

One further consideration of this partly biological, partly statistical, nature should be brought forward before passing from preliminary remarks to the consideration of actual data. When the individuals composing a group are measured or tested in several traits, it is found that those who rank high in one trait do not always rank high in others. On the whole, there is more correspondence than opposition; an individual who ranks well in one trait is rather apt to rank well in others. The correlation, as we say, is positive, but it is far from perfect. The individuals most gifted with ability in war are not altogether the same individuals who are ablest in government, or in art or literature, or in mechanical invention. This fact is not only of importance in reaching a just conception of a group, but it should be considered in comparing different groups. The circumstances surrounding a group call for certain special abilities, and bring to the fore the individuals possessing these abilities, leaving in comparative obscurity those gifted in other directions. Judging the group largely by its prominent individuals, we get the impression that the group is gifted in certain lines, and deficient in others. A nation whose circumstances call for industrial expansion and the exploitation of natural resources gives prominence to those of its members who are successful in these pursuits, and leaves in obscurity many who have native capacity for military leadership. Should war come to such a community, time and bitter experience are often necessary before the leadership can be transferred from the previously eminent men to those obscure and often despised individuals who are capable of doing best service in the new direction. This lack of perfect correlation between various abilities makes it difficult to judge of the capacity of a group of men by casual observation; and we must accordingly discount largely the appearance of specialization of mental traits in different peoples.

All in all, the discovery of true inherent differences between races and peoples is an intricate task, and if we now turn to the psychologist to conduct an examination of different groups, and to inform us regarding their mental differences, we must not allow him to present a hasty conclusion. His tests must be varied and thorough before we can accept his results as a serious contribution to this difficult subject. The psychologist may as well admit at once that he has little to offer; for, though the "psychology of peoples" has become a familiar phrase, and though books have been written on the subject, actual experimental work has so far been very limited in quantity.

One thing the psychologist can assert with no fear of error. Starting from the various mental processes which are recognized in his text-books, he can assert that each of these processes is within the capabilities of every group of mankind. All have the same senses, the same instincts and emotions. All can remember the past, and imagine objects not present to sense. All discriminate, compare, reason and invent. In all, one impulse can inhibit another, and a distant end can be pursued to the neglect of present incitations. Statements to the contrary, denying to the savage powers of reasoning, or abstraction, or inhibition, or foresight, can be dismissed at once. If the savage differs in these respects from the civilized man, the difference is one of degree, and consistent with considerable overlapping of savage and civilized individuals. The difference of degree calls for quantitative tests. But besides the traditional classification of mental powers, there is another of perhaps greater importance in studying differences between men. One individual differs from another not so much in power of memory, or of reasoning, or of attention, or of will, as in the sort of material to which he successfully applies these processes. One gives his attention readily to mathematics; he remembers mathematics easily; he reasons well on mathematical subjects; his will is strong in excluding distracting impulses when he is in pursuit of a mathematical goal. He may show none of these powers, in a high degree, in relation to music, or business, or social life; whereas another, totally inefficient in mathematics, may show equal powers of mind in another subject. The capacity to handle a given sort of subject matter is in part determined by native endowment, but is very responsive to training, and therefore is hard to test, because only individuals with equal training in any subject can be fairly tested and compared as to their native capacity to handle that subject. Thus it becomes hard to contrive a test for musical or mathematical or mechanical endowment which could fairly be applied to races having diverse trainings in these lines. This difficulty, moreover, infects our tests for such general powers as memory or reasoning, for a test has to deal with some sort of material, and success in passing the test depends on the familiarity of the material as well as on the power of mind which we design to test. We may suppose, indeed, that all of our tests, founded as they are on material which is familiar to us, will be more or less unfair to peoples of very different cultures and modes of life. The results of our tests need to be discounted somewhat—exactly how much we can not say—in favor of the primitive peoples tested.

We are now, it would seem, sufficiently entrenched in precautions and criticisms to admit the psychologist to our councils, and hear the results of his tests.

First, as to the senses. The point of special interest here is as to whether the statements of many travelers, ascribing to the "savage" extraordinary powers of vision, hearing and smell, can be substantiated by exact tests. The common opinion, based on such reports, is, or has been, that savages are gifted with sensory powers quite beyond anything of which the European is capable; though Spencer explains that this is a cause of inferiority rather than the reverse, because the savage is thus led to rely wholly on his keen senses, and to devote his whole attention to sense impressions, to the neglect and atrophy of his intellectual powers. Ranke, however, on testing natives of Brazil, a race notable for its feats of vision, found that their ability to discern the position of a letter or similar character at a distance, though good, was not remarkable, but fell within the range of European powers. The steppe-dwelling Kalmuks, also renowned for distant vision, being able to detect the dust of a herd of cattle at a greater distance with the naked eye than a European could with a telescope, have also been examined; and their acuity was indeed found to be very high, averaging considerably above that of Europeans; yet only one or two out of the forty individuals tested exceeded the European record, while the great majority fell within the range of good European eyes. Much the same result has been obtained from Arabs, Egyptians and quite a variety of peoples. Among the most reliable results are those of Rivers on a wholly unselected Papuan population. He found no very exceptional individual among 115 tested, yet the average was somewhat better than that of Europeans. I had myself, through the kindness of Dr. McGee, the opportunity of testing individuals from quite a variety of races at the St. Louis Fair in 1904, and my results agree closely with those already cited, though

I did not find any cases of very exceptional powers among about 300 individuals. There were a number who exceeded the best of the 200 whites whom I also tested under the same conditions, but none who exceeded or equaled the record of a few individuals who have been found in the German army. Indians and Filipinos ranked highest, averaging about 10 per cent. better than whites, when all individuals of really defective vision were excluded. The amount of overlapping is indicated by stating that 65-75 per cent. of Indians and Filipinos exceeded the average for whites. It did not seem possible, however, to assert anything like a correspondence between eyesight and the degree of primitiveness or backwardness of a people; since, for instance, the Negritos of the Philippine Islands, though much more primitive than the Malayan Filipinos in their mode of life, and, indeed, the most primitive group so far tested, were inferior to the Filipinos, and, in fact, as far as could be judged from the small number examined, no whit superior to whites. Nor does it seem possible, from results hitherto reported, to believe in a close correspondence between keen sight and dark skin, though it is true that pigment is important in several ways to the eye, and that therefore, as Rivers has suggested, the amount of pigmentation might be a factor in vision. But it does not seem to be specially the darkest races that show the keenest vision. We may perhaps conclude that eyesight is a function which varies somewhat in efficiency with difference of race, though with much overlapping. No doubt, however, the results as they stand need some qualification. On the one hand, inclusion of individuals with myopia and similar defects would lower the average of Europeans considerably more than that of most other races; so that the actual condition of eyesight differs more than the results show. On the other hand, it would not be fair to include near-sighted individuals, if what we wish to discover is native differences between peoples; for the different prevalence of myopia is certainly due to the differing uses to which the eye is put. And this matter of use may have considerable influence on the individuals not classed as near-sighted, and so admitted to the comparison. Rivers has made an observation in connection with the test for eyesight, which I am able to confirm, and which is perhaps of much importance. He found that when the letter or character used in his test, the position of which had to be recognized at the greatest possible distance, was removed from him beyond the distance at which he felt that he could judge it, he could still guess it right nearly every time, though without confidence. By such guessing, one's record in this test can be bettered considerably; and careful study enables one to see the slight and blurred indications of position which form the basis of the guessing. Now it may well be that the occupations of civilized life breed a habit of dependence on clear vision, whereas the life of those who must frequently recognize objects at a great distance breeds reliance on slight indications, and so creates a favorable attitude for the test of eyesight. When this possibility is taken in connection with the deterioration of many

European eyes from abuse, and in connection with the observed overlapping of all groups tested, the conclusion is not improbable that, after all, the races are essentially equal in keenness of vision. Even if small differences do exist, it is fairly certain that the wonderful feats of distant vision ascribed to savages are due to practice in interpreting slight indications of familiar objects. Both Rivers and Ranke, on testing some of the very individuals whose feats of keen sight seemed almost miraculous, found that, as tested, they had excellent but not extraordinary vision. A little acquaintance with sailors on shipboard is enough to dispel the illusion that such feats are beyond the powers of the white man.

The hearing of savages enjoys a reputation, among travelers, similar to that of their sight; but there can be little doubt that the cause is the same. In fact, the tests which have so far been made tend to show that the hearing of whites is superior. Such was the result of Myers on the Papuans, and of Bruner in his extensive series of measurements made at the St. Louis Fair. Only 15 per cent. of 137 Filipinos tested did as well as the average of whites; other groups made a somewhat better showing, but all seemed inferior on the average to whites. In spite of the experimental results, there is perhaps reason to doubt that the hearing of whites is essentially and natively much superior to that of other races. Civilized life protects the ear from some forms of injury to which it is exposed in more primitive conditions; and, then, the question of cleanliness must be considered in regard to the meatus. Besides, the ear is known to be highly susceptible of training in the perception of particular sorts of sound—as overtones and difference tones—and it is likely enough that the watch ticks and similar clicks used in the tests are not equally within the repertory of all peoples.

Much the same can be said regarding keenness of smell. On account of the high olfactory powers of dogs and some other lower animals, it has often seemed natural and proper that this sense should be highly developed among savages; and feats of primitive folk have been reported quite analogous to those already referred to under sight and hearing. No doubt here again, special interests and training are responsible, since what few tests have been made tend to show no higher acuity of smell among negroes and Papuans than among Europeans.

The sense of touch has been little examined. McDougall found among the Papuans a number with extremely fine powers of discrimination by the skin. The difference between two points and one could be told by these individuals even when the two points were brought very close together; on the average, the Papuans tested excelled Europeans considerably in this test. On the other hand, Indians and Filipinos, and a few Africans and Ainu, tested in the same manner, seem not to differ perceptibly from whites.

The pain sense is a matter of some interest, because of the fortitude or stolidity displayed by some races towards physical suffering. It may be, and has been conjectured, that the sense for pain is blunt in these races, as it is known to be in some individuals who have allowed themselves to be burned without flinching, and performed other feats of fortitude. The pain sense is tested by applying gradually increasing pressure to some portion of the skin, and requiring the person tested to indicate when he first begins to feel pain. Now, as a matter of fact, the results of McDougall on the Papuans, and those of Dr. Bruner and myself on Indians, Filipinos, Africans and Ainu, are in close agreeement on this point. Greater pressure on the skin is needed to produce pain in each of these races than in whites. This is the average result, but in this test the distribution of the cases is specially important. Though most whites feel pain at or about a certain small pressure, there is quite a respectable minority who give no sign till much higher pressures are reached, their results corresponding very closely to those of the majority of Indians. And similarly, a minority of Indians feel pain at much lower pressures than the bulk of their fellows, falling into the ranks of the white man. In each group, the distribution is bimodal, or aggregated about two points instead of one; but whites are principally aggregated about the lower center, and Indians and other races about the higher center. Introspection comes to our aid in explaining this anomaly, for it shows that there is some difficulty in telling just when the pressure becomes painful. If one is satisfied with slight discomfort, a moderate pressure will be enough; but if a sharp twinge is demanded, the pressure must be considerably increased. Most whites, under the conditions of the test, are satisfied with slight discomfort, while my impression in watching the Indians was that they were waiting to be really hurt. The racial difference would accordingly be one in the conception of pain, or in understanding the test, rather than in the pain sense.

On the whole, the keenness of the senses seems to be about on a par in the various races of mankind. Differences exist among the members of any race, and it is not improbable that differences exist between the averages of certain groups, especially when these are small, isolated and much inbred. Rivers has in fact found such small groups differing considerably from whites in the color sense. One such group showed no cases of our common color blindness or red-green blindness, while another group showed an unusually large percentage of color-blind individuals. In the larger groups, the percentage of the color-blind is, very likely, about constant, though the existing records tend to show a somewhat lower proportion among Mongolians than among whites. Very large numbers of individuals need, however, to be tested in order to determine such a proportion closely; even among Europeans, the proportion can not yet be regarded as finally established. We were able, at St. Louis, to try on representatives of a number of races a difficult color matching test, so different indeed from that of Rivers that our results can not be used as a direct check on his; with the result that all other races were inferior to whites in their general success in color matching. We also could find no correlation between ill success in this test and the degree of pigmentation. On the whole, the color sense is probably very much the same all over the world.

* * *

When we turn from the senses to other functions, the information which the psychologist has to offer becomes even more scanty.

Some interest attaches to tests of the speed of simple mental and motor performances, since, though the mental process is very simple, some indication may be afforded of the speed of brain action. The reaction time test has been measured on representatives of a few races, with the general result that the time consumed is about the same in widely different groups. The familiar "tapping test," which measures the rate at which the brain can at will discharge a series of impulses to the same muscle, was tried at St. Louis on a wide variety of folk, without disclosing marked differences between groups. The differences were somewhat greater when the movement, besides being rapid, had to be accurate in aim. The Eskimos excelled all others in this latter test, while the poorest record was made by the Patagonians and the Cocopa Indians—which groups were, however, represented by only a few individuals. The Filipinos, who were very fully represented, seemed undeniably superior to whites in this test, though, of course, with plenty of overlapping.

The degree of right-handedness has been asserted to vary in different races, and the favoring of one hand has been interpreted as conducive to specialization and so to civilization. We were, however, unable to detect any marked difference in the degree of right-handedness in different races, as tested by the comparative strength, quickness or accuracy of the two hands. The Negritos, the lowest race examined, had the same degree of right-handedness as Filipinos, or Indians, or whites.

We are probably justified in inferring from the results cited that the sensory and motor processes, and the elementary brain activities, though differing in degree from one individual to another, are about the same from one race to another.

Equitable tests of the distinctly intellectual processes are hard to devise, since much depends on the familiarity of the material used. Few tests of this nature have as yet been attempted on different races.

There are a number of illusions and constant errors of judgment which are well-known in the psychological laboratory, and which seem to depend, not on peculiarities of the sense organs, but on quirks and twists in the process of judgment. A few of these have been made the matter of comparative tests, with the result that peoples of widely different cultures are subject to the same errors, and in about the same degree. There is an illusion which occurs when an object, which looks heavier than it is, is lifted by the hand; it then feels, not only lighter than it looks, but even lighter than it really is. The contrast between the look and the feel of the thing plays havoc with the judgment. Women are, on the average, more subject to this illusion than men. The amount of this illusion has been measured in several peoples, and found to be, with one or two exceptions, about the same in all. Certain visual illusions, in which the apparent length or direction of a line is greatly altered by the neighborhood of other lines, have similarly been found present in all races tested, and to about the same degree. As far as they go, these results tend to show that simple sorts of judgment, being subject to the same disturbances, proceed in the same manner among various peoples; so that the similarity of the races in mental processes extends at least one step beyond sensation.

The mere fact that members of the inferior races are suitable subjects for psychological tests and experiments is of some value in appraising their mentality. Rivers and his collaborators approached the natives of Torres Straits with some misgivings, fearing that they would not possess the necessary powers of sustained concentration. Elaborate introspections, indeed, they did not secure from these people, but, in any experiment that called for straightforward observation, they found them admirable subjects for the psychologist. Locating the blind spot, and other observations with indirect vision, which are usually accounted a strain on the attention, were successfully performed. If tests are put in such form as to appeal to the interests of the primitive man, he can be relied on for sustained attention. Statements sometimes met with to the effect that such and such a tribe is deficient in powers of attention, because, when the visitor began to quiz them on matters of linguistics, etc., they complained of headache and ran away, sound a bit naïve. Much the same observations could be reported by college professors, regarding the natives gathered in their class rooms.

A good test for intelligence would be much appreciated by the comparative psychologist, since, in spite of equal standing in such rudimentary matters as the senses and bodily movement, attention and the simpler sorts of judgment, it might still be that great differences in mental efficiency existed between different groups of men. Probably no single test could do justice to so complex a trait as intelligence. Two important features of intelligent action are quickness in seizing the key to a novel situation, and firmness in limiting activity to the right direction, and suppressing acts which are obviously useless for the purpose in hand. A simple test which calls for these qualities is the so-called "form test." There are a number of blocks of different shapes, and a board with holes to match the blocks. The blocks and board are placed before a person, and he is told to put the blocks in the holes in the shortest possible time. The key to the situation is here the matching of blocks and holes by their shape; and the part of intelligence is to hold firmly to this obvious necessity, wasting no time in trying to force a round block into a square hole. The demand on intelligence certainly seems slight enough; and the test would probably not differentiate between a Newton and you or me; but it does suffice to catch the feebleminded, the young child, or the chimpanzee, as any of these is likely to fail altogether, or at least to waste much time in random moves and vain efforts. This test was tried on representatives of several races, and considerable differences appeared. As between whites, Indians, Eskimos, Ainus, Filipinos and Singhalese, the average differences were small, and much overlapping occurred. As between these groups, however, and the Igorot and Negrito from the Philippines and a few reputed Pygmies from the Congo, the average differences were great, and the overlapping was small. Another rather similar test for intelligence, which was tried on some of these groups, gave them the same relative rank. The results of the test agreed closely with the general impression left on the minds of the experimenters by considerable association with the people tested. And, finally, the relative size of the cranium, as indicated, roughly, by the product of its three external dimensions, agreed closely in these groups with their appearance of intelligence, and with their standing in the form test. If the results could be taken at their face value, they would indicate differences of intelligence between races, giving such groups as the Pygmy and Negrito a low station as compared with most of mankind. The fairness of the test is not, however, beyond question; it may have been of a more unfamiliar sort to these wild hunting folk than to more settled groups. This crumb is, at any rate, about all the testing psychologist has yet to offer on the question of racial differences in intelligence.

In the absence of first-hand study of the mental powers of different races, folk psychology resorts to a comparison of their civilizations and achievements. This is the method by which we habitually compare the intelligence of individuals judging capacity by performance, the tree by its fruits; and such judgments, though subject to occasional error, are probably in the main reliable. Why should we not extend the method to the comparison of groups, and say that a group possessing a high civilization has probably a high average intelligence, while a wild savage race is mentally poorly endowed? The first difficulty in employing the method is to obtain a just estimate of the cultures to be compared. First impressions regarding alien folk, derived from the reports of travelers, are usually wide of the mark. Only the patient and prolonged labors of the ethnologist can inform us as to what a tribe does and thinks; and where such studies have been made, it is found that a backward culture, such as that of the natives of Australia, has much more substance, and affords much wider scope for mental activity, than the early reports indicated.

The difficulty of inferring the mental endowment of a group from its stage of culture is well brought out by applying this method to the comparison of different epochs in the history of a nation. German culture today is much advanced from the days of Cæsar; shall we infer that the mental endowment of the Germans has advanced in like measure? Biologically, the interval, measured in generations, is not long, and from all biological considerations it is improbable that any advance in mental endowment has occurred. The difference in material civilization does not mean that the German of today is, on the average, gifted with more native inventiveness or business ability than his ancestors sixty generations ago. The difference in the arts and sciences does not mean that the German of today is naturally more studious, or scientific, or musical. The more settled condition of society does not imply greater native capacity for industry or government. The disappearance of old superstitions does not imply that later generations were born without the tendencies to superstition which characterized their fathers. We are still not many generations removed from witchcraft, curses, magic and the like savage beliefs and practices, and we can not reasonably believe our recent forefathers to have been naturally more savage than we are. When, for psychological purposes, we compare the culture of Europe with that of Africa, we should not leave out of account the Children's Crusade, or the Inquisition, or the Wars of the Roses. And if we attempt to use the state of civilization as a measure of racial intelligence, we must somehow adapt the method so that it shall give the same results, whether earlier or later stages in the culture of a group be taken as the basis for study.

In reality, the civilization possessed by a generation can not be used as a measure of the intelligence of that generation any more than an individual's property can be taken as a measure of his business ability. The greatest part of the civilization of a generation is bequeathed to it, and only the increase which it produces can be laid to its credit. If we could compare the rate of progress in different groups, this might serve as a measure of intelligence; and certainly some peoples are more progressive than others. Before adopting such a test, we should understand the mechanism of progress—a matter which belongs only in part to psychology.

Progress depends first of all on human inventiveness—so much will probably be allowed. Under the head of inventions should be included, not only mechanical devices, but works of art and government, business enterprises and changes in custom, so far as any of these demand originality in their producers. Science and all increase in knowledge should also be included, since the process of discovery differs but little from the process of invention. In both the essential mental act seems to be a bringing together of things that are found apart, or a pulling apart of what occurs together. In fact, both of these processes, the combining or associating, and the analytic or discriminating, go on together, since we see something new in a thing when we are reminded by it of something else and different. There is a suggestion of the accidental in all invention, since it depends on "happening to notice something," or "happening to be reminded of something." You can not be sure that a person will make a discovery, even when you supply him with the elements which would combine to produce it. Oftentimes, in reading the history of scientific progress, one is surprised that a certain discovery was not made by some man who had apparently everything before him to lead to it. Invention is of the nature of a spontaneous variation, and this accidental character is very important in understanding the mechanism of progress.

On the other hand, since one can not be reminded of things entirely unknown, invention depends on previously acquired knowledge, and the inventiveness of an individual must take a direction prepared for him by the social group among which he lives. A large share of the inventiveness of the Australian natives seems to be directed into the channels of magic and ceremony. The finished product of one mind's inventiveness becomes raw material for another, and invention of all sorts is distinctly a cooperative enterprise.

Invention is said to be mothered by necessity; and the proverb is no doubt true in the main, though curiosity and experimentation belong among the play instincts. But, in any case, the necessity must not be too dire, for some degree of leisure is demanded if anything novel is to be thought of, and rapid progress is only possible when individuals can be allowed to accumulate the special knowledge which may serve as the raw material for their inventive activity. Divisions of labor, guilds, universities, legislatures, investigating commissions, permanent research bureaus—each of which is, genetically, a series of inventions—are dependent for their existence on a certain degree of leisure, while they in turn provide more leisure and opportunity for further advance. They are inventions which accelerate the progress of invention. There are thus many factors besides the intellectual endowment of a generation which go to determine the progress which it shall make. The spur of necessity, the opportunity afforded by leisure, the existing stock of knowledge and inventions and the factor of apparent accident or luck have all to be considered.

A still further factor is the size of the group, which is deserving of renewed attention. Not only does a large group afford more opportunity for division of labor and special institutions for research, but the biological consideration already mentioned should be emphasized. The contributions to progress of the average man are small, the inventions of moment arising in the brains of a small fraction of the group. A large group provides a greater number of inventive minds, and it is rather the absolute number of such than their proportion to the whole population that determines the progress of invention within a group. The "group" needs to be redefined from the point of view of invention. If knowledge and inventions pass back and forth between two nations or races, the inventive minds of both are brought into cooperation, and the group is by so much enlarged. From the point of view of progress, however, the question is not simply how many inventive minds are brought into cooperation, but how free and rapid the communcation is between them. At the present time, a discovery originating anywhere in Europe or its colonies is quickly known by specialists in all parts, and may promptly fructify the mind of a distant investigator, leading to a fresh advance. The invention of printing and of rapid means of communication must be credited with a large share of the rapid progress which has been made by the last few generations. Much also must be credited to the invention of steam power, which has vastly multiplied the size of the European group, in an economic sense, and set free many minds of ability for productive thinking. The very idea of the advancement of science and invention as an end to be striven for is to be classed as an invention, and a rather recent one; and it too is an accelerator.

Such considerations provide at least a partial explanation of the different rates of progress in different generations, and among different races. Whether they explain everything could perhaps only be determined by a drastic experiment, which it will do no harm to imagine, though the question will never be settled in this convincing way.

Let two or more habitats, isolated from each other and from the rest of the world, and as nearly as possible alike, be chosen, and peopled by two equal groups of children, selected from some highly civilized nation, and so selected as to represent fairly the distribution of mental and physical traits among that nation. For every individual in the first group, let there be a practically identical individual in the second. Let these groups of children be introduced into their new homes in infancy, and, by some quasi-miraculous means, let them be all preserved to maturity, and then let them, and their descendants, be left entirely to their own devices, without fire, or a language, or other modern improvements. To watch such a spectacle from afar would be thrilling, if not too pitiful. We can readily grant that the infant communities would begin at the very zero of civilization, and that their progress, for many generations, would seem excessively slow. But the real point of the experiment is to inquire whether these two equal groups, alike in numbers, in heredity and in environment, would remain alike, and progress at equal rates. Probably they would not. We must allow for a large element of chance in the mating of males and females within each group, and consequently for changes and inequalities in the distribution and correlation of traits—changes which need not alter the average of either group. We must allow for spontaneous variation in the offspring, another accidental factor by virtue of which a really inventive and effective individual, or conjunction of such, would almost certainly arise in one group earlier than in the other, and give the advance of one group an impetus which might be felt through many generations, and carry this group far ahead of the other. And we must allow also for the accidental factor in invention. Even though the genius of one group was paired by an equal genius in the other, it is improbable that both would invent the same things. One might invent a hunting implement, and the other a fishing implement; and by this accident the direction of development might be settled for each group. If we closed the experiment after a thousand generations, we should probably find two peoples of different languages, different customs, and cultures divergent in many respects. The supposed result may be taken as an assertion of the importance of accident in determining the destiny of peoples. Obscure causes are no doubt at work beneath the accidents, but we can not trace them, nor reasonably state them in terms of racial superiority and inferiority.

It would seem that size of groups, and accidental factors, exert so much influence on the rate of advance in civilization that differences of culture could possibly be explained without supposing the mental endowments of the races to differ. Whether the existing races of men do or do not differ in such a trait as inventiveness is another and more difficult problem, the settlement of which must be left to time and educational experiments. The experiments must be continued for several generations, in order to equate social traditions. Regarding the negroes of the south, I am informed by a gentleman who has spent twenty years in educating them that a distinct advance is perceptible during this period, especially among the children of educated parents. These have more educational ambition, enter school earlier and have less to unlearn. The educational experiment, as far as it has gone, thus shows that much time will be needed before a clear result is reached.

Meanwhile it may be allowed to add one more general consideration by asking whether causes of a biological nature can be seen to be at work in human history, such as would differentiate the races intellectually, and, in particular, such as to raise up, in some part of the world, a race superior to the stock from which it sprang.

Natural selection has been suggested as such a cause. Life in the tropics, it has been said, is too easy to demand much inventiveness or forethought, but a migration to colder regions, where the banana does not grow, would make mental activity imperative, and select those individuals who were able to respond, so producing a superior race. There is a difficulty here, since we should expect natural selection to begin by lopping off the most poorly endowed fraction of the population, with the result, finally, that the lower range of intelligence should disappear from the higher races. The lowest grade of intelligence in Europe should accordingly be higher than the lowest grade in Africa. But this is probably not the case; the range of intelligence reaches as low in one as in the other. The distributions of intelligence in the two also overlap to quite an extent. Extensive experiment has shown that Africans can maintain existence in the temperate zone.

Sexual selection, or, more properly, mating customs, furnish a more promising factor. If a tendency could be detected in any population for the most intelligent members to mate with each other, the result would be, not indeed a raising of the average intelligence, since the less intelligent would also mate with each other, but an increase of the variability, and greater chance of the birth of very superior individuals. A caste system might operate in this way, since the founders of aristocratic families probably won admission to the caste partly by virtue of intelligence, and their descendants would tend, by heredity, to exceed the average intelligence of the population. Marriage confined to the caste would thus tend to mate superior individuals with each other, and might, in the course of generations, raise the upper limit of intelligence. Customs of mating within one's rank obtain among the aristocracy and royalty of Europe, and may have been a factor in increasing the number of superior intelligences. But too much can not be attributed to this factor, since the selection has been by classes, and not by individuals. Royalty, while marrying within its rank, has not usually chosen the most gifted individual available. Its selection has been relatively inefficient from the standpoint of royal eugenics. Certainly the upper reach of European intelligence has not been the result of breeding by castes; for, though royalty has indeed produced a disproportionate number of high intelligences, equally able individuals have, as a matter of fact, risen from humble birth. Moreover, marriage in all parts of the world is largely governed by considerations of family standing and wealth, so that the same sort of influence toward variability is everywhere operative. The dead level of intelligence, which is sometimes supposed to obtain among backward races, is not borne out by psychological tests, since individual differences are abundantly found among all races, and, indeed, the variability of different groups seems, from these tests, to be about on a par.

Selection by migration is also to be considered. When individuals leave their group and go to a new country, it would seem that those who emigrate must differ, on the average, from those who remain behind. An adventurous and enterprising spirit, perhaps, would be characteristic of the emigrants, and so of the new people which they helped to form. On the other hand, the ne'er-do-well and the criminal might also be induced to emigrate. The selective influence of migration would not be all in one direction, and the net result could not easily be predicted. Since we are now witnessing, though little comprehending, this process of migration as it contributes to form a people of the future, information regarding the kind of selective influence exerted by migration would have a practical value. Wisdom would dictate that the nation which is in process of formation should exert some selective influence on its own account, but, from all the facts in hand, the part of wisdom would be to select the best individuals available from every source, rather than, trusting to the illusory appearance of great racial differences in mental and moral traits, to make the selection in terms of races or nations.

This paper is of double interest in this volume. First, it is about a man who played a key role in the development of differential psychology. Second, the paper illustrates a technique developed by Terman to appraise the childhood intelligence of eminent men. The results of the investigation of 300 eminent men may be found in the book by Cox, Early Mental Traits of Three Hundred Geniuses. Terman's contributions to the study of intelligence rank second only to those of Binet, and his studies of genius are unsurpassed.

The Intelligence Quotient of Francis Galton in Childhood*

LEWIS M. TERMAN

1917

The writer does not remember to have seen Francis Galton classed among boy prodigies. Indeed, Galton's main contributions to science were given to the world at so late a date in his life that he is not infrequently mentioned as an illustration of late-maturing genius. *Hereditary Genius* was published in the author's fiftieth year; *Natural Inheritance* in his sixty-eighth year; and on the practical side the most important work of his life was not accomplished until he was more than eighty years of age.

In the recently published Volume I of Karl Pearson's *Life, Letters and Labors of Galton,* there is ample evidence that Galton was a boy of unusual attainments and that he was extraordinarily precocious. The biography in question departs radically from the usual type of biography by presenting documentary evidence regarding the more important events in the life of its subject, and that concerning Galton's childhood is especially full and significant. From the evidence given, one is justified in concluding that between the ages of three and eight years at least, Francis Galton must have had an intelligence quotient not far from double his actual age.

The significance of this will be apparent when we say that after diligent search in several cities and several counties in California—a search including many thousands of children in scope—the highest intelligence quotient we have yet found is 170. The number that we have found going above 150 can be counted on the fingers of one hand.

From early childhood Galton was under the instruction of his sister Adèle, herself a mere child. "She taught him his letters in play, and he could point to them all before he could speak. Adèle had a wonderful

* *The American Journal of Psychology*, 28 (1917), pp. 208-215. Reprinted by permission of the publisher.

power of teaching and gaining attention without fatiguing. She taught her-self Latin and Greek that she might teach him. She never had him learn by heart, but made him read his lesson, bit by bit, eight times over, when he could say it. He could repeat much of Scott's *Marmion* and understood it all by the time he was five." (Quoted by Pearson from Elizabeth Ann Galton's *Reminiscences*.)

Pearson further informs us that Francis knew his capital letters by twelve months and both his alphabets by eighteen months; that he could read a little book, *Cobwebs to Catch Flies*, when two and a half years old, and could sign his name before three years. The following letter from his fourth year has been endorsed by his mother, saying that Francis wrote and spelled it entirely himself;

My
dear
Uncle
We have
got Ducks. I know
a Nest. I mean
to make a
Feast.

The day before his fifth birthday he wrote the following letter to his sister:

My dear Adele,
I am 4 years old and I can read any English book. I can say all the Latin Substantives and Adjectives and active verbs besides 52 lines of Latin poetry. I can cast up any sum in addition and can multiply by 2, 3, 4, 5, 6, 7, 8, [9], 10, [11].
I can also say the pence table. I read French a little and I know the clock.

Francis Galton,
Febuary 15, 1827

The only misspelling is in the date. The numbers 9 and 11 are bracketed above, because little Francis, evidently feeling that he had claimed too much, had scratched out one of these numbers with a knife and pasted some paper over the other!

This document should have great interest for those who have worked with mental tests. That Francis at less than five years could read any Eng-lish book demonstrates beyond any possible doubt that he was as far ad-vanced at this time as the *average* English or American child at nine or ten years. It is an accomplishment which we do not believe is possible to a mental age of less than nine years with any amount of formal instruction. It is certain that our subject's accomplishments did not include merely the ability to pronounce words mechanically, for there is ample evidence from other sources that at this early age he read with understanding.

Again, at this age Francis had learned to do any sum in addition, and had learned all but the hardest part of the multiplication table. This in-dicates, at least, nine-year intelligence, for we have found that, however old a child and however much school instruction he may have had, the multiplication table is seldom mastered thoroughly much below the nine-year level. Further, his knowledge of the "pence table" indicates an acquaintance with the coins and their values such as children ordinarily do not have before something like eight years.

Besides informing us that Francis had, at this tender age, gotten quite a start in French and Latin, the above letter also tells us that he "knows the clock"; that is, presumably, he was able to tell the time of day by the clock. This performance has been definitely standardized at the mental age of nine to ten years, and it is almost never passed before the mental age of eight years.

The reader may raise the question whether it is safe to accept a child's own statements with regard to the above points. It would not be, of course, if there were no corroborative evidence. The fact that there is such evidence from many sources, and the fact that little Francis was known to be as remarkably conscientious as he was intelligent, justifies us in accepting the above statements without the slightest discount.

The fact that Francis' reading at the age of five years was intelligent and not of the mechanical kind is demonstrated by his ability at that age to offer quotations which would fit a given situation. For example, when he was five years old, a boy friend asked his advice as to what he ought to say in a letter to his father, who, it seems, was in danger of being shot for some political affair. Little Francis replied immediately from Walter Scott:

> And if I live to be a man,
> My father's death revenged shall be.

Again at the age of five, he was found holding a group of tormenting boys at arm's length, shouting meanwhile,

> Come one, come all. This rock shall fly
> From its firm base, as soon as I.

By six, under the tutelage of Adèle, he had become thoroughly conversant with the Iliad and the Odyssey. At this age, a visitor at the Galton home made Francis weary by cross-questioning him about points in Homer. Finally, the boy replied, "Pray, Mr. Horner, look at the last line in the twelfth book of the Odyssey" and then ran off. The line in question reads, "But why rehearse all this tale, for even yesterday I told it to thee and to thy noble wife in thy house; and it liketh me not twice to tell a plain-told tale."

It seems that Adèle also taught Francis a good deal about entomology, and at six and seven years he was active and persistent in collecting insects and minerals, which he is said to have classified and studied in more than a childish way. It has been shown by Mrs. Burk that collections of an analytical and classificatory type are not common before twelve or thirteen years. Here, again, we find evidence of an intelligence quotient not far from 200.

Pearson quotes the following letter written by a visitor at the Galton home on December 28, 1828:

The youngest child, Francis, is a prodigy. He is seven next February and reads 'Marmion,' 'The Lady of the Lake,' Cowper's, Pope's and Shakespeare's works for pleasure, and, by reading a page twice over, repeats it by heart. He writes a beautiful hand, is in long division, and has been twice through the Latin Grammar; all taught by Adèle.

At the age of eight, Francis was taken away from home to attend a boarding school. Here he was placed in a high class, although the boys in it ranged up to fifteen years. Since this was a private school attended by children of a superior social class, it is altogether likely that his fourteen- and fifteen-year-old classmates were themselves above the average mental level of that age; hence Francis must by this time have reached a mental level of not far from that which is median for sixteen years.

In his first year at this school, we find Francis writing to his father in these words; "I am very glad that you have left off being a banker, for you will have more time to yourself and better health." This little quotation certainly betokens a degree of filial solicitude by no means common to children of this age. Such altruism does not ordinarily develop so early. The words fit sixteen-year much better than eight-year intelligence.

Francis' interests at the age of ten are indicated by the following letter:

December 30, 1832.

My Dearest Papa:
    It is now my pleasure to disclose the most ardent wishes of my heart, which are to extract out of my boundless wealth in compound, money sufficient to make this addition to my unequaled library.

The Hebrew Commonwealth by John	9
A Pastor Advice	2
Hornne's commentaries on the Psalms	4
Paley's Evidence on Christianity	2
Jones Biblical Cyclopedia	10
	27

It is hardly necessary to comment on the above letter as an indication of the boy's mental maturity. It speaks for itself.

Francis' interests, however, were not wholly literary, for at the age of thirteen he gave us "Francis Galton's Aerostatic Project." It seems this was a series of drawings representing a flying machine. It was to work by large, flapping wings with a sort of revolving steam engine, and was supposed to carry five passengers, a pilot, and an engineer.

At the age of fifteen, we find the youth Galton expressing in his letters to his father serious opinions on mind training, the relative value of classics and English, and other matters of educational theory. These opinions were voiced by him again some sixty years later, substantially without change.

At the age of fifteen Francis was admitted to the general hospital at Birmingham as a medical student.

It is well known that, in general, a high correlation obtains between favorable mental traits of all kinds; that, for example, children superior in intelligence also tend to be superior in moral qualities. Francis Galton was no exception to this rule, as indicated by the following letter written by his mother when the boy was only eight years old:

Francis from his earliest age showed highly honorable feelings. His temper, although hasty, brought no resentment, and his little irritations were soon calmed. His open-minded disposition, with great good nature and kindness to those boys younger than himself, made him beloved by all his school fellows. He was very affectionate and even sentimental in his manners. His activity of body could only be equaled by the activity of his mind. He was a boy never known to be idle. His habit was always to be doing something. He showed no vanity at his superiority over other boys, but said it was a shame that their education should have been so neglected.

After Mr. Pearson has given us all the above significant information, it is astonishing to find him commenting upon it as follows:

The letters we have quoted from these early years may appear to the reader to contain little of note. They are, indeed, just what a healthy normal child would write, but it is that very fact that makes them essential human documents and gives them their fundamental interest. . . . Need we attempt to see signs of exceptional ability or to discover foreshadowings of future achievement in these outpourings of healthy childhood? I do not think we can say more than that Francis Galton was a normal child with rather more than average ability. . . .

Mr. Pearson's error is of a kind which is now coming to be generally recognized by those who work with mental tests; that is, an error due to the failure to take into account the significance of a mental performance *in terms of the mental age to which it corresponds.* Pearson did not know, and the average teacher does not fully appreciate, that a child of four years who is able to do the things characteristic of a child of seven or eight years is a genius of the first order. It is hard to get people to understand that what a child is able to do has no significance unless we take age into account.

The opposite error is no less common; that is, for a mentally retarded child in a grade far below his age to be considered perfectly normal and average in intelligence. One was only recently described as "slow to learn." The child in question was twelve years old and in the first grade, and we suggested to the teacher that in all probability the child was feeble-minded. We were met, however, with the most positive assurance that the little girl in question could not possibly be feeble-minded, that she was actually learning the work of the first grade, and that her normal mentality was shown by her motherly interest in her little six-year-old classmates. Without arguing the matter further, we urged the teacher to bring the child for a

Binet test, with the result that she was found to have a mental age of a little less than six years by the Stanford Revision. This child had been in school several years and had had every opportunity to learn, except the advantage of endowment. Experience has taught us that such a subject will never reach the mental level of seven years, however long she may live.

This teacher's error may seem to some almost incredible. In reality it is an error of about the same degree as that made by Mr. Pearson, though in the opposite direction. Similar errors, though perhaps not quite as great, are abundant even in the writings of psychologists on mental tests.

When the United States entered World War I, a group of dedicated psychologists saw the immense need for group intelligence tests. This group, under the direction of Robert M. Yerkes, assembled and tried out group tests based on the test ideas of Arthur S. Otis, drove them through to standardization, and convinced the armed forces that they could be useful. This dramatic story is told in detail in the reference below. The final forms of the group tests were called Alpha and Beta, and the enormous achievement of testing and classifying over 1,700,000 men firmly established intelligence testing in the American scene. Here we have reproduced the examiner's instructions and test material for one of the late forms of these famous tests.

Group Examinations: Alpha and Beta*

ARMY PSYCHOLOGISTS

1917–1918

Group Examination Alpha

1. Procedure

Examination alpha is to be given to all subjects who remain in the room after the elimination of illiterates. In giving the following directions examiner should speak rather slowly, distinctly, and with proper emphasis. *He should expect and demand perfect order and prompt response to commands.*

When everything is ready examiner proceeds as follows: "Attention! The purpose of this examination is to see how well you can remember, think, and carry out what you are told to do. We are not looking for crazy people. The aim is to help find out what you are best fitted to do in the Army. The grade you make in this examination will be put on your qualification card and will also go to your company commander. Some of the things you are told to do will be very easy. Some you may find hard. You are not expected to make a perfect grade, but do the very best you can.

"Now, in the Army a man often has to listen to commands and then carry them out exactly. I am going to give *you* some commands to see how well you can carry them out. Listen closely. Ask no questions. Do not watch any other man to see what *he* does.

"Look at your papers. Just below where you have been writing, there are several sets of forms—circles, triangles, and so forth. First you will

* The text is taken from Psychological Examining in the United States Army, *Memoirs of the National Academy of Sciences*, 15, Robert M. Yerkes, ed. (Washington, Government Printing Office, 1921). By permission of the National Academy of Sciences.

be told to do something with the circles at 1, afterward with the circles at 2, and so on.

"When I call 'Attention,' stop instantly whatever you are doing and hold your pencil up—so. Don't put your pencil down to the paper until I say 'Go.' (Examiner lowers his pencil.) Listen carefully to what I say. Do just what you are told to do. As soon as you are through, pencils up. Remember, wait for the word 'Go.' "

N. B.—Examiner: Give the following instructions very distinctly and at moderate speed. After giving the command "Attention," always notice carefully and have orderlies notice whether all pencils are up. Never proceed until they are. This is especially important in the beginning. Be careful to use the directions that fit the *form* of alpha booklet distributed. Be careful not to pause or to drop the voice in the course of a compound direction, e.g., in 2, before the words "and also." Raise your pencil whenever you say "Attention." Lower it promptly whenever you say "Go."

Test 1, form 5.

1. "Attention! 'Attention' always means 'Pencils up!' Look at the circles at 1. When I say 'Go' (but not before) make a cross in the first circle and also a figure 1 in the third circle.—GO!" (Allow not over 5 seconds.)

2. "Attention! Look at 2, where the circles have numbers in them. When I say 'Go' draw a line from circle 1 to circle 4 that will pass *above* circle 2 and *below* circle 3.—GO!" (Allow not over 5 seconds.)

3. "Attention! Look at the square and triangle at 3. When I say 'Go' make a cross in the space which is in the triangle but not in the square, and also make a figure 1 in the space which is in the triangle and in the square. GO!" (Allow not over 10 seconds.)

4. "Attention! Look at 4. When I say 'Go' make a figure 1 in the space which is in the circle but not in the triangle or square, and also make a figure 2 in the space which is in the triangle and circle, but not in the square.—GO!" (Allow not over 10 seconds.)

N. B.—Examiner: In reading 5, don't pause at the word circle as if ending a sentence.

5. "Attention! Look at 5. If a machine gun can shoot more bullets a minute than a rifle, then (when I say 'Go') put a cross in the second circle; if not, draw a line *under* the word NO.—GO!" (Allow not over 10 seconds.)

6. "Attention! Look at 6. When I say 'Go' put in the second circle the right answer to the question: 'How many months has a year?' In the third circle do nothing, but in the fourth circle put any number that is a wrong answer to the question that you have just answered correctly.—GO!" (Allow not over 10 seconds.)

7. "Attention! Look at 7. When I say 'Go' *cross out* the letter just before

C and also draw a line *under* the second letter before H.—GO!" (Allow not over 10 seconds.)

8. "Attention! Look at 8. Notice the three circles and the three words. When I say 'Go' make in the *first* circle the *first* letter of the *first* word; in the *second* circle the first letter of the *second* word, and in the *third* circle the *last* letter of the *third* word.—GO!" (Allow not over 10 seconds.)

9. "Attention! Look at 9. When I say 'Go' *cross out* each number that is more than 20 but less than 30.—GO!" (Allow not over 15 seconds.)

10. "Attention! Look at 10. Notice that the drawing is divided into five parts. When I say 'Go' put a 3 or a 2 in each of the two largest parts and any number between 4 and 7 in the part next in size to the smallest part.—GO!" (Allow not over 15 seconds.)

11. "Attention! Look at 11. When I say 'Go' draw a line through every even number that is not in a square, and also through every odd number that is in a square with a letter.—GO!" (Allow not over 25 seconds.)

12. "Attention! Look at 12. If 7 is more than 5, then (when I say 'Go') cross out the number 6 unless 6 is more than 8, in which case draw a line *under* the number 7.—GO!" (Allow not over 10 seconds.)

"During the rest of this examination don't turn any page forward or backward unless you are told to. Now turn over the page to test 2."

Test 2, arithmetical problems.

"Attention! Look at the directions at the top of the page while I read them. 'Get the answers to these examples as quickly as you can. Use the side of this page to figure on if you need to.' I will say stop at the end of five minutes. You may not be able to finish all of them, but do as many as you can in the time allowed. The two samples are already answered correctly.—Ready—GO!"

After 5 minutes, say "STOP! Turn over the page to test 3."

Test 3, practical judgment.

"Attention! Look at the directions at the top of the page while I read them.

" 'This is a test of common sense. Below are sixteen questions. Three answers are given to each question. You are to look at the answers carefully; then make a cross in the square before the *best* answer to each question, as in the sample:

"Why do we use stoves? Because

☐ they look well
☒ they keep us warm
☐ they are black

"Here the second answer is the best one and is marked with a cross.

"Begin with No. 1 and keep on until time is called.'—Ready—GO!"

After 1½ minutes, say "STOP! Turn over the page to test 4."

Test 4, synonym—antonym.

"Attention! Look at the directions at the top of the page while I read them." (Examiner reads slowly.)

" 'If the two words of a pair mean the same or nearly the same, draw a line under *same*. If they mean the opposite or nearly the opposite, draw a line under *opposite*. If you can not be sure, guess. The two samples are already marked as they should be.'—Ready—GO!"

After 1½ minutes, say "STOP! Turn over the page to test 5." (Pause.) "Now you have to turn your books around this way." (Examiner illustrates the necessary rotation.)

Test 5, disarranged sentences.

"Attention! Look at the directions at the top of the page while I read them." (Examiner reads slowly.)

" 'The words *a eats cow grass* in that order are mixed up and don't make a sentence; but they would make a sentence if put in the right order: *a cow eats grass,* and this statement is true.

"Again, the words *horses feathers have all* would make a sentence if put in the order *all horses have feathers,* but this statement is false.

"Below are 24 mixed sentences. Some of them are true and some are false. When I say 'Go,' take these sentences one at a time. Think what each *would* say if the words were straightened out, but don't write them yourself. Then, if what it *would* say is true, draw a line under the word 'true;' if what it would say is false, draw a line under the word 'false.' If you can not be sure, guess. The two samples are already marked as they should be. Begin with No. 1 and work right down the page until time is called.'—Ready—GO!"

After 2 minutes, say "STOP! Turn over the page to test 6."

Test 6, number series completion.

(N. B.—Examiner: Give these instructions very slowly.)

"Attention! Look at the first sample row of figures at the top of the page—2, 4, 6, 8, 10, 12; the two numbers that should come next are, of course, 14, 16.

"Look at the second sample—9, 8, 7, 6, 5, 4; the two numbers that should come next are 3, 2.

"Look at the third sample—2, 2, 3, 3, 4, 4; the two numbers that should come next are 5, 5.

"Now look at the fourth sample—1, 7, 2, 7, 3, 7; the next two numbers would, of course, be 4, 7.

"Look at each row of numbers below, and on the two dotted lines write the two numbers that should come next.—Ready—GO!"

After 3 minutes, say "STOP! Turn over the page to test 7."

Test 7, analogies.

"Attention! Look at the first sample at the top of the page: Sky—blue : : grass—table, *green,* warm, big.

"Notice the four words in heavy type. One of them—*green*—is underlined. Grass is *green* just as the sky is blue.

"Look at the second sample: Fish—swims : : man—paper, time, *walks,* girl.

"Here the word *walks* is underlined. A man walks and a fish swims.

"Look at the third sample: Day—night : : white—red, *black,* clear, pure.

"Here the word *black* is underlined because black is the opposite of white just as night is the opposite of day.

"In each of the lines below the first two words are related to each other in some way. What you are to do in each line is to see what the relation is between the first two words, and underline the word in heavy type that is related in the same way to the third word. Begin with No. 1 and mark as many sets as you can before time is called.—Ready—GO!"

After 3 minutes, say "STOP! Turn over the page to test 8."

Test 8, information.

"Attention! Look at the directions at the top of the page while I read them." (Examiner reads slowly.)

" 'Notice the sample sentence: People hear with the—eyes—ears—nose—mouth. The correct word is *ears,* because it makes the truest sentence. In each of the sentences below you have four choices for the last word. Only one of them is correct. In each sentence draw a line under the one of these four words which makes the truest sentence. If you can not be sure, guess. The two samples are already marked as they should be.'—Ready—GO!"

After 4 minutes, say "STOP! Turn over the page to test 1 again. In the upper right hand corner, where it says 'Group No. —,' put the number 101" (or 102, 103, etc., according to the number of this group in the examiner's series of groups).

Have all examination booklets and pencils collected immediately and before the men are allowed to leave their seats. Before dismissing the group, the number of booklets collected should be carefully checked with the number of men present and the number of booklets issued.

2. Directions for Scoring

General rules.

1. Each item is scored either right or wrong. No part credits are given.
2. In general, items evidently corrected stand as corrected.
3. In tests where the score is "number right," only wrong items need be

checked in scoring. In tests 4 and 5, where the score is "right minus wrong," wrong and omitted items must be separately checked.

4. Indicate the last item attempted by drawing a long line under that item and out into the margin.

5. Enter the score for each test in lower right-hand corner of the test page and encircle it. When the test has been re-scored, a check mark ($\sqrt{}$) may be made beside the circle.

6. Red or blue pencil increases accuracy of scoring.

Test 1.

(Score is number right.)

1. No credit is given for any item in which *more* is done than the instructions require.

2. In an item where something is to be written "*in*" a given space, give credit if a mark crosses a line from haste or awkwardness; give no credit if the position is really ambiguous.

3. Where something is to be underlined or crossed out, give credit if two or three underlinings are made in the required place, and give credit for any method of crossing out.

4. *Item 2.*—The pencil line must begin and end either on the circumference or within the circles indicated. It may touch the intermediate circles, but must not cut through them.

5. *Item 6.*—In the circle marked "not 12" there must be some number which is not 12, such as 5, 0, 27.

6. *Item 9.*—The proper numbers must be crossed out to receive credit.

7. *Item 10.*—In Form 5, "2" alone and "3" alone, but not "2 or 3," in each of the two largest parts; "5" alone and "6" alone, but not "5 or 6," in the next to the smallest part, are correct. Similarly for other forms.

8. *Item 11.*—The lines must cross, or at least touch, the proper numbers; they may or may not cut the accompanying letters. Mere indications of the square, triangle, etc., is not sufficient.

9. *Item 12.*—Underlining in place of crossing out is wrong.

Test 2.

(Score is number right.)

1. Answer may be written on dotted line or elsewhere near its problem.

2. If two answers are given to any problem, count as wrong.

3. If it seems clear that, by a slip, one answer has been put in the wrong brackets, and the next answers are all thus misplaced, give credit for the answers that are right even if misplaced.

4. Omission of dollar sign is permissible.

5. Omission of decimal point is permissible in items 2, 9, 13, and 14. Fraction may be expressed as decimal in item 15.

Test 3.

(Score is number right.)

1. Any clear method of indicating answer is given full credit—underlining, checking, etc.

2. If two answers are marked, count as wrong unless one is clearly indicated as final.

Test 4.

(Score is number right minus number wrong.)

1. Any clear method of indicating answer is given credit.

2. When both "same" and "opposite" are underlined, counts as *omitted*, not as wrong.

3. If only "same" is underlined right down the column, score for the test is zero. Similarly if "opposite" is underlined right down the column.

Test 5.

(Score is number right minus number wrong.)
Same rules as for test 4.

Test 6.

(Score is number right.)

1. If only one number is written, give no credit.

2. If only one of the numbers is right, give no credit.

3. If four numbers are written, as frequently happens with certain items (i.e., 33, 11 instead of 3, 3), give full credit.

Test 7.

(Score is number right.)

1. Any clear indication other than underlining receives full credit.

2. Underlining of any of the first three words of an item does not remove credit.

3. If two or more of the last four words are marked, give no credit.

Test 8.

(Score is number right.)
Same rules as for test 7.

3. Total Score and Rating

The result of examination alpha is expressed in a total score which is the sum of the raw scores of the several tests. The raw scores are obtained as follows:

Test	Method of scoring	Maximum raw score
1......................	R	12
2......................	R	20
3......................	R	16
4......................	R–W	40
5......................	R–W	24
6......................	R	20
7......................	R	40
8......................	R	40
Total...............	....	212

Letter ratings are assigned on examination alpha as follows:

Rating	Score
A	135–212
B.............................	105–134
C+............................	75–104
C.............................	45– 74
C–............................	25– 44
D	15– 24
D–............................	0– 14

All ratings above D − are entered and reported at once. Men whose scores are below D are recalled for examination beta. Ratings of D − may not be given in alpha, unless recall of the men for beta is impossible.

Group Examination Beta

1. Directions for Setting Up Apparatus

Beta materials are shipped in three packages.

1. Blackboard frame.
2. Blackboard chart.
3. (*a*) Cardboard pieces for test 7; (*b*) patterns for constructing cubes for test 2.

The *blackboard frame* consists of 8 fitted sections, 2 uprights which carry 2 rollers and 4 crossbars which are attached to the small crosspieces of the uprights. The blackboard should be set up so that the ends of the rollers to which the crank may be fitted come on the right-hand side. A piece of beaver board 30 by 40 inches should be nailed to the crossbars so as to give a rigid writing surface. This must be procured in the camps.

The *blackboard chart* is a continuous roll 27 feet long. Care should be used in attaching chart to rollers so that it will wind evenly. The chart must be kept as clean as possible at all times. The painting should be gone over from time to time with a white gloss paint.

The *patterns for constructing cubes for test 2* should be drawn on heavy cardboard on a scale such that the constructed model will appear to be made from 3-inch cubes. All cube edges, either real or imaginary, should be bordered in lines ⅛-inch thick painted with india ink. The models should be cut on the full lines and folded on the dotted lines as indicated in the patterns furnished. For these cube models a sloping shelf should be so arranged that the perspective from the center of the room will be the same as that of the models represented on the blackboard.

Chalk, eraser, pointer, and a curtain for covering beta apparatus are also necessary.

2. Procedure

It is most important that examination beta be given in a genial manner. The subjects who take this examination sometimes sulk and refuse to work. Examiner and his assistants will find it necessary to fill out most of the headings for the men before the examination begins. The time required for this preparatory work may be used to advantage in making the men feel at ease. As the demonstration preparatory to each test requires some time, the "pencils up" command is omitted in examination beta. The examiner's platform should be so high that he can readily see whether or not the subjects are working. Great care should be taken to prevent the overanxious from beginning work before the command "Go."

Seating conditions should be such that subjects can not copy from one another and the rule that copying shall not be allowed should be enforced strictly. The blackboard should at all times be kept clean so that the visual conditions may be excellent and constant. The blackboard figures for test 1 should be exposed when the subjects enter the examining room. *As soon as a test has been demonstrated and the men have been told to go ahead, the blackboard should be covered and kept covered until time is called.* It should not be turned to the next test until the men have been ordered to stop work on a given test. Care should be taken to have the physical conditions of examination reasonably uniform.

With the exception of the brief introductory statements and a few orders, instructions are to be given throughout by means of gestures instead of words. These gestures accompany the samples and demonstrations and should be animated and emphatic.

It is absolutely necessary that directions be followed closely and procedure kept uniform and definite. Variations of procedure are more likely to occur in beta than in alpha, and there is serious risk that if allowed they will lessen the value of results. Examiner should especially guard against using more or fewer gestures or words for one group than for another. Oral language should be rigidly limited to the words and phrases given in the procedure for the different tests.

Whether the men get the idea of the test and enter into it with the proper spirit will depend chiefly on the skill with which the examiner, the demonstrator, and the orderlies carry out their respective parts. Examiner and demonstrator especially should be selected with the greatest care. An examiner who succeeds admirably in giving alpha may prove to be entirely unadapted for beta. Both examiner and demonstrator must be adept in the use of gesture language. In the selection of a demonstrator the personnel office should be consulted. One camp has had great success with a "window seller" as demonstrator. Actors should also be considered for the work. The orderlies should be able to keep the subjects at work without antagonizing them and to keep them encouraged without actually helping them.

The demonstrator should have the single task of doing before the group just what the group is later to do with the examination blanks. The blackboard is his beta blank. Before examination beta can be given satisfactorily the demonstrator must be letter perfect in his part. Both examiner and demonstrator must be very careful to stand at the side of the blackboard in order not to hide the drawings.

As soon as the men of a group have been properly seated, pencils should be distributed and also examination blanks with test 8 up. While this is being done examiner should say "Here are some papers. You must not open them or turn them over until you are told to." Holding up beta blank, examiner continues:

"In the place where it says name, write your name; print it if you can. (Pause.) Fill out the rest of the blank about your age, schooling, etc., as well as you can. If you have any trouble we will help you." (The instructions given under segregation may be used for filling out the beta blank.) Examiner should announce the group number and see that it as well as the other necessary information is supplied. Before the examination proceeds each paper should be inspected in order to make sure that it is satisfactorily completed.

After the initial information has been obtained, examiner makes the following introductory remarks:

"*Attention.* Watch *this* man (pointing to demonstrator). *He* (pointing to demonstrator again) is going to do *here* (tapping blackboard with pointer), what *you* (pointing to different members of group) are to do on your *papers* (here examiner points to several papers that lie before men in the group, picks up one, holds it next to the blackboard, returns the paper, points to demonstrator and the blackboard in succession, then to the men and their papers). Ask *no questions. Wait* till I say 'Go ahead!' "

In general, when instructing the group to turn from test to test, examiner holds up a beta blank before group and follows his own instructions as he gives them. As soon as he has turned to desired test or page he says, "This is test X *here;* look!" (pointing to the page).

To suggest to the group the necessity of working rapidly the demonstrator, after proceeding very deliberately with the early samples of each test, hurries, as soon as he has worked out the last sample problem

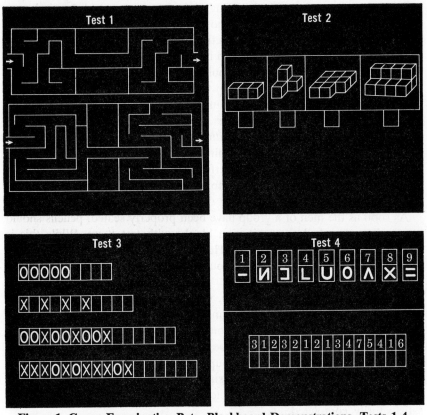

Figure 1. Group Examination Beta, Blackboard Demonstrations, Tests 1-4.

    (1) to record his response as fast as he can,
    (2) then to catch examiner's eyes for approval, and,
    (3) finally, to slip away from blackboard, drawing curtain as he does so.

After the personal data called for on page 1 of blank have been gathered and recorded, the orderlies' vocabulary in beta is rigidly restricted to the following words, or their literal equivalents in Italian, Russian, etc.: *Yes, No, Sure, Good, Quick, How many? Same, Fix it.* Under no circumstances may substitutional explanations or directions be given.

Test 1, maze.

"Now turn your papers over. This is test 1 *here* (pointing to page of record blank). Look." After all have found the page, examiner continues, "Don't make any marks till I say 'Go ahead.' Now *watch*." After touching

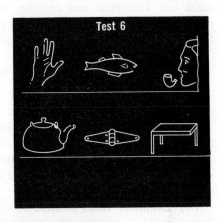

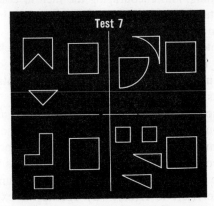

Figure 2. Group Examination Beta, Blackboard Demonstrations, Tests 5-7.

both arrows, examiner traces through first maze with pointer and then motions the demonstrator to go ahead. Demonstrator traces path through first maze *with crayon*, slowly and hesitatingly. Examiner then traces second maze and motions to demonstrator to go ahead. Demonstrator makes one mistake by going into the blind alley at upper left-hand corner of maze. Examiner apparently does not notice what demonstrator is doing until he crosses line at end of alley; then examiner shakes his head vigorously, says "No—no," takes demonstrator's hand and traces back to the place where he may start right again. Demonstrator traces rest of maze so as to indicate an attempt at haste, hesitating only at ambiguous points. Examiner says "Good." Then holding up blank, "Look here," and draws an imaginary line across the page from left to right for every maze on the page. Then, "All right. Go ahead. Do it (pointing to men and then to books). Hurry up." The idea of working fast must be impressed on the men during the maze test. Examiner and orderlies walk around the room, motioning to men who are not working, and saying, "Do it, do it, hurry up, quick." At the end of 2 minutes examiner says, "Stop! Turn over the page to test 2."

Test 2, cube analysis.

"This is test 2 *here*. Look." After everyone has found the page—"Now watch." The order of procedure is as follows:

(1) Examiner points to the three-cube model on the blackboard, making a rotary movement of the pointer to embrace the entire picture.

(2) With similar motion he points to the three-cube model on shelf.

(3) Examiner points next to picture on blackboard and asks, "How much?"

(4) Examiner turns to cube model and counts aloud, putting up his fingers while so doing, and encouraging the men to count with him.

(5) Examiner taps each cube on the blackboard and motions to demonstrator, asking him "How much?"

(6) Demonstrator (pointing) counts cubes on blackboard silently and writes the figure 3 in proper place.

In the second sample of this test, when examiner counts cubes of model he

(1) counts the three exposed cubes;

(2) touches the unexposed cube with pointer; and

(3) without removing pointer turns model, so that hidden cube comes into view of group. In other respects procedure with second and third samples is the same as with first.

In counting the 12-cube model, examiner (1) counts the top row of cubes in the model (left to right), (2) counts the exposed bottom row (right to left), (3) taps with pointer the end cube of hidden row, (4) turns the entire model around and completes his counting. Examiner then holds model in same plane as drawing and counts (in the same order as above) the cubes on blackboard, counting lines between front and top row as representing the hidden row. He then asks demonstrator "How much?" Demonstrator counts the cubes on blackboard (pointing but not speaking) and writes the response.

Throughout the demonstration the counting is done deliberately, not more rapidly than one cube per second.

At end of demonstration examiner points to page and says, "All right. Go ahead." At the end of 2½ minutes he says, "Stop! Look at me and don't turn the page."

Test 3, X-O series.

"This is test 3 *here*. Look." After everyone has found the page—"Now watch." Examiner first points to the blank rectangles at the end, then traces each "O" in chart, then traces outline of "O's" in remaining spaces. Demonstrator, at a gesture, draws them in. Examiner then traces first "X" in next sample, moves to next "X" by tracing the arc of an imaginary semicircle joining the two, and in the same manner traces each "X," moving over an arc to the next. He then traces outlines of "X's" in the proper blank spaces, moving over the imaginary arc in each case, and motions to demonstrator to draw them in. Demonstrator, at a gesture, fills in remaining problems very slowly, standing well to the right of the blackboard and writing with his left hand. Examiner points to page and says, "All right. Go ahead. Hurry up!" At end of 1¾ minutes he says, "Stop! Turn over the page to test 4."

Test 4, digit–symbol.

"This is test 4 *here*. Look." After everyone has found the page—"Now watch." Examiner points to first digit of key on blackboard and then points to the symbol under it. Same for all nine digits in key. Examiner then (1) points to first digit of sample, (2) to the empty space below digit, (3) points to corresponding digit of key, (4) points to proper symbol under digit in key, and (5) traces the outline of the proper symbol in the blank space under the digit in the sample. Same for first five samples. Demonstrator, at a gesture, fills in all the samples, working as follows: (1) Touches the number in the first sample with index finger of right hand; (2) holding finger there, finds with index finger of left hand the corresponding number in key; (3) drops index finger of left hand to symbol for number found; (4) holding left hand in this position writes appropriate symbol in the lower half of the sample.

Similarly with the other samples. While working, demonstrator should stand as far as possible to the left, doing all the samples from this side.

At the end of the demonstration examiner says, "Look here!" and points to key on page, repeating the gestures used in pointing on the blackboard at the beginning of the demonstration. Then, "All right. Go ahead. Hurry up!" Orderlies point out key to men who are at a loss to find it. At the end of two minutes, examiner says, "Stop! But don't turn the page."

Test 5, number checking.

"This is test 5 *here*. Look." After everyone has found the page, "Now watch." In this demonstration examiner must try to get "Yes" or "No" responses from the group. If the wrong response is volunteered by the group, examiner points to digits again and gives right response, "Yes" or "No" as the case may be. Examiner points to first digit of first number in left column, then to first digit, first number, in right column, then to second digit, first number, in left column and second digit, first number, in right column, nods head, says "Yes" and makes an imaginary cross at end number in right column. Motions to demonstrator, who makes an "X" there. Examiner does the same for second line of figures, but here he indicates clearly by shaking head and saying "No"—that certain digits are not identical. Examiner repeats for three more sets and after each, looks at group, says, "Yes?" in questioning tone and waits for them to say "Yes" or "No." He repeats correct reply with satisfaction. Demonstrator checks each after group has responded, or at signal from examiner if group does not respond. Demonstrator then works out remaining items, pointing from column to column and working deliberately. Examiner summarizes demonstrator's work by pointing to the whole numbers in each set and saying "Yes" (indicating X) or "No;" if "No," he shows again where numbers are unlike. Examiner then points to page and says "All right. Go ahead. Hurry up!" At the end of 3 minutes examiner says "Stop. Turn over the page to test 6."

Test 6, pictorial completion.

"This is test 6 *here*. Look. A lot of pictures." After everyone has found the place, "Now watch." Examiner points to hand and says to demonstrator, "Fix it." Demonstrator does nothing, but looks puzzled. Examiner points to the picture of the hand, and then to the place where the finger is missing and says to demonstrator, "Fix it; fix it." Demonstrator then draws in finger. Examiner says, "That's right." Examiner then points to fish and place for eye and says, "Fix it." After demonstrator has drawn missing eye, examiner points to each of the four remaining drawings and says, "Fix them all." Demonstrator works samples out slowly and with apparent effort. When the samples are finished examiner says, "All right. Go ahead. Hurry up!" During the course of this test the orderlies walk around the room and locate individuals who are doing nothing, point to their pages and say, "Fix it. Fix them," trying to set everyone working. At the end of 3 minutes examiner says, "Stop! But don't turn over the page."

Test 7, geometrical construction.

"This is test 7 *here*. Look." After everyone has found the page, "Now watch." Examiner points to the first figure on blackboard. He then takes the two pieces of cardboard, fits them on to the similar drawings on blackboard to show that they correspond and puts them together in the square on blackboard to show that they fill it. Then, after running his finger over the line of intersection of the parts, examiner removes the pieces and signals the demonstrator, who draws solution in the square on blackboard. The same procedure is repeated for the second and third sample. Demonstrator works out fourth sample, after much study, pointing from the square to the forms.

Demonstrator first draws two small squares in the upper half of the large square, then the two triangles in the remaining rectangle. Each small figure is drawn in by tracing its entire circumference, not merely the necessary dividing lines. While drawing each small figure in the large square, demonstrator points with index finger of left hand to the corresponding small figure at left of square, taking care not to obstruct the view. At the end of the demonstration examiner holds up blank, points to each square on the page and says, "All right. Go ahead. Hurry up!" At the end of 2½ minutes, "Stop! Turn over the page." Papers are then collected immediately.

3. Directions for Scoring

General rules.

1. In general, items evidently corrected stand as corrected. The only exception to this rule is in the maze test.

2. In tests where the score is number right, only wrong items need be checked in scoring. In test 5, where the score is right minus wrong, wrong and omitted items must be separately checked.

3. Enter the score for each test in lower right-hand corner of the test page and encircle it. When the test has been rescored a check may be made beside the circle.

4. Red or blue pencil increases accuracy of scoring.

Test 1.

1. One-half point for each correctly completely half of maze. A half maze is correct if drawn line does not cross any line of maze (except through awkwardness) nor an imaginary straight line across the opening of a wrong passage.

2. Allow much leeway in the cutting of corners.

3. Spur running into any blind passage counts wrong for that half-item, even though erased.

4. When two lines are drawn, one straight across the page, the other correct, full credit is given.

Test 2.

Score is number right.

Test 3.

1. Score is number right.

2. Any incomplete item receives no credit.

3. Count any item correct if intended plan is carried out. Disregard additional unnecessary marks, such as circles between the crosses of items 2 and 4 in first part of line, etc.

Test 4.

1. Score is one-third of number of correct symbols.
2. Use leniency in judging form of symbol.
3. Credit symbol for 2 even though reversed.

Test 5.

1. Score is right minus wrong (number of items checked that should be checked minus number of items checked that should not be checked).
2. If other clear indication is used instead of crosses, give credit.
3. If numbers which should not be checked are marked by some other sign than is used to check similar pairs, count as though not marked.
4. If all items are checked, the score for the test is zero.

Test 6.

1. Score is number right.
2. Allow much awkwardness in drawing. Writing in name of missing part or any way of indicating it receives credit, if idea is clear.
3. Additional parts do not make item wrong, if proper missing part is also inserted.
4. Rules for individual items:
Item 4.—Any spoon at any angle *in right hand* receives credit. Left hand, or unattached spoon, no credit.
Item 5.—Chimney must be in right place. No credit for smoke.
Item 6.—Another ear on same side as first receives no credit.
Item 8.—Plain square, cross, etc., in proper location for stamp, receives credit.
Item 10.—Missing part is the rivet. Line of "ear" may be omitted.
Item 13.—Missing part is leg.
Item 15.—Ball should be drawn in hand of man. If represented in hand of woman, or in motion, no credit.
Item 16.—Single line indicating net receives credit.
Item 18.—Any representation intended for horn, pointing in any direction, receives credit.
Item 19.—Hand and powder puff must be put on proper side.
Item 20.—Diamond is the missing part. Failure to complete hilt on sword is not an error.

Test 7.

1. Score is number right.
2. Allow considerable awkwardness in drawing.
3. Extra subdivisions, if not erased, make item wrong.
4. Rules for individual items.

Item 1.—Line of division may be slightly distant from true center, and need not be straight.

Item 3.—Lines of semicircumference must start from or near corners of square.

Item 4.—Line must not start from corner.

4. Total Score and Rating

The result of examination beta is expressed as a "total score," which is the sum of the raw scores of the several tests. The raw scores are obtained as follows:

Test	Method of scoring	Maximum score
1.............	Half point for each half maze.....	5
2.............	Number right...................	16
3.............	Number right...................	12
4.............	One-third of number right........	30
5.............	Right minus wrong.............	25
6.............	Number right...................	20
7.............	Number right...................	10
Total......	....	118

Letter ratings are assigned on examination beta as follows:

Rating	Scores
A	100–118
B.............................	90– 99
C+.............................	80– 89
C.............................	65– 79
C−.............................	45– 64
D.............................	20– 44
D−.............................	0– 19

All ratings above D − are entered and reported at once. Men whose scores fall below D are recalled for individual examination.

Ratings of D − may not be given in examination beta, unless recall of the men for individual examination is impossible.

FORM 5   GROUP EXAMINATION ALPHA   GROUP NO._____

Name_____ Rank_____ Age_____

Company_____ Regiment_____ Arm_____ Division_____

In what country or state born?_____ Years in U.S.?_____ Race_____

Occupation_____ Weekly Wages_____

Schooling: Grades, 1.2.3.4.5.6.7.8: High or Prep. School, Year 1.2.3.4: College, Year 1.2.3.4.

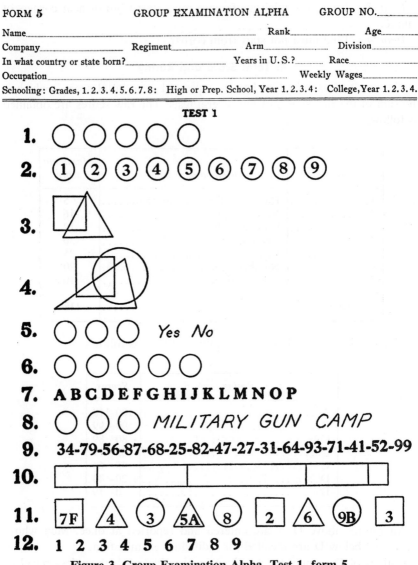

TEST 1

Figure 3. Group Examination Alpha, Test 1, form 5.

TEST 2

Get the answers to these examples as quickly as you can.
Use the side of this page to figure on if you need to.

SAMPLES
1 How many are 5 men and 10 men?...........Answer (15)
2 If you walk 4 miles an hour for 3 hours, how far do you walk?...........................Answer (12)

1 How many are 30 men and 7 men?.......................Answer (**37**)
2 If you save $7 a month for 4 months, how much will you save?
                                                  Answer (**$28**)
3 If 24 men are divided into squads of 8, how many squads will there be?..................................Answer (**3**)
4 Mike had 12 cigars. He bought 3 more, and then smoked 6. How many cigars did he have left?.......................Answer (**9**)
5 A company advanced 5 miles and retreated 3 miles. How far was it then from its first position?.......................Answer (**2**)
6 How many hours will it take a truck to go 66 miles at the rate of 6 miles an hour?.................................Answer (**11**)
7 How many cigars can you buy for 50 cents at the rate of 2 for 5 cents?..Answer (**20**)
8 A regiment marched 40 miles in five days. The first day they marched 9 miles, the second day 6 miles, the third 10 miles, the fourth 8 miles. How many miles did they march the last day?...Answer (**7**)
9 If you buy two packages of tobacco at 7 cents each and a pipe for 65 cents, how much change should you get from a two-dollar bill?..Answer (**$1.21**)
10 If it takes 6 men 3 days to dig a 180-foot drain, how many men are needed to dig it in half a day?.......................Answer (**36**)
11 A dealer bought some mules for $800. He sold them for $1,000, making $40 on each mule. How many mules were there? ...Answer (**5**)
12 A rectangular bin holds 400 cubic feet of lime. If the bin is 10 feet long and 5 feet wide, how deep is it?.............Answer (**8**)
13 A recruit spent one-eighth of his spare change for post cards and four times as much for a box of letter paper, and then had 90 cents left. How much money did he have at first?......Answer (**$ 2.40**)
14 If 3½ tons of coal cost $21, what will 5½ tons cost?......Answer (**$33.00**)
15 A ship has provisions to last her crew of 500 men 6 months, How long would it last 1,200 men?.......................Answer (**2½ mo.**)
16 If a man runs a hundred yards in 10 seconds, how many feet does he run in a fifth of a second?....................Answer (**6**)
17 A U-boat makes 8 miles an hour under water and 15 miles on the surface. How long will it take to cross a 100-mile channel, if it has to go two-fifths of the way under water? ......Answer (**9**)
18 If 241 squads of men are to dig 4,097 yards of trench, how many yards must be dug by each squad?.................Answer (**17**)
19 A certain division contains 3,000 artillery, 15,000 infantry and 1,000 cavalry. If each branch is expanded proportionately until there are in all 20,900 men, how many will be added to the artillery?..Answer (**300**)
20 A commission house which had already supplied 1,897 barrels of apples to a cantonment delivered the remainder of its stock to 29 mess halls. Of this remainder each mess hall received 54 barrels. What was the total number of barrels supplied? ...Answer (**3463**)

Figure 4. Group Examination Alpha, Test 2, arithmetical problems.

TEST 3

This is a test of common sense. Below are sixteen questions. Three answers are given to each question. You are to look at the answers carefully; then make a cross in the square before the best answer to each question, as in the sample:

SAMPLE {
Why do we use stoves? Because
☐ they look well
☒ they keep us warm
☐ they are black
}

Here the second answer is the best one and is marked with a cross. Begin with No. 1 and keep on until time is called.

1 Cats are useful animals, because
  ☒ they catch mice
  ☐ they are gentle
  ☐ they are afraid of dogs

2 Why are pencils more commonly carried than fountain pens? Because
  ☐ they are brightly colored
  ☒ they are cheaper
  ☐ they are not so heavy

3 Why is leather used for shoes? Because
  ☐ it is produced in all countries
  ☒ it wears well
  ☐ it is an animal product

4 Why judge a man by what he does rather than by what he says? Because
  ☒ what a man does shows what he really is
  ☐ it is wrong to tell a lie
  ☐ a deaf man cannot hear what is said

5 If you were asked what you thought of a person whom you didn't know, what should you say?
  ☐ I will go and get acquainted
  ☐ I think he is all right
  ☒ I don't know him and can't say

6 Streets are sprinkled in summer
  ☐ to make the air cooler
  ☐ to keep automobiles from skidding
  ☒ to keep down dust

7 Why is wheat better for food than corn? Because
  ☒ it is more nutritious
  ☐ it is more expensive
  ☐ it can be ground finer

8 If a man made a million dollars, he ought to
  ☐ pay off the national debt
  ☒ contribute to various worthy charities
  ☐ give it all to some poor man

☛ Go to No. 9 above

9 Why do many persons prefer automobiles to street cars? Because
  ☐ an auto is made of higher grade materials
  ☒ an automobile is more convenient
  ☐ street cars are not as safe

10 The feathers on a bird's wings help him to fly because they
  ☒ make a wide, light surface
  ☐ keep the air off his body
  ☐ keep the wings from cooling off too fast

11 All traffic going one way keeps to the same side of the street because
  ☐ most people are right handed
  ☐ the traffic policeman insists on it
  ☒ it avoids confusion and collisions

12 Why do inventors patent their inventions? Because
  ☒ it gives them control of their inventions
  ☐ it creates a greater demand
  ☐ it is the custom to get patents

13 Freezing water bursts pipes because
  ☐ cold makes the pipes weaker
  ☒ water expands when it freezes
  ☐ the ice stops the flow of water

14 Why are high mountains covered with snow? Because
  ☐ they are near the clouds
  ☐ the sun seldom shines on them
  ☒ the air is cold there

15 If the earth were nearer the sun
  ☐ the stars would disappear
  ☐ our months would be longer
  ☒ the earth would be warmer

16 Why is it colder nearer the poles than near the equator? Because
  ☐ the poles are always farther from the sun
  ☒ the sunshine falls obliquely at the poles
  ☐ there is more ice at the poles

Figure 5. Group Examination Alpha, Test 3, practical judgment.

TEST 4

If the two words of a pair mean the same or nearly the same, draw a
line under *same*. If they mean the opposite or nearly the opposite, draw a
line under *opposite*. If you cannot be sure, guess. The two samples are
already marked as they should be.

SAMPLES	{ good—bad	same—<u>opposite</u>	
	{ little—small	<u>same</u>—opposite	

1	wet—dry	same—<u>opposite</u>	1
2	in—out	same—<u>opposite</u>	2
3	hill—valley	same—<u>opposite</u>	3
4	allow—permit	<u>same</u>—opposite	4
5	expand—contract	same—<u>opposite</u>	5
6	class—group	<u>same</u>—opposite	6
7	former—latter	same—<u>opposite</u>	7
8	confess—admit	<u>same</u>—opposite	8
9	shy—timid	<u>same</u>—opposite	9
10	delicate—tender	<u>same</u>—opposite	10
11	extinguish—quench	<u>same</u>—opposite	11
12	cheerful—melancholy	same—<u>opposite</u>	12
13	accept—reject	same—<u>opposite</u>	13
14	concave—convex	same—<u>opposite</u>	14
15	lax—strict	same—<u>opposite</u>	15
16	assert—maintain	<u>same</u>—opposite	16
17	champion—advocate	<u>same</u>—opposite	17
18	adapt—conform	<u>same</u>—opposite	18
19	debase—exalt	same—<u>opposite</u>	19
20	dissension—harmony	same—<u>opposite</u>	20
21	repress—restrain	<u>same</u>—opposite	21
22	bestow—confer	<u>same</u>—opposite	22
23	amenable—tractable	<u>same</u>—opposite	23
24	avert—prevent	<u>same</u>—opposite	24
25	reverence—veneration	<u>same</u>—opposite	25
26	fallacy—verity	same—<u>opposite</u>	26
27	specific—general	same—<u>opposite</u>	27
28	pompous—ostentatious	<u>same</u>—opposite	28
29	accumulate—dissipate	same—<u>opposite</u>	29
30	apathy—indifference	<u>same</u>—opposite	30
31	effeminate—virile	same—<u>opposite</u>	31
32	peculation—embezzlement	<u>same</u>—opposite	32
33	benign—genial	<u>same</u>—opposite	33
34	acme—climax	<u>same</u>—opposite	34
35	largess—donation	<u>same</u>—opposite	35
36	innuendo—insinuation	<u>same</u>—opposite	36
37	vesper—matin	same—<u>opposite</u>	37
38	aphorism—maxim	<u>same</u>—opposite	38
39	abjure—renounce	<u>same</u>—opposite	39
40	encomium—eulogy	same—opposite	40

Figure 6. Group Examination Alpha, Test 4, synonym-antonym.

TEST 5

The words A EATS COW GRASS in that order are mixed up and don't make a sentence; but they would make a sentence if put in the right order: A COW EATS GRASS, and this statement is true.

Again, the words HORSES FEATHERS HAVE ALL would make a sentence if put in the order ALL HORSES HAVE FEATHERS, but this statement is false.

Below are twenty-four mixed-up sentences. Some of them are true and some are false. When I say "go," take these sentences one at a time. Think what each would say if the words were straightened out, but don't write them yourself. Then, if what it would say is true, draw a line under the word "true"; if what it would say is false, draw a line under the word "false." If you can not be sure, guess. The two samples are already marked as they should be. Begin with No. 1 and work right down the page until time is called.

SAMPLES	a eats cow grass......................	true..false	
	horses feathers have all................	true..false	
1	lions strong are...............................	true..false	1
2	houses people in live...........................	true..false	2
3	days there in are week eight a....................	true..false	3
4	leg flies one have only..........................	true..false	4
5	months coldest are summer the....................	true..false	5
6	gotten sea water sugar is from...................	true..false	6
7	honey bees flowers gather the from...............	true..false	7
8	and eat good gold silver to are..................	true..false	8
9	president Columbus first the was America of.......	true..false	9
10	making is bread valuable wheat for................	true..false	10
11	water and made are butter from cheese...........	true..false	11
12	sides every has four triangle....................	true..false	12
13	every times makes mistakes person at.............	true..false	13
14	many toes fingers as men as have.................	true..false	14
15	not eat gunpowder to good is.....................	true..false	15
16	ninety canal ago built Panama years was the......	true..false	16
17	live dangerous is near a volcano to it...........	true..false	17
18	clothing worthless are for and wool cotton........	true..false	18
19	as sheets are napkins used never.................	true..false	19
20	people trusted intemperate be always can........	true..false	20
21	employ debaters irony never.....................	true..false	21
22	certain some death of mean kinds sickness........	true..false	22
23	envy bad malice traits are and...................	true..false	23
24	repeated calls human for courtesies intercourse.....	true..false	24

Figure 7. Group Examination Alpha, Test 5, disarranged sentences.

TEST 6

SAMPLES	2	4	6	8	10	12	*14*	*16*
	9	8	7	6	5	4	*3*	*2*
	2	2	3	3	4	4	*5*	*5*
	1	7	2	7	3	7	*4*	*7*

Look at each row of numbers below, and on the two dotted lines write the two numbers that should come next.

3	4	5	6	7	8	*9*	*10*
10	15	20	25	30	35	*40*	*45*
8	7	6	5	4	3	*2*	*1*
3	6	9	12	15	18	*21*	*24*
5	9	13	17	21	25	*29*	*33*
8	1	6	1	4	1	*2*	*1*
27	27	23	23	19	19	*15*	*15*
1	2	4	8	16	32	*64*	*128*
8	9	12	13	16	17	*20*	*21*
9	9	7	7	5	5	*3*	*3*
19	16	14	11	9	6	*4*	*1*
2	3	5	8	12	17	*23*	*30*
11	13	12	14	13	15	*14*	*16*
29	28	26	23	19	14	*8*	*1*
18	14	17	13	16	12	*15*	*11*
81	27	9	3	1	⅓	*⅑*	*1/27*
20	17	15	14	11	9	*8*	*5*
16	17	15	18	14	19	*13*	*20*
1	4	9	16	25	36	*49*	*64*
3	6	8	16	18	36	*38*	*76*

Figure 8. Group Examination Alpha, Test 6, number series completion.

TEST 7

SAMPLES
$\left\{\begin{array}{l}\text{sky—blue :: grass— table } \underline{\text{green}} \text{ warm big} \\ \text{fish—swims :: man— paper time } \underline{\text{walks}} \text{ girl} \\ \text{day—night :: white— red } \underline{\text{black}} \text{ clear pure}\end{array}\right.$

In each of the lines below, the first two words are related to each other in some way. What you are to do in each line is to see what the relation is between the first two words, and underline the word in heavy type that is related in the same way to the third word. Begin with No. 1 and mark as many sets as you can before time is called.

1 gun—shoots :: knife— run <u>cuts</u> hat bird...................... 1
2 ear—hear :: eye— table hand <u>see</u> play...................... 2
3 dress—woman :: feathers— <u>bird</u> neck feet bill............... 3
4 handle—hammer ✕ knob— key room shut <u>door</u>............. 4
5 shoe—foot :: hat— coat nose <u>head</u> collar................ 5

6 water—drink :: bread— cake coffee <u>eat</u> pie.................. 6
7 food—man :: gasoline— gas oil <u>automobile</u> spark............ 7
8 eat—fat :: starve— <u>thin</u> food bread thirsty.............. 8
9 man—home :: bird— <u>fly</u> insect worm <u>nest</u>............. 9
10 go—come :: sell— leave <u>buy</u> money papers................... 10

11 peninsula—land :: bay— boats pay <u>ocean</u> Massachusetts........ 11
12 hour—minute :: minute— man week <u>second</u> short.............. 12
13 abide—depart :: stay— over home play <u>leave</u>................ 13
14 January—February :: June— <u>July</u> May month year........... 14
15 bold—timid :: advance— proceed <u>retreat</u> campaign soldier..... 15

16 above—below :: top— spin <u>bottom</u> surface side............... 16
17 lion—animal :: rose— smell leaf <u>plant</u> thorn.............. 17
18 tiger—carnivorous :: horse— cow <u>pony</u> buggy <u>herbivorous</u>...... 18
19 sailor—navy :: soldier— gun cap hill <u>army</u>................ 19
20 picture—see :: sound— noise music <u>hear</u> bark.............. 20

21 success—joy :: failure— <u>sadness</u> success fail work.............. 21
22 hope—despair :: happiness— frolic fun joy <u>sadness</u>............ 22
23 pretty—ugly :: attract— fine <u>repel</u> nice draw.................. 23
24 pupil—teacher :: child— <u>parent</u> doll youngster obey........... 24
25 city—mayor :: army— navy soldier <u>general</u> private........... 25

26 establish—begin :: abolish— slavery wrong abolition <u>end</u>...... 26
27 December—January :: last— least worst month <u>first</u>.......... 27
28 giant—dwarf :: large— big monster queer <u>small</u>............... 28
29 engine—caboose :: beginning— commence cabin <u>end</u> train..... 29
30 dismal—cheerful :: dark— sad stars night <u>bright</u>.............. 30

31 quarrel—enemy :: agree— <u>friend</u> disagree agreeable foe....... 31
32 razor—sharp :: hoe— bury <u>dull</u> cuts tree...................... 32
33 winter—summer :: cold— freeze <u>warm</u> wet January............ 33
34 rudder—ship :: tail— sail <u>bird</u> dog cat.................... 34
35 granary—wheat :: library— desk <u>books</u> paper librarian........ 35

36 tolerate—pain :: welcome— <u>pleasure</u> unwelcome friends give... 36
37 sand—glass :: clay— stone hay <u>bricks</u> dirt....................... 37
38 moon—earth :: earth— ground Mars <u>sun</u> sky.................... 38
39 tears—sorrow :: laughter— <u>joy</u> smile girls grin................. 39
40 cold—ice :: heat— <u>lightning</u> warm <u>steam</u> coat.................. 40

Figure 9. Group Examination Alpha, Test 7, analogies.

TEST 8

Notice the sample sentence:

People **hear** with the   **eyes**   **ears**   nose   mouth

The correct word is **ears**, because it makes the truest sentence.

In each of the sentences below you have four choices for the last word. Only one of them is correct. In each sentence draw a line under the one of these four words which makes the truest sentence. If you can not be sure, guess. The two samples are already marked as they should be.

SAMPLES { People **hear** with the   **eyes**   **ears**   nose   mouth
         { **France** is in   **Europe**   Asia   Africa   Australia

1 **America** was discovered by   Drake   Hudson   Columbus   Cabot.................... 1
2 **Pinochle** is played with   rackets   cards   pins   dice........................ 2
3 The most prominent industry of Detroit is   automobiles   brewing   flour   packing...... 3
4 The **Wyandotte** is a kind of   horse   fowl   cattle   granite..................... 4
5 The **U. S. School** for Army Officers is at   Annapolis   West Point   New Haven   Ithaca... 5

6 **Food products** are made by   Smith & Wesson   Swift & Co.   W. L. Douglas   B. T. Babbitt... 6
7 **Bud Fisher** is famous as an   actor   author   baseball player   comic artist............ 7
8 The **Guernsey** is a kind of   horse   goat   sheep   cow........................ 8
9 **Marguerite Clark** is known as a   suffragist   singer   movie actress   writer............ 9
10 "Hasn't scratched yet" is used in advertising a   duster   flour   brush   cleanser....... 10

11 **Salsify** is a kind of   snake   fish   lizard   vegetable 11
12 **Coral** is obtained from   mines   elephants   oysters   reefs..................... 12
13 **Rosa Bonheur** is famous as a   poet   painter   composer   sculptor................ 13
14 The **tuna** is a kind of   fish   bird   reptile   insect.......................... 14
15 **Emeralds** are usually   red   blue   green   yellow 15

16 **Maize** is a kind of   corn   hay   oats   rice.......................... 16
17 **Nabisco** is a   patent medicine   disinfectant   food product   tooth paste....,........... 17
18 **Velvet Joe** appears in advertisements of   tooth powder   dry goods   tobacco   soap..... 18
19 **Cypress** is a kind of   machine   food   tree   fabric........................ 19
20 **Bombay** is a city in   China   Egypt   India   Japan........................ 20

21 The **dictaphone** is a kind of   typewriter   multigraph   phonograph   adding machine.... 21
22 The **pancreas** is in the   abdomen   head   shoulder   neck...................... 22
23 **Cheviot** is the name of a   fabric   drink   dance   food...................... 23
24 **Larceny** is a term used in   medicine   theology   law   pedagogy................ 24
25 The **Battle of Gettysburg** was fought in   1863   1813   1778   1812.................. 25

26 The **bassoon** is used in   music   stenography   book-binding   lithography............. 26
27 **Turpentine** comes from   petroleum   ore   hides   trees...................... 27
28 The number of a **Zulu's** legs is   two   four   six   eight........................ 28
29 The **scimitar** is a kind of   musket   cannon   pistol   sword 29
30 The **Knight engine** is used in the   Packard   Lozier   Stearns   Pierce Arrow........... 30

31 The author of "**The Raven**" is   Stevenson   Kipling   Hawthorne   Poe.............. 31
32 **Spare** is a term used in bowling   football   tennis   hockey...................... 32
33 A six-sided figure is called a   scholium   parallelogram   hexagon   trapezium......... 33
34 **Isaac Pitman** was most famous in   physics   shorthand   railroading   electricity....... 34
35 The **ampere** is used in measuring   wind power   electricity   water power   rainfall...... 35

36 The **Overland car** is made in   Buffalo   Detroit   Flint   Toledo.................... 36
37 **Mauve** is the name of a   drink   color   fabric   food......................... 37
38 The **stanchion** is used in   fishing   hunting   farming   motoring.................. 38
39 **Mica** is a   vegetable   mineral   gas   liquid 39
40 **Scrooge** appears in   Vanity Fair   The Christmas Carol   Romola   Henry IV.......... 40

Figure 10. Group Examination Alpha, Test 8, information.

FORM 0   GROUP EXAMINATION BETA   GROUP NO.....................

Name.. Rank........................... Age.....................

Company............................ Regiment........................ Arm........................ Division.........................

In what country or state born?.................................. Years in U. S.?............ Race...........................

Occupation.. Weekly Wages.........................

Schooling: Grades, 1, 2, 3, 4, 5, 6, 7, 8: High or Prep. School, Year 1, 2, 3, 4: College, Year 1, 2, 3, 4.

Test 1

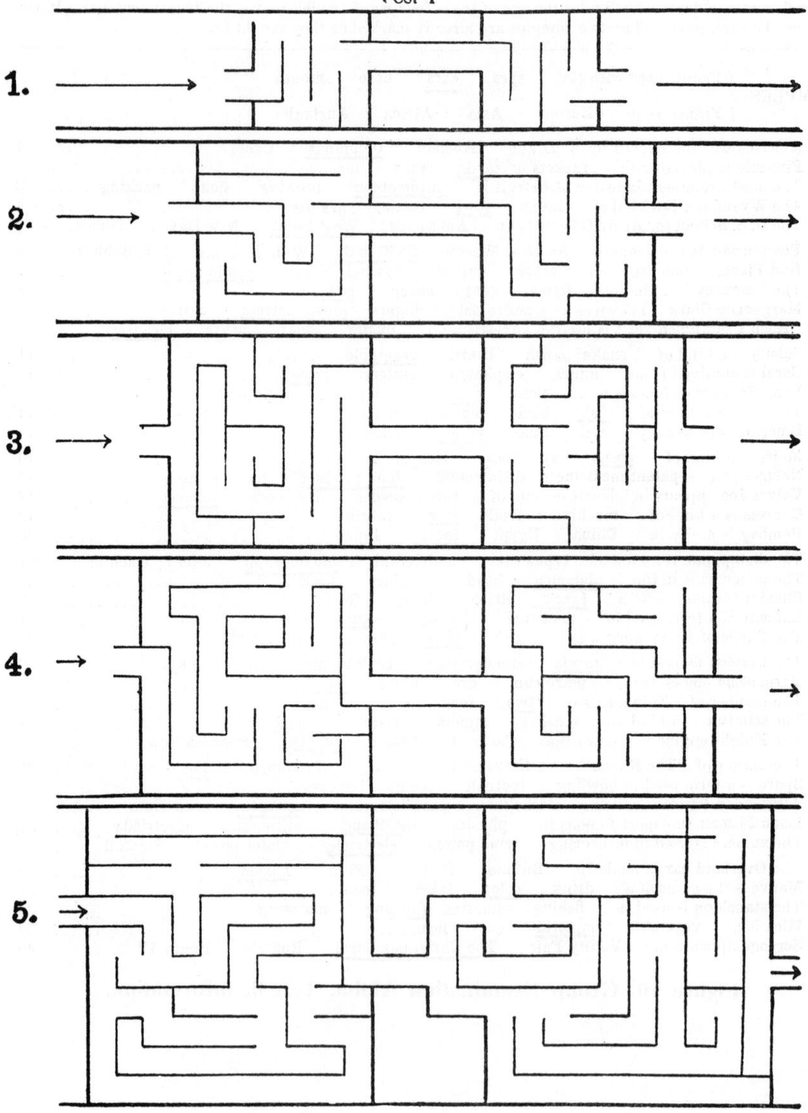

Figure 11. Group Examination Beta, Test 1, maze.

Test 2

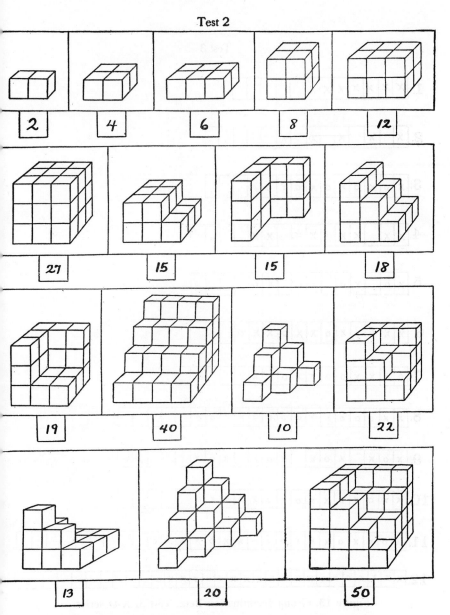

Figure 12. Group Examination Beta, Test 2, cube analysis.

168

Studies in Individual Differences

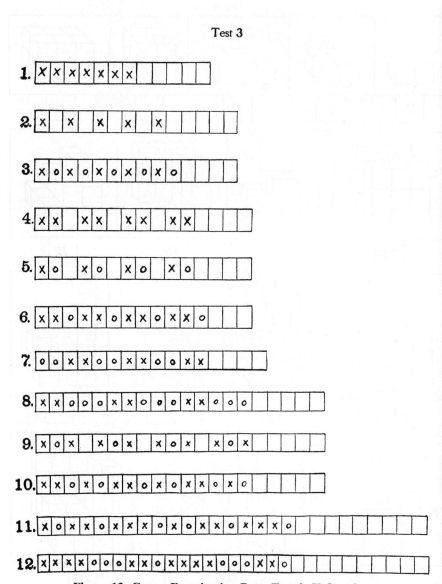

Figure 13. Group Examination Beta, Test 3, X-O series.

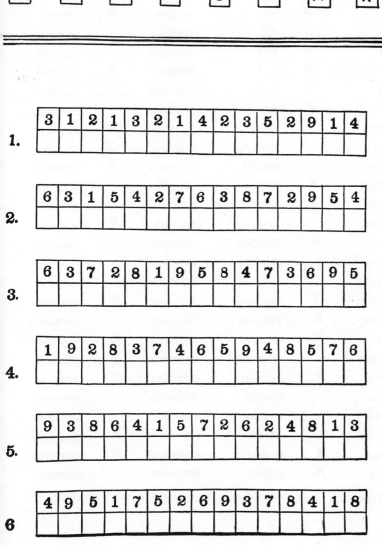

Figure 14. Group Examination Beta, Test 4, digit symbol.

Test 5

650	......X..... 650	10243586	....X...... 10243586
041	 044	659012534	 6590211354
2579	......X..... 2579	388172902	 381872902
3281	......X..... 3281	631027594	....X..... 631027594
55190	 55102	2499901354	 2499901534
39190	......X..... 39190	2261059310	 2261659310
658049	 650849	2911038227	....X..... 2911038227
3295017	 3290517	313377752	....X..... 313377752
63015991	 63019991	1012938567	....X...... 1012938567
39007106	.....X..... 39007106	7166220988	 7162220988
69931087	.....X..... 69931087	3177628449	 3177682449
251004818	 251004418	468672663	....X...... 468672663
299056013	.....X...... 299056013	9104529003	 9194529003
36015992	 360155992	3484657120	 3484657210
3910066482	 391006482	8588172556	 8581722556
8510273301	.....X...... 8510273301	3120166671	....X..... 3120166671
263136996	.....X...... 263136996	7611348879	 76111345879
451152903	.....X...... 451152903	26557239164	....X..... 26557239164
3259016275	 3295016725	8819002341	....X..... 8819002341
582039144	.....X...... 582039144	6571018034	....X..... 6571018034
61558529	 61588529	38779762514	 38779765214
211915883	 219915883	39008126557	 39008126657
670413822	 670143822	75658100398	....X..... 75658100398
17198591	.....X...... 17198591	41181900726	....X..... 41181900726
36482991	.....X...... 36482991	6543920817	 6543920871

Figure 15. Group Examination Beta, Test 5, number checking.

Test 6

Figure 16. Group Examination Beta, Test 6, picture completion.

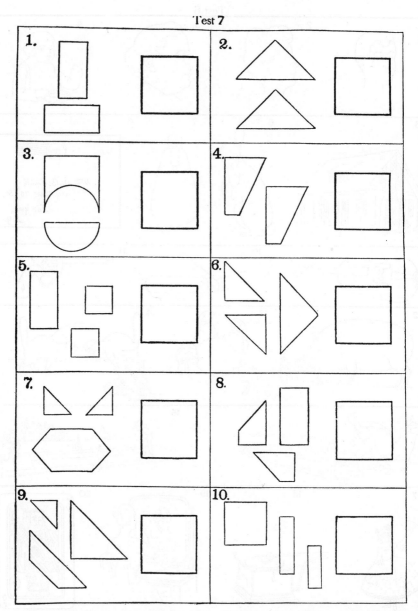

Figure 17. Group Examination Beta, Test 7, geometrical construction.

This is one example of how the Army data was used in applied psychology during the period immediately following World War I. Observe the extensive overlap of the occupational groups and note especially that the "Score Range" is from the 25th to the 75th centile, not the true range of each group—which is of course much greater.

Occupational-Intelligence Standards*

DOUGLAS FRYER
1922

With intelligence as a standard there are several definitely determined occupational levels *blocking* an individual into the field of his occupational achievement. The man who is vocationally unsuccessful and dissatisfied may find: (1) that he is attempting to succeed in an occupation demanding greater intellectual capacity than is his; or (2) that he is in an occupation which fails to make sufficient demands upon his intellectual capacity to keep him interested and at work. However, it should be noted in this connection that rather simple concrete mechanical processes are frequently enjoyed by men of superior intelligence during the period of apprenticeship, because then, during the time of learning, there is a greater demand upon the intelligence.

Occupational levels with intelligence as a basis for the grouping can be roughly classified as follows:

I. Professional occupational level (Superior intelligence required).
- A. Professional work with very high educational and professional standards.
- B. Professional work with slightly lower educational and professional standards.

II. Technical occupational level (High average intelligence required).
- Technical work; business promotion; clerical work; highly skilled mechanical work demanding leadership qualifications.

III. Skilled occupational level (Average intelligence required).
- Skilled mechanical work of concrete nature.

IV. Semi-skilled and low-skilled occupational level (Low average intelligence required).
- Mechanical work demanding some occupational skill.

V. Unskilled occupational level (Inferior intelligence required).
- Manual work demanding no skill.

* *School and Society,* 16 (1922), pp. 273-277. Reprinted by permission of the author and publisher.

The occupational territory of an individual is bounded by his intellectual capacity; he is blocked off into an occupational field with intelligence as the standard for classification. A classification of the occupations with intelligence as the basis for the groupings is essential information for a vocational office. Occupational levels have been clearly indicated by many studies of intelligence.

The intelligence rating secured through the intelligence examination compared with occupational-intelligence standards would appear to be a significant guide in the judgment of workmanship ability. (It must be remembered, however, that the intelligence rating as a guide to workmanship ability is limited by the fact that the examination is a measure of *instantaneous* capacity; the emotional qualities necessary to intellectual achievement, *i.e.,* success in intellectual work, contribute possibly 40 per cent to such intellectual achievement). Equally such occupational-intelligence standards may be of great assistance in the process of vocational counsel and in the selection of personnel.

It was in an attempt to furnish occupational-intelligence standards for the vocational counseling and occupational selection processes that this work was begun over two years ago in the vocational department of the Central Branch, Y. M. C. A., Brooklyn. A short list of occupations with their respective intelligence requirements was roughly assembled as a result of the study of a few hundred cases. When the results of the occupational studies made by the Division of Psychology S. G. O. became available these occupational-intelligence standards were corrected and amplified. Four studies were made by the Division of Psychology in army cantonments (Dix, Lee, Wadsworth and Devens) and a most exhaustive one was an assembling in the S. G. O. of data from sixteen army camps. All these studies totaled approximately 60,000 cases and dealt with more than 115 different occupations.

Consideration has necessarily been made of the fact that these studies by the Division of Psychology were returns from draft quotas which were slightly inferior in intelligence on the average to the civilian population. This would indicate that occupational-intelligence standards derived from draft quotas would be slightly lower than should be expected normally. The selective service act further influenced these results secured from draft quotas in that of the seven tenths of the men in the country between 21 and 31 who were given deferred classification 6.8 per cent of them received this deferment because they were skilled agricultural and industrial workers or highly specialized technical and mechanical experts. Undoubtedly these men were superior to the average intelligence for their occupation. Other factors influencing the exactness of the draft records as representative of a civilian standard were as follows: Probable exemptions of more men of high occupational skill than low occupational skill because of family dependents; prior enlistments of a higher mean intelligence than the civilian's population, which would have reduced the draft average; a lower rating of foreigners because of poor understanding of English than justified by their capacity; placing of students on record for clerical occupations; semi-skilled workers often classified as laborers, etc.

The correction process applied to this Army data was based upon a study of the records of over 3,598 personnel examinations made by the vocational department. Norms established by the Army studies have been verified, corrections applied, and additions made. The influences mentioned above have been considered in this correction process. It is thought now, however, with most of the records presented here that there is a tendency toward a slightly lower average than should be set for practical vocational purposes. Especially is this thought to be true with many of the mechanical occupations in the "C" and "C—" intelligence groups.

TABLE I

Occupational-Intelligence Standards
Intelligence Standard Index

96 Occupational Designations

Intel. group	Score ave.	Score range	Occupation
A	161	110–183	Engineer (Civil and Mechanical)
	152	124–185	Clergyman
	137	105–155	Accountant
B	127	107–164	Physician
	122	97–148	Teacher (Public Schools)
	119	94–139	Chemist
	114	84–139	Draftsman
	111	99–163	Y. M. C. A. Secretary
	110	80–128	Dentist
	109	81–137	Executive (Minor)
C+	103	73–124	Stenographer and Typist
	101	77–127	Bookkeeper
	99	78–126	Nurse
	96	74–121	Clerk (Office)
	91	69–115	Clerk (Railroad)
	86	59–107	Photographer
	85	57–110	Telegrapher and Radio Operator
	83	64–106	Conductor (Railroad)
	82	57–108	Musician (Band)
	81	59–106	Artist (Sign Letterer)
	81	60–106	Clerk (Postal)
	81	57–109	Electrician
	80	62–114	Foreman (Construction)
	80	56–105	Clerk (Stock)
	78	54–102	Clerk (Receiving and Shipping)
	78	61–106	Druggist
	77	59–107	Foreman (Factory)
	75	56–105	Graphotype Operator
	74	53–91	Engineman (Locomotive)
	72	54–99	Farrier
	70	46–95	Telephone Operator
	70	44–94	Stock Checker
	69	49–93	Carpenter (Ship)
	69	48–94	Handyman (General Mechanic)
	69	46–90	Policeman and Detective
	68	51–97	Auto Assembler
	68	47–89	Engineman (Marine)
	68	42–86	Riveter (Hand)
	67	50–92	Toolmaker
	66	45–92	Auto Engine Mechanic
	66	45–91	Laundryman
	66	49–86	Gunsmith
C	66	44–88	Plumber
	66	44–88	Pipefitter
	65	44–91	Lathe Hand (Production)
	65	43–91	Auto Mechanic (General)
	65	43–91	Auto Chauffeur
	65	42–89	Tailor
	65	44–88	Carpenter (Bridge)
	64	43–88	Lineman
	63	40–89	Machinist (General)
	63	46–88	Motor Cyclist
	63	41–86	Brakeman (Railroad)
	62	31–94	Actor (Vaudeville)
	61	40–85	Butcher
	61	44–84	Fireman (Locomotive)
	61	39–82	Blacksmith (General)
	60	38–94	Shop Mechanic (Railroad)
	60	36–93	Printer
	60	40–84	Carpenter (General)
	59	40–87	Baker
	59	39–83	Mine Drill Runner
	59	38–81	Painter
	58	37–85	Concrete Worker
	58	40–83	Farmer
	58	37–83	Auto Truck Chauffeur
	58	37–82	Bricklayer
	57	41–81	Caterer
C	57	39–71	Horse Trainer
	56	38–76	Cobbler
	55	35–81	Engineman (Stationary)
	55	34–78	Barber
	55	35–77	Horse Hostler
	52	38–96	Salesclerk
	52	33–74	Horse Shoer
	51	31–79	Storekeeper (Factory)
	51	26–77	Aeroplane Worker
	51	31–74	Boilermaker
	50	33–75	Rigger
	50	30–72	Teamster
	49	40–71	Miner (General)
	48	21–89	Station Agent (General)
C—	40	19–67	Hospital Attendant
	40	19–60	Mason
	35	18–62	Lumberman
	35	19–57	Shoemaker
	32	16–59	Sailor
	31	20–62	Structural Steel Worker
	31	19–60	Canvas Worker
	30	16–41	Leather Worker
	27	19–63	Fireman (Stationary)
	27	17–57	Cook
	26	18–60	Textile Worker
	22	16–46	Sheet Metal Worker
	21	13–47	Laborer (Construction)
D	20	15–51	Fisherman

Intelligence for achievement

In the table given above occupational-intelligence standards are listed for 96 occupational designations. These occupations are indexed numerically according to the average intelligence score. The score ratings are for Army Alpha. The mean for the occupation is presented as the "score average," and the "score range," indicating the range of intelligence within which can be expected success in the occupation, secures its limits (usually, but not always) from the first and third quartile. The scores are so presented as to indicate that in all probability an individual must have an intelligence rating within the "score range" for achievement in the occupation, with the further probability that he should be above the "score average" to be sure of sufficient intellectual capacity for the occupation.

This paper represents an interesting attempt to disentangle some of the variables which may have taken part in determining the average scores attained in each of the states on the Army test. You should of course be cautious in leaping from the fact of a correlation to a presumption of its causation. Also you should be wary of interpreting "correlation of averages" as meaning "correlation of the variables." A careful study of this article should raise questions in your mind on both these points.

A Comparison of the Ranks of American States in Army Alpha and in Social-Economic Status*

HERBERT B. ALEXANDER

1922

There is a widespread belief in the value of Alpha medians as indices of average differences in innate capacity among the occupational and other social groups to which this test was applied in connection with the army examinations. This belief has been disseminated without due regard to the social-economic environments which may conceivably have had large part in determining these medians.

In Chapter 5, Part 3, of the official report (Psychological Examining in the Army, *Memoirs of the National Academy of Sciences,* Vol. XIV 1921) distributions of scores are shown for a large number of men with respect to their residence among the American states. For those who took Alpha only, the total reported is 40,530. An introductory paragraph to this chapter reads as follows:

"It has been shown in the comparison of camps that there are decided differences from one camp to another and that these differences may depend to an unknown amount on differences in camp procedure or on other conditions that are not matters of actual intelligence of the men examined. In general, the staff feared to come to hasty conclusions upon the comparison of states with data of which the precision was so greatly affected by camp differences. On the other hand, as has been pointed out, many of these discrepancies between camps may be due to real differences in intelligence that in turn depend upon the different sections of the country from which the camps drew. It is quite possible, then, that a comparison of camps is in part a geographical comparison. The study of the distribution of intelligence by residential section in the United States is of prime importance and should

* *School and Society,* 16 (1922), pp. 388-392. Reprinted by permission of the publisher.

be made as soon as feasible. Its very importance, however, made its undertaking seem unwise with the limited time and statistical assistance available in the office of the Section of Psychology. The comparison could undoubtedly best be made in terms of the theoretical combined scale outlined in Chapter 2. . . ."

Pending the more exhaustive study anticipated in this paragraph, it has seemed worth while to make comparison of the state medians in Alpha only, with certain social phenomena distinguishing these states. It is possible that the Alpha medians taken by themselves may not be as representative of the mentality of the states as would be measures based upon all the tests used, but the use of the Alpha scores would seem to be not unfair to the states showing the lower medians, at least. The presumption is that those state contingents which, by reason of a greater degree of illiteracy, were compelled to make larger use of Beta and the other forms of individual examination, would send to the Alpha a more selected, and theoretically a more able group. The presumption here rests upon the prevailing belief that illiteracy tends to associate with a lower capacity on the whole. Whether the army draft as such was really representative of the civil population at large in ability, or was better or worse, the writer has no definite means of knowing. Apparently informed opinion varies on this head. Whether the several states were equally well represented by their several contingents is another relevant point of importance concerning which no positive evidence is at hand. The correlations reported below are made as between the actual achievement in Alpha, whatever its conditions, and the social phenomena in question.

The coefficients reported have been determined by Spearman's Method of Rank Differences (rho) and transmuted to r by table. Only white drafted men are involved in the state medians, and from such states only as had at least 500 representatives. The states eliminated are New Mexico, Wyoming, Arizona, and West Virginia.

The frequencies of the table (200) of the official report are distributed upon five-step intervals. Assuming that the median score is at the point within such an interval indicated by the relative position of the midmost measure of the total state distribution within the corresponding frequency, the rank-order shown in Table I is obtained.

It will be noted that Oregon's median falls in the lower portion of the C-plus interval on the well-known letter-scale while Mississippi's drops to the upper portion of the C-minus interval, a difference represented by the disparity between clerical workers as a group and common labor, on the occupational listing—a disparity including within its terms the medians of practically the whole body of skilled trades. The range is striking, and one immediately raises the question as to whether, in the light of the history of the American population, such differences can be set down primarily as

TABLE I

Showing the Rank-Order of the States in Alpha

State	Median score
1. Oregon	79.9
2. Washington	79.2
3. California	78.1
4. Connecticut	73.6
5. Idaho	73.5
6. Utah	72.2
7. Massachusetts	71.6
8. Colorado	69.7
9. Montana	68.5
10. Vermont	67.5
11. Ohio	67.3
12. Maine	67.0
13. Nebraska	66.2
14. Pennsylvania	65.1
15. New York	64.5
16. Iowa	64.4
17. Minnesota	64.0
18. Kansas	63.9
19. Illinois	63.8
20. Michigan	63.3
21. Rhode Island	62.9
22. New Hampshire	61.9
23. Missouri	59.5
24. South Dakota	58.3
25. North Dakota	57.1
26. Wisconsin	56.5
27. Virginia	56.3
28. Maryland	56.2
29. Indiana	56.1
30. Oklahoma	52.5
31. Texas	50.9
32. New Jersey	48.7
33. South Carolina	47.4
34. Tennessee	47.2
35. Alabama	46.3
36. Louisiana	45.2
37. North Carolina	43.2
38. Georgia	42.2
39. Arkansas	41.6
40. Kentucky	41.5
41. Mississippi	41.2

those of original endowment, as many commentators on the Alpha findings have been prone to assume.

COMPARISON WITH THE DISTRIBUTION OF DISTINGUISHED PERSONS

In the Appendix to his *Social Environment* Professor George R. Davies reports a number of rank-orders for the American states with respect to their comparative fertility in noted men. For certain of these he used the names of persons found in *Who's Who in America* for 1912. These men were born about 1860. One of his rank-orders is based upon the number of such persons born in those states which were in the Union in 1860, divided by the white population of these states according to the census of that year. The correlation with Table 1 (Alpha) involves 29 states and yields a coefficient of .79 ± .05. Whence it appears that the conditions, whatever they are, which obtained to bring about the rank-order for Army Alpha in these states from 1890 on, are not essentially different from those which produced distinguished persons during the decades just preceding.

NATIONALITY

Various opinions have been voiced as to the relative capabilities of the different stocks within the white population in America. When the states involved in the comparison are ranked according to the per cent of foreign-born in the total white population, from the census of 1910, the coefficient of correlation with Table 1 (Alpha) is found to be .65 ± .06. Placing the case in the negative, that is, according to the per cent of native-born of native parentage, we obtain the rank-order of states indicated in Table II. The coefficient of correlation for Table I with Table II is −.61 ± .07.

If the members of the draft were truly representative of the population of these states these correlations would place in question the common assumption that the unblemished native stock is superior to the newer immigrant stock, assuming that Alpha tests the endowment of these stocks. It tends to show, furthermore, that the state with a large population recruited from southern and eastern Europe is not necessarily inferior to the state with a far greater proportion of North European stocks. The southern states, for example, can trace almost their entire white population back to northern stocks established in this country years before the influx of industrial workers from Italy, Austria-Hungary, or Russia. Yet these states are found at the bottom of the Alpha list. Since, however, the foreign element tends to settle in cities, the high correlations may be explained by the fact that the states with great foreign populations are urban, and as we shall see, the correlation of urban states with Alpha is high.

TABLE II

Showing the Rank-Order of States in Per Cent of Native-Born of Native Parentage

State	Per cent
1. North Carolina	99.0
2. South Carolina	97.5
3. Georgia	97.2
4. Tennessee	96.7
5. Mississippi	96.3
6. Alabama	95.8
7. Virginia	95.4
8. Arkansas	95.3
9. Kentucky	91.9
10. Oklahoma	90.7
11. Louisiana	82.5
12. Texas	81.2
13. Indiana	80.7
14. Missouri	76.2
15. Kansas	73.9
16. Maryland	72.1
17. Maine	66.9
18. Ohio	65.2
19. Vermont	64.7
20. Idaho	63.8
21. Oregon	63.6
22. Colorado	60.6
23. Iowa	59.0
24. Pennsylvania	56.5
25. Nebraska	54.4
26. New Hampshire	53.6
27. Washington	52.8
28. California	49.0
29. Illinois	47.1
30. Utah	46.8
31. Montana	45.0
32. Michigan	44.0
33. South Dakota	43.6
34. New Jersey	41.3
35. New York } tied	36.0
36. Connecticut } tied	36.0
37. Massachusetts	33.2
38. Wisconsin	32.9
39. Rhode Island	30.0
40. North Dakota	28.5
41. Minnesota	27.9

ENVIRONMENT

If environment plays any part in the shaping of the individual, it is during the years, let us say, from two to eighteen. Since the average of the draftees in 1918 was 26 or thereabouts, we shall not be far wrong in placing the average birth year of these men in the neighborhood of 1892. The period of greatest susceptibility to environment would therefore be the years 1894-1910. Since the greater part of this period is between 1900-1910, the economic conditions reported in the census of 1910 will best serve to picture the forces of the environment which presumably moulded the lives of these draftees.

(A) Density of Population

Ranking the states according to the per cent of urban population from the census of 1910, the coefficient of correlation with Alpha is .62 $\pm$ .07. This finding coincides with those of Cattell, Clarke, Davis, and Nearing, who uniformly found the fertility in noted persons emphatically associated with urban centers.

(B) Economic Conditions

1. Homes: In a city the fact that one does not own his own residence is not an indication that he is poor. In the country, on the contrary, such may be said to be true. Rural life is relatively permanent in character, and it is a natural tendency for one to strive to own those things which will have use through a lifetime. By and large, therefore, dwellers in the country who do not own their own homes will be relatively less well-to-do. Using the ownership of a home as a crude index to the level of well-being we may rank those states with a rural population of over 50 per cent with respect to the ownership of dwellings. When this is done the coefficient of correlation with Alpha is found to be .68 $\pm$ .07. (Negroes omitted).

2. Farms: Tenantry is undoubtedly in general a lower economic status than farm-ownership. One who is a tenant-farmer may be said to be less independent than a farm-owner, and less capable of purchasing the means for self-culture and for the education of his children. Ranking the states according to the per cent of farms owned by white men and correlating with Table I the resulting coefficient is .70 $\pm$ .05. In urban states, however, the bad economic status of the farmer may not necessarily mean that the majority of the population, that is, the city dwellers, are in the same economic condition. When we confine the correlation to those states which are predominantly rural the coefficient is .66 $\pm$ .07.

3. Hired Men's Wages: Neither of the above economic conditions are perhaps as significant of the economic differences among the states as are the variations in the average wage without board paid to hired help on

farms. Since farm labor is chiefly unskilled and this unskilled labor competes with that of the cities, and since the wages of unskilled labor presumably reflects that of skilled labor, we may assume that the variations from state to state in the incomes of so large a class are in a general way indicative of the general standard of living, possible variations in the cost of commodities notwithstanding. The coefficient of correlation of the average wage for farm labor and Alpha is .83 ± .03. For states predominantly rural, .88 ± .03.

(C) Educational Efficiency

1. Literacy: Using this basic index to the distribution of cultural opportunity and correlating with Alpha a coefficient results amounting to .64 ± .06 (Negroes omitted).

2. Schools: Ayres (*An Index Number for State School Systems,* Sage Foundation, 1920) has arranged a rank-order of the school systems of the American states in terms of their efficiency as gauged by the following criteria:

1. Per cent of school population in daily attendance.
2. Average days attended by each child of school age.
3. Average number of days schools were kept open.
4. Per cent that high school attendance was of the total.
5. Per cent that boys were of girls in high schools.
6. Average annual expenditure per child attending.
7. Average annual expenditure per child of school age.
8. Average annual expenditure of teacher employed.
9. Expenditure per pupil for purposes other than teacher's salary.
10. Expenditure per teacher for salaries.

Since Table I is concerned with white persons only the fact that Ayres' ranking of state school systems applies to black and white alike might affect the correlation slightly. His ranking for 1900 is used because the average draftee was of school age at this time. The resulting coefficient is .72 ± .05. This result may be compared with that of Davies (*op. cit.*) for noted men.

CONCLUSION

Our study has given us ground for making three general inferences:

1. Population centered in cities is on the whole more intelligent than the population of rural districts.

2. States with the more favorable economic conditions tend to rank higher in intelligence.

3. States which afford their citizens better educational advantages tend to average higher in median Alpha scores.

It may be argued that the best blood tends to be attracted to the cities, that good endowment assures success in economic advancement, and that the states having the better stocks build the better schools.

On the other hand it may be maintained that it is the cultural institutions, excellent schools, the continued exchange of ideas and the varied associations of urban life that develop intelligence in youth; that favorable economic circumstances mean better home environments, opportunity for culture, leisure for study, better types of individual and group associations; and finally that an excellent educational system is a great factor in the unfolding of intelligence.

Such, briefly stated, are the contentions of the hereditarian and environmentalist respectively. Whatever one's inclinations may be, one fact stands out clearly, that where density of population, favorable economic conditions, and educational opportunities exist in conjunction, there will be found the better intelligence. The substantiation of this statement is as follows: When the average position for each of the forty-one states is found from the rankings for per cent of urban population, ownership of farms, average wage for farm labor, literacy, and Ayres' school systems and the correlation of this combined rank-order is made with Alpha, the resulting coefficient is .89 ± .02.

Our conclusion is that in so far as it applies to such large social groups as the American states, Army Alpha appears as a test of what *has* been learned rather than what *can* be learned.

This paper affords a clear demonstration of Binet's statement that ". . . retardation is a term relative to a number of circumstances which must be taken into account in order to judge each particular case." Hollingworth shows that special and economic considerations play an important part in the practical definition of feeblemindedness. Intelligence test scores have variable meanings in different societies, depending on the demands a society makes on the individual.

Differential Action Upon the Sexes of Forces which Tend to Segregate the Feebleminded*

LETA S. HOLLINGWORTH

1922

1. PREVIOUS OBSERVATIONS

It has often been stated that among individuals of the lowest two or three percentiles in the distribution of human intelligence there are more males than females. This statement has been based chiefly on the census of state training schools for mental defectives, and of special classes for subnormal children. Such enumerations practically always show a preponderance of males. Kuhlmann gives figures, which may serve us as fair samples, collected by him in 1915, as the result of a questionnaire returned from seven states in this country. In the state schools for feebleminded were 4,046 males (53.5%), and 3,518 females (46.5%). The United States Report for 1910 showed in institutions for the feebleminded 11,015 males (53.8%), and 9,716 females (46.2%).

Special classes for subnormal children in local school districts also show more boys than girls on the registers. The reports of the Inspector of Ungraded Classes, in New York City, show a ratio of more than two boys to one girl. Recent reports from England show three boys to two girls on the records of the special schools after-care committee of The City of Birmingham, a ratio "which is frequently found in the various special schools for the mentally defective."

From reports of which those cited are fair samples, inferences like the following are drawn. "Idiocy is almost everywhere recognized as more common in males than in females." "There is no doubt that there are more feebleminded boys than girls. There are more boys in the special classes in London, and in the Hilfschulen in Germany, and in the special

* Adapted from the *Journal of Abnormal Psychology*, 17 (1922-23), pp. 35-57. Reprinted by permission of the American Psychological Association.

classes so far found in the United States, and everything agrees with this."

In working among the children in the special classes for mental defectives in Philadelphia, Sylvester noticed that when mental tests were made by him, the girls of these classes were revealed as more defective than the boys, though fewer in number, and he commented as follows: "For reasons not of interest here, a relatively small number of girls are placed in the special backward classes. It is a matter of observation, confirmed by these results (in mental tests) that the girls of these classes as a group are more backward than the boys . . . Obviously the girls of a mental grade corresponding to the brighter boys in the backward classes, were left in the regular classes."

Reference should here be made to the findings of The Royal Commission of Great Britain, of 1904. This Commission sought to enumerate the feebleminded outside of institutions, by sampling certain sections of the country, and applying a social-economic criterion to the inhabitants. The definition of "feebleminded person" which they adopted was, "One who is capable of making a living under favorable circumstances, but is incapable from mental defect existing from birth or from an early age (a) of competing on equal terms with his normal fellows or (b) of managing himself and his affairs with ordinary prudence." Upon application of this criterion, the Commission found more feebleminded males than females, but there is every reason to suppose that this criterion applies unequally to the sexes. The same supposition holds for their definitions of "imbecile" and "idiot."

* * *

2. AIM OF THE PRESENT INVESTIGATION

The present investigation proposes (1) to throw additional light upon the question of the frequency of extreme deviations in intelligence, as related to sex, (2) to pass upon the validity of the census of the segregated, as a measure of sex differences in mental variation, and (3) to give an account of the extent to which segregation may be differential, as it affects boys and girls.

The method is to analyze large samplings respectively of those who are brought for mental examination because they are thought to be deficient, and of those who have been actually segregated. As preliminary to the collection of data, the following specific questions were formulated:

1. Are males and females brought in equal numbers from the general population, for examination as suspected mental defectives?

2. Are males and females committed in equal numbers to institutions for mental defectives?

3. Are males and females, brought for mental examination as suspected mental defectives, and those committed as such, equally distributed in birthday age?

4. Are males and females so brought, and those so committed, of equal birthday age, mental age for mental age?

5. Are males and females so brought, and those so committed, equally stupid, age for age?

6. What inferences are to be drawn from a census of the segregated, regarding the relative frequency of extremely low intelligence as related to sex?

3. MATERIAL OF THE PRESENT INVESTIGATION

1. In 1913, 1,000 consecutive cases of suspected mental deficiency were transcribed from the files of The Clearing House for Mental Defectives, at The Post Graduate Hospital, in New York City. This was a public clinic, from which children or adults, if found to be feebleminded, might be officially committed to appropriate institutions. Individuals of any age, from any borough of Greater New York, if suspected of inadequate intelligence, were admissible to this clinic, for mental examination.

Measurement of intelligence was made at that time by means of Goddard's Revision of Binet's Measuring Scale. The mental examinations were made by psychologists duly appointed to serve on this clinic, among whom was the present writer, who made about one third of the measurements recorded here. Of the 1,000 consecutive cases tabulated, 117 had no record of mental measurement, because of sensory defect, language difficulty, non-co-operation, and so forth.

2. In 1921, 1,142 cases were taken from the official files of The Psychological Laboratory, in the institution maintained by The Department of Public Welfare, of New York City, called The Children's Hospital, of Randall's Island. This is the municipal institution for the detention of the feebleminded. The mentally defective of the City are received here without limitations as to age, and receive training in the schools conducted there, though the institution is called The Children's Hospital, the great majority of inmates being children of school age, as will be seen from the data presented.

The data here used were obtained by transcribing all commitments, resident at any time since the establishment of The Psychological Laboratory, alphabetically by surname, through A, B, C, D, E, F, G, and H. All cases falling under these categories were transcribed in order, both those who were inmates at the time of transcription, and those who had been inmates, except epileptics, and those whose mental tests were incomplete. The latter were cases either just admitted to The Island, or too ill to be brought for mental examination, and were distributed in chance proportion between the sexes.

The method of mental measurement was the Stanford-Binet, in about 90 per cent of cases, the remainder having been measured by Goddard's Revision of Binet's Scale, by Pintner's Scale of Performance Tests, or by Kuhlmann's Extension of Binet's Measuring Scale. The last named was used in grading cases under 3 years mentally. The mental measurements were made by the psychologists duly appointed to serve in The Psychological Laboratory, after civil service examination, or by assistants directly under their supervision.

These two distinct collections of data may be regarded as "check samples" for each other. In each case the date (1913 or 1921) refers to the year in which the transcription of cases was made.

There are certain reasons for supposing that the results here obtained from the study of segregated cases might differ somewhat from those obtained from a study of all segregated mental defectives in the state. The institution studied is located in a city, and there probably is a tendency to send boys and men to country institutions, where they can work upon the land. More males than females are transferred to up-state schools, as the files show. It seems highly probable that more males may be sent to the country in the first place, since that is permissible. Again, the state maintains a separate institution for feebleminded women of child-bearing age, and this may affect somewhat the number of women of that age found in this study of inmates (1921 data).

These possible selective influences do not, however, affect the data from those brought for examination (1913), as these cases were uncommitted at the time of examination.

4. COMPARATIVE INCIDENCE OF MALES AND OF FEMALES IN THE SAMPLES STUDIED

Are males and females brought in equal numbers for mental examination, as suspected mental defectives?

Are males and females segregated in equal numbers in an institution for mental defectives?

Of the 1,000 consecutive individuals examined at The Clearing House for Mental Defectives, 568 were males and 432 were females. Of the 1,142 cases listed in the Randall's Island institution alphabetically, 603 were males and 539 were females.

The preponderance of males brought for examination is greater than the preponderance of males actually segregated here, probably for two reasons. The first of these is that already mentioned, namely that there may be a tendency to commit males to state schools, where agriculture is possible. The second probability is that considerable numbers of the males presented are not committed, because they are found on test to be of a status higher than that where commitment can be justified.

It is true that more males than females are born, in a proportion of about 106 to 100. Statistics of mortality, however, show a somewhat higher death rate among male infants, so that by adolescence the numerical equality of the sexes is usually considered to be established. No statistics are available to the present writer from which the exact numerical ratio of the sexes at each birthday age, in New York City, over the decade studied, can be learned. The federal census in 1910 gave a proportion of 1,029 males to 1,000 females, in New York City, and in 1920 gave the proportion as 998 males to 1,000 females. The preponderance of males examined, and the preponderance of males segregated, in New York City, is greater at any rate than the preponderance of males born, or living in New York City during the time studied, as follows:

Proportion of males to females born................... 106 : 100
    ,,   ,,   ,,   ,,   ,,   living in N. Y. C., 1910 ... 1029 : 1000
    ,,   ,,   ,,   ,,   ,,   ,,   ,,   ,,   1920 ...   998 : 1000
    ,,   ,,   ,,   ,,   ,,   examined, 1913 .... 130 : 100
    ,,   ,,   ,,   ,,   ,,   committed, 1921 .... 112 : 100

5. COMPARATIVE AGE OF MALES AND FEMALES IN THE SAMPLES STUDIED

Are males and females, brought for mental examination as suspected mental defectives, and those committed as such, equally distributed in birthday age?

*   *   *

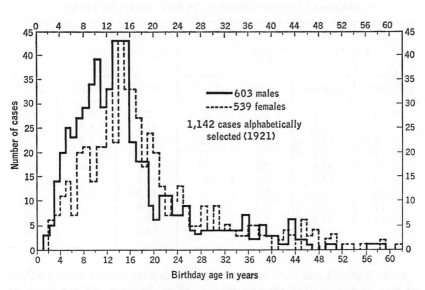

Figure 1. Showing the comparative frequency of males and females, among 1,142 individuals segregated as mental defectives, by birthday age.

From the data in **Figure 1** it is clearly seen that the preponderance of males is due to the presence of boys under 16 years of age. Males are brought for examination, and are segregated, at a relatively early age. Girls escape the pressure that brings about identification longer than do boys. It is obvious that many women who were in childhood of a status warranting segregation, escaped till the age of twenty or thirty years, or longer, in ways which were not open to the boys and men in question. Since many die before the age of 16 years, it follows that many females escaping examination and segregation at the ages when males are most frequently examined and committed, never come under those influences which cause the curves of distribution to cross at 16 years, because they have died in the meantime.

Also, there is no reason to suppose that factors which finally become operative to bring feebleminded girls for examination and commitment after 16 years of age, are equal in pressure to those which bring feebleminded boys before 16. Even if all the feebleminded lived to be just 70 years old, let us say, there is no reason to suppose that as many females as males would be ultimately identified by present social pressures.

Our second question relating to comparative age is this: Are males and females, brought for mental examination as suspected mental defectives, and those so committed, of equal birthday age, mental age for mental age?

TABLE I

Showing that Females are Older Chronologically, Mental Age for Mental Age, than are Males, Brought for Examination as Suspected Mental Defectives, in New York City (1913)

| Mental age, years | Birthday age at examination | | | | | |
| | Males | | | Females | | |
	Average	A. D.	Cases	Average	A. D.	Cases
0– 4	7.1	3.2	92	8.1	3.8	65
4– 5	9.2	2.4	29	11.4	4.3	16
5– 6	12.6	4.2	25	13.2	4.3	32
6– 7	11.4	2.9	42	15.8	6.0	40
7– 8	13.5	2.9	76	15.0	4.6	45
8– 9	12.9	2.5	82	17.2	5.1	56
9–10	14.0	2.7	70	17.3	4.3	53
10–11	15.2	2.7	57	18.5	5.4	46
11–12	14.2	1.0	20	17.7	2.5	27
12 +	13.0	0.0	4	16.8	2.9	6

From Tables I and II, it is clear that females who survive in the ordinary schools, and in society, till past the age of adolescence, do not do so because they are of better mentality than the corresponding males. Females

TABLE II

Showing that Females are Older Chronologically, Mental Age for Mental Age, than are Males, Committed to an Institution for Mental Defectives, in New York City (1921)

Mental age, years	Birthday age as examined in institution committed cases					
	Males			Females		
	Average	A. D.	Cases	Average	A. D.	Cases
Below 3	11.3	7.6	154	11.7	6.7	111
3– 4	14.0	8.5	66	16.5	9.6	47
4– 5	13.0	6.0	51	16.7	7.6	38
5– 6	18.7	9.4	42	19.2	9.1	52
6– 7	18.0	8.7	66	21.5	8.6	95
7– 8	16.2	5.5	72	22.7	9.3	64
8– 9	16.2	5.0	74	19.7	7.0	64
9–10	15.7	3.0	35	20.1	7.0	37
10–11	17.6	5.7	22	20.6	6.3	26
11 +	18.0	6.1	21	19.8	4.2	5

of any given mental age escape examination and segregation longer than do males of the same mental age,—this difference becoming very marked above the mental age of 6–7 years. A female with a mental age of 6 years has as good a chance to survive inconspicuously in the educational, social and economic milieu of New York City as has a male of a mental age of 10 years.

6. COMPARATIVE STUPIDITY OF MALES AND FEMALES IN THE SAMPLES STUDIED

Are males and females, brought for mental examination as suspected mental defectives, and those so segregated, equally stupid, age for age?

In seeking the answer to this question, the IQ's have been distributed by sex, and by birthday age, and the average IQ under each birthday age has been found for each sex separately. Also, the IQ's have been distributed by sex, disregarding birthday age. (IQ is here taken to mean the ratio between birthday age and mental age, by whatever scale of measurement was used.) In almost all of the cases here distributed, the scale was either Stanford-Binet (1921) or Goddard's Revision (1913).

In these tabulations a difficulty arises through the lack of exact measurement below the level of 3 years. As before stated, a few cases testing below 3 had been measured by Kuhlmann's method, and the IQ's for these can be included. All who remained unmeasured, being listed in the records simply as "below 3", were omitted from the distributions.

Very few of the children sufficiently stupid to be presented or segregated early, register as high as 3 mentally by their sixth birthday. Not enough children under 7 by birthday age registered 3 or more mentally, so that distribution of IQ's under that age would be worth while. The calculations begin, therefore, with the 7-year-olds.

There is no reason to suppose that the comparison would result differently, if all individuals below 3 mentally could be included in the distribution of IQ's. More males than females are below 3 in mental age, but this does not mean that there are more very low-grade intelligences among the males. More of the males than of the females below 3 mentally are relatively young children, so that their IQ's, when they have developed through the period of growth, may be relatively high.

By methods at present known, it is, of course, not possible to calculate the lowest existing IQ's. It is an interesting theoretical question as to how low IQ can run in the human species, and as to what "just not any intelligence," or zero intelligence, would be.

* * *

It will be seen that at the points which include the great majority of cases, namely among children of school age, the females have less intelligence than the males. After the age of 16 years, the difference disappears. For cases presented for examination after that age, the average IQ is 52, for both males and females. Among segregated cases the average IQ for adult females is 43 and for adult males, 45 with a large measure of unreliability.

It is interesting to see what the differences are between the presented, and the finally segregated. The IQ's of those presented run about ten points higher on the average than the IQ's of the actually committed. The difference in stupidity between the sexes is much more marked among those actually segregated, than among those presented for examination. A girl must be relatively more stupid than a boy in order to be presented for examination, in the first place, and she must be still more stupid, comparatively, in order that she may be actually segregated, as unfit for social and economic participation.

7. SPECULATIVE INTERPRETATIONS

The data here collected show that the pressures which bring about segregation of feebleminded school children are differential in their action upon the sexes, but they do not tell us what the pressures are. So far as the present study is concerned, interpretation of the nature of those pressures remains in the state of conjecture.

Girls segregated as mentally deficient are *more stupid* than boys segre-

TABLE III

Showing the Relative Stupidity of Males and Females, Presented for Mental Examination as Suspected Mental Defectives; Omitting Cases of Mental Age Below 3 (1913)

Birthday age, years	Males			Females		
	Av. IQ*	A. D.	Cases	Av. IQ	A. D.	Cases
7– 8	69	17.8	17	75	9.3	11
8– 9	65	14.5	21	58	15.9	16
9–10	70	15.4	30	70	16.2	14
10–11	71	14.8	41	67	12.6	18
11–12	70	14.3	43	66	12.5	16
12–13	66	10.2	52	57	12.6	38
13–14	67	11.3	52	67	11.0	24
14–15	61	11.5	55	60	12.4	22
15–16	53	9.9	45	57	8.0	33
16+	52	9.4	70	52	10.3	150

* To the nearest one half of one per cent.

TABLE IV

Showing the Relative Stupidity of Males and Females, Detained in an Institution for Mental Defectives; Omitting Cases of Mental Age Below 3, Except a Few Such Cases Examined by Kuhlmann's Method (1921)

Birthday Age, Years	Males			Females		
	Av. IQ*	A. D.	Cases	Av. IQ	A. D.	Cases
7– 8	60	14.5	14	62	18.3	17
8– 9	53	13.0	21	51	9.2	15
9–10	64	14.1	30	64	10.7	9
10–11	61	15.7	34	52	13.6	20
11–12	60	13.4	26	50	11.2	17
12–13	61	11.5	29	51	14.3	29
13–14	60	14.9	37	48	14.9	18
14–15	56	11.1	39	55	10.6	41
15–16	55	9.2	41	50	13.6	28
16–17	47	14.8	20	44	8.7	33
17–18	33	10.9	13	51	8.7	24
18–19	44	13.4	18	44	7.5	15
19–20	53	15.0	9	50	14.3	22
20–21	38	9.1	6	43	8.8	15
21–22	44	10.9	9	47	7.4	12
22–23	37	11.4	11	41	11.3	5
23–24	52	13.4	5	55	12.3	8
24–25	47	9.3	6	45	8.3	12
25+	41	1.2	64	43	9.7	103

* To the nearest one half of one per cent.

gated as mentally deficient; *fewer* girls than boys are segregated; and the girls who are segregated *escape longer* than do the boys.

These phenomena may possibly arise because (1) parents are more interested in their daughters than in their sons, and are more reluctant to part from them; (2) parents and other relatives are more interested in boys than in girls, and counsel is, therefore, more readily sought for deviating boys than for deviating girls; (3) girls and women have legal and customary means of economic survival, which boys and men do not have, and which require a low minimum of intelligence; (4) intelligence is not so important an element in the social-economic survival of girls and women, as it is in that of boys and men, so that girls who are extremely stupid do not give concern, and are not noticed, to the same extent as are boys of the same degree of actual stupidity; (5) boys, because they are less restricted, come more often into conflict with the law than do girls, and are thus scrutinized and referred more often by courts; (6) the subjective notion as to what constitutes intelligent behavior is different in the case of girls from what it is in the case of boys; (7) factors not included in any of these conjectures may be operative.

Data showing the social-economic status of the feebleminded over 16 years of age, among the cases presented for mental examination, are given herewith. They are suggestive as to a line of research which might prove fruitful, in an attempt to determine what are the forces, the differential action of which has been demonstrated.

The above tabulation shows that there is certainly a sex difference in the occupations followed by the feebleminded. Housework is the basis of survival for a very large percentage of feebleminded women. This may be for relatives, as paid domestics, as married women, or as common law wives. On the other hand, housework accounts for the survival of but one boy over 16 years of age.

Prostitution appears to offer the next most favorable basis for economic survival, among the feebleminded girls here found.

There seem to be no occupations which support feebleminded men as well as housework and prostitution support feebleminded women.

*   *   *

It is a matter of common knowledge that girls, as a group, are not expected continuously to follow competitive careers for a living. It is expected that their work will be in the household, domestic work and child-rearing, performed by the majority non-competitively (as wives or daughters) and without a stipulated wage.

Men, on the other hand, form a competitive group, working in rivalry with each other for a wage. This is true of even the simplest work that men do, such as digging with a pick, or loading sand on carriers. It would be

TABLE V

Vocational Status of Persons Over 16 Years of Age, Presented as Suspected Mental Defectives (1913)

Vocation	Males	Females
Housework at home	1	28
Housework for wage (av. $4 per mo. and board)	0	19
*Married	0	16
Prostitute	0	15
Still at school	0	5
Nursery maid	0	3
*Engaged to be married	0	2
*Common law marriage	0	2
Factory hand (unspecified)	0	2
Transfer from an institution	5	2
Scrubbing in hospitals	0	2
Feather worker	0	1
Cabaret singer	0	1
Bottle filler	0	1
Paper worker	0	1
Book binder	0	1
Laundry hand	1	1
Soldering lamps	0	1
Chamber maid	0	1
Cigar maker	0	1
Manicurist	0	1
Errand boy	3	0
Porter	1	0
Candy worker	1	0
Delivery boy	1	0
Gardener	1	0
Rag picker	1	0
Plumber's helper	1	0
Janitor	1	0
Umbrella mender	1	0
Helps father	1	0
Music student	1	0
Newsboy	1	0

* Marriage is listed as a vocation, since these women all did housework, and were in turn supported.

expected *a priori* that the boy who cannot compete would become an object of concern.

The girl who cannot compete mentally need not become an object of concern to the same extent, because she may drop into the non-competitive vocational life of the household, where she "naturally" performs many routine tasks, requiring but rudimentary intelligence, such as peeling vegetables, washing dishes, scrubbing, carrying fuel, and so forth. If physically unobjectionable, as may be the case, she may marry, thus fastening herself to economic support in a customary fashion. Or she may become a prostitute, for survival is possible in that pursuit at a low intellectual level. Thus feebleminded girls fit in with the existing folkways, in a relatively inconspicuous fashion.

It should be worth while, from the standpoint of school and society, to determine just what the forces are which act to bring about differential segregation, and what the relative weight of each force is.

*   *   *

8. CONCLUSIONS

From the foregoing study the following conclusions are drawn:

1. More males than females are brought in New York City for mental examination, as suspected mental defectives.

2. More males than females are committed to the municipal institution for mental defectives, in New York City.

3. Males and females brought for mental examination as suspected mental defectives, and those so committed, in New York City, are not equally distributed with respect to birthday age. From 0 years to 16 years of age, there is a decided preponderance of males. From the age of 16 years, the reverse is true. The frequency of cases after 16 years is greatly reduced, and almost no cases past the age of 40 are involved.

4. Males and females, brought for mental examination as suspected mental defectives, and those so committed, are not equally old, mental age for mental age. At all degrees of stupidity females survive longer without examination or commitment than do males of the same mental status.

Males and females suspected of being mentally defective, and those segregated as such, are not equally stupid, age for age. The females are of lower grade than the males, up to the age of about 16 years. Among the adults here studied, the segregated males have an average IQ of 42.6, and the females have an average IQ of 45.0, while among the adults presented for examination both males and females have an average IQ of 52.

Since the great majority of all cases falls under 16 years, the central tendency of IQ is lower for females than for males.

6. Institutional statistics, showing merely the numerical ratio of the sexes to each other among inmates, are invalid as an index of sex differences in frequency and amount of mental deviation, for the population at large. Such institutional statistics serve merely as an index of the extent to which it is comparatively easy and convenient for females who are extremely unintelligent to survive in the performance of their functions, in ordinary society.

9. IMPLICATIONS

The implications of this study are of interest for school and society. Among public school children there are probably more feebleminded girls than boys, since the girls corresponding to the higher grade boys under institutional supervision are evidently left in the population at large. Yet the registers of special classes for mentally deficient children show more boys than girls in such classes. Feebleminded girls will doubltess continue to drift with the regular classes, unless selection for special classes is made in a rigidly objective manner.

From the standpoint of society it is of interest to know that feebleminded girls fit into the existing social and economic order more conveniently than do boys of the same mental quality. Extremely stupid girls thus survive, and presumably reproduce their kind, more easily than do extremely stupid boys. The social order is such that survival for the former depends less upon intelligence than it does for the latter.

In so far as the preponderance of males among segregated feebleminded persons has been thought to support the theory of greater male variability in intellect, it must be said that a mere census of such persons is without validity as evidence.

This paper has a twofold interest for the reader. First, it points out the sometimes amazing capacities of the exceptionally brilliant child, and second, it deals thoughtfully with the bearing of data from identical twins on the nature-nurture controversy.

Mental and Physical Correspondence in Twins*

ARNOLD GESELL

1922

I. The Study of Twins

Twins have always captured the curiosity and imagination of man. They figure in myths, traditions, superstitions, in art, in humor and in advertising. They are written in the constellations. Recently they have become one of the problems of science. Ancient Assyrians, Babylonians, Egyptians, Indians, as well as Hottentots used to kill both or one of a pair of twins, on the theory that twins were omens of ill luck or a form of sin. Though we hold no such erroneous conception, now-a-days, there is still a great deal of romancing about twins.

* * *

The psychological aspects of the phenomenon of twins have not received their full share of attention. There are, however, two notable exceptions. The versatile Galton, who left few human problems untouched, made a suggestive, though rather leisurely, excursion into the subject in his *Inquiries into Human Faculty* in the year 1883. He used the questionnaire method and reported the returns of 80 cases of close similarity. Much of his material was anecdotal; but it was used to good advantage to prove the dominating influence of nature over nurture. He found only two cases of strong bodily resemblance being accompanied by mental diversity. He makes this characteristic suggestion: "It would be an interesting experiment for twins who were closely alike to try how far dogs could distinguish them by scent!"

In 1904, Thorndike published an important monograph entitled "Measurements of Twins," based on precise measurements of 50 pairs of unselected public school twins from 9 to 15 years old, in 6 mental traits, and 8 physical traits. "The arguments concerned the lack of differences in the amount of resemblance (1) between young and old twins, (2) between traits little, and traits much subject to training and (3) between mental and physical traits, and also the great increase in resemblance of twins over ordinary siblings. The resemblance of twins was found to be approximately

* Adapted from *The Scientific Monthly*, 14 (1922), pp. 305-331. Reprinted by permission of the author and *Scientific Monthly*.

.80 or .75 to .80 in amount." The author considers that his data was well-nigh conclusive evidence that the mental likenesses found in the case of twins and the differences found in the case of non-fraternal pairs, when the individuals compared belonged to the same age, locality and educational systems, are due, to at least nine-tenths of their amount to original nature.

"The form of distribution of twin resemblance seems to be that of a fact with a central tendency at about .80 and with a great variability, restricted towards the upper end by the physiological limit of complete identity. Such a distribution would be most easily explained by the genesis of twins as a rule from two ova and by a great reduction of the variability of contemporaneous germs and ova below that of germs and ova developed at different times." (Thorndike, p. 63.)

Thorndike therefore refuses to classify twins into the two classical divisions, duplicate and fraternal. He does not find two coherent species of resemblance; and he doubts that there are but two corresponding modes of genesis (monozygotic and dizygotic). He believes that there is considerable specialization of resemblance in all type of twins. Although he finds that resemblance in general appearance and countenance is correlated by no means perfectly with resemblance in other traits, his figures show a tendency toward such resemblance. The medians of resemblance in (1) three head measurements, (2) in three stature and arm measurements, (3) in perception, (4) in association,—of twins of the same sex (a) closely alike and (b) not much alike in countenance are as follows: 1. (a) 85, (b) 70. 2. (a) 86, (b) 59. 3. (a) 84, (b) 63. 4. (a) 94, (b) 70.

II. A Clinical Comparison of Duplicate Twins

We report herewith a case, or rather a pair of cases, which will serve as a basis for the consideration of the problem of resemblances in twins. We became interested in these two children, not because they were twins, but because of the exceptional superiority of their intelligence; and they were first studied from this point of view. Accumulating evidence, however, gradually convinced us that, regardless of their caliber, they presented a remarkable degree of correspondence in physical and mental constitution. It is this correspondence which is here emphasized. The facts have psychological interest, and may not be without some biological significance.

The twins will be referred to with an impersonal A and B, because there is no intention to publicly extoll them. We are not concerned to reveal their identity—except in the sense indicated by the term "identical twins!"

(A) DEVELOPMENTAL HISTORY

A complete family chart of the twin sisters A and B would show evidence of superior endowment in the immediate ancestry on both the maternal and paternal sides. Scientific and linguistic ability of high order and physical energy are some of the traits which are found in the two immediate generations. The trait of twinning likewise has a hereditary basis in this instance; for the mother also bore two boys, twins who died in infancy.

Their sisters A and B were born six years later, by Caesarian section, somewhat prematurely, weighing respectively 4.3 and 5.3 pounds. They thus escaped some of the hazard and strains which may accompany birth.

Their prematurity did not hinder precocity. At any rate, they very early showed unmistakable signs of more than ordinary alertness and attainment. At six months A startled her mother by rising suddenly into a sitting position in the mother's lap. Very soon after this B showed the same capacity. At 11 months they had both begun to walk and talk; indeed they were talking sentences, such as, "I see you, Auntie, * * *." They spoke clearly with less than the usual infantile lisping; and, according to report, with more than the usual degree of purposive, voluntary speech imitation. In October, 1915, at the age of three they began the study of French, and in less than a year (by April, 1916) they were reading elementary English, French and Esperanto. Their mother was a very constant companion; and stimulated this development by the aid of plays and games, but the children needed no prodding. They were distinguishing parts of speech with the aid of a Teddy Bear at the age of four; and at the same age one of them asked a searching question in regard to the Immaculate Conception. Formal arithmetic was begun at the age of six, and in less than a year they were solving mentally problems in fractions and percentage. They entered Grade III at the same age, and now at the age of nine, they are in Grade VII, doing Junior High School work. They are not prigs: they are attractive, animated, sociable children, with a bubbling sense of humor. They are popular with their playmates. They can take charge of a gymnasium class in which most of the members are two to four years their seniors, and preserve excellent attention and discipline. They speak mature but not pedantic English, and they speak French with the fluency of a native. They have read Genesis in Italian and are now speaking a little Italian. They have read the Book of Knowledge in its entirety in French; and a year ago embarked on Russian. They play duets on the piano; but not with rare distinction. They swim; they ride horseback; they write jingles, and they read by the hour. Their school work does not tax them; they do not worry about it; and they are far from fastidious in regard to the form of their written work.

In this brief general review of their developmental history it is impossible to make any noteworthy distinctions between A and B. They have been inseparable, and abreast. Physically as well as mentally there has been a correspondence. They have both escaped most of the children's diseases; and neither has suffered a physical setback. So that now, as when they were babies, they are practically interchangeable children. The general impression made by physique, countenance, demeanor, conversation is one of complete similarity. A rather thoroughgoing analysis does not seriously disturb this impression of underlying identity of psychophysical make up.

(B) PHYSICAL TESTS AND MEASUREMENTS

[Gesell recounts in detail twenty-five physical tests and measurements made on the twins. The correspondence is startling in all respects. The writer concludes his discussion with a last, fine similarity.]

* * *

Finally may be mentioned one permanent indication of underlying identity of constitution. This is a tiny pigmented birth mole on the upper lip, situated a short distance from the left outer corner of the mouth in both twins. So here "the standard mole of the penny-novelists" could not even be relied upon for the purpose of personal identification, because both twins have the self-same mole!

There are several very tiny pigmented areas in the facial skin which are limited to one twin; and there are no doubt other physical deviations which minute study would disclose. Even two hairs, each but a half inch in length, taken from the same head, would, as Wilder says, prove to be "absolutely unlike if magnified sufficiently to show the epidermic markings that cover the surface with a fine tracery." By such ultra refined standards, complete identity is a mathematical impossibility; but general, coherent correspondence and absolute identity are two quite different considerations. Our data compel us to recognize a basic developmental and physical correspondence in Twins A and B.

Since this correspondence has expressed itself in such structural details as teeth, skin patterns, birth moles, and cranial and carpal bones, it is not unreasonable to suppose that it should also assert itself in the general architecture and organization of the nervous system. We can gather some light on this point by inquiring into the mental correspondences, through the use of psychometric methods.

(C) MENTAL AND EDUCATIONAL MEASUREMENTS

The adjoined table summarizes the results of a group of intelligence, performance, and educational measurements of A and B which were made at the Yale Psycho-Clinic, and at the home of the children. The writer wishes to acknowledge the assistance of Dr. Margaret Cobb in the administration of these tests. The cooperativeness of the subjects who entered into all of the situations in the spirit of a game, enlivened with rivalry, aided us. The subjects deserve our especial thanks; for they were indispensable in this particular study.

TABLE I

Mental and educational test	A	B	A	B	Remarks
	Score*		Age norm.		
1. Binet, Age 7	188	181	13.5	13	⎫ Average I.Q.:
2. Binet, Age 8	179	185	14.75	15.25	⎬ A, 183+
					⎭ B, 183
3. Vocabulary, Age 7	50	50	14	14	
4. Vocabulary, Age 8	52	54	14+	14+	
5. Vocabulary, Age 9	67	65	16	16	
6. National Intelligence, Age 9	136	155	15	15+	
7. Porteus			12.25	11.25	A shows more foresight.
8. Ship	18	20	11	13	
9. Feature Profile	150 s	250 s	15	10	
10. Diagonal	195 s	70 s	6	10	
11. Triangle	25 s	30 s	14+	14	
12. Knox Cube	7	10	14−	18	
13. Healy A	205 s	135 s	9	10	
14. Seguin Form Board ...	28 s	30 s	7+	7	
15. Healy Coordination....	305	445			A more deliberate.
16. Opposites	40 s	80 s			B spent 45 sec. on last word.
17. Easy Directions	98 s	85 s			⎫ No errors; both
18. Hard Directions	175 s	155 s			⎬ showed intense interest and attention.
19. Symbol Digit	23.4	12.2	12	9	
20. Trabue Language Completion	13	13	13.5	13.5	
21. Kansas Silent Reading .	12.9	21.5	12.5	13.5	
22. Woody Fundamentals of Arithmetic	28	26	12.5	12.5	
23. Ayres Spelling	VIII	VIII	14.5	13.5	
24. Ayres Handwriting	60	60	13	13	Differentiation increasing.
25. Drawing (Thorndike) ..	10.5	10.5			
Accuracy (15)	90%	80%			
Average for combined tests			13.6	13.9	
Average for performance tests			11.75	12	
Standard deviation	2.83	2.91			
*S = second.					

The mental examinations were not, of course, all made at one sitting; but the twins were always submitted to the selfsame tests on the same days.

The results of these tests for which we have standardized age norms are plotted on the accompanying chart, in which the solid line stands for A's performance and the broken line for B's. It is hardly necessary to give mathematical expression to these curves. The two lines show a striking degree of cohesion. Note, for example, how they both plunge down on the formboard test, and how equally they rise on the vocabulary tests. The most pronounced disagreement is that shown in the feature profile test. Here there was apparently a more or less fortuitous circumstance, which disturbed B's attack of the problem. Indeed it is quite likely that not a few of the

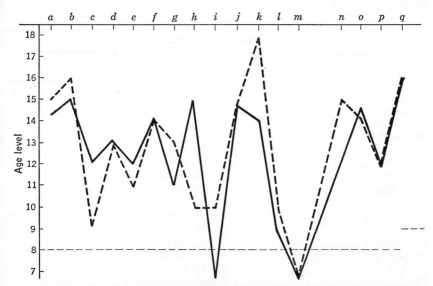

Figure 1. GRAPH SHOWING CORRESPONDENCE IN MENTAL MEAS-UREMENTS OF A AND B. The results are plotted on the basis of mental age scores, the heavy straight dotted line representing the chronological age. The tests in order are (*a*) *Binet*, (*b*) National Intelligence, (*c*) Symbol Digit, (*d*) Trabue Completion, (*e*) *Porteus*, (*f*) *Vocabulary*, (*g*) *Ship*, (*h*) *Feature Profile*, (*i*) Diagonal, (*j*) Triangle, (*k*) Knox Tube, (*l*) Healy A, (*m*) Seguin Form-board, (*n*) Kansas Silent Reading, (*o*) Ayres Spelling, (*p*) Woody Mixed Fundamentals of Arithmetic, (*q*) Vocabulary II.

minor disparities shown in the performance scores in various tests indicate variation in the conditions of the test, beyond our control, rather than fundamental differences in mentality. In view of this, the amount of psychological correspondence actually revealed by the tests is all the more significant.

* * *

It was possible to make a satisfactory comparison of the twins A and B by means of a vocabulary test. This test, Terman considers to have a far higher value than any other single test in the whole intelligence measuring scale. The test consists of 100 words derived by random selection from a

dictionary containing 18,000 words. An abbreviated series of 50 words of
increasing difficulty ranging from *gown* and *tap* to *shagreen* and *complot*
was given to both A and B. This virtually constituted a graded scale of 50
individual tests, and revealed a startling degree of resemblance; A failed on
16 of the test words; B failed on exactly the same words, and on only one
additional word, namely *harpy*. The calculated vocabulary score of A at
the age of 9 is 65 and for B it is 67, a standard equivalent to the average
adult level.

TABLE II
Vocabulary Test

	A	B		A	B
1. gown	+	+	26. Mars	+	+
2. tap	+	+	27. mosaic	+	+
3. scorch	+	+	28. bewail	+	+
4. puddle	+	+	29. priceless	+	+
5. envelope	+	+	30. disproportionate	+	+
6. rule	+	+	31. tolerate	+	+
7. health	+	+	32. artless	−	−
8. eye-lash	+	+	33. depredation	−	−
9. copper	+	+	34. lotus	+	+
10. curse	+	+	35. frustrate	−	−
11. pork	+	+	36. harpy	+	−
12. outward	+	+	37. flaunt	−	−
13. southern	+	+	38. ochre	−	−
14. lecture	+	+	39. milksop	−	−
15. dungeon	+	+	40. incrustation	−	−
16. skill	+	+	41. retroactive	−	−
17. ramble	+	+	42. ambergris	−	−
18. civil	+	+	43. achromatic	−	−
19. insure	+	+	44. perfunctory	−	−
20. nerve	+	+	45. casuistry	−	−
21. juggler	+	+	46. piscatorial	−	−
22. regard	+	+	47. sudorific	−	−
23. stave	+	+	48. parterre	−	−
24. brunette	+	+	49. shagreen	−	−
25. hysterics	+	+	50. complot	±	±

+, passed. −, failed.

This degree of correspondence is truly remarkable when we reflect that
this searching test, in a statistical sense, compasses the whole wide domain
of the English language. Although we must give due weight to the similarity
of verbal and academic environment to which A and B have been subjected, do not the results of the test testify even more eloquently to an underlying similarity of nervous constitution and organization?

Incidentally we may record a characteristic reaction which occurred in
the course of the first vocabulary test which I gave to the twins at the age

of 7. A encountered a word which sounded familiar, but for which she could frame no definition. The word was *civil,*—"Civil, don't know; can't say; and yet I think I know. O, that reminds me: it is like that story about space. A teacher asked his pupil to define *space*. The boy said, 'I can't tell you what it is, but I've got it in my head.'" Thereafter, whenever an unfamiliar word was presented, A smiled slyly, tapped her head and said, "I guess it's that space story again!" Even so, both girls at the age of seven had a vocabulary score of 50, equivalent to the mental age of 14. Moreover, they knew when they didn't know. Mentally inferior children venture wild definitions in the field of the unknown.

There are no satisfactory objective methods for directly measuring emotional and volitional traits. We, of course, secure data concerning them indirectly through so-called intelligence measurements; but we are chiefly dependent upon clinical inference and estimate. Even so, it would require a psychological Boswell to furnish a complete comparative picture of the temperaments and dispositions of A and B. Long continued and intimate observation might reveal some interesting disparities in the emotional sphere. The ordinary observer would probably develop a partiality for one of the twins on the ground that A or B is less assertive, more reasonable, more affectionate, than B or A. But this preference might indicate the inveterate selective and discriminative tendency of human perception, quite as much as a fundamental diversity in the twins.

Assuming that there is at present a high degree of correspondence in temperamental traits: does it follow that such will always be the case? Hardly so. To begin with these children have not as yet come into full possession of all of their mental inheritance. Adolescence brings with it many new psychic characters, and these may not be equally shared, or equally assimilated by A and B. And as we look down the future we must reckon with the differentiating power of differences in fortune, social position or professional career. We have noticed that one twin is definitely more dependent upon demonstration of affection by the mother; that one is becoming interested in the violin, the other, perhaps in poetry. Suppose that one should seek distinction in music and the other in letters. Even such a relatively small disparity in vocation might ultimately create by accretion a very decided difference in mental content, habits of thought, social attitudes, outlook upon life; so that the conditioned reflexes and complexes of A would become quite distinguishable from those of B; an interesting difference in vegetation, growing upon much the same soil. Personality in its higher expressions is always so conditioned by social and educational factors that it would be futile to deny the possibilities of differentiation even with "duplicate twins."

But we are concerned with the present status of twins A and B, age 8. At that age we gave them an opportunity to express some of their likes and dislikes on paper. It was a simple, almost impromptu test; but the results were amazing. They independently answered in writing a questionnaire, which is reproduced with their replies exactly as they gave them.

QUESTIONS ON LIKES AND DISLIKES, ANSWERED IN WRITING
INDEPENDENTLY BY A AND B

Question: If you had $1,000.00 to spend, how would you do it? Tell me about it on this page.
Answer: A. I would buy a painting outfit and learn to use it. Take Mother to Europe (because she wants so much to go).
B. I would buy a horse (like Black Beauty), a riding habit, the Universal Anthology for Mother and a barrel of sugar for my horse.
Question: What is the most unpleasant thing you have to do every day?
Answer: A. Practice on the piano.
B. Practice on the piano.
Question: What is the most agreeable thing you do every day?
Answer: A. Ride horse-back.
B. Ride horse-back.
Question: What is most likely to make you angry?
Answer: A. Our dog.
B. Rasputin. (The dog.)
Question: What is it your ambition to be when grown up?
Answer: A. An artist.
B. To teach.
Question: What game do you like best?
Answer: A. Play lady and dress up in Mother's clothes.
B. Mother.
Question: What was the most fun you had last summer?
Answer: A. Going in swimming.
B. Going in swimming.
Question: What is your favorite color?
Answer: A. Green.
B. Green.
Question: What is your favorite book?
Answer: A. Bible stories.
B. The Bible.
Question: What is your favorite song?
Answer: A. Red, White and Blue.
B. Home Sweet Home.
Question: What is your favorite study in school?
Answer: A. Reading.
B. Reading.

It would be easy to exaggerate the significance of these questionnaire results, and yet it is inconceivable that they would have been possible without a considerable degree of correspondence in personality traits. The same conclusion must be drawn from the results of the vocabulary tests made at seven, eight, and nine years of age. The close correspondence in mental level revealed by the Binet ratings is also undeniable. There were several points of difference in the I Q at the ages of seven and eight, but the average for the two testings was within one point,—183.

The I Q, or Intelligence Quotient, expresses the ratio of mental age to chronological age. If these two ages are the same in a given individual the I Q is 100. If the mental age is less than the chronological, the I Q is below 100. If the mental age is in advance the resulting I Q is above 100. Children with an I Q of 65 or less are usually feebleminded. Children with an I Q of 120 or more may be regarded as relatively superior. The psychological literature reports very few cases with an I Q as high as 180.

A comparative psychograph of the performances of A and B in the Binet tests gives a fair graphic picture of the degree of intellectual correspondence of these two children at the age of 8. The diagram is so drawn that success and failure are indicated in corresponding meridians. All the tests in the age levels below 12, were passed with great facility and are not included.

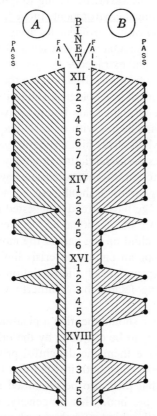

Figure 2. COMPARATIVE PSYCHOGRAPH Showing intellectual correspondence of Twins A and B at age 8. Forty-four graded intelligence tests were given. All the tests at the mental age levels of 8 to 12 inclusive were passed with facility.

One half of the psychograph proves to be almost a mirror image of the other.

(D) GENERAL CONCLUSION

Reviewing, then, the developmental history of A and B, and the results of scores of tests,—the physical, the anthropometric, the psychological, performance and educational measurements; and considering the collective weight and tendency of these findings, and the wider diversity which would have been shown by a similar study of ordinary siblings—it seems highly probable that this pair of twins were of nearly duplicated or identical genetic antecedents.

The general conclusion is inescapable that the consistent similarity between these two children is based upon a fundamental, inherent similarity in endowment. It would, however, be wrong to ignore the equalizing influence of a practically identical environment. Indeed, in studying the development of personality it is rather artificial to bring nature and nurture into rigid contradistinction. Personality represents the resultant cooperative product of both intrinsic and extraneous factors, and the interaction of these factors in highly dynamic relations. It is because these dynamic relations are so sensitive, that any marked psychological similarity even between co-twins at the relatively old age of eight years is impressive. It may even be usual that one of a pair of twins begins with or early acquires a physical or temperamental advantage which gives him a different status in the social situations of life; and initiates a differentiating process which waxes with what it feeds upon. But in the present instance, such a strong differentiating tendency has not become very apparent. I should not be willing to say that it will never come into power. We have already suggested the differentiating possibilities of a wide difference in vocational or social careers. Even now a consistent partiality for one child on the part of the mother, a physical accident or an unshared illness, or an emotional crisis limited to one child, might become the germ for a pronounced differentiation of personalities. But on the whole, the equalizing factors have hitherto with A and B remained dominant.

Among these factors we should mention a pleasant degree of jealousy and emulation. Neither wishes to be out done by the other. For example, when at the age of seven I gave them the delightful privilege of filling my hod with chunks of cannel coal, they both insisted that they be permitted to put on the big gloves and that they also be permitted to put exactly the same number of chunks into the hod. This propensity, which fundamentally is hereditary, has preserved a kind of balance of power and has helped to impress a certain identity on their respective personalities. Neither has become a leader of the other.

The argument that similar experiences have made these children similar does not bear close scrutiny; experience, after all, is a descriptive term for the reactions of an organism to its environment. As Dewey puts it, the combination of what things do to us in modifying our actions, and what we can do to them in producing new changes constitutes experience. From a clinical point of view, the experience argument begs the question. What we really wish to know is to what degree have these children actually had similar experiences. Our conclusion is that they have manifested similarity of experience to a remarkable degree, due primarily to the structural parity of the nervous system with which they were endowed. A similarity of environment has developed a corresponding functional parity. But here again the considerations become involved; for this so-called similarity of environment has consisted not only in the same house, similar beds, similar clothes, similar food and identical instruction; but the twins have had each other, and each has carried around much the same environment, because each apparently assimilated much the same things for her milieu. There has at least been a high degree of reciprocity between nature and nurture!

During the 1920's intelligence tests came in for violent criticism. The myth of the "child mind" of the American adult, fostered by an uncritical view of the Army test data, was ridiculed; critics, notably Walter Lippmann, lambasted psychologists for pretending to test what they could not even define. Boring's paper was an attempt to communicate to a popular audience what the psychologist was doing and what a score on an intelligence test meant.

Intelligence as the Tests Test It*

EDWIN G. BORING

1923

If you take one of the ready-made tests of intelligence and try it on a very large number of persons, you will find that they succeed with it in very different degrees. Repeat the test, and you will find that they cannot, with the best will in the world to do well, alter their scores very greatly. Then give the same group another intelligence test, and you will discover that the differences among individuals are approximately, although not exactly, the same. And you can go on. You will find that an adult, after continued exposure to his social and educational environment, does not greatly alter his score on a given test; that children, however, do steadily improve their performances until somewhere between ten and twenty years old; that the average age at which improvement stops is about fourteen years; but that children while improving tend to maintain the same individual differences, so that in a given group every child would keep about the same rank within the group. These are basic observational facts of the psychology of intelligence. What do they mean?

WHAT THE TESTS TEST

They mean in the first place that intelligence as a measurable capacity must at the start be defined as the capacity to do well in an intelligence test. Intelligence is what the tests test. This is a narrow definition, but it is the only point of departure for a rigorous discussion of the tests. It would be better if the psychologists could have used some other and more technical term, since the ordinary connotation of intelligence is much broader. The damage is done, however, and no harm need result if we but remember that measurable intelligence is simply what the tests of intelligence test, until further scientific observation allows us to extend the definition.

* *The New Republic* (June 6, 1923), pp. 35-37. Reprinted by permission of E. G. Boring and *The New Republic*.

An observational method for extending knowledge of intelligence as the tests test it is the method of statistical correlation. The relation to intelligence of any measurable capacity at all can be determined by comparing the relative performances of a large number of persons in an intelligence test with their achievement in the measure of capacity in question. If the correlation is considerable, yet not perfect, say 60 percent, we say that the particular capacity is partly dependent upon intelligence and partly independent of it. We shall not be far wrong if we think of such a capacity as complex, involving 60 percent of intelligence and 40 percent of some special ability that is not intelligence.

The method of correlation gives us at once some insight into the nature of intelligence as the tests test it. No satisfactory intelligence test exists at present which employs a single type of mental operation. Most tests for intelligence, like the army tests, consist of batteries of single tests, every one of which appears, on inspection, to test some special ability, like arithmetical ability, or an appreciation of verbal relations or of logical relations. When one obtains the correlations among the different tests that make up the battery called an intelligence test, one finds that the separate tests do not correlate with one another so very highly—not so highly as a rule as does one combined intelligence test with another. These results are explained by saying that the separate tests are really tests of separate abilities, and that each of these abilities involves, in part, intelligence, which is a factor common to all the tests, and in part a special ability, which is not intelligence and which therefore explains the failure of the tests to correlate very highly. When the separate tests are combined in a total score, the special abilities, being unrelated, are supposed to cancel out, leaving the score to represent the "common factor," intelligence.

Thus we see that there is no such thing as a test for pure intelligence. Intelligence is not demonstrable except in connection with some special ability. It would never have been thought of as a separate entity had it not seemed that very different mental abilities had something in common, a "common factor."

A CONFUSION OF MEANINGS

One of the most frequent reasons for the misunderstanding of the tests is the fact that the existence and importance of these special abilities are usually lost sight of. The psychologists themselves are very apt to forget them and it is no wonder that their lay audiences are scarcely aware of them. Yet it is not even possible to understand the nature of the tested intelligence without considering them. They are forgotten in part because the "common factor" has seemed especially important and the interest of the testers in the last decade has centered in it. Words, however, have also helped to obscure their existence. The tested intelligence of an individual is often called his "mental age"; the increase of intelligence in childhood is generally called "mental growth." In this way psychologists have inadvertently equated the "intelligent" to the "mental," overlooking in their terminology the vast number of special abilities that help to make up the "mind." It is high time for a change of words here. The present usage requires us to say that the average adult has a "mental age" of about fourteen and that "mental growth" on the average stops at fourteen. Nothing could be more untrue. The statement can be true only of intelligence as the tests test it. The special abilities, which make up skill and knowledge, continue to cumulate presumably throughout all adult life.

A very useful conception of intelligence, and one that is approximately correct in the light of our present knowledge, is that intelligence is like "power" as the physicist uses the word: the amount of work that can be done in a given time. All intelligence tests involve the maintenance of time-limits to some extent, and most tests are "speed" tests where all the work is performed against time. We may think, then, of intelligence as power and of a special ability as a machine that utilizes the power for a particular purpose. No machine can operate without power, and power is actually demonstrable only when it has a machine through which to operate. It is idle to speculate as to which is the more important, the power or the adaptive device for the utilization of the power; and it is folly to bet one's fortune on the power, forgetting the machine.

UP THE HILL ON LOW

A frequent complaint made of the tests is that they place too much emphasis upon speed. It is argued that some people, who do poorly in the intelligence tests, are persons who naturally work slowly but very accurately, and that the tests penalize them unfairly. If, however, intelligence is like power, this contention is not an argument. If these people have less power, they have to go up the hill on low gear and it takes them longer; that is all. Of course they "get there" just the same, but when they "get there" their powerful rivals are on and somewhere else. If they ride more smoothly as they go, that is an entirely different matter from the one under discussion; they have a special ability which is not intelligence as the tests test it. They probably never would have complained at all if they had not been misled into thinking that the intelligence-rating characterized their entire mental make-up. There were, for instance, competent surgeons in the army who rated low in the tests. There was no question about their value to the army; they had the requisite knowledge and skill. The conception of intelligence as power implies merely that they had gained their professional competence relatively late.

There has been much public concern since the war over the discovery of the army psychologists that the average "mental age" of Americans is about fourteen years. This concern is founded on ignorance, although it must be admitted that some psychologists have shared it. Before the war less adequate investigations had led the psychologists to suppose that the average "mental age" was about sixteen. No one was concerned on account of this tenet, largely because it did not get public attention. Now the army results correct the earlier finding, and everyone exclaims: "We are a nation of fourteen-year-olds!" Well, with respect to stature we are a nation of twenty-year-olds. There is no reason for concern because it is discovered that a given mental capacity, intelligence, attains its maximal development in adolescence. If there were some reason to believe that we ought to be sixteen or that other nations are on the average sixteen, there might be some cause for alarm, but there is not. We ought to be congratulating ourselves that we now have a more accurate knowledge concerning one mental capacity, and hoping that success in the field of intelligence promises eventually a detailed knowledge of the special abilities, which are equally important factors in mental life and in the value of the individual to American civilization.

The place where observation often yields too readily to inference is in the answer to the question: Is intelligence inherited? Psychological belief has been that it is, though recently some psychologists have been doubting. The question cannot be answered with assurance until there are observational correlations between parents and their offspring. It may well be that only a tendency toward intelligence is inherited, just as a tendency toward some diseases is inherited, and in such a case we should need to state, in terms of a correlation, the strength of the tendency. Experiments upon animals are in progress, but the results can hardly settle the problem for human beings. The test of intelligence in an animal is a maze to learn or a puzzle-box to open. Such a performance measures a special ability along with the "common factor," and it cannot be considered as a test of intelligence, as we have been using the word, unless observational correlation establishes a relationship. The positive answer therefore still lies in the future, and the person who states dogmatically that the man who consistently scores low in intelligence tests has only his ancestors to blame is not stating an irrefutable fact.

INTELLIGENCE IS LARGELY PREDETERMINED AT FIVE

It is obvious, however, that the intelligence which the tests test is at some time predetermined. If it stops developing in adolescence, it is predetermined for the adult as much as is stature, and no man by taking thought can add ten percent to his intelligence quotient. The intelligence tests begin to be fairly accurate at about five years of age, and we have seen that the child's relative position in intelligence with respect to other children of his age does not alter greatly as he grows up. This fact is expressed by saying that the intelligence quotient of the child (the ratio of his tested intelligence to his physical age) does not usually vary greatly. It would seem then that intelligence is predetermined at five years of age.

We are left with several possibilities. The actual time of the predetermination may be in infancy, in utero, or in the germ-plasm. The Freudians have shown the importance of infantile life in its effect upon adult life, and it might not seem strange if the predetermination occurred then. Psychologists, however, do not generally regard this argument seriously because the Freudian mechanisms are all of the order of the special abilities. Almost nothing is known about prenatal determinants, but one psychologist has recently suggested them as accounting for his seeming failure to obtain high correlations between the intelligences of children of the same family. Predetermination by inheritance is supported most strongly by the family histories of the feeble-minded: the Jukes, the Kallikaks, and similar studies. These cases, however, are not conclusive against environment in infancy as a determiner. Degenerate strains naturally grow up in an environment of degeneracy. Strangely enough the argument from correlation is sometimes inverted. Bright parents have a stupid son, and it is suggested that this is just what would sometimes happen if a Mendelian law applied to intelligence. There is no doubt that the argument from authority is for the inheritance of intelligence. It is better, however, to wait upon more research.

If we agree, then, to define intelligence as what the tests of intelligence test, there is a good deal that we can say about it. We can say everything that has been experimentally observed. We can say that it is a "common factor" in many abilities, that it is something like power, that it can be measured roughly although not very finely, that it is only one factor among many in the mental life, that it develops mostly in childhood, that it develops little or not at all in adult life, and that it is largely predetermined at five years of age. Only with more observation and less inference shall we eventually know much more about both intelligence and the special abilities.

These excerpts give only a minimal view of this 58-page monograph, but they are sufficient to provide a contrast with the earlier study by Thorndike. The results add evidence that, psychologically as well as biologically, there are two kinds of twins which differ appreciably in degree of resemblance. The "like-sex" twins here include both identicals and fraternals and hence underestimate the true resemblance of identicals, as Merriman indirectly points out in the last sentence of his conclusion.

The Intellectual Resemblance of Twins*

CURTIS MERRIMAN

1924

Three possible sources of data presented themselves for consideration. First, it was necessary to secure data on the intellectual behavior of each twin when he worked alone. It was immediately evident that the Stanford-Binet was the most desirable instrument for this purpose. Second, it seemed desirable to have some kind of estimate given by some one who knew the members of the twin pair intimately. For this it was decided to obtain a teacher rating on a number of traits which are commonly accepted as primarily intellectual in nature. Third, it was desirable to supplement both of the above by group tests. For this purpose two types were used, The National Intelligence Test, and a modified form of the Army Beta. The latter was used to get as far away as possible from the verbal factors represented in the other tests.

In the collection of the data, every known precaution was taken to insure the validity of the results. Of these precautions the following may be mentioned:

1. All tests were given by trained examiners. Besides having studied the books and manuals on testing, each person had given a considerable number of tests under the personal supervision of a psychologist. It is believed, therefore, that the procedure was as nearly uniform as it was possible to make it.

2. In almost all cases the Stanford-Binet test was given to the two members of a twin pair by the same person, the test of the second twin following immediately upon that of the first.

3. All group tests were given to both members of a pair at the same sitting.

4. Extreme care was taken to make sure that the children were actually

* Adapted from *Psychological Monographs*, 33, No. 5, Whole No. 152, 1924. Reprinted by permission of the author and the American Psychological Association.

twins. Strangely enough, two cases were found of children who were passing as twins, but were not twins.

5. The twin population tested was limited to those found in the eight grades of the elementary schools. This was done because of the inadequacy of some of our tests when used above or below certain age ranges. For example, the National Test was not designed to measure beyond a level represented by the brighter children in the eighth grade. The limitation of the survey to the eight grades also made it possible to avoid certain undesirable selective factors.

6. Every possible effort was made to secure data upon every twin pair in a given school population. All the schools included in this study are co-educational. This made it as easy to locate twins of unlike sex as twins of like sex. Extreme care was taken on this point. The school principal or city superintendent cooperated by calling teachers' meetings. Statements were made before the entire school. Diligent inquiry was made of the children themselves on the playgrounds. It was announced in the newspapers that a search was being made for twins. It is believed, therefore, that factors which could have produced a systematic tendency to overlook cases which were not in the same grade, or which did not resemble, were pretty completely eliminated. In a later part of the study, data will be presented on the number of twins that appear in a general population, and on the relative number of like sex and unlike sex pairs. It is interesting to note that in the populations covered by this study the actual number of twins found agrees closely with the observed frequency in the general population. The same is true as regards the relative number of like and unlike sex pairs. These facts give added weight to the statement that there was present no systematic tendency to overlook any cases.

* * *

General Summary of Purposes, Data, and Results

1. *Purposes.* This study of the intellectual resemblance of twins has sought to answer three questions:
   a) What is the effect of environment upon the amount of intellectual resemblance of twins?
   b) Does the fact of twin origin and birth operate in any way to lower the intellectual level of a twin population?
   c) What light do the psychological data throw upon the current biological belief that there are two distinct types of twins, fraternal and duplicate?
2. *Data.* Individual and group material was collected as follows:
   Stanford-Binet tests for . . . . 105 pairs

      Teacher estimates for .... 90 pairs
      Army Beta tests for .... 76 pairs
      National Intelligence tests for .... 143 pairs

3. *Treatment of Data.* These data were studied from many different angles. Young pairs were compared with old pairs. Like-sex pairs were compared with unlike-sex pairs. Boys were compared with girls, etc., etc. In making these various comparisons four methods of treatment were used:

    a) Pearson correlations between various groups.
    b) Difference in gross scores.
    c) Curve plotting and fitting to determine character of population.
    d) Empirical study of correspondence between psychological data and judgment of friends as to the resemblance of certain pairs.

4. *Findings.* The results of the study are presented in the form of answers to the three questions asked at the outset. For convenience, all the correlation results are assembled in Table 1. The reader will find it very helpful to refer frequently to this summary.

    a) Environment appears to make no significant difference in the amount of twin resemblance. Table 1 shows twenty pairs of correlations on the basis of young twin pairs versus old twin pairs. Of these twenty pairs there are 15 that show either very slight changes or changes that can be explained on the basis of small population. The larger changes of the teacher rating comparisons are explained on the basis of better acquaintance with the older pairs and over emphasis of slight differences.

    b) Twins suffer no intellectual handicap. This is shown in various ways:
       1) Mean and median I.Q. practically same as for general population.
       2) Mental level of boys same as girls.
       3) Like-sex pairs same mental level as unlike-sex pairs.
       4) No significant differences in variability of sexes.
       5) Young pairs show slightly higher mental level but this is explained by the fact that Stanford-Binet is more difficult for older children.

    c) The data show quite conclusively that there are two distinct types of twins. This is shown in various ways:
       1) In every case where like-sex pairs are compared with unlike-sex pairs, the correlation of the like-sex pairs is significantly higher. Table 1 shows in groups 2 and 5 the twenty-four correlations that provide the evidence for the statement just made.
       2) When sibling data are compared with twin data, the correlations lie much nearer the unlike-sex pair twin data than to the like-sex pair data. This is in harmony with the biological claim that genetically speaking fraternal twins are siblings.
       3) All the curves and curve fitting tests used in the study indicate clearly a difference between like and unlike-sex pair twins.

4) The empirical study of verbal reports on "similar pairs" tends
strongly to show that curve differences are to be largely accounted for by the like-sex pairs that show great intellectual and
physical similarity, and that presumably belong to the "duplicate"
type.

TABLE I
Summary of Correlations

	Binet		Beta		N.I.T.		Teacher	
	r	N	r	N	r	N	r	N
All twin pairs	.782 ± 2.05	105	.841 ± .022	76	.891 ± .011	143	.512 ± .053	90
Pairs, 5 to 9 yrs.	.809 ± .032	47	.784 ± .049	28	.797 ± .034	54	.686 ± .057	39
Pairs, 10 to 16 yrs.	.757 ± .037	58	.664 ± .054	48	.875 ± .017	89	.373 ± .081	51
Like-sex pairs	.867 ± .020	67	.908 ± .017	45	.925 ± .009	92	.654 ± .053	53
Like-sex 5 to 9	.882 ± .028	29	.921 ± .025	16	.946 ± .012	31	.788 ± .053	23
Like-sex 10 to 16	.865 ± .027	38	.842 ± .036	29	.865 ± .022	61	.568 ± .083	30
Girl-girl pairs	.857 ± .029	40	.866 ± .033	25	.928 ± .012	61	.645 ± .071	30
Girl-girl 5 to 9	.915 ± .026	19	.709 ± .112	9	.965 ± .009	24	.913 ± .030	14
Girl-girl 10 to 16	.814 ± .050	21	.896 ± .032	16	.919 ± .021	37	.521 ± .123	16
Boy-boy pairs	.877 ± .030	27	.938 ± .015	20	.925 ± .018	31	.605 ± .090	23
Boy-boy 5 to 9	.800 ± .078	10	.934 ± .049	7	.921 ± .041	7	.534 ± .161	9
Boy-boy 10 to 16	.890 ± .034	17	.747 ± .080	13	.895 ± .027	24	.715 ± .089	14
Unlike-sex pairs	.504 ± .081	38	.732 ± .056	31	.867 ± .025	51	.266 ± .102	37
Unlike-sex 5 to 9	.774 ± .064	18	.519 ± .147	12	.753 ± .066	23	.681 ± .090	16
Unlike-sex 10 to 16	.298 ± .137	20	.643 ± .091	19	.834 ± .044	28	.072 ± .141	21

Terman's brilliant longitudinal study of gifted children is one of the great contributions to the psychology of intelligence. In these brief excerpts from the first volume of Genetic Studies of Genius we have tried to give you a glimpse of his intensive preparation for this work and of its first fruits. One of the several follow-up studies (The Promise of Youth) is represented by a later reading in this book, but these fragments can only suggest the wealth of information to be found in this series. The most recent summary of the progress of the gifted children will be found in Volume V, published by the Stanford University Press in 1958.

Mental and Physical Traits of a Thousand Gifted Children*

LEWIS M. TERMAN

1925

History and Description of the Investigation

PRELIMINARY EXPLORATION

This research may be said to have had its beginning during the years of the writer's graduate study, 1902–1905. He first became interested in the psychology of genius in a study of leadership which he made in 1902–1903 under the direction of Professor E. H. Lindley, of Indiana University. While a student at Clark University he reviewed in 1903–1904 the medical-psychological literature on precocious children and the following year carried out as a doctor's dissertation an experimental study of some of the mental processes of seven bright and seven dull boys.

However slight the positive contribution of these studies, they at least introduced their author to the literature on the psychology of genius and gave a keen realization of the fact that the field was a promising one for experimental investigation. When in 1910 it became possible for the writer to return to the problem, the progress which Binet and others had made in the field of mentality testing had created an entirely new situation. For certain ages, at least, it was at last possible to determine with some degree of approximation the brightness of a given child, compared with that of unselected children of his own age.

* Reprinted from *Mental and Physical Traits of a Thousand Gifted Children*, Vol. I, *Genetic Studies of Genius*, by Lewis H. Terman, et al. with the permission of the publishers, Stanford University Press. Copyright 1925 and 1926 by the Board of Trustees of Leland Stanford Junior University.

The importance of Binet's work for later studies of intelligence can hardly be overestimated. It has not yet received and possibly may never receive from psychologists the appreciation which it deserves. Critical ability, unfortunately, is far more common than ability to create, and to the critical psychologist the imperfections and crudities of Binet's methods, both in their practical and in their theoretical aspects, have often been more evident than their remarkable originality. More than anyone else, it was Binet who taught us where to search among mental functions for significant intellectual differences. It was he who gave us our first successful intelligence scale and demonstrated the actuality of an age development through successive "hierarchies of intelligences." That the term "mental age" which resulted from the latter concept has often been misinterpreted and misused, does not detract from the importance of his contribution. The fact is that previous to the publication of Binet's 1908 scale the significance of age differences in intelligence was very little understood. Psychologists were not aware of the extraordinary and detailed similarity that may exist between a dull child of twelve years and a normal average child of eight. No one recognized the significance, for future mental development, of a given degree of retardation or acceleration. As one who had worked experimentally upon the diagnosis of intellectual differences in the pre-scale period, the present writer had perhaps more reason than most psychologists to appreciate the value of Binet's contribution. He is willing to admit that after spending four or five hours a day for several months in administering an extended series of well selected intelligence tests individually to fourteen boys, he was unable, notwithstanding the large individual differences in performance which these tests clearly revealed, to render a judgment as to the prognostic significance of the differences found. By the Binet scale it would have been possible to make a more meaningful diagnosis after a one-hour test of each child; and it would now even be possible to do so after a single hour spent in testing the fourteen boys by a group test. This advance is due (1), to the demonstrated validity of the concepts of mental "retardation" and mental "acceleration;" and (2), to the convenient and readily comprehensible method suggested by Binet for evaluating degrees of retardation and acceleration in terms of normal mental age units. Previous to 1908 it was impossible for any psychologist, after devoting any amount of time to intelligence tests of ten or twenty children of different ages, to make a valid comparison of the intellectual abilities found. This is now possible for even a well-trained normal school graduate.

The value of the Binet method in the identification of the intellectually gifted became immediately evident to the writer when with Mr. H. G. Childs he made trial of the 1908 scale. It was obvious that children who showed marked acceleration in mental age were, by any reasonable criterion, brighter than children who tested at or below their chronological age. A little later Stern's suggestion looking toward the use of an intelligence ratio, or quotient, refined still further the method of Binet and made possible more accurate comparisons of children of different ages.

In 1911 more or less systematic work was begun at Stanford University in the collection of data on children who had made exceptionally high scores in a mental test. In 1913–1914 three schools in San Francisco were sifted for bright children, and in 1915 certain data were published on 31 cases testing above 125 intelligence quotient (IQ). Ratings on several traits were secured from the teachers, who also filled out a brief information schedule for each child. Some of the results of this explorative study were out of line with the writer's expectations and in contradiction to earlier views which he had published on the supposed evils of precocity. It was obvious that these children did not, as a group, possess the traits which had been popularly supposed to characterize intellectually precocious children, such as sickliness, eccentricity, one-sidedness, and lack of social adaptability. In passing it may be noted that one of the bright children tested in 1911 has taken his Ph.D. degree and is (1924) an instructor in a great western university; that another has just completed his work for the degree of Sc.D.; and that another is studying in the universities of Europe.

In 1916 the methods used were considerably revised. The teacher's information schedule was enlarged, a similar information schedule was prepared for the parent to fill out, and ratings on twenty traits were secured both from parents and from teachers. With the assistance of Margaret Hopwood Hubbard, data were collected on 59 cases, most of whom had an intelligence quotient above 140. The main results of this study have been published elsewhere and need not be summarized here. The writer's tentative conclusions of 1915 were fully supported.

The establishment by Stanford University of a research fellowship for the study of gifted children, in 1919, was the occasion for further revision of method and a stimulus to renewed search for cases. The information schedules were materially improved and an interest blank was arranged for the child to fill out. By the spring of 1921 approximately 150 cases testing for the most part above 140 IQ had been located, and for 121 considerable supplementary data had been secured. The results for these 121 cases have not been published, but it may be stated that they suggested the following tentative conclusions:

1. There is probably a somewhat higher incidence of intellectual superiority among boys than among girls.

2. In physical growth and general health gifted children as a group excel unselected children of the same age.

3. Gifted children who attend school are on the average accelerated about a year and a half, compared with unselected children, but on an average they are about two grades below that which corresponds to their mental development.

4. Only a very small minority of intellectually gifted children have been

subjected to forced culture or otherwise "pushed" in their development.

5. Heredity is superior. Fifty per cent of the fathers belong to the professional groups; not one to the unskilled group.

6. There is an apparent excess of Jewish cases and a deficiency of cases from the Italian, Portuguese, and Mexican groups living in the vicinity of Stanford University.

7. Trait ratings and social data give no evidence that gifted children tend more often than others to be lacking in social adaptability or leadership. However, they are probably less superior in social, emotional, and psychophysical traits than in intellectual and volitional traits.

During the academic year 1920–21, Mrs. Jessie Chase Fenton served as full time assistant on the gifted children fellowship. Her services did much to lay the foundation for the more extensive investigation which was to follow. Besides collecting considerable data on the social traits of a group of 100 intellectually superior children, she assisted in the preparation of a report on a gifted young poet, and in a summary of recent literature on genius.

Perhaps the most valuable thing gained from the work to this point was the experience. Intimate acquaintance with a considerable number of gifted children had shown the need of certain kinds of home and school data, and successive revisions of information schedules for the use of parents and teachers had shown what methods were likely to be most dependable in gathering such data. As for conclusions having a statistical basis, none could be established except on a far larger number of cases. This is especially true of comparisons involving age, race, school grade, occupational class, etc. It was clear that for such purposes it would be necessary to locate 500 or 1,000 cases by a method which would insure that the group selected would be reasonably representative of intellectually gifted children.

THE PRESENT STUDY

The task of locating the desired number of cases and of securing the necessary tests and supplementary data was of course far too costly to be financed out of the ordinary budget of a university department. Fortunately, early in 1921 the directors of the Commonwealth Fund made a grant of $20,300 to Stanford University to continue and extend the research. The purposes of the grant as indicated in the formal application which the author submitted under date of February 23, 1921, were as follows: (1) to increase the number of gifted subjects to approximately 1,000; (2) to secure at least two intelligence tests of each subject; (3) to secure measures of school achievement in at least four or five of the school subjects; (4) in the case of a small number of cases to give tests of specialized ability; (5) revision of the methods of securing trait ratings and social data; and (6) follow-up of the subjects for a period of at least ten years. In 1922, before the end of the first year's work, an additional grant of $14,000 was received from the Commonwealth Fund for the purpose of extending the study along medical, anthropometric, and psychological lines. This sum was supplemented by a contribution of $8,000 in money and $6,000 in services from Stanford University. The money cost of the study here reported, apart from services contributed, was therefore $42,300. The contribution of services by the University has exceeded the amount stipulated and would bring the total cost of the study to more than $50,000.

The second Commonwealth grant made it possible to secure for our main group of subjects anthropometric measurements, medical examinations, character and personality tests, and interest tests; and, in addition, to carry out a parallel biographical study of the early mental traits of three hundred men and women of genius.

The first grant was made available in May, 1921. May, June, and July were devoted by the writer to the preparation of plans, tests, and information blanks and to securing the necessary help. The research staff to begin with was as follows:

Assistant Director:

Dr. T. L. Kelley, Stanford University.

Field Assistants:

Florence Fuller, M.A., University of Minnesota.

Florence Goodenough, M.A., Columbia University.

Helen Marshall, M.A., Ohio State University.

Dorothy H. Yates, Ph.D., University of California.

Office Assistant:

G. M. Ruch, Ph.D., Stanford University.

It will be evident that the success of an undertaking of the kind here described depends in no small measure upon the qualifications of the field assistants secured. In the search for suitable assistants the leading universities of the country were canvassed by the writer in person. Every selection made proved to be a happy one. Dr. Yates had recently completed a Ph.D. dissertation on gifted high school pupils; Miss Goodenough had worked extensively in mental tests and clinical methods with Dr. Leta S. Hollingsworth; Miss Marshall had worked with Dr. Rudolf Pintner in mental surveys of school children; and Miss Fuller had assisted Dr. M. E. Haggerty for a year in a survey of gifted children in Minneapolis. All had had extensive training in the use of tests, all had taught in public schools, and all were especially interested in the proposed investigation. The assistance of Dr. Ruch in the work carried on at the University was extremely valuable. During 1921–1922 this had to do largely with the preparation of tests, especially the achievement and general information tests.

On August 8th the four field assistants began a course of five weeks of intensive training at Stanford University in preparation for their year's work. Professor L. L. Burlingame of the Department of Biology, Stanford

University, gave instruction on heredity; Dr. J. Harold Williams, Director of the California Bureau of Juvenile Research, on methods of collecting field data; Dr. Maud Merrill, instructor in psychology, Stanford University, on Binet test procedure; the writer, on the literature of genius. Dr. Ruch assisted in shaping the plans, and in the preparation of information schedules and a general information test.

The data to be collected for each child chosen for study included the following:

1. Two intelligence tests (Stanford-Binet and National B)
2. A two-hour educational test (The Stanford Achievement Test)
3. A fifty-minute test of general information in science, history, literature, and the arts
4. A fifty-minute test of knowledge of and interest in plays, games, and amusements
5. A four-page interest blank to be filled out by the children
6. A two-months reading record to be kept by the children
7. A sixteen-page Home Information Blank, to be filled out by the parents, including ratings on twenty-five traits
8. An eight-page School Information Blank to be filled out by the teachers, including ratings on the same twenty-five traits as were rated by the parents
9. When possible, ratings of the home on the Whittier Scale for home grading.

*   *   *

Conclusions and Problems

It will be recalled that the primary purpose of the investigations which have been recounted in this volume was to determine, if possible, what traits may be said to characterize children of markedly superior intellectuality. "Superior intellectuality" is here arbitrarily defined as ability to make a high score on such intelligence tests as the National, the Terman Group, and the Stanford-Binet. It is not necessary to assume that the criterion of intellectual superiority is wholly adequate, or that the superiority itself is either hereditary or abiding. The adequacy of the criterion and the degree of permanence of the superiority which has been found can later be judged in the light of follow-up studies in which the promise of youth is compared with the performance of manhood and womanhood.

Regardless of the results which such follow-up studies may yield, it is unquestionably a matter of considerable importance to ascertain the *present* traits of children earning high intelligence scores. The nature of many of these traits has been indicated in considerable detail in preceding chapters, and the numerous chapter summaries render an inclusive summarization at this point unnecessary. It remains only to bring together a few of the outstanding results of the study and to suggest problems for further investigation.

First, however, the reader is cautioned to bear in mind the variability which obtains in the so-called gifted group with respect to the various traits that have been rated or measured. The group has been described throughout in terms of the deviation of its average from the average of unselected children. It does not follow that what is true of the group is true of all its individual members. Where it could be done without unduly extending the report, complete distributions of both the gifted group and the control group have been given. Where this was not feasible the amount of dispersion from the central tendency has ordinarily been indicated. In most cases the amount of overlapping of the two groups can readily be computed from the data given, where such computations have not already been made.

* * *

The validity of the generalizations made regarding the traits which characterize gifted children hinges upon the representative nature of the group studied. We have been at considerable pains to insure that the group would not be to any considerable extent unrepresentative of that entire portion of the child population which is capable of earning an intelligence quotient of 140 or above. We believe that our efforts in this direction have been reasonably successful. It is unlikely that more than 20 per cent of the cases have been missed, out of the total number of children who could have qualified in the school population canvassed. The loss may not have exceeded 10 per cent. Granted that the cases missed might for some traits have yielded distributions differing appreciably from those actually found, there is no likelihood that their inclusion would have modified in any important respect the nature of the conclusions that have been drawn. So far as the traits which have been measured are concerned, one is justified in believing that the characterizations which hold for the experimental group hold for gifted children in general.

It is perhaps more important to bear in mind the limits of the field covered by the various tests and measurements that have been applied. For example, it cannot be supposed that the intelligence of our subjects has been measured in all its aspects by the two intelligence tests used, that the full scope and depth of interests have been measured by the interest data, or that the available samplings of character and personality traits tell all it would be worth while to know about this group of trait-complexes. The twenty-five traits which have been rated by the parents and teachers are so many out of possible hundreds, although it is hoped they are among the most important. The physical measurements and medical examinations were exceptionally complete, but they leave altogether untouched a great many things that one would like to know about the physical correlates of superior mentality.

Nevertheless, incomplete and fragmentary as our data are when compared with the many-sided richness of a child's total mental and physical equipment, it may justly be claimed that they carry us well beyond the bounds of previously established fact. Character analyses and case descriptions based upon the subjective evaluation of the best data to be had from ordinary observation can never take the place of quantitative measurements even of the cruder sort. If our data are incomplete, they are at any rate, for the most part, objective and verifiable. No degree of completeness could possibly make good the fault of subjectivity and unverifiableness. If the methods that have been employed have at times led to erroneous conclusions, these in time will be discovered and corrected. One who suspects error at any point has only to apply the same or demonstrably better objective methods to test the justness of his suspicions. It is to be hoped that sooner or later all our conclusions will thus be put to trial. The ultimate value of our study will be measured more by the investigations which it stimulates or provokes others to make than by the amount of its factual data that later experiments may verify.

What are the outstanding characteristics of this group of gifted children? Space is available for mention of but a few, and the temptation to extended discussion must be resisted.

The group contains an unexpectedly large proportion of cases in the upper IQ ranges. Assuming the standard deviation of the IQ distribution for unselected children to be between 15 and 18, there is an appreciable excess of 150 IQ cases, or better, over and above the theoretical expectation. Above 160 IQ the number of cases found increases out of all proportion to the theoretically expected number and by IQ 170 exceeds it several times. Unless this discrepancy can be explained as due to the imperfection of the IQ technique it would appear that the distribution of intelligence in the child population departs considerably from that described by the normal probability curve.

The group contains a significant though not overwhelming preponderance of boys. This finding is not in harmony with any expectations that could be based upon a comparison of the mean scores earned in intelligence tests by unselected boys and girls of corresponding age. No thoroughly convincing explanation can be formulated from the data at hand, although an examination of various hypotheses suggests that the cause may possibly lie in the greater variability of boys. The fact that the excess of boys over girls is far greater in the high school group than in the younger gifted group raises the question whether the mental growth of boys tends to continue somewhat beyond the level which marks the mental maturity of girls.

In physical growth and in general health the gifted group unquestionably rates on the whole somewhat above par. There is no shred of evidence to support the widespread opinion that typically the intellectually precocious child is weak, undersized, or nervously unstable. Insofar as the gifted child departs at all from the average on these traits it is pretty certainly in the other direction, but the fact seems to be that his deviation from the norm on physical traits is in most cases very small indeed in comparison with his deviation in intellectual and volitional traits. Even the slight superiority that he enjoys with respect to physical equipment may or may not be due primarily to endowment. It might be accounted for mainly if not entirely by such factors as diet, medical care, and other environmental influences.

To explain by the environment hypothesis the relatively much greater deviation of our group from unselected children with respect to intellectual and volitional traits appears difficult if not impossible. Our data, however, offer no convincing proof, merely numerous converging lines of evidence. There is a marked excess of Jewish and of Northern and Western European stock represented. The number of highly successful, even eminent, relatives is impressively great. The fact that in a State which justly prides itself on the equality of educational opportunity provided for its children of every class and station an impartially selected gifted group should draw so heavily from the higher occupational levels and so lightly from the lower, throws a heavy burden upon the environment hypothesis. In spite of all our effort to equalize educational opportunity, the 10 year old child of the California laborer competes for high IQ rank no more successfully than the laborer's son competed for the genius rank in Europe a hundred years ago. This statement is based upon a comparison of the relative number in our group and in the Galton-de Candolle-Ellis genius-groups of individuals whose parents belonged to the unskilled or semi-skilled labor classes. Previous studies had only demonstrated the superiority of the higher occupational and social class with respect to the number of finished geniuses produced, and it was only natural that many should prefer to explain this superiority on the ground of educational opportunity. We have demonstrated that the superiority of the same occupational and social classes is no less decisive when the compared offspring are at an age at which educational opportunity is about as nearly equalized as an enlightened democracy can make it.

Two possible environmental causes of the intellectual superiority of our gifted group are definitely excluded by the data that have been presented: (1) formal schooling, and (2) parental income. It has been shown that within a given age group, the intelligence and achievement scores earned are totally uncorrelated with length of school attendance. The median family income does not greatly exceed that for the general population of the cities in question. The families of some of our most gifted subjects are in financial circumstances below the level of moderate comfort.

In a majority of cases the superiority of the gifted child is evidenced at a very early age. Among the most commonly mentioned indications are intellectual curiosity, wealth of miscellaneous information, and desire to learn to read. The frequent presence of such traits among our subjects in the pre-school period suggests strongly the influence of endowment. Although in a small minority of cases attempts at forced culture may have contributed to the result, it is manifestly impossible to account for the general superiority of the group by any such influence.

There are, nevertheless, many persons who believe that intelligence quotients can be manufactured to order by the application of suitable methods of training. There are even prominent educators and psychologists who are inclined to regard such a pedagogical feat as within the realm of possibility, and no one knows that it is not. If it is possible it is time we were finding it out. Conclusive evidence as to the extent to which IQ's can be artificially raised could be supplied in a few years by an experiment which would cost a few hundred thousand or at most a few million dollars. The knowledge would probably be worth to humanity a thousand times that amount.

Although a majority of our children have had the advantage of superior cultural influences in the home, their more formal educational opportunities have been entirely commonplace, in no way superior to those enjoyed by the children from the humblest families of Los Angeles, San Francisco, and Oakland. At school they have studied and played with the children of the generality. The school has provided for them no special program of instruction. It has given no form of individual treatment except an occasional extra promotion. Such promotions have usually been doubly or trebly earned, for it has been demonstrated by reliable and extensive achievement tests that the average child of our group had already mastered the subject matter of the curriculum two or three grades beyond that in which he was located. More accurately, this promotional "slack" amounts on the average to about 25 per cent of the child's age. Perhaps because of this fact, the superiority of the group in achievement is only two-thirds or three-fourths as great as its superiority in intelligence. It is evidently a rare experience for a gifted child to be given work of a grade of difficulty commensurate with his intellectual abilities.

The excess in achievement above the norm for the gifted child's actual grade status is general rather than special, although it is somewhat less marked in spelling and arithmetic than in general information, reading, and language. The amount of specialization or unevenness in the abilities of our group was made the subject of extended study by Dr. De Voss. His results show that in respect to measurable disparity of abilities the gifted child differs little if at all from children in general. The "one-sidedness" of precocious children is mythical. The fact is that a considerable proportion of all children show appreciable specialization in their achievements. The gifted child has only his share of this common human trait. Nevertheless, the measurable disparities found are such as to show clearly the necessity of taking them into account in any scheme of vocational or educational guidance for children of every grade of intelligence. It will be one of the important problems in the follow-up of these gifted children to work out the degree of correlation between the specialized achievement in adult life and the special aptitudes discovered in this investigation.

The matter of interests was deemed of sufficient importance to warrant investigation from several angles. As would be expected, the interests of gifted children reflect in many ways their intellectual superiority. The school subjects which they like best are for the most part the subjects which unselected children find the most difficult. The vocations which they prefer rank fairly high in the occupational hierarchy with respect to the intellectual demands they make.

The reading of gifted children surpasses that of unselected children both in quantity and quality. The typical gifted child of seven years reads more books than the unselected child reads at any age up to fifteen years. Gifted children have more than the usual interest in books of science, history, biography, travel, and informational fiction, and less in books of adventure, mystery, and emotional fiction.

The common opinion that intellectually superior children are characterized by a deficiency of play interests has been shown to be wholly unfounded. The mean play-information quotient of the gifted group is 136. The typical gifted child of nine years has a larger body of definite knowledge about plays and games than the average child of twelve years. If he devotes somewhat fewer hours per week to play activities it is because his play interests must compete with a wealth of other interests which are no less compelling. Another finding of considerable importance in this connection is that the play interests of the gifted boy are above rather than below the norm in degree of "masculinity."

The experiment carried out for the purpose of measuring the strength of interests along intellectual, social, and activity lines is perhaps one of the most significant reported in the entire study, whether considered from the point of view of methodology or results. It is probable that the type of instrument which Mrs. Wyman designed for this purpose will be found capable of unlocking many hitherto inaccessible regions of human personality and interest. Adaptations of her method might be devised which would aid in the discovery of special aptitudes and in the diagnosis of pre-delinquent and pre-psychotic tendencies. In the present instance the Wyman test has given a fairly precise measure of three important aspects of interest. It has shown that in strength of intellectual interest 90 per cent of our gifted children surpass the average of a control group, that the superiority of the gifted in strength of social interests is well-nigh as great, and that in activity interests the two groups are practically indistinguishable.

That our gifted surpass unselected children in tests of honesty, trustworthiness, and similar moral traits, will probably surprise no observant judge of human character. Few have ever denied that there is at least a certain amount of positive correlation between intelligence and character. The Cady-Raubenheimer tests show that it is considerable. Considering total score on the seven character tests used, one can say that the gifted child of nine or ten years has reached a stage of moral development which is not attained by the average child until the age of thirteen or fourteen. Approximately 85 per cent of the gifted surpass the average of unselected children. The test results on this point are confirmed by the testimony of special class teachers of gifted children. The tests in question are measures of untrustworthiness, of dishonesty of report, of tendency to overstatement, of objectionable social-moral attitudes, and of interest in questionable books and questionable companions.

A modification of Woodworth's test of psychotic tendencies showed approximately 75 per cent of the gifted above the average of unselected children. Comparison of later mental troubles and conduct disorders with the results of these tests will be of surpassing interest.

It should be emphasized, however, that one could find in the gifted group numerous exceptions to the general rule with respect to character, personality, and emotional stability. The gifted are not free from faults, and at least one out of five has more of them than the average child of the general population. Perhaps one out of twenty presents a more or less serious problem in one or another respect.

The ratings secured from parents and teachers on the twenty-five mental, moral, social, and physical traits are of value chiefly in their confirmation of the results secured by the method of test. These ratings undoubtedly have a very low reliability for an individual subject, but when used as a basis for comparing the relatively large gifted and control groups they yield reasonably dependable results. For example, one can say with considerable assurance that gifted children excel the average most of all in intellectual and volitional traits, next in emotional and moral traits, and least in physical and social traits.

The purpose and form of this report have tended almost inevitably to center attention upon the traits of the gifted group rather than upon the control groups with which they have been compared. To an extent this is unfortunate. A volume could well have been devoted to fuller treatment and discussion of the data collected for unselected children, including sex and age differences in each of the following: scholastic and occupational interests, play interest and play information, reading interests, teachers' ratings of scholastic abilities, interest tests, character and personality tests, and ratings by teachers and parents on the twenty-five selected traits. The reader who is interested may assemble for himself the most essential data on these points from the various chapters of this report; lack of space has prevented our performing this service for him. Special attention is called to the significance of such data as the age and sex differences disclosed by the interest and personality tests and by the twenty-five trait ratings. On these and other traits important data are to be found on the relative variability of the sexes. . . . Examination of these data will show that the evidence on variability is inconsistent and therefore inconclusive.

A study of superior talent inevitably raises a host of pedagogical problems. It has been no part of our purpose, however, to exploit any theory as to the educational methods best adapted to the gifted child. About the culture of genius next to nothing is known, although new light may in time be expected from the rapidly increasing experimentation with differentiated curricula, classification by ability, and methods of individual instruction. Traditional methods have ignored the problem; their influence is negative rather than positive; the best that can be hoped for them is that they may not be as bad as they seem. The present neglect of superior talent is sufficiently indicated by the inability of teachers to recognize it. One of the most astonishing facts brought out in this investigation is that one's best chance of identifying the brightest child in a schoolroom is to examine the birth records and select the youngest, rather than to take the one rated as brightest by the teacher.

Follow-up data covering the first two years after the subjects were located are encouraging. Grade progress and quality of school work indicate that general ability is being fully maintained. The previous good record of school deportment has been improved, and difficulties in the field of social adjustment are clearing up. It is probably very significant that the children who received the greatest number of extra promotions are in general the ones whose school work has most improved in quality.

Prediction as to the probable future of these children would be profitless. We can only wait and watch. It should be pointed out, however, that to expect all or even a majority of the subjects to attain any considerable degree of eminence would be unwarranted optimism. In the first place, eminence is a poor measure of success. In the second place, success even in the best sense is largely a product of fortunate chance combinations of personal merits and environmental circumstances. In the third place, the group itself, although far superior to the average, is nothing like as highly selected as the groups of genius-adults studied by Galton, de Candolle, Ellis, Castle, Cattell, and others. Each of Galton's subjects, for example, ranked in eminence at least as high as the first in four thousand adults of the general population. To qualify for our gifted group it was only necessary for a child to rate as high as the first in two hundred. Only about one of our subjects in twenty, or about fifty in the group of one thousand, would rank as the first in four thousand of a random selection. About one man in a thousand in the generality finds his way into *Who's Who*. Twenty per cent of our boys rank as high in IQ as the first in a thousand taken at random, but we should hardly expect so large a proportion to attain *Who's Who* distinction. Perhaps no one would contend that this or any similar type of eminence is more than moderately correlated with general intelligence. In a city of 25,000 population there are, say, 5,000 males above the age of thirty years. It is with the most distinguished 25 to 50 of such a group that our gifted boys could be most fairly compared a few decades hence.

It is hoped that some of the later volumes which are planned for this series of *Genetic Studies of Genius* will add at least something to our

Psychologists themselves were looking critically at intelligence measurement during this period. In this paper Thurstone attempts to persuade his colleagues to abandon the mental age concept. His first argument is actually weaker than it appears here because the two kinds of mental ages are more similar in a well-standardized test than they appear to be in his argument. The clear exposition of the different regression lines is valuable, however. His second argument, concerning adult intelligence, is much more persuasive and, in the main, his line of thought has won out in adult measurement.

The Mental Age Concept*

L. L. THURSTONE

1926

It is the purpose of this article to show that the mental age concept is a failure in that it leads to ambiguities and inconsistencies. In discussing the logic of the mental age concept, we shall have occasion to describe two definitions of mental age, both of which are in use and both of which lead to the same ambiguities.

The two definitions of mental age which are either stated or implied in current mental test work are as follows:

1. The mental age corresponding to any given test performance is that chronological age for which the test performance is the average.

2. The mental age corresponding to any given test performance is the average chronological age of people who make that test performance.

These two definitions of mental age do not have the same numerical values. Since they are inconsistent, it is essential, if we insist on using mental ages, that we specify rather definitely which of the two possible kinds of mental age we are using. They are not interchangeable. Both of them may be defended, but the first definition is the one usually followed.

In order to set out in relief the difference between these two definitions of mental age, we may recall the meaning of the two regression lines on a correlation table and their application in this case. When you step on the scales at the drug store, you notice a little table with two columns, heights and weights. You ordinarily read it by saying that your height is so and so. You find this height in the table, and next to that entry you read the average weight of people with your height. You have used the record of a regression line. But now suppose that when you have ascertained your weight, you try to find the average *height* of people who have your *weight*.

* *Psychological Review*, 33 (1926), pp. 268-278. Reprinted by permission of the American Psychological Association.

Your impulse is to find your weight in the same table and to read the height next to it. But that doesn't work. Another table would have to be used which would be constructed from another regression line. One of these tables shows the average *weight* of people with given *heights*. The other table would show the average *height* of people with given *weights*. It is the former table in which we are ordinarily interested.

Now, if the same reasoning is applied to a correlation table for test performance and chronological age, we shall have two regression lines here also. One of these lines, or tables, will show the average test performance for children of given age. The other line, or table, will show the average chronological age for children of given test performance. But these two lines are different and the two tables cannot be used interchangeably. Their practical use would be illustrated as follows. If the age of the child is known and we want to know the average or expected test performance, we use the regression 'test performance on age.' If, on the other hand, the test performance is known and we want to guess the child's chronological age, we should use the regression 'age on test performance.' When we test children's intelligence, we nearly always have access to their chronological age. We don't need to guess at that. But we need to do a lot of guessing about the child's intelligence. Therefore one of these regressions is of considerable interest and practical importance whereas the other one is of practically no importance. The important regression line in this correlation table is therefore the regression of 'test performance on age.' It can be used to ascertain the test performance that is to be expected of the average child of a given or known age.

Figure 1 will assist in making clear this distinction. Let it represent the correlation table for test performance and chronological age. Let test performance be measured in any terms or units. In the vertical column, *x*, are represented all the children of age *x* who took the test, and their test performances are indicated by the dots in that column. The average test performance of all these children of age *x* is indicated at *A*. If a similar column is erected at each age we should of course find that the older children have higher average test performances than the younger children. If the average test performance is located in each column, these average performances will constitute the regression 'test on age.' By means of this regression line we can ascertain the average or expected test performance for a child of any given age within the limits of the table. In fact, by the more customary definition of mental age, each of these average test performances is designated as the mental age of the column in which it is found. Therefore, the test score, or performance *A* is designated as the mental age *x* because *A* is the average test performance or score for children of age *x*. This is the first of our definitions of mental age and it is the customary one.

But in the same table it is also possible to draw another regression line.

Suppose that we have collected all the test records with the score A. All of these children will be represented in the correlation table of Fig. 1 in the horizontal row at the level A. Each child is represented in such a table by a dot or other suitable mark. Now we may determine the average chronological age of all the children who get that particular score A. Let that average age be represented by x' in Fig. 1. We may of course do likewise for every class interval of test performance, and that will give us a set of horizontal rows, each with its own average age. It is to be expected that as we increase in test performance, the average chronological age will also increase. If these average ages of the successive horizontal rows be connected, we shall have the regression line 'age on test.'

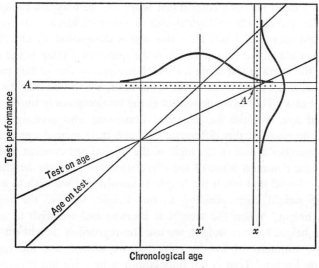

Chronological age

Figure 1

What is the significance of these two regression lines in our definition of mental age? Let us attempt to define just what we mean by a mental age of eight. If we have tabulated our data for age and test score in the form of a correlation table like Fig. 1, we shall have two alternatives which refer to the two regression lines. Suppose that the x-column represents the eight-year old children and their test scores. We can then determine the average test score for these eight-year old children. We may designate that average test score, A, as the normal performance for eight-year old children and we may argue that this test performance should therefore be called the mental age of eight. When a child attains this test performance, A, we should say that the child has a mental age of eight.

But there is another consideration that makes this interpretation look awkward, although it is the customary one. Suppose that we consider in one group all the children who have this test performance, *A*. What is their average chronological age? It is certainly not eight unless there is a perfect correlation between chronological age and test performance, which is an impossibility. We therefore find that the average test performance of eight-year olds is not the same as that test performance, the average age for which is eight. We may, however, select one of these analyses as basic for a definition of mental age. We might say, for example, that a certain test performance is to be regarded as a mental age of eight if the average age of all the people who get that score is eight. That is the second definition of mental age. According to this definition the test performance *A* would be assigned a mental age at *x'* in Fig. 1.

In the practical situation we might proceed along either of these two lines. When a child makes a certain test score, *A,* we may ask the question, "What is the average chronological age of other children who make this particular test score, *A*"? In Fig. 1 this age is designated *x'*. On the other hand, we may ask about that same child the question, "What is the chronological age, the average test score for which is equal to that of this particular child"? Then, if the child made a test score of *A,* we should find the answer at *x* and not at *x'*. This latter definition is the one commonly implied by the term mental age, but the usage is not consistent and investigators may possibly be unaware of this difference between their mental age norms.

There is another aspect of the logic of the mental age concept which goes contrary to the common sense of the correlation table. In the height-weight example, we found that when the height is known and we wish to ascertain the average weight corresponding to our height, we use the regression 'weight on height.' When the weight is known, and we wish to ascertain the average height for our weight, we use the regression 'height on weight.' This can be summarized by the rule that we always use the regression 'unknown on known.' That is not only common practice but it is also common sense in the use of the correlation table.

But when this reasoning is applied to the correlation table for test score and chronological age, it leads to the less popular definition of mental age. When a child has attained a certain test score, it is the test score that is known and if any estimate is to be based on the test score, we should be estimating the chronological age by the test score. In other words, we should be using the regression 'age on score.' We should then define the mental age of a child as the average chronological age of all children who make the test score of this particular child. According to this definition, a child would be at par mentally if its test performance is such that the average age of all people who make that test score is equal to the child's age. That is our second and less popular definition of mental age.

So far we have considered some of the inconsistencies which are the result of using two definitions of mental age. However, either one of these definitions might be adopted and universally used so that we should always know which is which. Some other name might be adopted for the other definition if it were found advisable to use both measures of brightness or test intelligence. My main argument is, however, that both of these definitions of mental age lead to ambiguities when applied to the adult years, and that the mental age concept should therefore be discarded in favor of a more direct and simpler measure of brightness which does not lead to logical somersaults like those of mental age.

In Fig. 2 I have represented schematically the same correlation table as in Fig. 1, except that the age range has been extended into the adult years. It represents an analysis of the first definition of mental age as it appears in the adult ages. At *a* we have the distribution of test performance for age *a*. The average test performance at that age is at *a'* and the distribu-

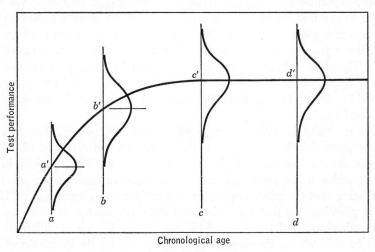

Figure 2

tion of test performance ranges above and below the performance *a'* as a mean. For our present purpose the question of the normality or symmetry of this distribution does not matter. At a higher age, *b,* we have similarly a distribution of test performances which range above and below the mean test performance at *b'*. Naturally we should expect the mean performance *b'* to be higher than the mean performance at *a',* because *b* represents a higher chronological age than *a*. At the age *c* which is somewhere in the teens, or perhaps as high as twenty, we have the maximum test performance which our mental age tests can differentiate. The highest mean test performance, *c',* is attained at the age *c*. But now the difficulty arises in applying the mental age concept. If we inspect the distribution of test performance at the adult age *d,* which may be age 40, for example, we find that its mean test performance *d'* is no higher than the mean test performance already attained at the age *c*. If the age *c,* at which the maximum mean test performance is attained, is found experimentally to be at 16, for example, then it will automatically be impossible to attain a mental age beyond that age. The reason may be in the limitations of our tests which do not measure mental development beyond adolescence, or the reason may be in the possible conclusion that intelligence does not develop beyond that age. At any rate we must deal with the fact that a group of 40-year olds would make a mean test performance which would be no higher than the mean test performance at 16. Now let us look at the first definition of mental age which we are here trying to interpret. It states that the mental age corresponding to any given test performance is that chronological age for which the test performance is the average. It will readily be seen that since the mean test performances c' and d' are equal, we shall have an indefinite number of mental ages assigned to this particular test performance. We have a right to say that the test performance c' should be given a mental age of 40 because a group of 40-year olds would make a mean test performance of c'. But a group of 16-year olds would also make this mean test performance. Therefore this definition of mental age is entirely ambiguous. A mental age of 40 is the same as a mental age of 16 or of any other age beyond the 16- or 18-year level. The only way out is to revise the definition of mental age.

This difficulty is well known to all mental test people. The solution usually given is arbitrarily to call the mean test performance of 16- or 18-year old children the adult level. Walter Lippman in his articles in the *New Republic* a few years ago, drove home rather effectively the absurdity of insisting that the adult population has an average mental age of 12 or 13 by pointing out that the Army test data constituted as valid an age standardization as the few hundred tests given to school children. We might be able to save the mental age term by revising the definition so that the mental age corresponding to any given test performance is *the lowest* chronological age for which the test performance is the average. But why use age at all as a scale for mental development when the relation between intelligence and age is imperfect and non-linear? Why not specify test performance on any convenient scale directly related to the test performance itself, instead of twisting it into some sort of age?

But there remains the second alternative definition of mental age which may be interpreted for the adult years. In Fig. 3 I have represented again the correlation table for test performance and chronological age. In this figure the horizontal section a represents all the people who have the test performance a. They vary in age, of course, and the distribution of age is represented diagrammatically by the frequency distribution with its mean a'. In the same manner the horizontal section b represents all the subjects whose test performance is b and their ages are diagrammatically represented by the frequency distribution with its mean at b'. But what about the distribution of ages for the test performance c? Since this is the mean of the adult test performance the age distribution stretches over the whole range of life. The mean age c' would be perhaps 35 or higher. Even if we should decide to determine this mean age, we should find it impossible to do so without ambiguity because the mean age for this distribution, and for those immediately below it, is largely determined by the number of individuals that we should select at each age. Should we select the same number of people at each age in this distribution? Or should we select such a frequency of individuals at each age that the distribution of age corresponds to the frequency of each age in the general population? Such a distribution might be determined from the mortality tables. Since the mental

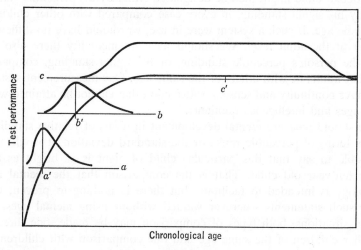

Figure 3

age scale is intended as a scale of mental development, there is no sense in translating test performance into age with all these entirely unnecessary troubles. In the case of the first alternative definition of mental age, we found that the term could be saved from absurdity, if we must have it, by redefining it. But in the nature of the case, there is probably no way in which the second alternative meaning of the term may be redefined so as to avoid ambiguity.

All of these difficulties would be avoided entirely if we should discard the awkward mental age concept and proceed instead as follows. When a child has been given a mental examination of the Binet type, or any other, we might ascertain the child's chronological age. Then we might consult our norms and say that this child's mental development, compared with other children of the same age, has a percentile standing of, say, 70. This would be extremely simple. It would mean that this child is a little above the average in intelligence among children of its own age. It would mean that 30 per cent of the children of the same age are brighter, and that 70 per cent are less bright. The intelligence quotient would be discarded along with the mental age concept on which it depends and the percentile standing of the child would be used instead. Such questions as the constancy of the intelligence quotient would still be with us but we should use the percentile standing of the child among others of its own age as the index, instead of the intelligence quotient. We should be inquiring whether a child keeps his relative standing among other children of the same age as he grows older.

For many statistical studies it might be preferable to use the sigma standing of the child instead of the percentile standing. The test performance of any particular child might then be designated either by his percentile standing or by his sigma standing, in every case compared with other children of the same age. If such a system were in use, we should have no difficulty whatever at the adult level. We should measure mentality there also by stating the person's percentile standing, or his sigma standing, compared with other adults or with others of the same age. Our measurement system would have continuity and sense, a satisfaction that cannot be attained with mental ages and intelligence quotients.

If we should measure mental development in terms of relative standing, either in terms of percentile ranks or the standard deviation, it would still be possible to say that this particular child of eight is as bright as the average ten-year old child. That is the comparison that the mental age terminology is intended to facilitate, but there is nothing to prevent our making such statements wherever wanted without using mental ages. In practical situations, both types of comparison may be made, one directly with other children of the same age and one comparison with children of any other given age. Then a given eight-year old child's mentality would be described by a percentile of, say, 70 for his own age, and he could also be compared with ten-year old children by saying that he would have a percentile of, say, 50 among them and so on. The child could be compared with children of other ages by the same set of tables or norms.

Binet may still be given credit for having introduced certain types of objectivity in mental measurement but his invention of the mental age concept was an awkward and unfortunate one. It is of course possible to retain the terminology of mental ages and intelligence quotients and to limit these terms to tests for children. But since these terms become nonsense when applied to adults, there would always be the question as to what age shall be the practical limit for their use. Would it not be better to discard mental ages and intelligence quotients and to adopt a measuring system, already universally known, which is extremely simple and which has the advantage of continuity so that it may be used for all ages?

In his remarkable book, The Abilities of Man, Spearman cleared the way for his concept of general intelligence by summarizing and amplifying the criticisms of current approaches to the measurement of intelligence. Two chapters of this criticism have been adapted for use here. They are followed by the chapter presenting Spearman's "two-factor" theory and the criterion of tetrad differences. His work was instrumental in preparing the way for the general development of factor analysis which was to follow.

The Abilities of Man*

C. SPEARMAN

1927

PRESENT DOMINANCE OF THIS DOCTRINE

Universal acceptance in popular usage. In considering the scientific doctrines on human ability, exceptionally great importance must be attributed to the popular view of the matter. For this view has become ossified into current language, and thus has come to constitute a rigid shell within which the layman and the expert alike seem to be fixedly encased.

Now, paramount among the lay beliefs is that which assumes mental ability to lie under the sovereign rule of one great power named "intelligence." In distinction from other doctrines which will be discussed in later chapters, this credence in a single ruling power may be characterised as "monarchic."

Judgments about intelligence conceived in this manner are made everywhere and by everyone—for the most part with much fluency and confidence. In degrees of it we habitually rate all the persons with whom we come into contact. . . .

Such estimates are formed with peculiar abundance and emphasis in the sphere of education. From the kindergarten up to the university, the pupil is continually being subjected to ratings of this nature, whether set forth in official reports, or reserved for private guidance. But hardly less prominent is the part played by similar estimates in connection with industry. Hardly an employee is selected—from the office boy up to the general-manager—but that the chief motive (as regards ability) consists in an opinion as to whether he is or is not intelligent.

Here, then, is an outstanding fact by which even the expert psychologist does not and cannot escape being profoundly influenced; all the more so,

* Adapted from Chapters II, V, and VI of *The Abilities of Man* (London, The Macmillan & Co., Ltd., 1927). Reprinted by permission of the publisher.

perhaps, when this influence remains subconscious. Any doctrine put forward will sooner or later be faced by the choice between docilely accepting this popular belief so firmly entrenched in current speech, or else hardily attempting to tilt against it.

Introduction into science by biologists. This ascendancy of popular over scientific psychology has in its support, not only the prestige always attaching to the *vox populi,* but even, it would seem, a priority of authorship. For at least as far back as the fifteenth century, we find that estimates were commonly made in ordinary life about a man's "intelligyens." Whereas in the systematic psychology of modern times, the concept does not seem to have attained to prominence earlier than the work of Herbert Spencer. By him, as might have been expected, it was brought in for the purposes of biology, at the period when this latter was being immensely stimulated by the then novel theory of evolution. Life was taken by Spencer to consist essentially in "the continuous adjustment of internal relations to external relations"; and to "intelligence" it was that he credited the making of such adjustments in so far as these are mental.

* * *

From Spencer, who took into consideration animals in general, it was but a short step to those authors who were interested in differentiating the human from the lower species. The essential distinction between the respective powers of these two was now declared to lie in the fact that man alone is gifted with the prerogative of being intelligent. In order to explain how, nevertheless, the lower animals manage their affairs in such an effective manner as they undoubtedly do, the further power of "instinct" was brought forward as their endowment instead. Man also, indeed, was credited with some of this instinctive kind of knowing, but only for employment in such actions as had (with the human species) become mere routine. For new and individual emergencies he has recourse, it was said, to his sovereign power of intelligence.

In truth, however, the preceding doctrine was not so much a novelty as a revival. It really represented the most ancient of all known views about cognitive ability. After long ages of neglect, it had now been rummaged out of the psychological lumber-room and hastily furbished up to meet the latest scientific requirements.

Adoption for mental tests. High as was this status attained by the concept of intelligence in biological territory, it later on became quite eclipsed by the reputation which the concept won for itself in the domain of mental tests. During a prolonged incubatory period, these had been cultivated in the seclusion of several psychological laboratories. Then, suddenly, Binet transformed such theoretical work into live practice. The success was astounding. Teachers found in tests of intelligence something that they could handle; and the public got what it believed it could understand.

In a very few years there followed the tremendous feat of testing the intelligence of nearly two million men in the American Army. And even this, unsurpassable as a single event, was eventually outdone by the cumulative amount of testing effected in schools, universities, and other institutions.

The brilliant outlook. But the whole total of what has actually been accomplished seems as nothing compared with what looms in the not distant future, or has even already begun to be set on foot. How high the hopes are running may perhaps be illustrated by the following passage from a writer of well deserved authority:

> Two extraordinarily important tasks confront our nation; the protection and improvement of the moral, mental, and physical quality of its people and the reshaping of its industrial system so that it shall promote justice and encourage creative and productive workmanship.

These are the opening words of a recent book on the results to be obtained through the tests of intelligence; such tests are taken to supply an instrument capable of largely aiding the "two extraordinarily important tasks."

Nor can these hopes easily be accused of exaggeration, when we consider that an accurate measurement of every one's intelligence would seem to herald the feasibility of selecting the better endowed persons for admission into citizenship—and even for the right of having offspring. And whilst in this manner a suitable selection secures a continual rise in the intellectual status of the people taken in mass, the same power of measuring intelligence should also make possible a proper treatment of each individual; to each can be given an appropriate education, and thereafter a fitting place in the state—just that which he or she demonstrably deserves. Class hatred, nourished upon preferences that are believed to be unmerited, would seem at last within reach of eradication; perfect justice is about to combine with maximum efficiency.

RISE OF DOUBT AND CRITICISM

Repeated recourse to symposia. Curiously jarring with all these signs and messages of the happy new era, however, there has been sounded in certain places a note of solicitude, of suspicion, and even of downright hostility. Still more strange is it that such scepticism towards the testing of intelligence, instead of quietly subsiding under the influence of its apparently so victorious career, would seem on the contrary to be always gathering more and more force.

*   *   *

In a resolute effort to clear up the situation, recourse was had to a symposium of several pre-eminent British authorities. And as was inevitable from such an assembly, many thoughts were uttered of high interest and suggestiveness. But in respect of the main purpose, the result can hardly be regarded as other than disappointing. On not one of the disputed matters does any approach seem to have been made towards better mutual understanding.

Some years later, even greater embarrassment was felt, now among the mental testers in America. To meet it, another symposium was convoked; here no less than fourteen leading authorities took part. But this time the task undertaken was far more restricted. Instead of attempting to settle the relations of intelligence to instinct—or to anything else—all efforts were concentrated upon describing its own nature. As before, such a distinguished gathering could not fail to beget many an observation bearing the stamp of brilliancy. But as for the essential aim, that of supplying the psychology of intelligence with a generally acceptable analysis, there appears to have been no success obtained. Each speaker gave his own opinion; almost all of these turned out to differ widely; and reconciliation between them was not even attempted.

Eventually, yet another symposium on intelligence was called together, this time at Oxford in 1923. But the situation became even more perplexed than at the previous meeting. For then the problem had only been as to the nature of the single thing, intelligence. But now there appeared in the field many different "intelligences," each presenting as hard a problem of its own!

Increasingly serious attacks.   Alongside of all such symptoms of hesitation and anxiety, there has also arisen a more actively destructive criticism. Already, in 1912, Kirkpatrick had ventured to say: "I do not believe that the Binet tests or any other tests likely to be devised within the century will serve as a reliable measure."

And ten years later, this voice crying in isolation suddenly swelled into a chorus. Thus Trabue, who had himself been among the most active constructors of mental tests, veered round towards scepticism. He told of a woman who, although making a very bad record with the tests, nevertheless became "the housekeeper at one of the finest Fifth Avenue hotels, where she successfully directed the work of a corps of approximately 50 maids, three carpenters, two decorators, and a plumber."

By this achievement on her part he was moved to conclude as follows: "In spite of the evidence of the tests, I insist that she is intelligent."

A different but no less damaging line of criticism was about the same time adopted by Viteles. He complained that although the current tests "are all called tests of 'general intelligence' . . . the mental ability measured by each is not the same."

Another assault was headed by Woodworth, who declared that the tests really touch neither the lower nor the higher ranges of intelligent behaviour.

*   *   *

And openly disdainful is the verdict of W. Lippmann:

Psychologists have never agreed on a definition (of intelligence). . . . The intelligence tester cannot confront each child with the thousand and one situations arising in a home, a workshop, a farm, an office, or in politics, that call for the exercise of these capacities which in a summary fashion we call intelligence. He proceeds, therefore, to guess at the more abstract mental abilities which come into play again and again. By this rough process the intelligence tester gradually makes up his mind that situations in real life call for memory, definition, ingenuity, and so on. He then invents puzzles, which can be employed quickly and with little apparatus, that will acording to his best guess test memory, ingenuity, definition and the rest. . . . The tester himself guesses at a large number of tests which he hopes and believes are tests of intelligence. . . . These puzzles may test intelligence, and they may not. They may test an aspect of intelligence. Nobody knows.

* * *

THE WORD "INTELLIGENCE" CANKERED WITH EQUIVOCALITY

Present prevailing chaos. Now, what, if anything, has really gone wrong? Much of the criticism we have been quoting may be vague and contradictory; it may suggest a disgruntled mood, rather than reasonable objections. But through it all—continually waxing in both clearness and emphasis—runs at least one theme that cannot be overlooked; this urges from many standpoints that the very concept of "intelligence" is unsatisfactory.

Let us, then, submit this concept to some examination. And for this purpose, we shall not have to plunge into any profound arguments—as was done at the symposia—but may content ourselves with simply asking what the word "intelligence" is really intended to mean.

Take, to begin with, that very wide class of mental operations that are commonly included under the heading of memory. Is or is not this intended to come within the meaning of the word? To our confusion, half of the authorities say yes, but the other half no. And this contradiction not only pervades the theoretical discussions, but equally so the practical framing of the tests. In the famous American Army set, as also in such standardized sets as those of Otis, of the Presseys, of the Illinois University, etc., all memorizing is excluded. But in other sets that likewise stand in highest repute—from Binet's earliest to Thorndike's latest—it is expressly introduced. Not even one and the same constructor of tests appears to maintain any uniformity in this respect. Thus Thorndike, although he admits memorizing into the tests which he has made for the purposes of matriculation, still leaves for it no place in the "National" series for which also he seems to be more or less responsible. Terman, again, retains memorizing in his tests for individuals taken singly, but excludes it from those which he has designed for groups. Binet, despite his free acceptance of memory in his test-scale, nevertheless explicitly says that it is really not intelligence but only the "great simulator" of this. Nor is the consistency better on turning from the expert psychologist to the "plain man." With one breath he will say, "How intelligent of you to remember that"; with the next, he will excuse a lapse as not being one of intelligence but merely of memory.

Nor is this all. Rivalling even memory in scope are the operations usually attributed to the "imagination." Shall or shall not these, then, be taken to fall within the domain that is to be assigned to intelligence? Few psychologists appear to face this obvious question at all. But two of the leaders, Stern and Claparède, do with their customary thoroughness deal with it; and they both declare that this power lies not inside but outside the domain. Yet many other eminent psychologists adopt the contrary view, both in theory and in practice. For example, the test-scale of Yerkes—which has substantially the same composition as that of Binet—contains out of twenty components six that are expressly assigned by their author to "imagination."

The list of such contradictory interpretations of the word intelligence can be extended indefinitely. Take the case of language. In the eyes of some writers, the great part played by this in current tests is only right and proper, on the ground of language being just that wherein human intelligence is most specifically manifested. But other writers, on the contrary, are always complaining of the influence of language in the tests as being irrelevant and disturbing. Or take the power of attention. Is this wholly, or partly, or not at all the same as intelligence? All three views are widely held in current literature. Take even motor ability. By many experts this is unhesitatingly rejected from the scope of intelligence. Yet others as confidently declare that the power of co-ordinating movements has just as much right to be called intelligent as that of co-ordinating ideas.

Surely, however, the strangest fact has yet to be mentioned. If such terms as "intelligence" or "intellect" have—by right of general usage and long history—secured for themselves any unalienable core of meaning at all, this certainly lies in their being opposed to and contrasted with mere sensation. Yet even this last piece of seemingly solid ground for the word is beginning to tremble. Already Binet wrote: "A sensation, a perception, are intellectual manifestations as much as reasoning is."

And such a view continues to find advocates. Thus, Haggerty declares that: "Intelligence" is "a practical concept connoting a group of complex processes traditionally defined in systematic psychologies as sensation, perception, association, memory, imagination, discrimination, judgment and reasoning."

Chaos itself can go no farther! The disagreement between different testers—indeed, even between the doctrine and the practice of the selfsame tester—has reached its apogee. If they still tolerate each other's proceedings, this is only rendered possible by the ostrich-like policy of not looking facts in the face. In truth, "intelligence" has become a mere vocal sound, a word with so many meanings that finally it has none. . . . The present devotion to the term recalls unpleasantly the old saying of Hobbes: "Words are wise men's counters, but they are the money of fools."

In a similar vein J. S. Mill writes:

The tendency has always been strong to believe that whatever receives a name must be an entity or being, having an independent existence of its own. And if no real entity answering to the name could be found, men did not for that reason suppose that none existed, but imagined that it was something peculiarly abstruse and mysterious.

*   *   *

ATTEMPTED REMEDY BY DEFINITION

Definitions distinguished from mere statements.   The way to mend matters might seem obvious enough. If the word has become so disastrously equivocal, why not simply supply it with a definition? Indeed, one might easily think that this has been done many times already. The symposia themselves could be taken to have furnished a whole treasury of definitions.

*   *   *

Favourite definition on a biological basis.   Looking round for some proposition to fulfil the requirement, the one which seems likely to win for itself far the largest number of votes comes from Spencer and his modern biological followers, especially Stern and Claparède. Here, intelligence is said to be that mental power which produces "conscious adaptation to new situations."

Now, so long as this saying is only taken in the sense of a "statement about" intelligence, we may be confident—from the very names of their authors—that it admits of being interpreted in a valuable manner. But may it, furthermore, be taken to supply our present necessity, that of a genuine unequivocal definition?

To this question the answer cannot but be in the negative; the proposition would be equivocal through and through. Consider first the key word in it, "adaptation." With Spencer, this signified the furtherance of racial life. But with Stern it seems to have become the fulfilment of purpose. Other writers employ it in even more disparate senses, such as the discovery of truth. So too "situation" is sometimes made to mean the entire surroundings of a person as they really are, but sometimes only his very limited and fallible perceptions and thoughts about them. Even when restricted to the latter sense, the word may still be interpreted in varying manners. Thus, Stern seems to understand by it any task with which a person may be confronted, so that it must of course include all tests he has to undergo. But Porteus, adopting another and not less natural sense of the word, has been able to urge that the power to deal with new situations is just what the current tests do *not* call into exercise.

Even supposing that some good fairy were to conjure away the ambiguousness of this definition, it would still only tell us what purpose intelligence serves, not what it is. For no general agreement exists as to what kind of mental operation really does produce "adaptation." Almost the sole detailed effort to settle this point was that made originally by Spencer; and he concluded in favour of associative reproduction. But Stern and Claparède appear to have in view almost anything rather than this. In truth, possibly no kind of operation ought to be held exclusively responsible. Mind and body alike have evolved under conditions of survival which must have led to much adaptability in general. But what constituent of either mind or body has actually achieved this end, and how perfectly or imperfectly it does so, these are points not to be assumed *a priori* but ascertained by laborious investigation. There may perhaps be scope for operations of *every* kind.

On the whole, then, what superficially looked like an almost unanimous acceptance of this biological definition has shown itself to be at bottom little more than verbal jugglery. Psychologists have "found a formula" with which everyone can agree—provided that each interprets it differently!

Pedagogical and kindred definitions. There has been another much favoured attempt at defining intelligence, this time not so much in biological as in pedagogical interest. The power is said to consist in educability, or the capacity to learn. But this time we can be very brief—for almost all the preceding considerations about the biological view occur here over again.

According to the dictionary, "to learn" means "to acquire skill or knowledge." But this fairly intelligible meaning of the word is far from being adhered to by those who are using it to define intelligence. Their writings often imply that just the acquirement of skill, and even the absorption of knowledge, does *not* belong to it.

Moreover, we must here again ask, What mental processes do produce skill or knowledge? On this point, as in the previous case, opinions are very discrepant. And perhaps the truth is that in learning, just as before in adaptation, every sort of mental process finds some or other useful work to do. In short, although to call intelligence the capacity to learn may perhaps supply a valuable "statement about" it, nevertheless as an attempt to furnish it with a definition such a proceeding can only render the confusion worse.

There are several further modern versions of "intelligence" to which similar comments apply. Among the most notable are the following: "The power of good responses from the point of view of truth" (Thorndike). "The ability to act effectively under given conditions" (Buckingham). "That which can be judged by the degree of incompleteness of the alternatives in the trial and error life of the individual" (Thurstone). "A biological mechanism by which the effects of a complexity of stimuli are brought together and given a somewhat unified effect in behaviour" (Jos. Peterson). Here must also be classed the important attempt of Ebbinghaus, followed by Ziehen, de Sanctis, and others, to characterize intelligence as the power of "combination." So, too, its treatment by Bergson and Wildon Carr. Many of these may make most valuable "statements about" it; but as definitions they would plunge us back again in the old paralyzing equivocality.

* * *

The call back to Scholasticism. Contrasting with all these attempts to use the word intelligence in some characteristically modern signification, is that which harks back to the usage of the mediaeval Schoolmen. Foremost in this movement, naturally, is the neo-scholastic school itself, which in late years has made extraordinary strides towards becoming better appreciated. Here, intelligence is defined as the operation of thinking in abstract or universal terms. Such thinking has usually, but not always, been taken to fall into the following three specific manifestations—conception, judgment, and reasoning.

As an instance of return, even among experimentalists, towards this time-honoured view may be cited the statement of Terman that "An individual is intelligent in proportion as he is able to carry on abstract thinking."

Now, if ever a concept can fairly lay claim to the title of intelligence, surely it is this one, so faithfully preserved for so many centuries by the Schoolmen. To the labour of these it is that the name really owes its prestige (which the other schools are now trying to annex for themselves). And in addition to possessing such titular right, this ancient doctrine even lends itself moderately well to the hard task of furnishing a definition; its criterion, abstractness, although not so free from being ambiguous as might be desired, is at any rate far freer than any such notions as adaptability, educability, and so forth.

DOUBT AS TO POSSIBILITY OF MEASUREMENT

A further and worse difficulty. But even now, we are far from out of the wood. Bravely suppose all the preceding obstacles to have been somehow conjured away—let the word intelligence be interpreted in congruence with the best of psychological doctrines, let it be defined in some fashion that really precludes ambiguousness, and let this purified rendering of it be compliantly accepted by every leading authority—still even in this ideal case, we have not yet passed the worst part of the road which has to be traversed before establishing the current doctrine that confronts us in the present chapter.

For up to this point, we have only examined the matter from its qualitative aspect. There remains its aspect of quantity, particularly as involved in any test or measurement. In order to support effectively the monarchic doctrine, the intelligence must not only be definite in nature, but also single in function; it must constitute a genuine "behaviour-unit."

But where is the evidence for this? Very competent psychologists, notably

Whipple and Colvin, tell us just the contrary; they report that what we measure by the current mental tests includes many different functions more or less uncorrelated with each other. The obtaining of a high total score in these tests, they say,

fails to get anywhere in our real inquiry as to just which ones of the various mental functions are possessed by the extraordinarily heightened efficiency. Is it memory span, or capacity for concentrated attention, or ability to handle symbols, or apprehension of abstract relations, or acute perceptive capacity, or lively imagination, or originality, or breadth of associative tendencies, or speed of learning, or what, that demarcates such a child from other children?

With different authors, the intelligence is analysed on different lines; but the consequence that several measurements are requisite remains unaffected. Thus, Abrahmson demands that, for testing purposes, the intelligence should be divided up into such separate powers as "abstraction," "critical sense," "invention," and "recognition."

Especially interesting in this respect is the interpretation of intelligence as the power of adaptation. Stern himself explicitly analyses this into many different kinds. When he throws all together under the name of intelligence, his aim is only classification; he is far too clear-sighted to suppose that thereby he necessarily obtains a single ability measurable by a single value. Similar perhaps is the position of Claparède, when he divides the adaptation into three steps, viz. the posing of a question, the invention of a hypothesis, and the ensuing verification. To explain each of these he postulates a different mental power.

Even the Scholastic doctrine of intelligence, as we have seen, divides up its manifestations into three sorts; conception, judgment, and reasoning. Each, then, would appear to require its own measurement.

What, finally, shall we say of Binet? He wrote (as late as 1909) that "the mental faculties of each subject are independent and unequal; with a little memory there may be associated much judgment. . . . Our mental tests, always special in their scope, are each appropriate to the analysis of a single faculty." Why did not he then, why do not his avowed followers, measure (for each year of age) each of these independent faculties, memory, judgment, etc., one by one? To have made no attempt in this direction seems inconceivably illogical.

CONCLUSION

On the whole, the chronicle of the modern "intelligence" has been dramatic. The first act shows it rapidly rising to a dazzling eminence. But in the second, there begin to be heard notes of criticism, which soon swell into an insistent hostile chorus. The most ethusiastic advocates of the intelligence become doubtful of it themselves. From having naïvely assumed that its nature is straightway conveyed by its name, they now set out to discover what this nature really is. In the last act, the truth stands revealed, that the name really has no definite meaning at all; it shows itself to be nothing more than a hypostatized word, applied indiscriminately to all sorts of things.

Moreover, even on supposing that some cure could be invented for this blight of equivocality, there has been found a further and even worse objection to the monarchic doctrine. For this takes the intelligence to constitute a unitary function or single behaviour-unit, measurable by a single value. Whereas really, there seems to be no escape from regarding it as divisible into several different functions more or less uncorrelated with each other, and therefore each needing a measurement of its own.

Such an admission would appear to break up the very foundations of both theory and practice as now largely current. If, then, the great edifice of mental testing with all its fair promises is not to collapse like a house of cards, at least some other doctrinal support seems needed for it than is supplied by the current concept of a monarchic "intelligence."

Anarchic Doctrine: "General Level," "Average," or "Sample"

DOCTRINE OF INDEPENDENCE

Crude view that all abilities are independent.   The trend of the preceding chapter was once more towards further analysis. Already in the two previous chapters, we had been compelled to break up the sovereign "intelligence" into several different ruling faculties or types. All these were found to need separate treatment—and especially measurement—since they appeared to be more or less independent of one another. And then this same fate befell the faculties and types themselves; each of these, also, had to be further broken up; for it covered a variety of mental operations which, so far as could be seen, were more or less independent.

To what point, then, must all this sub-division be eventually carried? No stopping place seems to present itself short of the most elementary processes; every one of these may derive from a separate and independent ability. Such a movement over into the doctrine of all-round independence —or the "anarchic" doctrine, as it may be called—was taken at once by Herbart and his followers. Having demolished all defence for the view that ability is tied up into a few great separate faculties, they naturally enough went on to proclaim that ability is really subdivided into innumerable independent parts.—Volkmann, as we saw, roundly declared that every idea possesses its own memory, its own imagination, and so forth.

And a similar view appears to have been advanced even in quite recent times. It may be found, for instance, in some of the earlier writings of no less an authority than Thorndike. He expresses his opinion that "the mind is a host of highly particularized and independent faculties."

And indeed, at the moment when he made this statement, it was fully warranted by the most exact research then known. For shortly before (1901) there had been published a momentous investigation by Cattell and Wissler. These authors had devised tests for no less than 22 different mental powers and had tried them upon 325 university students. Furthermore— for the first time in psychology—the degree of dependence between one ability and another had been submitted to definite quantitative measurement, the means employed being the then little known "correlational coefficients." The issue was blankly negative; the tests displayed no appreciable correlation, either among themselves, or with success in academic work. So manifest was the superiority of this research to anything done previously, that to be incredulous would not have been wise but rather the reverse.

Unfortunately, however, these investigators had fallen victims to their own insight and enterprise. They had rightly grasped the immense value of the new mathematical tool invested by statisticians; but they had no means of knowing that this tool was still vitiated by a fatal flaw, that of "attenuation" (see appendix, p. i). After this flaw had been detected, such negative results never again made any appearance. On the contrary, sets of tests almost always produced high—and often very high—inter-correlations.

Later view that all abilities are correlated. Not infrequently, certain authors—notably Ziehen and Thorndike—are still cited as championing the aforesaid crude doctrine of independence. But in all such passages as have come under the notice of the present writer, there are to be found some explicit reservations. Ziehen does indeed declare that "the intellectual aptitude falls into numerous aptitudes"; but he quickly adds the qualifying clause that the latter "stand in complicated connection with one another." So also Thorndike does appear to continue to assert the existence of many different abilities; but now he carefully proceeds to note that these are more or less inter-correlated.

By the aid of these safeguards, the doctrine may indeed be said to have been rendered absolutely irrefutable. Beyond all reasonable doubt, human ability does admit of being regarded as being made up of very numerous particular abilities that are mutually correlated. But has not this security been purchased at the price of significance? The collapse of the earlier and crude view, that all different abilities are independent, had come from establishing just this fact of their inter-correlation. Thereafter, the whole problem at issue was to discover some aspect from which the inter-correlation could be rendered intelligible. And towards solving this problem, such statements as we have been considering do not appear to make even a commencement; the bare proposition that the intellectual aptitudes stand in complex relations to one another says nothing wrong only because it says almost nothing at all. . . .

Hypothesis of independent elementary factors. Yet a road for progress lay open obviously enough, namely, by pursuing the analysis still further.

This in the preceding view comes naïvely to an end at each distinct mental operation. But with far greater likelihood every concrete operation itself— even the simplest—depends upon numerous abstract influences, or "factors" as they have been called in psychology. This is obvious even in the physical world; not the smallest movement of the smallest particle of matter can occur but that a part is played by many different factors, such as weight, heat, or electricity.

If so, then the correlation displayed between any different concrete operations admits after all of being readily explained. For it may well be due to these operations having one or more of their elementary factors in common. It is these basic factors, then, not the entire concrete operations however simple, to which the doctrine of independence should naturally be applied. And when so applied, all the objections that we have hitherto seen against it become void.

Interestingly enough, this is the very road that has led to the general mathematical theory of all correlation. The original work of Bravais himself was fundamentally established upon the basis of assuming that each single observable correlated magnitude is a function of multiple unobservable uncorrelated elements. And his successors have had to content themselves with following in his footsteps. Recently, definite proof has been supplied by Garnett, that such an analysis is always mathematically possible. Any number of total magnitudes however correlated with each other— he shows—can always be expressed as functions of elements that are themselves uncorrelated.

Had but this more finely analytical direction of thought been followed by the advocates of independence, their theory could scarcely have failed to merge eventually into the one that will chiefly occupy us later on (ch. vi.).

DOCTRINE OF A "GENERAL LEVEL" OR "AVERAGE"

Origin of the doctrine. This promising line in which to pursue the doctrine of independence, however, appears to have escaped notice. We arrive now, instead, at that view which among those who are actively engaged in mental testing is probably having the greatest influence. For the belief in a monarchic "intelligence" (ch. ii.) seems not to affect the actual testing so much as the conclusions drawn from its result. The assumption of unitary faculties (ch. iii.) or types (ch. iv.) is most prominent in theoretical discussions; its supporters usually drop them again on getting down to the actual testing. But the doctrine to which we now turn appears to be pre-eminently that which inspires confidence in the tester when busy at his work. It consists in regarding that which is measured by the tests as the "general level," the "average," or a "sample" of the person's abilities.

Now, there is some reason to suppose that this way of thinking started from a suggestion of the present writer. He—almost alone at that time, it would seem—had been much impressed by the difficulty of submitting the individual differences to any genuine measurement at all. To every one of the current doctrines there had appeared to exist some insuperable objections. In each case, the fatal flaw had lain in assuming the existence of some correlation that was unsupported—or even contradicted—by the available evidence. The remedy seems to be necessarily based upon some deepening of the theory of correlations. An attempt was actually taken in this direction, with the result of finding that there does indeed exist something measurable which might possibly be entitled general intelligence. But the procedure which the theory indicated for obtaining the measurement was of a most curious kind. For up to now the trend that we have been examining has always been towards finer and finer analysis. Seemingly flouting all this, the procedure dictated by this correlational theory was to take almost at random very numerous tests quite different from each other and to throw all the scores for them indiscriminately into one common pool.

A little more than a year afterwards appeared the great work of Binet and Simon. Here, this paradoxical recommendation to make a hotchpot was actually adopted in practice. Nevertheless the elaborate correlational theory which had in point of fact generated the idea, and had supplied the sole evidence for its validity, was now passed over. The said authors employed a popular substitute. "Intelligence," as measured by the pool, was depicted as a "general level" of ability. So far as doctrine is concerned, this is the only thing introduced by them that was novel. And most surprisingly Binet, although in actual testing he took account of this "general level" alone, still in all his theoretical psychology continued to rely altogether upon his old formal faculties, notwithstanding that these and the "general level" appear to involve doctrines quite incompatible with each other.

Interpretation of "general level" as average or sum.   Such a replacement of an elaborate correlational theory by the simple concept of a "general level" was—if valid—a remarkable achievement. But before being finally accepted, it needs at least some critical examination.

To begin with, what is intended to be the meaning of this term "general level" (or any other term taken to involve this, such as "mental age" or the "I.Q.")? Really, a person's abilities will in the ordinary course of events be most *un*level; with everybody, some kinds of ability very much surpass others. The level, then, must be taken as some theoretical line or plane, not necessarily coinciding with any of the actual abilities at issue, but bearing some general relation to them all. Where is any such thing to be found?

* * *

We are compelled to interpret the person's general level of ability as being some theoretical *central* altitude, whilst his different actual abilities lie, on the whole, as much above as below it. And the most natural value to take as central is the *average*.

Accordingly, this does appear to have been the view of all or almost all writers (including Binet himself) who used the term "general level," and even of many who employ "general intelligence" or "general ability." Some are careful to state as much. Others, instead, write of the "sum" of abilities, or of the "total efficiency"; but this comes to the same thing; for an average is, of course, only the sum or total divided by the number of cases. Many more make no definite statement as to what they intend such terms to mean, but the interpretation in the sense of an average seems best to accord with their context.

This concept of an "average," then, we will adopt as the basis for the following considerations. But, as may readily be seen, our arguments would apply just as well to any other kind of central value (as median, mode, geometric mean, harmonic mean, etc.).

Violated postulate of unequivocal domain. Now, speaking broadly, there can be no doubt but that averages are not only a legitimate statistical device, but one of extremely great value. Even in ordinary life, their use is frequent and very convenient, as for example, when calculating an average weekly expenditure. And in science, they are used for almost every value of importance. As for psychology, in this even more than in physics, the procedure of averaging dominates all quantitative work; an average is determined of reaction times, of memory spans, of errors committed, of "right and wrong cases," and so forth without limit.

Nevertheless, we must venture to raise the question as to whether this procedure of averaging, so widely and so successfully employed in other cases, may also be employed in the special case here interesting us. That the average score can be calculated for *all the tests* applied to any person is, of course, obvious. But can the value so obtained ever be regarded as the average of *all the person's abilities?*

In order to answer this question, let us consider what postulates are indispensable, if any genuine average is to be obtained. One, evidently, is that the domain should be settled within which the averaging is intended to run. It would be absurd, for instance, to pretend to give the average rainfall for Burma without having first said whether it referred to Lower Burma (which has about 200 inches) or to Upper Burma (which has only about 40). But then analogously idle must be any averaging of a person's "intelligence," unless there has first been some settlement as to whether motor ability, sensory perception, memory, imagination, etc., are to be counted in or not.

* * *

Violated postulate of comparable cases. Another fundamental requirement in order to obtain any genuine average is that the cases to be averaged should be equivalent to one another, or at any rate in some way comparable. It would be ridiculous to try to take the average expenditure for a number of periods, if some of these happened to be weeks, some months, and others of unknown duration. Yet just such arbitrariness and uncertainty vitiate any attempt to average abilities. . . .

Violated postulate of no repetition. Equally futile must be any averaging where the same items are introduced repeatedly. In the instance of weekly expenditure, no valid result would be expected if, say, Xmas week were brought in several times. . . .

Violated postulate of no omission. This is the converse of the preceding requirement. Its indispensability is no less obvious. What would be the use of a man averaging his expenditure, if those weeks were omitted in which he paid his rent? Yet no one can seriously believe that any scale of tests is able to escape making grave omissions. . . .

On the whole, there appears to be no possibility of satisfying a single one of the postulates which—for any genuine averaging—are indispensable.

Pleas in defence. From all these criticisms that can be brought against the doctrine of measuring a general level in the sense of an average value, let us turn to what can be said in its defence.

As one plea, it might be urged that all these difficulties may be removed simply by virtue of psychologists coming to some agreement. Let only a World Court of them settle upon any definite number of definite traits. Thenceforward, there need be no equivocality of domain, no incomparable cases, no repetitions, and no omissions. But this pleasing prospect quickly shows itself to be delusive. For if the lines of agreement are to be arbitrary, then science becomes none the better for it; the value obtained can be no more significant than would be that got from any list made of desirable traits of body; it would at best be comparable with some average mark derived from an individual's height, weight, strength of grip, soundness of heart, capacity of lungs, opsonic index, and so forth *ad lib*. How can any such concoction of heterogeneous traits, bodily or mental, be taken seriously?

Another possible plea is that our postulates are too rigorous, too subtle, too refined, too pedantic, for ordinary practical purposes. But this suggestion would be quite intolerable. Every one of the said postulates is acknowledged and fulfilled throughout the entire range, not only of physical science, not only of psychological science, but even of every-day domestic economy. Shall the scientific treatment of "intelligence," with its elaborate mathematics of standardizations, calibrations, frequency distributions, mental ages, mental ratios, achievement ratios, correlational coefficients, reliability coefficients, multiple and partial coefficients, measures of skewness, curve fittings, and so forth—with its aims at reforming education, at revitalizing industry, at re-shaping the laws of immigration, at dictating the right to have children, at upsetting the very constitution of society—shall all this be founded upon a quantitative basis that would not be good enough to estimate the spendings of the humblest housewife?

Only one other plea seems to have been hitherto forthcoming. It is that the theory of a general level or average has actually led to approximately valid results, since the different test-series—whatever else may be said about them—undeniably do show fairly high correlations with each other. But against even this plea must be answered that no such theory of a level or average ever *led* Binet to his hotchpot procedure; for, in truth, his theoretical views were entirely alien to anything of the sort (still immersed, as he was, in "faculties"). He only took up the general "level" as an after-thought, a "rationalization," to account for a procedure which he really had adopted from elsewhere.

In any case, the fact that the hotchpot test-series have high correlations with one another, or in any other way actually "work," is no proof whatever that they do this by virtue of any impossible "levels" or averages. As is much more natural, every virtue possessed by the hotchpot procedure will find its genuine explanation in the doctrine from which this procedure really emanated.

DOCTRINE OF SAMPLING

Recurrence of the same violations.   There remains open a recourse to the allied doctrine of "sampling." The test-scale, it may be conceded, does not in itself supply any general level, average, or sum of a person's abilities, but it does furnish instead a sample of these. And herewith we reach, probably, the position that among the most active testers can boast of the largest number of adherents.

Now, what does the term sample mean? The dictionary tells us, a part or group selected at random as representative of the whole. And the introduction of the word "representative" seems to indicate that the chief relative quantities of the sample and those of the whole must be approximately similar; any way, such similarity is absolutely essential, if the sample is to fulfill any scientific purpose. But to secure this representativeness, in what sense are we to take the words "at random?" This certainly cannot mean that the selecting may be done anyhow at haphazard. All who have studied sampling know full well that *to obtain any part or group fairly representative of the whole is usually a most difficult matter.*

On examination as to where such difficulty lies, it will be found to consist in fulfilling just the same fundamental postulates as before. To begin with, there is the need of settling the precise limits of the domain over which the sampling has to run. For instance, before any one started to sample the weight of Americans, he would have to decide whether he meant by this the population of the United States. Then, he would have to settle whether to include all immigrants, or only persons who had resided in the country for some particular period, or only such as had been born there, or perhaps only those whose parents had been born there. Similarly, he would have to settle whether negroes were to be included; whether both sexes, or only one. Again, he would have to fix the age limits for the persons to be taken into account. And so on, for a large number of vital points.

Turning back to mental ability and asking analogous questions, we once more come up against the equivocalities in the concept of "intelligence." Shall or shall not our sample be made to include memory, imagination, motor activity, and so forth? In our illustrative test-scale, more than half of the sub-tests are involved in this fatal dilemma.

After the need of marking out the domain from which to draw the sample, comes that of letting every case, or sort of case, have its proper chance of being drawn. For example, any sampling of the consumption of beer by Germans would be illusory if most of the persons included in the sample were taken from the specially beer-drinking region of Bavaria, or from the specially schnapps-drinking East Prussia, or from the specially wine-drinking Rhine districts. Instead, each region should contribute its due quota. But here we come up against the second great postulate that is not possibly fulfilled by any selection of the mental abilities to be tested. For, as we have seen, there exists no rational way of deciding what quota of these should be taken respectively from judgment, imagination, and so forth.

The preceding requirement, that each sort of case should be given its proper chance of being drawn in the sample, involves also the third and the fourth of our postulates. Obviously, we should not be sampling a regiment fairly if we took one quota from those who were officers and another from those who were catholics. For in this way, two chances would be given to the catholic officers, one each to the protestant officers and to the catholic rank-and-file, and no chance at all to the protestant rank-and-file. But in respect of mental abilities, both repetitions and omissions are, as we saw, present to a degree that touches the outrageous.

New difficulties superadded. Not only do all the obstacles to averaging thus re-appear in sampling, but the latter procedure adds on new difficulties of its own. For no sample will in general be representative, unless it contains cases in such large numbers as to smooth away accidental irregularities. Now, is this really achieved in respect of abilities? Take the scale of Binet himself. Only a small portion of it is applied to any particular child, the easier components being taken as unquestionably within his power and the harder components as unquestionably not within it. Central in the portion actually used are the components that belong to the year of his "mental age." Let us, then, consider as typical this main year (what will be said applies equally to the others also). Now, for the age of three years the component tests are five in number, and two of them deal with "memory." For the age of seven years, there are four tests, of which memory gets none at all. For the eleventh year, there are five tests, and again memory is left out altogether. But for the twelfth year, memory once more gets two out of five. To advance such a meagre and vacillating sample as scientific and representative seems a strange claim.

Shall, then, the claim of effective sampling be renounced for this Binet series, but still maintained for other series where the components are more numerous? Surely this would be a logical fallacy. The Binet series succeeds just as well as those others, in spite of its making no approach towards genuine sampling. And the same may be said even more forcibly of other series, as that of Wyatt, which has been conspicuously successful despite having only three components altogether. Such success as is at present obtained, therefore, can by no means be accredited to any bare virtue of sampling.

* * *

Inconsistency with actual practice. The worst about this theory of sampling, however, has yet to be mentioned. It is that, in actual practice, the procuring of a genuine sample has not really even been attempted.

One of the many indications of this is the prevalent procedure, in the construction of a series of tests, of trying out a large number and then selecting those which exhibit the highest correlations with all the rest. Such a procedure seems to have been more or less influential, directly or indirectly, in the framing of all generally accredited series at the present day. It has been formally designated as the "principle of coherence."

But who, when attempting to get a fair sample of Americans, and finding in his preliminary selection the majority to be Easterners, would thereupon proceed to eliminate even such Westerners as he had already obtained? Or who, on gathering together what was meant to be a representative sample of some mixed wheat for sale and on noticing that the larger part happened to be of his best quality, would proceed to weed out even such representatives of the inferior quality as were present—on the ground of making his sample "coherent"? Not improbably, such a procedure would bring him within reach of the law. In order to obtain a genuine sample, one carefully retains, and even adds to, the sorts which were at first little represented, and which therefore tend to be *least* correlated with, the remainder.

CONCLUSION

To summarize this chapter, every version of the "anarchic" doctrine has failed to make good. To maintain that the abilities for different operations are independent of each other is now, by universal admission, untrue. To say that they stand in complicated inter-relations is true but sterile.

As for the prevalent procedure of throwing a miscellaneous collection of tests indiscriminately into a single pool, this—whether or not justifiable by the theory which gave birth to it—certainly cannot be justified simply by claiming that the results give a "general level," an "average," or even a "sample." No genuine averaging, or sampling, of anybody's abilities is made, can be made, or even *has really been attempted*. When Binet borrowed the idea of such promiscuous pooling, he carried it into execution with a brilliancy that perhaps no other living man could have matched. But on the theoretical side, he tried to get away too cheaply. And this is the main cause of all the present trouble.

Eclectic Doctrine: Two Factors

DISCOVERY OF THE "TWO FACTORS"

History. Next to examine will be that doctrine from which the notion of pooling together a miscellaneous lot of different tests really emanated. This doctrine was based upon what we have all along been finding of such paramount importance, namely, the correlations between abilities. . . .

Criterion of "tetrad differences." The start of the whole inquiry was a curious observation made in the correlations calculated between the measurements of different abilities (scores for tests, marks for school subjects, or estimates made on general impression). These correlations were noticed to tend towards a peculiar arrangement, which could be expressed in a definite mathematical formula. And the formula thus originally reached has ever since been maintained without any essential change. Only from time to time, for convenience, it has been converted from one form to some other that is mathematically equivalent.

The form recently preferred is given below. In it, as usual, the letter r stands for any correlation, whilst its two subscripts indicate the two abilities (tests, school marks, etc.) that are correlated.

$$r_{ap} \times r_{bq} - r_{aq} \times r_{bp} = 0.$$

This formula has been termed the *tetrad equation* and the value constituting the left side of it the *tetrad difference*.

An illustration may be afforded by the following imaginary correlations between mental tests (actually observed correlations will be give in abundance later on):

		Oppo-sites	Com-pletion	Memory	Discrim-ination	Cancel-lation
Opposites	1		.80	.60	.30	.30
Completion	2	.80		.48	.24	.24
Memory	3	.60	.48		.18	.18
Discrimination	4	.30	.24	.18		.09
Cancellation	5	.30	.24	.18	.09	

For instance, let us try the effect of making:

a denote Opposites.

b "   Discrimination.

p "   Completion.

q "   Cancellation.

From the table of correlations above, we see that r_{ap} will mean the correlation between Opposites and Completion, which is .80. Obtaining in a similar fashion the other three correlations needed, the whole tetrad equation becomes—

$$.80 \times .09 - .30 \times .24 = 0.$$

which is obviously correct. And so will be found any other application whatever of the tetrad equation to this table.

The Two Factors.   So far, the business is confined to matters of observation; we simply try out the tetrad equation on any table of actually observed correlations and examine whether it fits. The next step, however, is not observational, but purely mathematical; we have to ask how, if at all, this equation between the correlations bears upon the individual measurements of the correlated abilities. The answer is that there has been shown to exist a very remarkable bearing indeed. It is to the effect that, whenever the tetrad equation holds throughout any table of correlations, and *only* when it does so, then every individual measurement of every ability (or of any other variable that enters into the table) can be divided into two independent parts which possess the following momentous properties. The one part has been called the "general factor" and denoted by the letter g; it is so named because, although varying freely from individual to individual, it remains the same for any one individual in respect of all the correlated abilities. The second part has been called the "specific factor" and denoted by the letter s. It not only varies from individual to individual, but even for any one individual from each ability to another. The proof of this all-important mathematical theorem has gradually evolved through successive stages of completeness, and may now be regarded as complete.

Although, however, both of these factors occur in every ability, they need not be equally influential in all. On the contrary, the very earliest application of this mathematical theorem to psychological correlations showed that there the g has a much greater relative influence or "weight" in some of the abilities tested than in others. Means were even found of measuring this relative weight. At one extreme lay the talent for classics, where the ratio of the influence of g to that of s was rated to be as much as 15 to 1. At the other extreme was the talent for music, where the ratio was only 1 to 4.

Here at once we have before us the essence of the whole doctrine, the seedling from which all else has sprung. But notice must be taken that this general factor g, like all measurements anywhere, is primarily not any concrete thing but only a value or magnitude. Further, that which this magnitude measures has not been defined by declaring what it is like, but only by pointing out where it can be found.

It consists in just that constituent—whatever it may be—which is common to all the abilities inter-connected by the tetrad equation.

Such a defining of g by site rather than by nature is just what was meant originally when its determination was said to be only "objective." Eventually, we may or may not find reason to conclude that g measures something that can appropriately be called "intelligence." Such a conclusion, however, would still never be the definition of g, but only a "statement about" it.

Suggested universality of g.   The vital problem, in respect of empirical observation, is as to how far and how regularly our tetrad equation actually holds good. In the original work, an extremely wide generalization was adventured. The suggestion was made that "all branches of intellectual activity have in common one fundamental function (or group of functions), whereas the remaining or specific elements seem in every case to be wholly different from that in all the others." Here, then, lies the justification for attributing so much importance to g, despite its purely formal character. The view is put forward that this g, far from being confined to some small set of abilities whose inter-correlations have actually been measured and drawn up in some particular table, may enter into all abilities whatsoever.

Such a universal law could only be advanced very tentatively. The express caution was added that "it must acquire a much vaster corroborative basis before we can accept it even as a general principle and apart from its inevitable corrections and limitations."

This caution was the more imperative, seeing that the law not only had such a tremendous scope, but moreover came into sharp conflict with the most authoritative psychology then prevailing, the latter being at that time wedded to the doctrine of independence.

Utility of the doctrine in practical testing.   The preceding doctrine—as we shall see later—admits of usage throughout almost every kind and description of problem within the whole domain of individual differences of ability. For the present, however, we will only allude to two of the most obvious of these applications.

The one consists in the power conferred of measuring any individual in a genuine manner (instead of giving a pseudo-average or level, see ch. v.). We can determine the magnitude of his g which will tell us nearly everything about some of his abilities and something about nearly all of them (see p. 75). And then we can do the same as regards any of his s's, one for each distinct kind of performance: this supplements and completes the information supplied by his g.

The other immediate application of the doctrine is in the construction of mental tests. We are enabled to ascertain just the degree of accuracy with which any given test, or series of them, will measure either a person's g or any of his s's. Further, we learn how this degree of accuracy may be raised to its maximum.

We can already see, too, that some crude approach towards measuring g can be obtained by the seemingly unscientific course of throwing very miscellaneous tests into a common hotchpot. So doing does not indeed supply an average, or even a representative sample, of the person's abilities; anything of the sort seems to be for ever precluded by the impossibility of fulfilling the necessary postulates. What the pooling does effect is to make the influences of the many specific factors more or less neutralize each other, so that the eventual result will tend to become an approximate measure of g alone.

DISCREPANCIES BETWEEN THEORY AND OBSERVATION

Effect of sampling errors.   Although we have above suggested that the range of g as indicated by the tetrad equation is really universal, this must not be taken to mean that the said equation is under all conditions well satisfied. To expect this would be as absurd as to infer from the law of conservation of energy that the distance a man can walk is always proportional to the amount of food he eats. The manifestations of all such laws, whether mental or physical, are bound to be more or less intermingled with, and modified by, further influences. For such influences, then, all due allowance must be made. In order to verify the law of Two Factors, actual experiment should *not* satisfy the equation exactly, but instead should present exactly the right departure from it. If a marksman wishes to hit the bullseye, he does not aim plump at it but more or less to one side, according to the direction and strength of the wind.

Now, all such inevitable complications of the theorem will be treated in detail later on. But about two of them—to obviate gross misapprehensions —a few words may be said forthwith. One such complication derives from the "errors of sampling." In any actual investigation only a limited number of individuals—ranging generally from 50 to 1,000—can actually be measured; these have to be accepted as a representative sample of the entire class of persons under consideration. But between the correlation found for any such mere sample and that truly holding for the entire class, there must naturally be expected some random discrepancy. The general size of this for any single correlation has long been ascertained; about half of the discrepancies will be greater and about half less than a calculable value called the "probable error" of the correlation. Every table or correlation must, then, be looked upon as consisting of the true values peppered over with, and more or less disguised by, random positive or negative additions; the general size of these, however, will bear a predictable relation to that of the said "probable error."

Such disturbances of the correlations cannot but exercise some effect upon our "tetrad differences," since the latter are constructed out of the former. Consequently, if the true value of the tetrad differences is always zero as shown in the tetrad equation (p. 73), then the actually manifested values ought *not to* be always zero, but instead should present some deviations from this. We need to ascertain how large these deviations should tend to be.

To discover this—or more broadly speaking, to make allowances for the disturbance of the correlations by their errors of sampling—has been the greatest trouble in the whole development of the doctrine. In the earlier investigations, the degree of allowance was left for anybody to estimate as high or as low as he pleased. Such a procedure, of course, is unscientific and misleading. Later on, the artifice was devised of replacing the tetrad equation by another criterion, which would at any rate be approximately correct and which did admit of calculating the allowance to be made for the errors of sampling. This substitute criterion was called that of "intercolumnar correlation." Quite recently, however, this long-standing grave defect in the doctrine has at last been overcome. Means have been discovered for evaluating the effect of the disturbance in the case of the true criterion, the tetrad equation itself. Knowing (as we always do) the probable errors of the four correlations that enter into the tetrad difference we can now deduce from these the probable error of the tetrad difference as a whole.

Overlap between specific factors.   As mentioned, there is another conspicuous limitation to the doctrine we are considering. Obviously, the specific factors for any two performances can only be independent of each other when these performances are quite different. When, on the contrary, two performances are much alike, their respective specific factors will necessarily cease to be mutually independent.

For example, take as one test the cancellation of all the a's in a printed page, and as another test the cancellation of all the e's. These two performances, being so extremely alike, may naturally be expected not only to have the g factor in common, but also to present a large overlap in respect of the s factor. The case may be symbolized in the following figure, where the vertical shading (top left and the bottom circles) stand for the s and the g in cancelling a's, whilst the horizontal shading (top right and the bottom circles) stand for the s and g in cancelling e's. Whenever such cases are introduced, then our tetrad equation must in general *cease* to be valid.

But where, it may be asked, shall the line be drawn between those performances which are and those which are not "quite different." The answer must be that this is not a point to settle intuitively, but to ascertain by experiment. Performances should be regarded as quite different—in the present signification of this phrase—so long as the tetrad equation is satis-

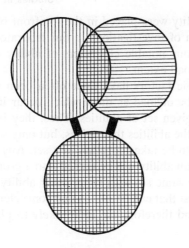

fied and no longer. To give some notion, however, of how this rule pans out in actual practice, it may at once be said that the most striking instance of such an overlap was afforded by just these two tests that both consist of cancelling letters and only differ as to which letter should be cancelled. Another instance of likeness found to produce marked overlap was that between counting dots one at a time and doing so three at a time. A somewhat different instance was found in school subjects; the correlation between marks for Latin Grammar and those for Latin Translation proved far too large to fit into our tetrad equation.

Evidently, such overlaps are akin to the "common elements" which have been taken by Thorndike, Judd, Sleight, and others to account for any "formal training" that may exist. But our overlaps might also derive, it was found, from various more or less accidental circumstances. Thus, some of the children had been learning Latin for a longer period than the others, and therefore naturally enough tended to excel at both the Grammar and the Translation. By this fact, of course, the correlation between the two abilities must have been increased beyond the amount due to g alone.

In general, the early investigations indicated that the cases of appreciable overlap are surprisingly scarce: that is to say, it appeared only to link together abilities that were allied very obviously. But already at this early period an exception was announced. It consisted in the overlap found between the memorizing of syllables and that of numbers. This observation was said "to indicate the possibility of a rather extensive group of performances being so nearly related, that they might be gathered together as a more or less unitary ability under the concept of 'memorization.'"

And the point was again emphasized in 1912. Herewith, then, was actually encountered something at least akin to the formal faculties or the types.

After this discovery, such broad factors capable of embracing very extensive ranges of ability were placed in the forefront of enquiry. There has been a steady stream of investigations in our laboratory devoted to ascertaining whether various notable characters of ability do or do not act as specific factors of broad extent.

Overlapping specific factors have since often been spoken of as "group factors." They may be defined as those which occur in more than one but less than all of any given set of abilities. Thus, they indicate no particular characters in any of the abilities themselves, but only some kinship between those which happen to be taken together in a set. Any element whatever in the specific factor of an ability will be turned into a group factor, if this ability is included in the same set with some other ability which also contains this element. The most that can be said is that some elements have a broader range than others, and therefore are more *likely* to play the part of group factors.

In the opening chapter of his book, Crossroads in the Mind of Man, Kelley signals the departure of the American factor analysts from the model provided by Spearman. Though still saddled with an unwieldy technique, Kelley has found evidence for group factors rather than g, the general factor. While no data are presented in this introduction, both Kelley's criticisms of Spearman and his own line of thought emerge clearly.

Group Factors*

T. L. KELLEY

1928

The study of the nature and scope of mental traits is as broad as the entire field of psychology, and just about as evasive as the all-pervasive ether. He who dedicates his services to "human welfare" is rather less likely to ease the progress of mankind than, say, an ear doctor who limits his attention to a narrower field. Nevertheless it is necessary to envisage an entire realm in order to maintain a proper perspective, to keep poised in the turmoil of separate schools, neo-schools, and counter-schools. Each separate school is generally willing to ignore the others with the fine tolerance of the wise toward the harmlessly demented. If perchance a behaviorist takes issue with a psychoanalyst, the latter blandly informs him that he does not know the facts and the principles of the latter's study, and in this he is probably right. How, then, as each school becomes more specialized in technique, more confined within its self-made walls, and more dependent upon the rapidly increasing fruits of its own garden, is there any chance for helpful criticism of school by school, or any prospect of co-ordination of their several doctrines? . . .

It would seem that just two things are necessary to a comparative and co-ordinative study: First, a technique that is universal in its applicability in the sense that it serves not only at the crossroads, but along the remote stretches where no other highway is near. And, second, the will and the opportunity on the part of someone to apply this technique to the divergent and convergent paths of modern psychology. The technique that is necessary is to be merely deductive, for its object is to test the validity of claims made and supported by sundry schools, and it is not primarily interested in the way these various claims happen to have been conceived in the first instance.

This single method of valuation applies to all schools of psychology, because in one important regard they all do the same thing, in that each ad-

---

* Adapted from Chapter I in *Crossroads in the Mind of Man: A Study of Differentiable Mental Abilities* (Stanford, Stanford University Press, 1928). Reprinted by permission of the author.

vances certain psychological elements as underlying its particular system—the behaviorist has his original tendencies and "given" nervous structure, the gestalt psychologist his configurations and *e pluribus unum* doctrine, the Freudian his underlying sexual urges, and so on. Without expressly so stating, the very postulation of these different elements constitutes a claim that each is an entity in itself and is entitled to an independent status in the field of mental life. Thus all that is needed in the way of technique by him who would investigate the entire field is a device for testing the independence of any given element from all others or at least from such as may be thought to be somewhat similar to it.

Before such testing there must be a definition of the element, and the school of psychology in question is obligated to supply this. This definition must be invariable, and expressible in terms of conduct. Certainly it would be in reason to demand as much in any other field. If a certain doctor maintains that hives are caused in one person by tomatoes, in some other individual by any sort of protein, and in a third person by some particular protein, unless caused by the lack of some protein, his very comprehensive formulation is not subject to experimental test. About all that can be done with such a formulation, whether in psychology, medicine, astrology, economics, or any other department of human activity is to let it alone and see that it does not intrude upon more promising hypotheses.

The multiplicity of causes put forward by certain psychoanalysts for a single outcome nearly precludes the subjection of their claims to scientific inquiry. If it is claimed that one performance is consequent to one certain capacity, the matter may be readily tested. Even if the performance is a compound of two capacities, check-up is possible. As the number of possible causes increases to three, four, or more, the possibility of check-up rapidly vanishes, and science goes through pseudo-science to speculation or to charlatanry. The trouble is not primarily in postulating several contributing causes but in doing this antecedent to the development of a method of proof. In any true science the formulation and the means of at least partial verification, generally by noting necessary objective consequences, run hand in hand.

Thus, in the field of psychology, if a designation of some trait or capacity, as a category of mental life, is to be given serious consideration, it must be such as to reveal itself as a measurable difference in conduct, that is, as a measurable difference in the same individual at different times, or in different individuals at the same time. Does a trait like introversion meet these conditions? The number of different verbal statements of the meaning to be attached to this term falls but a little short of the number of people using it in writing. Many of these meanings are so subjective as to lead one to doubt whether differences of conduct can be related to them. No method of verification can be hoped for or in fact desired that will investigate the reality of so indefinite a concept. If one or more of the users of the term state that they mean thereby high scoring on a designated test which is definite, administered in a standardized manner, and which yields an objective score, then, and practically only then, can the matter be subjected to test.

This demand that a concept be subjected to objective measurement before it is worthy of serious consideration as an independent category of mental life, though sweeping, is not too sweeping, if we limit objective measurements to such as are definable and verifiable. How about the large class of concepts which are definable only in a rough way and verifiable only in part? Suppose we define "honesty" in the following manner: "It is a trait possessed in varying amounts by school children and recognized by teachers, with the result that when teachers rank their pupils on the basis of honesty, a measure of the trait is obtained." Let us first note that in this statement no precise distinction has been made between honesty itself and the measure of it. To determine whether such a lack of distinction is justified we should attempt to verify the measure. If a second equally trustworthy teacher having equal familiarity with certain pupils gives a rank order which is the same as a first teacher's, and if a third teacher, a fourth teacher, etc., all do the same, then the measure is verified and there is no need of distinction between the trait and the measure of it. Such a situation would arise in practice if height instead of honesty were the trait in question. We say, "John is four feet eight inches tall," and do not quibble over the fact that "four feet eight inches" is merely some person's measurement of John. If there is complete agreement the measurement is the trait for all practical purposes. In the case of honesty there would be no complete agreement but partial agreement only. Does such a measure provide a basis for scientific investigation? It seems to the writer that it does, provided (1) the degree of agreement of a measure in hand with a second equally trustworthy measure is known, (2) the technique adopted takes the unreliability of the measure into account and allows for it so that no systematic error is introduced, and (3) the technique adopted guards, by drawing tentative conclusions where necessary, against any chance error which may be introduced due to this unreliability of the measure.

These are necessary qualifications, but when these precautions are taken it would seem that objective measures in the sense earlier insisted upon may be derived from sources no more specific than the judgments of acquaintances. Though this is true, it is surely the part of wisdom to utilize performance records which are independent, or nearly independent, of human judgments whenever possible and when dealing with the more far-reaching issues.

Some very suggestive studies of mental capacity based upon judgments have been made. . . . After exercising all possible care there remain ambiguities in the interpretation of judgment measures. Should ten, twenty, or even one hundred acquaintances give judgments, which, pooled, characterize a person as one standard deviation above the average for his age, in honesty, still no one knows just what is meant by them, and probably never can know, for he has no way of discovering how his independent concept agrees or disagrees with the average concept of these judges. On the other hand, if honesty is defined as a trait tending toward higher scores on a designated test, when administered and scored as directed, then any particular student can study the relationships of this "honesty," even though he might individually misinterpret the purport of the test question.

A few years ago Garnett made an analysis of Webb's study based upon judgments, and concluded that there is a mental factor "cleverness." Certainly to understand this, "cleverness" is to be interpreted as by Garnett, but this we can only approximate. And further, Garnett deduced his "cleverness" from "quickness," "profoundness," "common sense," "originality," etc. (of 48 mental traits investigated, 43 came from judgments), which were traits appraised by Webb's judges. The meaning of these traits is certainly to be interpreted as by the average of Webb's judges, but as to these meanings both we and Garnett can secure only rough approximations, so that our final belief in "cleverness" as a factor must be most uncertain. Still more serious is the fact that it is incapable of verification, for we cannot duplicate by reproduction of the investigation, step by step, our own interpretation of Garnett's interpretation of Webb's judges' interpretation of the traits of the unknown subjects. All these difficulties except the last—differences in supposedly similar populations—are avoided when a trait is defined in terms of an objective measure which is capable of being duplicated and thus verified.

Definition and reproducibility are essential characteristics of the psychological data to be dealt with. Having data with these characteristics, and having purposes as unified as is the case with investigators, there is provided a situation which is amenable to a single type of analysis. The avowed purposes of psychologists sound quite different, but this need not deter us from approaching all investigations with a single comparative technique, because there is a fundamental underlying unity in these purposes. The determination of some difference is the object of every psychological formulation. For convenience these differences may be characterized as of three types, or of some composite of the three. Thus the difference may be chiefly affected by a change in time, as in the case of growth and fatigue, chiefly affected by spatial consideration, as are all of our sensory and motor functions, or chiefly related to differences in type of central nervous activity, as are the emotions and the several intellectual modes of thought, reasoning, memorizing, etc.

The technique of Spearman based upon tetrad differences for determining the discreteness of mental phenomena, and that used by the writer, involving much of Spearman's technique but also a considerable extension of it, is entirely adequate to determine whether two things, say a set of visual and a set of auditory measures, are basically the same or different. The case cited is so simple that its solution seems obvious. Much simpler devices than tetrad differences are available here, as perhaps in the case of all differences affected by spatial considerations, which enable one to establish that the auditory and visual phenomena are disparate. It would be ridiculous to measure both the visual and the auditory acuity of a large number of people, measure still other traits, and then calculate a lot of tetrad differences to see if they would warrant the conclusion that visual and auditory acuities are different things. Also, dealing with a single individual, it would be absurd to measure the sensitivity to light, to sound, to heat, etc., of different areas of the body surface, calculate tetrad differences and conclude that visual and the other sensitivities are not the same. However, this could be done, and by this technique each measurable sensory and motor trait of mankind that does stand alone could be so proved. We thus see that the technique in question is much broader in its applicability than one might judge from the field to which it has been applied. However ponderous the tetrad-difference method is in the case of these sensory and motor traits, it seems to be the only way, other than that of introspection, available in connection with purely mental phenomena. Apparently the reason is that the usual concomitants of sensory and motor traits, namely, space and time, are not conditions of mental life. One's reasoning power has not been localized in any particular end organ, and it is approximately timeless, operating with equal facility yesterday, today, and tomorrow. Mental phenomena are not entirely devoid of temporal characteristics, as will be discussed at greater length in connection with growth, but in so far as they are independent of it they are not amenable to study by the simple procedures which suffice with sensory and motor traits.

We may characterize the entire realm of psychological thought by saying that it is concerned (a) with differentiating between traits, or more broadly, though without a change in meaning, with studying the relationship between traits; (b) with determining changes in single traits (growth, fatigue) as time changes; and (c) with modification as locus (end-organ) changes. From a different point of view, the first of these is to be recognized as a study of individual differences. Of these three problems of difference, we are here concerned only with the first, for a trait must be determined as independent before it is very useful to attempt to determine its growth, if it does grow, or its locale, if it has one. Further, as to differentiating between traits we are here concerned only with those the independent status of which is open to question—memory, analysis, persistence, etc., but not visual acuity, righthand grip, etc.

* * *

We have noted that mental traits which we wish to study with a view to differentiating between them are of the class not readily localized in space and time. Even so the field is very extensive and includes what are commonly called the higher mental processes. Our problem is difficult because of the complexity of these processes and because of their number, for they cannot be studied singly. A single mental trait can be studied with reference to growth without any attention to other traits, but obviously when the issue is the difference between traits, it must be studied in conjunction with other traits.

It is here argued that such an approach should logically precede all detailed studies of a trait. Professor Spearman argues that "perseveration," as measured by G. E. Müller, is the same as "introversion," as proposed by Jung. Surely so vital an issue as this could well be made a matter of first importance, even if the investigator is studying merely the one or the other trait, and not primarily trying to see things in proper perspective. If this latter is the object, then not only should introversion and perseveration be studied together, but also along with many other traits, of which some will probably be related to these two and some will be entirely independent. A comprehensive study of this last sort has never been made. The experimental work of the present volume has dealt jointly with general ability (probably, in the main, maturity), manipulation of spatial relationships, facility with numbers, facility with verbal material, memory, mental speed, and certain other less clearly defined traits. Professor Spearman and his students have studied these same abilities, except facility with verbal material as here defined, and other traits, but his studies have not been of all the traits at once. Generally speaking they have been investigations of the independence of each of the traits singly, from Spearman's general factor "g." These studies have been most fruitful in indicating real differences between certain traits and certain g's (the writer does not quite subscribe to the view that the thing called "g" in all of these investigations is the same throughout), and in suggesting differences between these; but the much-needed comprehensive examination of relationships between many differently labeled, derived, measured, and variously sponsored mental traits is still to be made. Certainly such an investigation should take into consideration the following factors: (a) maturity; (b) sex; (c) race; (d) manipulation of spatial relationships in so far as independent of differences in visual acuity, etc.; (e) manipulation of auditory relationships in so far as independent of auditory acuity, etc.; (f) verbal facility; (g) number facility; (h) memory—one or more kinds; (i) mental speed; (j) one or more traits involving general motor organization and skill; (k) purpose or purposes; (l) ebullience or cleverness; (m) perseveration or intro-extraversion; (n) oscillation or variability in performance; (o) one or more traits connected with social interest and activities; (p) any remaining general factor not included in the preceding. The only adequate attack is to study all of these at once upon the same population, as otherwise certain relationships, perhaps of great importance, will be missed. Owing to previous work, mainly that of Spearman, the list as drawn up is very select and very promising for future study. The writer believes that the techniques herein employed are adequate for such a study and rather more comprehensive than those of Spearman, in spite of the fact that Spearman's have already yielded rich return.

In the study of independent mental capacities, Spearman has in the past utilized quite a number of different criteria. Though he claims that these early criteria are sound, because in harmony with results based upon what he now considers his final technique, there is considerable room for argument. If Technique B is sound and leads to a certain conclusion, then it does not follow that Technique A is sound because in some given instance it leads to the same conclusion. We are, however, not concerned at this time with Spearman's earlier techniques. His last one, for which he claims finality and universality, must be carefully scrutinized.

It is readily shown that if four variables have one, and only one, common factor running through them (in, the writer would add, a linear manner) then every tetrad difference involving the correlation coefficients of these four variables will be equal to zero. In the notation of this text, tetrad differences are denoted by the letter t with appropriate subscripts, and are defined as follows:

$$\left.\begin{array}{l} t_{1\,2\,3\,4} = r_{12}r_{34} - r_{13}r_{24} \\ t_{1\,2\,4\,3} = r_{12}r_{34} - r_{14}r_{23} \\ t_{1\,3\,4\,2} = r_{13}r_{24} - r_{14}r_{23} \end{array}\right\} \dots\dots\dots\dots\dots[1]$$

The equality of these tetrads to zero in the case when one general factor is sufficient was first pointed out by Spearman. It is very easily proved in a number of ways.

If there are more than four variables, if one general factor only runs through the variables, and if they contain no group factor, i.e., a factor found in a number of the variables but not all of them, then every tetrad will equal zero. The converse of this is also readily proved, namely, if every tetrad does equal zero, then the variables may be thought of as having one general factor and no group factors. With this as a starting-point Spearman argues that if the distribution of obtained tetrad differences shows a variability no greater than would be expected as a matter of chance, then one and only one factor, other than factors specific to the separate variables, may be looked for in the several measures. To carry this argument into effect the distribution of tetrads must be made (based on all the possible tetrads resulting from the variables employed), and its standard deviation must be calculated and compared with the theoretical standard deviation in case all tetrads deviate from zero merely as a matter of chance. This line of reasoning and the execution of it must be examined very critically, for it constitutes Spearman's major technique and, according to him, the only technique which is adequate. First as to the execution of it: The formula which Spearman and Holzinger have derived for the standard deviation of the distribution of a population of tetrad differences is

$$\sigma = 2 \left\{ \frac{r^2(1-r)^2 + (1-R)s^2}{N} \right\}^{\frac{1}{2}} \dots \dots \dots [2]$$

wherein r is the mean of all the r's and s^2 is their variance, and

$$R = 3r\frac{n-4}{n-2} - 2r^2\frac{n-6}{n-2}$$

In these equations n is the number of variables and N is the size of the population.

The writer has criticized the earlier formula, now replaced by this one, and of the use of this later formula Spearman writes: ". . . . although on some theoretical points still awaiting further elucidation, in practice at any rate [it] appears to be far more convenient, and even more reliable than [Spearman and Holzinger's formulas giving the probable errors of single tetrads]." The proof of this very critical Formula 2 has not as yet appeared in print.

Formula 2 may be called not merely a critical formula, but *the* critical formula. Professor Spearman states: ". . . . whenever the tetrad equation holds throughout any table of correlations, and *only* when it does so, then every individual measurement of every ability can be divided into two independent parts . . . . [a general and a specific factor]." Formula 2 is the final criterion that Spearman uses to determine if the tetrads throughout the entire table are merely chance deviations from zero. He writes: "To begin with, a note of warning must be sounded against all attempts to replace the rigorously demonstrated criterion by anything else. Many writers have tried to invent a new one for themselves; others have declared that so many are in the field as to produce a difficulty in choosing between them. Against this, we must formally declare that no other rigorous criterion than that demonstrated here (including mere equivalent conversions of it) has ever been proved *or ever can be*." Professor Spearman is presumably referring to the tetrad difference formula, $r_{12}r_{34} - r_{13}r_{24} = $ O, but we must note that the crux of the matter is not in the proposition that all tetrad differences equal zero, but in the standard errors of their actual values, which deviate by chance or otherwise from zero. According to Spearman's method this leads back to Formula 2. Clearly it is the basic formula in the entire treatment. If we grant that Formula 2 is correct, we may still question the use made of it, for Spearman assumes that chance would yield a normal distribution of tetrad differences with this standard deviation. This assumption of a normal distribution, even in situations where one general factor only is present does not seem reasonable, for the chance errors in the correlation coefficients are known to be correlated, so that we may expect the chance errors in the tetrads also to be correlated, and to an appreciable extent, for they are only functions of four correlation coefficients and the products of correlation coefficients in pairs are repeated many times in the total population of tetrad differences. This would yield a non-normal distribution, of just what form the writer does not know. The obvious way of using the chance standard deviation of a population of tetrad differences would be to compare it with the obtained standard deviation, find the difference between the two, and the standard error of this difference. This standard error, which will certainly be very small, is not known, and it probably cannot be determined by any means sufficiently simple to be serviceable. Should one object to this proposed method of interpretation on grounds similar to those just raised, namely, that the distribution of differences between these two standard deviations will not be normal and thus not readily interpretable, it can be shown that the point, though not without foundation, is much less material here than in the former case.

How material this particular criticism of Spearman's use of Formula 2 is, is not known. It may be quite trivial. A more important criticism from the writer's point of view is the fact that the situations in which one is really interested are not those to which it can usefully be applied. According to Spearman's latest conclusions there are no less than three general cognitive factors—g, oscillation, and perseveration—and a much larger number of group factors, including memory, a spatial factor, a conjunction factor (probably identical with what the present writer calls a number factor), a music factor, etc., as well as "conative" factors. All that Spearman's criterion could tell us would be that one factor was or was not sufficient to explain a given situation. All of the writer's data do show, and he ventures to prophesy that all of the forthcoming as well as much of the earlier data from Spearman's laboratory will show, the need for more than a single factor; thus Spearman's tool proves inadequate. We are no longer concerned with the first step, "Does one factor suffice?" but with the later steps, "How many and what factors suffice?" The writer presents herein the complete solution of the adequacy of two factors in the case of variables up to the number five, but he has found even this to be inadequate, for there are found in his data more than two general or group factors. Finally, the writer presents an iteration method for handling the problem when more factors and more variables are present. This method seems to be a powerful analytical device. It calls, however, for a wider use and more detailed mathematical scrutiny than it has as yet received. As to the needed mathematical scrutiny, it can, in brief, be said that the writer has been using an iteration method and obtaining a convergency in a series without having first proved that convergency is a mathematical necessity.

The fundamental technique of Spearman has been supplemented by him by a partial correlation procedure. When he has found that one independent factor was insufficient, he has partialed out g and by a study of the residual correlations has found additional factors. This procedure depends upon the ability to obtain a measure of g uncontaminated by other factors. The difficulty of doing this is great, because of the special hazards involved in partialing out just what is needed and no more when dealing with measures having large chance elements in them, and perhaps also having disconcerting specific and group factors in them. The writer has not attempted to follow carefully all of this partial correlation treatment, because Spearman's populations have been very small, the partial correlations very small, and the resulting probable errors very large and, most unfortunately, unknown. He would, however, express the belief that in spite of these special hazards the method has much to commend it.

Though certain shortcomings in the tools used by Spearman have been pointed out, nevertheless the writer believes that on the whole he has used them with rare judgment and has determined the existence of many important mental factors. In short, as Spearman's technique and point of view with reference to the significance of differences seems too rigorous, or, in other words, unfavorable to the discovery of factors in addition to g, we may place rather special confidence in the reality of such special factors as he does report. The very thorough review of these to be found in his *Abilities of Man* (1927) makes it unnecessary to give more than a brief discussion of them here. Professor Spearman clearly distinguishes cognitive, conative, and affective traits, as well as various other traits, for example, retentivity and fatigue. It does not seem to the writer that he has established by his own method of tetrad differences the independence of these things. We will therefore, even at the risk of not doing full justice to his view, make no attempt to preserve his classification of traits and capacities. We will list those that he has found disparate, but we should bear in mind that in the main, by his technique, differences of each from g are established rather than complete difference of each from each other.

First in this list is Spearman's g. As measures of it, which involve nothing else except specific factors, are the "usual sets of mental tests." The number of specific tests which could here be mentioned is very great, including in addition to many others, opposites, synonyms, classification, completion, questions, analogies, paragraphs, meanings, memory, abstract thought, accuracy, inferences and likelihood. Owing to the universality of g, Spearman states that "any test will do just as well as any other, provided only that its correlation with g is equally high." The saturation of measures with g is not markedly affected by any differences in the fields of cognition. Again, "g proved to be a factor which enters into the measurements of ability of all kinds, and which is throughout constant for any individual, although varying greatly for different individuals. It showed itself to be involved invariably and exclusively in all operations of eductive nature, whatever might be the class of relation or the sort of fundaments at issue. It was found to be equally concerned with each of two general dimensions of ability, Clearness and Speed. It also applied in similar manner to both the dimensions of span, which are Intensity and Extensity. But it revealed a surprisingly complete independence of all manifestations of Retentivity. Whether there is any advantage in attaching to this g the old mishandled label of 'intelligence' seems at least dubious." In brief, Spearman's concept is that g is the ability to deduce relations and correlates, and is dependent upon a central fund of energy.

The experimental results reported in later chapters hardly support this concept, because there seem to be two, and perhaps three, traits combined in this one concept. First, there is a factor making for correlation between variables due to maturity, race, sex differences, and differences of antecedent nurture. That these things would strongly tend to introduce a general factor is shown in this book, and that Spearman pays far too little attention to them is very obvious to one going over the various experimental investigations that have been made in his laboratory and under his direction. In fact, he writes, "Also worthy of mention, though hardly of prolonged examination, is the taking of g to have reference only to children, being in fact no more than a measurement of their maturity. One child does better at the tests than another of the same age, it is said, only because of being more precocious." Though this statement implies the comparison of children of the same age, Spearman's groups typically have not been children of the same age, and he has not resorted to a partial correlation technique to reduce his data to a constant age basis. Certainly race and nurture have not been partialed out, and only very occasionally has sex been experimentally treated as a separate factor. It is regrettable that this very fundamental matter of maturity has not been thought worthy of prolonged examination. On *a priori* grounds why should one consider it of less significance in connection with intellect than with bodily structure?

The second factor which the writer finds clearly indicated in his own data, and which is undoubtedly present in the tests measuring g, is a verbal factor, for the tests that Spearman regularly uses as the better measures of g are very similar to those in which the writer has found a large verbal factor. One might say that this is merely quibbling over terms, and that what the present writer means by a verbal factor is what Spearman means by g. This does describe the situation in part, though the writer finds that the verbal factor is more limited in its scope than the statements of Spearman would indicate his g to be. It is nevertheless probably true that fully one-half of Spearman's g is represented by what is here called a verbal factor.

* * *

Finally, there may be a third factor—not variability, in maturity, in sex, in race, in nurture; and not verbal—present in Spearman's g. The writer believes that if such a residual factor remains, after an allowance for the things mentioned, it is very small. A general factor, not verbal, is found by the writer throughout his work, but as he has not allowed for sex, race, or nurture, and probably not adequately for maturity, it is truly an open question whether any g factor at all would exist if these things had been properly taken into account.

The data which most adequately take into account maturity and sex are the Army Alpha data quoted very disparagingly by Spearman. As to the facts we can all agree that a single general factor is not indicated. As to the cause, Spearman writes that by the procedure followed, "the subjects, and still more so the testing, must have become heterogeneous to the last degree." Knowing something of the care with which this testing work was done, the writer does not believe the second of these charges is justified. As to the first charge, it is true that the group was rather heterogeneous, but this fact would introduce a g factor, not take out one already there. In brief, these data, almost unique in that they allow for maturity and sex, for the group consisted of adult men, do not yield a comprehensive g factor.

The relationship pictured by Spearman between education and g is stated in the following words: "On the whole, the most reasonable conclusion for the present appears to be that education has a dominant influence upon individual differences in respect of s (specific factors), but normally it has little if any in respect of g." The writer has shown in an earlier study that there is a great community of function between general intelligence and general scholastic achievement. If Spearman is correct in his statement, then general scholastic achievement is of necessity little affected by education. Though this may be so to an extent not ordinarily suspected, at least in certain respects it has been found by the writer not to be the case. . . .

From Spearman's great dependence upon a central fund of intellective energy as a highly important category of mental life to a view wherein no general factor exists is indeed a far step, but one quite within the realm of possibility, judging by all the data at hand.

The nurture element earlier mentioned as a source of a general factor would be a general nurture, i.e., a tendency of the environment to stimulate or repress all intellectual development. Over and above this there may be a nurture operating on particular phases only of intellectual life, for example, an environment tending to stimulate or repress number ability. In either case there is no way, except by studying different age groups, to differentiate between native and acquired traits. Accordingly, with reference to the group traits found, we must, while noting Spearman's findings, be content to be concerned with the question of their existence rather than of the original or acquired nature of their origins.

A trait designated "perseveration" is considered by Spearman to be a universal factor. It is an expression of his fundamental "law of inertia." The sensory tests (speed of rotation of a color disk to cause fusion; seconds needed for adaptation to darkness) employed by Wiersma showed rather systematic differences in the case of 11 maniacs, 9 normals, and 18 melancholics. Heymans and Brugmans with these same tests and with others obtained, in the case of 15 normal subjects, such low correlations that no very likely conclusion is indicated from their data. Next, Wynn Jones tested "77 children about 12 years of age" with tests, all of which involve motor activity and habits. The attempt was made to eliminate the motor factor by employing other motor tests not involving "perseveration," but this should surely be called unsuccessful, because the inter-correlations were very low, averaging .09, which we may expect to have been due largely to the unreliability of the tests. Spearman writes, "nothing of this diminutive size could possibly account for—or even by being eliminated sensibly diminish—the correlations shown in the foregoing table." This is true but altogether insufficient, as the author of the correction for attenuation should know, for one cannot partial out a motor factor by partialing out the scores on motor tests of very low reliability. Finally, there is the study of Lankes involving 47 students in the Islington Day Training College (ages and sex not indicated). His array of tests is quite extensive, but his inter-correlations are so low, running from $-.05$ to .51, and averaging .22, and his population so small, that probable errors are very large. The data are hardly servicable in proving the existence of a perseveration factor. From the Wiersma, Heymans and Brugmans, Jones, and Lankes data, Spearman not only deduces a "perseveration" factor, but he defines many of its characteristics. These data are surely a feeble foundation for so imposing a superstructure. The writer believes that factors other than g are indicated by these data, but that it is hazardous to say more than this.

A trait called "oscillation" is presented as a third universal cognitive factor. Its experimental foundation is perhaps a trifle more adequate than in the case of "perseveration," for the largest population studied consisted of "about 80 children aged about 12 years." Here the inter-correlations ranged from .00 to .44, with an average of .21. Somewhat more adequate intelligence measures were available for this group.

One further general factor, this time connected with the field of conation, is considered to be present. This is Webb's "persistence of motives," and Garnett's "purpose" factor. The difficulty of establishing this is greatly increased by the fact that it is deduced from personal judgments and not from objective test scores. However, the population was large, "200 students with an average age of 21 years," and the evidence quite clear-cut that there is more than one factor present—the factors being g and "persistence of motives" according to Webb, and g, "purpose," and "cleverness" according to Garnett. A thing much to be hoped for is the measurement of these factors in a more objective manner, and a more exact establishment of their place in mental life.

Let us now note briefly other factors which Spearman calls group factors, because he considers them of less universality than the general factors. There has been no criterion established justifying, say "perseveration" as a general factor, and "memory" as a group factor. In either instance, and also in the case of g, the evidence of the generality of the factor depends upon the measures employed in the investigation. With reference to a designated set of measurements through all of which runs a certain factor *A,* through several of which runs a factor *B,* and in one of which is a factor *C,* the writer sees a value in the terms general, group, and specific; but this value is only in the descriptive power of these terms for the particular situation which is being investigated. Given other tests, the *A* factor might become specific, the *B* factor become general, and the *C* factor become a group factor. To determine factors which are not thus dependent upon a particular set of tests, it is necessary to utilize many measures at once, thus making a very exhaustive survey of the mental ability of the subjects tested. In noting factors reported by Spearman additional to those already mentioned we will not draw a distinction between general and group factors.

There is a memory factor certainly extending to different sensory fields and to verbal material.

One of Spearman's "ideal" relations is "conjunction," and he finds a factor of this nature. The writer prefers to call it a "numbers" or "arithmetical" factor as being more descriptive of the content and nature of the tests revealing it.

There is a constructive mechanical ability factor which may be related to that characterized by the writer as "manipulation of spatial relationships."

Dealing with this trait, McFarlane reports that the factor is found in the case of boys and not in that of girls. Certain other evidence of sex differences is cited, but no extensive treatment of sex as a factor in mental life is undertaken by Spearman. . . .

The reader must not conclude because of the criticisms that have been made of Spearman's technique and interpretation that there is wide disagreement between his findings and those of the present writer. On the whole the two sets of findings are quite remarkably in harmony, the agreements being in the matter of a spatial, a numerical, a memory, and even a general factor, though this last is differently interpreted, and also in the conclusion that a large number of specific motor (probably also sensory) factors exist. There is scarcely a disagreement in the matters of music, purpose, cleverness, and sex, though here the data are inadequate. There does seem to be a real disagreement in the importance and extent of a verbal factor and in that of a mental speed factor.

*   *   *

It is admitted that the treatment of the present chapter and related treatments by the writer are an inadequate discussion of psychological points of view, varied both as to phenomena dealt with and methods employed. They may, however, suffice to emphasize the variety of mental activity of which man is master and to outline a picture of mental life which future study will fill in. In brief, the boundaries of mental traits are ruts, not far-flung indefinite fringes of consciousness. Mental life does not operate in a plain but in a network of canals. Though each canal may have indefinite limits in length and depth, it does not in width; though each mental trait may grow and become more and more subtle, it does not lose its character and discreteness from other traits.

The differentiation of kinds of intelligence measures became progressively clearer as researchers explored the relations of intelligence to other variables. Here Hollingworth shows differential changes in intellectual subtests with increasing age in an adult population.

Changes in Mental Capacity after Maturity*

H. L. HOLLINGWORTH

1928

Very few experimental data or measures are available on the mental changes after the period of early maturity. For one thing, it has been difficult to assemble unselected cases of middle age or senescence, for such examinations as experiments of this type require. The writer once had occasion to examine 534 adults, ranging in age from below twenty years to forty-five years. In the following table the scores for these men are given in age groups, there being thus about 100 men in each age level.

TABLE I

Changes with Age, after Maturity (Hollingworth)

Age level	Completion	Naming opposites	Word building	Digit span	Substitution
Below 20 years	31	12	10	6.0	68
20 to 25 years	32	12	10	5.5	64
25 to 30 years	32	11	9	6.0	60
30 to 35 years	32	12	10	6.0	58
35 to 45 years	34	12	12	6.0	57

The scores in Digit Span, Word Building, Naming Opposites, and Completion, do not change with age. But ability in the Substitution test falls off regularly with increasing age. The fall from a score of sixty-eight at age twenty to fifty-seven at forty years or thereabouts, is very significant. This is a loss of eleven points, and is equivalent, in terms of mental age, to a fall from an age of sixteen to that of eleven years, from a postadolescent to a preadolescent ability.

The Substitution test is the only one of these that calls for the establishment and exercise of new associations. The remaining tests involve es-

---

* Taken from pages 310-314 in the Chapter "Senility" in Hollingworth's book, *Mental Growth and Decline* (New York, D. Appleton and Company, 1928). Reprinted by permission of Appleton-Century-Crofts, Inc.

sentially the quick and ready use of bonds already established, or the ordinary mental efforts of attention and intelligent observation. And these records go only up to the age of forty-five years, before the changes commonly associated with senescence appear. The results seem to confirm the statement of Paton that "generally speaking, the acquisition of new facts

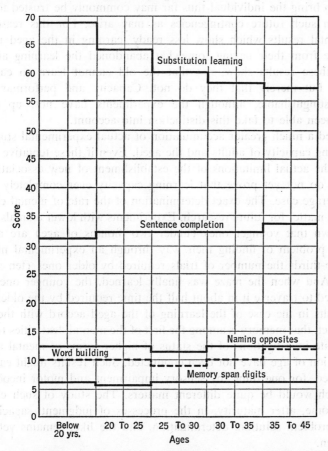

Figure 1. SHOWING CHANGES IN ABILITY TO DO VARIOUS KINDS OF MENTAL WORK, WITH INCREASING AGE. The higher the score, the greater the efficiency. Ability in Substitution Learning declines with age, while the other processes remain unchanged, or else slightly improve.

and intellectual expansion in the individual do not continue after the fiftieth year." At least our results suggest that such acquisitions will proceed with greater difficulty. We may suppose that actual changes in brain organization underlie this specific loss in capacity for ready learning. In general the fact seems to be that with increasing age, after maturity, learning capacity declines while general alertness and ability to utilize facts already acquired are still at their maximum.

It is however to be recognized that adults, and especially the aged, are little called upon to make new adjustments, or are temperamentally indisposed to do so. For one thing, the learning of new things commonly implies a forward-looking interest which is less characteristic of age than of youth. Again, the established habits and accumulated knowledge which have sufficed to bring the individual thus far may commonly be trusted to serve as well in such future contingencies as may arise. For this reason the experimental results which show less ready learning in the aged may in part come from their having somewhat abandoned the learning attitude. Perhaps these results show, not that the old cannot learn so easily as formerly, but merely that they do not. Capacity and performance are surely distinguishable, although the experiments have not, up to the present, been able to take this distinction into account.

We need a much greater accumulation of actual experimental studies of the learning capacity of adults and the aged. Even if these tentative results point to the actual limitations of the establishment of new associations in age, they do not yet prove that learning capacity ever completely ceases in the average case. The exact determination of the rate of mental changes in age is a matter for future research. Experiments with lower animals (rats) have shown that younger ones (under two months of age) are able to learn the problem of finding their way through an experimental maze in about two-thirds the number of trials required by older ones (ten months in age). And when the maze was finally learned, the younger ones were accustomed to traverse it in about half the time required by the older ones. Such results in the case of the learning of the aged accord with the other general fact, that memory is among the first of the mental dexterities to fail.*

Adequate investigations of the status of higher forms of mental activity as a function of age have not been conducted. Such results might easily be complicated, for one thing, by sensory impairment and motor incoördination, which would be quite different matters. The study of such changes as may come, after maturity, in the processes of judgment, sagacity, inference, problem solution, determination, and the like, remains yet to be undertaken.

* One of my former students, in 1924, measured a small group of old people ranging from sixty-three to eighty-three years of age. "The old groups equals the army men on Knox Cube Test and Memory Span for digits. There is a decline on the Porteous Maze Test, a very marked decline on the Substitution Test and complete failure on the Paired Associates Test." (From Helen Werner, unpublished master's essay, Department of Psychology, Columbia University, 1924.)

· This article is actually a critique of intelligence testing. Its somewhat misleading title stems from the fact that Brigham in 1923 published a comparison of national and racial groups in America based on the Army data from both group and individual testings converted to a "combined score." In his work with college entrance examinations, he came more and more to distrust results of heterogeneous tests combined to yield a single score. This paper in effect serves as a retraction of his earlier work.

Intelligence Tests of Immigrant Groups*

CARL C. BRIGHAM

1930

A number of articles and books have appeared reporting the results of the psychological examination of immigrants in the United States. In the present article, the general trend of the current studies will be summarized or interpreted without extensive citation of references. This summary may be regarded as in the editorial form, and is not a systematic review of the literature on the subject. The articles in question are practically all in the following form: the Blank test of intelligence was given to n children in x grades of a certain school system; the average test scores of children of nationality $A, B,$ and C were as follows. Our inquiry will disregard questions of sampling, methods of treating data, and the like, and will direct itself to the more fundamental problem of the meaning of test scores.

Psychologists have been attacked because of their use of the term 'intelligence,' and have been forced to retreat to the more restricted notion of *test score*. Their definition of intelligence must now be 'score in a test which we consider to measure intelligence.' The ordinary test includes several different types of sub-tests for which varying time allowances are made. Each test battery, or collection of sub-tests, is a closed system which may be studied in its own right, first by the method of correlation with independent criteria, and second by various internal criteria of reliability and self-consistency.

The diversion of psychologists from general debates on the question of the nature of intelligence to the more careful analysis of test scores has resulted in several important advances. The question immediately arises as to whether or not the test score itself represents a single unitary thing. This question is crucial, for if a test score is not a unitary thing it should not be given one name.

* *Psychological Review,* 37 (1930), pp. 158-165. Reprinted by permission of the American Psychological Association.

Professor Spearman of the University of London has for many years advocated the two factor theory of intelligence, which is to the effect that there is a general factor, 'g,' underlying performance in sub-tests of diverse sorts, and special factors, 's's,' unique to each type of sub-test. Two similar sub-tests within one test battery may give rise to a 'group factor' which is not g. Earlier discussions concerning the validity of this hypothesis revolved around a technical issue on the validity of a certain method of proof. Another method has more recently been advanced by Spearman, and this method has been elaborated by Professor Kelley of Stanford University. The present discussion in this field is no longer concerned so much with the validity of Spearman's theory as it is with the proper statement of the number of factors into which a test score may be resolved. The issues here are very involved, as it has been found that the correlations between sub-tests depend on time allowances, and on the difficulty and validity of single test items making up the sub-tests. Until some of the variables are more adequately controlled, no satisfactory answer will be found.

While these investigations are in progress and no guess can yet be made as to their probable outcome, there are many findings which effectively challenge certain interpretations of test results made in the past. For the sake of illustration, one may consider that an 'intelligence' test battery containing six sub-tests and an 'achievement' test battery also containing six sub-tests have been given to the same group of people. If one should regard this as one battery of tests, and should study all 66 of the possible bonds between pairs of sub-tests, one could hardly expect to find the dichotomy in the names of the two tests revealed in such an analysis of their nature. A safe procedure is to disregard what a psychologist calls his test, and to study the test itself as an instrument more or less adequate to its purpose. Most psychologists working in the test field have been guilty of a *naming fallacy* which easily enables them to slide mysteriously from the score in the test to the hypothetical faculty suggested by the name given to the test. Thus, they speak of sensory discrimination, perception, memory, intelligence, and the like while the reference is to a certain objective test situation.

A far-reaching result of the recent investigations has been the discovery that test scores may not represent unitary things. It seems apparent that psychologists in adding scores in the sub-tests in some test batteries have been doing something akin to adding apples and oranges. A case in point is the Army Alpha test.

All of the methods of analyzing the army test data were evolved from a statistical study of a special experimental group of 1047 cases. Spearman has analyzed the army test data and finds that they do not fit his hypothesis. His explanation follows:

"In the endeavour to procure fairly representative samples of the Army, the plan had been conceived of sending round to twelve different camps, asking each that the tests should be given to 'approximately 100 relatively unselected men.' Nine of the camps responded, their contributions of men ranging from under 20 to over 200. But by such a procedure the subjects, and still more the testing, must have become heterogeneous to the last degree. For instance, when in any camp the testing or marking happened to be more generous than in others with respect to any of these tests, then the men here would tend to shine in these particular tests; the result must be to generate additional correlation between these tests quite independently of any resemblance or psychological connection between them. And the cumulative result of such influences could scarcely fail to produce the highly irregular character that we actually find."

Kelley has criticized the above interpretation as follows:

"The data which most adequately take into account maturity and sex is the Army Alpha data quoted very disparagingly by Spearman. As to the facts we can all agree that a single general factor is not indicated. As to the cause, Spearman writes that by the procedure followed, 'the subjects, and still more so the testing, must have become heterogeneous to the last degree.' Knowing something of the care with which this testing work was done, the writer does not believe the second of these charges is justified. As to the first charge, it is true that the group was rather heterogeneous, but this fact would introduce a g factor, not take out one already there. In brief, these data, almost unique in that they allow for maturity and sex, for the group consisted of adult men, do not yield a comprehensive g factor."

There were eight tests in the Army Alpha battery as follows:

1. Directions
2. Arithmetical reasoning
3. Practical judgment
4. Synonym-antonym
5. Disarranged sentences
6. Number series
7. Analogies
8. Information

There are certain difficulties involved in the analysis of the army test data which have been summarized adequately by Kelley:

"The special study of the inter-correlations between the eight sub-tests of the Army Alpha Test, conducted by the Division of Psychology of the Surgeon General's Office, provides data upon a large population of American white English-speaking adults in nine different army camps. The special merits of these data are that they cover a large population, sex is constant, and maturity substantially constant. The defects are that racial homogeneity is not attained, the tests separately have low reliability, and a technique of treatment was followed which makes it impossible to calculate the probable errors of the correlation coefficients or of the tetrad differences. The number of cases examined was 1047, and it was found that the distribution of a number of sub-tests gave undistributed extreme scores, zero, or perfect scores. Accordingly, all correlations were corrected for these undistributed scores, to obtain estimates of the correlation maintaining if the tests had permitted lower or higher scoring as required. Though the writer sees no reason to believe that these very carefully made corrections either introduced or took out any general or group factors, still it is true that the corrections are of such magnitude that ordinary probable-error formulas may not be used for the determination of reliability."

Kelley has analyzed the army test data from the special experimental sample and has designated in words the probable nature of bonds found between pairs of tests. He finds what he calls a numerical factor common to tests 1 and 2, tests 1 and 6, and tests 2 and 6; a verbal factor common to tests 3 and 4, tests 3 and 8, and tests 4 and 8. He also notes a factor common to tests 5 and 7, and a factor common to tests 6 and 7.

The present writer has made a similar analysis introducing the Stanford-Binet examination as another test (called 9) in the series. This study shows the same bonds noted above with the addition of another bond (5-8) which Kelley might have included, and another possible bond (4-9) about the size of the 1-2 bond. Because of certain inadequacies in such studies arising from the defects of the original data, and the methods which it was necessary to use in calculating the coefficients of correlation between the sub-tests, it is, perhaps, not worth while to attempt a more systematic study of the data from the Army Alpha test. After puzzling over the situation longer than the data warrant, the writer offers the following not entirely satisfactory solution.

The assumption is made that people taking the Alpha test adopted two different attitudes or sets, viz., a 'directions attitude,'—an attitude of careful attention to the examiner's instructions without looking at the test questions while the directions were read; and a 'reading attitude,'—partially or completely ignoring the examiner's instructions while studying the test questions during the time in which the examiner was reading. The adoption of the first attitude would tend to give the individual higher scores in test 1 (entirely oral directions), test 6 (an unusual form of mathematical test), and in test 7 (a novel type of verbal test). On the other hand, a person adopting the second attitude might quickly find out what was required in tests 3, 4, 5, and 8, and his score would be better if he ignored what the examiner was reading and studied the test questions during the period of instruction. The adoption of this reading attitude, while tending to make scores higher in tests 3, 4, 5, and 8, might make for lower scores in tests 1, 6, and 7. The writer's analysis shows nothing inconsistent resulting from the combination of tests 1, 6, 7, and 9 (the Stanford Binet), nor from the combination of tests 3, 4, 5, and 8, while all of the sixteen possible bonds between the two groups of four tests are negative except 4-9 and 5-7. A fairly good case may therefore be made for the directions attitude in tests 1, 6, 7, and 9, and for the reading attitude in tests 3, 4, 5, and 8. There is also evidence of what might be guessed to be a mathematical factor in tests 1, 2, and 6, the directions attitude making for still higher scores in tests 1 and 6. The mathematical factor in tests 1, 2, and 6 is independent of the 3, 4, 5, and 8 complex, and all twelve cross bonds are negative here except 2-3 which is slightly positive. The only remaining positive bonds not accounted for appear between tests 5 and 7, and between tests 4 and 9.

The report of the army examiners shows that scores in different sections of the Alpha scale were derived from different tests. One may estimate, for example, that tests 4 and 7 would rarely enter into a total score around 30 points, while persons scoring at the upper end of the scale, as high as 190, would normally get 60 or 70 points from these two tests. At the various levels of scores, different sub-tests contribute to the total in varying amounts so that Alpha was not a consistent test even from this standpoint. This fact together with the facts previously noted which suggest disparate group factors within the test show that the eight tests of Army Alpha should not have been added to obtain a total score, or, if added, similar total scores should not have been taken to represent similar performances in the test.

If the Army Alpha test has thus been shown to be internally inconsistent to such a degree, then it is absurd to go beyond this point and combine Alpha, Beta, the Stanford-Binet and the individual performance tests in the so-called 'combined scale,' or to regard a combined scale score derived from one test or complex of tests as equivalent to that derived from another test or another complex of tests. As this method was used by the writer in his earlier analysis of the army tests as applied to samples of foreign born in the draft, that study with its entire hypothetical superstructure of racial differences collapses completely.

Kelley, in compiling a list of traits which he has found to be more or less independent of each other, enumerates:

"(1) Verbal intelligence, or the ability which in the main underlies facility in naming opposites, coördinates, subordinates, supraordinates, predicates; and found in tests of mixed relationships, practical judgments, vocabulary, written directions, sentence completion (textual matter of literary content), sentence meaning, paragraph meaning, word meaning, and logical selection.

"(2) Quantitative intelligence, or the ability in the main underlying facility in computation and other situations involving numbers as content.

"(3) Spatial intelligence, or the ability in the main underlying facility in handling form boards, geometrical forms, and right- and left-hand, Knox cube, and other similar tests." He states that verbal intelligence "can be determined by school achievement tests of the reading and vocabulary sorts and by general intelligence tests or such portions of them as are of a verbal nature and do not include numbers and spatial relations as content."

These findings of Kelley as to the probable existence of independent

Binet's teaching that intelligence is a psychological rather
than a physical affair has never served to discourage investigators who pursue the elusive goal of a physical measurement
which will predict intellectual status. In this paper Paterson
presents a brief review of such attempts and evaluates their
progress. A complete account of this work may be found in
his book Physique and Intellect. Interestingly, the state of the
field today is almost exactly as it was in 1930.

Intelligence and Physique*

DONALD G. PATERSON

1930

I. Introduction

Modern techniques in the measurement of mental development make
possible a new attack upon the age-old problem of the relation between
bodily and mental traits. This problem received attention long before anyone dreamed of measuring objectively either the growth of intellect or the
relation between this growth and specific physical characteristics. Indeed,
Aristotle is credited with having produced the first systematic treatise on
physiognomy wherein are described the physical signs and symptoms of
mental traits. Physiognomy, palmistry, and phrenology survive to this
day as pseudo-scientific, non-scientific, and even anti-scientific formulations
of the assumed dependence of personality upon physical development and
physical type.

The scientific approach to the problem busied itself with concrete,
quantitative studies of one or another physical character, always seeking
to relate each physical measurement to some criterion of mentality. At first
attention centered on the more obvious structural characteristics of the body
such as height, weight, and especially head diameters and proportions.
Measurements of these features were then brought in line with such
available evidences of mental ability as teachers' estimates and scholastic
standing. Of course in recent years these studies have more frequently
utilized standardized intelligence tests.

Toward the end of the first decade of the present century, a fascinating
field of research emerged, in which subtle aspects of physical status were
probed in an effort to find crucial indices of the physical traits that would be

* Adapted from Personality and Physique, Chapter III, in J. Arthur Harris, R. E.
Scammon, D. G. Paterson, and C. M. Jackson, *The Measurement of Man*, copyright
1930, University of Minnesota. Reprinted by permission of D. G. Paterson and the
University of Minnesota Press.

more intimately related to mental traits than those hitherto mentioned. The phenomena associated with the onset of puberty were seized upon as highly significant of physiological status, and it was hoped that these would afford a physical basis for mental classification. The discovery of the Roentgen rays opened up the possibility of measuring the progress of ossification of the skeletal bones, and straightway many experiments were undertaken to prove that these indices are of great importance in connection with normal mental development. Standards for interpreting the significance of the time of teeth eruption were also drawn up with the claim that dentition would be found to be associated with mental growth. Finally, efforts were made to develop a suitable index of body build in the belief that relative physical proportions would prove to be definitely related to mental efficiency and temperament.

Throughout the history of all these efforts to find a physical basis for mental traits, the hypothesis was maintained that mind is dependent upon or conditioned by physical growth and status. That is, if physical development be accelerated, then mental development would be facilitated, whereas if physical growth be delayed or impaired in any way, there would be a corresponding retardation or impairment in mental growth. Furthermore, there is a suggestion that these varied approaches were made under the influence of a conviction that some sort of unitary factor dominates all phases of growth; and hence the search always aimed to discover that single physical trait which would best reveal this guiding principle.

The foregoing statement sketches in broad outlines the problem before us. It remains to fill in details with sufficient refinement to indicate the present status of scientific knowledge on the subject. In a rough way, we propose to follow the chronological sequence of discovery, since, in fact, scientific knowledge emerges from the cumulative efforts of many workers, many of whom perforce must grope somewhat blindly.

II. Non-Scientific and Pseudo-Scientific Attacks on the Problem

1. POPULAR BELIEFS

Belief in the mental significance of particular physical features has long dominated the thoughts of mankind. The prevalence of such phrases as "long-headed" or "high brow" in popular speech testifies to the survival of physiognomic beliefs among persons many of whom may even be unaware that systematized treatises on physical characterology exist. It is worth noting that the phrase "long-headed" connotes primarily something psychological, such as shrewdness or farsightedness. It is difficult to recognize the metaphor and realize that the term literally describes the dolichocephalic head shape. Likewise, "high brow" now connotes superior intellect and learning, with scarcely any immediate physical reference to actual height of forehead.

Our playwrights and novelists are greatly aided in their attempts at character delineation by the existence of similar widespread beliefs. The villain must be a brunette, with shifty eye, and smooth, oily manner. The fickle coquette, of course, is most generally blond, small of stature, with the bloom of youth upon her cheek. The stooping miser inevitably possesses long, bony fingers. Herr Professor, in shiny frock coat, is round-shouldered, nearsighted, and somewhat anemic in appearance. The successful business man strides forth, alert and energetic, smooth shaven, hair graying at the temples. The vampire is the extreme brunette, with lustrous eyes half-concealed under purple lids. Of course, the jolly and carefree bachelor, who wins his way by means of wit and fun, simply must be somewhat rotund so that when he laughs he laughs all over. Then there is the sharp-tongued neighborhood gossip or busybody, thin to the point of emaciation, with long beak-like nose, and altogether plain and unprepossessing, if not down-right ugly. There is no end to these human stereotypes from Chaucer to Hollywood. Perhaps Shakespeare more than anyone else has set the stage: prodigious Falstaff; distrusted Cassius with "lean and hungry look"; Hamlet cloaked in black, slow in movement, saturnine in countenance; and a hundred others.

Analogical reasoning has contributed much to the establishment of belief in the essential unity of physical and mental qualities. By analogy, men possessing physical traits similar to certain animals are endowed with the behavior characteristics known to be possessed by those animals. The person with the bulldog jaw is assumed to be tenacious, persevering, and relentless in carrying out plans and purposes; or witness the hangdog look of the wrongdoer suddenly exposed; the sheepish look, the foxy face, the cow-like expression—each example brings emphasis to the point.

2. PHYSIOGNOMY, ANIMAL AND HUMAN

A long section of Lavater's four-volume work on physiognomy (second edition, published in 1804) is devoted to demonstrating that there is a science of animal physiognomy as well as human physiognomy. A few quotations selected here and there from the second volume will illustrate the extent to which analogical reasoning has run riot in this field. "If any one would endeavor to discover the signs of bravery in man, he would act wisely to collect all the signs of bravery in animated nature, by which courageous animals are distinguished from others." "It cannot be doubted but that the human head, here annexed, has something of the ox; though it appears to me rather to partake of the ox and lion, than the ox singly." "The skull of the ox expresses patience, resistance, difficulty of being moved, a great desire of feeding." "Whoever contemplates the middle line of the mouth of the living hyena, will there discover the character, the very index, of the most inexorable malignity." "As the characters of animals are distinct, so are their forms, bones, and outlines. From the smallest winged insect to the eagle that soars and gazes at the sun, from the weakest worm, impotently crawling beneath our feet to the elephant or the majestic lion, the gradations of physiognomical expression cannot be mistaken. . . . Were the lion and lamb, for the first time, placed before us, had we never known such animals, never heard their names, still we could not resist the impression of the courage and strength of the one, or of the weakness and sufferance of the other." "Each species of beast has, certainly, a peculiar character, as it has a peculiar form. May we not hence, by analogy, infer that predominant qualities of the mind are as certainly expressed by predominant forms of the body, as that the peculiar qualities of a species are expressed in the general form of that species?"

The argument from analogy is not restricted to the animal realm as may be seen from the following quotations from the same source. "May not souls also have a determinate capacity, proportionate to the form and organization of the body? (Water which takes the form of the vessel.)" "Large oranges have thick skins, and little juice. Heads of much bone and flesh have little brain. Large bones, with abundance of flesh and fat, are impediments to mind."

To men of science the absurdity of such physiognomic assertions is no less evident than is their quaint ingeniousness to the sophisticated and realistic layman of today. Certainly no obligation rests upon any of us to consider seriously their possible validity, based as they are upon opinion derived from unsystematic and casual observation with no shred of supporting quantitative evidence.

Modern physiognomic "doctors" (a flourishing profession even in the twentieth century) go far beyond Lavater to include characteristics such as blondness, voice quality, texture of skin, bodily build, posture, hardness or softness of muscles, gait, handshake, gestures, clothing, etc. Katherine Blackford, perhaps, holds first rank among modern exponents of physiognomy. Her system of character analysis is based upon nine fundamental physical variables: (1) color, (2) form, (3) size, (4) structure, (5) texture, (6) consistency, (7) proportion, (8) expression, and (9) condition.

We may gain a good idea of her system by selecting her exposition of the so-called law of color as illustrative. In describing blond versus brunette characteristics, she states: "In brief, always and everywhere, the normal blond has positive, dynamic, driving, aggressive, domineering, impatient, active, quick, hopeful, speculative, changeable, and variety-loving characteristics; while the normal brunette has negative, static, conservative, imitative, submissive, cautious, painstaking, patient, plodding, slow, deliberate, serious, thoughtful, specializing characteristics." Furthermore, Dr. Blackford assures us on the same page that her law of color is simple and straightforward. To quote: "In applying this law of color to people of the white race, the method is simple. The less the pigmentation in any individual, the more marked will be the characteristics of the blond in his physical, mental, and psychical nature; the greater the degree of pigmentation, the more marked the characteristics of the brunette."

It occurred to the writer that such positive assertions might well be put to a quantitative test and, in collaboration with Dr. Katherine E. Ludgate, an attempt at verification was undertaken. We held that if blonds as a group, always and everywhere, possess or exhibit traits that are positive, dynamic, driving, etc., then blonds individually should possess such traits. If such is the case, then at least a majority of blonds should be rated by intelligent, educated judges as being the possessors of those traits. Furthermore, a large majority of blonds should be rated as being deficient in the brunette traits. The opposite results should hold, of course, in securing ratings on brunettes.

Accordingly we prepared a rating sheet on which were listed the twenty-six traits in random order. Each of ninety-four judges was asked to select from among his acquaintances two pronounced blonds and two pronounced brunettes and to rate them with respect to the presence or absence of each trait or characteristic. In this way we secured ratings on 187 blonds and 187 brunettes.

The ratings for blonds and brunettes were tabulated separately and the percentage of blonds rated plus (+) in each trait and the percentage of brunettes rated plus (+) in each trait was then computed. A graphic representation of the facts is shown in Figure 1. It is obvious that these so-called blond and brunette traits fail to differentiate real flesh-and-blood blonds and brunettes. The percentage of brunettes possessing the blond traits is approximately as high as the percentage of blonds possessing blond traits. Likewise the percentage of blonds possessing brunette traits is also very similar to the percentage possessing brunette traits. Such a result is at complete variance with the result to be expected if Dr. Blackford's generalization were true.

The same experiment was repeated by Kenagy of the Carnegie Institute of Technology, who secured the cooperation of sales managers in some forty national organizations in rating 152 highly successful salesmen (82 blonds and 70 brunettes). The results are almost identical with our results, thus disposing of Blackford's claims with reference not only to the so-called law of color but incidentally also to her application of the method in the selection of salesmen.

One other attempt to verify experimentally one of Blackford's assertions may be mentioned in passing. Hull reports the work of one of his students (Alice L. Evans) on "convex" versus "concave" profiles. Blackford has

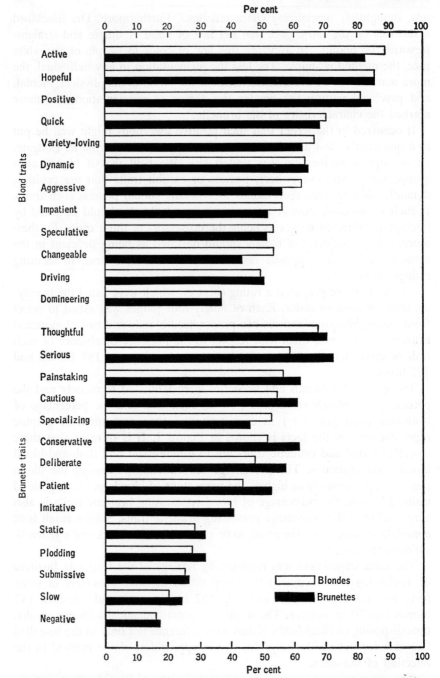

Figure 1. Bar diagram showing percentages of blonds and brunettes rated plus (+) in each of Blackford's so-called blond and brunette traits. (Paterson and Ludgate)

stated: "The significance of the pure convex type is energy, both mental and physical. Superabundance of energy makes the extreme convex keen, alert, quick, eager, aggressive, impatient, positive, and penetrating. . . . The pure concave, as might be expected, is the exact opposite. . . . The keynote of his character is *mildness*. . . . He is slow of thought, slow of action, patient in disposition, plodding." By means of an ingenious measuring device, Hull and Evans carefully measured the precise degree of convexity of the profiles of each of twenty-five members of a university sorority. Five different measurements of convexity were obtained. These measurements were then correlated with a series of character-trait ratings secured by having each sorority member rate the others. Character traits rated were optimism, activity, ambition, will power, domination, and popularity. With such a small number of subjects the resulting coefficients of correlation would naturally have very high probable errors and hence would fluctuate within rather wide limits. As a matter of fact the thirty coefficients ranged from $-.27$ to $+.39$, sixteen being negative and fourteen positive. The best indication of the real relationship between convexity of profile and these character traits would seem to be an average of the thirty coefficients. This, when computed, turns out to be $+.01$, a figure that is as close to zero as would be expected if chance alone were operating.

In her 1918 book, *Reading Character at Sight,* Blackford gives only one bit of quantitative evidence and this happens to bear upon the convex-concave profile. Asserting that the convex profile indicates quickness in seeing, thinking, deciding, and acting, she holds that, since taxicab drivers must possess just such mental traits, they must also possess convex profiles. It is reported that one of her students began classifying the profiles of taxicab drivers with the result that the great majority were actually found to possess the convex profile. However, later on in her book she set at naught the quantitative proof of her theory by inadvertently stating that the majority of the people in the United States have convex profiles. Thereby, she merely proved that, in respect to profile, taxicab drivers constitute a fair sampling of the American population. It is obvious that satisfactory scientific evidence would have required: (1) actual measurement of the degree of concavity or convexity of the profile of each taxicab driver; (2) actual measurement of the same feature for another group of men of similar age, schooling, race, and economic and social class, but engaged in work that does not involve such mental qualifications; and (3) demonstration of a statistically significant difference between the two groups in the measurements secured. Needless to say, no physiognomist adopts such laborious and tedious methods of proof.

Perhaps the most elaborate attempt to verify physiognomic claims is to be found in the work of Cleeton and Knight. One hundred and twenty-two physical measurements were considered in testing the hypothesis that judgment, intelligence, frankness, will power, ability to make friends, leadership, originality, and impulsiveness are revealed by various physical characteristics. Ratings of these character traits as exhibited by the thirty subjects employed in the experiment were secured from intimate associates and pooled in such a manner as to yield an unusually reliable index of those traits. These pooled ratings were then correlated with each of the physical measurements, with the net result that the average of 201 correlations between variations in physical traits and variations in character traits (presumed by character analysts to be closely related to the physical traits) is exactly zero. Here is a beautiful statistical refutation of the sweeping claims indulged in by devotees of physiognomy.

It is true that carefully controlled experiments have not yet been performed utilizing as working hypotheses all of the seductive assertions put forth by physiognomists. Such studies as have been made, however, yield monotonously negative results. Nevertheless, scientific caution compels us to admit the possibility of extracting a few kernels of truth from these pseudoscientific systems. Even a rigorous thinker like Kelley cautiously states of physiognomy: "None of these methods has established itself as having more than the faintest suggestion of validity. The writer finds it hard to believe that this will always be so and in truth expects that some day the analysis of mental ability and of emotional characteristics will be clearly furthered by quantitative and qualitative measures, facial contours, and expressions."

Woods, who is best known for his study of mental and moral heredity in the royal families of Europe, seems to have shown a positive correlation between size of nose and ability. He assembled photographs of both eminent and nondescript persons, and although dependent on estimates of nose length, he showed that a significant difference in respect to that characteristic obtains between superior and ordinary mortals, concluding, "The majority of great men have large or long noses, the remainder nearly always have noses of at least average size." It is possible, of course, that an accidental linkage in heredity between this particular physical characteristic and ability in some of the families in his sampling of eminent persons gave rise to the apparent significant correlation. That there is no necessary or inevitable relationship between size of nose and intelligence is shown by Sommerville in his study of the physical and mental characteristics of about one hundred Columbia University students. The correlations between various facial measurements and the Thorndike three-hour intelligence examination for high school seniors and college students hover around zero. The detailed results are shown in Table I. It is difficult to see how such slight relationships as are demonstrated by Sommerville can be interpreted in any other way than as tending to refute current physiognomic claims. Negative results emerging from actual measurements seem to throw doubt upon Wood's conclusions supported by less accurate methods.

The failure of physiognomical assertions to meet the test of actual measurements is beautifully illustrated in an incidental investigation undertaken by Sir Charles Goring, whose monumental labors culminated in a complete overthrow of the Lombrosian school of criminal anthropology. This incidental study was an inquiry regarding the validity of belief in the intellectual significance of a high or a low brow.

TABLE I

Coefficients of Correlation between Various Facial Measurements and Thorndike Intelligence Test Scores of 105 Columbia University Students
(After Sommerville)

Thorndike intelligence test score and	r	PE_r
Nose length	+.10	.06
Length of lower jaw (horizontal ramus)	+.09	.06
Nose length ÷ length of lower jaw	+.01	.06
Face length	−.05	.06
Face width	+.09	.06
Height of lower face (infradental-menton)	−.05	.06
Distance between eyes (interpupillary space)	−.04	.06
Distance between eyes ÷ face width	−.13	.06
Palpebral index: width of eye opening ÷ length of eye opening...	−.12	.06
Gonial angle	−.14	.06

He secured for each of 300 convicts official ratings or estimates of (a) intelligence and (b) height of forehead. Four grades of intellect: "intelligent," "unintelligent," "weak-minded," and "imbecile" were distinguished in the rating scale. Since the raters had had ample opportunity to observe the behavior of these convicts in the process of assigning each to a suitable occupational task, there is good reason to believe that the estimates of intelligence submitted by them were fairly accurate.

Analysis of the results seemed to indicate a marked tendency for the more intelligent to have high foreheads and the less intelligent to have low foreheads. Of those judged "intelligent," 20.5 per cent were also judged to have high foreheads, whereas only 8 per cent of those judged as "imbecile" were judged to have high foreheads. Conversely, 46 per cent of the imbecile group as contrasted with 20.5 per cent of the intelligent group were judged to have low foreheads. Results for the other two intermediate intelligence groups were in line with this trend.

Thereupon Goring actually measured the height of the foreheads of these 300 convicts. These actual measurements plotted in relation to the four intellectual grades revealed an astonishing reversal of the supposed trend. The median height of forehead for the intelligent group was 50 mm.; for the unintelligent group 52 mm.; for the weak-minded group 54 mm.; and for the imbecile group 53 mm. Fourteen of the most intelligent group were found to have lower foreheads than any of the imbeciles!

How can we account for the discrepancy in results? Apparently the convict known to be intelligent was judged to have a high forehead and the known weak-minded convict to have a low forehead, in utter disregard of what would be the findings by precise measurement. Apparently the error in the estimation of height of foreheads arose as a result of belief on the part of the raters in the intellectual significance of a high brow or a low brow.

We are indebted to Goring for his convincing demonstration of the non-validity of the "high brow, low brow" superstition. Goring's proof that human judgment may be seriously in error in estimating such a simple, observable physical characteristic as height of forehead throws grave suspicion on all character-analysis schemes that rely upon casual observation instead of precise physical measurements.

3. PHRENOLOGY

Phrenology, originated by Gall and Spurzheim toward the close of the eighteenth century, exhibits the same sort of anecdotal evidence in behalf of the intimate causal nexus in which physical and mental are presumed to be involved. Early discoveries concerning brain localization encouraged the hypothesis that every trait of character and every mental aptitude had its own assigned localization in the brain. The law of exercise was invoked to assist in the determination of these specific brain areas, on the assumption that if a given mental trait were much used, then its corresponding brain part would be enlarged through exercise. As a particular portion of the brain became enlarged, it was supposed to press against the skull, thus causing an enlargement or protuberance at that point. Thus reading character through the bumps on the head becomes a simple matter—simply look over the skull, note bumps, and instantly you know just what parts of the brain are unusually developed and hence what mental characteristics predominate in that person's total make-up. Complicated and minute maps of the surface of the skull were drawn to represent each important mental or moral trait, or faculty, as it was originally called. Present-day phrenological maps differ little from the original maps of Gall and Spurzheim in spite of the progress that has been made in neurology during the past one hundred years.

Brain localization as now accepted is very tentative. The latest findings place emphasis increasingly upon the quantity of nervous tissue available and stress the reaction of the brain as a whole, even in simple mental functions. The sense of color was localized by the phrenologist immediately behind the eye, whereas we now know that the visual area is located in the occipital lobe. In this instance the phrenologists were as far wrong geographically as it was possible to be. And yet their placement of the color sense immediately behind the eye must have seemed reasonable enough at the time as an illustration of the principle that nature is always frugal and economical. The mental faculty of "worship," which we now recognize only as a very general label applicable to a variety of attitudes rather than as a unitary mental function, was localized in what corresponds to the pre-Rolandic area. As a matter of fact, the function of this particular area is wholly motor and controls such activities as wiggling the toes. Readers versed in modern neurology will be amused at many similar grotesque errors committed by the phrenologists. That there could be any point-for-point correspondence between unevennesses on the skull and similar variations in the contour of the brain likewise seems most fanciful to modern brain specialists. The type of mental analysis indulged in by Gall, Spurzheim, and their successors is known as faculty psychology, long since discredited by experimental psychology.

As an example of the sort of evidence marshaled in behalf of phrenology may be mentioned an investigation of 160 deaf children undertaken by Fowler. He believed that "causality" and "comparison of ideas" would be the two mental traits developed to an unusual degree in the deaf because their physical handicap would necessitate the compensatory development of reflective thinking in the absence of normal opportunities for social contacts. When the heads of deaf children were examined, we are seriously told that in truth their foreheads bulged to an unusual degree exactly over those brain areas in which "causality" and "comparison of ideas" are localized. Here is the example par excellence of "The wish is father to the thought," since psychological testing of the deaf has established the fact that they are most seriously handicapped in language ability, surely a basic requisite for "comparison of ideas," whatever the phrase may mean.

A chief phrenological tenet holds that the greater the intellect, the larger the brain and, hence, the larger the skull. This belief in a close relationship between size of skull and intellect was so widespread in scientific circles that Karl Pearson, as recently as 1906, undertook to put the belief to a crucial test. He collected data for some 4,500 twelve-year-old boys and girls and for 1,010 Cambridge University students, showing for each subject certain cranial measurements together with his intellectual standing as determined by teachers' estimates and scholastic grades. When cranial measurements were correlated with intellectual ability, the absence of a close relationship was immediately apparent as may be seen from Table II. As Pearson points out, these correlations do indicate the existence of a slight but sensible relation between size of head and intelligence. The relationship is so slight, however, that it is impossible to make use of such a correlation in attempting to predict the intelligence of any individual person

on the basis of head measurements. A quotation from Pearson will emphasize the fact that even up to most recent times the phrenological belief
concerning head size and intelligence still had a foothold in scientific
circles: "It is impossible to use head size as a basis for judgment as to
intelligence. Of course, all this is merely stating in other words what is
obvious to the biometrician when he finds a low correlation, but possibly,
although I am hardly hopeful, it may help convince the anatomist and
old school anthropologist that head measurements are not of real service

TABLE II

Correlation Ratio between Certain Cranial Measurements and Estimates of Intelligence
(After Pearson, '06)

Correlation ratio between intelligence and	1,011 Cambridge Univ. graduates	2,290 boys, age 12 yrs.	2,165 girls, age 12 yrs.
Cephalic index.............	−.06 ± .02	−.04 ± .01	+.07 ± .01
Length of head	+.11 ± .02	+.14 ± .01	+.08 ± .01
Breadth of head	+.10 ± .02	+.11 ± .01	+.11 ± .01
Height of head	—	+.07 ± .01	+.06 ± .01

as intelligence tests." The lack of significance attaching to head measurements can be more fully realized when we note in this same study that
eye color and hair color are related to intelligence as closely as are head
diameters. We may conclude that head measurements are related positively
to intellect to only a very slight extent—no more closely, in fact, than is
eye color or hair color.

4. LOGICAL FALLACIES UNDERLYING PHRENOLOGICAL AND PHYSIOGNOMIC BELIEFS

To the psychologist these systems of character analysis are of interest,
not so much from the standpoint of verification or refutation, but rather
from the point of view of the psychological and logical factors underlying
such false beliefs. It is quite evident that belief in physical and psychological
discontinuity is implicit in much, if not all, of the thinking of the character
analyst. That is, he tends to pigeonhole mankind into distinct physical and
mental classes or types as if physical traits and mental traits exist in discrete
steps or grades. As a matter of fact, biometric research regarding the distribution of human traits, whether physical or mental, clearly shows all such
traits to be continuous, for the most part distributed in a manner approximating the normal probability curve. This belief that traits are discon-
tinuous, and that their interrelation is relatively simple, admirably illustrates
the fallacy of false simplicity.

This failure of character analysts systematically to verify their pronouncements through follow-up studies is natural in view of the confidence most people have in their own judgments of human character. The fact that the degree of confidence we have in passing judgment upon the other fellow is no guarantee of the correctness of this judgment was forcibly brought home to the writer some years ago when making psychological examinations of all new patients entering the Ohio Institution for the Feeble-Minded. On a particular morning a beautiful child, apparently five or six years of age, was brought into the psychological laboratory for examination. Large, bright brown eyes, fine black hair neatly combed, beautiful olive complexion, together with a freshly laundered, pretty dress combined to produce an immediate judgment—"Somebody has made a horrible blunder; surely this child has no business being in a feeble-minded school." An animated and attractive smile on the girl's face converted this impulsive judgment into a profound conviction. Had the writer seen this girl in a street car or on the playground, he would have immediately concluded that she was an unusually bright youngster. Furthermore, if further opportunity for observing this child in action had not been granted then, this passing judgment, rendered so confidently, would have remained unchallenged. To obtain a psychological rating, however, it was necessary to proceed with the examination.

When the child was asked, "What is your name?" there was no response. The thought flashed through my mind, "This child is deaf—someone has failed to distinguish between deafness and feeble-mindedness." So I stepped behind her and clapped my hands. She responded by turning toward the noise. Then I surmised that she was suffering from some sort of speech difficulty. This judgment called for the abandonment of the usual Binet tests and for resort to non-language performance tests. One of the simplest form boards was placed before her with the simple gestures that usually suffice to bring satisfactory response even from an untutored deaf child. Her response was woefully inadequate—aimless fumbling with the blocks. It then for the first time dawned upon me that in truth she was seriously deficient mentally. The reader can imagine my surprise when I gave her the choice of a piece of wood and a piece of milk chocolate to find that she chose the wood, put it into her mouth, and attempted to chew it up. I finally wrapped a piece of chocolate in a piece of paper and offered it to her. She grabbed it, put it in her mouth, paper and all, and proceeded to eat it, thereby demonstrating an incapacity even to eat discriminatingly. The diagnosis was "idiot" with a mental level of less than one year.

On that same day another patient was brought into the laboratory, assisted solicitously by a nurse because of great difficulty in walking. This patient, a girl of fifteen, was partially paralyzed and succeeded in dragging herself to a chair beside my desk only with the greatest difficulty. Her skin was rough, dark, and leathery in appearance. Her eyes were crossed, adding to a marked distortion of the face through asymmetry of facial contour. When asked her name, she replied slowly and with evident difficulty in manipulating her tongue, jaws, and lips. I immediately judged her to be a low-grade imbecile and hence began the examination with tests suitable for the ordinary three- or four-year-old child.

To the first question, "Point to your ears," she failed to respond. Apparently my first impression was fully confirmed. But there was something in her expression that indicated displeasure. The examination was therefore temporarily discontinued pending re-establishment of favorable rapport. I asked her where she lived and to my surprise she answered by giving her street address as well as the name of her home town. I then asked her if she had any brothers or sisters, and she replied by giving me a complete account of the members of her family. All of this was volunteered, although with great difficulty in speaking. It dawned upon me at last that I had previously insulted her intelligence by asking her to do such an absurd and easy thing as pointing to her ears. I then renewed the examination by asking some of the more difficult questions in the Binet Scale, and she answered them in a most satisfactory manner. When the examination was finally over and her mental age was computed, I discovered that she had earned one of the highest ratings of any inmate I had examined. My first judgment was wholly in error.

Such experiences as these make the psychologist distrust his ability to estimate intelligence from appearance or superficial observation. Binet recognized this limitation upon most judgments of intelligence, and he therefore proceeded to develop objective, standardized tests to replace impressionistic estimates. The availability of such a device as a mental test makes it possible for the psychologist to check the correctness of first impressions, and since so often first impressions are found to be widely erroneous, it is natural for psychologists to hold that the claims of character analysts should be heavily discounted, especially when it appears that they have neglected to develop any satisfactory techniques for detecting or recording instances of false judgment.

This preceding review of non-scientific and pseudo-scientific notions regarding an intimate relationship between physical and mental characters has been necessary in order that we may approach the scientific studies of the problem properly inoculated with an attitude of "suspended judgment." Such negative evidence as has emerged from the above considerations need not close our eyes to satisfactory proof, although it certainly constitutes an argument for extreme caution.

III. Scientific Studies of Physique in Relation to Mental Traits

1. STRUCTURAL CHARACTERISTICS—HEIGHT AND WEIGHT

From the time of Galton's observations that men of genius tend to be above the average in height and weight down to the present, many studies have been reported asserting or denying a close correlation between these two structural characteristics on the one hand and intellect on the other. Galton's pre-eminent position as one of the founders of modern biometry adds to his views the weight of authority.

* * *

Galton's observations admittedly were unsatisfactory to some degree in view of the lack of precise comparative data. More recently, Gowin supplied height and weight data for a group of 1,037 American executives—governors, senators, mayors, university presidents, bishops, merchants, manufacturers, and presidents of insurance and railroad companies. The average height is reported as 71.4 inches and the average weight as 181.1 pounds—figures obviously above the average for the population at large (the average height of one million U.S. Army recruits is 67.5 inches). An interesting and rather significant comparison of the average height and weight of what we may designate as major and minor executives within each of a series of similar lines of work is also given by Gowin. A summary of

TABLE III

Comparison of Major and Minor Executives with Respect to Average Height and Average Weight

(After Gowin)

Class	Average height	Difference	Average weight	Difference
Bishop..........................	70.6⎫	1.8	176.4⎫	17.0
Preachers in small towns	68.8⎭		159.4⎭	
University presidents	70.8⎫	1.2	181.6⎫	17.6
Presidents of small colleges	69.6⎭		164.0⎭	
City school superintendents	70.4⎫	0.7	178.6⎫	21.0
Principals in small towns...........	69.7⎭		157.6⎭	
Salesmanagers	70.1⎫	1.1	182.8⎫	25.8
Salesmen.......................	69.1⎭		157.0⎭	
Presidents of railroad companies	70.9⎫	1.5	186.3⎫	31.7
Station agents in towns of 500 population	69.4⎭		154.6⎭	

these comparisons is shown in Table III. In every case the difference is in the same direction, and hence may be accepted as indicative of a definite trend. Although Gowin places great stress upon the findings as demonstrating the importance of height and weight factors in the personalities of the more successful executive, we must remember that the data were collected by the questionnaire method, which sometimes produces biased results through lack of random sampling in returns. Of course if people in general *believe* that large stature adds to the prestige of a man in power, it would follow that governing boards would tend to select "big" men for important executive positions. For these reasons we must examine the evidence that height and weight are significant indications of intelligence in quantitative studies of these traits as they exist in a random, unselected sample of a total population. It may be that data on school children representative of all social and economic classes in a given community would afford a better opportunity for studying this question than would studies of particular groups of adults in universities, in executive positions, or in any other positions of outstanding importance.

*   *   *

In the early 1890's the importance of studying the relationship between physical and mental development among children was clearly recognized. It so happens that the original study by Porter of 33,500 St. Louis school children seemed to afford a sound basis for concluding that stature and weight are both closely related to intelligence. He used age-grade location in school as a criterion of brightness and dullness. That is, the nine-year-old in the first grade is assumed to be mentally retarded, whereas the nine-year-old in the fourth grade is assumed to be mentally accelerated. When tables showing average height and average weight for the two sexes separately for each age in each grade were constructed, the relationship between physical development and mental development appeared to be quite definite. For example, the median weights for nine-year-old boys in the various grades were as follows: 55.87 for those in grade I; 57.64 for grade II; 59.66 for grade III; and 61.75 for grade IV. It is clear that the brighter nine-year-old boys (in grades III and IV) are on the average distinctly heavier than the duller nine-year-old boys (in grades I and II). Porter believed that these data established a physical basis of precocity and dullness.

Many workers, employing this same method of analysis, have repeated Porter's investigations, always confirming his results. Unfortunately, demonstration of a trend in averages was interpreted as indicating a *close* relationship between physical development and mental development, whereas the method of averages could, at best, indicate nothing more than the presence of a trend for children in the mass.

We now know that if the modern method of correlation had been available when Porter undertook his investigation, its use would have demonstrated the presence of only a slight relationship. Had such a conclusion been reached in this first important study, subsequent investigators would not have perpetuated the misleading exaggeration that has persisted until within the past few years.

It so happens that Porter, for illustrative purposes, presented a small fragment of his data in the form of what we now designate as a correlation scatter diagram. These data (reproduced as Table IV) show the grade location of each of 2,169 nine-year-old boys in relation to weight. The writer computed the Pearson coefficient of correlation for this scatter diagram, obtaining an r of $+0.06 \pm 0.01$. If this be taken as the probable amount of relationship present in Porter's data as a whole, it is so slight as to invalidate the great emphasis placed by him and by many subsequent investigators upon physical status as a basic factor conditioning mental development.

For those unfamiliar with correlational data the result just reported must be surprising, especially when it is remembered that the averages for nine-year-old boys in the various school grades reported four paragraphs back

TABLE IV
Scatter Diagram Showing Relation between Weight and Grade Location of 2,169 Boys, Aged 9

(After Porter)

Weight in pounds	School grade					Total
	I	*II*	*III*	*IV*	*V*	
86–90...................	—	2	—	—	—	2
81–85...................	1	2	3	—	—	6
76–80...................	—	10	8	2	—	20
71–75...................	8	24	15	4	1	52
66–70...................	17	93	36	6	—	152
61–65...................	99	236	90	13	1	439
56–60...................	155	334	91	10	—	590
51–55...................	169	343	81	6	1	600
46–50...................	86	122	21	3	—	232
41–45...................	29	25	5	—	—	59
36–40...................	5	1	5	—	—	11
31–35...................	1	3	2	—	—	6
Total	570	1195	357	44	3	2169
Median	55.87	57.64	59.66	61.75	65.00	57.75

$$r = +.06 \pm .014$$

were derived from the data that are given in Table IV. Of course by restricting one's attention to the *averages alone,* the trend appears to be quite pronounced, but we have long since, in dealing with measurements of mankind in the mass, discovered that we must scrutinize our data with respect to variability as well as central tendency. As may be seen from Table IV, the overlapping is tremendous. The distribution of weight for each of the grades is very similar.

Without boring the reader with detailed presentations and criticisms of findings of such workers as Gilbert, Boas and West, De Busk, Smedley, Arnold, Stewart, Pyle, Baldwin, and Brooks, we may cite as evidence for the position of this paper with respect to height and weight, the work of Murdock and Sullivan in Honolulu, who adopted an exceptionally satisfactory scientific approach to the problem.

Their investigation differs chiefly from the work of predecessors in utilizing on a large scale minutely graduated measures of intelligence. Standard intelligence tests such as the Otis Primary Test for grades I-III, the National Intelligence Test for grades III-IX, and the Terman Group Test of Mental Ability for grades IX-XII were used—all tests being administered by Katharine Murdock, who was serving as school psychologist. The physical measurements were made by Louis R. Sullivan, anthropologist representing the American Museum of Natural History in New York. In a sense it is fortunate that the physical data and the mental data were obtained in entire independence of each other and for other purposes than that of correlating the two. The subjects were some 600 pupils of old American, British, German, or Scandinavian descent, constituting a "fairly homogeneous race group."

Scores on the mental tests were converted into *IQ's* (intelligence quotients obtained by dividing mental age by chronological age) and in similar manner the absolute physical measures were converted into relative measures by expressing each as a quantitative deviation from the average of each age-sex group. Both techniques thus eliminate the age factor, permitting direct comparison for all subjects.

The main correlations emerging from their work are as follows:

r between weight and *IQ* = $+0.16 \pm 0.03$ ($N = 595$),
r between height and *IQ* = $+0.14 \pm 0.03$ ($N = 597$).

There is thus shown to be a slight positive correlation between height, weight, and intelligence. Recomputation of the correlation between weight and intelligence for boys and girls separately did not reveal any effect from lumping the two sexes together in the original computations.

The precarious basis for individual predictions afforded by such slight correlations as have been cited is also present even when we attempt the far easier task of group predictions. It will be remembered that Professor Jackson, in the present series of lectures, cited comparative figures on height, weight, etc., for Yale University students and for University of Minnesota students. His data show the latter to be superior, on the average, to the former in a series of physical measurements. Presumably such physical superiority should indicate mental superiority as well. But available facts indicate quite the reverse. The median score of Yale freshmen on the Army Alpha Intelligence Test was reported as being 159.5 (slightly higher than the median score of 157 made by Ohio State University graduate students!), whereas the median score of University of Minnesota freshman men was reported as being 129 on the same test. Approximately 89 per cent of the Yale freshmen exceeded the median Minnesota student. Only 11 per cent of the Yale freshmen made a score as low as, or lower than, the median for Minnesota freshmen. These figures bear eloquent testimony in behalf of the success of Yale's selective admission scheme in recruiting mentally superior freshmen. The results are in striking contrast to those secured by the admission plan of a state university. But Yale's policy definitely fails to secure physical superiority as well. Here is convincing evidence of the almost complete independent variability of physical and mental traits. The two are so slightly related that selective factors may easily operate to produce two contrasting mentality groups that differ physically in the reverse direction.

We may summarize the general trend of results of all the more important investigations by stating that a slight positive correlation seems to exist between physical development as indicated by height or weight and mental development. From one point of view, we would emphasize the fact that the relationship is definitely positive even though slight. From the point of view of the exaggerated notions, which have been current in the past and which exist even at the present time, it would be well to emphasize the fact that physical status and mental status are to a great extent independent of one another. That is, knowing a child's height or weight enables you to predict his mental capacity with an accuracy only a little better than a chance guess.

2. ANATOMICAL AGE AND MENTAL AGE

Closely following upon Alfred Binet's brilliant discovery of the possibility of measuring mental growth in terms of mental age, a series of American studies introduced a similar concept in regard to physical growth, namely, anatomical age. Scientific workers interested in child development quickly recognized the possibility of an intimate connection between mental age and anatomical age, and a number of research studies undertook to demonstrate this relationship.

Rotch, in a series of papers published from 1905 to 1910, described investigations of skeletal development designed to measure stages in the ossification of the eight carpal bones in the wrist. An excellent summary of this work is to be found in Woodrow's *Brightness and Dullness in Children*. Rotch was able by means of X-ray photographs to discriminate thirteen typical stages of skeletal development. The series of X-ray pictures affords a sort of standard developmental scale whereby from the photograph of any given child's wrist bones its stage of development might be inferred.

In vigorously defending the thesis that anatomical age and mental age

are intimately interrelated, Rotch asserted that in cases where there is
delayed mental development there is delayed skeletal development as well.
Illustrative cases are cited in proof.

It is clear from the work of Rotch and others that marked individual
differences in rate of skeletal development exist, just as there are marked
individual differences in rate of mental development. The crucial question
concerns the extent to which these two types of growth actually parallel
each other in the individual child.

The work of the late Bird T. Baldwin and of Woodrow and Lowell
suggested that the relationship was far less close than Rotch had supposed.
Three further elaborate studies from the laboratories of Harvard, Chicago,
and Columbia Universities appeared almost simultaneously, pointing most
definitely to an absence of any very close connection.

Because of the comprehensive character of Gates's investigation we may
select his presentation as typical of the general findings regarding the intellectual significance of variations in anatomical age. Indeed, it is Gates's
work that permits us, for the first time, to portray the intercorrelations of
the various measures that have been proposed as suitable indices of physical
development. Furthermore, his work throws light on the correlation between these several physical indices and mental, emotional, social, and
educational maturity ratings. Although his study involved only 115 pupils
at the fourth-grade level and in the kindergarten, nevertheless the age
factor was so well controlled through experimental selection and partial
correlation technique that we may accept his results with unusual confidence in their validity.

The principal correlations are presented in Table V. X-ray pictures of
wrist-bone development correlates with Stanford-Binet mental age to the
extent of +.11. It correlates with the other maturity indices only slightly
more. Indeed the correlation between X-rays and physical vigor is only
+.15. The conclusion of this study, supported by the other studies mentioned, is that the correlation between anatomical age and mental age or
any other feature of mental, emotional, or social development is definitely
positive but very, very slight. Not only is there an absence of appreciable
relationship between wrist-bone ossification and mental age but also there
is an equally impressive absence of marked relationship between any of the
other six physical traits and mental age.

It is rather astonishing to discover from this table of correlations that
no single physical measurement yields what might be termed a reasonably
high positive correlation with physical vigor. If we assume that the physical
vigor ratings are highly reliable and valid—and there is every reason to
believe that they do faithfully portray the physical efficiency of the children
—then what are we to say about the relatively low correlation between
each of the physical traits and vigor ratings? Implicit in the whole literature
on physical development is the assumption that any one physical trait is as

good an index of development as any other. This assumption is based in turn upon the assumption that all phases of physical development are closely interrelated, hence any one may be used as a suitable index of physical status taken as a whole. Now, if these assumptions are correct, we must conclude that physical vigor, stamina, and efficiency in participating in day-by-day school activities are not conditioned to an appreciable extent

TABLE V

Coefficients of Correlation between Physical Traits and Various Maturity Indices

(After Gates)

Physical traits	Stanford-Binet MA	Mental maturity	Social maturity	Educ. maturity	Educ. achievement	Emotional maturity	Physical vigor
X-rays of wrist bones† ..	.11	.15	.24	.15	.16	.20	.15
Height	.06	.11	.11	.07	.01	.15	.18
Weight	.10	.13	.09	.17	.07	.17	.25
Chest girth	.09	.09	.15	.14	.03	.17	.19
Lung capacity	.09	.09	.12	.06	.00	.11	.22
Grip	.06	.07	.08	.15	.15	.05	.31
Nutritional status‡......	.13	.15	.18	.17	.15	.15	.37

The various maturity indices

NOTE: Each r is the average of four r's computed for each of four homogeneous sex and school groups, in each case age being held constant. $N=115$.

* Mental maturity=teacher's estimates of common sense, critical attitude, initiative, perseverance, and responsibility in mental activities. Social maturity=teacher's estimates of responsibility for own acts, property, and hygiene; and cooperation, leadership, and respect for law and order. Educational maturity=teacher's estimates of school success. Educational achievement=objective, standardized subject-matter test scores. Emotional maturity=teacher's estimates of presence or absence of excessive emotionality, proper responsiveness, evenness of responsiveness, and emotional maturity verus babyishness. Physical vigor=teacher's estimates of health, vitality, stamina, and efficiency in the day-by-day school activities.

† X-rays taken by Department of Roentgenology of the Vanderbilt Clinic. Pictures were taken at exact natural size and were measured by a planimeter permitting computation of the ratio of ossification of wrist bones to total wrist bone area.

‡ Actual weight subtracted from the norm as found in the Thomas D. Wood Height and Weight Table.

by such physical factors as skeletal status, chest development, lung or vital capacity, strength of grip, or nutritional status. Such a conclusion would be quite out of line with our notions of the physical determinants of vigor and stamina.

The explanation of this unfamiliar picture is of the utmost importance to pediatricians, child hygienists, directors of physical education, and others charged with responsibility for the physical welfare of children. As Gates points out, the true explanation lies in the simple fact that these physical traits are not closely related one to the other, and hence no one physical feature is an adequate index of either physical status or physical vigor. An adequate index would require a combination of several aspects of physical development. This is shown most clearly by the fact that when these physical measurements were properly weighted and combined by multiple correlation technique into a single index of physical development, the index obtained correlated to the extent of $+.61$ with the physical vigor ratings.

The above explanation provides us with definite and new insights into developmental problems, demonstrating as it does that physical growth is specialized and has many phases or aspects, no one of which adequately portrays the physical fitness of the child. This conclusion suggests the urgent need for an extensive cooperative research program designed to explore thoroughly the possibility of measuring physical vigor or stamina through utilization of every conceivable physical test (including such tests of incipient psychasthenia and neurasthenia as may be perfected) and through proper combinations of them to derive a single index of the greatest possible validity. Here is a pressing problem that will require the combined services of anthropometrists, pediatricians, and biometricians, especially those who have become expert "test statisticians," if satisfactory results are to be secured.

To go back now to the relation between these physical traits and mental development. Since multiple correlation technique applied to the physical measurements yielded a physical index that correlated $+.61$ with physical vigor ratings, it might well be suspected that when these same traits were properly weighted and combined they would thereupon yield a fairly high correlation with mental age. But when Gates attempted this, the maximum correlation turned out to be $+.21$. In other words, no method of statistically manipulating the physical measurements will bring about appreciable correlation between physique and intellect. We may conclude, therefore, that physical development and mental development are to a large extent independently variable, mental growth proceeding in relative independence of physical factors. However, this conclusion must not blind us to the fact that there is a slight positive correlation between the two, demonstrable for children in the mass.

3. BODY BUILD AND INTELLIGENCE

Interest in body build as a conditioning factor in disease, temperament, and intellect has long been manifested. Even Hippocrates differentiated between the "habitus apoplecticus" and the "habitus phthisicus." Data from Italy were cited in a preceding lecture by Professor Jackson indicating that there is a demonstrated susceptibility of these two body types (the stout vs. the thin) to apoplexy and circulatory disturbances, on the one hand, and to tuberculosis, on the other. More recently, Viola and also Naccarati describe the "macrosplanchnic type" in which the trunk is proportionately larger than the extremities. The "microsplanchnic" has extremities predominating over the trunk, while in the "normosplanchnic" the trunk and extremities are harmoniously developed. Sigaud emphasizes the "digestive," "muscular," "respiratory," and the "cerebral" body types. Mills recognizes the "hypersthenic," the "sthenic," and the "asthenic" types. And Kretschmer differentiates between the "pyknic" type exhibiting a tendency toward rotundity with a barrel-shaped trunk and relatively short extremities, the "asthenic" type in which the extremities are relatively long in proportion to a relatively small trunk, the "athletic" type in which the various parts of the body are well developed and in proper proportions, and a "dysplastic" type composed of those not fitting into any of the three main classes. As Wertheimer and Hesketh point out, there is a marked similarity between these various schemes of body-type classification in spite of differences in terminology.

Of immediate concern to the psychologist are Naccarati's researches designed to demonstrate a morphological basis for intellect. Believing that no single anthropometric measurement, such as height, would solve the problem of the physical correlate of intelligence, he proposed to utilize a complicated morphological index that would be definitely related to intelligence since it is a composite of many elementary physical traits. This morphological index is the ratio of the length of the limbs to the volume of the trunk

$$\left(MI = \frac{\text{length of extremities}}{\text{trunk volume}} \right).$$

A high index is indicative of microsplanchny and a low index of macrosplanchny. This scheme recognizes continuity of variation from the one extreme to the other. In the absence of all of the necessary measurements, Naccarati authorized, and indeed chiefly employed in his own work, a simple substitute for the MI, namely, the height-weight ratio $\left(\dfrac{\text{height}}{\text{weight}} \right)$.

Rather elaborate reasoning based on certain physiological facts primarily concerned with the functions of the endocrine glands led Naccarati to assume that microsplanchnics are more intelligent than macrosplanchnics. In order to verify this thesis, he conducted a number of experiments with Columbia University students correlating their indices of body build with scores on various standard intelligence tests. In all, thirteen coefficients of correlation between these two factors were reported in his various papers, the average being $+0.26$. Such a value would seem to indicate that there is a closer relation between body build and intellect than between intelligence and any isolated physical trait, such as height, weight, or ossification ratio. However, the experimental groups yielding these correlations in several instances were too small to preclude the possible effects of chance in producing moderately high correlations. Furthermore, these experimental groups sometimes contained both men and women, a somewhat questionable procedure since there are marked sex differences in body build. A further complicating factor may have been the inclusion of Jewish students in disproportionately large numbers. If Jewish students tend to be brighter than non-Jewish students and if they also tend toward microsplanchny to a greater extent, the result would be a correlation spuriously raised because of a racial factor. One of my graduate students is now investigating this possibility.

Five attempts to verify Naccarati's results were promptly made by psychologists—Heidbreder, Stalnaker, Sheldon, Garrett and Kellogg, and Sommerville. They all produced negative results. Heidbreder's experiment is perhaps the most significant, since her attempt at verification was based upon 1,000 white, native-born American students, with adequate controls as regards sex, reliability and validity of intelligence tests employed, and careful physical measurements of height and weight. The mental and morphological heterogeneity of her subjects (freshmen in the University of Minnesota) as compared with the Columbia University subjects should of course yield higher correlations than Naccarati's, provided there is as great a relationship between the height-weight ratio and intellect as he announced. But the actual correlations approximate zero. In a similar manner, the other four attempts to verify Naccarati's conclusions culminated in negative results, the trend of the correlations pointing to a very slight positive correlation.

Just as with height, weight, and anatomical age, so with morphological index, the experimental evidence warrants the view, at present, that physical status and mental status are largely independent of one another. From the viewpoint of man in the mass, there is a definite, though slight, correlation between physical development and mental development. From the point of view of individuals, the connection between physical characters and intellectual traits is so slight as to make it quite impossible in any given case to predict mental status, knowing physical status, and vice versa. In other words, so far as these researches go, we have as yet to discover a physical basis for solving this twentieth-century and empirical "mind-body" problem.

*   *   *

4. PHYSICAL CONDITION AND INTELLIGENCE

Space limitations forbid more than brief reference to this important topic. Its importance arises from the prevalence of the view that the enormous range of individual differences in intellect among children and adults is to be explained in terms of differential opportunities for developing a strong physique. Our friends with strong leanings toward explanations in terms of environment have not failed to promulgate the doctrine that physiological impairment would necessarily have a deleterious effect upon normal intellectual development. Indeed, the presumption that malnutrition, diseased tonsils and adenoids, enlarged glands, dental caries and impacted teeth, etc., prevent normal mental growth is so strong that most investigators approach the problem, not with the idea of discovering whether or not such conditions adversely affect mental development, but rather to determine just how extensive is the havoc wrought by these deleterious influences.

However, negative results reported by David Heron from an application of the precise biometric techniques of the Galton-Pearson laboratory should make us extremely skeptical of the usual assertions put forth by physician and layman alike. His investigation dealt with 4,286 boys and 4,474 girls in a dozen different schools in England. A large number of correlation

TABLE VI

Summary of Mean Coefficients of Correlation between Teachers' Estimates of Intelligence and Various Physical Traits

(Heron, 1910)

Mental capacity and	Mean of partial coefficients of correlation for constant age	
	Boys	Girls
Height	.10	.07
Weight	.06	.03
Condition of teeth	.08	.09
Nutrition status	.01	.08
Cervical glands	.09	.08
Tonsils and adenoids	−.01	.11

coefficients between intelligence, judged by school teachers, and physical condition, reported by medical examiners, were computed. These are summarized in Table VI. It is to be noted that his results for height and weight are in harmony with our critical review of the available evidence on this relationship. Negative results regarding the alleged deleterious consequences arising from bad teeth, impaired nutrition, enlarged cervical glands, and diseased tonsils and adenoids will doubtless be received by many with surprise. But the connection between such conditions and mental capacity is here demonstrated to be very slight indeed, as shown by correlations consistently ranging right around zero.

Our previous discussion of height, weight, and body build in relation to intelligence should have prepared us to find little or no demonstrable effect of malnutrition on intellect, since this condition is diagnosed on the basis of percentage deficiency in weight in relation to standard height-age norms. Furthermore, the results secured by Gates and reported in Table V showed only a slight positive correlation between nutritional status and Stanford-Binet mental age. Moreover, additional investigations concerning the alleged injurious effect of malnutrition upon mental development, could be cited pointing definitely to the same conclusion, namely, that there is but a slight connection between malnutrition and variations in mental capacity of children of a given age.

It would appear that mental development proceeds apace, little influenced by undernourishment. If we assume that our measures of intelligence reflect the condition of the higher centers of the central nervous system, we would be forced to conclude that nature has thrown safeguards around the central nervous system adequate to guarantee the continuance of mental development even in spite of adverse physical conditions. This view receives strong support from the observations reported by Professor Scammon in the concluding paper in this symposium to the effect that although gross malnutrition may exist sufficient greatly to retard physical growth or even to arrest it, yet the nervous system continues to grow, apparently at the expense of the bodily tissues themselves.

Assertions regarding the harmful mental effects of diseased tonsils and adenoids continue to be made in spite of Heron's demonstration to the contrary. These assertions frequently are accompanied by extravagant claims regarding mental improvement after removal of infected tonsils and adenoids. Perhaps citation of the careful investigation of Rogers will serve to confirm Heron's results and so provide a convincing answer to popular belief and unscientific medical opinion.

Rogers arranged to have a group of 530 school children examined by a school nurse or physician and then subdivided into two groups, one composed of those in whom the diseased condition of tonsils was pronounced enough to warrant medical treatment, the other composed of those in whom the tonsils were normal or so slightly defective as not to demand treatment. The Stanford-Binet IQ's of these two groups of children were then compared, the median IQ of the 237 children in the diseased-tonsil group being 95.3 and the median IQ of the 294 children in the normal-tonsil group being 95.6. The difference is almost imperceptible. Furthermore, when the IQ percentage distribution curves are plotted, the two curves are almost identical, justifying the conclusion that the presence of diseased tonsils in the infected-tonsil group in no way impaired their mental development.

A more crucial test was reported by Rogers wherein a comparison of the IQ before and after removal of diseased tonsils was made for 28 children. A control group of 28 children was also formed, each one of whom suffered from diseased tonsils but was not operated upon. The children in the operated group and in the control group were retested six months later. The average gain in *IQ* for the operated group was 2.25. But the control group, in the meantime, gained, on the average, 3.28 *IQ* points! To insure that these negative results were not due to shortness of time elapsing between operation and retest, a third mental test was applied after an interval ranging from ten to seventeen months following operation. The average gain in *IQ* for the operated cases was 3.0, whereas the average gain in *IQ* for the control cases was 6.2. It must be remembered that the control children, during this whole period, continued to possess infected tonsils. It seems safe to conclude that no substantial improvement in *IQ* is discernible as a result of the removal of diseased tonsils either after six months or after an interval of one year. This conclusion might have been anticipated from the preliminary survey comparison, since there was no evidence that diseased tonsils had produced any mental retardation from which operated children could have recuperated.

When disease processes directly involving the central nervous system are studied for their possible mental sequelae, a very different picture is disclosed. For example, sleeping sickness (encephalitis lethargica) is now known to affect mental development profoundly in the great majority of cases, bringing about an apparently permanent arrest of mental growth. Undoubtedly similar positive findings would be disclosed were intelligence tests applied to children suffering from spinal meningitis and other germ diseases attacking the brain. There is urgent need for cooperative research projects in this field—psychologist and physician combining forces to discover the precise effect upon intelligence of various disease processes and of such remedial techniques as gland-extract feeding, artificial sunbaths (Alpine lamp treatments), scientific vitamin diets, etc.

IV. Summary

Man's search for an intimate connection between inner function and outer structure seems merely to reflect his universal tendency to think in terms of positive, rather than negative, relationships. The history of science itself shows there has been far keener interest in establishing a new relationship than in discovering the absence of a relation previously assumed to exist. Many there are who insist upon the scientific value of positive findings and deny, or at least disparage, the issue of negative results. With this in mind, the writer is quite prepared to see his audience somewhat crestfallen and disillusioned at the trend toward negative evidence manifest throughout our discussion of the relation between physical and mental development.

With the possible exception of physical factors associated with temperamental characteristics and of disease processes involving the higher centers of the central nervous system, our survey has demonstrated that prevalent notions regarding an intimate relation between bodily traits and mental development have been greatly exaggerated. Structural characteristics such as height and weight seem to be correlated with intellect to only a slight extent. Even precise X-ray measurements of skeletal development fail to show marked dependence of mental growth upon physical development. Indeed the evidence reveals that physical growth itself is far from being uniform. It appears that growth is highly specialized, with individual phases far less interdependent than most thinkers have assumed. Likewise, hope of finding positive relationships of greater magnitude by employing complicated morphological indices of body build seems to vanish when carefully controlled statistical investigations are actually pushed through to completion. And finally, ordinary physical defects and certain presumably deleterious physical conditions seem to be relatively unrelated to the enormous range of individual differences in intelligence to be seen on every hand.

Of course, it must be understood that our presentation makes no pretense of deriving final answers to the questions before us. The initials P.U., standing for *plus ultra,* should be appended to every scientific formulation as an admission of its provisional character. Here we have merely tried to set forth as faithfully as possible the present state of our knowledge. Improved statistical techniques, discoveries of now unthought-of physical indices, invention of new modes of mental and physical diagnosis—all of these may at any time lead to positive findings contrary to those we now believe to be true. Furthermore, our available evidence has come wholly from investigations upon children of school age or upon adults, a fact that definitely precludes direct conclusions as to the facts for children less than six years of age. Therefore, the possibility that a closer connection between physical development and mental development may be discovered during the preschool period of childhood must constantly be borne in mind. In fact, the writer would urge those now investigating infancy and early childhood to repeat upon their subjects all the investigations reviewed in this paper in order to amass scientific knowledge concerning the period when physical growth and mental growth are proceeding at their maximum acceleration.

No more appropriate closing sentence for our present discussion could be found than Pearson's comment on the negative character of the results that he secured in investigating one single aspect of our problem, "Much of science is the verification or refutation of impressions and opinions, and the mainly negative conclusions of this paper place at any rate on a sounder quantitative basis the view that even for the mass, and therefore much more for the individual, little can be judged as to intelligence from the more obvious anthropometric measurements."

This volume presents the results of the first general follow-up of the gifted group described in the first book of the series, Mental and Physical Traits of a Thousand Gifted Children. Of particular interest is the finding that substantial changes in I.Q. do occur and that a sizeable sex difference appears at the high school level.

The Promise of Youth*

BARBARA S. BURKS

DORTHA W. JENSEN

LEWIS M. TERMAN

1930

More than fifteen years have passed since the researches set forth in these volumes of *Genetic Studies of Genius* were first definitely planned; it is twelve since the senior author began devoting each year a portion of his salary to the collection of data on bright children in the hope that once a beginning had been made funds would somehow be found for a realization of the larger plan. Although the undertaking entered upon so long ago is still far from completed, the first stage has been compassed, and it may not be unprofitable to cast a backward glance of appraisal over the problem that has been set, the labors that have been expended, and the factual information that has been garnered. There is further reason for such a review in the fact that the additional volumes which are in prospect can probably not appear until several more years have elapsed.

* * *

SPECIFIC AIMS OF THE PRESENT RESEARCHES

It is with the brightest four or five out of a thousand that Volumes I and III of this series are concerned. It is their characteristics—physical, intellectual, social, and moral—which we have attempted to delineate, their development which we have attempted to trace. The investigations which have been carried out for this purpose, although purely scientific in their immediate aim, have in their ultimate end been motivated by considerations of practical import, as is doubtless true of the majority of scientific investi-

* Reprinted from *The Promise of Youth: Follow-up Studies of a Thousand Gifted Children*, Vol. III, *Genetic Studies of Genius* by Barbara S. Burks, Dortha W. Jensen, and Lewis M. Terman with the permission of the publishers, Stanford University Press. Copyright 1930 by the Board of Trustees of Leland Stanford Junior University.

gations in every field. In this case the purpose has been to build up a foundation of pertinent and verifiable factual material upon which improved educational methods can at some time be securely based.

What, can it be reasonably claimed, has been accomplished toward this end? At best, certainly, not more than a modest fraction of the total that is needed. Perhaps the author and his co-workers should be content if it can be said that an honest beginning has been made and that the foundation stones they have set will not have to be torn away and replaced. That much, they would fain believe, has been accomplished.

DEFINITION OF THE GROUP FOR WHICH THE CONCLUSIONS ARE VALID

In advance of a final discussion of results it may be well to remind the reader once more that the generalizations to be offered can be held to apply only to a group selected as this group was selected, namely, on the basis of a Stanford-Binet IQ of 140 or higher; also that possibly 10 or 15 per cent of the total number who could have qualified according to this criterion were missed by the methods of sifting employed. Although it is impossible to say how those who were missed would have differed from those who were identified, the number of these was fortunately not large enough to distort conclusions seriously. It is more important to bear in mind the arbitrariness of the line set for inclusion of subjects and the probable error of the intelligence score through which the line was drawn. Many children whose found IQ's were appreciably below 140 may have had higher IQ's than some whose test scores satisfied the criterion. There is roughly one chance in seven that a child whose measured (found) Stanford Binet IQ is 135 has a true Stanford-Binet IQ of 140. There is roughly one chance in sixteen that a measured IQ of 130 should really have been as high as 140. There are corresponding chances that measured IQ's of 145 or 150 should not have been above 140. These estimates are based upon a probable error of 4 IQ points for Stanford-Binet test scores. The probable error is somewhat less than this in the mental age range of five to ten years, but at the levels above twelve or fourteen is probably greater. In any case it cannot be claimed that the group studied is composed of all the children above a certain (true) level of intelligence and of none but those. Because the selective method is fallible, the result is only an approximation to this. The criterion set is one which is satisfied by about 4 children in 1,000 of the urban pre-high-school population of California. This is at the rate of 1,000 in 250,000.

SEX RATIO IN THE GIFTED GROUP

As the sex ratio in the pre-high-school groups of subjects is about 116 boys to 100 girls, a gifted group of 1,000, selected as ours was selected, contains about 538 boys and only 462 girls. At the high-school level a method of selection somewhat similar to that used in the elementary grades but employing the Terman Group Test instead of the Stanford-Binet as the final criterion gives a sex ratio of 212 boys to 100 girls, or 680 boys to only 320 girls in a group of 1,000.

These facts are very challenging, especially when considered in connection with the fact that among historic geniuses, eminent living scientists, and other outstanding groups the large majority (usually above 90 per cent in any group) are males. In Volume I four hypotheses were examined in the search for possible explanations: biased selection; sex ratio in families of the gifted children; differential death rate of embryos; and sex difference in variability. Analysis of the data seemed to rule out the first two explanations and to suggest the possibility that either or both of the last two may have been to some extent accountable. The vastly greater excess of boys at the upper age levels than at the lower was at the time explained as possibly due to the difference in method of selection of subjects in the upper and lower age ranges.

The follow-up study sheds no further light on the sex ratio in the younger group, but suggests another explanation of the greater excess of boys at the upper age levels; namely, that gifted girls do not maintain their intellectual superiority in adolescence as well as boys do. Whether this is to be thought of in terms of decreasing variability of the girls with increasing age, or as an earlier cessation of intellectual growth on the part of the girls, the result is the same. It is probable that all the facts regarding sex ratios are accounted for as follows: (a) a slightly greater male variability, explaining the relatively small difference in the number of boys and girls found in the pre-high-school grades; and (b) an earlier cessation of mental growth on the part of the girls, resulting in the large sex difference in numbers of gifted children at the high-school level.

COMPOSITE PORTRAIT OF THE GIFTED CHILD

A large part of both Volume I and Volume III has been devoted to a delineation of the characteristic traits of gifted children considered as a group. This seemed necessary because of the large amount of erroneous opinion that has been disseminated in connection with this aspect of the problem. Further justification for making this one of the major objectives of the research is found in the fact that the educational issue as to what the school should or should not do with gifted children hinges largely on their group characteristics. We believe that the data secured have enabled us to delineate these characteristics faithfully, at least so far as the main outlines are concerned. There is probably no part of the study which has yielded conclusions less likely to be materially modified by further investigation. It seems to have been satisfactorily demonstrated that:

1. Gifted children come predominantly from family stocks of decidedly superior intellectual endowment and of slightly superior physical endowment;

2. These family stocks have greatly decreased in fecundity during the last two generations and have already reached the point where they are not maintaining themselves;

3. The mean IQ of siblings of children who are in the IQ range above 140 is about 123, or almost exactly what would be expected if the correlation between siblings in the general population were in the neighborhood of .45 or .50;

4. Intellectually gifted children, either because of better endowment or better physical care, or both, are as a group slightly superior to the generality of children in health and physique and tend to remain so;

5. Children above 140 IQ are not as a group characterized by intellectual one-sidedness, emotional instability, lack of sociality or of social adaptability, or other types of maladjusted personality;

6. Indeed in practically every personality and character trait such children average much better than the general school population;

7. In social-intelligence ratings, social interests ,and play activities, gifted children as a group are either normal or superior;

8. In mental masculinity and femininity gifted boys rate on a par with unselected school boys of corresponding age, while gifted girls deviate significantly from the norm of their sex in the direction of greater masculinity;

9. In the character traits measured by the Raubenheimer-Cady tests the typical gifted child of nine years is on a par with unselected children of thirteen or fourteen years;

10. In trait ratings by teachers, gifted children show their superiority to the average most of all in intellectual and volitional qualities and least in physical and social traits;

11. In school progress the typical gifted child is accelerated by 14 per cent of his age, but in actual mastery of the school subjects (as shown by achievement tests) he is accelerated by more than 40 per cent of his age;

12. At the age of ten years there is no correlation between achievement test scores and the number of years gifted children have attended school;

13. As a rule gifted boys maintain or almost maintain their relative superiority to the common run in intelligence, at least through the period of adolescence;

14. Girls somewhat more often than boys show a drop in the IQ as adolescence is approached, or soon thereafter;

15. School achievement as a rule continues through high school and college to be in line with the IQ originally found in 1921–22;

16. Subject failures in high school are practically never incurred by children of this grade of intelligence;

17. Nearly three-quarters of the total marks earned in high school by

gifted girls, and nearly half of those earned by gifted boys, are of A grade;

18. Gifted children of the senior high-school year test on the average above the 90th percentile of the general run of high-school seniors on the Iowa High-School Content Examination, or from 1.5 to 2.0 S.D.'s above the mean of high-school seniors in general;

19. More than 90 per cent of gifted boys and more than 80 per cent of gifted girls (in this group) go to college, most of them remaining to graduate;

20. Those who graduate from high-grade universities win Phi Beta Kappa or other graduation honors about three times as frequently as do the general run of graduates from such institutions.

The twenty generalizations in this list could have been multiplied several times, but they are among the more significant features of the portrait. A few of them are more or less specific to this group of subjects, but the large majority will in all probability be found to hold for any gifted group selected from the school population of any city or country by means of any of the better forms of intelligence tests when the criterion for admission to the group is set in the neighborhood of 140 IQ. There is every reason to believe that they will be found valid, though in somewhat less degree, for representative groups of children in the IQ range of 120 to 140.

It is to be hoped that the superstitions so commonly accepted relative to intellectually superior children have been permanently swept away by the factual data these studies have presented. It is simply not true that such children are especially prone to be puny, over-specialized in their abilities and interests, emotionally unstable, socially unadaptable, psychotic, and morally undependable; nor is it true that they usually deteriorate to the level of mediocrity as adult life is approached. Educational reforms in the direction of special classes, special curricula, and special classroom procedures can now be confidently formulated upon this foundation of established truth. If special classes and special procedures are to be opposed, it must henceforth be upon other grounds than those which have been most commonly alleged. One would like to believe that the stage is set for one of the most important educational reforms of the century; a reform that would have for its end the discovery, conservation, and intensive cultivation of every form of exceptional talent.

RELATIVE PERMANENCY OF THE CHARACTERISTIC TRAITS OF GIFTED CHILDREN

The most important single outcome of the follow-up investigation is the abundant and conclusive evidence that for the group as a whole the picture did not greatly change in the period that elapsed between the studies summarized in Volume I and Volume III. With minor exceptions, what was true of these children in 1921–22 was true of them in 1927–28. During this period, however, there were changes in the background of the picture which are likely at times to deceive the reader. What is here referred to is the fact that the school population with which it is necessary to make our comparisons was a much more highly selected population at the time of the follow-up study than in 1921–22. This has been alluded to many times in the exposition of the findings, but it cannot be too often emphasized. There are few who appreciate how much the composition of a class of high-school seniors has been affected by the retardation and elimination of their less-gifted fellows. This holds true, though to a less marked degree, of high-school freshmen, and of course to a far greater degree of students enrolled in superior universities.

Moreover, it is constantly necessary to make allowance for the fact that the gifted group usually averages some two years younger than the school population with which it is compared. In 1921–22 the comparisons in school achievement were in most cases age comparisons; in 1927–28 they were of necessity grade comparisons, because of the absence of age norms for achievement tests at higher levels. In 1921–22 less than one child in a hundred of the general school population rated as high in achievement as the typical gifted child of the same age. In 1927–28 about one high-school senior in ten rated as high in achievement as the typical gifted child of the same grade but two years younger. The latter showing is approximately as favorable as the former, although it might not appear so to one not fully cognizant of all the factors entering into the comparison.

INDIVIDUAL CHANGES IN RATE OF INTELLECTUAL GROWTH

The composite portrait method is useful, just as concepts and generalizations are useful in the shorthand of thinking. Nevertheless, the composite portrait, like any other kind of average, has its limitations. In telling what is true of a group, it fails to convey any sense of the uniqueness that is to be found in each of those who compose the group. In the present instance too exclusive concentration of attention upon what is true in general hinders us from recognizing the variety of trait combinations that the fact of personality necessarily implies, and obscures all those characteristics which are exceptions to the rule. It is in giving a more vivid impression than did Volume I of the "exceptions to the rule" that the present volume makes one of its most important contributions.

For example, it is true that the gifted subjects as a group have held their own intellectually, but it is no less true that some of them have changed significantly in their intelligence ratings. In interpreting the findings on this point the reader will need to bear in mind the factors which complicate the issue: the probable error of a Stanford-Binet score, the fact that the Stanford-Binet as at present standardized yields scores with older subjects which are too low, and the fact that the tests in the scale which measured the younger subjects in the original survey do not test exactly the same functions as those in the upper ranges which measured the same subjects at the time of the follow-up study. The same factors are involved in greater or less degree in the case of retests by other intelligence scales. The Herring-Binet not only lacks "top," but because of faults of standardization it yields IQ's much below those of the Stanford-Binet. The Terman Group Test measures in part other functions than those measured by either the Stanford-Binet or the Herring-Binet, and like both of these it is inadequate to measure the brighter half of our adolescent subjects.

For the reasons just given, and others, it is impossible to make a quantitative statement of the exact degree to which IQ's tend to maintain themselves. Considering the evidence from all sources, including intelligence tests, achievement tests, school marks, etc., it appears that the IQ's of boys tend to remain constant and those of girls to decrease. One finding out of harmony with this conclusion is that at all ages girls retain a certain superiority over boys in school marks, but it has long been known that for one reason or another, or for several reasons, girls make a far better showing per unit of intelligence than boys do in the matter of class marks.

Making due allowances for complicating factors in measuring IQ constancy, one can hardly avoid the conclusion that there are individual children in our gifted group who have shown very marked changes in IQ. Some of these changes have been in the direction of IQ increase, others of them in the direction of decrease. The important fact which seems to have been definitely established is that there sometimes occur genuine changes in the rate of intellectual growth which cannot be accounted for on the basis of general health, educational opportunity, or other environmental influences. The opinion has often been advanced that something like this is true, but convincing evidence has hitherto been lacking, previous data having been limited entirely to retests by a single fallible intelligence measure without supporting evidence.

OTHER DEVIATIONS FROM CENTRAL TENDENCIES OF THE GROUP

The group studied shows far more variability in other traits than in constancy of IQ. One finds among the subjects extreme deviation from the group average in every physical, mental, and personality trait: size, strength, athletic ability, health, scientific ability, artistic ability, literary ability, mental masculinity and femininity, fair-mindedness, social and activity interests, vocational interest, social intelligence, leadership, interest in school work, ambition, and moral dependability. One member of the group became definitely psychopathic and committed suicide; one is serving time in a state reform school after an extended career as a delinquent. The group in fact contains disharmonic personalities of almost every type. Several cases of these have been described. Other behavior and adjustment problems include cases showing inferiority complexes, inordinate conceit, "wildness," disobedience, untruthfulness, social deficiency, dishonesty, and extreme laziness. There are several cases of marked inversion with respect to mental masculinity and femininity, though it must be said that the significance of such inversion is not yet fully understood. A considerable number of the subjects are so lacking in ambition, or in ability to work consistently toward even a moderately distant goal, that after leaving school they either remain content with inconsequential positions or drift aimlessly from job to job.

The other side of the story would take longer to tell, because there are so many more instances of extreme deviation in the direction of personality balance, stability of character, and successful accomplishment. Examples of heroic self-sacrifice and of courageous struggle against such handicaps as ill health, poverty, parental ignorance, race prejudice, and other unfavorable circumstances of environment have been described, and the list of such case studies could have been greatly extended. The group contains several musicians of genuine promise, one of whom has already taken rank as one of the outstanding musical composers and musical theorists of America. Among the subjects are at least a half-dozen who have produced literary juvenilia comparable to the best produced by eminent authors at corresponding age. Three or four have shown unusual promise in art. The number who have evidenced exceptional ability in science is so large that it will be surprising if thirty or forty years hence the group is not well represented in starred lists of the type illustrated by Cattell's 1,000 American men of science.

In a highly original manner this study reinvestigates the
question of the relation of mental traits to physical characteristics. Specificity of traits seems to win the day, however.

Is Mental Resemblance Related to Physical Resemblance
in Sibling Pairs?*

BARBARA S. BURKS

RUTH S. TOLMAN

1932

The conception that mental processes are closely related to physical structures, particularly of the central nervous system, is necessary unless we wish
to imagine ourselves as completely dualistic beings in which mind and
body pursue independent paths that meet only by coincidence. Although
most experimental attempts to establish the presence of correlations between
normal variations in mental and structural traits have failed, the results far
from disprove that close interdependence exists. They only demonstrate
that the problem is a resistant one, and that associations have not yet been
sought in the domains where they actually reside.

Phrenology and various other "systems" of character analysis are the
outlawed progeny of dignified speculations that began in the armchairs of
philosophers, and continued in the modern laboratories of psychologists.
If logical grounds alone do not answer the bizarre claims of these "systems,"
such experiments as those of Paterson and Ludgate, Kenagy, Cleeton and
Knight, Sheldon, and Hull and Evans do so most adequately. These investigators have reported zero correlations between reliable pooled ratings
of personality traits and the features of head and face on which various
"systems" pin their faith.

Pronounced relationships between anatomical structures and mental and
personality characteristics will probably never be found as long as they are
sought with utter disregard of the intrinsic functions of physical organs. To
expect generosity with a wide mouth, or a calculating disposition with small
ears, is as reasonable as to look for the cause of color-blindness in the ali-
mentary canal. . . .

It is not unlikely, however, that genetic linkages may be discovered within
family groups between disparate human traits whose only bond in common
is the chromosome in which their determiners lie. Many such linkages have
been found between unit characters in the lower animal forms, especially in

* *Journal of Genetic Psychology*, 40 (1932), pp. 3-15. Reprinted by permission
of Ruth S. Tolman and The Journal Press.

Drosophila. With the exception of "sex-linked" characters such as hemophilia or color-blindness, however, no clear case of simple linkage has yet been reported in man. Since there are only a few human traits which behave as unit characters, one's best chance of discovering linkages is probably to examine variable traits determined by several or many genes.

PROBLEM

The present study investigates the possibility that some of the genes for mental ability and general physical appearance are linked. There is a widespread impression that this is the case. In lay circles in which the principles of genetic inheritance are unknown, the comment is frequently made that this child "takes after" his father's side of the house, that another child is "exactly like his mother's people," while still another "is just his older brother all over again." The family commonly expects these children to grow up with the mental and personality traits of the relatives they most resemble in appearance, and is fearful if a child in its midst looks too much like some unfortunate black sheep whose portrait has been turned to the wall.

There is a sound theoretical reason why the amount of physical resemblance which a child bears to his father or to his mother should not influence in the least the amount of his resemblance to either parent in hereditary mental traits. Each parent always contributes half of the 48 chromosomes which determine within more or less narrow limits the course of a child's mental and physical development. If the child happens to inherit, for example, the brown eyes of one of his parents, this does not mean that the child has received a "larger share" of heredity from the parent in question. The other parent has also contributed a chromosome in which is located a gene for eye color—possibly for blue. As brown happens to be a dominant color, this blue-eye gene is temporarily lost to view, only to reappear later among some of the child's descendants in the absence of genes for a dominant color. If some mental trait, such as musical ability, should happen to have one of its genes located in the same chromosome, it does not follow that the parent whose gene for eye-color was dominant over that of the other parent should show a similar dominance for musicality. On the contrary, it is a matter of pure chance which parent, if either, should do so. Many genes, like those for color in the blue Andalusian fowl, do not exhibit the phenomenon of dominance to any appreciable extent, but display, instead, a blending effect when combined.

In the case of siblings, the situation is altered. Though each sibling receives a full set of 48 chromosomes (24 from each parent), it is a matter of chance which 24 of the 48 chromosomes per parent will fall to his lot. On the average, a pair of siblings, unless they are duplicate twins, share only half their chromosomes in common; but the number of shared chromosomes may vary, according to the law of normal probability, from 48 to zero. When the number of shared chromosomes is less than 6, the relationship of siblings, genetically speaking, is less close than that of ordinary first cousins.

It is reasonable to suppose that siblings who resemble one another very closely in physical appearance have received an unusually large chance number of chromosomes in common, and that siblings who impress an observer as showing little or no family resemblance have an unusually small overlapping of chromosomes. If the particular chromosomes involved in the traits under scrutiny should happen also to contain genes for certain mental traits, we might expect the siblings who looked most alike to be the most alike psychologically, and those who looked least alike to show unusually large mental differences.

NOMINATION OF CASES

In the investigation, which was carried out in Pasadena, every public school was provided with nomination blanks upon which to note the names of pairs of brothers and pairs of sisters who resembled one another unusually much or unusually little in general appearance. Teachers and others who filled out the blanks were not told that the study would later be concerned with the mental traits of these children, for we wished to avoid as far as possible any bias of selection that might distort results. We asked simply for the names of pairs (not twins) "who look so much alike that a person acquainted with one child but not with the second would, on meeting the second, instantly recognize him as belonging to the same family as the first," and of pairs "who are so different in appearance that a stranger would scarcely believe they belonged to the same family."

All siblings nominated from the junior high school and senior high school grades (7 to 12) were rated for general resemblance on a 9-point scale independently by the two writers. In addition to siblings nominated from the elementary schools, *all* like-sex sibling pairs attending two representative elementary schools were seen and independently rated. The latter group, consisting of 141 pairs, was used for computing the reliability of the ratings, and for determining the proportions of random sibling pairs which display physical resemblance of varying degrees. In this group, as in the group of nominated pairs, children meeting certain criteria to be described were selected for further study.

In order to simplify interpretation, only white English-speaking children of north-European or mixed "American" descent were included in the statistical treatment which follows. Half-siblings were, of course, excluded. It is believed that the results are free from selective influences other than those always attendant upon studies of siblings taken from a school population, and that the correlations can, therefore, be fairly compared with those reported by other investigators.

THE RATINGS

The following scale was used by the writers in making their ratings:
1. Almost as much alike in general appearance as identical twins
2. Very marked family resemblance
3. Marked family resemblance
4. Slight family resemblance
5. No noticeable resemblance
6. Slight difference in type
7. Marked difference in type
8. Very marked difference in type
9. As different as two people of the same race could be

The writers carefully agreed upon the significance which they would assign to the scale, and made several practice ratings before beginning their field work. Their independent ratings of (a) the siblings nominated from the junior and senior high schools, (b) the siblings nominated from the elementary schools, and (c) all like-sex sibling pairs attending two elementary schools (including some from b) gave the following correlations:

	r	$P.E._r$	N
a	.71	.04	80
b	.75	.04	67
c	.67	.03	141

The fact that correlations a and b are slightly higher than the third is due to the presence of a larger number of extremely similar or dissimilar pairs among the nominated cases than among the random cases. If correlation c is corrected by the Spearman-Brown formula to give the reliability of the average of two ratings in an unselected group, the result is .80.

Average ratings were distributed in the group of 141 unselected sibling pairs as in Table I.

COLLECTION OF DATA

The original plan of the experimenters was to administer the Stanford-Binet test to the like-appearing siblings of the elementary schools whose average rating of resemblance was 2.0 or better. Only 3.5 per cent of the unselected siblings received so high a rating. As this boundary netted only 17 cases, it was extended to include siblings whose average ratings were distributed as in Table II. The 34 cases of Table II include 11 pairs of brothers and 23 pairs of sisters. In 24 pairs the older child was tested by the junior author and the younger child by the senior author, in 2 cases Miss

TABLE I

Resemblance Ratings of Unselected Sibling Pairs

Rating interval	Boys	Girls	Total	Percentage reaching or exceeding
1.5–1.99		3	3	2.1
2.0–2.49	4	4	8	7.8
2.5–2.99	5	10	15	18.4
3.0–3.49	15	14	29	39.0
3.5–3.99	23	18	41	68.0
4.0–4.49	15	5	20	82.2
4.5–4.99	5	4	9	88.6
5.0–5.49	4	2	6	92.8
5.5–5.99	3	1	4	95.7
6.0–6.49	1	2	3	97.8
6.5–6.99		1	1	98.5
7.0–7.49		1	1	99.3
7.5–7.99	1		1	100.0

TABLE II*

Resemblance Ratings of Elementary School Like-Appearing Pairs

Average rating	Percentage of unselected siblings reaching or exceeding	Number of pairs tested
2.0 or higher	3.5	17
2.25	7.8	6
2.5	15.6	11
		——
		34

* The sisters in one of the 34 pairs were attending a junior high school, but as both children were under fourteen years of age they were given the Stanford-Binet as well as the Terman Group Test.

Natalie Raymond and the senior author each tested one member of a pair, and in 8 cases the senior author tested both members of each pair.

Limitations of time prevented the testing of a comparable group of elementary school unlike-appearing sibling pairs. Four pairs of brothers whose average ratings ranged from 5 to 7 were tested, however, with interesting results.

Terman Group Test scores were obtained for all sibling pairs nominated and rated at the junior and senior high schools. The distribution of average ratings of resemblance in these pairs is shown in Table III. In approximately 60 per cent of the cases the Terman Group Test was administered

TABLE III
Resemblance Ratings of Junior and Senior High School
Nominated Pairs

Rating interval	Boys	Girls	Total
1.5–1.99		1	1
2.0–2.49		2	2
2.5–2.99	1	3	4
3.0–3.49	4	6	10
3.5–3.99	12	11	23
4.0–4.49	5	9	14
4.5–4.99	4	6	10
5.0–5.49	2	5	7
5.5–5.99	2		2
6.0–6.49	1	4	5
6.5–6.99	2	1	3
7.0–7.49	3		3
	36	48	84

by the writers. Scores upon this test were obtained for the remaining cases from the school files. The ratings were made before the tests were scored or obtained from the files, and nearly all the tests were scored by a third person who was unfamiliar with the ratings. Four pairs are included in Table III who were rated by only one of the experimenters.

Tables I, II, and III all indicate that the standards employed by the writers in rating the girls were somewhat more lenient than those used in rating the boys, for more girls than boys received high ratings.

TREATMENT OF DATA

1. In the group of 34 elementary school like-appearing siblings the IQ of the older member of each pair was correlated against the IQ of the younger member.

2. In the junior and senior high school group of 84 pairs, the following subdivisions were made:

   a. 20 like-appearing pairs whose ages were less than 15-0 (rating 3.5 or better)

   b. 23 unlike-appearing pairs whose ages were less than 15-0 (rating less than 3.5)

   c. 32 like-appearing pairs of all ages, including those of (a) (rating 3.5 or better)

   d. 52 unlike-appearing pairs of all ages, including those of (b) (rating less than 3.5)

   e. 20 cases with highest ratings of resemblance, regardless of age (rating 3.5 or better) *f.* 20 cases with lowest ratings of resemblance, regardless of age (rating 5.0 or less)

Terman Group Test IQ's were computed for Groups *a* and *b* in the usual way. In groups *c* and *d* certain empirical assumptions were made—that the average IQ of the children in age groups above fourteen was equal to that of the children of lesser age, and that it took the same number of points on the test to equal one point of IQ among children above fourteen as it did among children of fourteen. These assumptions are probably only approximately accurate, but give "estimated" IQ's whose values are more reasonable than those yielded by a MA/CA ratio in children over fourteen. As in the case of Group 1, the IQ of the older child was correlated against that of the younger child of each pair.

RESULTS

Table IV summarizes the correlation coefficients between the IQ's of the sibling groups just described.

TABLE IV
Correlations between IQ's of Like- and Unlike-Appearing Pairs

	r	P.E.$_r$	N
Group 1, elementary school, likes	.45	.09	34
Group 2, junior and senior high school			
a. Likes under 15–0	.78	.06	20
b. Unlikes under 15–0	.31	.13	23
c. Likes of all ages	.67	.07	32
d. Unlikes of all ages	.61	.06	52
e. Pairs most like	.61	.09	20
f. Pairs most unlike	.63	.09	20

The IQ's of the childen in Groups 1 and 2 had means and standard deviations as shown in Table V, in which the mean chronological ages are also listed.

TABLE V
Measures of Central Tendency and Dispersion of IQ's

	Mean IQ	S.D.	Mean CA	N
Group 1 (likes)				
Older of pair	101	14	9–9	34
Younger of pair	106	12	7–5	34
Group 2 (likes)				
Older of pair	101	15	14–4	32
Younger of pair	107	14	12–8	32
Group 2 (unlikes)				
Older of pair	101	12	14–9	52
Younger of pair	106	14	13–1	52

With the exception of correlations *a* and *b* for Group 2, the correlations reported in Table IV are fully in accord with those found by other investigators for groups of siblings of similar grade range measured upon tests similar to those used in this study. Upon individual tests (chiefly the Stanford-Binet), various investigators have reported sibling correlations as follows:

Rensch (1921)	.45
Elderton (1922)	
using Gordon's data	.54
using Drinkwater's data	.38 to .53
Hart (1924)	.40 to .46
Madsen (1924)	.63
Hildreth (1925)	.41
Jones (1928)	.49

Thorndike has reported correlations of .66 and .73 between I.E.R. group test scores (interpreted in terms of age norms) of siblings attending high schools.

Since correlations *a* and *b* for Group 2 (Table IV) are based upon only a small number of cases, and are not checked by any of our other correlations, we are not justified in attributing significance to the difference between them. Correlations *c* and *d*, based upon larger numbers, display a difference that is insignificant in the light of its probable error. In correlations *e* and *f*, what slight difference occurs is in favor of the unlike group! The correlation, .45, between the like pairs of Group 1 is certainly no higher than would be expected on the basis of previous work with siblings tested on the Stanford-Binet. In this connection, it is interesting to compare the differences found between the Stanford-Binet IQ's of four pairs of very unlike-appearing brothers. The average IQ difference for the four pairs was 9.5 as against 13.4 for the 34 like pairs, and 12.0 for a group of siblings differing less than two years in age who were studied by Tallman. The present study, then, offers no evidence in support of linkage between intelligence and general physical appearance of siblings.

It is possible that the siblings considered in this study were not selected rigorously enough to show linkage if it exists. To gain a little light on this possibility, we examined the records of four pairs of siblings who resembled one another so closely in appearance that only their differences in size served to distinguish them for the casual observer. The IQ's of these pairs were as follows:

1. Brothers of ten and seven, IQ's 103 and 105
2. Sisters of eleven and ten, IQ's 92 and 91
3. Sisters of eleven and eight, IQ's 128 and 95
4. Sisters of seven and five, IQ's 87 and 116.

Two pairs were very similar in IQ, but the other two pairs showed differences in IQ that were exceeded by only one other pair of Group 1.

Fingerprints were taken by the writers for Cases 1, 2 and 4, but not for Case 3 because of the illness of one of this pair. The patterns are indicated below. The friction ridge patterns of duplicate twins have proved to be so amazingly similar that Newman and others use them for one of the chief criteria in distinguishing between fraternal and duplicate twins. The writers believed that friction ridge patterns might be of great assistance in determining the amount of overlapping in sibling inheritance.

In Case 1, which is really the most striking case of physical resemblance among all the pairs studied, only two pairs of corresponding fingers have the same patterns. Yet the IQ's of these brothers differ by only two points. In Case 2 there is a high degree of correspondence between the finger patterns of the two sisters, and also a close correspondence in their IQ's (difference of only one point).

TABLE VI

	Left digits					Right digits				
	1	*2*	*3*	*4*	*5*	*1*	*2*	*3*	*4*	*5*
Case 1										
Oldest	W.	L.P.	L.P.	W.	L.P.	U.	L.P.	L.P.	W.	U.
Youngest	U.	R.	T.A.	U.	U.	U.	T.A.	U.	U.	U.
Case 2										
Oldest	U.	T.A.	U.	U.	U.	U.	T.A.	U.	U.	U.
Youngest	U.	T.A.	U.	U.	U.	U.	U.	U.	U.	U.
Case 4										
Oldest	U.	U.	U.	U.	U.	U.	R.	U.	U.	U.
Youngest	U.	U.	U.	U.	T.A.	U.	A.	T.A.	U.	U.

But the fact that most of the patterns are ulnar loops deprives this comparison of some of its significance, since the ulnar loop has the highest incidence of all patterns in the general population. In Case 4, which shows the large difference of 29 points of IQ, 7 of the 10 pairs of fingers have the same pattern (though all seven are ulnar loops). While it is possible that palm patterns, which were not taken, would have yielded results of positive significance, the fingerprint comparisons seem to furnish no explanation of the mental resemblance of Cases 1 and 2, nor of the disparity of Case 4.

SUMMARY

The study investigates the possibility that some of the genes involved in mental ability and general physical appearances are linked. A rating scale of physical resemblance was devised for use in selecting cases for mental tests. The average of two ratings on general resemblance had a reliability of .80 in a group of 141 white, English-speaking, like-sex sibling pairs attending elementary schools.

Intelligence tests were administered to a group of 34 elementary school sibling pairs showing strong physical resemblance, and to 84 pairs of junior high school and high school sibling pairs subdivided into groups showing much and little physical resemblance. The resulting correlations do not support the view that siblings who look most alike are most alike psychologically, or that those who look least alike show unusually large mental differences.

Of four elementary school pairs whose physical resemblance was extremely close (within the top 2 per cent of random pairs), two pairs were very similar in IQ, but two pairs showed differences in IQ that were exceeded by only one other pair of the elementary school series. Fingerprint comparisons obtained in three of these four cases failed to shed light on the causes of IQ resemblance and disparity.

Although a number of studies have been directed toward observing the effects of age on intelligence test scores, sampling has always been a difficult problem. Here Miles and Miles sampled from clubs, organizations, and church groups, paid their subjects for participation, and were successful in testing almost all of the subjects they worked with. The sample is at least specifiable, though far from random. The hazards of a cross-sectional study (of which they were well-aware) are, of course, present in full force. It is now known that longitudinal studies of bright samples show quite a different picture from the one sketched here. Nevertheless, the cross-sectional study provides a description of the population sampled at the time. The great difficulty that arises is in "causal" explanations. In this regard Kuhlen's paper, later in the book, is of interest.

The Correlation of Intelligence Scores and Chronological Age from Early to Late Maturity*

CATHERINE COX MILES

WALTER R. MILES

1932

The high correlation between intelligence age and chronological age during childhood and youth is a well-demonstrated fact. Intelligence scores or mental age norms based on the results of adequately validated tests are available for each year, often for each month of each year from the period of school entrance up to 'adulthood.' Adult levels are further differentiated into 'average' and 'superior' or even into IQ or corrected IQ ratios as in the Stanford-Binet test; into 'intelligence ratings' A, B, C, D, with their plus and minus subdivisions, as in the Army Alpha tests; into 'brightness indices' or derived IQ, as the Otis group tests; or into percentiles of adult performance, as in the Otis Tests, the National Tests, and the Thorndike Intelligence Examination for High School Graduates. Studies of intelligence have for the most part been made on the more available people: school children, college students, or comparatively young adult groups, such as institutional groups or the draft army and its sub-groups. Studies of occupational groups, drawn generally from younger adult populations, sometimes include intelligence ratings, but only very rarely is it possible to discover the age ranges or age means for these groups. Comparatively little has been reported con-

* Abridged from The Correlation of Intelligence Scores and Chronological Age from Early to Late Maturity, *The American Journal of Psychology*, 44, 1932, 44-78. Reprinted by permission of the authors and the publisher.

cerning the intelligence of older adults. In test standardization a plateau of ability 'adult intelligence' is generally assumed extending onward from the high point reached somewhere between the ages of 13 and 20 years.

*   *   *

Plan of present study.   In the following pages, tables and curves are presented and described which indicate the trend from childhood to old age of intelligence scores in samplings from the populations of two American towns. In order to find the relation between age and intelligence score throughout the life span, and especially in maturity, the intelligence was measured of persons from every decade and semi-decade beginning with the 'teen' age and continuing to senescence.

An effort was made to secure a sampling of the literate citizens in each of the two towns that would (1) present sufficiently large numbers at each age decade and semi-decade for statistical reliability and that would (2) be homogeneous in general mental character from age to age. Conclusive evidence regarding the relation of age to intelligence test score will, of course, not be available until scores have been obtained year after year from childhood until old age from the same members of large representative populations. In the meantime, if as far as possible the older, the middle aged and the younger members of the same social groups can be tested in sufficient numbers and selected in sufficient numbers at each point on the age scale a substitute comparison of some value can be made. The present study is an attempt in this direction. To what extent the trend in the populations examined is characteristic of the expected trend in a representative 'general population' will be indicated as far as possible by an analysis of the characteristics of the particular groups investigated.

Subjects.   The results presented are based on the scores of 823 *S*s from two cities, A and B. In City A (a manufacturing, industrial, and banking town, population about 12,000, situated in an agricultural community, the capital of its county) usable intelligence test scores were obtained from 122 adults (36 male, 86 female), ages 50 to 90. In City B (a residential and banking town, population about 15,000, also situated in an agricultural region, the seat of several private schools and near a university) usable scores were obtained from 134 children and youths (48 male and 86 female), ages 7 to 19 inclusive, and from 567 young adults and adults (249 male and 318 female), ages 20 to 94 inclusive.

Test instrument.   The test used was a specially printed form in large type (12-pt. Antique) of the first 60 items in the Otis Self-Administering Test of Intelligence, Higher Examination Form A given as a 15-min. test. We have found that scores on Form A with a 15-min. limit correlate $+ 0.86 \pm .02$ with scores on the same form used as a 30 min. test in the limited range of superior ability represented by 121 university students. Fifteen-minute scores of the same students correlate $+ 0.90 \pm .01$ with their 20-

min. scores on the same test. Fifteen-minute scores of 394 eighth grade pupils correlate $+ 0.971 \pm .003$ with their 20-min. scores. The scores for split halves of the 15-min. test correlate $+0.96 \pm .005$ for the university students. The 15-min. scores of 55 university students correlate $+ 0.71 \pm .05$ with their scores on the Thorndike Intelligence Examination for High School Students.

Each test was given individually and the time measured by stopwatch. The group of 823 persons whose scores have been found usable worked for exactly 15 min. each. Of these, 4 persons finished the test, having tried all 60 items. The score used is the number of correct responses.

Procedure.   The Otis 15-min. test was administered as part of a program of psychological experiments designed to investigate the mental abilities and capacities of normal persons in youth and maturity. The fact that this particular test was intended to measure 'intelligence' was not stressed. In our special printing (4-page booklet) of the first 60 items of the Otis S-A, Form A, in large type the word 'intelligence' was omitted from the title.

Every *S* was tested separately.

*   *   *

RESULTS

The mean scores for decades and semi-decades in the populations of the two cities appear in Tables I-IV inclusive. Fig. 1 gives the unsmoothed intelligence score curves based on the means for the 5- and 10-yr. periods. The scores from City B extend from the earliest age testable by this type of examination throughout the life span. Those from City A extend only through later maturity, from 50 to 90 yrs. of age.

TABLE I

**Otis S-A Intelligence Scores, by Semi-Decades, of 124 Adults,
Both Sexes, from City A**

		Otis 15-min. S-A scores		
No. cases	*Semi- decades*	*Means*	*σ*	*D/σ diff.*
18	50–54	30.94	8.92	
25	55–59	22.86	10.16	2.76
24	60–64	22.18	6.82	0.28
25	65–69	19.10	9.40	1.32
20	70–74	21.30	10.24	−0.74
5	75–79	16.90	8.08	1.02
6	80–84	15.82	10.28	0.20
1	85–89	5.50		

TABLE II

Otis S-A Intelligence Scores by Decades and by 20-yr. Periods of 124 Adults, Both Sexes, from City A

		Otis 15-min. S-A scores		
No. cases	*Period*	*Mean*	σ	*D/σ diff.*
43	50–59	26.2	10.6	
49	60–69	20.6	9.8	2.62
25	70–79	20.4	9.7	.84
7	80–89	14.5	10.0	1.55
92	50–69	23.3	10.5	
32	70–89	19.1	10.2	1.98

TABLE III

Otis S-A Intelligence Scores, by Semi-Decades, of 617 Adults, Both Sexes, from City B

		Otis 15-min. S-A scores		
No. cases	*Semi-decades*	*Means*	σ	*D/σ diff.*
51	15–19	38.50	8.04	
40	20–24	38.10	7.04	0.25
40	25–29	39.22	8.20	−0.66
43	30–34	35.26	10.32	1.94
44	35–39	35.06	8.44	0.09
48	40–44	33.82	11.36	0.59
42	45–49	34.50	11.04	−0.29
63	50–54	30.98	11.64	1.80
56	55–59	28.74	9.04	1.41
50	60–64	27.94	11.16	0.41
53	65–69	24.22	9.64	1.87
42	70–74	23.78	10.48	0.21
26	75–79	20.46	8.56	1.42
13	80–84	14.50	9.40	1.98
5	85–89	15.30	9.60	−.016
1	90–94	15.50	0	

TABLE IV

Otis S-A Intelligence Scores, by Decades, and by
20-yr. Periods of 616 Adults, Both Sexes,
from City B

		Otis 15-min. S-A scores		
No. cases	*Period*	*Mean·*	*σ*	*D/σ diff.*
51	15–19	38.5	8.0	−.11
80	20–29	38.7	7.9	2.53
87	30–39	35.1	9.6	.17
90	40–49	34.2	9.2	3.27
119	50–59	29.9	9.7	2.86
103	60–69	26.1	10.6	2.05
68	70–79	23.1	8.7	3.54
18	80–89	14.7	9.3	
131	15–29	38.6	7.9	3.84
177	30–49	34.7	10.4	6.51
222	50–69	28.1	10.4	5.48
86	70–89	20.9	10.2	

For discussion we have divided the curve into three somewhat arbitrarily selected periods: (1) The period of growth, from 7 or 8 to 18 or 19 yr.; (2) the period of early maturity, from 20 to 49 yr.; and (3) the period of later maturity, from 50 to 89 yr. It is not always possible to conduct the discussion strictly within the limits of this classification, but we have done so as far as was practicable. The results for these periods are presented in sequence.

Childhood and youth. The period of growth extends here to the age of 18 yr. The correlation between age and score from the earliest age tested until the maximum mean score is reached for this population (ages 7 to 17 yr. inclusive) is + 0.80 ± .023. This coefficient indicates the usual amount of agreement between score and age expected in groups of this size for the period in question and the score scatter shows no special selection of more or less superior individuals in one age as compared to another. The degree of brightness in the younger group and the homogeneity of mental talent for the early period is found in a comparison of the IQ at successive age levels, and in a comparison of the average scores (using 30-min. equivalents) with Otis' norms for the ages in question. . . .

The mental age equivalents for the three age levels, 12, 14, and 16 yr., are respectively 14·8, 16·2, and 17·4 yr. . . .

During the period of growth we are then dealing with a superior and homogeneous population whose Otis IQ approximates 115 and whose

mental development follows the usual upward trend in score expressed in
the coefficient + 0.80 ± .023.

Early maturity.   This period we count as extending from the third to
the fifth decade. The curve of intelligence score averages maintains almost

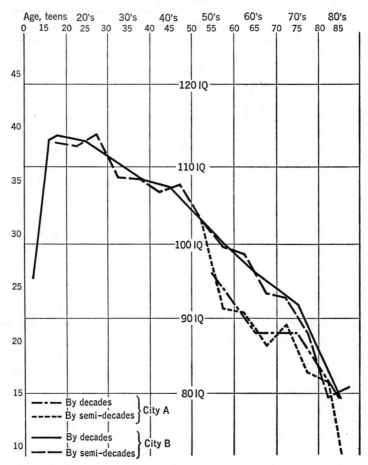

**Figure 1. The mean intelligence score plotted by decades and semi-decades for
the populations over 12 years of age studied in two cities with results for both
sexes combined.**
   Initial rise during the period of growth shows Pearson r, + 0.80.
   Decline from early to late maturity, r, −0.30 and −0.39.

the same level throughout the twenties. It drops very slightly in the 'thirties,' and but little more in the 'forties.' The average for the 'twenties' has
an equivalent mental age of 17 yr. 3 mo. (Otis IQ 114). The population is,
therefore, approximately equal in mental level to the 17-18 yr. old group
and in brightness to the other groups representing the period of growth.

Homogeneity of mental talent seems therefore to be demonstrated up to this point as far as this population is concerned.

* * *

From the values in Table IV it may be seen that the mean score and mental age for the 'twenties' is not lower than that for the previous semi-decade. The equivalent mental ages are the same, 17 yr. 3 mo., and the Otis IQ of 114 registered by both is approximately the same as the average for the members of the population under 20 yr. of age. The drop from the third to the fourth decade mean is represented by a decline of 7 mental age months, from 17 yr. 3 mo. to 16 yr. 8 mo. The difference between the two means is two and a half times its σ and therefore of possibly true significance. Between the 'thirties' and the 'forties' the drop is only one mental age month and the decline can not be regarded as in the least significant. From the 'forties' to the 'fifties,' however, a drop of 11 mental age months is registered and the difference between the two means is more than three times its σ and, therefore, very probably significant statistically.

* * *

The Otis IQ in the decade periods between 20 and 50 yr. of age are as follows: 114, 109, 107. If the population groups represented at the successive 10-yr. periods are homogeneous it appears from these IQ that within the age period in question a drop of about 7 IQ points has taken place. The Otis IQ for the 'fifties' shows a further drop to 102, five IQ points below the 40-yr. level.

The coefficient of correlation between life age and score during this period gives a further measure of the decline in scoring ability. The coefficients for various parts of the age span and for the total range from the late teens to the 'nineties' appear in Table V. . . .

From the peak, mental age 17 yr. 5 mo., of the intelligence score curve reached at approximately the age of 18 yr. the trend is first almost level, then it gradually declines to a point at the age of 50 yr. some 15 or 16 mental age months lower (mental age 16 years 1 month). The decline in Otis IQ points is from 115 to 104.5 and the correlation coefficient indicating the relation of score to age is -0.283 for males and females combined.

Later maturity.   This we have considered as covering from the sixth to the ninth decade. From the age of 50 yr. onward scores for two populations, Cities A and B, are available. It is obvious from the intelligence score curves for these two cities (Fig. 1) that A and B represent different levels of intelligence. It is therefore necessary to consider them separately and not as a single larger population except where trend during the age period of 50 to 90 yr. is being considered. However, it is equally clear that the score curves for both follow approximately the same downward course. The average population of one city registers at successive decades mean scores

TABLE V

Correlations between Age and Intelligence Score in the Age Range 15 to 95 Years

Age range	Sex	City A No. cases	Product-moment r	Sex	City B No. cases	Product-moment r
15–55				M & F	368	−.283 ± .031
30–55				M	106	−.108 ± .065
30–55				M & F	249	−.191 ± .040
15–95				M & F	620	−.528 ± .021
20–95				M	250	−.465 ± .032
20–95				F	319	−.532 ± .026
20–95				M & F	569	−.504 ± .021
30–95				M	207	−.371 ± .040
30–95				F	282	−.520 ± .028
30–95				M & F	489	−.455 ± .023
40–95				M	166	−.381 ± .044
40–95				F	234	−.489 ± .033
40–95				M & F	400	−.447 ± .026
50–95	M	36	−.302 ± .103	M	128	−.392 ± .051
50–95	F	86	−.367 ± .064	F	183	−.392 ± .042
50–95	M & F	122	−.343 ± .055	M & F	311	−.385 ± .032

	City A and City B combined		
Age range	Sex	No. cases	Product-moment r
50–95	M	166	−.387 ± .045
50–95	F	267	−.370 ± .036
50–95	M & F	433	−.372 ± .028

regularly divergent from those of the other and this divergence is always in the same direction, *i.e.,* City A is always lower than City B. The significance of the differences is as follows for the 'fifties,' 'sixties,' 'seventies,' and 'eighties': 2.01, 3.18, 1.21, 0.55. For the combined period of 50–69 yr. the ratio of difference to σ diff. is 3.75 and for the total period, 50–90 yr., it is 3.48.

The decade and semi-decade scores for City B, forming the curve which we have followed up to this point, show about the same rate of decline from the 'fifties' onward as was indicated from the 'forties' to the 'fifties.' From the 'forties' to the 'seventies' the decade scores describe a straight line, from the 'seventies' to the 'eighties' the curve is steeper. The loss in scoring power from the 5th to the 6th decade was 11 mental age months. From the 6th to the 7th decade it was 12 mo., from the 7th to the 8th there is a drop of 9 mo., and from the 8th to the 9th, 28 mo. The differences are respectively 3.2, 2.9, 2.0, and 3.5 times their σ and, therefore, possibly or probably of statistical significance. The semi-decade drops are always less than twice the σ diff.; they range in amount, for the successive groups having more than 10 members, from 2 to 18 mental age months and average 8.5 mental age months. The total mental age loss from the age of 50 yr. (M.A. 16–1) to the age of 85 yr. (M.A. 11–7) is 54 M.A. months or 4.5 M.A. years. The Otis IQ for the 6th to 9th decades are as follows: 102, 96, 92, 79. From the age of 50 yr. (IQ 104.5) to the age of 85 yr. (IQ 79) the loss is 25.5 IQ points. The relation between scoring ability and age in later maturity (City B) is indicated further by the correlation coefficients (Table IX); for the period from 50 to 95 yr. of age, r = $-0.385 \pm .032$ (both sexes combined) and -0.392 for either sex separately.

In City A the trend is similar but the curve is, as already noted, at a lower level. The decade populations are smaller than those for City B and the differences between levels are therefore correspondingly less significant statistically. The decade drops are respectively 2.6, 0.8, and 1.6 times the σ diff. Those for the semi-decades are with one exception (early to late 'fifties' 2.8) never even possibly of statistical significance. But gradual though they are, they total for the period from the beginning of the 6th to the middle of the 9th decade a loss of 52 mental age months or $4\frac{1}{3}$ mental age years, which is exactly the amount of loss suffered in City B in the same age period. The difference between the mean score for the 'fifties' and the mean score for the 'eighties' is 5.9 σ diff. The degree of correlation between score and age in City A from 50 to 95 yr. of age is $-0.343 \pm .055$, for the sexes combined; $-0.302 \pm .103$, for the males alone; or $-0.367 \pm .064$, for the females alone.

From the means for the populations in the two cities the decline in scoring power is seen to persist and even to increase from the beginning to the end of the period of late maturity. Differences, insignificant as the mean scores for successive 5-yr. periods are compared, become highly significant as they accumulate and the loss for the total period is found to be 7.48 σ diff. for the two cities combined. The correlation between intelligence score and age for the combined group, age 50 to 95 yr., is $-0.372 \pm .028$.

Summary. From a maximum score at the age of 18 yr. the curve of intelligence maintains almost a plateau through the 'twenties,' begins then to fall, and persists in its downward course, at first slowly, then more rapidly until the end of the life span. The drop in intelligence from the age of 18 to the age of 85 yr. (City B) measured in 15-min. scores on the Otis S-9 test is 24 points, 62% of the original high score; in mental age months it is 70 (5 yr. 10 mo.), in Otis IQ points it is 36. The correlation between age and score from the age of 20 to the age of 95 yr. is approximately

$-0.50 \pm .02$, and the difference between the average score in the 'twenties' (City B) and that in the 'eighties' (City B) is 9.9 σ diff.

* * *

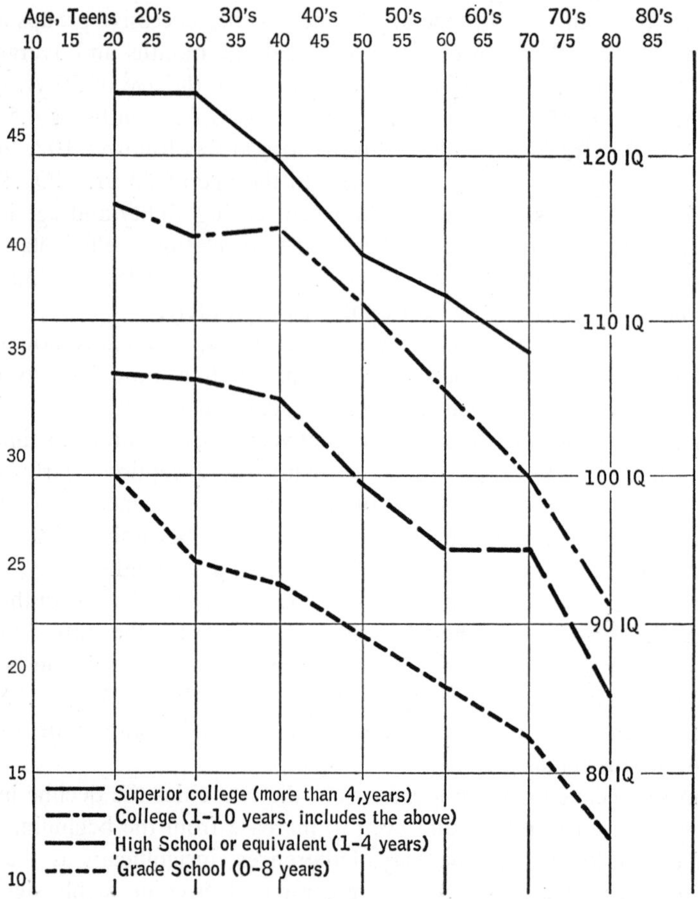

Figure 2. Decade distributions of mean intelligence scores for groups representing 4 educational levels (data from both cities combined).

For the same age period there were 289 persons who could be so classified. The percentage of Ss in each of the classes was as follows:

	City A	City B
Grade School	60%	27%
High School	26%	44%
College	14%	29%

This striking dissimilarity in the constitution of the two groups and the resultant divergence of the curve of one from that of the other suggested the desirability of analysing both populations in terms of educational status.

In deriving mean scores for the three educational levels decade by decade the results from the two cities are combined. . . . Plotted curves for the three contrasted groups appear in Fig. 2. Here in addition to the college group as represented in the tables we have set off a superior (more than 4 yrs.) college population.

It is strikingly evident, first of all, that the same tendency for increasing age to be associated with intelligence score decrement is a characteristic of each of the educational groups. In IQ points lost from the 'fifties' to the 'nineties' there is little to choose between the three, the people of grade school education lose 26 points, those with high school training 28, and those with college opportunity 27. The correlations suggest that there is a slightly stronger relationship between score and age the higher the educational class.

TABLE VI

Correlations between Age and Intelligence Score in the Age Range 20 to 95 yr. at Three Educational Levels
(Cities A and B combined)

Educational level	Sex	No. cases	Product-moment r
Grade School	M	74	−.401 ± .065
(0–8 Grades)	F	92	−.361 ± .061
	M & F	166	−.394 ± .045
High School	M	64	−.413 ± .070
(9–12 Grades)	F	175	−.509 ± .038
and N. and B.	M & F	239	−.403 ± .037
College	M	121	−.436 ± .050
(1–10 years)	F	103	−.544 ± .047
and S. Coll.	M & F	224	−.439 ± .036

The decrement from decade to decade within the three educational levels is not large. No one of the differences is statistically significant for our comparatively small groups. But the fall is almost regularly continued whatever the degree of education and the result is a loss of 4 to 5 mental age years during the period of maturity.

The striking feature of the present comparison is the practical advantage of the person of greater education and higher initial IQ over the person of lesser education and poorer initial mental equipment. The individual who starts with the ability that measures during the period of growth at or near the average falls to the 6th intelligence score percentile for adults by the time he reaches age 75. The person who starts near the upper quartile falls during the same period to the low average score indicated by the 33rd percentile. The person whose rating during the period of growth registers at the 93rd percentile scores even in the eighth decade at the 50th intelligence score percentile which is the average for adults in general and an average based in large part on groups in the early maturity age range. Individuals having at this later period in life an intelligence scoring ability that is average or above for active adults and combined with it a great wealth of experience, easily maintain their eminence and leadership in the affairs of men and may successfully continue their business and professional activities to very advanced age.

*   *   *

DISCUSSION

The results presented in this paper we have qualified because of the size of the samples and the character of the populations studied, but we have no reason to surmise that the findings would be significantly different if the investigation were to be repeated on a larger scale in several communities representing different social and economic strata. We have been careful to describe and discuss our data as measures of intelligence in the form of scores on the 15-min. Otis S-A Higher Examination. While not inclined to weave a halo about this test we are nevertheless bound to express some confidence in it as an indicator. For the practical purpose in hand we know of no better present-day instrument. The examination was administered with great care as to procedure and detail and under ideal conditions. It bore the caption, "Good-Judgment Question Series," with no mention of "intelligence" or "mental ability." It was not forbidding, in fact the contrary, as proven by the record that only 3 people out of 856 for any subjective reason balked at trying. A positive score could be made by practically everybody from 7 years of age to the oldest persons who could leave their homes, while at the same time only 4 members of the rather large group examined were able to finish, having tried all 60 items offered. The trustworthiness of the 15-min. test score compared to a similar test of 20- or 30-min. duration has been amply demonstrated, as well as in comparison with much longer examinations.

We examined intelligence by what is called a speed test in distinction to a power test. The circumstances of the experimental program seemed to demand this technique. Of course it may be objected that aging is itself a biological slowing down and that effective intelligence in the mature is not necessarily a thing that, to work well, must function at whip-cracker speed.

This common observation on the decreasing speed of the old is doubtless a popular way of recognizing and naming the progressive decrement discussed in this paper. While the speed test may seem to some unfair to the old, we can not close our eyes to the strong probability indicated by many well conducted studies, which we need not discuss now, that speed and power in mental operations are closely related and at base may well be dependent on the same conditions.

The factor of disuse or practice we have to been able to analyze or equate in the successive decade groups. It seems probable that the test items are not greatly at fault in this respect, as evidenced by the very wide applicability of the test. Subjects did not complain of inability to understand the wording of the items nor did they claim that the questions were unfamiliar in form or substance. Naturally some of those in the 'teens' were more familiar with being tested but there was probably little difference in this respect for all adults over 30 years of age.

Taking all of these things into consideration we see no conditions requiring that a special discount be levied against our findings nor, on the other hand, should they be considered beyond criticism. To use a phrase from Claude Bernard, "The investigator should have a robust faith and yet not believe." We have tried to do both of these things in the present study. But it is our opinion that anyone who works with a large or moderately large body of data, representative of normal human intelligence throughout the life-span, is certain to be impressed with the general regularity of the results and the characteristic course taken by the mean values for the successive ages.

SUMMARY

(1) The correlation of intelligence scores with chronological age during childhood and youth is well-known and has often been demonstrated. Hypothetical curves for the course of intelligence in later life have been drawn, usually from studies on more or less atypical groups and with relatively few data for ages beyond 50 years. The correlation coefficients previously reported have ranged from -0.011 to -0.35.

(2) The relation between age and intelligence throughout the life span was investigated in the present study by securing intelligence scores on samplings (from two fair sized American towns), for every decade and semi-decade from 7 to 92 years of age.

(3) All the intelligence tests for both children and adults, males and females, were made by means of a large type edition of the first 60 items of the Otis Self-Administering Test of Intelligence, Higher Examination, Form A, given as a 15-min. test. Such a 15-min. test has been found to correlate $+0.86 \pm .02$, with scores on a similar 30-min. test in the limited range of superior ability represented by 121 university students. The test was administered individually under ideal conditions. Only 3 people out of a total of 856 for any reason objected to taking the examination, which passed under the name of "Good-Judgment Question Series." Only 4 people of the entire group were able to complete the test in the 15-min. period.

(4) For the age span 7 to 17 years inclusive the coefficient found be-

tween age and score was $+0.80 \pm .023$. The age group ranging from 15 yr. 0 mo. to 16 yr. 11 mo. registered a mental age of 17·4, and the next 2-yr. group, which represents the peak of ability in these findings, exceeds this level by only one month (17·5).

(5) From the high point in the intelligence score curve represented at about 18 yrs. of age the trend is at first almost level, then gradually declines, dropping 15 or 16 mental age months by the chronological age of 50 years. In this period covered by the 3rd to the 5th decade the decline in Otis IQ points is from 115 to 104.5 and the correlation coefficient indicating the relation of score to age is -0.283 for males and females combined.

(6) The drop in intelligence score from age 18 to age 85 (City B) amounted to 62% of the original high score and in mental age months to a decline of 5 yr. and 10 mo. The correlation between age and score from the age of 20 to 95 years is approximately $-0.50 \pm .02$ and the difference between the average scores in the 'twenties' and in the 'eighties' (City B) is 9.9 σ diff.

(7) Distribution of the Otis 15-min. scores in terms of the Army brightness classification, A to E, shows that the Classes A and B progressively decrease with increasing age, and disappear altogether in both populations in the 9th decade. Groups $C-$, D, and E, practically non-existent in the earliest adulthood in our population, include altogether 35% in the 8th and 55% in the 9th decade.

(8) The downward trend of intelligence scores as age increases is shown to be definitely a characteristic of both sexes. In 3 or 4 comparisons out of 5 the men demonstrate somewhat better ability to score on the test, but this superiority is not regular throughout the life span and may be attributable chiefly to errors in sampling.

(9) The two cities studied exhibited considerable average difference in educational level, but the curves for decline of score with age were found to follow parallel courses. When classified according to educational level all groups exhibited the same tendency for increasing age to be associated with intelligence score decrement. From 50 to 90 years people of grade school education lost 26 Otis IQ points, those with high school training 28, those with college opportunities 27 points.

(10) The correspondence between the degree of education and the degree of brightness was prominent. There was a slightly stronger relationship between score and age in the highest educational class, but the great advantage of the individual who starts with high initial ability is evident. The person who registers, in youth, at the 93rd percentile score, according to the rate of decline found, would be in the 50th intelligence score percentile for average adults on reaching the 8th decade of life.

In this small lithoprint monograph, Thurstone set forth the theory of multiple factors and the first technique he devised for calculating the factors. Although the calculational techniques were soon changed, the comments on the "meaning" of factor analyses and the introduction to the theory are still fresh and clear. You will find that a careful reading of even these few pages will help you greatly in understanding the basic language of factor analysis and the applications of this powerful technique.

The Theory of Multiple Factors*

L. L. THURSTONE

1932

Introduction

These notes have been prepared for teaching purposes in a course on "The Theory of Psychological Measurement" at the University of Chicago. Most of the literature on the factor problem revolves about the Spearman single common factor method and its interpretation and much of it is beside the essential points. The literature on this subject has tended temporarily to obscure the significance of Professor Spearman's contributions to psychological method. It is a powerful tool that Spearman has invented for us and it is our present purpose to generalize it so that factor methods may be used on those many problems in psychology and social science in which the single factor pattern of Spearman is too simple and for which several independent factors must be postulated.

The student who begins his study of the factor problem should read Spearman's early papers. His book, "The Abilities of Man", has its main content in the appendix which should have been expanded to be the book itself. Holsinger's lithographed monograph on the tetrad difference criterion contains a description of the tetrad difference method and several probable error formulae. The principal contribution to the multiple factor problem is Kelley's "Crossroads in the Mind of Man". Most recent writers on the factor problem have used the tetrad difference method. In these notes we have described several methods of dealing with the factor problem which are not based on the tetrad difference. The tetrad difference method is shown to be a special case of the multiple factor methods here described. But even when only one factor is to be investigated it is not necessary to

* Excerpts from the introduction and first chapter, pp. i-vi and 1-9, of *The Theory of Multiple Factors*, Louis Leon Thurstone (published and copyrighted by the author, 1933). Reprinted by permission of Thelma G. Thurstone.

compute tetrads in order to obtain the least square single factor solution for a table of intercorrelations.

Before the student turns to the controversial papers in the journals he might be warned about several points. These points are: 1) the distinction between Spearman's contribution to quantitative method and his hypothesis concerning a common factor "g" in intelligence; and 2) the nature of uniqueness in the factor problem and in scientific proof generally.

If you were asked whether you "believe" in the Spearman two factor theory you could not give an answer unless you knew what was meant by the inquiry. Confusion can be avoided by interpreting the question before answering it. Spearman's two factor method refers to two factors, namely, a factor common to all of the tests or variables, and a factor that is specific for each test or variable. It would be less ambiguous to refer to Spearman's method as a single factor method because it deals with only one common or general factor. If there are five tests that have a single common factor and a specific for each test, then Spearman's method involves the assumption of one common and five specific factors, or six factors in all. We shall refer to his method less ambiguously as a single factor method.

We must distinguish next between Spearman's method of analyzing the intercorrelations of a set of variables for a single common factor and his theory that intelligence is such a common factor which he calls "g." Much of the confusion in the controversial literature on this subject is caused by a failure to see this distinction clearly. If we start with a given table of intercorrelations it is possible by Spearman's method, and also by other methods, to investigate whether the given coefficients *can* be described in terms of a general or common factor plus specifics and chance errors. If the answer is in the affirmative, then we *can* state each test performance as a sum of the effects of 1) a common factor, 2) a factor specific to each test, and 3) chance errors. In factor theory, the last two are combined because they are both unique to each test. Hence the analysis yields a summation of two factors, namely, 1) a common factor, and 2) a factor unique to each test. About this aspect of Spearman's single factor method there can be no debate because it is straight and simple logic.

But there can be debate by those who *do not want* to describe the tests by a single factor even though Spearman's criterion is satisfied. Here we have the worst confusion in the whole subject. It is in a sense an epistomological issue. Even though a set of intercorrelations *can* be described in terms of a single factor it is possible, if you like, to describe the same correlations in terms of two or three or ten or any number of factors. The trouble here is that the debaters talk as though the factors were some sort of reality, that the factors should be searched for and tagged when found but this is the same troublesome illusion that appears elsewhere in science. An example or two from physics will illustrate the point. Consider Coulomb's inverse square law of electrical attraction. The force is expressed as a function of the separation of the charges. Now, if the charges were to be personified, they would probably be much surprised that we humans describe their activities in terms of their linear separation. There is no string between the charges and the linear separation would be to them perhaps a very trivial aspect of that which is happening and which constitutes their identity. The point is that the same effects *could* be described in terms of other coordinates but it is *convenient* for us to state the relation in terms of their separation. We are the ones who introduce the fiction of a linear separation as a convenient frame for our thinking.

But the force is also such a fiction. Nobody has ever seen or touched a force. If a particle moves we describe the situation with an arrow-head in the direction of motion, but if it suits our convenience we put two arrow-heads or more so that the observed motion may be expressed in terms that we have already been thinking about such as the x and y axes. Whether an observed acceleration is to be described in terms of one force (one arrow) or two forces parallel to the x and y axes is entirely a matter of convenience for us. In exactly the same manner we may postulate two or more factors in a correlation problem instead of one even when one factor would be sufficient. The only criterion here as elsewhere in science is that we shall have peace of mind about the phenomena that we are studying. If our schemes are inconsistent or if the phenomena are inconsistent with our schemes, then in order to regain peace of mind, we must either reinterpret the phenomena according to our scheme or else change the scheme to fit our experiences. But we try to save our scheme first. To ask whether there "really" are several forces when one is sufficient or to ask whether there "really" are several factors when one is sufficient is foolish because it is in the last analysis only a matter of preference and convenience anyway. If the situation is such that one factor is not adequate while two factors would be adequate, then you may think of two factors but you may state the problem in terms of more than two factors if your previous training or habits make that preferable. This point of view will save the student much useless labor.

Spearman believes that intelligence can be thought of as a factor that is common to all the activities that are usually called intelligent. Perhaps the best evidence is that if you make a list of stunts, as varied as you please, which all satisfy some common sense criterion that the subjects must be smart, clever, and intelligent to do the stunts well and that good performance does not depend primarily upon muscular strength or skill or upon other non-intellectual powers, then the inter-stunt correlations will all be positive. It is quite difficult to find a pair of stunts, both of which call for what would be called intelligence, as judged by common sense, which have a negative correlation. This is really all that is necessary to prove that what is generally called intelligence can be regarded as a factor that is conspicuously common to a very wide variety of activities. Spearman's hypothesis that it is some sort of energy is not crucial to the hypothesis that it is a common factor in intellectual activities.

In proving intelligence as a common factor in a quantitative way we meet a rather simple sort of difficulty about which more has been written than necessary. It is customary to postulate a single common factor (Spearman's "g") and to make the additional but unnecessary assumption that there must be nothing else that is common to any pair of tests. Then Spearman's single factor method is applied and it usually happens that a pair of tests in the battery has something else in common besides that which is common to all of the tests. For example, two of the tests may have in common the ability to write fast, facility with geometrical figures, or a large vocabulary. Then Spearman's criterion is not satisfied and the conclusion is then one of two kinds, depending on which side of the fence the investigator is on. If the investigator is out to prove "g," then he concludes that the tests are bad for one should not have tests that measure more than one factor! If the investigator is out to disprove "g," then he shows that Spearman's criterion is not satisfied and that therefore there is no "g." Neither conclusion is correct. The correct conclusion is that more than one general factor must be postulated in order to account for the intercorrelations, and that one of these general factors *may* still be what we should call intelligence. But the technique for multiple factor analysis has not been available and consequently we have been stumbling around with "group factors", as the trouble making factors have been called. A group factor is one that is common to two or more of the tests but not to all of them. We see therefore that Spearman's criterion, limited as it is to a single common factor, is not adequate for proving or disproving his own hypothesis that there is a conspicuous factor that is common to all intelligence tests. If his criterion gives a negative answer it simply means that the correlations require more than one common factor but only indirectly does it throw light on the extent and nature of the several factors, some of which may be common factors of minor importance. We do not need any factor methods at all to prove that a common factor of intelligence is a legitimate postulate. It is proved by the fact that all intelligence tests are positively correlated.

There is a rather general preference for a set of tests in a battery to contain only one common factor. A battery of tests is criticized when it is found that there are group factors present or that more than one general factor is needed to account for the intercorrelations. This idea is defensible in some situations and not in others. If the investigator is assembling a set of tests for the prediction of college scholarship, then the criterion of success is of course the prediction of scholarship. If he succeeds in doing that, then the battery of tests is a good one, quite irrespective of whether it requires more than one factor to describe the intercorrelations. There is nothing intrinsically good or bad about the presence of more than one common factor. If, on the other hand, the investigator is trying to assemble a battery of tests that shall measure a single mental trait, then he prefers to have them so constructed that one general common factor shall be conspicuous. But group factors may still be present without doing any harm whatever. Suppose that two of the tests in such a battery contain a factor in common, namely, that they both require a large vocabulary. The tests may contain the principal common factor which the group of tests represents but in addition the two tests may have a group factor also in common, the vocabulary. Spearman's criterion would not be satisfied and some of his students would be inclined to throw out one of the two tests in order to avoid having the group factor of vocabulary represented in two tests. They would be willing to have this factor represented in one of the tests but not in two of them because they want all of the tetrad differences to vanish! If the same set of tests were investigated with a multiple factor pattern it might be discovered that a conspicuous common factor runs through all of the tests and that in addition there are group factors of minor importance. The verification of the principal common factor "g" would still be satisfactory and the battery would be as good with the presence of minor common factors. In neither of the two cases considered is there anything intrinsically good or bad about the presence of group factors or factors which extend only to two or three tests.

The situation would be quite different if it were found that the tests contain two factors that are common to most of the tests in the battery. Then there would be justification for splitting the battery into two parts or in revising the tests so that each battery might represent only one principal factor. It should be remembered that if two factors are common to all of the tests in the battery they do not necessarily combine into a single factor. But this is not usually the debated case. Usually, the investigator merely wants all of the tetrads to vanish and in order to do so he throws out some of the tests that have minor common factors. This is not necessary even in those situations where it is desired to have a battery of tests with a conspicuous single common factor.

The "probable error phobia" is a mental disease which afflicts psychologists particularly. Its principal symptom is a fear of numbers that do not have probable error appendages. Perhaps it should be described as a compulsion neurosis. The patients refuse to write down interesting numbers just because they don't know how to compute the probable errors. They even refuse to think about numbers without the entanglement of probable errors and consequently their style is much cramped. This serious condition impedes progress. A healthier attitude is to regard probable errors in their true light, as aids in judging the order of magnitude of chance errors in numbers—when we can compute them conveniently. But the patients insist that the probable errors be a substitute for common sense and that is unfortunate. The student should be warned that it is really not a crime to give a correlation coefficient without a probable error. As a matter of fact, the fluctuations from one sample to another are much larger than the probable error. The probable error fits only the experimental case in which chance, and chance alone, is allowed to enter. But biased or constant errors are usually larger than chance errors.

These notes are divided into three sections which have been condensed from manuscript four or five times the present length. The first section is a description of the problem and the development of concepts that are useful in dealing with the problem. The second section is a generalized least square solution which is rather illuminating but exceedingly laborious in application. The fundamental factor theorem is there stated, namely, that *the number of factors required to account for a table of intercorrelations is the rank of their matrix*. The third section describes a least square solution by successive approximation that is applicable to any number of variables, to any number of factors, and to any required degree of accuracy. Special data sheets have been prepared for the computing. As an example, we have included the application of these methods to a table of intercorrelations of nine tests, from which three successive factors are extracted.

Tetrad differences need no longer be computed. Instead, we can get the first factor loadings or coordinates of the tests and these constitute the correlations between the tests and the most conspicuous common factor which may be called "g" if the variables are tests of intelligence. Group factors constitute no problem here. The theoretical coefficients obtained by the first factor loadings may then be compared directly with the obtained coefficients. If these discrepancies are small, we simply proceed to find the second most important factor and so on by the same procedure until we are satisfied that the residuals are small enough so that they can be ignored or until they are comparable with the probable errors of the given cofficients.

The development of factor methods will require that we study more mathematics, and as far as I am able to judge, the subjects that will help us most are vector analysis, the geometry of hyperspace, matrix theory. These subjects will help us more than the statistical theory by which we may be able to write more probable errors. It is the development of patterns for thinking about the complexities that are represented by a table of intercorrelations that we need first and these may lead to a realignment of the principal variables in terms of which we set up and think about psychological and social problems.

Theory of Multiple Factors

NATURE OF THE PROBLEM

One of the psychological problems that has engaged the attention of investigators for many years is the problem of isolating traits or separate mental abilities. This is a challenging problem in view of the fact that, in the nature of the case, we cannot observe a mental ability in isolation. The observations that are used in factor theory are practically always correlation coefficients or some comparable measure of association between pairs of performances. In this discussion we shall talk about tests, but the theory of multiple factors can be applied equally well to a table of correlation coefficients which represents other variables. We shall show in illustrative examples how the factor methods may be applied not only to psychological tests but also to such different variables as psychotic symptoms, vocational interests, physical measurements, and personality traits.

The data with which we start consist of a table of intercorrelations of a set of tests or other variables. The correlation coefficients may be product moment coefficients that have been computed from measurements of some kind or they may be tetrachoric correlation coefficients that are computed from records of the mere presence or absence of each of a pair of traits. We shall assume that in the usual case, every one of the variables has been correlated with every other variable, but this is not an absolutely necessary condition. It is, of course, preferable to have the table of correlation coefficients complete.

If a series of psychological tests has been intercorrelated, the questions which we try to answer by means of the factor methods are: 1) How many factors must we postulate in order to account for the observed correlations between the variables? and 2) How much of each factor is represented by each of the tests or variables?

In all of our present work on factor theory we shall assume that the factors combine in a linear manner in order to produce the total performance in a test. This is the assumption of the usual regression equation. The general pattern that we shall follow in factor analysis can be illustrated by a linear equation for two general factors as follows.

$$S_a = a_1 x_1 + a_2 x_2 \tag{1}$$

in which

S_a = standard score in test A.
x_1 = standard score in ability no. 1.
x_2 = standard score in ability no. 2.
a_1 and a_2 are coefficients.

The two abilities are assumed to be uncorrelated. The performance S_a, on a test, is here expressed as a function of the scores in the two general abilities. If the value of a_1 is large and the value of a_2 is small, then we should interpret the equation by saying that test A calls for much of ability number 1 but very little of ability number 2.

Inspection of equation (1) shows that a good performance S_a, on a test, may be accounted for by superiority in either of the two abilities that the test demands, or else by fair ratings on both of the abilities. The same reasoning may be extended, of course, to the situation in which a test performance is determined by three, four, or more abilities. Hence, a good performance on a test does not prove that the subject has superior rating on any one ability except in the case in which a test is assumed to represent only one ability. The latter is the special case to which Spearman and his students have given much attention.

The coefficients a_1 and a_2 are essentially properties of the test in that these coefficients indicate the extent to which test A calls for each of the abilities 1 and 2. We shall see that these coefficients have certain very definite restrictions in possible magnitude. The values of x_1 and x_2 are attributes of the individual subject who makes the performance S_a.

We shall consider the combination of equation (1) which refers to test A with a second similar equation for another test B. We have then

$$S_a = a_1 x_1 + a_2 x_2 \qquad (1)$$

$$S_b = b_1 x_1 + b_2 x_2 \qquad (2)$$

in which

$S_b =$ standard score in test B.

b_1 and b_2 are the factor loadings for test B that correspond to a_1 and a_2 for test A.

The variance of the performance of a group of subjects in test A may be written as follows,

$$\sigma_a^2 = \frac{\Sigma S_a^2}{N} = 1 \qquad (3)$$

since S_a are standard scores by definition. The size of the sample is designated N. Also by (1)

$$\sigma_a^2 = \frac{\Sigma(a_1 x_1 + a_2 x_2)^2}{N} \qquad (4)$$

$$= \frac{1}{N}\Sigma(a_1^2 x_1^2 + a_2^2 x_2^2 + 2a_1 a_2 x_1 x_2) \qquad (5)$$

$$= a_1^2 \frac{\Sigma x_1^2}{N} + a_2^2 \frac{\Sigma x_2^2}{N} + 2a_1 a_2 \frac{\Sigma x_1 x_2}{N} \qquad (6)$$

But $\quad \dfrac{\Sigma x_1^2}{N} = \dfrac{\Sigma x_2^2}{N} = 1 \qquad$ since x_1 and x_2 are standard scores. $\qquad$ (6a)

We shall assume that the two abilities are entirely independent so that if a man has, let us say, a high rating in one of the two abilities, we can make no guess whatever as to how he will rate in the other ability. If this assumption were not made, then we should be dealing with an analytical situation in which the two abilities would have something in common, they would not be truly separate abilities, and the solution would be as awkward as the usual multiple correlational problems. While it is possible to handle the problem in terms of abilities that are not distinct, it is certainly simpler to postulate a set of abilities that are distinct. Then the cross products conveniently disappear so that

$$r_{12} = \frac{\Sigma x_1 x_2}{N\sigma_1 \sigma_2} = O \text{ or } \Sigma x_1 x_2 = O \tag{7}$$

Hence by equations (3), (6) and (7) we have

$$a_1^2 + a_2^2 = 1 \text{ in which } a_1 \text{ and } a_2 \text{ are factor loadings of } A. \tag{8}$$

and we shall find that this simple relation is quite useful in factor theory. It shows a necessary limitation in the magnitudes of a_1 and a_2 that enter into equation (1). By analogy with (8) we write the corresponding relation for test B, namely

$$b_1^2 + b_2^2 = 1 \tag{9}$$

We shall see that this relation can be extended to any number of abilities or factors, that is, *the sum of the squares of the factor loadings in a test must equal unity.*

GEOMETRICAL INTERPRETATION

These equations (8) and (9) determine the same circle with center at origin. We can represent the two test performances vectorially with inter-

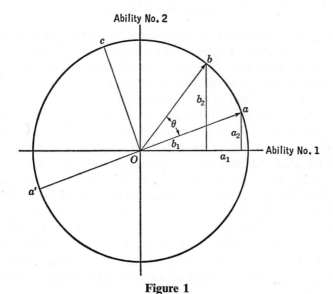

Figure 1

esting results. In *figure 1* let the two coordinate axes represent the two abilities respectively. Then, since a_1 and a_2 are the coefficients for test A, we may represent this test as a vector $\overline{oa}$ and test B may be represented by the vector $\overline{ob}$. Or we may think of the tests as represented by points in the periphery of a circle. If we were dealing with a three factor system we should have the tests represented as points on the surface of a three dimensional sphere and, in fact, the same reasoning may be extended by analogy to a sphere of a number of dimensions equal to the number of factors or abilities.

Let us now consider a geometrical interpretation of the correlation between the two tests. Since S_a and S_b are both standard scores, their respective standard deviations are both unity and the correlation then reduces to

$$r_{ab} = \frac{\Sigma S_a \cdot S_b}{N} \tag{10}$$

By (1) and (2)

$$S_a \cdot S_b = (a_1 x_1 + a_2 x_2)(b_1 x_1 + b_2 x_2) \tag{11}$$

$$= a_1 b_1 x_1^2 + a_2 b_2 x_2^2 + a_1 b_2 x_1 x_2 + a_2 b_1 x_1 x_2 \tag{12}$$

$$\frac{\Sigma S_a \cdot S_b}{N} = a_1 b_1 \frac{\Sigma x_1^2}{N} + a_2 b_2 \frac{\Sigma x_2^2}{N} + a_1 b_2 \frac{\Sigma x_1 x_2}{N} + a_2 b_1 \frac{\Sigma x_1 x_2}{N} \tag{13}$$

But the cross products vanish because the abilities are uncorrelated. Hence by (6a)

$$r_{ab} = a_1 b_1 + a_2 b_2 \tag{14}$$

Equation (14) shows that the correlation r_{ab} is the cosine of the angle between the two vectors in *figure 1*. If we have a table of intercorrelations of n variables or tests, then these n tests could be represented as points on the periphery of a circle when only two factors are operative. The intercorrelations are the cosines of the central angles.

It should be carefully noted that a table of intercorrelations gives us the angular separations of the tests but no information whatever as to where the coordinate axes should be located. Thus, in *figure 1*, the fact that the cosine of the angle between the two vectors a and b is known does not tell us anything about the locations of the principal axes. An analogous situation in linear measurement would be the case in which the differences in elevation between pairs of points were known. No amount of such information can tell us anything at all about absolute elevations. It is just as well to face the philosophical problem involved here by frankly acknowledging that absolute elevations refer, necessarily, to some conventional datum such as sea level. And just so we must acknowledge that when the intercorrelations are known for a series of tests, we have no basis for locating any sort of absolute coordinate axes, absolute factors, or absolute mental abilities. They can be located anywhere you please so long as they agree with our definition that they should be orthogonal.

*   *   *

The geometrical interpretation of the correlation coefficients can be made clearer, perhaps, by one or two additional examples. A test C in *figure 1* would be expected to have a zero correlation with test A because the central angle between these two tests is $90°$, and consequently the cosine of the central angle is zero. An angular separation greater than $90°$, but less than $270°$ would represent two tests that are negatively correlated since the cosine of such an angle is negative. The two factors are independent by definition, their intercorrelation is zero and their angular separation is therefore $90°$. The two tests A and A' which are separated by $180°$ would have a correlation of -1 since the cosine of that angle is -1. Such relations are seldom found in mental tests, because the very abilities that produce a good performance in test A would have to produce a poor performance in test A', and such pairs of tests are certainly rare if they can be found at all. But this type of relation is found in other traits such as the two traits "to like spinach" and "to hate spinach" or between the traits "tactful" and "tactless."

So far we have treated the correlations between the tests as though they were free from chance errors, i.e., as though the tests were perfectly reliable. The chance error factor will now be introduced. Let

N = size of sample
X_a = obtained raw score in test A.
X = true score in the test
x_a = raw deviation score
x = true deviation score
m = mean raw score for a large group of subjects.

By assuming the group to be large, we may ignore the chance error in the mean, m. Then

$$X_a = m + x_a \tag{15}$$

and

$$X = m + x \tag{16}$$

Therefore the absolute amount of the chance error for an individual subject is

$$X_a - X = x_a - x = e \tag{17}$$

The standard deviation of the distribution of absolute errors in the individual scores is therefore

$$a_e = \sqrt{\frac{\Sigma e^2}{N}} \tag{18}$$

in which a_e is the standard error of the raw test scores. The total variance in the test performance of a group may be expressed, therefore, as

$$a_1^2 + a_2^2 + a_3^2 + \cdots \cdots a_n^2 + a_e^2 = 1. \tag{19}$$

This is merely an extension of equation (8) to cover n factors and to include that part of the total variance which is due to chance errors, namely a_e^2. The sum of the several variances is equal to unity in (19) because it is assumed that the performances have been reduced to standard form.

If we write equation (8) with the addition of the term a_e^2 for variance due to chance, we have

$$a_1^2 + a_2^2 + a_e^2 = 1 \tag{20}$$

This equation shows that test A can be represented as a point on the surface of a three-dimensional sphere, that two of the principal axes represent factors or abilities while the third represents variation due to chance error. If we write the corresponding equation for test B, we have

$$b_1^2 + b_2^2 + b_e^2 = 1 \tag{21}$$

The test B can be represented also as a point on the surface of a sphere, and the coordinates of the point will then be $(b_1 \ b_2 \ b_e)$. But both of these tests, A and B, cannot be represented on the same three-dimensional sphere because while a_1 and b_1 refer to the same coordinate axis, and while a_2 and b_2 both refer to a second coordinate axis, the projections a_e and b_e must be represented on two orthogonal coordinate axes. While both of these projections a_e and b_e refer to chance errors, they are, in the nature of the case, uncorrelated and hence their angular separation must be $\pi/2$. However, we can represent these two tests as two points on the surface of a *four-dimensional sphere* in which the four coordinate axes represent the two mental abilities and the two uncorrelated chance errors.

The correlation between these two tests is the cosine of the central angle between them in space of four dimensions. The equations for the two test scores, assuming two general mental abilities and chance error in each test, are then as follows.

$$S_a = a_1 x_1 + a_2 x_2 + e_a \tag{22}$$

in which e_a refers to the error in the individual standard score S_a. Also

$$S_b = b_1 x_1 + b_2 x_2 + e_b \tag{23}$$

Hence

$$a_1^2+a_2^2+a_e^2=1 \qquad \text{(Similar to equation (8) except for} \qquad (20)$$

$$b_1^2+b_2^2+b_e^2=1 \qquad \text{introduction of chance errors)} \qquad (21)$$

and the correlation between the two tests is

$$r_{ab}=a_1b_1+a_2b_2 \qquad (24)$$

Note that the product $e_a e_b$ is not included in (24), because the chance errors in the tests are supposedly uncorrelated, and hence they must be represented as projections on two orthogonal axes. Equation (24) is identical with (14), but (24) represents the situation in which $a_1\ b_1\ a_2\ b_2$ are depressed because of the introduction of chance errors, while (14) represents the situation in which errors of measurement are assumed to be absent. We must deal in the multiple factor problem with methods of handling obtained coefficients for variables that are subject to considerable errors of measurement.

Equation (24) may be used to investigate the reliability coefficient. If two parallel tests A and A' are correlated, then, we have the following arrangement of the coordinates.

Test	1	2	3	4	
A	a_1	a_2	a_e	o	Coordinates with four
A'	a_1	a_2	o	a'_e	orthogonal axes

$$r_{aa} = a_1^2 + a_2^2 \qquad (25)$$

But

$$a_1^2+a_2^2+a_e^2=1 \qquad (20)$$

and since the tests are parallel, it is assumed that

$$a_e=a'_e \qquad (26)$$

Hence

$$r_{aa}=1-a_e^2 \qquad (27)$$

If the test has a reliability coefficient of, say, $r_{aa}=.90$, then $a_e^2=.10$. In other words, a reliability coefficient of .90 means that one tenth of the total variance is to be attributed to errors of measurement. But when $a_e^2=.10$, then $a_e=.32$ so that, in the geometrical interpretation, the test has a projection of about one third of the unit vector for the errors of measurement. This is a considerable deviation from the vector that would represent an absolutely self-consistent test of the same abilities and it should be noted that the reliability coefficient in this example is as high as .90.

It is convenient to use a special name and notation for a factor or ability which is unique for a test so that its loading is zero in all the other tests in the correlation table. Such a factor is called a *specific factor*. The total variance of the standard scores in test A can therefore be described as follows

$$a_1^2 + a_2^2 + a_3^2 + \cdots \cdot a_n^2 + a_e^2 + a_s^2 = 1 \tag{28}$$

in which the subscripts 1, 2, 3, ---n refer to factors or abilities common to two or more of the tests, the notation a_e^2 refers to the variance caused by chance errors, while a_s^2 is that part of the variance which is attributable to a factor unique in test A. If we write the correlation between two parallel tests A and A', for two common factors, we have

$$r_{aa} = a_1^2 + a_2^2 + a_s^2 \tag{29}$$

But by (28) we have

$$r_{aa} = 1 - a_e^2 \tag{27}$$

as before. The difference between the variance due to chance errors a_e^2 and that which is due to the specific or unique factor a_s is that the self correlation of the test includes the specific factor but not the chance factor. This is readily seen if we consider the actual repetition of the test. The chance errors on the two occasions are uncorrelated while the specific ability is, of course, called for in both performances. We shall find it convenient to combine these two variances into a single term so that

$$a_e^2 + a_s^2 = a_o^2 \tag{30}$$

This is done because in analyzing a table of intercorrelations we may discover that a certain variance a_o^2 is unique for test A but we can not ascertain how much of this variance should be attributed to chance errors that are unique for the one particular occasion or performance and how much of it is due to some specific ability unique for test A and not called for in the other tests of the table. The separation of these two variances a_e^2 and a_s^2 can be effected experimentally by the usual methods of determining the reliability of a test. However, both a_e and a_s drop out of the expression for the correlation between two tests because the two specifics are uncorrelated by definition as well as the chance errors in the tests.

The relation between the factor loadings, the variance due to chance errors, the specific factor, and the reliability coefficient of a test, and the intercorrelation between two tests may be summarized as follows. Let us consider the two tests A and B and their comparable tests A' and B'. These four tests are defined by the following loadings.

	Factor 1	Factor 2	Specifics		Errors	of	Measurement	
Test A	a_1	a_2	a_s	o	a_e	o	o	o
Test A'	a_1	a_2	a_s	o	o	a'_e	o	o
Test B	b_1	b_2	o	b_s	o	o	b_e	o
Test B'	b_1	b_2	o	b_s	o	o	o	b'_e

The two parallel tests A and A' represent the same loading of the first factor and therefore the term a_1 is recorded for both of them. The two parallel forms B and B' also require the first ability or factor. This is represented by the loading b_1 for both of the B tests. If the two tests A and B do not require the first ability or factor to the same extent, then a_1 and b_1 will be to that extent numerically different. The same reasoning applies to the second factor loadings in the four tests.

Assume that test A contains a specific factor that is not found in any of the other tests with which it is compared. The loading of this specific factor in the performance on test A is represented by a_s and it is of course the same in the two parallel forms of the test, namely A and A'. The same reasoning applies to test B. Let the chance errors in test A be represented by a_e. Since the chance errors in tests A and A' are uncorrelated in the nature of the case, these two chance errors must be orthogonal and they are therefore represented as two uncorrelated factors. The same reasoning applies to the chance errors in the two parallel forms of test B.

The correlation between any two of these tests may be found, by analogy with equation 24. The reliability coefficient of test A is the correlation between the two parallel forms of the test, namely,

$$r_{aa'} = a_1^2 + a_2^2 + a_s^2 + a_e \cdot o + a'_e \cdot o$$
$$r_{aa'} = a_1^2 + a_2^2 + a_s^2 \tag{31}$$

This shows that the reliability of a test is determined by the first and second factor loadings in the test and by the specific factor which is of course also present in both forms of the test. Since we assume that the scores have been reduced to standard form, the total variance must be unity, but the total variance is

$$a_1^2 + a_2^2 + a_s^2 + a_e^2 = 1$$

Hence

$$r_{aa} = 1 - a_e^2$$

The correlation between two different tests A and B is written in the same manner.

$$r_{ab} = a_1 b_1 + a_2 b_2 + a_s \cdot o + b_s \cdot o + a_e o + b_e \cdot o$$
$$r_{ab} = a_1 b_1 + a_2 b_2$$

It is evident that the specific factor for test A is by definition absent in test B and vice versa and hence the correlation between the two tests is written in terms of the common factors only.

The part of the variance of a test which is due to factors common to other tests with which it is compared is *smaller* than the reliability of the test. We shall find it convenient to use a separate name for this part of the variance of a test. It will be called the *communality* of the test with reference to the given set of tests. These concepts can be summarized in the following definitions.

The total variance of a test is unity since the scores are reduced to standard form.

The reliability is the variance of a test with the error factor (errors of measurement) eliminated.

The communality is the variance of a test with both the error factor and the specific factor eliminated. The complement of the communality will be called the uniqueness of the test.

These definitions can be summarized for n factors in terms of our notation as follows.

$$\text{Total variance} = a_1^2 + a_2^2 + a_3^2 + \ldots a_n^2 + a_s^2 + a_e^2 = 1$$

$$\text{Reliability} \quad = a_1^2 + a_2^2 + a_3^2 + \ldots a_n^2 + a_s^2 \qquad = r_{aa} = 1 - a_e^2$$

$$\text{Communality} = a_1^2 + a_2^2 + a_3^2 + \ldots a_n^2 \qquad\qquad = h^2 = 1 - (a_e^2 + a_s^2)$$

$$\text{Specificity} \quad = \qquad\qquad\qquad\qquad\qquad a_s$$

$$\text{Uniqueness} \quad = \qquad\qquad\qquad\qquad a_s^2 + a_e^2 = a_o^2$$

The two terms a_s and a_e are unique for one test on one occasion and, for convenience, they will be combined so that

$$a_s^2 + a_e^2 = a_o^2$$

and hence the communality is written

$$h^2 = 1 - a_o^2$$

THE SPEARMAN TETRAD DIFFERENCE EQUATION

It may be shown that the present analysis is an extension of Spearman's methods for a single common factor. In fact, the tetrad difference equation of Spearman is a special case of the multiple factor methods that we are here describing. Consider the equation for the correlation between two tests A and B.

$$r_{ab} = a_1 b_1 + a_2 b_2 + a_3 b_3 + \cdots \cdot a_n b_n \qquad (31)$$

Impose Spearman's restriction that there shall be only one factor common to the tests and let that be factor No. 1. Then if $a_2 \neq 0$, b_2 must be zero or if $b_2 \neq 0$ then a_2 must be zero, for otherwise there would be two common factors. By the same reasoning the remaining terms drop out. Hence, with Spearman's restriction to one common factor, we have

$$r_{ab} = a_1b_1 \qquad \text{and by analogy}$$
$$r_{ac} = a_1c_1 \qquad\qquad\qquad (31a)$$
$$r_{ad} = a_1d_1$$
$$r_{bc} = b_1c_1$$
$$r_{bd} = b_1d_1$$
$$r_{cd} = c_1d_1$$

Then, evidently,

$$r_{ab} \cdot r_{cd} - r_{bc} \cdot r_{ad} = a_1b_1c_1d_1 - b_1c_1a_1d_1 = 0$$

This is Spearman's tetrad difference and it is thus seen to be a special case of the multiple factor problem.

It has long been realized that any differences observed in the United States between persons coming from different racial stocks or different countries may not be related to differences between similar groups who have remained abroad and so have not been subject to selective migration and altered environmental factors. No data were available for comparison until this study was performed. You should note that the age differences within each group are not analyzed. Is there significant information here?

Race Differences Studied in Different Environments*

ROSE N. FRANZBLAU

1935

PURPOSE OF THIS STUDY

The main purpose of this study was to discover whether there are any differences in intelligence between North and South Europeans when these groups are compared in their native habitat as well as in the United States.

* * *

THE RACIAL GROUPS INCLUDED

The blonde-haired, blue-eyed North Europeans represent as sharp a contrast to the black-haired, brown-eyed South Europeans as we can find within the Caucasian race. The climate in which these two groups live also differs greatly. For this reason these two contrasting groups were selected as the basis of this study.

The Danes were selected as representative of the North European group and the Italians were chosen as representative of the South European group. In each case, only such children as conformed to the racial type were chosen, *i.e.,* only blonde-haired, blue-eyed Danes and brown-haired, dark-eyed Italians. Samplings of these groups were selected from the population of the capital city of each country (which is also the largest city in each country).

To facilitate the study of physical maturity, which was one of the subsidiary investigations, only girls were included in the samplings. For obvious reasons, only those twelve years old or older were chosen.

* Adapted from Race Differences in Mental and Physical Traits: Studied in Different Environments. *Archives of Psychology*, No. 177 (New York, 1935). Reprinted by permission of the author and *Archives of Psychology*.

The groups were gathered in each case from schools drawing their enrollment from the upper and lower middle classes. In both cases, approximately one-half of the group were pursuing an academic course, and the other half were pursuing a commercial course.

The Danish group thus consisted of approximately 300 school girls over 12 years of age, having blonde hair and blue eyes and coming from middle class homes in the city of Copenhagen. Correspondingly, the Italian group consisted of approximately 300 school girls over 12 years of age, having black hair and dark eyes and coming from middle class homes in the city of Rome. As an added precaution, the parentage of all children was investigated and only those born of two native Danish or Italian parents, respectively, were selected.

In choosing comparable American samplings, the endeavor of the investigator was to match the European samplings as to racial type, age, social status, schooling and so forth. The problem of selection was, therefore, more difficult in the United States than it had been abroad. The samplings had to be taken, of course, where they could be found most abundantly.

For the Italian American group, New York City was chosen as the source because of its large Italian population. Only native children born of two immigrant Italian parents, and only those who had the characteristic hair and eye coloring, were included. To match the social levels of the European group as far as possible in the changed environment, girls were selected from schools on the lower East Side and from Walton High School on the one hand, and from Evander Childs High School on the other hand, giving, respectively, a lower and an upper middle class component. The age-range from which the group was selected was the same as in the case of the European samplings.

The assembling of the Danish American sampling presented much greater difficulty. One of the largest settlements in the United States is concentrated largely in Racine, Wisconsin, and the neighboring communities. Despite this fact the total number of Danish inhabitants is relatively small. When it is borne in mind that the sampling was to be limited to girls above 12 years of age who are natives born of two immigrant Danish parents, and who have blonde hair and blue eyes, the difficulty will be realized. However, with the valuable cooperation of the school authorities of Racine, Wisconsin, and Waukegan, Illinois, careful search of the Racine schools and those of all of the outlying communities yielded a group of approximately 300 girls who, with but few exceptions, measured up to all of the specifications. While all of the girls in this group fulfilled our age requirements, it was necessary to include a number of girls who were considerably older than the average of the other three groups. The requirements as to parentage were also somewhat relaxed. Although all the children in our samplings are natives born of Scandinavian immigrant parents and although the vast majority of these parents were Danes, a sprinkling of Swedes and Norwegians had to be included to bring the group up to the required numbers. All of the latter conformed, however, to the blonde-haired, blue-eyed racial type. The only other respect in which this group differs from the other group is that the city in which they live is considerably smaller than Copenhagen, Rome, or New York. With respect to the schooling factor, this group matched the other groups.

The study thus includes four fairly comparable groups, each of approximately 300 girls twelve years old or older, drawn from the same social stratum and conforming to certain definite racial types; namely, a North European group (Danes); a South European group (Italians); a North European American group (largely Danish Americans with some Norwegian and Swedish Americans); and a South European American group (Italian Americans).

The only respect in which these groups differ notably from each other is in average age. The average age of the Danish group is 13 years, 9 months; that of the Italian group is 14 years, 1 month; that of the Italian American group is 13 years, 11 months; but that of the Danish American Group is 15 years, 7 months.

We shall show in our analysis of the intelligence of the groups that this difference in age in no wise affects the results.

THE DATA USED IN THIS STUDY

The measure of intelligence used in this study was the International Intelligence Test, Form B. This is a non-verbal test consisting of eight subtests which includes counting of cubes, associations, similarities, judging of facial expression, mazes, rhythms, analogies, and recognition of sequences in pictured narratives. The eight tests are divided into two test-booklets. A practice booklet containing the first few pages of each of the subtests is given before the test proper. The test requires accurate stop-watch timing and takes, in all, about three hours to administer.

Since this is the first time that the International Intelligence Test was used on the Danish and Italian groups in Europe, it was deemed advisable to determine the reliability of the test for these groups. This was done by the split-halves method, correlating the sums of the odd and of the even items of the test, respectively.

The correlation of the odds with the evens among the Danes was .823 ± .013, which, by the Spearman-Brown formula, gives the test a reliability of .903 for this group. Among the Italians the reliability was even higher. The odds-evens coefficient was .958 ± .003 and the reliability was .979.

Among the American groups the test showed a reliability of .955 for the Danish Americans and .972 for the Italian Americans. It seems apparent that the International Intelligence Test is a highly reliable instrument.

This test was admirably suited for use in the present study for many reasons. The fact that it is a non-verbal test made it possible to use it for all four groups alike, without regard to language differences. This afforded a direct basis of comparison between the groups. The simplicity of the terms in which the directions for administering the test are couched made it easy to translate them into Danish and Italian. The universal nature of the pictures used in the test itself reduced to a minimum the environmental factors which might be prejudicial to the attainment of a satisfactory score by any child. The test is also of sufficient length and diversity to afford an adequate sampling of the mentality of the children. Finally, the use of the practice book helped to familiarize the children with the technique of responding to the test and allowed for an adequate warming-up period. This proved to be a decided advantage in handling the European groups, who are not at all as familiar with intelligence tests as are the American school children.

* * *

RESULTS OF THIS STUDY

Comparison of our racial groups with reference to their average total scores on the International Intelligence Examination revealed the findings set forth in Table I.

It will be noted from Table I that reliable differences exist between the average of the North and South European American samplings. In line with the findings of other investigators in this field, we find the American Danes definitely superior in intelligence to the American Italians.

TABLE I
Comparison of Mean Total Scores of the Four Groups

Group	Mean total score	σ	$\dfrac{d}{\sigma d}$
Danish American	609.40	59.70⎫	14.65
Italian American	530.57	69.63⎭	
Danes	512.85	87.78⎫	−.71
Italians	517.80	75.60⎭	
Danish American	609.40	59.70⎫	15.18
Danes	512.85	87.78⎭	
Italian American	530.57	69.63⎫	2.10
Italians	517.80	75.60⎭	

However, when we compare these groups in their native countries this difference disappears. It will be seen from Table I that the average total score of the Danish sampling from Copenhagen is not reliably different from that of the Italian sampling from Rome. The difference is only $-.71$ times its standard error, proving the Italian to be quite as intelligent, according to the International Intelligence Test, as the Dane.

This finding points to the conclusion that the differences which have so frequently been found between samplings of these racial groups in the United States are due to the operation of other factors than inherent racial inequality. It is possible to explain these differences on the basis of two alternate hypotheses; they may be the result either of the selective factors which are involved in the migration of groups from one country to another or of the environmental influences exerted upon these groups in their changed habitat in this country.

Since the Danish and Italian groups are equal in intelligence in their native countries, it may be argued that the apparent superiority of the Danes in the United States is attributable to the fact that a superior element of the population migrated to this country. This is substantiated by our finding of a marked difference between our American and European Danes. The superiority of the Danish Americans over their countrymen in Europe is quite as marked as over the Italians in America. The reliability of the difference between the American Danes and the Danes is 15.18.

While our findings, according to this hypothesis, indicate the superiority of the Danish immigrant over the general population in the home country, they fail to substantiate the commonly held assumption that the Italian immigrant to this country is inferior to the general population in his home country. The average scores of our American and European Italian samplings were not reliably different from each other. The reliability of the difference is only 2.10, as is shown in Table I. If we accept the first hypothesis, we must conclude from this that the Italians who migrated to this country were very similar in intelligence to the rank and file of the population in the home country.

The other hypothesis, namely, that the difference which we have found between the American groups is attributable to environmental influences exerted upon them in this country, finds some support in an analysis of these environmental influences. The Danes were transplanted from one Nordic environment to another; the Italians had to adjust to a radically different environment from that in their home country. The cultural similarities between the Danish civilization and our own are much greater than between the Italian and our own. The English language is not only closer to Danish than to Italian, but it is spoken and taught in the schools of Denmark to an incomparably greater degree than in those of Italy. If we add to these facts the alleged inferiority of the Italian in general language ability and the greater prevalence of conflicts between the home and the child which is said to exist within the Italian group in this country, we might well feel that the total explains the difference which we have found between the two groups.

In other words according to this hypothesis the Danes achieve superior scores on our test because they adjust more rapidly and more fully to our American environment. The environmental influences in this country being more favorable to them, they show up much better than the Italians to whom this country presents a less favorable environment.

Which of these two hypotheses represents the correct explanation of our findings, it is impossible to say on the basis of our data. Against the "selective migration" hypothesis stands the fact that we have no real evidence as to whether the American groups originated from superior or inferior elements of the population of the home country. This could be determined only by research tracing American immigrants of both races back to their native cities and studying their blood relatives there. Against the "environmental influence" hypothesis stand the facts, first, that the International Intelligence Test is a non-verbal test constructed for the purpose of equalizing environmental differences, second, that we have no scientific evidence, beyond mere inferences, that the American environment is more favorable, *ipso facto,* to Danes than to Italians, and third, that the conditions of our study were not such as to make its findings admissible in controversion of the mass of existing evidence that intelligence is not influenced by environment. This entire problem would probably prove a fertile one for future research. For the present we can merely present our findings and suggest, without proof, the two most likely hypotheses on the basis of which they might be explained.

Our findings are, of course, predicated on the assumption that we have compared equivalent groups in the various countries. It would therefore be well to discuss this aspect of our samplings briefly. Denmark is a democratic country having a socialist government. It has very few private schools, the vast majority of the child population attending the public schools. In our samplings of children in Copenhagen were included, for example, the daughters of the Minister of Finance and of the Chief Musical Director as well as the children of many other government officials. School attendance is compulsory from seven to 14 years of age. This also operates towards a superior group attending school after this age. Our sampling came from middle class neighborhoods which were regarded by the school authorities as typical of the population as a whole, and included academic and vocational schools to preclude the possibility of selection on a purely academic basis. We feel therefore that our Copenhagen sampling is representative of the population of this democratic middle class country.

In Italy also only 1/25 of the school population of over four million attends private schools. Education is compulsory here also until the age of fourteen. In Rome, too, the sampling was drawn from both academic and vocational schools.

For these reasons it is our belief that the Copenhagen and Roman samplings may be regarded as representative of the populations from which they were drawn. We may add that the selection of schools was made in both cases with the cooperation of the school authorities and the psychologists who assisted in this study, with this objective definitely in mind.

One objection to our findings which it may be desirable to anticipate is the assumption that the averages of the American groups are apt to be too high because of the comparative familiarity of American children with testing procedures and materials. We would point out first, that the International Intelligence Test is a non-language test, differing in this respect from the vast majority of the tests which are commonly given in our schools, and secondly, that the form of the subtests and the materials which they include are wholly unlike anything which the average American child, no matter how "test-wise," ever encounters in his experience with tests. Even trained psychologists are often puzzled at first sight of this test. Furthermore, the time limits on this test are sufficiently generous to permit every child to show his full mental stature before time is called. This eliminates the speed element, to which the American child is perhaps better adjusted.

We would conclude from all of this that the familiarity of American children with tests and testing procedures was not a factor of sufficient weight to mask or distort the true facts relative to our inquiry.

We have already stated that the American Danish group was considerably older than any of the other groups. This raised the question whether the age factor was distorting our findings. The four groups were divided according to age and the total score on the International Intelligence Test was computed for each group. Table II sets forth these results.

The reliability of the differences between the comparable age groups in all four racial groups is set forth in Table III.

To read Table III locate one of the groups to be compared at the top

TABLE II

Average Total Score for Comparable Age Groups Within the Four Groups Studied

Age	Danes	Italians	Danish Americans	Italian Americans
12–6	484.14	513.25	600.00	518.36
13–0	488.43	505.20	599.20	496.25
13–6	474.57	543.70	603.40	513.08
14–0	520.77	507.65	600.10	546.08
14–6	564.66	518.15	591.40	542.72
15–0	575.22	521.65	594.40	563.57

and the other down the side. At the intersection of the column and row, the reliability of the differences for the respective age groups will be found. For example; the reliability of the difference between total scores of thirteen year old Danish Americans and Italian Americans is +.353.

It will be noted that the only reliable differences which are found are between the Danish American group and the other three groups. The two

TABLE III

Reliability of Differences in Total Score Between Comparable Age-Groups Within the Various Racial Groups

Racial Groups	Age	Italian American	Italian	Danish American
Danes	13–0	−0.26	−0.56	−3.60
	13–6	−1.10	−1.85	−3.55
	14–0	−0.93	+0.39	−2.84
	14–6	+0.52	−1.33	−0.81
	15–0	+0.42	+1.76	−0.65
Danish American	13–0	+3.53	+3.24	
	13–6	+3.01	+1.83	
	14–0	+2.30	+2.98	
	14–6	+1.40	+2.05	
	15–0	+1.11	+2.38	
Italian	13–0	+0.32		
	13–6	+0.98		
	14–0	−1.26		
	14–6	−0.93		
	15–0	−1.45		

European groups show no reliable difference at any age; neither do the two Italian groups here and abroad. This indicates that the findings which we have reported for the groups as a whole, are equally valid when similar age-groups within the races are compared.

* * *

The main findings of the study are as follows:

1. While reliable differences in intelligence were found between the American samplings of Danes and Italians these differences disappeared completely when the samplings studied in the home countries were compared, indicating that there are no inherent race differences between these racial groups.

2. The Danish Americans are just as superior to the Danes in Europe as they are to the Italians in the United States and in Italy. This may be due either to the factor of selective migration or to environmental influences which operated more favorably on one group than on another.

This is, in our opinion, the best and most carefully controlled of the studies of foster children. It was undertaken in an attempt to resolve the different results obtained by two previous studies, the earlier Freeman-Chicago Study and the Burks-Stanford Study. Give special attention to the criteria of selection for the two groups of children and homes. You should also attend to the correlational indices and mean differences in intelligence shown in the various comparisons. Less than half of the monograph has been reprinted here; the interested reader will find further valuable details in the complete account.

Nature-Nurture and Intelligence*

ALICE M. LEAHY

1935

THE PROBLEM

Variation in human intelligence is universally recognized. But experimentation to discover the causes which affect this variation has moved slowly. The reasons are obvious. First, conditions which permit the control of either heredity or environment are difficult to secure, and secondly, our tools for measurement are limited and crude. Although identical twins provide an absolute control of heredity, their separate location in diverse environments is rare. Experimentation involving the control of environment, on the other hand, is not entirely possible. Measures are available for only certain of its features. For its dynamic attributes we have no measures. Hence, what may appear to be similar environments are only approximately identical. However, the individual mental examination has been demonstrated to be fairly reliable of what may be called test intelligence.

The present investigation approaches the problem by a comparison of two groups of children living in approximately identical environments. In one group, the children are unrelated by blood or marriage to the persons shaping the environment. They are adopted children. In the other group, the children are the offspring of the persons who have shaped the environment. Both heredity and environment are operative in the latter group, while in the former, only environment.

Resemblance as expressed by means of the correlation between attributes in the home and test intelligence of child will constitute one type of analysis.

* *Genetic Psychology Monographs*, Vol. 17, No. 4 (1935), pp. 241-305. Reprinted by permission of The Journal Press.

Presumably the magnitude of the correlation between adopted children and their foster homes is a function of environment. In the case of parents and true children, it is a function of heredity and environment combined.

A comparative analysis of mean intelligence with cultural levels will constitute a second type of analysis. Since, as will subsequently be shown, the mean intelligence of the two groups of children is almost identical, marked contrasts in intelligence under constant environmental conditions would place the burden of causation on heredity.

If random placement of adopted children exists in each social stratum then variation from the mean intelligence of the group may be assigned to environmental diversity. . . .

It should be emphasized that whatever trends and conclusions can be found in this study are valid only for populations as homogeneous in racial extraction, social standards, and educational opportunities as that from which our subjects are taken. The distribution of homes of the children in this investigation are probably somewhat skewed toward a superior level. Adoptive homes of even the lowest occupational and economic levels are undoubtedly superior in respect to other traits, since society's control and imposition of standards on this type of home is much greater than on the ordinary home. The educational requirement adhered to in matching our adoptive homes with homes in the general population would tend to raise the environmental and genetic level of the homes of the latter group. This would be particularly true in the lowest occupational groups. In the main, the homes were as variable in essential features as homes of an American urban white population. Clearly they were not as variable as if the homes of southern negroes and poor mountain whites had been included. In consequence, home environment cannot be expected to have as large a proportional effect upon the mental differences of the children studied as though they were being reared in unselected families.

However, attention should also be drawn to the fact that the distribution of inheritable mental capacity of the children in this investigation was probably skewed toward a superior level. No children of the idiot or imbecile grade are included. The true parents of the adopted children were somewhat superior in cultural status to parents of dependent children in general. Hence, heredity cannot be expected to contribute as large a proportional influence to the mental differences of the children as though a greater variation in genetic intelligence was included. Since environment was equally variable in both the experimental and control populations, and since our sample of parents and true offspring (control population) consistently yielded coefficients of resemblance of .50, it is fair to assume that no serious understatement of the general influence of environment exists in our experimental data.

* * *

PRESENT STUDY

In the formulation of the present investigation the problem of mental resemblance between foster parent and child resulting from selective placement received first consideration. Could it be controlled? Obviously if reliable preplacement tests were available the part that selective placement plays in the choice of a home for a child or a group of children could be definitely determined. Moreover, the actual measurement of gains and losses in performance on standard tests of mental ability accordingly as a child is exposed to extremes in environmental stimulation would then be possible. However, such an experiment would assume not only reliable preplacement tests of the child but equally reliable measures of environment. Neither are available. The files of child placement agencies reveal that only a small number of adopted children are tested in advance of placement. Out of a total of 2449 children adopted in Minnesota between the years 1918-1928, only 98 had been given mental tests. Most of these were tested subsequent to placement. In fact, failure to adjust in the new home generally prompted the examination.

Despite the absence of prognostic tests of mental ability it is highly probable that intellectual promise judged from overt behavior and family history enters into a social agency's recommendations for adoption. The questionnaire replies of 22 child placement workers revealed that 18 regarded *probable intelligence* as of *very great* significance in their judgments of the fitness of a child for an adoptive home, two regarded it of *great* importance, and two of *slight* significance on a scale of five descriptive levels, namely: very slight significance, slight, moderate, great, very great significance. Certainly such judgments would fall farthest from the mark in the case of infants. More accurate prediction of future development on the basis of overt behavior could conceivably be made for older children. Indeed very careful placement might result in striking similarity in the intellectual level of foster parents and their adopted children.

The problems that confront the investigator in a research population of untested children placed at older ages are two. First, he must know what elements of history and behavior contributed to the judgment of the child's mental ability and, secondly, whether the bases entering into the judgment were common for the entire group of children studied. Unfortunately, agency records do not reveal in any consistent manner the bases for their decisions. Hence, the inclusion of children placed at older ages would introduce serious disturbing factors in a research population. Further, any research on adopted children placed at older ages involves the measurement of the influence of the environment previous to the adoptive or foster one under consideration. Because of these reasons it was clear that our experimental population must be composed of children placed in their adoptive homes at as near zero age as possible. Only with such a population could we hope to secure random placement of children and thus reduce the operation of the unmeasurable influence of selective placement. It was recognized, nevertheless, that judgments of intellectual promise on the basis of family history still remained. The ideal experimental population would include only those children whose age at the time of placement is so young as to preclude prediction of future mental development and for whom no evidence of family history is available to agencies or persons placing the children. The complete elimination of family history is impossible, since the number of foundlings is relatively small. However, when the complexity of human inheritance is considered, as well as the infinite variety of factors that enter into the determination of socio-economic status in a competitive society, it is clear that inferences as to the mental ability of an individual from isolated facts of family history are highly unreliable. General trends, however, in mass evidence have been found to be consistent. For example, the progeny of college-trained professional people are generally above the average in mental ability, while the children of the unschooled laborer are somewhat inferior. A judgment as to the intelligence of a particular infant from a knowledge of his family background nevertheless would be very unreliable. The child may fall far below or far above the average of his parental group. Yet if child placing agencies pursued a consistent policy of relating cultural status of background to that of the adoptive home in all placements, a definite resemblance between foster parents and children would result. The contribution of family history to a judgment of the intellectual level of our experimental children and its consequent weighting of the observed resemblance between adoptive parent and child will be discussed below.

The imperative need of a check upon our methods committed us to a control group of true parents and offspring from the very inception of the study. Only from a study of a group of children who had been given the same tests and measures as the adopted children could we hope to attach any meaning to the results observed in the adoptive group. High or low correlations between adoptive parents and children, for example, might well be said to be the result of factors peculiar to our measuring instruments. The behavior of any particular group of human beings has meaning only in so far as we know how human beings in general behave. With measurable environment identical for both groups of children, differences in the relationship of child's intelligence to environment obviously must be the result of the presence of a common heredity in the case of true parents and offspring and the result of the absence of hereditary likeness in the case of adopted parents and their children.

SOURCE OF SUBJECTS

Once the decision was made to limit the investigation to children placed in their adoptive homes at a very early age, it was apparent that the records of adopted children deposited in the Children's Bureau of the State Board of Control would be our most complete source for subjects, since the adoption records of the entire state are available there.

Due to the relatively small number of legitimate children that are available for adoption in early infancy, it was deemed better to limit our subjects to illegitimate children. An additional point of significance in favor of illegitimate children was the greater probability of securing a population whose intelligence would be normally distributed. Legitimate children are ordinarily available for adoption only because of serious intellectual and economic inadequacies in their parents or immediate relatives. Illegitimate children, on the other hand, are relinquished for many reasons, namely: the youth of the parents, the social stigma attached to the illegitimacy situation, economic inadequacy of parents, and intellectual incompetency of the parents. The economic inadequacy of unmarried parents is frequently associated with youth, while the economic inadequacy of married parents generally arises from intellectual and personality deficiencies. In general, a population of legitimate dependents appears to come from a narrow socio-economic range, while illegitimate dependents come from a more variable family background.

Our first step, then, in anticipation of our research project was the tabulation of the factual items of family history for the illegitimate children adopted in Minnesota during the period 1918-1928. This period was chosen because it would provide children who would be not less than 5 nor more than 14 years of age at the time of the field investigation, 1932-1933. Records were available for 2449 children. Our transcript included information on the personal history of the child, the true parents and the foster parents.

Experimental Group, Criteria of Selection

In order that the least possible ambiguity exist in our results, the experimental group was limited to:

1. *Children placed in their adoptive homes at the age of 6 months or younger.* (The mean age of placement was 2.5 months.) At this early age precise judgments of mental ability on the basis of test performance, physical development, or overt behavior are highly improbable. Further, this criterion assures from early infancy an environment that is no more or less changing in character than that enjoyed by children in general. Moreover, it definitely avoids the difficulties which would arise in attempting to measure the influence of environment previous to the adoptive one under consideration.

2. *Only those adopted children who were known to be of white race, non-Jewish, north-European extraction.* This prerequisite tends to reduce the possibilities of a fortuitous resemblance between adoptive parent and child on the basis of racial regression. In addition it minimizes the possibility of a spurious heterogeneity arising from uncontrolled factors relating to race. Further, it limits the group to one which is similar in composition to the one on which the Stanford-Binet test was standardized.

3. *Children who were not less than 5 nor more than 14 years of age at the time of investigation.* This age range is conceded to give the most reliable test results.

4. *Children reared in communities of 1000 or more.* In this way we attempted to equalize the influence of such environmental factors as churches, clubs, and schools. No farm children are included. Ninety-five per cent of the group have been reared in communities of over 10,000.

5. *Children who were legally adopted by married persons.* Thus we secured a group where the legal relationship and responsibility between parent and child was the same as that of true parent and offspring.

6. *Adoptive parents who were of white race, non-Jewish, north-European extraction.* With this criterion we attempted to reduce the possibility of adventitious resemblance and further reduced the possibility of securing non-English-speaking homes.

By adhering rigidly to the foregoing criteria it is believed that we have controlled the element of selective placement to a point beyond the facilities of earlier investigators and to the highest possible degree that present day child adoption permits. Fitting the child to the home on the basis of coloring, physique, and religious faith, all of which occur, could hardly give rise to mental resemblance. Selective placement upon the basis of cultural status, however, is still possible. But since the preadoptive records did not reveal the facts on this point, we can only infer its existence or nonexistence from an analysis of the relationship of certain indices of cultural status.

In our earliest considerations of a population we conceived a research group which would sample the population of adoptive homes distributed from a socio-economic standpoint as male occupations are distributed in the general population. Because of the limited number of children placed in homes of the laboring class this plan had to be abandoned. In its place we accepted all children available in the two lowest occupational groups and secured at least 40 children at every other level. With these numbers we have not only obtained a fair picture of environmental differences contingent on occupational status, but have also secured a fair sample of the selective placement that may operate on the basis of cultural status. A small number at any level might give a distinctly distorted picture.

Control Group, Criteria of Selection

With the primary purpose of a control group serving as a check upon the validity of our methods, each *adopted* child was matched with an *own* child as follows:

1. *For sex.*

2. *Within an age range of plus or minus 6 months.*

3. *Whose fathers' occupations fell in the same group on the Minnesota Occupational Scale.*

4. *Whose fathers' school attainments agreed within plus or minus one school grade level.*

5. *Whose mothers' school attainments agreed within plus or minus one school grade level.*

6. *Whose parents were white race, non-Jewish, north-European extraction.*

7. *Whose residence has been in communities of 1000 or more.*

*   *   *

In matching cases for occupation and education, we employed the two most objective indices of cultural status that are available. In 12 cases the educational criterion was not adhered to. It was necessary to be content with agreement in education for one parent. In these cases, however, the educational disparity between the other adoptive parent and his control was held within the ordinary school groups of elementary, high school, or college level.

A typical match is illustrated by the following example. A lawyer, in the person of an adoptive father who had completed college and whose wife had finished the eleventh grade in high school, might be matched with an electrical engineer of not less than three or more than five years of college and whose wife had completed at least the tenth, but not more than the twelfth grade in high school, provided the sex and age of their respective children agreed.

If environment is dominant, it would seem that the trend of any trait concerning the children and their environment would be similar in direction and magnitude for both the adopted and control populations. Certainly, our adopted children should clearly reveal the relationship of environment to attributes which are not reciprocally affected by the innate tendencies of the child. For example, the occupation of the adoptive father is obviously not a function of the intelligence of the adopted child, while the number of children's books in the adoptive home and the intelligence of the child are reciprocally dependent. The books may be in the home because intelligent children enjoy books. Or the children may be more responsive and alert because the books are in the home. When the age of our children at the time of the test is considered, it is apparent that there are many factors in the adoptive home whose existence is entirely independent of the child and, therefore, whatever relationship exists between these factors and the child may be regarded as a measure of the influence of environment. The relationship between parent and true offspring, however, is a complex of environment and heredity. Here, for example, the child's intelligence may be not only the result of the quality of the environment that the parents have provided, but also an inherited characteristic from the parents. From the adopted population we should be able to get a measure of the influence of environment; from the control population a measure of the influence of environment re-enforced by heredity. Whatever unreliability exists because of imperfections in our measuring instruments will be similarly existent in both populations. Further, whatever the accumulated effect of environment may be, it will be operative in both populations in the same direction since both have enjoyed what might be termed an ordinarily continuous environment.

* * *

TESTS EMPLOYED AND THEIR ADMINISTRATION

The tests and measures used for both the adoptive and control families were the following:

1. A set of three blanks entitled *The Child and His Environment* covered the family and personal history of the child. Space was provided for specific information as to the identity of the child, the condition of his health, the cultural background of his true parents and for the replies to 88 questions relative to the cultural, economic and social status of the adoptive home. This last category of information constitutes our quantitative measure for environment. All replies were directly recorded in the mother's presence. . . .

The second blank permitted a description of the home as gleaned from informal conversation with the mother. The child's personality, behavior, his school progress, and a narrative of the circumstances surrounding his selection were the topics usually discussed. These data were recorded subsequent to the interview, but as soon after as possible.

The third schedule designed to contribute to our knowledge of family and personal history was the interest interview with the child. This was usually administered after the mental examination and covered the child's educational and social activities. The questions were asked directly and the replies were recorded immediately.

2. The Stanford Revision of the Binet-Simon Tests as described in Terman's "The Measurement of Intelligence" was administered to all the children. The procedure recommended by its author was rigidly adhered to, i.e., the testing was carried down to a level at which all tests were passed and up to a level at which all tests were failed. For those children who

exceeded the limits of the test the correction worked out in connection with the Stanford Study of gifted children was applied. In order to minimize errors contingent on the personal differences of examiners, a single examiner administered all of the tests to the adopted children. Similarly in the case of the control children a single examiner was used. All tests were checked and rescored by the mental test division of the Institute of Child Welfare.

3. The Woodworth-Mathews "Personal Data Sheet," a questionnaire of 75 questions designed to reveal psychotic tendencies, was given to all children age 10 years and over. Two questions (44 and 45) which pertain to adopted children were blotted from the booklets. According to the author the total number of unfavorable responses provides an index of an individual's emotional stability. . . . No claims are made for the validity or reliability of the questionnaire. It is simple to administer and supplies a ready instrument for comparative analysis.

4. The Otis Self-Administering Test of Mental Ability—Intermediate Form A, was given to the parents. The Intermediate examination, designed for grades 4 to 9, was chosen instead of the higher examination designed for high school and college students because of the great difficulty exhibited by 20 parents who tried the higher examination. They found the illustrative questions imposing and in general their "set" to the test situation was one of anxiety. And although our social data subsequently showed the mean schooling of the adoptive parents to be eleventh grade and that of the control parents, tenth grade, the average older adult is unfamiliar with the test situation and "shys off" anything of this nature that appears difficult. The fact that the test results were to be used primarily for comparative purposes further justified the use of the simpler form.

*   *   *

5. The Stanford-Binet Vocabulary Test was given to the parents. Total vocabulary score was calculated on the basis of the subject's responses to the first list of words. Definitions were carefully checked according to the directions in Terman, *The Measurement of Intelligence.* This test was included in our program because of its high correlation with the whole Binet scale and, secondly, because it had been used by Burks in her study of nature-nurture and intelligence.

6. A transcript of the social agency's record of the child and his true parents was made. The items of education and occupation of forbears were rechecked with the original record in order to have available the most reliable information possible on the cultural level of the child's background.

*   *   *

MAIN RESULTS OF THE STUDY

The relationship between test intelligence of children and various attributes of their home environment is shown in Table I. Since intelligence and age of child have been demonstrated to be negatively correlated (in these data, age and IQ for adopteds correlated from $-.17$ to $-.19$, for controls from $-.13$ to $-.18$), age has been partialled out and the relation-

TABLE I

Child's IQ Correlated with Other Factors

Correlated factor	Adopted children			Control children		
	r	P.E.	N	r	P.E.	N
Father's Otis score	.15	.05	178	.51	.04	175
Mother's Otis score	.20	.05	186	.51	.04	191
Mid-parent Otis score	.18	.05	177	.60	.03	173
Father's S.B. vocabulary	.22	.05	177	.47	.04	168
Mother's S.B. vocabulary	.20	.05	185	.49	.04	190
Mid-parent S.B. vocabulary	.24	.05	174	.56	.03	164
Environmental status score	.19	.05	194	.53	.03	194
Cultural index of home	.21	.05	194	.51	.04	194
Child training index of home	.18	.05	194	.52	.04	194
Economic index of home	.12	.05	194	.37	.04	194
Sociality index of home	.11	.05	194	.42	.04	194
Father's education	.16	.05	193	.48	.04	193
Mother's education	.21	.05	192	.50	.04	194
Mid-parent education	.20	.05	193	.54	.03	194
Father's occupational status	.12	.05	194	.45	.04	194

ships are expressed in product moment correlations. Because it was not possible to obtain full information for all the persons participating in the study, the number of cases varies for each correlation.

Although the difference between corresponding correlation coefficients in the Adopted and Control group is consistent and striking, their comparability must be determined before any interpretations are made. The test of comparability is equal variability. A re-examination of the data in Section V shows almost perfect agreement in the variability of environmental factors entering our correlational table. Equal variability does not exist for test intelligence, however, in the two sets of data. In the case of the Adopted children it is 12.5, for the Control children, it is 15.4. Although the difference is not large, correction should be made if two equally comparable series of coefficients are desired. Since the nature of the curtailment is known and exists in only one trait, the correction evolved by Pearson may be applied. The corrected correlations are presented in Table II.

Despite the severity of the correction the absolute change in magnitude of our correlations is not great. The greatest single increase is .05; on the average the correlations are increased .038 points. Note that the difference between corresponding coefficients in the Adopted and Control series con-

TABLE II

Child's IQ Correlated with Other Factors

(*r* corrected for unequal range in child's IQ)

Correlated factor	Adopted children			Control children		
	r	*P.E.*	*N*	*r*	*P.E.*	*N*
Father's Otis score	.19	.06	178	.51	.04	175
Mother's Otis score	.24	.06	186	.51	.04	191
Mid-parent Otis score	.21	.06	177	.60	.03	173
Father's S.B. vocabulary*	.26	.06	177	.47	.04	168
Mother's S.B. vocabulary	.24	.06	185	.49	.04	190
Mid-parent S.B. vocabulary	.29	.06	174	.56	.03	164
Environmental status score	.23	.06	194	.53	.03	194
Cultural index of home	.26	.06	194	.51	.04	194
Child training index	.22	.06	194	.52	.04	194
Economic index	.15	.06	194	.37	.04	194
Sociality index*	.13	.06	194	.42	.04	194
Father's education	.19	.06	193	.48	.04	193
Mother's education	.25	.06	192	.50	.04	194
Mid-parent education	.24	.06	193	.54	.03	194
Father's occupational status	.14	.06	194	.45	.04	194

tinues. For the Adopted children they are consistently low, about .20. In the Control group they maintain the level usually found for hereditary physical characteristics, .50. In the case of the latter group heredity and environment are both operative. Hence variance in intelligence is accounted for by variance in heredity and environment combined to the extent of about 25 per cent (square of *r* .50). In the Adopted group, however, where environment is functioning independently of heredity, variance in intelligence is accounted for by variance in environment only to the extent of about 4 per cent (square of *r* .20). If we neglect whatever artificial heredity selective placement of adopted children may have introduced into the data, these coefficients are clear evidence of maximum variance in intelligence with variance in environment. Apparently environment cannot compensate for the lack of blood relationship in creating mental resemblance between parent and child. Heredity persists.

A second type of analysis of our data appears in Table III, where the mean intelligence quotient of Adopted children in each successive occupation level is compared with the intelligence quotient of Control children similarily classified according to occupation of father. Note the constancy

TABLE III

Comparative Analysis of Intelligence of Adopted and Control Children and Environmental Status of Homes Classified According to Occupation of Father

Occupation of father	Adopted children					Control children				
		Intelligence quotient		Environmental status			Intelligence quotient		Environmental status	
	N	M	S.D.	M	S.D.	N	M	S.D.	M	S.D.
I Professional	43	112.6	11.8	194.6	27.2	40	118.6	12.6	180.4	29.1
II Business manager	38	111.6	10.9	171.3	40.2	42	117.6	15.6	160.7	31.1
III Skilled trades	44	110.6	14.2	133.2	35.2	43	106.9	14.3	106.3	43.4
IV Farmers	—	—		—		—	—		—	
V Semi-skilled	45	109.4	11.8	94.0	30.3	46	101.1	12.5	77.6	37.4
VI Slightly skilled and	24	107.8	13.6	74.7	28.7	23	102.1	11.0	40.1	26.7
VII Day labor										

of the IQ of Adopted children, irrespective of occupational level. Its progression is insignificant. When variability in IQ within each occupational group is considered, the children in the lowest level almost completely overlap the children in the highest group. The same is true when occupational groups V and I are compared. The difference is entirely effaced between occupational classes III and I. If we ignore the very lowest occupational bracket (VI and VII) in which the number of cases is considerably less than in the other levels, a difference of only one IQ increment exists between the successive occupational classes of Adopted children.

The Control children, on the other hand, advance conspicuously in mean level of intelligence with fathers' occupation. The difference in IQ between the lowest occupational levels and the middle group (III, skilled workmen, clerks, etc.) is as great as the difference in IQ between the lowest and highest occupational group of the Adopted children. Although the children in the two highest occupational classes (business managerial and professional) are undifferentiated they are widely separated from the children of the middle group (about 12 IQ points). The absolute difference in child's IQ between the extreme occupational levels in the Control group is three times as great as the difference between the extreme levels of Adopted children. The fact that the children of each occupational group are almost identical in age should be borne in mind. If the children in the highest occupational levels were younger than those in the middle and lowest groups, then their superior rating in IQ might be said to be a function of age. It will also be recalled that each Adopted child was matched with a Control child of the same age and whose father's occupation was in agreement with that of the adoptive fathers. Hence, cross-comparisons are entirely valid.

The probability of differences in IQ continuing in the same direction with occupational status in the case of similarly chosen populations as those observed here is shown in Table IV. Apparently none of the differences

TABLE IV

Comparative Analysis of the Probability of Differences in IQ of Children Expressed by D/σ_{diff}, Continuing in the Same Direction as in the Experimental Populations Classified According to Father's Occupation

Occupational groups	Adopted children				Control children			
	II	III	V	VI & VII	II	III	V	VI & VII
I	.40	.72	1.27	1.45	.32	3.96	6.45	5.43
II		.36	.88	1.15		3.29	5.44	4.66
III			.43	.80			2.03	1.52
V				.49				.34

for the Adopteds are reliable. Reversal of direction might occur in another population; while in the Control population the differences between the two highest groups and every other group are clear and dependable. The probability of a difference in the same direction between the middle and the lowest level is greater for the Controls than the probability of the recurrence of any single difference in the Adopted population. Clearly, environment as typified by occupational status does not compensate for the absence of blood relationship between parent and child.

The foregoing observations take on added significance when the environmental status scores of the successive occupational levels are studied. We note that in both populations environmental status score increases with occupation and further that the magnitude of each successive difference is more than 2.6 times its standard error (Table V). It should also be noted

TABLE V

Comparative Analysis of the Probability of Differences in Environmental Status Scores Expressed by D/σ_{diff}, Continuing in the Same Direction as in the Experimental Homes Classified According to Father's Occupation

Occupational groups	Adoptive homes				Control homes			
	II	III	V	VI & VII	II	III	V	VI & VII
I	3.02	9.12	16.40	16.70	2.96	9.19	14.32	19.43
II		4.53	9.74	11.02		6.65	11.37	16.41
III			5.63	7.40			3.33	7.65
V				2.61				4.79

that at all levels the mean score of the Adoptive homes is higher than that of Control homes. If intelligence progresses with environment independently of heredity then as great increases in IQ should be expected in the Adopted group as in the Control group.

Considering test intelligence and vocabulary scores of parents, measures which may be more reflective of innate capacity than environmental status score, the same tendency of progression with occupation is noted for both Adoptive and Control parents. (Table VI.) In the case of Control parents the occupational levels appear about equally spaced in respect to test intelligence and vocabulary scores. In the Adoptives the two lowest levels are undifferentiated in score as are also the two highest. Yet both extremes are equally spaced from the middle occupational group and at a greater distance than the Controls. If the dynamic quality of the environment is in proportion to the intellectual level of the parents, then one would conclude that the Adoptive and Control homes are similar in stimulation potential. The

TABLE VI

**Comparative Analysis of Adoptive and Control Mid-Parent
Scores on the Otis Test of Mental Ability and the S.B.
Vocabulary Test, Classified According to
Occupational Status**

Occupational group	Adoptive parents				Control parents			
	Otis test		S.B. Vocab.		Otis Test		S.B. Vocab.	
	M	S.D.	M	S.D.	M	S.D.	M	S.D.
I	59.6	8.0	74.0	6.4	64.6	5.4	74.9	7.8
II	59.6	6.7	73.4	7.2	57.1	10.0	67.8	8.3
III	49.6	11.9	64.6	11.4	51.8	11.5	62.0	9.3
IV	—	—	—	—	—	—	—	—
V	39.7	12.3	59.1	11.6	44.0	11.5	55.7	9.6
VI & VII	38.4	11.2	54.5	9.2	38.3	9.0	48.7	9.1

difference, however, in intelligence of Adoptive children is only 1 IQ point in either direction, while the difference for the Control children is 5.8 points between occupational groups III and V and 10.7 points between groups III and II. The failure of Adopted children to attain levels of intelligence corresponding more exactly to those of the Control group would appear to be due to a factor or factors other than environment.

When the most stimulating environment was arbitrarily defined to exist in those homes that possessed all of the environmental traits at a level beyond 1 SD of the mean of the entire group, very interesting contrasts in mean IQ of the children of these homes appear. The seven Adopted children found in such homes had a mean IQ of 113.3±6.0. The eight Controls who were so located had a mean IQ of 127.5 ± 9.5. These Controls are 17.8 IQ increments above the mean (109.7) of their entire group; the Adopteds so classified are only 2.8 IQ points in advance of their mean (110.5). Despite the small number of cases involved, the ratio of the difference in IQ of these selected children to its standard error is 3.52. When the definition is reversed for the least stimulating environment, i.e., the homes located below minus 1 SD for every trait, no cases were found.

If we widen our definition of a stimulating environment so as to include the homes that were at the mean and above for every trait, 58 Adopted and 52 Control children are found. Here again the Control children surpass the Adopteds. The mean for the Controls is 119.4 ± 14.9, for the Adopteds 112.3 ± 10.8. The ratio of the mean difference to its standard error is 2.8. Hence, irrespective of attempts to equalize environments, the Controls from the upper levels are distinctly superior in intelligence to the Adopted children at the same levels.

When the children in the least stimulating environment (defining the latter to include the homes that score below the mean on every trait) are considered as a group the Adopteds secure a mean IQ of 106.0 ± 10.2, the Controls 99.5 ± 10.9. Although the numbers involved in this analysis are relatively small, 11 Adopteds and 16 Controls, and the ratio of the mean difference to its standard error is only 1.5, the results are consistent with the comparisons made on the basis of occupation. Whether the impact of a poor environment is responsible for the lowered IQ is, of course, problematic. Note that the Adopteds fall 4.5 IQ points below the mean of their entire group, while the Controls drop 10.2 points below the mean of their group. If environment is dominant one would expect the same amount of depression in IQ for both groups. It should also be noted that the difference between Control children of the upper and lower environmental levels as defined above is 19.9 IQ points. The difference in the case of the Adopteds is 6.3.

What is the explanation of the difference in IQ with variation in environment in these two sets of children? The marked similarity of the children in age, school grade, and mean IQ will be recalled. Similarity in other respects, also, exists. Vocabulary and IQ correlate .64 for Adopteds, .63 for Controls; Woodworth-Mathew scores of emotional stability and IQ correlate .02 for Adopteds, .06 for Controls. To what extent our results may be due to personality factors of which we have no measure it is impossible to say. We have no reason to believe that such attributes as self-confidence, industry, "drive" or their converse are differently distributed in the two groups of children. Nor have we any reason to believe that the emotional environment provided by the parents of the Control children is more stimulating than that provided by Adoptive parents. To the extent that coefficients of assortative mating (Table VII) are an index to qualitative factors in

TABLE VII
Coefficients for Assortative Mating

	Adoptive parents			Control parents		
	r	P.E.	N	r	P.E.	N
Height	.26	.05	178	.27	.05	146
Education	.59	.03	192	.71	.02	193
Father's occupation and mother's education	.58	.03	192	.64	.03	194
Otis score	.57	.03	177	.41	.04	173
Vocabulary	.61	.03	174	.43	.04	164

the home influencing the child's response to his environment there are no differences in our two sets of homes.

If selective placement is entirely absent in the Adopted population, variation in environment may be said to be accountable for changes in IQ to the magnitude of about plus or minus 3 to 5 points. If, as previously stated, adoptive parents in the higher occupational, educational, and social levels secure children of greater promise than the adoptive parents in the lower levels, then the observed differences are clearly a function of genetic diversity rather than a function of environmental variation. Evidence relative to selective placement will be presented in the following section.

*   *   *

SUPPLEMENTARY DATA

If environment is dominant we should expect that unrelated children in the same household would agree markedly in ability. The contrary was found as may be seen by the following:

	r	PE	N
IQ of Exper. Adopteds and Own Children	.06	.14	25
IQ of Unrelated Adopteds in Same Household	.12	.22	10
Vocab. of Exper. Adopteds and Own Children	.06	.13	25

Although the number of cases is small the results suggest that the children are widely different in intellectual ability, regardless of their common environment.

In 20 cases of own children of Adoptive parents, IQ of own child and mid-parent Otis correlated .36. This correlation follows the expected familial pattern.

Although our single measure of the emotional stability of the children is probably not sufficiently reliable to permit any conclusions about personality differences, the similarity in the relationship between Woodworth-Mathews' scores and home environment for both groups of children is striking. As indicated below, Woodworth-Mathews' scores correlate:

  .10 for Adopteds, .13 for Controls with mid-parent Otis Score
−.04 for Adopteds, .07 for Controls with mid-parent Vocabulary
  .06 for Adopteds, .13 for Controls with Cultural index of home
  .11 for Adopteds, .18 for Controls with Child Training Index of home
−.04 for Adopteds, .07 for Controls with Occupation of father.

Clearly the fact of either blood relationship to person shaping the environment or its absence makes no difference. Adopted children, where presumably only environment is operative, behave in a manner similar to own children where both heredity and environment are operative. These results are in distinct contrast to our observations on the relationship of intelligence to home environment. They are based on the tests of 72 Adopteds and 77 Controls and give support to the theory that heredity plays a less significant role than environment in the variation observed for traits other than intelligence.

* * *

SELECTIVE PLACEMENT

The extent to which our results are free from selective placement of children on the basis of cultural similarity between adoptive and true parents determines the limits of the influence of environment on intelligence. If selective placement is entirely absent, then our results stand as evidence of the maximum influence of environment. If selective placement exists then our results overstate the influence of environment on intelligence.

In Table VIII the relationships of cultural background of true and adoptive parents are shown. All of the coefficients are low. Only three are reliable. The majority, however, are positive. In general, they offer weak evidence for selective placement in our data. Nevertheless, further analysis was applied for an appraisal of the point.

TABLE VIII

Factors in Adoptive Home Correlated with Factors in the Background of Child as Reported by Social Agency

	True father's occupation			True mother's occupation			True mother's education		
	r	P.E.	N	r	P.E.	N	r	P.E.	N
Adoptive father's occupation	.09	.07	89	.20	.07	89	.23	.06	96
Adoptive father's education	.24	.07	88	.21	.07	88	.20	.07	95
Adoptive mother's education	.10	.07	88	.38	.06	88	.25	.07	94
Adoptive mid-parent Otis score	.11	.07	79	.12	.07	83	.20	.07	89
Adoptive mid-parent vocabulary test	−.02	.08	76	.07	.07	79	.08	.07	86
Social status of adoptive home	.20	.07	89	.29	.06	89	.23	.06	96

One check involved an analysis of the replies of 22 placement workers to a questionnaire which asked the importance of certain attributes in judging the fitness of a child for a home. Most of the workers who answered the questionnaire had been engaged in child placing in Minnesota during the period from which our cases were drawn. Eighteen of the 22 regarded *probable intelligence of child* as of very great importance. The group, however, was evenly divided on the significance of education and occupation of true parents in judging *probable intelligence of child*. Eleven regarded education of true mother of slight or moderate importance and 11 held it to be of great or very great importance. The ratings for education of true father followed the same pattern. The judgments on the significance of occupation of true parents were similarly divided. Obviously if these placement workers behave in accordance with their replies the possibility of selective placement in a group of adopted children on the basis of education and occupation of true parents is nil.

The second check consisted in holding background constant in the correlation between child's IQ and adoptive home. This, clearly, is the crucial test. Time permitted the analysis for only a limited number of traits of the adoptive home. The traits selected, however, and presented in Table IX,

TABLE IX

Comparative Correlations between Child's IQ and Adoptive Home

	Background factor held constant			Zero order r background not constant
	True father's occupation N = 89	True mother's occupation N = 89	True mother's education N = 96	Entire group
Adoptive father's occupation	.18	.03	.05	.12
Adoptive father's education	.12	.13	−.02	.16
Adoptive mother's education	.18	.16	.13	.21
Adoptive mid-parent Otis score	.26	.10	.09	.18
Adoptive home environment score	.19	.16	.02	.19

are the most generally used indices of environment; namely, occupation, education, test intelligence of parents, and home rating.

An examination of this table shows that the correlations between child's IQ and attributes in the adoptive home are not greatly different from those for the entire group except when true mother's education is held constant. Then the correlations drop for each correlated factor. What may we infer? Clearly, for the populations involved, true mother's education appears to be a basis of selective resemblance between the adoptive home and its child, while true parent's occupation does not. Whether the population for whom no background history is available would support or refute these findings is problematic. Certainly the correlations reported in Table II may be regarded as no understatement of the relationship between child's IQ and home environment. From evidence of family background reported by adoptive parents on 50 of our cases, mental resemblance due to selective cultural likeness seems highly probable and therefore our correlations for child's

IQ and environment tend to overstate the influence of nurture. Because of the possibility of retrospective falsification in reports of this kind, these data may be ignored and the correlation of .20 be regarded as a general characterization of the relationship of child's IQ and environment.

CONCLUSIONS

By methods which allowed the effects of environment to be studied separately from those of heredity in combination with environment, this study attempted to discover the influence of environment and heredity on intellectual variation. As stated in the opening section, the tendencies observed in this study are valid only for populations which are similar to the experimental population in composition. However, the consistency with which a coefficient of .50 was secured for parent and offspring suggests that the restricted range in both the hereditary and environmental variables was reciprocal and hence no serious distortion in our results exists. The main conclusions are as follows:

1. Variation in IQ is accounted for by variation in home environment to the extent of not more than 4 per cent; 96 per cent of the variation is accounted for by other factors.

2. Measurable environment does not shift the IQ by more than 3 to 5 points above or below the value it would have had under normal environmental conditions.

3. The nature or hereditary component in intelligence causes greater variation than does environment. When nature and nurture are operative, shifts in IQ as great as 20 IQ points are observed with shifts in the cultural level of the home and neighborhood.

4. Variation in the personality traits measured in this study other than that of intelligence appears to be accounted for less by variation in heredity than by variation in environment.

Following many indications that the structure of intelligence changes with age, these investigators use factor analysis as an appropriate tool for a more careful study of the question. The paper argues both for change and for specificity of traits, which places it in the tradition of Columbia investigators.

The Age Factor in Mental Organization*

H. E. GARRETT

ALICE I. BRYAN

RUTH E. PERL

1935

SECTION I. THE PROBLEM AND METHOD

1. Introduction

The purpose of this study was to investigate the relationships of certain selected abilities at three stages in the growth curve. Previous investigations clearly indicate a tendency toward greater differentiation in mental abilities as age increases. Thorndike, for example, has reported an r of .52 between tests of arithmetic ("number ability") and vocabulary ("verbal ability") in a group of 126 fifth grade pupils; while Garrett has reported an r of only .21 between arithmetic and vocabulary in a group of 338 college freshmen women. At the pre-school level, Bryan found that various tests of memory were as closely related to tests of verbal ability and general intelligence as to each other. Bryan's results were obtained with a group of 200 children (100 boys and 100 girls) between the ages of 5 and 6 years. Each child was given 11 tests of memory for various kinds of visually presented material as well as a vocabulary test and the Stanford-Binet intelligence examination. In contrast to Bryan's results, Anastasi found that at the college level immediate memory for various types of material (words, colors, geometric forms) broke away sharply from both verbal and number ability. Anastasi obtained an average r of .06 between her battery of 8 immediate memory tests and vocabulary, and an average r of .15 between the same memory battery and arithmetic reasoning. The average intercorrelation of the memory tests was .40. These results were obtained with a group of 225 men college students, and were later checked upon a group of 140 women college students.

It appears that somewhere in the course of mental development there occurs a marked specialization of mental abilities as measured by psycho-

* Adapted from *Archives of Psychology*, No. 176 (New York, Jan. 1935). Reprinted by permission of the authors and *Archives of Psychology*.

logical tests. Various influences both intrinsic and extrinsic may contribute toward this result. As children grow older, simpler functions mature earlier than more complex. Specificity of function, therefore, may be effected through differential rates of growth and subsequent differences in time of maturation. Again it seems probable that specificity in achievement may result from increasing divergences in training, interests, and incentives. The adaptive behavior of a young child is more amorphous (more nearly on the same performance level) than is that of the adult. Furthermore, a child's school achievements depend to a greater degree upon facility and understanding in reading (and hence are less variable) than do the achievements of a college student in whom reading habits have become highly mechanized. All of these factors probably operate in the direction of specificity, *i.e.,* of reducing the *r*'s among tested abilities. It is worth noting, too, that in studies of college students one always deals with highly selected groups. The factor of selection, with the resultant narrowing of the ability range, would alone reduce the intercorrelations at the upper age levels even if there were no real tendency for abilities to become specialized with age.

To avoid the danger of greater selection at upper than at lower age levels, it seemed wise in the present study to work with groups not too widely separated in age. At the same time, since we were concerned with the effect of age change upon abilities, we wanted to employ groups far enough apart on the growth curve to make age a real factor. Three groups made up of boys and girls in approximately equal numbers were finally chosen from age levels 9-10, 12-13, and 15-16. These children were given a battery of 11 tests constructed so as to sample a wide range of ability and hence be applicable to all three age groups. Use of the same tests at all age levels enabled us to compare the correlations among the same abilities from one age level to the next, and in this way to reveal any tendency toward closer or more divergent relationships as age increased.

2. Subjects

Our subjects were children in the public schools of Kearny, New Jersey, an industrial and residential town of about 40,000 inhabitants, situated 8 miles west of New York City. The school system of this town has seven elementary schools, two junior high schools, and one senior high school. In order to obtain as unselected a sampling as possible, we took our subjects from all nine of these schools. . . . The 9 year old children were obtained from the seven elementary schools of the town, and were drawn from grades II to V inclusive, with grade IV furnishing the largest proportion. The 12 year old group was obtained from the two junior high schools, plus a small retarded group that was still in the elementary schools and another small advanced group that had reached the senior high school. The 15 year old group was obtained from the senior high school, plus a small retarded group still in the junior high schools. We believe that our 15 year old group is an unusually representative sampling of the population of 15 year olds. These subjects were drawn from all courses and included a number of children who in more prosperous times would undoubtedly have left school long since to take jobs.

As regards nationality, the fathers of our subjects represented twenty different national or racial groups, more than a third being American-born. With few exceptions, the children themselves were born in this country, and a large proportion of them were born either in Kearny or in neighboring towns and cities. A wide range of parental occupations and socio-economic levels was represented, with about one-third of the fathers engaged in skilled labor of various sorts.

Our entire group included originally 750 children, each age group containing 250 subjects, with an equal representation of boys and girls. After we had discarded all subjects whose records were incomplete in some respect, our total group was reduced to 646, of whom 340 were girls and 306 boys. In the 9 year group there were 225 children, 117 girls and 108 boys; in the 12 year group 196 children, 100 girls and 96 boys; and in the 15 year group 225 children, 123 girls and 102 boys. All 9 year old children were between 9 and 10; all 12 year old children between 12 and 13; and all 15 year olds between 15 and 16.

3. The Tests

In the process of selecting our tests, we first tried out a battery of 14 tests on four different groups of children in New York City. These groups were made up as follows: (1) Five bright 9 year olds, (2) Twelve bright 16 year olds, (3) Twenty-five dull 9 year olds, and (4) Twenty-five bright 16 year olds. The latter two groups were obtained from the Hebrew Orphan Asylum. Preliminary testing was chiefly for the purpose of establishing correct ranges of difficulty. We wanted our tests to contain items so easy that dull 9 year olds could make a score, and at the same time items so difficult that bright 15 year olds could not make a perfect score. It was necessary, also, to standardize time limits, directions, and other procedures.

* * *

Three tests were discarded and one test added as a result of this preliminary testing. The revised battery contained 11 tests, of which 7* were classified as "memory" tests, and 4 as "non-memory" tests. This two-fold division does not imply that the memory tests were taken to be measures of memory ability only, or that the non-memory tests were assumed to be entirely unrelated to memory. To be sure, our "memory" tests were designed to be measures primarily of the fixation process, *i.e.,* of immediate memory for material just presented. But we expected general intelligence, attention, previous acquaintance with and interest in numbers, words, geo-

* One memory test was later discarded because of its low reliability.

metrical forms, etc., to play an important rôle in their performance. That this was true is shown clearly in the correlations of these measures with the non-memory tests.

The following tests were selected for use in the present experiment:

A. *"Non-Memory" Tests.*

1. *Making Gates:* This was a simple motor speed test. The subjects were provided with lined paper and instructed to make rows of little "gates" with their pencils. These consisted of four vertical lines with a diagonal line drawn across them. The children were instructed to make as many as they possibly could in the time allotted. "Time" was called every half minute and the subjects then drew a line to show how far they had gone. *Time:* 2 minutes. *Score:* Number of gates completed. *Reliability:* 1st and 3rd quarters versus 2nd and 4th quarters.

2. *Vocabulary:* The subjects were given mimeographed sheets containing 60 items. Each item consisted of a word to be defined, with a group of five other words. The subjects were instructed to draw a line under the one word in the group which meant the same or nearly the same as the test word. The items were selected from the Thorndike CAVD vocabulary test, 5 items being drawn from every level from F to Q inclusive. *Time:* 8 minutes. *Score:* Number correct. *Reliability:* Odd versus even items.

3. *Arithmetic:* The subjects were given mimeographed sheets containing 40 problems in arithmetic and were instructed to do as many as they had time for. The problems were taken from the Thorndike CAVD arithmetic test, 5 problems each being drawn from levels H, I, J, K, L and M, and 3 each from levels F, G. N, O, P, and Q. *Time:* 20 minutes. *Score:* Number correct. *Reliability:* Odd versus even problems.

4. *Form Board Test:* The Likert-Quasha Revision of the Minnesota Paper Form Board Test was used as a measure of spatial ability. In order to make this a power test rather than a speed test, an ample time limit was allowed. *Time:* 25 minutes. *Score:* Number correct minus one-fifth number wrong. *Reliability:* Odd versus even items.

B. *"Memory" Tests.*

5. *Logical Prose:* The selection entitled "The Marble Statue," used originally by Shaw and later by Whipple, was revised for our purposes. We divided the selection into two equivalent halves, each containing 38 ideas or phrases. . . . The halves were then mimeographed on separate sheets of paper and were given separately with other tests intervening. The procedure was as follows: The children were told that they were going to read a story and that they would then be asked to write out as much as they could remember. The sheets containing the first half were passed out with instructions to keep them face down. At the experimenter's signal, they turned over the sheet. The experimenter then read the story out loud, at a uniform rate, while the subjects followed on their sheet, silently. As soon as she had finished, the sheets were collected and the subjects wrote

all that they could remember on blank sheets of paper. The second half was given in the same way, the subjects being told that it was the sequel to the first story—"what happened next." *Time:* 4 minutes were allowed for recall of each half. *Score:* Number of ideas correctly recalled for the whole story. *Reliability:* First half versus second half.

6. *Word-Word:* White cards, 6 x 20 inches long, each containing two four-letter words. Willson's black gummed letters, 4 inches high, were used for making the words. A sample set of 3 cards was given first, and then two sets of 10 cards each. The cards were first shown to the subjects with both words exposed, then the order was changed and the cards were shown again with only the first word of each pair exposed. The subjects wrote down the missing words as the cards were shown the second time. *Time:* 10 minutes. *Score:* Number right. *Reliability:* First set versus second set.

7. *Word Retention:* Cards containing single four-letter words were shown, one at a time, in two sets of 20 each. The subjects were then given paper and asked to write down all they could remember. The order did not matter. The two sets were separated by other tests. *Time:* 10 minutes. *Score:* Number recalled. *Reliability:* Set I versus Set II.

8. *Digit Span:* White cards containing 4 inch black digits. Two sets were used, each containing a series of from 3 to 13 digits inclusive. The combinations were made up in accordance with Locke's findings. The cards were shown one at a time at a speed approximating 1 second per digit for exposure and 1 second per digit for writing. *Time:* 15 minutes. *Score:* Weighted span, number of digits on the last card perfectly reproduced before an error was made, plus 1 point for any card completely correct thereafter. The averages presented in this study are computed from the total scores for both sets. To get the actual weighted span, divide by 2. *Reliability:* First set versus second set.

9. *Picture-Number:* Cards containing pairs of pictures and two-place numbers. This test proved so unreliable that the results were discarded.

10. *Geometrical Forms:* This test was devised by Jones and is described in detail by Woolley. A series of fifteen white cards, 9 x 12 inches, each containing a geometrical form drawn in black ink, was shown to the subjects. Another set of twenty cards, ten of which contained duplicates of drawings in the first set and ten of which contained different but similar designs, was then shown. The subjects were required to place a plus or minus sign opposite the number of each card in the second set, as it was shown, to indicate whether or not they had seen it before. The list of numbers was mimeographed on slips of paper which were passed out to the subjects. *Time:* 5 minutes. *Score:* Number correctly recalled as having been seen or not seen. *Reliability:* Odd versus even items.

11. *Objects:* This test was based on one used by Cornell and modified by Bryan. Two sets of fifteen objects each were used. The objects were chosen for their familiarity and interest to the subjects and for their visi-

bility, and included such things as a small American flag, a small doll, a glove, a pipe, a necklace, a toothbrush, etc. The objects were arranged attractively on two sheets of heavy white card board, 22 by 30 inches, and fastened securely by glueing and sewing them to the card board. Each card was exposed for 30 seconds, and the subjects were required to write down all they could remember of the 15 objects that had been shown. The second set of 15 objects was presented in the same way. *Time:* 10 minutes. *Score:* Total number of both sets correctly recalled. *Reliability:* Set I versus Set II.

As indicated in the descriptions of the tests, all material was presented visually. Subjects were tested in small groups of from 35 to 40 children at a time, by the same two experimenters working as a team and following a standardized routine. Testing covered a period of about three weeks during the Spring of 1934, and was completed about a month before the final school examinations began. Interest and cooperation on the part of the children were good throughout.

SECTION II. EVALUATION OF TESTS; AGE AND SEX DIFFERENCES

1. Evaluation of Tests

The means, standard deviations, and reliability coefficients for all of the tests employed in this study are reported for the three age groups, and for the combined age groups, in Tables I, II, III, and IV. Reliability co-

TABLE I

Means, Standard Deviations, and Reliability Coefficients for 117 Girls and 108 Boys, 9–10 Years of Age

	Means		S.D.'s		Reliability	
Variables	*Girls*	*Boys*	*Girls*	*Boys*	*Girls*	*Boys*
1 Making Gates	48.18	44.11	11.30	11.39	.87	.87
2 Vocabulary.........	16.73	16.28	4.69	5.36	.80	.84
3 Arithmetic	9.86	10.93	4.05	4.16	.90	.88
4 Form Board........	20.96	19.13	10.61	8.69	.91	.83
5 Logical Prose.......	31.29	28.19	9.06	10.25	.75	.75
6 Word-Word........	3.56	4.13	2.21	2.71	.51	.67
7 Word Retention	11.89	11.14	3.84	3.84	.62	.56
8 Digit Span	11.09	10.58	2.44	2.66	.55	.63
10 Geometric Forms ...	14.48	14.42	2.54	2.85	.61	.78
11 Objects	14.61	13.44	3.32	4.17	.66	.75

efficients were obtained by the split-half method. Tests No. 5 (Logical Prose), No. 6 (Word-Word), No. 7 (Word Retention), No. 8 (Digit Span), and No. 11 (Objects) were so constructed as to yield two equivalent forms. In tests No. 2 (Vocabulary), No. 3 (Arithmetic), No. 4 (Form

TABLE II

Means, Standard Deviations, and Reliability Coefficients for 100 Girls and 96 Boys, 12–13 Years of Age

	Means		S.D.'s		Reliability	
Variables	Girls	Boys	Girls	Boys	Girls	Boys
1 Making Gates	71.25	62.29	10.62	12.87	.58	.72
2 Vocabulary........	25.42	24.41	5.49	6.00	.89	.87
3 Arithmetic	18.24	18.23	4.66	5.04	.84	.88
4 Form Board	35.43	31.91	12.41	10.73	.93	.88
5 Logical Prose	47.00	41.36	7.31	10.74	.65	.77
6 Word-Word	6.14	5.46	3.19	3.27	.56	.54
7 Word Retention ..	20.19	16.58	5.22	5.10	.62	.68
8 Digit Span	13.67	12.91	2.89	2.47	.72	.59
10 Geometric Forms .	15.65	15.29	1.71	2.28	.31	.52
11 Objects	21.19	18.84	3.16	3.57	.52	.59

Board), and No. 10 (Geometric Forms), odd items were correlated against even and the reliability of the whole test estimated by the Spearman-Brown prophecy formula. The time limits in tests No. 2, 3, and 4 were long enough to make these tests measures of power rather than of speed; hence the split-half method was applicable. In test No. 1 (Making Gates), which was clearly a speed test, the time allotted to the whole test was divided into four parts and the number of items completed in the 1st and 3rd quarters correlated against the number completed in the 2nd and 4th quarters. Test No. 9 (Picture-Number) proved to be so unreliable that it was discarded.

TABLE III

Means, Standard Deviations, and Reliability Coefficients for 123 Girls, 102 Boys, 15–16 Years of Age

	Means		S.D.'s		Reliability	
Variables	Girls	Boys	Girls	Boys	Girls	Boys
1 Making Gates	80.27	73.09	12.46	10.86	.87	.74
2 Vocabulary.......	29.16	30.10	5.94	6.12	.84	.85
3 Arithmetic	19.74	22.59	3.82	3.38	.82	.59
4 Form Board	35.92	37.63	10.27	9.81	.86	.86
5 Logical Proce.....	45.37	43.98	6.98	7.73	.72	.46
6 Word-Word	6.07	6.59	3.02	3.26	.63	.66
7 Word Retention ..	17.97	17.62	4.06	4.32	.58	.51
8 Digit Span	13.80	13.41	2.12	2.26	.62	.59
10 Geometric Forms .	15.40	15.65	1.76	2.19	.16	.44
11 Objects	20.93	19.11	3.13	3.11	.55	.52

TABLE IV

Means, Standard Deviations, and Reliability Coefficients for 340 Girls, 306 Boys, 9–12–15 Year Olds

Variables	Means		S.D.'s		Reliability	
	Girls	Boys	Girls	Boys	Girls	Boys
1 Making Gates	66.56	59.43	18.02	16.87	.90	.88
2 Vocabulary.......	23.78	23.41	7.59	8.19	.92	.92
3 Arithmetic	15.89	17.09	6.07	6.46	.93	.92
4 Form Board	30.61	29.28	13.09	12.51	.93	.91
5 Logical Prose	40.99	37.56	10.56	11.84	.84	.80
6 Word-Word	5.22	5.36	3.07	3.24	.63	.65
7 Word Retention ..	16.52	15.00	5.58	5.29	.75	.70
8 Digit Span	12.82	12.25	2.78	2.77	.71	.70
10 Geometric Forms .	15.15	15.10	2.11	2.53	.42	.67
11 Objects	18.82	17.02	4.43	4.52	.78	.77

2. Sex Differences

If we take a D/SD_d of 2.5 or more to indicate a reliable difference, the girls are reliably superior to the boys on Tests No. 1 (Making Gates) and No. 11 (Memory for Objects) at all three age levels; and on Test No. 5 (Logical Prose) and Test No. 7 (Word Retention) at age 12. In two of these tests the superiority of the girls may, perhaps, be attributed to the nature of the material. The logical prose selection (The Marble Statue) probably appeals more to 9 and 12 year old girls than to boys of the same age; while the objects used in test No. 11, being mostly household articles, were perhaps more familiar to the girls. The only reliable difference in favor of the boys appeared on the arithmetic test at age 15.

The boys were somewhat more variable than the girls in 67% of the 30 comparisons possible at the 3 age levels; but reliably more variable only on Test No. 5 (Logical Prose) and Test No. 10 (Geometric Forms) at age 12.

3. Age Differences

The 12 and 15 year old boys and girls were reliably superior to the 9 year olds on all of the tests. The 15 year old boys and girls were superior to the 12 year olds on Making Gates, Vocabulary, Arithmetic, and Form Board (boys); but were not reliably superior on the 6 tests designed to measure memory. The age-progress curves for the tests of memory, vocabulary and arithmetic are shown in Figure 1. The leveling off of progress between 12 and 15 years suggests that immediate memory for symbolic material, as well as those elementary aspects of reading, attention, perception, etc., operative in tests of the sort employed here, reach their peak during the pubescent period. It is interesting to note that the boys' curve on the memory tests rises very slightly between 12 and 15, while the girls' curve drops very slightly. In those abilities sampled by tests of vocabulary and arithmetic, both girls and boys continue to improve up to 15 years. The girls, however, make relatively less progress after 12 years than the

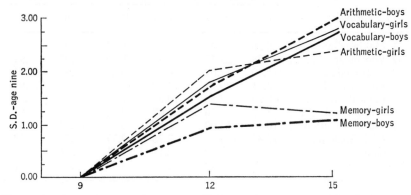

Figure 1. Comparison of Boys and Girls on the Memory, Vocabulary, and Arithmetic Tests at Three Age Levels, Nine, Twelve, and Fifteen Years. Differences between Means are Expressed in Terms of the S.D. of the Nine Year Old Group.

boys in both tests. In all of these comparisons the apparent earlier maturity of the girls is in accord with the established fact that girls reach mental and physical maturity earlier than do boys.

There is no consistent tendency for variability to increase or decrease with age. In 20 comparisons of 9 and 12 year olds the three significant differences are in two cases in favor of the older, and in one in favor of the younger group. Two of the seven significant differences between 9 and 15 year olds are in the direction of the older, and five in the direction of the younger children; while all four of the significant differences between 12 and 15 year olds are in the direction of the younger children. The lack of a significant tendency towards restricted variability with increase in age augurs well for the lack of special selection in our groups at years 12 and 15. We regard this as particularly important, since, as we have pointed out, the often drastic restriction in range at the upper age levels renders invalid comparisons of correlation coefficients from one age level to another.

SECTION III. THE CORRELATION OF TEN MENTAL TESTS AT THREE AGE LEVELS. MULTIPLE FACTOR ANALYSIS

1. Correlations of Ten Mental Tests at Ages 9, 12, 15

Tables V, VI, VII, VIII present the intercorrelations of all of our tests computed separately for boys and girls at each of the three age levels, as well as for the two combined groups of boys and girls. Entries above the diagonal refer to girls, those below to boys. Table IX summarizes in several ways the correlations in these tables. All of these average *r*'s were computed with the aid of R. A. Fisher's z-function, since individual *r*'s varied widely.

TABLE V

Intercorrelations of Ten Tests—9 Year Old Groups
(Girls above diagonal, boys below)

	1	2	3	4	5	6	7	8	10	11
1 Making Gates		.304	.371	.269	.395	.185	.218	.342	.159	.254
2 Vocabulary.........	.232		.400	.239	.523	.237	.160	.339	.056	.284
3 Arithmetic	.181	.516		.462	.489	.273	.306	.318	.292	.217
4 Form Board	.149	.013	.238		.248	.214	.140	.310	.289	.185
5 Logical Prose	.242	.407	.531	.236		.337	.379	.457	.233	.425
6 Word-Word	.201	.211	.066	-.115	.283		.388	.288	.148	.290
7 Word Retention	.175	.427	.432	.190	.412	.322		.307	.203	.364
8 Digit Span	.150	.078	.298	.061	.137	.177	.221		.267	.207
10 Geometric Forms ...	.241	.198	.350	.099	.220	.267	.165	.046		.129
11 Objects	.253	.520	.600	.108	.626	.411	.566	.320	.316	

TABLE VI

Intercorrelations of Ten Tests—12 Year Old Groups
(Girls above diagonal, boys below)

	1	2	3	4	5	6	7	8	10	11
1 Making Gates		.289	.131	.231	.308	.048	.183	.101	.039	.104
2 Vocabulary.........	.251		.550	.456	.472	.247	-.101	.156	.128	.156
3 Arithmetic	.345	.610		.421	.373	.214	.175	.193	.125	.302
4 Form Board	.391	.404	.490		.330	.192	-.003	.315	.094	.224
5 Logical Prose	.356	.637	.625	.483		.333	.093	.119	-.006	.175
6 Word-Word	.081	.185	.330	.286	.256		-.007	.132	.100	.258
7 Word Retention	.161	.098	.315	.285	.222	.246		.276	.042	.298
8 Digit Span	.209	.284	.313	.131	.362	.082	.094		-.063	.193
10 Geometric Forms ...	.261	.262	.194	.301	.161	.151	.125	.051		.198
11 Objects	.119	.221	.430	.403	.351	.316	.451	.100	.213	

The outstanding fact in Table IX is the fairly consistent tendency for the average *r*'s to decrease with age. This decrease does not occur for the boys between 9 and 12 (perhaps because of their slower development) but is quite clear-cut for both boys and girls between 9 and 15 and between 12 and 15. The average *r*'s for the same test groups computed from *r*'s corrected for attenuation show exactly the same picture as appears here, except that the corrected *r*'s are regularly about .10 higher. These results

TABLE VII

Intercorrelations of Ten Tests—15 Year Old Groups
(Girls above diagonal, boys below)

	1	2	3	4	5	6	7	8	10	11
1 Making Gates		.210	.253	.203	.361	.119	-.021	.017	.165	.160
2 Vocabulary.........	.182		.545	.296	.421	.212	.070	.212	.092	.005
3 Arithmetic	.055	.366		.406	.318	.126	.003	.171	.178	-.025
4 Form Board	.223	.119	.049		.080	.029	.002	.068	.132	.088
5 Logical Prose	-.021	.263	.070	.056		.192	.119	.031	.047	.133
6 Word-Word	.117	.280	.136	-.095	.191		.375	.094	.069	.251
7 Word Retention	.223	.083	.181	.149	-.029	.035		.081	.118	.224
8 Digit Span	.164	.277	.052	-.023	.141	.028	.271		.057	.074
10 Geometric Forms ...	.078	.185	.168	.117	-.052	-.131	-.198	.008		.172
11 Objects	.126	.024	.034	.021	.059	.088	.122	.250	-.032	

TABLE VIII

Intercorrelations of All Variables—Combined Age Groups
(Girls above diagonal, boys below)

	1	2	3	4	5	6	7	8	10	11
1 Making Gates		.657	.665	.525	.651	.357	.472	.426	.244	.589
2 Vocabulary.........	.615		.749	.563	.681	.414	.393	.453	.205	.531
3 Arithmetic	.643	.765		.636	.677	.407	.506	.468	.300	.577
4 Form Board	.593	.544	.621		.494	.318	.347	.425	.274	.470
5 Logical Prose	.539	.656	.685	.542		.450	.527	.451	.249	.604
6 Word-Word	.310	.374	.355	.224	.363		.401	.309	.181	.446
7 Word Retention	.490	.448	.524	.479	.470	.318		.429	.241	.585
8 Digit Span	.425	.439	.475	.321	.421	.216	.386		.200	.416
10 Geometric Forms ...	.286	.292	.315	.258	.229	.160	.149	.126		.272
11 Objects	.498	.541	.634	.471	.609	.380	.584	.432	.277	

point directly to a greater emphasis upon specific ability-factors, and a lessening of the influence of "general ability," as age increases from 9 to 15. This result is all the more significant since the drop in correlation at the 12 and 15 year levels, as compared with the 9, cannot be explained away as due to restriction in range at the two upper age levels.

From Table IX it is clear that the average correlation of the "memory" tests *inter se* is no greater (for boys less) than the average correlation of the "memory" and "non-memory" tests. This is true for each of the three age levels as well as for the combined groups of boys and girls. By employing a form of the correction for attenuation formula, we have computed the r between "what is common" to the memory and non-memory tests at each age level, boys and girls kept separate, and for the combined groups.

TABLE IX

Average Intercorrelations of Various Groups of Tests

	Girls 9	12	15	Age groups combined	Boys 9	12	15	Age groups combined
All Tests	.29	.20	.16	.46	.27	.29	.09	.45
"Memory" tests with all others	.28	.17	.13	.43	.28	.26	.07	.41
"Non-memory" tests with all others	.29	.23	.17	.50	.25	.33	.10	.50
"Memory" tests with "memory" tests	.30	.15	.14	.40	.31	.22	.05	.35
"Non-memory" tests with "non-memory" tests	.35	.35	.33	.64	.23	.42	.17	.64
"Memory" tests with "non-memory" tests	.27	.18	.13	.45	.26	.30	.09	.45
Averages by Age Groups:	.30	.21	.18	.48	.27	.30	.10	.47
Averages Boys and Girls Combined:					.29	.26	.14	.48

TABLE X

Correlations Between What is Common to Six Memory Tests and Four Non-Memory Tests at Each of Three Age Levels, and for the Combined Age Levels, Boys and Girls Separate

Ages:	9	12	15	Combined Ages
Girls	.82	.90	.54	.87
Boys	.96	.94	.82	.90
Average	.89	.92	.68	.89

These results, as reported in Table X, show that the two groups of tests, memory and non-memory, are measuring in large part the same common ability or abilities.

The fact that two groups of tests which differ in name, at least, seem to measure essentially the same common function is most reasonably explained, perhaps, in terms of Thorndike's "quantity hypothesis" of ability. Thorndike found that in a group of 250 eighth grade children, tests of association and information (largely routine memory) correlated with tests of reasoning and relation finding (so-called "higher" or intellectual abilities) as highly as either battery correlated *inter se*. He concluded from these data that the difference between a "good" intellect and a "poor" one lies in the number and variety of available responses, rather than in differences in their quality or kind. Garrett found that in a group of 158 college students the average intercorrelation of a group of 8 simple memory-learning tests was .25, and the average correlation of these tests with the Thorndike Intelligence Examination was .24. But the multiple correlation of the 8 memory-learning tests with the Thorndike Examination was .60; a result which indicates that simple memory-learning tests are measuring essentially the same ability as an extensive test of general level, even though the area covered by each single test is small.

Further evidence against the existence of a broad factor of retentivity distinct from general intelligence has been presented by Anastasi, who found no common factor running through a group of tests designed to measure memory for tones, pitch differences, movements, words, nonsense syllables, and prose passages. Anastasi interprets the memory factor which she found in an earlier study of college groups as representing a relatively narrow ability, namely, immediate memory for fairly difficult symbolic material, visually presented. The rote character of the material and similarities in the techniques utilized in fixation and recall are also suggested as contributing to the common factor. As already pointed out, Bryan found no essential differences in relationship between intelligence and memory tests in her group of 200 five year olds. Spearman also cites the results of several studies from his laboratory, all of which fail to reveal a special group factor of memory. These studies agree with the results which we have obtained.

2. Multiple Factor Analysis

In order (1) to differentiate more precisely, if possible, the factors operating to produce our correlations, and (2) to examine the changes in these factors with age, we have analyzed each table of correlations by Thurstone's Multiple Factor Method. Tables XI, XII, XIII, XIV present the first 4 factor loadings for each test at each age level, boys and girls being kept separate. The column headed "h^2" gives the percentage of the variance of each test which is attributable to the 4 factors taken together. The entries in the $\dfrac{K^2}{N}$ rows show the percentage of the variance of the test battery which (on the average) is attributable to each of the 4 factors.

At every age a fairly large first factor was found, the loadings being positive for all tests. In the 9 year olds, the weight of this first factor is .31 for both girls and boys; in the 12 year old groups it is .24 for the girls and .32 for the boys; in the 15 year old groups it is .19 for the girls and .13 for the boys. Clearly, the first factor accounts for progressively less of the variance of the 10 tests (except at age 12, boys) as age increases. This substantiates our findings based upon average correlations that abilities become more specific with increasing age. When the three age groups are

TABLE XI

Multiple Factor Analysis of All Variables
9 Year Old Groups

Variables	Girls					Boys				
	I	*II*	*III*	*IV*	*h²*	*I*	*II*	*III*	*IV*	*h²*
1 Making Gates	.527	.031	−.166	−.038	.308	.392	.081	.217	−.074	.213
2 Vocabulary.......	.559	−.140	−.372	.095	.479	.589	−.119	−.148	.254	.448
3 Arithmetic	.659	.183	−.150	.103	.501	.719	−.378	−.020	.177	.692
4 Form Board......	.513	.392	−.037	.245	.478	.230	−.241	.201	−.351	.275
5 Logical Prose.....	.730	−.215	−.163	−.106	.617	.702	−.227	−.024	.007	.545
6 Word-Word......	.500	−.151	.220	.012	.321	.422	.540	−.086	.102	.487
7 Word Retention ..	.519	−.170	.354	−.118	.438	.656	−.002	−.200	−.064	.474
8 Digit Span	.600	.065	−.052	−.314	.466	.341	.161	.002	−.117	.156
10 Geometric Forms .	.377	.341	.212	−.101	.314	.425	.062	.487	.418	.596
11 Objects	.506	−.331	.157	−.147	.412	.820	.054	−.247	.109	.748
Σ K²	3.098	.536	.462	.237	4.333	3.141	.598	.456	.439	4.634
Σ K²/N	.310	.054	.046	.024	.434	.314	.060	.046	.044	.463

TABLE XII

Multiple Factor Analysis of All Variables
12 Year Old Groups

Variables	Girls					Boys				
	I	*II*	*III*	*IV*	*h²*	*I*	*II*	*III*	*IV*	*h²*
1 Making Gates	.332	−.037	−.215	−.082	.165	.469	.066	−.393	.088	.387
2 Vocabulary.......	.750	.223	−.058	−.295	.703	.656	.500	.126	−.222	.745
3 Arithmetic	.648	−.085	.005	−.072	.432	.781	.127	.182	.008	.659
4 Form Board	.657	−.023	−.018	−.171	.462	.669	−.175	−.143	−.212	.544
5 Logical Prose.....	.600	.141	−.249	.095	.451	.747	.270	.092	.059	.643
6 Word-Word	.450	.066	.105	.400	.378	.413	−.175	.171	−.061	.234
7 Word Retention ..	.159	−.670	−.477	.176	.733	.447	−.415	.183	.140	.425
8 Digit Span	.286	−.214	−.138	.096	.156	.363	.248	−.024	.285	.275
10 Geometric Forms .	.186	−.136	.365	−.102	.190	.369	−.129	−.225	−.373	.343
11 Objects	.390	−.428	.178	.197	.406	.558	−.337	.270	−.028	.499
Σ K²	2.381	.779	.528	.387	4.076	3.216	.769	.419	.350	4.754
Σ K²/N	.238	.078	.053	.039	.408	.322	.077	.042	.035	.475

TABLE XIII
Multiple Factor Analysis of All Variables
15 Year Old Groups

Variables	Girls					Boys				
	I	II	III	IV	h^2	I	II	III	IV	h^2
1 Making Gates	.436	−.192	−.129	−.359	.372	.304	−.256	.245	.151	.241
2 Vocabulary.......	.623	−.319	.005	.294	.576	.705	.058	−.214	−.236	.602
3 Arithmetic	.602	−.396	.239	.137	.595	.486	.279	−.083	.045	.315
4 Form Board......	.408	−.222	.298	−.090	.313	.178	−.042	.352	−.060	.162
5 Logical Prose.....	.507	−.210	−.469	−.039	.523	.329	.049	−.182	−.444	.340
6 Word-Word	.440	.357	−.236	.211	.421	.282	−.521	−.785	−.028	.068
7 Word Retention ..	.321	.471	−.093	.145	.355	.013	−.724	.247	−.018	.585
8 Digit Span	.243	.071	.146	.184	.119	.297	−.261	.157	.155	.205
10 Geometric Forms .	.289	.099	.163	−.183	.153	.242	.279	.168	.063	.169
11 Objects	.319	.365	−.056	−.282	.318	.230	−.264	.074	.067	.127
ΣK^2	1.905	.886	.498	.456	3.745	1.237	1.162	1.001	.315	3.714
$\Sigma \dfrac{K^2}{N}$	.191	.089	.050	.046	.375	.124	.116	.100	.032	.371

TABLE XIV
Multiple Factor Analysis of All Variables
Combined Age Groups

Variables	Girls					Boys				
	I	II	III	IV	h^2	I	II	III	IV	h^2
1 Making Gates	.772	.169	−.119	−.145	.660	.753	−.061	.222	−.013	.620
2 Vocabulary.......	.792	.346	−.115	.085	.767	.812	−.290	−.095	.140	.772
3 Arithmetic	.842	.238	.060	−.028	.770	.863	−.177	−.026	.114	.760
4 Form Board......	.688	.158	.277	.012	.575	.698	−.133	−.370	.024	.642
5 Logical Prose.....	.802	.074	−.220	.004	.697	.776	−.017	−.112	.102	.625
6 Word-Word	.548	−.163	−.114	.219	.388	.460	.063	−.153	−.140	.259
7 Word Retention ..	.659	−.343	−.094	−.262	.629	.662	.380	.150	.048	.607
8 Digit Span	.594	−.037	.079	−.041	.362	.555	.070	−.011	.124	.328
10 Geometric Forms .	.363	−.103	.187	.009	.177	.359	−.175	.034	−.334	.272
11 Objects	.748	−.184	−.157	−.012	.618	.756	.219	−.186	−.043	.656
ΣK^2	4.824	.425	.244	.148	5.641	4.719	.369	.290	.194	5.572
$\Sigma \dfrac{K^2}{N}$	.482	.043	.024	.015	.564	.472	.037	.029	.019	.557

combined, the first factor is .48 for the girls and .47 for the boys, this increase in size being undoubtedly the result of age heterogeneity.

We interpret the first factor to be general ability to perform mental tasks of the kind presented by our tests. The reasons for this view are (*1*) that such typical general intelligence tests as arithmetic and vocabulary have on the average the highest correlations with factor 1; (Logical Prose, which ranks third, is certainly as much a measure of ability to read and understand as to retain) (*2*) while the six memory tests correlate with factor 1 on the average about .10 less than the 4 non-memory tests, the lack of evidence in factors 2, 3, and 4 for a distinctive memory factor makes it probable that factor 1 represents whatever common ability there is in the memory tests. . . .

Multiple factor analysis of all of our tests checks with the analysis of average correlations. Between 9 and 15, abilities of the sort here measured become more and more specific, general mental ability apparently playing a more important rôle before puberty than later on.

3. Multiple Factor Analysis of the Memory Battery Alone

We have made a factor analysis of the memory tests apart from the other tests in our battery, in order to identify more precisely, if possible, the character of the first factor. At the same time, we wished to investigate the possible presence of other bonds—verbal, spatial, etc.—within the memory group.

* * *

For the 9 year olds, the first factor accounts for .32 of the variance of the 6 tests for the girls and .36 for the boys. At age 12, the average weight of the first factor is .18 for the girls and .25 for the boys; and at age 15, it is .18 for the girls and .12 for the boys. Here, as was true of the whole battery, the first factor decreases in weight with increasing age, the largest decrease coming between 9 and 12 for the girls, and between 12 and 15 for the boys. For the combined age groups, the first factor weights are .42 for the girls and .39 for the boys.

The average correlation between first factor weights for the 6 memory tests alone and for the same tests when treated as part of the battery of 10 is .80. This substantial agreement is further evidence that the ability common to the 6 memory tests is the ability common to the whole battery. There is no evidence of a specific retentivity apart from general ability, the data thus supporting our argument for the "quantity" hypothesis.

The weights of the second, third, and fourth factors are small for both boys and girls at all three age levels. The evidence for a break as between the "spatial" tests (Nos. 10, and 11) and the "verbal" tests (Nos. 5, 6, 7) is very slight, and any conclusion as to group factors in these tests would be extremely precarious.

SECTION IV. SUMMARY AND INTERPRETATION

1. Three groups, composed of 9, 12, and 15 year old children, each age group containing about 250 boys and girls in equal proportions, were given a battery of 10 mental tests. These children were, to a greater extent than is usual in such groups, representative of their populations.

2. Our battery consisted of 6 tests designated as "memory" tests, and 4 tests designated as "non-memory" tests. The memory tests were designed to measure, primarily, the ability to reproduce visually presented material; and the non-memory to measure speed of response, verbal, numerical, and spatial abilities. Analyses of intercorrelations, however, indicate that all of the tests measure much the same ability, and do so about equally well.

3. The memory tests taken alone exhibited reliable increases from years 9 to 12, but no significant increase from 12 to 15. The tests of verbal ability (vocabulary) and number ability (arithmetic) showed increases up to 15 years, the increase from 12 to 15 being relatively greater for the boys than for the girls.

4. Few reliable sex differences appeared. The boys were reliably superior to the girls at the 15 year level in arithmetic; the girls were reliably superior in the speed test (Making Gates) and in several of the memory tests at all age levels.

5. With increases in age, the abilities measured by our tests tend to become more and more specific. This is shown by a study of the average intercorrelations of groups of tests, and by multiple factor analysis of the correlations. Four factors were calculated from the intercorrelations of the ten tests, and from the intercorrelations of the six memory tests alone. Of these factors, only the first was large enough to account for any appreciable share of the variance of the battery. This first factor exhibited a consistent decrease as age increased from 9 to 15 years, paralleling the drop in average correlation. The correlation of the first factor weights as found by analysis of the battery of ten tests, and from analysis of the six memory tests alone, was .80, indicating a single common ability in all of the tests. No distinctive memory factor appeared in either analysis.

As a tentative explanation of the drop in correlation with age, it is suggested that in young children ability is amorphous to a greater degree than during later growth periods. The first factor, then, may be taken to represent an earlier achievement in the growth process. At the younger ages, this factor differentiates individuals because of their unequal maturity; but at age fifteen all are mature with respect to it, and consequently differ less in this function than before. As an illustration, speed of locomotion is a strong factor in the simple directions test ("Go get that doll and lay it on the table") at the age when some children are walking and others still creeping; but this factor has little value at later ages when all are walking.

As children grow older, variation in levels of maturation, differentiation in interests, the development of special aptitudes, and selection by the schools of the more gifted lead to a greater emphasis upon specific abilities as opposed to general mental alertness. The representative character of our twelve and fifteen year old groups seems to answer fully the objection that specialization with age is entirely an artifact of selection. The two older groups were not significantly less variable than the nine year olds; and decrease in correlation could hardly have been brought about solely through restriction in range.

The identification of the general factor common to all of the tests as being essentially the same factor common to the group of memory tests suggests an explanation in terms of Thorndike's "quantity hypothesis." If intellect or general intelligence is homogeneous, the only difference between a good intellect and a poor one being in the extent and variety of possible responses, it would seem logical to expect our memory tests (which clearly demand intelligence as well as retentivity) and our non-memory tests (which clearly demand retentivity as well as intelligence) to express the same common ability. Our inability (1) to separate retentivity from general intelligence at the three age levels which we have investigated; and the finding (2) that the rôle of general ability is minimized in favor of special abilities as age increases, are the most significant results of this study.

In selecting a control group for their studies of aphasia the writers hit upon the happy idea of using a mentally normal hospital population. Their discussion of why they chose this sample is informative. They then discovered that their control group looked like average Americans in education, employment, socio-economic status, and so on, so they proceeded to study age differences in this surprisingly representative sample. Their findings, briefly summarized here, stress again the differential effects of age on specific mental tasks.

Changes in Adult Intelligence*

THEODORE WEISENBURG

ANNE ROE

KATHERINE E. McBRIDE

1936

SELECTION OF THE GROUP

a. Problems Involved

In selecting normal adults to serve as a control group in the study of aphasia, the first requirement was to obtain subjects similar in age and in educational, occupational, and cultural status. Survey of the possible sources for such a group showed that the most nearly similar sample of the population, and therefore the best control, was to be found in the patients admitted to the same hospitals in which the aphasic patients were studied but not suffering from any nervous disorder or any condition known to affect mental functioning. Permission was therefore secured to study patients in the wards of the hospitals in which the majority of the aphasic patients were being examined: the Orthopedic Hospital and Infirmary for Nervous Diseases, the Graduate Hospital, and the Philadelphia General Hospital. Samples from the wards of these hospitals were satisfactory as controls because almost all the aphasic patients were also ward cases.

The advantage of this method of selection is immediately obvious. The patients admitted to one department of a hospital are more likely to be similar to those admitted to another department in all factors except the type of disease which required their admission, than is any other limited group of the population which could be studied. The disadvantage, when the purpose is the study of mental functioning in *normal* adults, is also obvious, for a number of hospital patients certainly cannot be considered

* Adapted from the book *Adult Intelligence: a psychological study of test performance* (New York, The Commonwealth Fund, 1936). Reprinted by permission of Anne Roe, Katherine McBride, and The Commonwealth Fund.

normal either mentally or physically. At the same time there are many patients whose hospitalization is enforced by the need for some particular treatment rather than by a serious protracted illness or general debilitation, and who, in the opinion of the authors, would be accepted by both medical men and psychologists as normal from the point of view of mental functioning. The problem in the selection of the normal control groups therefore resolved itself into the choice of those patients whose disorders were least likely to have any effect on the functions required in the various mental and educational achievement tests.

Neurological conditions were immediately excluded from the normal control group and in addition it seemed wise to reject all cases of glandular disorder, tuberculosis, or syphilis. Aside from these, few types of disease had been studied with regard to possible mental changes and there was little material available to determine the choice of patients. Data from tests of intelligence in cases of children with diseased adenoids and tonsils were not of immediate value because patients coming in for treatment for these conditions had not been hospitalized long enough to be studied thoroughly. Many of the subjects finally accepted had had tonsillectomies at some previous time; very few showed diseased tonsils or adenoids at the time of the examination.

In view of the fact that orthopedic cases were available for study and were particularly suitable because they were in good working condition and had unlimited time, the study of crippled children made by Fernald and Arlitt was of special interest. These investigators found an average Stanford Binet I.Q. of 82.35 for a group of 194 children, a figure which would seem to indicate somewhat inferior intelligence. Analysis showed that this mean I.Q. was lowered by the inclusion within the group of 27 cases of spastic birth paralysis (mean I.Q. 69.11) and 15 cases of central nervous system involvement, including congenital lues (mean I.Q. 75.93). The groups of poliomyelitis, tuberculosis, nutritional disorders including rickets, infections not involving the central nervous system, and trauma ranged from 83.79 to 86.53 in I.Q. These groups were still slightly inferior, but apparently not because of the disease conditions, for similar ranges in I.Q. were characteristic of the siblings of the crippled children. In short, it seemed probable that the crippled children, who were all institutional cases, were drawn from inferior family groups in which I.Q.'s of about 85 would be typical.

Another study of interest in view of the large number of gastro-intestinal cases available for examination was Paulsen's report on mental and motor efficiency in cases of intestinal toxemia. The group under treatment for intestinal toxemia gained 16 per cent more than the control group on reexamination by a battery of mental tests and tests of steadiness, motor control and coordination. The author concluded that this net gain represented the increase in mental and motor efficiency resulting from the treatment. This conclusion might well be questioned, however, in view of certain unsatisfactory conditions in the experiment. The test group was selected on the basis of the presence of harmful bacteria in sufficient numbers in the feces, and the majority when questioned "confessed" the symptoms of intestinal toxemia. The control group was matched as nearly as possible in chronological age, test intelligence, training, and environment; but no attempt was made to determine the presence or absence of intestinal toxemia in these cases. A further, though probably less important, defect in the experimental conditions is a difference of motive in the two groups: the test cases were promised assistance in bettering their intestinal conditions in return for work on the tests while the controls "entered the experiment as a matter of interest and desire to be of assistance to the examiner."

As these reports indicate, there was little evidence at the beginning of this research as to the effect on intelligence of disease, other than glandular disease or disorders of the central nervous system. During the course of the work, however, there appeared a very important study by Dawson and Conn, which is more extensive and more decisive than any previous investigation. An intelligence test, the Burt Revision of the Binet, was given to over a thousand children suffering from types of disease which included pneumonia, rheumatism, nephritis, glandular disorders, epilepsy, encephalitis lethargica, and other brain conditions. The findings show clearly that non-brain cases made scores on intelligence tests equivalent to those made by the healthy population to which they belonged, while the brain cases were on the average inferior. In other words, disease, apart from disease of the brain or ductless glands, "does not appear to have any appreciable effect on the intelligence." An interesting analysis of mental test performance in acute, non-acute, and chronic conditions revealed the fact that the average scores were actually higher for patients examined when fevered and acutely ill; they were slightly lower for patients classified as chronic than for those in the afebrile but non-chronic group, but the difference was not significant.

The subjects selected for this research were studied during periods of less serious illness than those whom Dawson and Conn examined. With so little positive data on the problem, however, it was considered safest to restrict the cases to patients with bone fractures or dislocations and to patients recuperating from some surgical treatment and in good working condition at the time of the examination.

b. Criteria for Selection

For the reasons discussed above, the normal adults were chosen from the orthopedic and surgical wards, with further limitations which would make them satisfactory as controls for the aphasic group. These limitations were as follows:

1. Freedom from any present or earlier neurological, mental, or glandular disease

2. Satisfactory vision and hearing
3. Age under sixty years
4. English as the native tongue.

c. Method of Approach

When cases which seemed to fill the requirements had been selected from the hospital records, or the physician's report, the examiner proceeded very informally to explain the problem and ask for the patient's cooperation. He was told that studies were being made of patients who had speech difficulties resulting from a "stroke" or injury to the brain, and that these studies were handicapped by lack of knowledge as to just how much the average man remembered of his schooling, or how much he had learned without schooling. It was further explained that we were as yet unable to do a great deal for the aphasic patient because we did not know how the ordinary man worked on tests of reading, writing, and arithmetic. Two points were always made as clear as possible: 1) that the "ordinary man" was the one we wanted to study, not the well-educated man; and 2) that while each person must do his best, it was not his individual score, but the general results for the group which interested us. Sometimes one of these points was more useful in clinching the bargain, sometimes the other; and occasionally our objectives were attained when our explanations did not seem to be comprehended at all.

All investigators report a certain number of refusals; Miles and Miles speak of the "difficulty which we and others have encountered with adult subjects in administering intelligence tests." In this work, of the total number of patients asked to take the examinations, only 21 per cent refused.

The motives which led to acceptance in the remaining 79 per cent of the cases are of some interest. Three types were distinct, but all of these were probably present to some degree in most cases. The first was a willingness to do anything which would help someone else. The second was boredom; the patient welcomed any occupation to fill in time. The third was more personal, arising from a reluctance to say "no" to the examiner and pride at being selected. At the Philadelphia General and Orthopedic Hospitals, where work was carried on over long periods of time, there was some good-natured banter about "taking lessons," but this publicity was an advantage rather than a disadvantage; patients felt that there was a certain amount of prestige attached to taking the examination, and a number who had not been selected offered themselves as subjects.

It will have been evident that in approaching the patient, the emphasis was placed rather upon achievement in reading, writing, and arithmetic than upon intelligence. During the course of the examination, a few of the patients asked if some of the tests were intelligence tests, but were not disturbed upon being told that they were.

Whether the tests were designed for group or individual application they were all given as individual tests, a very important point since individual work enabled the examiner to become well acquainted with each patient, to observe his methods of work, and to ensure his steady cooperation. Occasionally a patient was reluctant to try some particular test; if he objected seriously the test was omitted, but in most cases he could be persuaded to attempt the work, and once persuaded, he seemed to take pride in doing his best. Cooperation was splendid, and the contact between patient and examiner all that could be desired. The advantages which accrue from a favorable personal relation cannot be overemphasized.

*   *   *

CONCLUSIONS

This research has tapped a new and valuable source for the study of adult intelligence. Too little advantage has yet been taken of the opportunity the hospital offers for detailed psychological studies of adults from the middle levels of the population. Within the hospital group there are undoubtedly many types and degrees of abnormality in mental functioning, but there are also patients who may safely be said to be "normal" mentally. Among them there are cases requiring hospitalization for two weeks or longer, and such patients are practically unique among adult subjects in that their time is comparatively unlimited and most of them are willing to spend a large amount of it on the examinations. They may be given not one but many tests, with the result that a much more complete knowledge of the individual's mental functioning can be obtained than is usually the case. Furthermore, they may be given repeated examinations without fear that their interest will flag; when the studies are properly conducted, interest in the examinations as well as friendliness with the examiner usually increases steadily throughout the work. It is true that individual studies are costly, but they are rewarded by the certainty that the tests have served their purpose fully and that they have yielded not only a score value for the particular performance, but an opportunity for observing how that performance was carried through and what difficulties stood in its way.

The hospital group as a whole is the only single group which comprises all social and economic strata. The ward patients, who formed the subjects in this research, constitute a more limited sample, but a sample which has every indication of being truly representative of the middle levels of the population. It has been shown to have approximately the same occupational distribution as the population of Philadelphia; it seems to be close to the average of the Army population with regard to the grade of intelligence required by the occupations represented; and it shows a distribution for education similar to the Army distribution.

The correlation between intelligence and the predisposition to disease or environmental conditions favorable for disease is still an unknown quantity. If it is negative the consequence would naturally be that hospital patients, because of the disease conditions, tended toward inferiority in intelligence. It is probable that such a tendency, if it exists, is more marked in certain diseases than in others, and notably in those diseases in which neglect or poor living conditions are etiological factors. Again the problem resolves itself into proper choice among the hospital patients; and, granted this, it seems clear that any slight selective factors which may exist because of a relationship between intelligence and disease are of little weight in comparison to the advantage the hospital group offers as a random sample of the middle levels of the adult population.

Because the purpose of this research was a study of normal adults as a basis for work with aphasic and non-aphasic cases of cerebral lesion, every effort was made to select only patients who would be generally accepted as mentally normal. Many were rejected whose performances on the tests might well have been normal, for example, the diabetics, but with so little knowledge of the characteristics of mental functioning in various diseases, risks had to be cut to a minimum. It goes without saying that there is a large field for work on the problem of intelligence and disease, and that beginnings should be made in accumulating cases which are clear-cut from the diagnostic point of view.

When one considers the problems of adult intelligence and the various studies contributing to the knowledge on the subject, it seems clear that the average level of so-called general intelligence and the characteristics of its course with age have been fairly well established. Within recent years there have also been reports on specific types of test performances, but many of the activities which are important for a knowledge of mental functioning in the adult years have as yet been little studied. In this research a certain number of these activities have been investigated. The groups examined were comparatively small so that the actual norms obtained are no more than tentative. It is believed, however, that they are highly trustworthy: the individual nature of the work ensured maximum effort from all ages and types of subject, the group is apparently typical of the middle levels of the population, and the findings themselves are consistent.

With regard to the particular tests of the battery and their use with adults, the most important conclusions may be listed as follows:

1. The sentence completion test is undoubtedly one of the most important types of so-called language test for adults. The one used in this research, the Kelley Trabue Completion Exercise Beta, proved satisfactory from every point of view and would probably be difficult enough for a group slightly superior to this.

2. Vocabulary tests are well suited for work with adult subjects and readily accepted by them. In use with the normal subjects in this research there was little to choose between the two vocabulary tests from the point

of view of their discrimination within the group or their relation to other tests. The Stanford Binet Vocabulary, however, naturally had the advantage over the Thorndike Test of Word Knowledge in providing an opportunity for study of the patient's reactions and attitudes.

3. The mixed analogies test in the forms arranged in this research differentiates fairly well among "average" adults, is readily accepted by them, and because of its apparent relationships with the non-verbal tests and its marked decline with age is one of the most interesting theoretically.

4. The absurdities test is also well adapted for use with adults, but is not satisfactory in the forms employed with these subjects and needs further development.

5. Many of the educational achievement tests employed were satisfactory in their existing forms. Both tests of reading comprehension, the Thorndike McCall and the Chapman, were adequate from the point of view of their discriminative power, but the former suffered a little in use with adults because of too childish content. Both the arithmetic tests, the Stanford Achievement Computation and the Reasoning, were found to be very satisfactory in discriminating among these adults. The Gray Oral Reading Test, the Gates Oral Spelling, and the Stanford Dictation each showed a piling up of scores at the upper end of the scale, probably not so much because the tests were too easy as because the activities involved are fairly well acquired by adult subjects, even by those of only moderate education and ability. The Morrison McCall Spelling Scale was obviously too simple for adults from the middle levels of the population, but it is well adapted for work with low-grade or pathological cases.

6. Many of the non-verbal or performance tests at present available fail to discriminate among normal adults. Most of the tests of the Pintner Paterson Performance Scale fall in this class. The data on these tests will not be useful in connection with further studies of normal adults, but have a definite value in studies of deteriorated adults whose level is low enough to require comparatively simple tests and whose deterioration may be estimated roughly by reference to the median and quartiles for normal adults.

7. Other non-verbal tests, notably those of the Pintner Non-Language, are more satisfactory in differentiating among "average" adults and contribute data on abilities which are important at adult as at childhood levels. There are not enough of these tests, however, or rather they do not cover all the types of performance which should be studied, for example, form or picture analogies.

8. The Goodenough Drawing Test presented an assignment unwelcome to many adults, and was undoubtedly a different type of problem for them than for the child, with success on the test much less closely related to intelligence than among children. Experience with the test of Drawing a Chair indicated that this too was a difficult problem, and suggested that

studies of drawing in adults run up against very variable factors, emotional as well as intellectual, and must be interpreted with caution.

The analysis of the results for their bearing on the question of age and test performance is one of the most interesting sections of the work. The first conclusion is that by far the greatest extent of mental development as indicated by these test performances has occurred before the twenties, and that from this decade through the fifties there is little further gain and comparatively little decline. While the magnitude of the development before twenty far outweighs any change between twenty and sixty, smaller changes do occur in the adult period. As they appear in specific types of mental activities, these changes are comparatively little known, but are none the less important, for example, in estimating the relative value of the worker in a given occupation at twenty and at fifty, or the value of educational projects for the "average man" in earlier or later decades. The results of this study show clearly that the peak of development and the course with age are different for different performances. A survey of the findings suggests two conclusions which may be briefly stated as follows:

1. The abilities sampled by most of the so-called language tests are well maintained through the thirties and in the majority of cases show only slight declines thereafter. The abilities sampled by the vocabulary tests show little or no decline through the fifties.

2. The abilities sampled by another group of tests show an early peak, probably falling either in the twenties or before, with successive declines in the thirties, forties, and fifties. These declines are not significant at any one-decade or two-decade interval, but most of them are significant for the interval between twenty and fifty or for the larger age groups twenty through thirty-four and forty-five through fifty-nine. A point of great interest is that all but one of these tests are of the non-language type, while the tests which do not show a drop in mean score before the thirties are language or arithmetic tests. The only "language" test in the group characterized by steady declines with age is the Printed Analogies, which repeatedly manifested a close relationship to the non-language tests. Declines with age on some of the non-language tests probably reflected the generally accepted declines in simpler motor and perceptual abilities and particularly in those in which speed was a dominant factor. Declines in others, notably the Porteus Maze and the more complex tests of the Pintner Non-Language Scale, and also in the Printed Analogies, could not be explained on this basis. Furthermore, they were apparently not to be attributed to a greater difficulty among the older subjects in adapting to the test situations, for such difficulty was not observed in the situation itself. It is suggested rather that these tests probably involve spatial factors and that the declines are to be understood on this basis.

From the point of view of the relation of education and test performance, the findings indicated that the amount of formal schooling was probably not such an important factor as it is generally supposed to be. An analysis of individual cases revealed that the intelligent men with poor school training had effected some compensation by adult life, while the dull individuals who had received more training in the fundamental school subjects than their intelligence warranted either had never profited by it or had forgotten most of what they once knew. It would not be wise to lay too great stress on this point in view of the small size of the group, and also in view of the fact that at least one performance, arithmetic computation, showed a slightly closer relation to education than to test intelligence. It is important to note, however, that scores on all the other "educational achievement" tests analyzed bore a closer relation to the test intelligence than to the school grade completed, and that this relationship held even for the spelling tests, the skills involved in which are definitely school trained. The results furnish additional proof, though such is hardly necessary, of the wisdom which lies in studying the mental abilities of the school child and making the nature and extent of his training fit his potentialities for development.

A study of test performance in relation to the occupational classes of the Taussig Scale indicated a condition which is easily accepted on the basis of common observation, namely that the professional and business groups excel the others in the abilities sampled by the Sentence Completion, the Stanford Binet Vocabulary, and the Thorndike McCall Reading Scale. It is noteworthy that these tests are all verbal, and that none of the non-verbal tests showed a relationship to any of the groups of the Taussig Scale. It would seem that the abilities involved in these non-language tests either are not those in which the skilled laborer excels the professional or business man, or that the abilities shown by the skilled laborer in different trades are in themselves so diverse that group analysis obscures the general trend.

Survey of the results led to the conclusion that sex differences on the test performances studied were negligible. No significant difference was found for any test performance, and the slight inequalities appearing for a few probably resulted from fluctuations of sampling.

Analysis of the relationship between various performance levels in the individual case showed that adults who did well with some test performances usually did well with others, while those who had difficulty with some also had difficulty with others. This condition represents only the general trend, however, and there were large variations in some cases. Within the limits of the ten language and non-language tests studied, these variations revealed only a few cases of marked constellations in mental abilities, with some groups of tests falling at very different levels from others.

There is no doubt that one of the most important problems in the study of adult intelligence, and indeed in all studies of intelligence, is the analysis of mental abilities and their relationship. With groups as small as those in this research, statistical analyses such as those developed by Spearman, Kelley, or Thurstone promised little, and have not been carried through, so that it is impossible to arrive at any conclusions on this basis as to the particular mental abilities in the adult or their interrelationship. Without throwing caution to the winds entirely, however, it is possible to discuss certain interesting leads which appear from the correlational and other data for the normal group and from the findings for the abnormal subjects examined, notably the cases of cerebral lesion with and without aphasia.

The study of the normal shows positive correlations between almost all tests, but much higher correlations in general between the so-called language tests than between language and non-language or within the non-language group. Naturally rigid lines of division do not hold: one striking instance of a crossing of the line is the Printed Analogies Test, which obviously involved verbal material, but is apparently as closely related to the arithmetic and non-verbal as to the verbal tests. The Arithmetic Computation Test also occupies a sort of mid-way position.

The evidence for a distinction between different groups of mental abilities gains additional support from the findings for the pathological groups studied by the same tests. Cases of right-sided cerebral lesion without aphasia or history of it were found to resemble the normal most closely in sentence dictation, oral spelling, and oral vocabulary, and to be significantly inferior to the normal only on the arithmetic and some of the non-language tests. These non-aphasic cerebral cases represent a sample inferior to the normal, but this condition does not explain the marked inequalities in their performance levels. Language abilities are apparently well maintained while the abilities required by the arithmetic and most non-language tests show evidences of deterioration.

The distinction between language and non-language is more pronounced in typical cases of aphasia; and here the opposite condition is to be found, that is, the language activities are more seriously affected than the non-language. Interestingly enough, the arithmetic activities usually stand in between. Some few patients whose language processes are extremely limited or confused so that they speak and understand only a few words correctly nevertheless do better than the average of the normal group on non-language tests, and may also do moderately well in arithmetic. Others, the great majority, show some deterioration in non-language activities and in arithmetic, but far less than in language. Only a few aphasic patients have anything like as great difficulty in non-language as in language work. In short, aphasia is a deterioration which usually extends beyond language processes and involves activities which do not require overt verbal responses, but the changes in non-language performances are less marked than those in language and in some cases the differentiation is clear enough for one to say that the aphasic patient has lost one form of intelligent response, the verbal, and retained other forms which do not require language.

Uncertain as reasoning from the pathological to the normal must be, it seems probable that the characteristics of cases of cerebral lesion, with and without aphasia, give certain new cues for an understanding of normal mental functioning. Despite the positive correlations found for the normal group between almost all the many activities studied and despite the fact that analyses of individual cases revealed few marked constellations of mental test performances, there are in all probability more or less independent groups of mental abilities. The typical normal adult does not show great differences in the development of these different abilities; in so far as performances on tests of intelligence and educational achievement may be taken as indices, the various abilities all fall at fairly similar levels. In cases of brain disease, however, or at least in cases of localized brain disease, they may be affected unequally. As to the nature of these groups of mental abilities and their interrelationships, there is still little precise knowledge and it may well be that groups as yet undefined will have to be postulated to explain results such as those found in this research. For the present it seems clear from this study and others, however, that there is probably a verbal ability of a rather extensive nature. Numerical and spatial abilities have also been indicated, particularly in Kelley's work, and the necessity for some such groups as these is suggested by the findings for both normal and pathological subjects.

This interesting little study raises the question of the effect of speed on test scores of older subjects and suggests a technique for evaluating the extent of this influence. Further work confirms the findings reported here on the growth of vocabulary in the upper intelligence groups during maturity.

Growth of Vocabulary in Later Maturity*

ALICE M. CHRISTIAN

D. G. PATERSON

1936

Practically all studies dealing with the effect of later maturity on verbal ability indicate that age has a detrimental effect. In contrast, the present note reports a study in which growth in range of vocabulary recognition appears to exist up to and even beyond age 60.

Comparability of older and younger subjects was attained by testing University of Minnesota Freshmen on the one hand and parents and relatives of University of Minnesota students on the other. Thus social-economic status and educational opportunity were held relatively constant for older and younger subjects.† Data on this point are available and are clear cut.

Sub-test A of the University of Minnesota College Ability Tests was used. This consists of 120 vocabulary items taken systematically from Thorndike's "Teacher's Word Book" so that approximately one-third of the words are drawn from the eight-thousand word level, one-third from the nine-thousand word level, and one-third from the ten-thousand word level. The time limit is 15 minutes, which permits about 75 per cent of college freshmen to attempt all the items.

The total number of items correct for college students and for parents and relatives of college students show, on the average, a slight but steady decline up to and beyond age 60. See Table I. The difference between the mean score made by the college freshmen (18 year olds) and the mean scores made by parents and relatives grouped in ten-year age intervals are

* *The Journal of Psychology*, 1 (1936), pp. 167-169. Reprinted by permission of the authors and The Journal Press.

† It is possible that parents and relatives of college students who are willing to be tested represent a selection of the more able and competent. If this be so, then an increase in vocabulary score from age 18 to age 40 is a function of selection and not of growth in vocabulary. A more extensive investigation is now under way to check on this point. Even so, the study reported here affords clear cut evidence that when "rate of work" is held constant, an apparent decline in range of vocabulary becomes an actual increase.

TABLE I

Recognition Vocabulary Tests Scores of College Freshmen
(18-Year-Olds and Parents and Relatives)

(120-item test)

Age group	N	M	σ	Range
18-year-olds	200	87.5	16.7	41–115
40–49-year-olds	50	84.2	22.2	40–116
50–59-year-olds	49	81.9	25.9	25–115
60–69-year-olds	30	79.3	28.7	10–114

not statistically significant. Nevertheless, the trend is toward lower scores with advancing age.

The increased variability for the older age groups (σ and range) suggested that their slightly lower mean scores might be due to a slowing up effect of age. In other words, parents and relatives may work at such a slower rate that their total scores might be reflecting decrease in rate of work rather than decrease in range of vocabulary knowledge. Analysis of the number of items attempted by the various groups revealed a marked slowing up in rate of work with advancing age. See Table II. The difference

TABLE II

Number of Items Attempted in the Recognition Vocabulary
Test by College Freshmen and Parents and Relatives

(120-item test)

Age group	N	M	σ	Range
18-year-olds	200	116.7	11.2	76–120
40–49-year-olds	50	101.5	19.6	55–120
50–59-year-olds	49	100.6	20.3	51–120
60–69-year-olds	30	92.9	28.2	24–120

in rate of work between freshmen and parents and relatives is statistically significant.

Further inspection of the papers showed that most of the older subjects attempted all of the first 60 items. This fact permits a comparison of college entrants and parents and relatives on the basis of range of vocabulary knowledge with the speed factor eliminated by simply obtaining accuracy scores for the first 60 items. When this was done, a reversal in trend appeared,—there is a definite increase in vocabulary score of parents and relatives as compared with college freshmen. See Table III. Furthermore, there is no evidence that range of vocabulary knowledge decreases during

TABLE III

Recognition Vocabulary Test Scores of College Freshmen and Parents and Relatives

(60-item test)

Age group	N	M	σ	Range
18-year-olds	200	43.4	7.1	21–58
40–49-year-olds	50	48.8	7.3	25–59
50–59-year-olds	49	48.6	9.6	16–60
60–69-year-olds	30	49.9	8.1	24–58

the 60's as compared with the 40's and 50's. Actually, a slight increase appears, . . .

Admittedly, the number of adults tested is inadequate for purposes of generalization. Nevertheless, the evidence is such as to indicate the wisdom of eliminating the speed factor from ability tests when older and younger subjects are to be compared. When this is done, it is probable that vocabulary knowledge will be found to remain intact even up to age 70. Furthermore, it is even likely that range of vocabulary will be found to show a steady increase from age 18 up to age 40 with a possible slight increase up to age 60 or even 70. Such a finding, however, may not hold for average or below average groups since the findings in this study were derived from testing relatively superior adults.

In this paper, Lorge took up directly the question of the effect of speed on the intelligence-test performance of older people. His findings were striking and helped modify the widely spreading opinion that intelligence declined rapidly after early maturity.

The Influence of the Test Upon the Nature of Mental Decline as a Function of Age*

IRVING LORGE

1936

The measurement of the relationship of age to ability is dependent largely upon the manner in which ability and age are defined. Age is generally defined as chronological age (and whatever it may involve in terms of physiology, education and experience). Ability is defined in two ways: (1) The level of difficulty of a task or a series of tasks that a person can do successfully, or (2) the number of tasks of equal difficulty that a person can complete successfully in a unit time. Regardless of definition, ability is measured usually by a series of tasks which are of varying difficulty, and which tasks are to be attempted within a unit time. The ability as measured is an undifferentiated mixture of power and speed; power representing the sheer ability to complete tasks successfully, and speed being a measure of the number of tasks that can be completed in a unit time.

Assuming that age is measured by chronological age, then the relationship between age and ability will depend upon the ability and the test used to measure it. The fact that a high correlation exists between a power test of ability and a speed test of ability is not sufficient to indicate that each measures the same thing. It is only in the event that the correlation between power and speed tests of ability equals unity, that the equivalence of two measurements can be assumed. Although, in our studies, the IER Intelligence Scale CAVD, a test of power with unlimited time allowance, and the Otis Self-Administering Tests of Mental Ability (Higher Examination), a test of speed and power with a twenty-minute time allowance, are correlated .85, the relationship of each to age differs markedly.

In order to determine the relationship between age and various tests of mental ability, eleven tests were administered to a group of adults ranging in age from twenty to over seventy years. The total population of one hundred forty-three took the following tests:

* Adapted from the *Journal of Educational Psychology*, 27 (1936), pp. 100-110. Reprinted by permission of the author and Warwick and York, Inc., publisher.

428

1. IER Intelligence Scale CAVD (usually levels *M* to *Q,* although some were oriented at lower levels) [given with unlimited time allowance].
2. Army Group Examination Alpha, either Form 5 or Form 7 [standard timing].
3. Bregman Revision of Army Alpha Examination [standard timing].
4. Wells Revised Alpha Examination, Form 5 [standard timing].
6. Otis Self-Administering Tests of Mental Ability (Higher Examination), Form *B* [twenty-minute time allowance].
7. Thorndike Intelligence Examination for High-school Graduates.

In addition, eighty of the total population took the following tests:

5. Otis Self-Administering Tests of Mental Ability (Higher examination), Form *A* [twenty-minute time allowance].
8. Pressey Senior Verification Test.
9. Pressey Senior Classification Test.
10. Psychological Corporation Test VI Form *A.*
11. Psychological Corporation Test VI Form *B.*

The usual order of administration of the tests was one, two, three, four, six and seven; then after a lapse of several months, five, eight, nine, ten, and eleven were given. Usually a subject took five alternate forms of (1) the IER Intelligence Scale CAVD before he was given the remainder of the testing battery. In the event that a subject had taken more than one form, his score was considered as the arithmetical mean of all of his performances. The IER Intelligence Scale was given without time restrictions —the subjects took from four to thirty hours to complete a single form. Test (7), the Thorndike Intelligence Examination for High-school Graduates, was given in many forms. Usually the score used in this study was the mean of scores for five different forms of the test.

In Table I are reported the means and standard deviations for two subgroups and for the total population for each of the tests taken, and for age. In Table II are reported the coefficients of correlation between age and the various tests of intelligence for the sub-groups and for the total population. It is apparent that the relationship of ability to age varies as the test used to measure the ability. The penalty that age imposes upon a measure of ability can be estimated from the size of the correlation coefficients. The range of the correlation coefficients is from − .27 to − .48—the higher the negative correlation, the greater the penalty that age imposes upon the measurement. All other things being equal, the IER Intelligence Scale CAVD penalizes older persons less than the Otis Self-Administering Test *A.* The correlation between these last two tests is + .83. Yet the correlations of each with age are −.27 and − .48 for CAVD and Otis Self-Administering *A,* respectively. The correlation of Army Group Examination Alpha with CAVD is + .87 and with age −.36. A high correlation between two measures of ability still allows for considerable variation in the relationship of each test to age. The sharp separation between the relationship of age and the IER Intelligence Scale CAVD, and age and each of the

TABLE I

**The Means and Standard Deviations for a Battery of Eleven
Tests of Intellectual Ability by Sub-groups and
by Total Population**

Variable	Group I, $n = 80$		Group II, $n = 63$		Total, $n = 143$	
	M	SD	M	SD	M	SD
1. CAVD	408.49	15.73	397.87	18.28	403.81	17.70
2. Army Alpha	143.58	38.76	126.41	42.63	136.01	41.39
3. Bregman Alpha....	149.89	39.39	121.90	40.23	137.56	42.12
4. Wells Alpha.......	149.48	37.99	125.05	44.79	138.71	42.88
5. Otis A	48.31	12.77				
6. Otis B	41.85	15.24	33.13	15.11	38.01	15.79
7. Thorndike H. S. ...	64.30	19.86	54.08	19.72	59.80	20.44
8. Verification	69.71	18.22				
9. Classification	67.38	20.00				
10. Bureau A	114.46	34.03				
11. Bureau B	100.21	37.63				
12. Age (months)	428.73	148.93	451.42	150.90	438.72	150.23

TABLE II

**The Correlation between Each of the Tests of Intellectual
Ability and Age by Sub-groups and by Total Population**

Age and	Group I, $n = 80$	Group II, $n = 63$	Total, $n = 143$
1. CAVD.............	−.2747	−.3338	−.3047
2. Army Alpha	−.3656	−.4463	−.4086
3. Bregman Alpha	−.3842	−.4793	−.4266
4. Wells Alpha	−.4198	−.5000	−.4586
5. Otis A	−.4858		
6. Otis B	−.4521	−.4753	−.4639
7 Thorndike H. S.	−.4326	−.5170	−.4725
8. Verification.........	−.3787		
9. Classification	−.2816		
10. Bureau A	−.4398		
11. Bureau B	−.4805		

other tests seems corroborative of the fact that the CAVD is a measure of power, whereas the other tests of the battery measure a mixture of power and of speed.

The regression equation of each of the tests of mental ability and age would show the rate of decline of mental ability with age. Experimentally this rate of decline could be shown (perhaps more vividly) by equating three groups of different age-levels on the basis of a power test so as to determine the rate of decline on speed tests. In order to evaluate experimentally the rate of decline on speed tests, three groups of age-levels (1) between 20.0 and 25.0, (2) between 27.5 and 37.5, and (3) over 40.0 years were equated person by person on the basis of the CAVD scale. The matching was made from among the total sample of one hundred forty-three persons and yielded three groups each of twenty-three persons who were matched for CAVD, and who then could be compared for scores on the Army Group Examination Alpha, the Bregman Revision of Army Alpha, and the Wells Revision of Army Alpha, as well as for scores on the Otis Self-Administering Test *B* and on the Thorndike Intelligence Examination

TABLE III

The Means and Standard Deviations for a Battery of Six Tests of Intellectual Ability and for Age by Three Different Groups Equated on the Basis of Altitude Score on the IER Intelligence Scale CAVD

Means

Group	Age-range	Age (months)	CAVD	Army Alpha	Bregman Alpha	Wells Alpha	Otis SA (twenty minutes) B	Thorndike High-school graduates
I	20.0 to 25.0	274.04	405.25	149.61	149.39	158.35	44.39	66.92
II	27.5 to 37.5	384.04	405.66	142.26	149.13	147.04	39.26	60.28
III	over 40.0	604.70	405.51	128.70	132.43	129.83	33.39	53.03

Standard deviations

Group		Age (months)	CAVD	Army Alpha	Bregman Alpha	Wells Alpha	Otis SA (twenty minutes) B	Thorndike High-school graduates
I	....	15.28	12.75	32.66	27.61	32.28	12.86	14.81
II	....	34.05	13.19	26.27	29.79	29.51	10.64	14.59
III	....	89.85	13.05	32.33	31.36	31.31	12.29	16.91

for High-school Graduates. In Table III are reported the means and standard deviations for each of the three matched groups for the six tests of mental ability and for age. The penalty of age is significantly a function of the test of mental ability. The three groups equated on the basis of sheer power to perform mental ability tasks reveal important differences on the basis of tests which measure an undifferentiated mixture of speed and of power. The penalty can be assayed by considering the difference in score as a ratio to the difference in age. For instance, the penalty in Army Group Examination Alpha for age groups of equal mental ability power would be $\frac{149.61 - 142.26}{384.04 - 274.04}$ and $\frac{149.61 - 128.70}{604.70 - 274.04}$ which yields .0668 and .0632 Army Alpha points per month of chronological age. Averaging these two determinations gives a penalty of .065 Army Alpha points per month, or .780 Army Alpha points per year. If mental ability is measured in terms of Army Alpha, persons over twenty years of age would, other things being equal, be penalized approximately three quarters of a point for every year of chronological age beyond twenty.

Jones and Conrad have reported on mental decline with age of a homogeneous population. Using Army Alpha as the basis for the measurement of mental ability, they find that the rate of growth or decline "may be summarized as involving a linear growth to about sixteen years, with a negative acceleration beyond sixteen, to a peak between the ages of eighteen and twenty-one. A decline follows, which is much more gradual than the curve of growth, but which by age fifty-five involves a recession to the fourteen-year level." This imputed recession, in our belief, is not a loss of mental power as such, but rather an inability to work as fast with mental tasks. Yerkes reports that the Army Group Examination Alpha sub-tests "are neither principally 'speed' tests nor 'power' tests but tend to show the characteristics of a 'power' test more at the low levels than they do at the high levels." He also states "In all tests but test two more than sixteen per cent are through in double time and are, therefore, scored too low" in single time. We agree with Brigham when, in reference to the Army Alpha, he states "at least in our consideration of the army tests, we may definitely discard the opinion that we are testing speed rather than intelligence." Our agreement, however, is one of changed stress. The Army Alpha measures intelligence and speed in amounts that are undifferentiated. It is not that the Army Alpha measures power intelligence or speed intelligence, but rather that the test reports a score which is a mixture of both.

If the corrections determined from our matched group data were applied to the Jones and Conrad results, corrections from 0.39 to 29.25 Army

TABLE IIIa

The Application of a Correction for the Penalty That Is Imposed by Age on Measurements with the Army Group Examination Alpha: Data of Jones and Conrad

Age groups	Jones and Conrad obtained mean	Correction of .780 points per year of age after 20.0	Adjusted Jones and Conrad means
19–21	100.7	0.39	101.0
22–24	91.8	2.73	94.5
25–29	90.5	5.85	96.4
30–34	87.0	9.75	96.8
35–39	85.1	13.65	98.8
40–44	92.2	17.55	109.8
45–49	80.7	21.45	102.2
50–54	81.3	25.35	106.7
55–59	78.6	29.25	107.9

Alpha points would be added to the obtained average scores on different age-levels. The application of the correction is shown in Table IIIa.

The adjusted Jones and Conrad means do not show the same gradual decline exhibited in their obtained scores. The correction for the penalty of age, indeed, may be a correction for slowness, for remoteness from school, for disutility of function, for lack of motivation or for other physiological, educational or psychological changes. In mental decline, however, the power to cope with mental tasks must be considered freed from the influence of other factors or traits that may obscure it. In our opinion, speed obscures sheer mental power in older adults.

Miles and Miles also have reported a study concerned with the decline of mental ability with age of a group of adults in two communities. Using a form, specially printed in large type, of the first sixty items of the "Otis Self-Administering Test of Intelligence, Higher Examination Form A" as a fifteen-minute test, they found that "From the high point in the intelligence score curve represented at or about eighteen years of age the trend is at first almost level, then gradually declines dropping fifteen or sixteen mental age months by the chronological age of fifty years." Our results provide the data for the determination of the penalty of age on the Otis Self-Administering Test of Mental Ability (Higher Examination) Form B, which is an alternate form of the curtailed examination used by Miles and Miles. Our population was given the Form B of the Otis on the twenty-minute time interval. For them the penalty of age may be estimated as $\dfrac{44.39 - 39.26}{384.04 - 274.04}$ and as $\dfrac{44.39 - 33.39}{604.70 - 274.04}$ or as .0466 and .0333 Otis (twenty-minute) points per month. Using the average of these two estimates of age penalty, the probable correction should be .0400 Otis (twenty-minute) points per month, or .480 Otis (twenty-minute) points per year. By estimating the probable twenty-minute score from the fifteen-minute score of the Miles and Miles material from the data in their Table II, a table can be constructed to show the influence of the estimated correction for age and slowness on the mean score of the city B population. In Table IIIb are reported the adjustments for Miles and Miles scores.

The correction for the penalty that a test of mental ability (which is an undifferentiated mixture of power and speed) places upon age changes the curve of mental decline to a curve of mental plateau, or even to a curve of mental growth. Mental growth in the later age brackets may be more the result of a special selection of death than of true growth. If this be true, an apparent rise in the curve of intellectual status would not be so much an indication of growth as it would be of the fact that the poorer members of the population were being eliminated, either by death or disease. Death, indeed, may come earlier to the mediocre. Thorndike *et al.,* in

TABLE IIIb

The Application of a Correction for the Penalty That Is Imposed by Age on Measurements with the Otis Self-administering Tests of Mental Ability (Higher Examination): Data of Miles and Miles

Age group	Miles and Miles		Correction of .480 points per year of age after 20.0	Adjusted Miles and Miles means (20 minutes)
	Obtained means (15 minutes)	Estimated means (20 minutes)		
15–19	38.50	44.50	0	44.5
20–24	38.10	44.10	1.2	45.3
25–29	39.22	45.22	3.6	48.8
30–34	35.26	40.26	6.0	46.3
35–39	35.06	40.06	8.4	48.5
40–44	33.82	38.73	10.8	49.5
45–49	34.50	39.50	13.2	52.7
50–54	30.98	34.98	15.6	50.6
55–59	28.74	32.74	18.0	50.7
60–64	27.94	31.91	20.4	52.3
65–69	24.22	27.22	22.8	50.0
70–74	23.78	26.78	25.2	51.2
75–79	20.46	22.69	27.6	50.3
80–84	14.50	16.50	30.0	46.5
85–89	15.30	17.30	32.4	49.7
90–94	15.30	17.30	34.8	52.1

a study of the persons who died or were seriously ill before age 22.0, state "The general psychological theorem that all positive traits are correlated positively is here demonstrated in reverse; negative traits are correlated negatively. Death, contrary to the widespread old wives' tale, does not select the good or the gifted. Death comes earlier to the mediocre, to the inferior, to those not fully equipped for life's battles."

The correction applied to the Jones and Conrad data may be too large since in our material the Army Alpha average scores were one hundred forty-nine, one hundred forty-two, and one hundred twenty-eight, which are significantly higher than the high average of 100.7 in their data. The correction, however, may also be too small, since the influence of age was left in the CAVD scores used to equate our matched groups. The correction applied to the Miles and Miles data may also be too small for the same reason (since their means were very much like ours).

The influence of age may be subtracted from the CAVD scores by computing that part of the CAVD score which is freed from the influence of age. The regression equation gives the CAVD score that can be predicted from age. The difference between a person's obtained CAVD score and his regressed CAVD score from age gives a score for CAVD independent of age (the statistical symbolism for this expression is CAVD·Age = CAVD − CAVD$_{age}$. Any person's raw score may be considered as made up of two parts: One part for that amount of the CAVD which can be predicted from a regression equation of CAVD on age; the other part as the residual, or difference, between the amount of CAVD predicted from the regression equation and the obtained raw score. The residual represents the error made in estimating a person's CAVD score from a knowledge of age alone. This error of estimate is a score which is independent of age from which the regressed score was predicted. For each of the one hundred forty-three persons in our material we computed a CAVD score independent of age (CAVD·Age); that is, we computed the residual between a person's raw score and his CAVD score predicted from age. With these age-independent-CAVD scores as criteria, we matched three new groups in the age ranges: 20.0 to 25.0, 27.5 to 37.5, and, over 40.0 years. These three groups were matched, person by person, on the basis of the CAVD·Age score; that is, matched on the basis of the residuals. In Table IV are reported the data

TABLE IV

The Means and Standard Deviations for a Battery of Seven Tests of Intellectual Ability and for Age by Three Different Age-groups Equated on the Basis of an Altitude Score Freed from the Influence of Age (the IER Intelligence Scale CAVD Score-age)

Means

Group	Age-range	Age (months)	CAVD Age +100	CAVD	Army Alpha	Breg-man Alpha	Wells Alpha	Otis SA (twenty minutes) B	Thorndike high-school graduates
I	20.0 to 25.0	271.39	101.68	411.50	159.22	159.78	165.09	49.74	72.42
II	27.5 to 37.5	392.09	101.69	407.00	140.65	147.65	14.943	39.17	63.50
III	over 40.0	603.50	101.68	400.38	124.52	125.78	123.65	31.65	50.82

Standard deviations

Group		Age (months)	CAVD Age +100	CAVD	Army Alpha	Breg-man Alpha	Wells Alpha	Otis SA	Thorndike
I	....	15.71	14.24	14.08	27.78	24.63	24.33	13.57	15.68
II	....	40.27	14.00	14.34	31.07	32.44	32.86	11.36	17.06
III	....	95.96	14.65	14.17	38.07	35.30	40.94	13.51	17.58

resulting from this new matching on the basis of an altitude score, freed from the influence of age. The correction for the Army Alpha may be esti-mated from $\dfrac{159.22 - 140.65}{392.09 - 271.39}$ and from $\dfrac{159.22 - 124.52}{603.50 - 271.39}$ as .1539 and .1045 Army Alpha points per year. Averaging these two estimates gives a correction of .1292 Army Alpha points per month, or 1.5504 Army Alpha points per year, which contrasts sharply with the correction of .780 Army Alpha points per year estimated from groups equated on the basis of an altitude score in which the influence of age had been left in the score. The correction for the Otis Self-Administering Test of Mental Ability (Higher Examination) may be estimated from $\dfrac{49.74 - 39.17}{392.09 - 271.39}$ and from $\dfrac{49.74 - 31.65}{603.50 - 271.39}$ as .0876 and .0545 Otis (twenty-minute) points per month. Averaging the two estimates gives a correction of .0716 Otis (twenty-minute) points per month, or .8592 Otis (twenty-minute) points per year, which contrasts sharply with the correction of .480 Otis (twenty-minute) points per year estimated on the basis of scores from the group equated for altitude with age left in the score.

By any reasonable evaluation of the estimated correction for the penalty that age imposes upon persons by a test which is an undifferentiated mixture of power and speed, it is clear that reported curves of mental decline with age are exaggerated. While it is recognized that a follow-up of mental power scores of individuals from a time shortly after birth through senescence, is the only technique for a definitive answer to the actual measurement of the relationship of mental ability to age, the results reported in this paper are suggestive in cautioning against the imputation of loss of mental power as a function of advancing age, especially when such inference is based upon scores from tests that are a mixture of power and speed functions.

The facts concerning the slowing up of reaction time and of coördination speed with advancing age, reported by Miles, and by Bellis, showed that simple and complex reaction times are slower in older adults than in younger adults. Ruger, in an elaborate and painstaking analysis of the measurements collected by Sir Francis Galton in his first anthropometric laboratory at the Health Exhibition in South Kensington in 1884, finds that the dynamic or motor characters (strength of pull, hand grip, swiftness of blow and vital capacity) show "a rapid rise in childhood, a pubescent dip at about fifteen years, a prime or maximum at about twenty-four or twenty-five years, and senescent decadence following the maximum." Further, for sensory acuity (vision and limit of audible pitch) he shows that decadence begins earlier than for motor characters.

It may be true that decadence of any one character may not significantly hamper performance in a test of mental ability which is a mixture of speed and of power. Yet decline in visual acuity, in auditory acuity, in strength, in speed of reaction, in speed of coördination as well as disuse of function, remoteness from school, and preoccupation with life's problems cumulatively must have a retarding influence upon the performance of an older individual in a test of mental ability which partakes of aspects of both power and speed.

Our study demonstrates that the reported facts of mental decline as a concomitant of age are, at the least, exaggerated. The power to do mental tasks or to solve those of life's problems which must be approached mentally, probably does not deteriorate as a function of age. The reported deterioration is more apparent than genuine. It lacks genuineness in the sense that the test used to measure mental ability is not a genuine measure of mental power. Contaminating power with speed measurements among older adults obscures the true relationship of intellectual power to age. The inference of mental decline is an unfortunate libel upon adults.

Following the publication of the findings of the Army intelligence tests relating to race differences, it was widely
assumed that there were basic racial differences in intelligence.
During the 1920's and 1930's this view came under attack
on many grounds. In this article, comparisons within the
"Negro" group are studied to see what light they shed on the
nature of the differences. You should follow the argument
closely and especially note the assumptions on which the "corollaries" rest. Note also that the differences in test score between the Negro and white populations are not at issue here.

Intra-Race Testing and Negro Intelligence*

PAUL A. WITTY

MARTIN D. JENKINS

1936

Shortly after the inception of objective testing in America "race differences" in intelligence were established "scientifically." Typical procedure
was to test contiguous samples of white and of Negro populations and to
compare the mean scores: generalizations followed and inferior intelligence
was assigned the Negro, since Negro groups invariably made low *average*
scores. To the student of psychology the results and conclusions of such
studies are well known. Pintner, after citing representative investigations,
concludes:

In the case of the Negro and perhaps in the case of the Indian we have a race of
inferior intelligence as measured by our present intelligence tests when compared
with American whites. The greater the amount of white blood entering the
various mixtures of the two races, the greater is the intelligence of the resulting
progeny, and this takes place because of the inheritance of mental ability.

The conclusion cited above is considered tentative by many, since test
scores reflect cultural opportunities as well as innate factors. Results from
extensive and thorough research involving inter-race testing have demonstrated, of course, that there are *differences between the races, and in sub-
groups within each race, in test performance—not that there are true racial
differences in innate or inherited intelligence.*

The statement that "the greater the amount of white blood . . . the
greater the amount of intelligence" deserves more careful analysis. Psychologists are frequently little cognizant of the degree of miscegenation in the
American Negro population. Competent anthropologists estimate that only

* *The Journal of Psychology,* 1 (1936), p. 179-192. Reprinted by permission of
the authors and The Journal Press.

about one-fourth of the total American Negro population is of unmixed Negro ancestry.

Even the most casual observer must have noticed the heterogeneity of our Negro population (from superficial observation of differences in pigmentation). Since, in America, the term "Negro" has been accorded a sociological rather than an anthropological connotation, Negroes range from "pure" Negro to practically "pure" white. Therefore it appears that this distribution would provide a favorable basis for testing the hypothesis which assigns inferior intelligence to the Negro. If Negro ancestry affects mental test performance, this effect should be directly evidenced in the test performance of Negroes of varying degrees of white blood. Furthermore, this *intra*-race approach should be free of many of the inherent weaknesses of the *inter*-race approach.

In this paper, the two logical corollaries of the hypothesis that Negroes are inferior to whites in mental ability will be examined: 1. Mental test scores of Negroes should increase in proportion to the amount of white ancestry, and 2. Negroes who make the very highest scores on mental tests should be those who come from admixtures predominantly white. The first corollary will be evaluated in terms of the results of published studies, and the second in terms of the writers' findings with a group of Negro children of superior intelligence.

COROLLARY 1

Herskovits points out that if the Negro is inferior in intelligence the following corollary is logical:

That in a mixed-Negro group such as we have in the United States those individuals having the largest amount of White ancestry should, on the average, stand higher in tests, other things being equal, than persons of total or large amounts of Negro ancestry.

In general, this statement is acceptable, providing one could define "other things." Among "other things," the following item is of significance: in order to make valid comparisons of two races, the norms or average test scores should be based upon adequate and truly representative samplings of the total population of *both* races. One must have a reliable norm for the "pure" Negro as well as for the typical American. In addition, in order that comparisons be strictly valid, it is necessary to know whether the intelligence of the white forebears is superior, typical, or inferior. Insofar as the writers can ascertain, the probable intelligence of the white ancestry of the American Negro has not been objectively studied—probably it can not be. It may be that the white ancestry is above average. The American Negro has been found to come from North European and British stock (Herskovits); these groups stood high on the Army Alpha intelligence tests.

Whether miscegenation during the slavery era was more frequent among those of high or of low intelligence in either or both races is unknown. It is held by some that in such miscegenations the white stock was inferior. This assumption, similar to the first, is unverified.

Another factor is of significance if intra-racial comparisons are to be valid. One must take into account adequately the relative opportunities for cultural and social acquisitions among Negroes of varying degrees of white ancestry. Speculation is rather futile at this point: however, several observers have noted the relatively favorable social and cultural opportunities for Negroes whose color and general appearance approach those of the American white person.

Only a few studies of groups of Negroes of various degrees of racial admixtures are now available. There are, it appears, but ten published studies which deal with the relationships of Negro-white ancestry to standing on intelligence tests. Typically the procedure followed in those studies has involved separating the Negro subjects into groups on the basis of skin color and comparing the average intelligence-test scores of the groups. This method has serious limitations since it has been amply demonstrated that the racial composition of the individual Negro cannot be determined accurately by the degree of pigmentation. Nevertheless, it seems that when too fine discriminations as to color are not demanded, judgment of degree of mixture on the basis of pigmentation may be useful in providing a basis for valid *group* comparisons. This assumption is not wholly defensible, but one may logically assume that, for example, if one compares one hundred "light-skinned" Negroes with one hundred "dark-skinned" Negroes the lighter group undoubtedly has the greater amount of white ancestry. It must be recognized that this procedure necessitates subjective judgment in which skill and honesty are requisite in the judges.

Evidence for Hypothesis I. Ferguson's early investigation is perhaps the best known study in this field; the influence of his findings is still evident in the writing of many psychologists. Ferguson classified 271 Negro school children of Richmond, Virginia into four groups: *pure, three-fourths Negro, mulatto,* and *quadroon,* on the basis of "color of skin, hair texture and general facial and cranial conformation, the main emphasis [however], being placed upon color." A "mixed relations and completion" test was then administered. The average standings of the various color-groups follow:

(1) Pure 69.2%	(2) 3/4 73.2%	Combined 1 and 2 70.8%	(3) Mulatto 81.2%	(4) Quadroon 91.8%	Combined 3 and 4 83.6%

It may be observed that there is a consistent increase in score with decrease in pigmentation. Ferguson attributes this condition "to the greater inherent capacity of Negroes of lighter skin." The findings here seem convincing because of the consistent inverse relationship between test scores and degree of pigmentation. This result is precisely that which one should predict if the hypothesis of Negro inferiority were valid.

Analysis of Ferguson's data, however, reveals that certain selective factors were not fully taken into account. Approximately two-thirds of his group were girls (181 girls and only 90 boys); in an unselected population of elementary school children there should be approximately equal numbers of boys and girls. The exact influence of this unequal sampling is, of course, unknown: the condition suggests that representative populations of Negro boys and girls could not have been included in the relatively small numbers assigned to each of the smaller "color" groups. A second factor also causes one to be skeptical of the representative nature of Ferguson's study. Fifty per cent of the group were judged to be "of one-half or more white ancestry." This percentage is higher than estimates for typical Negro populations. Furthermore, Ferguson gives no information about the social status of the groups. The observed differences, therefore, may be attributable in part to differences in the social status of the "color" groups rather than to innate racial factors. This rather detailed attention has been given Ferguson's study because the results are at variance with those of several other investigations in this field. At this point another study by Ferguson will be scrutinized. In 1919 Ferguson published a widely-read report concerning the intelligence of Negroes at Camp Lee, Virginia. The men of eight companies were classified as "lighter" or "darker" in skin color. "In the main those classed as darker were pure Negroes; those classed as lighter were mulattoes, quadroons or Negroes with some other proportion of white blood." In *Examination a* (an experimental form which preceded the *Army Alpha Test*) the lighter Negroes made a median score of 51, and the darker Negroes, 40. This investigation was extended by Ferguson and his assistants who classified 1156 other Negroes as *black, brown,* or *yellow.* The median scores of these groups on *Examination a* follow: *block,* 39; *brown,* 45; *yellow,* 59.

Here again one observes that the lighter Negroes made the highest scores. Ferguson points out that the darker group contained a far greater percentage of illiterates than did the lighter group, although the standard for literacy (being able to write one's name) was low. The greater literacy of the lighter Negroes doubtless enabled them to make a superior record on *Examination a.* Indeed, Ferguson states (although not in this connection) that, "The northern negroes were considerably less illiterate than the southern and they obtained considerably higher scores." Differences in median scores therefore could readily be attributed to factors other than inherited tendencies, although Ferguson emphasizes the latter. Certainly, such a presentation cannot be interpreted validly or intelligently unless one has detailed data concerning the social-economic *milieu* of the groups. And the genetic psychologist would insist, we believe, that case studies (and rather complete family histories) would illumine (perhaps explain) the differences in the test-score averages.

Another study similarly restricted in plan and scope, was made by Young, who administered the *National Intelligence Test* to 282 white and 277 Negro children of Baton Rouge and Lake Charles, Louisiana. Principals and teachers assisted in labelling the Negro subjects: *lighter* and *darker*. Thirty-three subjects who "looked light when put with the negroes and black when placed among the light group" were classified as "miscellaneous negroes." Young found a "noticeable decrease of intelligence as we go from the white children to light negroes and then to dark negroes." The lighter group was 19.7 per cent better on the test than was the darker group. The absence of measures of variability makes interpretation of Young's figures difficult. Moreover, nothing is said about the social status of the lighter and darker subjects, but Young concludes,

That the light negroes were on the average 19.7 per cent more intelligent than the dark negroes . . . may be explained by the hypothesis that *their white blood makes them more intelligent than the dark Negroes"* (Italics not in the original).

Evidence Against Hypothesis I. Herskovits' anthropometric study of Howard University males reported in 1926 appears to be the first rather thorough approach to the problem of the relationship of Negro-white mixture and mental test ability. Measures of differentiating physical traits such as width of nostril, lip thickness and pigmentation (gauged by the Milton-Bradley Color Top) were correlated with scores on the *Thorndike College Entrance Examination*. The following coefficients of correlation (Pearsonian), based on 115 cases, are reported:

Between score and width of nose, $r = +.014$
Between score and thickness of lips, $r = -.198$
Between score and black element, $r = -.144$
Between score and white element, $r = +.172$

Herskovits concludes:

the relationship between test scores and physical traits denoting greater or less amounts of Negro blood is so tenuous as to be of no value in drawing conclusions as to the comparative native ability or relative intelligence of the Negro when compared to the white.

The validity of Herskovits' generalization has been critized because his subjects were university students among whom the darker subjects might be more highly selected than lighter Negroes. Herskovits, however, gives convincing evidence showing that his group of university students is quite similar in physical traits and pigmentation to several other unselected samplings of the American Negro. Moreover, the study of Peterson and Lanier corroborates Herskovits' conclusion. The *Otis S-A* examination was given to ninety-one college people and the *Myers Mental Measure* to forty-nine students. Degree of pigmentation was estimated on the Von Luschen color scale. Correlations between test ability and skin color follow:

Between Otis S-A and skin color, $r = +.044$ $\pm.067$
Between Myers Mental Measure and skin color, $r = -.18$ $\pm.091$

This study, similar to that of Herskovits, led the authors to conclude, "There is no significant relation between lightness of skin color in the Negroes and intelligence."

Price mentions Mathaisen's unpublished study of 760 Hampton Institute students; apparently these were high school and college students. Entering students were classified in eight sections according to skin color and facial characteristics. The *Menti-Meter* intelligence test was administered and coefficients of correlation were computed between skin color, test score and grade quotient. The results follow:

Between skin color and Menti-Meter score, $r = +.09$ $\pm.0003$
Between skin color and grade quotient, $r = +.05$ $\pm.003$

Strong, employing a different experimental method, classified 122 children of Columbia, S. C., into dark, medium, and light, using skin color estimates as a criterion in classification. The performance of these groups on the *Goddard Revision* (1911) of the Binet examination follows:

TABLE I

Color	Number	Tested below age	Tested at age	Tested above age
Dark	34	14.4%	76.7%	8.8%
Medium	45	31.1	62.2	6.6
Light	43	44.2	44.2	11.6

This study, one of the earliest, is frequently neglected. Although the method may be criticized (because of limitations similar to those mentioned in connection with Ferguson's conclusion), it is noteworthy that herein one finds that the darkest children tested higher than the lighter!

In 1928 Davenport essayed to determine the effect of race-crossing upon intelligence test performance. The study was conducted in Jamaica, where, it was thought, groups could be more reliabily equated in social status than in the United States. The *Army Alpha* test was given to 100 "pure" blacks, 100 browns (Negro-white mixture), and 100 whites (Caucasoids). The groups were presumably of similar socio-economic levels, although with respect to education the brown group, which included some college students, probably was superior. The groups made the following mean scores on Army Alpha: black, 9.64; brown, 7.95; white, 10.23. The "pure" group made better scores than the mixed. Certain discrepancies are cited by

Davenport who reports that the brown children of ages ten to sixteen made better scores than either the black or the white of similar ages.

Two hundred New York City school children and 139 West Virginia rural children were studied by Klineberg. The New York subjects were classified into four groups according to skin color: Group I apparently being pure Negro and group 4 having evidently a good deal of white mixture. . . . Groups 2 and 3 were intermediate. The groups made the point scores on three form boards (the *Mare and Foal, Casuist,* and *Healy A*), as in Table II. The highest median score was made by the *NNW* group (more

TABLE II

Group	N	Md.	Q	Range
(1) Pure Negro	89	86	28	24–176
(2) Less N than (1)	57	116	31	50–172
(3) Less N than (2)	32	102	28	46–164
(4) Least N	22	90	31	38–148
(1) and (2) combined	146	97	30	24–176
(3) and (4) combined	54	99	89*	38–164

* This figure appears in the original table although it is obviously much too large; it is probably a typographical error.

Negro than white) and the highest individual score was made by a member of the *N* group.

Klineberg determined the degree of pigmentation of the West Virginia group by means of the *Milton-Bradley* color top. The subjects were divided into three sections on the basis of pigmentation: the darkest 25 per cent, the middle 50 per cent and the lightest 25 per cent. The performance of these groups on the Pintner-Paterson Performance Scale is given in Table III.

TABLE III

Group	N	Md. score	Q	Range	Av. score
Darkest, ←25%	36	293.5	47	154–421	288.1
Middle, ←50%	67	313.0	74.5	114–476	297.8
Lightest, ←25%	36	304.5	47.5	92–463	301.2

The middle group made the highest median score, and the lightest group made the highest average. Inspection of the variability of the groups, however, reveals that there is no significant difference between the middle and the lightest groups. The highest score was earned by a member of the middle group. Klineberg correlated certain anthropometric data with the Pintner-Paterson IQ. The coefficients of correlation are as follows:

Between intelligence and thickness of lips,	$r = .11$
Between intelligence and thickness of lips, age constant,	$r = -.10$
Between intelligence and black pigmentation,	$r = -.096$
Between intelligence and black pigmentation, age constant,	$r = -.12$
Between intelligence and nose width, age constant,	$r = -.06$

It will be observed that the coefficients, although negative, are negligible in statistical significance.

The contradictory results in these studies seem difficult to reconcile. Investigators have found (a) that the pure Negro group is superior, (b) that the *NNW* group (more Negro than white) is superior, and (c) that the *NWW* group (more white than Negro) is superior. Nevertheless, the more complete, careful, and recent investigations consistently indicate that intelligence test performance is not conditioned by the degree of Negro-white mixture. Investigations which have reported a direct positive relationship between test ability and amount of white ancestry should be evaluated with full recognition of the fact that cultural factors were not considered and samplings were incomplete or unrepresentative. Investigations in which the anthropometric approach is utilized suggest a negative but insignificant relationship between mental test performance and Negroid characteristics.

A *crucial* study of *Corollary 1* would involve study of a large number of unselected subjects, the utilization of anthropometric and genealogical data, and a very clear and complete statement of the socio-economic status of the groups compared. No study cited above conforms to these requirements. Nevertheless, it seems that *Corollary 1* is at present indefensible. One must conclude, tentatively, therefore, after examination of available data, that superior intelligence test ability is *not* exhibited by those Negroes having the largest amount of white ancestry.

COROLLARY 2

If the hypothesis that the Negro is of inferior intelligence is valid, then the American Negroes who make the very highest scores on intelligence tests should be those of predominantly white ancestry.

The writers tested this hypothesis in connection with a study of Negro children of superior intelligence. A systematic appraisal of the intelligence of 8000 Negro school children in grades 3 to 8 of the Chicago public schools resulted in the selection of 103 children of Stanford-Binet *IQ* 120 or above. The racial composition of sixty-three of these children (of *IQ* 125 or above) was determined from genealogical data secured from parents. The weaknesses inherent in this approach are recognized. In some instances individuals are unable to ascertain accurately their own degree of racial mixture. Deliberate inaccuracy in report and failure to account for total ancestry are other limitations. That such an approach is fairly valid is demonstrated by Herkovits who, after checking such data reported by Howard University students against anthropometric criteria, observed:

> This is of particular methodological interest for it indicates that more use can be made of Negro genealogical material than has hitherto been thought possible. ... (I believe) that for a given group for which genealogies are taken, such use can be made of their statements as to ancestry as can be made of statements from any other element of our population that lacks written records of ancestry.

The following procedure was utilized in determining the racial composition of the children of superior test intelligence: the mothers and fathers reported their own racial mixture insofar as they were able, in sixteenths. From these data, subjects were then classified into four categories: N (those having no white ancestry), NNW (those having more Negro ancestry than white), NW (those having about an equal amount of Negro and white ancestry), and NWW (those having more white ancestry than Negro). Cross classifications of this character tend to eliminate minor errors in fine estimates.

Table IV shows the numbers and percentage of subjects in each of the four classifications used by Herskovits. Almost one-half of the group (46.1 per cent) is found in the NNW category while slightly less than one-

TABLE IV

Racial Composition of 63 Negro Children of Superior Intelligence Compared with That of 1551 Cases Reported by Herskovits

Classification	Number	Superior Negro children Per cent	Herskovits' population Per cent
N	14	22.2	28.3
NNW	29	46.1	31.7
NW	10	15.9	25.2
NWW	10	15.9	14.8

quarter is in the N category. Thus more than two-thirds of the group is of Negro or predominantly Negro ancestry. The NW and NWW classifications include 15.9 per cent of the cases, respectively. Twenty-two subjects or 35 per cent of the group have some Indian ancestry.

These percentages may be compared with those of the Negro population in the United States. In commenting upon the degree of mixture in the Negro population, Hooton observes:

In the population rated as "Negro" by the gatherers of the United States census, not more than one-quarter, or at most one-third may be approximately full-blooded Negroes. Indeed this is a most liberal estimate.

Herskovits similarly found less than 30 per cent of American Negroes to be unmixed. His conclusions are based on anthropometric and genealogical data secured from samplings of the population of several different rural and urban communities.

After comparing the racial composition of Negro children of superior intelligence with that of the general American Negro population, one finds that the *NNW* group includes more than its quota of superior children, the *NW* group includes less, and the *N* group slightly less. The *NWW* section conforms closely to the general population percentage. Of course, the variations (which are not large) may be caused by chance errors, since the group of Negro children of superior intelligence is relatively small. Despite discrepancies, the similarity is a noticeable feature of the two distributions.

Twenty-eight of the subjects were "gifted" children (*IQ* 140 and above). It is interesting that the racial composition of this group, Table V, is about the same as that of the total group. The highest *IQ,* 200, was earned by a girl whose parents report no knowledge of any white ancestry.

TABLE V

Classification	Number of "gifted"	Per cent
N	6	21.4
NNW	12	42.8
NW	6	21.4
NWW	4	14.3

These data show that whatever the provenance of the superior mental-test ability of these Negro children may be, it certainly is not attributable to white ancestry. One is led also to doubt the validity of the hypothesis that Negro ancestry *per se* is a limiting factor in the matter of high intelligence test ability.

CONCLUSION

Numerous comparisons of the intelligence test performance of contiguous white and Negro groups have shown that the white group almost invariably makes the superior average score. Therefore, it is generally concluded that racial differences in intelligence have been demonstrated, and that the American Negro is inherently inferior to the American white. If this hypothesis is valid then the following corollaries should hold:

1. *In a mixed group such as we have in the United States those individuals having the largest amount of white ancestry should on the average stand higher in tests, other things being equal, than persons of total or large amounts of Negro ancestry.*

2. *Negroes who make the very highest scores on intelligence tests should be those who emanate from admixtures predominantly white.*

In this paper *Corollary 1* was evaluated in terms of the results of published studies. It was found that investigators have set forth dissimilar conclusions, but the weight of experimental evidence clearly indicates that intelligence test performance is not conditioned by the relative proportions of Negro and white ancestry. The results of the most comprehensive, careful, and recent studies indicate that there is a negative but insignificant relationship between mental test performance and Negroid characteristics. On the basis of the evidence *Corollary 1* appears untenable.

The validity of *Corollary 2* was estimated by considering data from a recent study of Negro children of superior mental-test ability. Two-thirds of the superior Negro children were of pure Negro or predominantly Negro ancestry; this proportion held both for the superior group (Stanford-Binet *IQ* 120 and above) and for the "gifted" group (*IQ* 140 and above). These superior Negro children ($n = 103$) have even less white ancestry than is found in the general American Negro population. Moreover, the very highest *IQ* was earned by a subject of allegedly "pure" Negro ancestry. It is apparent that these findings indicate that *Corollary 2* is undemonstrated.

The hypothesis of Negro inferiority must stand or fall in respect to its consonance with logical corollaries such as those stated above. Since these corollaries appear undemonstrable, one may conclude tentatively that the differences in the average test scores of American whites and Negroes are not to be attributed to differences in inheritable intelligence. Furthermore, one may conclude that the technique involving test score comparison is at present specious as a definitive single approach in racial studies.

If there is a standard for American intelligence tests, it is most certainly the Stanford version of the Binet test. The first Stanford-Binet was developed in 1916, and its revision in 1937 was an important event in the history of intelligence testing. Excerpts are given here to illustrate some of the many difficulties encountered and the great care taken in building the revision. The complete text is strongly recommended as valuable reading.

Measuring Intelligence*

LEWIS M. TERMAN

and MAUDE A. MERRILL

1937

Essential Features of the Revision

The major faults of the original Stanford-Binet scale have long been recognized. Although affording a satisfactorily valid and reliable measure over a fairly wide intermediate range, it was especially defective at both extremes. Abilities below the mental level of four years or above that of the average adult were very inadequately sampled. In the range from five to ten years the standardization was surprisingly correct, considering the rather small number of subjects on which it was based, but above ten it yielded scores that were progressively too low. A number of tests in the scale were unsatisfactory because of low validity, difficulty of scoring, susceptibility to coaching, etc. The instructions both for administration and scoring in numerous instances lacked the precision which is necessary to insure objectivity and comparability of results. Finally, one of the severest limitations to the usefulness of the scale was the fact that no alternative form was available for use in retesting or as a safeguard against coaching.

In the revision here offered we have provided two scales which differ almost completely in content, but are mutually equivalent with respect to difficulty, range, reliability, and validity. The scales are designated as Form L and Form M. In content Form L bears greater resemblance to the original Stanford-Binet, but neither form can be recommended above the other. Both, we believe, are relatively free from the grosser faults of the old scale. They cover a far wider range, they are more accurately standardized throughout, the tests provide a richer sampling of abilities, and the

* These excerpts are taken from the first three chapters of the book, *Measuring Intelligence* (Boston, Houghton Mifflin Co., 1937). Reprinted by permission of Dr. Merrill and the Houghton Mifflin Company.

procedures have been more rigidly defined. On the whole they are somewhat less verbal than the old scale, especially in the lower years.

The revision utilizes the assumptions, methods, and principles of the age scale as conceived by Binet. There are of course other systems of tests which are meritorious, but for the all-round clinical appraisal of a subject's intellectual level the Binet type of scale has no serious rival. It is not merely an intelligence test; it is a method of standardized interview which is highly interesting to the subject and calls forth his natural responses to an extraordinary variety of situations. The arrangement of the tests in year groups makes the examination more interesting to the examiner by enabling him to grasp the evidence as it comes in. There is a fascination in the use of an age scale that does not fade out with experience. Each examination is a new adventure in which every step is interesting and meaningful. The variety provided by the ever-changing tasks insures the zestful cooperation of subjects and is at the same time based upon what we believe to be sound psychological theory. It is a method which, to paraphrase an oft-quoted statement by Galton, attempts to obtain a general knowledge of the capacities of a subject by the sinking of shafts at critical points. In our revision we have greatly increased the number of shafts and have sunk them at points which wider experience with tests has shown to be critical.

The scale devised by Binet contained fifty-four tests, and the first Stanford revision increased the number to ninety. Each form of the new revision contains 129 tests. Below the five-year level tests are now located at half-year intervals, the gaps which existed at years eleven and thirteen have been filled, and the scale has been given more top by the addition of two supplementary superior adult levels. In the selection of tests we have tried to correct such inadequacies of the old scale as its too verbal character at the lower levels and its too great dependence upon rote memory at the upper. For the younger subjects the scale has been made incomparably more interesting and also more valid by the liberal use of diminutive objects, brightly colored cubes, wooden beads, and other attractive materials. In general, however, the content of the new scales resembles that of the old and includes such well-known tests as comprehension, absurdities, word-naming, drawing designs, memory for digits, giving differences and similarities, defining abstract terms, etc.

Our efforts to increase the number of non-verbal tests were successful chiefly at the lower levels. Like other investigators we have found that it is extremely difficult to devise non-verbal tests for the upper levels which satisfy the requirements of validity, reliability, and time economy. At these levels the major intellectual differences between subjects reduce largely to differences in the ability to do conceptual thinking, and facility in dealing with concepts is most readily sampled by the use of verbal tests. Language, essentially, is the shorthand of the higher thought processes, and the level at which this shorthand functions is one of the most important determinants of the level of the processes themselves.

One of the important aims of the revision was to secure greater objectivity of scoring. Where judgment is involved in evaluating responses to an item, definite principles and classified illustrations have been given to guide the examiner. Ease and objectivity of scoring have in fact often played a crucial rôle in the selection and rejection of test items. The part played by subjective judgment cannot be wholly eliminated from a test of the Binet type, but we have tried to bring it as near as possible to the irreducible minimum.

Hardly less important than the selection of suitable tests has been the selection of subjects for use in the standardization of the scales. We have devoted more than ordinary effort to secure a representative sampling of the white child population in the United States between the ages of two and eighteen years. Besides increasing the number of subjects tested to 100 at each half-year level below six, to 200 at each age between six and fourteen, and to 100 at each age from fifteen to eighteen, we have made a stubborn attempt to avoid sampling errors inherent in age, grade location, nationality, and geographical distribution. We do not flatter ourselves that we have been entirely successful, but our data represent a much closer approximation to an unbiased sampling than has heretofore been attained in the standardization of any scale for individual examining. The fact that the same subjects were used in the standardization of Form L and Form M has made it possible to guarantee almost perfect equivalence of the scores yielded by the two scales.

Development and Standardization of the Scales

PRELIMINARY SELECTION OF TESTS

Work on the revision was begun with a survey of the literature on the old Stanford-Binet and a study of every kind of intelligence test item that had been used or suggested. The search for suitable material yielded thousands of test items, some of them of unknown value and most of them of unknown difficulty. The first principle of sifting was to give preference, other things equal, to types of test items that experience had shown to yield high correlations with acceptable criteria of intelligence. Such items were assembled in as great variety as possible and with special attention to promising types of non-verbal tests. Practical considerations which had to be taken into account included ease of scoring, appeal to the subject, time requirement, and convenience of administration. For one or another of these reasons a large number of otherwise excellent tests had to be rejected.

Prominent among tests which have universally proved their worth are analogies, opposites, comprehension, vocabulary, similarities and differences, verbal and pictorial completion, absurdities, drawing designs from copy and from memory, memory for meaningful material and for digits, etc.

* * *

After the mass of test items had been assembled and critically examined, the material which seemed to be the most promising was selected for experimental trial. This tryout was preliminary rather than final and was intended to effect the elimination of the least satisfactory tests and to give the approximate age location of those retained for further trial. It utilized about a thousand subjects in the vicinity of Stanford University for whom mental ages had been determined by the original Stanford-Binet scale.

* * *

This preliminary tryout provided the necessary data for the selection of tests for the provisional scales. As we have already stated, the retention or rejection of items was based upon several criteria. In order of importance these were: (1) validity, (2) ease and objectivity of scoring, and (3) various practical considerations such as time economy, interest to the subject, the need for variety, etc.

Validity in turn was judged by two criteria: (1) increase in the percents passing from one age (or mental age) to the next, and (2) a weight based on the ratio of the difference to the standard error of the difference between the mean age (or mental age) of subjects passing the test and of subjects failing it. The use of such a weighting scheme was prompted by the obvious advantage of being able to utilize the data for all of the subjects who were tested with a given item. Since this weight is based upon the total number of successes and failures for the item in question, and because it is a unitary index, it affords a better basis for judging the relative validity of items than a series of percents passing.

Increase in percents passing at successive chronological ages is indirect but not conclusive evidence of validity. Height, for example, increases with age, but is known to be practically uncorrelated with brightness. Increase in percents passing by mental age is better, but exclusive reliance upon this technique predetermines that the scale based upon this criterion will measure approximately the same functions as that used in selecting the mental age groups. In the present case this was not objectionable, since the purpose of the revision was to provide scales closely comparable to the old with respect to the mental abilities tested.

FORMATION AND USE OF THE PROVISIONAL SCALES

When the sifting process described above had been completed, a sufficient number of promising tests remained to make up two provisional scales for final tryout. In order to insure having the requisite number of surviving tests to make two complete scales, it was necessary to provide a margin of safety in the provisional batteries by the inclusion of more tests than would be ultimately needed. This margin of safety had to extend throughout the entire range. Provisional Form L contained 209 tests and provisional Form M 199. As we have stated in Chapter I, the number of tests in the completed scale is 129 in each form, only a small number of which are identical in the two forms. The margin of safety allowed (about 30 per cent) was none too large.

* * *

THE SELECTION OF SUBJECTS

In order to secure a representative group of school children, we chose them from different sections of the country, trying to avoid selective factors due to social and economic status. We chose average schools, and, as far as possible, recruited the pre-school group from the siblings of school cases. All subjects are American-born and belong to the white race. There has been no elimination of any particular nationality groups.

Geographical distribution. Seventeen different communities in eleven states were sampled to secure the 3184 subjects upon whom our final standardization was based. During the first year devoted to testing, three of the examiners worked in different communities in California, one in Nevada, one in New York, one in Colorado, and one in Kansas. During the second year testing was done in two communities in California, two in Virginia, one in Vermont, one in Texas, two in Minnesota, and a number of communities (chiefly rural) in Indiana and Kentucky. The same examiners were employed. The selection of localities for the second year's testing was based upon certain considerations in regard to the sampling which had resulted from a study of the socio-economic levels of the first 1500 subjects.

Socio-economic status. Four estimates of the socio-economic status of the subjects tested during the first year were made in an effort to appraise the group and to guide in the selection of next year's subjects.

The Sims Questionnaire was given to two grade groups, between the fifth and the eighth, in each school that supplied subjects for the revision standardization. Our data indicate no such reliability for the questionnaire as Sims reports (a correlation of .94 between paired siblings), and, as the published norms are inadequate to serve as a criterion for our sampling, we have been able to make but little use of this estimate of social and economic level.

Classifications of the occupations of fathers of the first 1500 cases were made according to the Barr rating scale, the Taussig five-grade grouping, and a grouping arranged by Goodenough based on the census classification and affording a basis for comparison with the occupational distribution of employed males in the United States in 1930.

The mean Barr rating on occupational status of fathers was 9.34 for a population of 1572 cases. Terman found a mean Barr rating of 8.88 for employed adult males of the general population of the United States based on figures reported in the 1920 census. The mean of 8.88 for the general population corresponds to the Barr rating of gardener; the mean of 9.34 for fathers of our group to a Barr rating of carpenter (9.37).

The Taussig classification gave:

    I. Professional 8.79%
 II(a). Semi-professional and higher business 15.21
 II(b). Business and clerical 18.49
  III. Skilled labor 42.08
   IV. Semi-skilled labor 6.7
    V. Unskilled labor 8.72

The Goodenough classification, which afforded a basis for comparison with the 1930 census figures, was as follows:

TABLE I

Occupational Group	Percentages of Employed Males in U.S.	Percentage Distribution of Known Occupations of Living Fathers of Revision Cases		
		1st Sample	2d Sample	Total
I	3.1	7.5	1.2	4.5
II	5.2	11.1	4.2	7.8
III	15.0	28.3	22.4	25.5
IV	15.3	6.3	24.2	14.9
V	30.6	31.8	31.0	31.4
VI	11.3	8.8	9.9	9.4
VII	19.5	6.2	7.1	6.6
Total N	38,077,804	1438	1319	2757

Group I is professional; Group II, semi-professional and managerial; Group III, clerical, skilled trades, and retail business; Group IV, farmers; Group V, semi-skilled occupations, minor clerical positions, and minor businesses; Group VI, slightly skilled trades and other occupations requiring little training or ability; and Group VII, day laborers (urban and rural).

All of the figures indicate that the first year's sampling is least adequate in the case of the rural group. Accordingly we took care to include several additional rural communities in the selections for the following year. Two of the examiners spent the entire year testing in rural districts, one in country schools in southern Indiana and Kentucky, the other in a country village in Vermont. A third spent three months testing in a rural community in Minnesota and another about the same amount of time testing the child population of a backwoods village of Virginia.

Our rural sampling is still inadequate. Following the census classification, according to which areas having a population density of less than a thousand per square mile are listed as rural, about thirty per cent of our cases are drawn from rural communities as against fifty per cent of the population of the United States under nineteen years of age. The figures in Table 1 for the total 2757 cases (cf. column five) indicate that class VII (urban and rural day laborers) includes a disproportionately small number of cases.

It is also apparent from the table that the distribution is slightly skewed in the direction of superiority of occupational status. This deviation from the census figures probably represents a trend in the right direction inasmuch as the census figures for employed males over ten years of age include Negroes, who, of course, represent on the whole a lower occupational group. Though the lower occupational groups tend to have larger families than those of higher occupational status, this differential birthrate factor tends to be offset by the inclusion in the lower occupational groups of more of the *young* men unskilled by reason of lack of experience and training, who have not yet established families.

Selection of school cases. Schools of average social status were selected in each community. Then in each school our examiners tested all of the children between the ages of six and fourteen who were within one month of a birthday in whatever grade enrolled. Our data include 200 such cases, 100 boys and 100 girls, at each age level from six to fourteen.

The advanced group, aged fifteen to eighteen, presented the greatest difficulties of selection. Dozens of studies have shown that the regular academic high school is highly selected, how highly depending on the nature of the community and on various other factors. In some localities the presence of factories tends to withdraw children from school as early as the law permits. The laws in the various states differ with respect to the compulsory school age and there are differences in the degree of rigor of enforcement of the existing laws. Certain communities have continuation or part-time schools and technical high schools which are usually attended by less highly selected groups. The indications are that the industrial depression in these years, 1930-32, operated to keep the older children in school since there were fewer jobs available to withdraw them.

Only a hundred cases were to be tested at each of these upper age levels, according to our schedule, fifty boys and fifty girls. There were many different kinds of secondary schools to choose from and there was more selective elimination. Instructions to the examiners were intended to insure that the advanced group would be as nearly as possible continuous with the intermediate, with no break between fourteen and fifteen years. The compulsory school age was taken into account, the general character of the population, and the type of secondary education that was offered. In each community the school census was consulted to determine the amount of elimination after age fourteen. We made certain that some of the twelve-, thirteen-, and fourteen-year-olds who had gone on to high school were included, also some of the slow fifteen-and sixteen-year-olds who were still in the intermediate school. A few cases who had graduated from high school were included and a few who had dropped out of school without completing high school. These out-of-school groups were sampled by choosing siblings of school children in numbers proportional to the amount of elimination at ages above fourteen. However, the number of out-of-school cases tested falls somewhat short of the actual proportions chosen by reason of limitation of time and the difficulty of locating the desired cases.

Selection of the pre-school subjects. In order to make sure that our pre-school group, too, was a continuation of the same distribution, we chose as far as possible younger sibs of the school groups. The chief sources through which these younger children were secured were: (1) birth records; (2) school census; (3) school siblings; (4) kindergartens; (5) well-baby clinics of city or county health centers; (6) day nurseries; (7) nursery schools conducted by settlement houses; and (8) personal report. When the field work was first begun, the pre-school children of one community were secured largely through the agency of the local parent teacher association, ladies' aid society groups, and personal report. But the cases chosen in this way made up such a highly selected sample that we found it necessary to eliminate the whole group. Needless to say this error was not repeated.

The extent to which various sources were utilized in selecting our cases differed widely from one community to another, depending upon the local conditions. In some of the rural counties in Indiana and Kentucky, birth records were almost unknown and a school census non-existent, while in other communities birth records and school census reports yielded practically complete lists of the pre-school children of the community to which the other sources added but little. Great care was exercised in the large population centers to include representative groups; if a school in a suburban district which had been chosen as average on the advice of superintendent and counselors seemed to include too large percentage of higher occupational groups it was offset by a tenement district center.

* * *

Since a number of our pre-school subjects were attending kindergarten, we made a comparison between this group of 132 children aged four and a half to five and a half and a group of 115 children of the same age who were not in kindergarten, in order to determine the effect of selection in the kindergarten group. The average I.Q. of 132 kindergarten children was found to be 102, while that of the same age group not in kindergarten was 103.

*   *   *

Nationality of descent. The subjects of our group were all American-born white children. In the case of the pre-school group the parents also were American-born, but we made no effort to control the selection in regard to nationality of descent. In fifty per cent of the cases both parents were born in the United States.

DERIVATION OF THE FINAL SCALES FROM THE STANDARDIZATION DATA

The primary tasks in arranging the final scales were two: (1) elimination of the less satisfactory tests, and (2) the achievement of an age arrangement of the retained tests which would make the mean mental age of each age group of subjects identical with mean chronological age, giving a mean I.Q. as close as possible to 100.

*   *   *

The "correct" standarization of an age scale depends, of course, upon the age location of the separate tests and upon the amount of credit (months of mental age) allowed for passing them. Other factors, such as the inter-correlation of the tests and the shapes of the curves of percents passing, are also involved. It is at present not possible to lay down, in advance, rules which if followed will cause the scale to yield a mean I.Q. of 100 at each level. In the present revision, as in the original Stanford-Binet, it has been necessary to work empirically by revising and re-revising until an arrangement of the tests was formed which achieved the desired goal.

*   *   *

UNITS OF MEASUREMENT

Indices of developmental level. Three indices of developmental level have been used by psychologists: mental age, point (or raw) score made up of admittedly unequal units, and a statisticised point score composed of units allegedly equal. In practice the first two reduce to one, for raw point scores are commonly converted at once into age norms and thus become in effect mental age scores. The choice is accordingly between a mental age score and an "altitude" score composed of supposedly equal linear units ranging upward from an established zero point in the manner of a yardstick. Only one intelligence scale of the latter type has been fully worked out, that for Thorndike's CAVD test. The advantage of a scale which starts at zero and increases by equal units is that it permits one to add, substract, multiply, and divide scores. As measured by such a scale, a subject who scores 20 is presumed to be twice as intelligent as one who scores 10, and half as intelligent as one who scores 40.

However, the CAVD technique is open to criticism from a number of points of view. One may first of all raise the question whether such expressions as "A is twice as intelligent as B," or "half as intelligent as C," have any real psychological meaning. Thorndike has tried to give them meaning by positing a theory of intelligence which explains intellectual differences as solely a function of the *number* of established neural bonds, but for reasons we cannot here enter into, we are unable to accept his proof that area and altitude of intelligence are perfectly correlated. His view seems to us an over-simplification of the complex and in direct opposition to most of the recent trends of psychological theory.

Secondly, the only available statistical procedure for making an equal-unit scale rests on the assumption that in an unselected population the distribution of intelligence follows strictly the normal curve. This may or may not be true. There are biological characters for which it is not true, and intelligence may conceivably be one of them. The question could be answered for intelligence if we had an equal-unit scale to begin with, but we are in the unfortunate position of having to assume the answer in advance in order to derive the equal-unit scale. It is the old problem of lifting oneself over the fence by one's bootstraps.

The expression of a test result in terms of age norms is simple and unambiguous, resting upon no statistical assumptions. A test so scaled does not pretend to measure intelligence as linear distance is measured by the equal units of a foot-rule, but tells us merely that the ability of a given subject corresponds to the average ability of children of such and such an age. This was all that Binet claimed to accomplish, and one can well doubt whether the voluminous output of psychometric literature since his day has enabled us to accomplish more. We have accordingly chosen to retain this least pretentious of units for the estimation of mental level.

There are, however, certain characteristics of age scores with which the reader should be familiar. For one thing, it is necessary to bear in mind that the true mental age as we have used it refers to mental age on a particular intelligence test. A subject's mental age in this sense may not coincide with the age score he would make in tests of musical ability, mechanical ability, social adjustment, etc. A subject has, strictly speaking, a number of mental ages; we are here concerned only with that which depends upon the abilities tested by the new Stanford-Binet scales.

Another characteristic of the mental age unit is that we do not need to assume for it uniformity of magnitude from year to year. Indeed the unit appears definitely to decrease with age, if we can judge by the ease or difficulty with which adjacent mental ages can be discriminated. For example, the difference between one-year and two-year intelligence is so great that any one can sense it, while even a psychologist might have difficulty in discriminating between the mental levels of twelve years and thirteen years on the basis of ordinary observation. Certaintly the magnitude of the mental age unit shrinks rapidly as mental maturity is approached, just as annual increments in height decrease as the child approaches physical maturity. The difference in intellectual ability between the average child of fifteen and the average child of sixteen is so small that it can barely be detected by the most elaborate mental tests. Probably not one twelve-months-old child in a million has reached the mental level which is normal to the average child of two years, but almost half of the fifteen-year-olds have reached the level which is average for sixteen years. Increments beyond this point have not been clearly demonstrated for unselected subjects.

Finally, the reader should understand that mental ages at the upper end of the Stanford-Binet scales are not true "mental ages," but instead are more or less arbitrary scores designed to permit the computation of I.Q.'s of superior older subjects. The magnitude of these units in score points has been adjusted in such a way as to give approximately the same distribution of I.Q.'s for adult subjects as is found for children. The adjustment assumes that in terms of an absolute scale (if we had one), the distribution of brightness scores of adult subjects would follow the same curve as the distribution for unselected children of a given age.

The index of brightness. We want to know not only the intellectual level (mental age) of a subject, but also his brightness or dullness in comparison with others of his age. As already stated, we have continued to use the I.Q. for this purpose. Alternative units which might be considered in this connection are percentile scores and standard scores.

* * *

From the statistical point of view, every advantage is in favor of the standard score. Why, then, have we not discarded the I.Q. index of brightness in favor of some kind of standard score index?

One reason is that the majority of teachers, school administrators, social workers, physicians, and others who utilize mental test results have not learned to think in statistical terms. To such a person a rating expressed as "+2 sigma" is just so much Greek. They have, however, gradually accumulated considerable information in regard to the educational and behavioral correlates of various grades of I.Q. They know, for example, that an I.Q. of 80 signifies a particular grade of dullness, one of 50 a particular grade of mental deficiency, etc. If necessary they could in the course of time acquire an equal amount of information about the concrete significance of standard scores. It has taken twenty years for the groups of workers in question to reach their present stage of skill in the interpretation of I.Q.'s; it would probably take another twenty years to reach the same stage in the interpretation of standard scores.

* * *

As it has turned out, the I.Q.'s yielded by the new Stanford-Binet scales are themselves standard scores within a reasonably small margin of error. This comes from the fact that the S.D.'s of the I.Q. distributions of the different age groups show a marked tendency to cluster in the neighborhood of 16 I.Q. points, from which it follows that an I.Q. of 116 corresponds fairly closely to a standard score of +1; an I.Q. of 132 to a standard score of +2, etc. One can therefore say that, so far as practical uses of the scales are concerned, the I.Q.'s which they yield are about as free from objectionable features as true standard scores.

Whatever index of brightness is used, some will claim too much from it and others too little. The uninformed will read meaning into it which it does not connote and the overenthusiastic will, in too exclusive dependence upon it, ignore other lines of information which should be taken into account. The hypercritical, on the other hand, will continue to oppose its use on grounds which are largely irrelevant: because it is often misunderstood or misused; because it is influenced by environment as well as by endowment; because it does not measure social adaptability; because it does not always predict accurately success in school or success in life, etc.

There are psychologists who so dread the misunderstanding and misuse of their concepts that they would prefer to keep them strictly esoteric, as theologians once did and as physicians still sometimes try to do, but one can hardly take seriously the suggestion that the results of mental age tests should be reported exclusively in terms intelligible only to the psychometrician. The sensible alternative is to employ the simplest indices available and as rapidly as possible acquaint teachers, school counselors, social workers, and physicians with their significance and their limitation.

* * *

STATISTICAL ANALYSIS OF SCORES

Figure 1 gives the distribution of the composite of the adjusted L-M I.Q.'s for the standardization group in terms of the per cent of cases at each of the ten-point I.Q. intervals. In view of the effort made to secure a representative standardization group, and in view of the accuracy with which the scales have been adjusted for difficulty throughout the age range, the curve shown in Figure 1 probably gives the clearest picture available of the intellectual differences which obtain among American born white children of the ages in question.

* * *

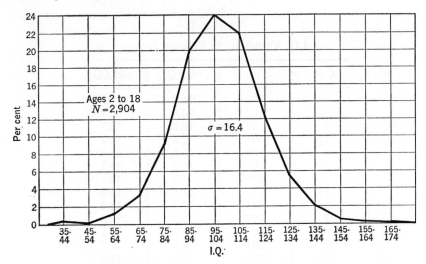

Figure 1. Distributions of composite L-M I.Q.'s of standardization group.

I.Q. VARIABILITY IN RELATION TO AGE

The use of I.Q. scores rests on the assumption that variability in terms of I.Q. remains approximately constant from age to age, or, stating it in another way, that variability in terms of mental age is directly proportional to chronological age. Only to the extent that this assumption is true does the I.Q. score have consistent meaning, as otherwise a given I.Q. at one age might be equivalent to a much higher or lower I.Q. at another age. Numerous investigations have shown that scales of the Binet type when carefully standardized do show a marked tendency to yield constant I.Q. variability, at least from fairly early childhood to the adolescent period. Thus, for example, the proportion of four-year-olds with a mental age of five years (I.Q. 125) agrees closely with the proportion of eight-year-olds who test at ten or of twelve-year-olds who test at fifteen. Similarly, the proportion of five-year-olds who test at four (I.Q. 80) agrees closely with the proportion of ten-year-olds who test at eight.

* * *

Table II, which presents the data with respect to I.Q. variability and age, shows that the standard deviations of I.Q.'s fluctuate around a median value slightly in excess of 16 points, and that at each age the values agree closely for the two scales. Since inspection of the values reveals no marked relationship between I.Q. variability and C.A. over the age range as a whole, we may accept 16 points as approximately the representative value of the standard deviation of I.Q.'s for an unselected population. Attention, however, should be drawn to ages six and twelve, where the relatively low

TABLE II
I.Q. Variability in Relation to Age

C.A.	N	σL I.Q.	σM I.Q.
2	102	16.7	15.5
2½	102	20.6	20.7
3	99	19.0	18.7
3½	103	17.3	16.3
4	105	16.9	15.6
4½	101	16.2	15.3
5	109	14.2	14.1
5½	110	14.3	14.0
6	203	12.5	13.2
7	202	16.2	15.6
8	203	15.8	15.5
9	204	16.4	16.7
10	201	16.5	15.9
11	204	18.0	17.3
12	202	20.0	19.5
13	204	17.9	17.8
14	202	16.1	16.7
15	107	19.0	19.3
16	102	16.5	17.4
17	109	14.5	14.3
18	101	17.2	16.6

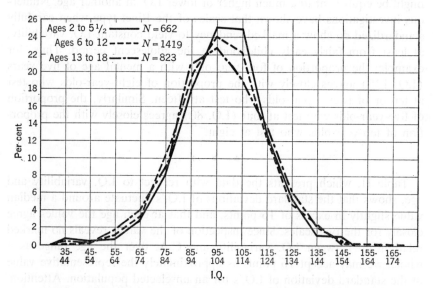

Figure 2. Distribution of composite L-M I.Q.'s at three age levels.

and high values respectively are deviations too extreme to be explained as purely chance fluctuations. The high variability at age twelve might conceivably be ascribed to the differential age of the onset of pubescence, although it has yet to be demonstrated that pubescence is significantly related to the rate of mental growth. Whether the atypical I.Q. variability at age six resides in the character of the sampling at that age, or whether it is perhaps an artifact of the nature of the scale at that level cannot be determined from the available data. In the lack of positive proof to the contrary, we are probably justified in assuming that the true variability is approximately constant from age to age. Repeated tests of the same subjects from early childhood to maturity will be necessary to determine whether this assumption is in accord with the facts.

Figure 2 shows the distributions of the adjusted composite L-M I.Q.'s for three age levels: 2 to 5½, 6 to 12, and 13 to 18. It is evident from inspection of these curves that I.Q. variability as measured by the new scales is approximately the same for the three levels.

* * *

PRACTICE EFFECTS

Inasmuch as both scales were administered to all the subjects with an interval of from one to a few days between testings, it has been possible to determine the practice effect with considerable accuracy. The mean increase in I.Q. on the second test is the same from L to M as from M to L. The amount of increase shows no noticeable trend in relation to size of I.Q., but varies according to the age of the subjects. Table III summarizes the data on practice effect.

TABLE III
Practice Effects in Relation to Age

Age Group	Mean increase in I.Q. on second test
2 and 2½ years	2.6
3 and 3½ years	4.4
4 and 4½ years	2.5
5 and 5½ years	2.0
6 and 7 years	2.1
8 and 9 years	2.1
10 and 11 years	2.2
12 and 13 years	2.4
14, 15, and 16	2.1
17 and 18 years	4.0

RELIABILITY OF THE SCALES AND PROBABLE ERROR OF SCORES

The reader should not lose sight of the fact that a test with even a high reliability yields scores which have an appreciable probable error. The probable error in terms of months of mental age is of course larger with older than with young children because of the increasing spread of mental

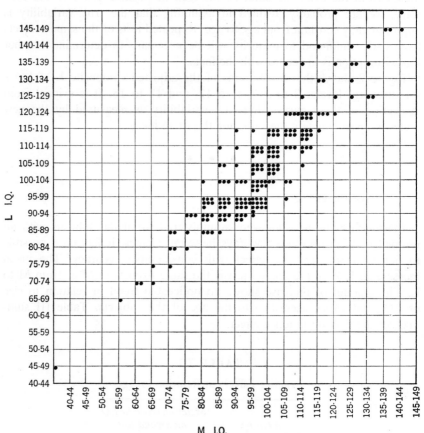

Figure 3. Scatter plot of correlation between L and M I.Q.'s at C.A. 7.

age scores as we go from younger to older groups. For this reason it has been customary to express the P.E. of a Binet score in terms of I.Q., since the spread of Binet I.Q.'s is fairly constant from age to age. However, when our correlation arrays were plotted for the separate age groups they were all discovered to be distinctly fan-shaped. Figure 3 is typical of the arrays at every age level.

From Figure 3 it becomes clear that the probable error of an I.Q. score is not a constant amount, but a variable which increases as I.Q. increases. It has frequently been noted in the literature that gifted subjects show greater I.Q. fluctuation than do clinical cases with low I.Q.'s—a phenomenon which has usually been ascribed to scale defects, faulty standardization at the upper levels, or the alleged instability of gifted children. However, we now see that this trend is inherent in the I.Q. technique itself, and might have been predicted on logical grounds. It is reasonable to expect that a subject's fluctuation in mental age score will be proportional, not to the variability of his chronological age group, but to the variability of his mental age group. Thus, the probable error of a test-score of an eight-year-old boy with a mental age of twelve should resemble the typical probable error of that group characterized by a mental age of twelve—viz., the twelve-year group.

It follows that the P.E.$_{\text{I.Q.}}$ must be expressed as a function of the I.Q., a procedure which is empirically verified by the observations summarized in

TABLE IV

Average Difference Between L and M I.Q.'s

(as empirically observed)

	Ages 3–18 combined	
I.Q. Level	N	Av. Diff.
130 and over	154	5.92
110–129	872	5.55
90–109	1291	5.09
70–89	477	4.35
Below 70	57	2.49

Table IV. It follows equally that the reliability coefficient is inadequate for I.Q. data unless reliabilities are derived separately for various I.Q. levels. From the average differences listed in Table IV, we may derive the standard error of a test score for the corresponding I.Q. levels, and from these values we can deduce the appropriate reliability by solving the equation $\sigma_{\text{I.Q.}} = \sigma_{\text{dist}} \cdot \sqrt{1 - r_{11}}$ for r_{11}, assuming the standard deviation of the I.Q. distribution as 16.4, the most typical value.

It will be seen from Table V that in general P.E.$_{\text{I.Q.}}$ is approximately .03 times the I.Q. The chances are even that a score which falls in the I.Q. range 90 to 109 does not differ from the true score on such a scale by more than 3 points, and the chances are five to one that it does not differ from the true score by more than 6 points, or twenty-two to one that it is not in error by more than 9 points. The probable error of a score above 130 I.Q. is approximately 3.5 points, and for a score below 70 I.Q. it is only about 1.5 points. The chances are twenty-two to one that a score

TABLE V

Errors of Measurement and Derived Reliabilities for Various I.Q. Levels

I.Q. Level	$\sigma_{I.Q.}$	$P.E._{I.Q.}$ (derived from av. diff. between L. and M I.Q.'s)	Equivalent to reliability of
130 and over	5.24	3.54	.898
110–129	4.87	3.29	.912
90–109	4.51	3.04	.924
70–89	3.85	2.60	.945
Below 70	2.21	1.49	.982

below 70 on one of these scales is not in error by more than 4.5 points. The extreme accuracy of the scales at the lower I.Q. levels will be gratifying to those who make frequent use of the test for clinical purposes and who are rightly concerned with the dependability of their findings. The probable errors just given represent the situation for the scale as a whole. When different age levels are treated separately it is found that the situation for the age range above 6 is appreciably more favorable than this, and for the range 2 to 6 appreciably less favorable. The probable errors for the abbreviated scales composed of the starred tests are about 20 per cent greater than those for the unabbreviated.

The last column of Table V gives the reliabilities which correspond to the average differences between L and M I.Q.'s as given in Table IV. It will be seen that these reliability values range from .98 for subjects below 70 I.Q. to approximately .90 for subjects above 130 I.Q. For subjects near 100 I.Q. the reliability is .925.

The above reliabilities are unquestionably more meaningful than the reliabilities that would be found by correlating Form L against Form M. However, the latter were computed, separately for the twenty-one age groups, and were found to range from .85 to .95, with a median of .91. The median for ages 2 to 6 was .88 and for the ages above 6 it was .93[1]

[1] It should be mentioned, in this connection, that the foregoing coefficients cannot be directly compared with the reliabilities customarily reported for intelligence tests. Since the subjects were all within four weeks of a birthday or half-birthday, the spread of ability at each level is restricted to the variability of a single-age group. If reliabilities had been computed by correlating mental age score on L against mental age score on M for several age groups combined, as is often done in establishing mental-test reliability, the coefficients so obtained could have been sharply (but spuriously) increased. Doubling the standard deviation of mental age score in this fashion would raise an r_{11} of .909 to .977. Even basing the reliabilities on a twelve months' age range, instead of the range of two months which was employed, would have raised the median figure from .91 to approximately .915. Basing them on school grade groups (grade 1, grade 2, etc.), as is customary in computing reliabilities of achievement tests, would have raised the value still higher. Therefore, our median reliability of .91 is probably as good as, or better than, a majority of coefficients of .92 to .95 which one finds reported in the literature of psychometrics.

A great deal has been written about selective migration, but such studies as exist are for the most part subject to serious errors which throw a cloud over the whole issue. The best American study is clearly this one. You should be cautioned, of course, against assuming that all migration is selective for high intelligence. Nothing of the sort is implied by the authors. Changing conditions change the selective variables. This study is valuable both as a description of rural-urban migration in Kansas at that time and because it is the most generally useful model for such research.

Intelligence as a Selective Factor in Rural-Urban Migration*

NOEL P. GIST

CARROLL D. CLARK

1938–1939

Migration of rural peoples to urban centers has been one of the important features of our national development. Quantitatively this population movement is a matter of fairly detailed historical record. From the qualitative angle, however, there is a paucity of reliable data, although the movement itself has stimulated no little speculation as to its selective character and the probable consequences to rural society. . . .

More recently the problem of social selection in rural-urban migrations has been attacked in a more thoroughgoing fashion. Intelligence tests have been given to groups of rural and urban children and the results compared. Although the tests have almost invariably shown a higher "intelligence" of city children, the lower ratings of the rural children may reflect nothing more than lack of adequate educational opportunity. Using a different research technique, Wilson Gee and his associates found that in certain rural areas of Virginia the city was exerting a greater pulling-power on the upper classes than on the less privileged segment of the population. A similar study of the Carolina Piedmont areas, however, revealed no evidence of strong association between social and economic status and migrations to cities. On the basis of studies conducted in Minnesota, Sorokin and Zimmerman reached the conclusion that no evidence exists to show that cities are attracting "those who are better physically, vitally, mentally,

* Reprinted from "Intelligence as a selective factor in rural-urban migration," *American Journal of Sociology*, 44 (1938-39), pp. 36-58, by Noel P. Gist and Carroll D. Clark by permission of the authors and the University of Chicago Press.

morally, or socially." The investigations of Lively and Beck in Ohio seem to corroborate the conclusions of Sorokin and Zimmerman.

The main impression that one derives from these studies is the dearth of adequate data on which to base reliable generalizations concerning the selective character of migrations. Natural resources, demographic traits, climatic conditions, cultural patterns, and economic organization are all factors which undoubtedly influence the trend of population movement. Accordingly, it is reasonable to suppose that qualitative as well as quantitative differences may be manifest in migrations from different rural sections of the country. To suggest, as do Sorokin and Zimmerman, a "net law of rural-urban social selection" in which "cities attract the extremes and the farms attract the mean" seems premature, to say the least.

For the most part the studies thus far made have failed to control satisfactorily the numerous cultural factors involved. If the traits of urban residents who migrated from rural communities are measured and then compared with the same traits of their former neighbors who remained in rural communities, the results may show marked differences existing in the two groups, but such differences are likely to reflect the influence of the different environments since migration occurred. Even where deliberate effort has been made to control such factors as education, occupational status, and income, there is no assurance that the more subtle cultural influences pervading the urban and rural environments may not affect the results.

From a methodological standpoint, however, a satisfactory control of the cultural factor would be achieved *if the traits of the groups to be compared had been measured when both were living in the same rural communities, before migration to cities had occurred.* If the traits of a rural population could be thus measured and the data filed away until members of the group had had opportunity to migrate, we would then be in a position to learn how far the migrating group excelled or fell short in any given trait, and hence to appraise the strength of various factors presumed to have a selective influence free from the interference of cultural differences operating since the time of migration.

In the present study, which seeks to determine the operation of certain selective factors in rural-urban migration, the essential condition stated above has been followed. This paper, however, is limited to a discussion of the results obtained for a single measured trait, viz., intelligence as indicated by a standard group test. The method employed was briefly as follows. During the academic year 1922-23 standardized Terman intelligence tests were given under the supervision of the school of education at the University of Kansas to a large number of high-school students in rural communities scattered widely over the state. The test scores, together with the names and ages of the students, were made available to the writers for use in this study. In 1935, approximately thirteen years after the tests were given, steps were taken to secure further information on as many as possible of the individuals originally tested, the chief purpose being to ascertain which of them had migrated to cities and which had remained in rural communities. Cases originating in towns so large as to approach the census definition of urban, as well as those from communities so near cities as to be subject to pronounced influences of urbanization, were discarded. As finally completed, the sample of former high-school students on which the present study is based was drawn from forty communities, all essentially rural not only as determined by the technical United States Census criterion but as judged by the writers, both of whom have lived a long time in the state.

Most of the communities in the eastern half of the state were visited by research assistants, and the data were secured either directly from the former students themselves, if they were still living in the community and could be interviewed, or from local residents likely to have the desired information, such as the postmaster, schoolteachers, storekeepers, relatives of the former students, and others. Wherever possible, the present residence of a migrant was ascertained in the form of a definite post-office address. In those cases where a former student was known to have moved away but no definite knowledge of his whereabouts could be obtained, the schedule was discarded. Frequently it was found possible to verify the facts entered on a schedule by reference to several sources of information.

In the case of some communities located in the western part of the state and too far away to be easily accessible to the field workers, the data were secured through the co-operation of certain key-persons in these communities who were qualified and willing to assist in the study. Schedules sufficiently complete to serve the purpose of the investigation were obtained for a total of 2,544 persons. As a means of checking on the accuracy of the crucial facts, particularly to determine whether those listed as having migrated to the cities actually had done so, calls were made at the addresses reported in the schedules for about one hundred of these migrants in Topeka and Wichita. In a high percentage of cases the former student either was found to be living at the address reported or had moved from that address some time previously.

When the intelligence tests were given in 1922-23, the median age of the students was around sixteen; therefore the median age at the time when residential data were obtained was approximately twenty-nine. Inasmuch as migrations from country to city are largely recruited from the younger-age groups, it seems reasonable to suppose that the bulk of the urbanward movement from this sample of 2,544 persons had taken place prior to the time of obtaining residential data. Even if this assumption should prove erroneous, the findings on the selective nature of the intelligence factor presently to be reported would probably not be greatly altered.

After the data relating to the place of residence were assembled, a classificatory residential scheme was decided upon. Former students still living in communities under 2,500 were classified as rural, in accordance with the basis of classification employed by the Bureau of the Census; whereas all found to be residing in communities of 2,500 or over were classed as urban. The rural residents were again subdivided into farm and nonfarm groups, the latter referring to residents of towns or villages, or to persons engaged in nonagricultural pursuits. The urban residents, on the other hand, were subdivided into four categories based on the size of the cities in which they lived. The first category included all cities from 2,500 to 9,999; the second, cities from 10,000 to 24,999; the third, cities from 25,000 to 99,999; the fourth, cities of 100,000 or over. In order to avoid errors relating to place of residence, the informants were asked not only to indicate the name of the community but also the street address (or rural mail route) and the occupation of the person concerning whom information was sought. Thus it was possible to classify properly any rural person such as a farmer whose post-office address referred to an urban rather than a rural community.

Most of the communities supplying the sample of former high-school students included in the study are small country villages with only a few hundred inhabitants. Only four had a population exceeding one thousand. Inasmuch as the student bodies of rural high schools in Kansas are ordinarily recruited from both villages and farms, the persons included in the sample probably represented a fair cross-section of youthful farm and nonfarm population in rural Kansas. It is not known, however, what percentage of the students lived on farms and what percentage lived in villages at the time the tests were made, since the students were not originally so classified.

It may be observed at the outset that heavy migrations occurred from all the forty communities. Of the 2,544 students included in this study, 1,783, or 70.08 per cent, were living in other communities at the time the data were gathered. Several who took the tests could not be located and hence were necessarily excluded from consideration. The figures given for the number and percentage of migrants would probably be an understatement if data on all originally tested were available, since the individuals about whom no information could be obtained had undoubtedly left the community.

Of the total actually studied, 964, or 37.89 per cent, were residing in urban communities; 819, or 32.19 per cent, had moved to some other rural community; while 761, or 29.92 per cent, remained where they had attended school. Viewing the migrants alone, 54.05 per cent, or slightly more than half, went to cities, whereas 45.95 per cent moved to other rural areas.

* * *

With information concerning the I.Q., sex, and place of residence for each of the 2,544 persons, it was possible to proceed upon an analysis of

TABLE I

Distribution of Intelligence Scores of 2,544 Rural
High-School Students in 1923 According to
Present Rural and Urban Classification

I.Q.	Urban		Rural	
	No.	Per cent	No.	Per cent
55– 64	1	0.10	0	0.00
65– 74	8	0.83	32	2.03
75– 84	111	11.51	282	17.85
85– 94	258	26.77	518	32.78
95–104	326	33.82	472	29.87
105– 14	190	19.71	209	13.23
115– 24	60	6.22	57	3.61
125– 34	10	1.04	9	0.57
135– 44	0	0.00	1	0.06
Total	964	100.00	1,580	100.00
	Summary			
Under 95..............	378	39.21	832	52.66
95–104	326	33.82	472	29.87
105 and over	260	26.97	276	17.47
Total	964	100.00	1,580	100.00

selection in so far as the results of the intelligence tests might indicate a
selective process. Table I presents the distribution of the intelligence quotients of the 2,544 former high-school students classified according to their
present (1935) rural or urban residence. The superiority of the urban
group as indicated by these data is at once apparent. The modal I.Q. class
for the rural group falls in the interval 85-94; for the urban class, in the
interval 95-105. Over half (52.66 per cent) of the group comprised of
those remaining in rural areas had I.Q.'s below 95, as compared with two-
fifths (39.21 per cent) of the group migrating to cities. In each of the
superior classes (those above 105) the urban group is represented by a
higher percentage, 26.97 per cent of its total cases falling in these classes
as compared with 17.47 per cent of the total rural cases (see Fig. 1).

The mean I.Q. of the rural group is 94.78, with a standard deviation of
11.36 and a probable error of ± 0.193; the mean for the urban group is
98.26, with a standard deviation of 11.52 and a probable error of ± 0.250.
The probable error of the difference between these means is ± 0.316, or
less than one-tenth the computed difference, 3.48. The chances are overwhelming that the observed difference in the means of these samples is a

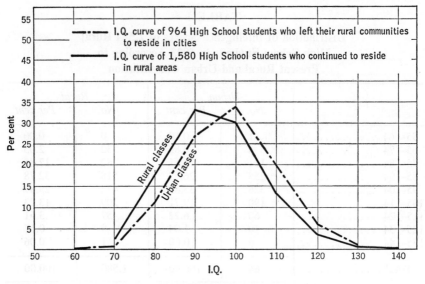

I.Q. curve of 964 High School students who left their rural communities to reside in cities

I.Q. curve of 1,580 High School students who continued to reside in rural areas

Figure 1

true difference and not to be explained as arising from the accidental conditions of sampling.

In Table II the rural group is further classified as to present farm or nonfarm (village) residence. The superiority of the nonfarm group over the farm group is almost as striking as that of the urban group over the rural group as a whole. Nearly three-fifths (57.88 per cent) of the farm I.Q.'s fall in the range below 95, while less than half (47.72 per cent) of the nonfarm cases fall in this range. In the upper range (over 105) the ratio of the percentages is about 3:2 in favor of the nonfarm cases. The mean of the nonfarm group is 96.14 (S.D. 10.40, P.E. ± 0.248) and that of the farm group 93.38 (S.D. 11.06, P.E. ± 0.269), a difference that is likewise highly reliable.

A comparison of the data in Tables I and II brings out even more effectively the differences in intelligence quotients of the urban, rural-non-farm, and rural-farm groups. Highest in the scale is the urban group, with the rural nonfarm next, and the rural farm at the bottom. The data are summarized in Table III.

So far, the urban category has included all persons living in communities having a population of 2,500 or more. Table IV shows the distribution of intelligence quotients according to the four classes of cities as based on numerical size. For communities falling within Class I, that is, from 2,500 to 9,999 in population, the modal group is in the 85-94 interval, whereas the modal group in the other three classes is in the interval 95-104. The

TABLE II

Distribution of Intelligence Quotients of 1,580 Former Rural High-School Students According to Present Farm or Nonfarm Classification

I.Q.	Rural farm		Rural nonfarm	
	No.	Per cent	No.	Per cent
55– 64...............	0	0.00	0	0.00
65– 74...............	15	1.95	17	2.10
75– 84...............	168	21.85	114	14.06
85– 94...............	262	34.07	256	31.57
95–104...............	222	28.87	250	30.82
105– 14...............	77	10.01	132	16.28
115– 24...............	20	2.60	37	4.56
125– 34...............	4	0.52	5	0.61
135– 44...............	1	0.13	0	0.00
Total	769	100.00	811	100.00
	Summary			
Under 95..............	445	57.87	387	47.72
95–104...............	222	28.87	250	30.80
105 and over	102	13.26	174	21.46
Total	769	100.00	811	100.00

TABLE III

Summary of Distribution of Intelligence Quotients of 2,544 Former Rural High-School Students Classified as to Urban, Rural-Nonfarm, and Rural-Farm Residence

I.Q.	Urban		Rural nonfarm		Rural farm	
	No.	Per cent	No.	Per cent	No.	Per cent
Under 95.......	378	39.21	387	47.72	445	57.88
95–104.........	326	33.82	250	30.80	222	28.87
105 and over....	260	26.97	174	21.46	102	13.25
Total	964	100.00	811	100.00	769	100.00

TABLE IV

Distribution of Intelligence Scores of 964 Former Rural High-School Students According to Class of Urban Community in Which They Reside at Present (1935)

I.Q.	Class I		Class II		Class III		Class IV	
	No.	Per cent	No.	Per cent	No.	Per cent	No.	Per cent
55– 64	0	0.00	1	0.46	0	0.00	0	0.00
65– 74	0	0.00	3	1.38	3	1.68	2	0.57
75– 84	30	13.76	21	9.68	23	12.85	37	10.57
85– 94	70	32.10	60	27.65	46	25.69	82	23.43
95–104	69	31.66	72	33.18	58	32.41	127	36.29
105– 14	36	16.51	48	22.12	36	20.11	70	20.00
115– 24	10	4.59	9	4.15	13	7.26	28	8.00
125– 34	3	1.38	3	1.38	0	0.00	4	1.14
135– 44	0	0.00	0	0.00	0	0.00	0	0.00
Total	218	100.00	217	100.00	179	100.00	350	100.00
			Summary					
Under 95....	100	45.87	85	39.17	72	40.23	121	34.57
95–104	69	31.65	72	33.18	58	32.40	127	36.29
105 and over.	49	22.48	60	27.65	49	27.37	102	29.14
Total	218	100.00	217	100.00	179	100.00	350	100.00

differences are even more apparent when a comparison is made of the percentages falling within the "low" and "high" intelligence groups. For Class I, the percentage of persons having I.Q.'s below 95 was 45.87; for Class II (10,000 to 24,999), 39.17; for Class III (25,000 to 99,999), 40.22; and for Class IV (100,000 or over), 34.57. Thus the smallest class of city had 11.3 per cent more persons in the low I.Q. group than did the metropolitan class. The differences between communities are much the same for the superior groups. In Class I only 22.48 per cent of the persons had I.Q.'s of 105 or over, whereas percentages for Classes II, III, and IV were 27.68, 27.37, and 29.14, respectively. It may thus be observed that the metropolitan type of community had 6.66 per cent more persons in the superior category than the small city.

These differences may also be shown by comparing the mean I.Q.'s of the persons residing in the four types of communities. For the small cities, Class I, the mean was 97.02 (S.D. 11.20, P.E. $\pm$ 0.511); for Class II, 98.16 (S.D. 10.17, P.E. $\pm$ 0.466); for Class III, 97.82 (S.D. 11.45, P.E. $\pm$ 0.554); and for Class IV, 99.31 (S.D. 11.52, P.E. $\pm$ 0.415). When the mean I.Q. of Class I is compared with that of Class IV, an observed difference of 2.29 is found. The probable error of the difference between these means is ± 0.654, or approximately one-fourth the computed difference. It may be concluded, therefore, that on the basis of statistical probability the difference between these two means is reliable. As between the other classes, the differences are less pronounced. The computed difference of the means of Class II and Class IV is 1.49, or only twice the probable error of the difference between the two means. For Classes II and IV the observed difference of the means is 1.15, only slightly more than the probable error of the difference. For Classes I and II the observed difference of the means is 1.14, or less than twice the probable error of the difference between the means of the samples. The computed difference of the means of Classes II and III is less than half the probable error, indicating a high degree of unreliability.

The foregoing data show a tendency for the intelligence quotients to be graduated upward as the size of the community increases. In other words, the large communities have tended to attract a disproportionate share of superior persons in the total sample. The exception to this tendency is Class II, which has a slightly lower mean I.Q. than the smaller cities falling in Class II. (The difference, as just noted, is unreliable and may be due to the accidental conditions of sampling.) It is possible that communities of the size indicated by these two categories are so similar in occupational opportunities, cultural resources, and other features that their drawing-power on rural migrants is much the same.

Of the total number of migrants, 489 left the state of Kansas. A comparison of the intelligence quotients of these 489 persons with those of the 2,055 persons who remained in Kansas reveals a selective process in the out-of-state migrations. Table V shows the distribution of 2,544 persons classified according to residence in or out of the state. The modal I.Q. class the out-of-state migrants falls within the 95-104 interval; for the group remaining in Kansas it lies in the interval 85-94. Approximately half (49.2 per cent) of those residing in the state were in the I.Q. classes under 95, while only two-fifths (40.1 per cent) of the out-of-state migrants were in the same category. One-fifth (20.1 per cent) of the Kansas residents were in the superior I.Q. classes as compared with slightly more than one-fourth (26.4 per cent) of the migrants. The mean I.Q.'s for the two groups, Kansas residents and out-of-state migrants, were 95.68 and 97.79, respectively, or an observed difference of 2.11. The probable error of the difference between the two means is ± 0.392, or less than one-fifth of the computed difference. It may be concluded that the difference noted has a high degree of reliability.

The data from Table V, then, are indicative of a selective process in favor of out-of-state communities. Owing to the fact that a majority of out-of-state migrants have gone to urban rather than to rural communities, this I.Q. differential is not surprising. As noted above, the cities are tending to attract a disproportionate share of those from the superior I.Q. classes.

TABLE V

Distribution of Intelligence Quotients of 2,544 Former Rural High-School Students Classified According to Residence in Kansas or Out of the State

I.Q.	Leaving state No.	Leaving state Per cent	Remaining in state No.	Remaining in state Per cent
55– 64	0	0.00	1	0.05
65– 74	4	0.82	36	1.75
75– 84	62	12.68	331	16.11
85– 94	130	25.58	644	31.34
95–104	164	33.54	631	30.70
105– 14	94	19.22	311	15.13
115– 24	31	6.34	85	4.14
125– 34	4	0.82	15	0.73
135– 44	0	0.00	1	0.05
Total	489	100.00	2,055	100.00
Summary				
Under 95	196	40.10	1,012	49.20
95–104	164	33.50	731	30.70
105 or over	129	26.40	415	20.10
Total	489	100.00	2,055	100.00

It is interesting to note that no significant differences exist between the mean I.Q.'s of the males and females in the study. Moreover, when the two sexes are classified as to rural or urban residence the differences are very slight, the rural females having a slightly higher mean I.Q. than the rural males, and the urban males exceeding by a very narrow margin the urban females. Table VI shows that 53.77 per cent of the rural males

TABLE VI

Sex and Distribution of Intelligence Quotients of 1,580 Former Rural High-School Students as to Residence

I.Q.	Males Rural No.	Males Rural Per cent	Males Urban No.	Males Urban Per cent	Females Rural No.	Females Rural Per cent	Females Urban No.	Females Urban Per cent
Under 95	413	53.77	176	39.46	419	51.60	202	38.99
95–104	223	29.04	148	33.18	249	30.67	178	34.36
105 or over	132	17.19	122	27.36	144	17.63	138	26.65
Total	768	100.00	446	100.00	812	100.00	518	100.00

were in the inferior group below 95 as compared to 51.60 per cent of the rural females— a difference of 2.17 per cent. Similarly, 17.19 per cent of the rural males fell within the superior group as compared with 17.73 per cent of the rural females, the difference being only about one-half of 1 per cent. The data show also that 39.46 per cent of the urban males and 38.99 per cent of the urban females were in the low category; in the high group the percentages were 27.36 and 26.64, respectively. These differences between the sexes, it would seem, are so small as to suggest the probability that they may have arisen from accidental conditions of the sampling procedure.

Somewhat more pronounced is the difference in the migratory tendencies of the two sexes. Of the 1,214 males, 446, or 36.74 per cent, moved to the city, while 518 of the 1,330 females, or 38.95 per cent, changed from rural to urban residence. This difference of 2.21 per cent in favor of the females is not large, although it does conform to the prevailing trend of rural-urban migrations in this country.

By way of summarizing the results here presented, brief consideration may be given to the significance of the data themselves and the possible social consequences of the selective process. For one thing, there is a difference of opinion as to the meaning and validity of intelligence tests as a basis for social investigation. The present study has merely taken the tests for what they may be worth, and anyone is free to place his own interpretation thereon. The writers have nowhere assumed that the tests are reliable measurements of innate capacity, since it would hardly be possible to measure something the exact nature of which is unknown.

What the tests apparently do measure, however inadequately, is a composite of the social experiences and backgrounds of the individuals, the richness or drabness of their home environments, their intellectual interests, their attitudes and values, the character of their emotional life, their ambitions, energy, and zeal, or the lack of these qualities. That hereditary factors profoundly influence these conditions or traits there can scarcely be a doubt. It may be further suggested that the individual's later career, his choice of occupation, his success or failure in that occupation, his leisure-time activities—in a word, the general character of his social adjustment—is significantly affected by these factors concerning which the tests seem to furnish a rough index. If, then, the tests represent something of a gauge of the individual's mental ability as influenced by hereditary, social, and psychological conditions, we have good reason to infer, on the basis of the results here presented, that the urban environment is exerting a stronger pull upon the abler and more favored rural individuals than upon those less able and less favored.

It may be noted here that the tests were given to a sample of persons who had already undergone a selective process in the educational system. That is, many of those exhibiting marked evidence of inferiority were undoubtedly weeded out before they reached high school. Hence this sample could not be considered representative of the entire youthful population in the forty communities. Whether the same selective tendencies observed in this study would be present if the total population was included there is no way of knowing. A similar method of investigation using tests given to children in the lower grades might yield results even more significant than those of the present study.

In so far as the tests are indicative of ability, therefore, the superior persons in the sample are tending to migrate more frequently to the cities than those in the inferior or average classes. On the basis of these data two questions logically suggest themselves: (1) Is such qualitative selection characteristic of rural-urban migrations in general? (2) What are the possible consequences of such selectivity to community life? As was noted earlier in this paper, sufficient data are not available for any broad generalizations concerning the qualitative selection of migrations, either for the country as a whole or for any of its major divisions. Until more evidence on the subject is provided by research, the question can only be formulated as a hypothesis. The answer to the second question cannot, of course, be stated until the answer to the first is found.

But if the country is losing to the city a disproportionate number of those from the upper I.Q. range, as appears from this study to be the case, such selection does not necessarily have any genetic significance. That is to say, the progeny of the rural population may be quite as adequately endowed by nature as the children of the urban migrants. On the other hand, it is entirely possible that the traditional conservatism of the country, the lack of effective rural organization in many areas, and the shortage of qualified leaders may be in part the consequence of selective migrations.

Enough has already been said in this book about cross-sectional studies, and a sufficient number of them has been presented, to make the relevance of this article plain. Most of us are aware of social change, but although we make a passing nod to it in planning studies, few of us realize that the differences are as striking as Kuhlen points out.

Social Change: A Neglected Factor in Psychological Studies of the Life Span*

RAYMOND S. KUHLEN

1940

Investigators in the field of adult life (and their number is increasing) are faced with problems especially serious in studies involving a wide age range. When older and younger people are compared, how are differences to be interpreted? Are they due primarily to the process of aging, to disuse of functions, to motivational differences or perhaps to sampling errors? These possibilities have received some attention, but too little notice has been directed toward social change as a possibly significant factor.

The usual procedure in studies of adult years is to obtain test results or other measures from adults of all ages, to compare the results for older and younger persons and (if sampling seems reasonably representative of the age groups) to interpret any differences as due primarily to aging. The basic assumption here seems to be that the groups are largely homogeneous with respect to all significant variables except age. This note argues that the rapid social change of recent decades (in itself widely recognized) is far more important in studies of the life span than is usually considered, since differences in background conditions of life thus caused may result in the observed differences between older and younger adult groups independently of the age factor. Certain data are presented which lend weight to this conclusion.

Consider first in Table I the issue of intelligence-test scores. They decline from age group to age group, thus suggesting a decline in intelligence in old age. While other data on learning in adult years support this interpretation, the test scores themselves are seriously inadequate. Evidence from a variety of sources points out that such scores vary with general and educational background, and it so happens that the cultural change of the past few decades has been such that, compared to modern standards, the older

* *School and Society*, 52 (1940), pp. 14-16. Reprinted by permission of the author and *School and Society*.

TABLE I

Age Differences in Certain Characteristics as Revealed by Cross-section Studies of Adult Life.

Figures Have Been Rounded

	Age group					
	20–29	30–39	40–49	50–59	60–69	70–79
Intelligence test scores	39	35	34	30	26	23
Bridge (per cent indicating liking for)	63	54	40	31	—	—
Movie attendance (per cent never attending).....................	18	33	50	61	72	80
Height (employed men, in centimeters)	171	169	168	167	166	—

the age group the more "inferior" the background. This becomes clearly apparent in Table II, which presents data indicating certain social and cultural changes through the years, data which describe childhood conditions for those in the various age groups to-day.

TABLE II

Data Indicative of Social Changes in the United States Since 1890. Note that Columns for 1890–1900 Describe Conditions in Which To-day's 50- and 60-year-olds Developed; More Recent Years Describe Conditions of Youth for Younger Adults

	1890	1900	1910	1920	1930
Per cent of those of secondary school age in secondary school.....................	7	12	16	33	51
Illiteracy rate (census data)	13	11	8	6	4
Magazine circulation (per 100 population)..	—	9	20	21	27
Per cent of total population in towns over 8,000	29	33	39	44	49
Life expectancy (males in yrs.)	—	48	50	54	57

To be more specific, the 60-year-old was born at a time when white illiteracy was nearly three times as prevalent as to-day, when school curricula were meager, attendance irregular and age of leaving school early. To-day's 10-year-old, on the other hand, was born into a culture where compulsory education laws required school attendance, where schools were versatile in their offerings and where opportunities for broadened intellectual horizons (through books, magazines, movies, automobiles) were plentiful. Not only do the older age groups have fewer years of schooling to their credit on the average, but such as they do have is far from equivalent (as regards length of term and versatility of offerings) to a comparable number of years in present schools. Thus to match age groups as regards length of schooling by no means removes the inequalities in educational background—inequalities which would lead one to expect *a priori* that the older the age group the lower would be the test scores.

The other items in Table I may be treated more briefly, but should also be considered with reference to Table II. People in the older age brackets have grown up in a culture devoid of many amusements of our technological age (radio programs date from 1920), and at a time when many modern recreational practices were disapproved. Surely these influences, and the early habits so engendered, affect later life—and may contribute much to the "decline" of interest in movies and bridge noted. Even physical measurements (of height for example) obtained by the "cross section" procedure may be similarly criticized. Recent studies suggest the younger generation to be perhaps an inch and a half taller than the last. (Increasing life expectancy shown in Table II implies the better health conditions which may account for this trend.) Thus the average 60-year-old to-day may be found to be noticeably shorter than the average 20-year-old if he has not shrunk one iota!

It is not the writer's intention to imply that social change is to be held accountable for all age trends observable in cross-section data from the life span (very probably in old age intellectual alertness does decline, height decrease), but it is argued that such change is of sufficient psychological importance to warrant more consideration in the interpretation of these studies. Cross-section studies do give insight into age changes, but they make a more specific contribution to the understanding of age groups within the present population than to the prediction of behavior changes present-day youth will undergo. Since to-day's young folk are living and developing in an environment different from that of their fathers or grandfathers, it is to be expected that in their old age they will differ somewhat from the old of to-day—and their old age adjustments will be made to a culture different still.

In conclusion three suggestions are offered to help obviate the difficulties mentioned above: (1) Greater use of a technique such as used by Miles who tested adult groups and retested them two years later, comparisons among age groups being made in terms of *amount of change* in this period. (2) More frequent follow-up of individuals already tested in schools and colleges (much important pretest data are now simply stored), with appropriate control groups to check on cultural change. (3) Analysis of test data with reference to individual items and allowance then made for social change, the influence of which is apt to be more evident when individual responses are examined. In a very real sense sociological and population data constitute background data for the psychology of adult life.

This probing study is a model of its kind. The author has attempted to consider her subjects' background and status in detail and has employed several instruments in order to give various hypotheses concerning Negro-white differences in intelligence a fair trial. Although the results do not by any means "settle" the questions of race differences definitively, the reader is made more aware of the nature of the differences and more wary of easy and casual "explanations" of either the environmental or hereditary kind. The complete monograph is well worth careful study.

Factors Affecting Intelligence Test Performance of Whites and Negroes in the Rural South*

MYRTLE BRUCE

1940

The problem of this study was the localization of factors that (1) differentiate between White and Negro groups, and (2) are responsible for the subnormal intelligence quotients in the rural South.

The method employed was (1) a statistical comparison of a White and a Negro sample on the Kuhlmann-Anderson Group Tests, Terman's (1916) revision of the Binet-Simon Intelligence Test, the Grace Arthur Point Performance Scale, and the Sims Socio-Economic Scale; and (2) a statistical and qualitative analysis of scores on the three intelligence tests and their component subtests and items, in order to determine the relative difficulty of the "new situation" tests versus the "information" tests, and of "speed" tests versus "power" tests for White and Negro children in the rural South.

BACKGROUND OF SUBJECTS

Physiography and Agriculture

The locality subjected to this investigation lies in the Southside section of Virginia. In this Piedmont area yellow flue-cured cigarette tobacco is cultivated by White and Negro tenant farmers, or "sharecroppers." The highlands not devoted to raising tobacco are covered with second growth forests. These forests are rapidly being depleted by migratory sawmills. Periodic floods destroy crops of corn and wheat raised for local consumption. These crops are planted on the narrow alluvial plains because this is the only soil in the community that does not require artificial fertilizers.

* Abridged from *Archives of Psychology*, Vol. 36, No. 252 (1940). Reprinted by permission of the author and *Archives of Psychology*.

Population

The county under consideration was populated by the descendents of colonists from the British Isles,* who landed on the shores of Virginia throughout the seventeenth century. According to one' authority these colonists represented a typical cross-section of English society at that time (2). Throughout its history, Virginia has produced men of outstanding ability, such as Jefferson, Madison, Marshall, Stonewall Jackson, Woodrow Wilson, and Carter Glass. On the other hand, a law passed in Virginia in 1671 forbidding the further importation of criminals from England indicates that these colonists represented many undesirable characters as well as political offenders and debtors. The importation of Negroes from Africa began in 1619.

Today within an area of 814 square miles there is a population of 41,283, of whom 54.1% are Native White, 45.7% Negro, and 0.1% foreign born. This population is almost entirely rural. The combined populations of all incorporated towns total only 5,903 inhabitants. One town with a population of 4,841 is the only community in the county having more than 1,000 inhabitants. This town, with its eight tobacco warehouses, is the trade center of Southside Virginia.

Approximately 86% of the total population of the county live on farms. Of those engaged in agriculture, 66% cultivate land that does not belong to them. Half of these landless farmers are Negroes. In Virginia as a whole, most of the farm laborers and tenants, and from 25 to 50% of the White landowners and 75% of the Negro landowners belong to the marginal population group (*i.e.,* having a family income of $600 or less in 1929).

Taxes

An enormous difference between White and Negro economic status is indicated in the 1936 report on local taxes in the county. Although Negroes constitute 46% of the population, and pay 40% of the adult head tax, they pay only 17% of the personal property tax. Only 13% of the land taxed is owned by Negroes. These figures represent a fair comparison between the total White and Negro groups; but they do not offer a fair comparison between the median White and Negro inhabitant, due to the considerable concentration of wealth in the hands of a few Whites. It must not be forgotten that there are as many landless White farmers as there are landless Negro farmers.

Socio-Economic Status

Another index of the economic status of the county was obtained from the Sims Socio-Economic Scale, which was administered to representative

* Bean estimates that approximately 95% of the settlers of this county were of British descent. [See Bean, Robert Bennett. The Peopling of Virginia, Boston, Chapman and Grimes Inc. 1938 (p. 146).]

samples consisting of 87 White and 72 Negro children used in this investigation. The resulting scores indicate the lowest social status yet recorded in the United States for either White or Negro groups. The reason why the averages are below those recorded for Alabama may be due to the fact that the Alabama results were obtained from sixth grade students, while the results of this study were based on an age range from 6.0 through 12.9 years. Sixth grade students undeniably constitute a select sample, since many children drop out of school before they reach the sixth grade.

The White and Negro distributions of socio-economic scores show a heavy piling up of scores at the lower end of both distributions. In spite of enormous overlapping, the White range is almost double that of the Negro range.

* * *

[A detailed discussion of educational provisions, socio-economic data, daily activities of the children, and so on, must be omitted. The following conclusion seems well-documented, however.]

Relative to the background of the subjects, evidence has been summarized from marginal population studies, tax reports, teachers' salaries, "Sims Socio-Economic Scale," and a "Daily Life of the Child" questionnaire. It may be concluded that there is a very low economic level for both the White and the Negro groups, with a distinct advantage for the White group in every instance except in the external appearance of unconsolidated rural schools.

Procedure

SELECTION OF SUBJECTS

For this investigation of intelligence in the rural South, nine White and nine Negro schools were chosen on the basis of their wide distribution throughout the county. Each pair of White and Negro schools was situated in the same locality, and matched in respect to ratio of pupils to teachers. Eight of the nine pairs were unconsolidated schools having only one or two teachers, except in one instance where there were three teachers. The pair of consolidated schools was situated at approximately the center of the county, in a village of 473 inhabitants.

In these selected schools all the children included within the age range of 6.0 through 12.9 years were to take part in this investigation. The total number of cases involved included 521 Whites and 432 Negroes. The Negroes represented 45% of the combined samples—approximately the same as the proportion of Negro children to White children in the county as a whole, namely 49%.

MATERIALS EMPLOYED

1. "Kuhlmann-Anderson Group Tests" (grades 1 through 8).
2. Terman's "Stanford Revision of the Binet-Simon Intelligence Test." (1916 edition.)
3. Grace Arthur's "Point Scale of Performance Tests" (a derivative of the Pintner Paterson Performance Scale).
4. Sims Socio-Economic Scale.

METHOD OF COLLECTING DATA

During the fall term of 1935 Kuhlmann-Anderson Group Tests were administered to all children between the ages of 6 and 13 in the nine pairs of selected schools.

During the spring term of 1936, representative samples of 87 Whites and 72 Negroes were selected from the two original groups. The selection was made on the basis of I.Q. distribution on the Kuhlmann-Anderson Group Tests. For example, all the children in a single school who took the Kuhlmann-Anderson Group Test during the fall term were ranked in order of their I.Q.'s. From this ranking, a representative sample of 20% of the total group was taken by selecting the child at each end of the distribution, and every fifth child between the two extremes. These selected samples, White and Negro, were to be retested on Binet, the Grace Arthur Performance Scale, and the Sims Socio-Economic Scale.

The average chronological age of the total White group is 9 years 6 months; the Negro average is 9 years 9 months. This difference is exactly the same as the difference in average age of enrollment of the two groups. In the case of the selected samples the White average is lowered one month, while the Negro average remains constant.

* * *

TREATMENT OF DATA

The results of this investigation are analyzed under the headings below, in the chapters that follow:

I. White and Negro Group Differences
II. Comparison of the Three Intelligence Tests
III. Subtest Analysis
IV. Item Analysis

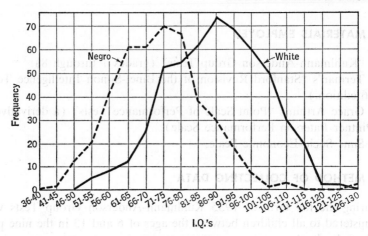

Figure 1. Comparison of 521 Whites and 432 Negroes on the Kuhlmann-Anderson Group Test.

Negro-White Difference

The statistical results from the administration of the Kuhlmann-Anderson Group Tests to the total White and Negro samples are outlined below (see also Figure 1):

Kuhlmann-Anderson

(group intelligence test)

	White	*Negro*
Number of Cases	521	432
Range of I.Q. Scores	129 − 52 = 77	130 − 39 = 91
Average I.Q. Score.................	88.10	71.80
Median I.Q. Score	88.48	71.64
Standard Deviation	13.60	12.43
Skewness*	−.31	+.49

Range from 130 to 51 includes 100% of the Whites and 97% of the Negroes.

Critical ratio between Negro and White averages = 19.31. Ten percent of the Negroes equal or surpass the White Median.

The Kuhlmann-Anderson Tests give the average White child of this study an I.Q. of 88, while the average Negro child has an I.Q. of 72. Thus the Whites are rated as "dull" in relation to the norm of the United States; and the Negroes as borderline. The difference between the White and Negro averages is statistically significant in spite of the considerable overlap. A range from 130 through 51 includes 100% of the Whites and 97% of the Negroes. The highest Negro score of 130, at 4.70 sigma of the Negro

* The formula used to measure skewness was $Sk. = \dfrac{P_{90} + P_{10}}{2} - P_{50}$. (P=percentile.)

distribution, is one point higher than the highest White score of 3.0 sigma of the White distribution. The White median is equalled or surpassed by 10% of the Negroes.

To show that the Negro-White differences in the case of the selected samples are practically the same as those of the total White and Negro groups from which they were chosen, the results of the Kuhlmann-Anderson tests administered to the selected sample are outlined below:

Kuhlmann-Anderson
(group intelligence test)
Sample Group

	White	Negro
Number of Cases	87	72
Range of I.Q. Scores	129 − 52 = 77	130 − 39 = 91
Average I.Q. Score	88.23	73.49
Median I.Q. Score	89.25	72.64
Standard Deviation	16.61	15.79
Skewness	−1.06	+1.59

Range from 130 to 51 includes 100% of the Whites and 93% of the Negroes.

Critical ratio between Negro and White averages = 5.72. Seventeen percent of the Negroes equal or surpass the White Median.

The White average remains constant, while the Negro average is raised 1 point. The White average is still significantly higher than the Negro average. The ranges remain constant, but overlap is somewhat increased; the White median is equalled or surpassed by 17% instead of 10% of the Negroes.

The Binet test results are listed below:

Binet
(individual intelligence test)
Sample Group

	White	Negro
Number of Cases	87	72
Range of I.Q. Scores	130 − 51 = 79	127 − 50 = 77
Average I.Q. Score	90.07	76.33
Median I.Q. Score	90.00	74.17
Standard Deviation	15.66	14.22
Skewness	−.75	+3.73

Range from 130 to 51 includes 100% of the Whites and 99% of the Negroes.

Critical ratio between Negro and White averages = 5.79. Seventeen percent of the Negroes equal or surpass the White Median.

The Stanford Binet Test raises the average White I.Q. 2 points to 90, and the average Negro score 3 points to 76. The White average is 14 points higher than the Negro average, and statistically significant. Again, as in the Kuhlmann-Anderson group tests, the ranges of the White and the Negro scores are almost identical, with 17% of the Negroes equalling or surpassing the White median.

The results of the Grace Arthur Performance Scale are summarized below:

Grace Arthur
(performance test)
Sample Group

	White	Negro
Number of Cases	87	72
Range of I.Q. Scores	173 − 46 = 127	116 − 48 = 68
Average I.Q. Score	94.21	77.10
Median I.Q. Score	93.25	74.73
Standard Deviation	22.11	14.08
Skewness	−2.40	+2.52

Range from 120 to 46 includes 92% of the Whites and 100% of the Negroes.

Critical ratio between Negro and White averages = 5.91. Eleven percent of the Negroes equal or surpass the White Median.

The Grace Arthur Performance Scale yields the highest I.Q.'s of the three intelligence tests, but the difference is only slight. The average White score is 94, only 4 points higher than the score of the Binet test; and the average Negro score is 77, only 1 point higher than that of the Binet test. As in the case of the other two intelligence tests, the difference between the White and the Negro groups is statistically significant. Owing to a few extremely high scores in the White distribution, the White and the Negro ranges are not nearly so similar as they are for Kuhlmann-Anderson and Binet. A range from 120 through 46, however, includes 92% of the White and 100% of the Negroes; and 11% of the Negroes equal or surpass the median of the Whites.

A comparison of the White and the Negro distribution of scores on the Sims Socio-Economic Scale yields the following results (see also Figure 2):

Sims Socio-Economic Scale
Sample Group

	White	Negro
Number of Cases	87	72
Range of Soc. Status Scores	30 − 1 = 29	18 − 1 = 17
Average Soc. Status Score	7.52	4.39
Median Soc. Status Score	6.00	3.50
*Standard Deviation	5.71	2.69
*Skewness	+2.63	+1.14

Range from 18 to 1 includes 95% of the Whites and 100% of the Negroes.

Critical ratio between Negro and White averages =4.54. Twenty-one per cent of the Negroes equal or surpass the White median.

* This measure cannot be considered in its usual sense, because we cannot assume that social status is distributed according to the normal curve.

When the White and the Negro groups are compared on the Sims Socio-Economic Scale, it is seen that there is a significant difference in social status between them. However, the meaning of this measure is unknown since the formula used is based on the normal distribution curve which cannot be assumed in relation to social status. From an inspection of the White and Negro distribution of socio-economic scores it can be seen that the two groups show greater similarity on this scale than on the three intelligence tests. The range from 18 through 1 includes 95% of the Whites and 100% of the Negroes. The White and the Negro modes fall on the same interval; and 21% of the Negroes equal or surpass the White median. Although the socio-economic scores are piled up at the lower end of the scale all cases are above zero.

Correlations between social status and intelligence test scores appear in Table I:

TABLE I

	White	Negro
Correlation K.A. and Soc. Status	.55 ± .05	.50 ± .06
Correlation Binet and Soc. Status	.57 ± .05	.51 ± .06
Correlation G.A. and Soc. Status	.46 ± .06	.44 ± .06
Correlation av. IQ and Soc. Status	.52 ± .05	.52 ± .06

The correlations for both groups range from .44 to .57, being slightly higher for the Whites in most instances.

Since there is a considerable difference between the White and the Negro average social status, it seemed advisable to compare the intelligence quotients of a White and a Negro group that had been equated or matched according to their Sims Socio-Economic Scores. The method of equating the White and the Negro group was as follows: First all of the White cases receiving socio-economic scores above the Negro range were eliminated. The remaining White and Negro cases were then paired on the basis of their socio-economic scores. No arbitrary selections were made, for where there were two or more children of the same socio-economic status to be matched with one child of the other group, the average of their intelligence quotients was used rather than the I.Q. of any one of them. The White and the Negro equated groups may be compared in the following outline of their I.Q. distributions on each of the three intelligence tests:

When the White and the Negro equated samples are compared on the three intelligence tests, the following effects are noted. The White averages are lowered from 4 to 5 points; the Negro averages remain constant. Nevertheless, the differences remain statistically significant, with all three critical ratios slightly over 3. In the case of the Whites the upper ranges are lowered: the Kuhlmann-Anderson test 14 points, the Binet test 5 points.

Kuhlmann-Anderson
Equated Group

	White	Negro
Number of Cases	49	49
Range of IQ Scores	$115 - 51 = 64$	$130 - 41 = 89$
Average IQ Score	83.31	73.20
Median IQ Score	84.00	72.09
Standard Deviation	14.76	15.29
Skewness	-1.0	$+3.85$

Range from 115 to 51 includes 100% of the Whites and 94% of the Negroes.

Critical ratio between White and Negro averages = 3.33. Twenty percent of the Negroes equal or surpass the White Median.

Binet
Equated Group

	White	Negro
Number of Cases	49	49
Range of IQ Scores	$125 - 51 = 74$	$130 - 51 = 79$
Average IQ Score	85.76	76.88
Median IQ Score	86.89	74.67
Standard Deviation	13.85	14.30
Skewness	-2.45	$+3.33$

Range from 125 to 51 includes 100% of the Whites and 98% of the Negroes.

Critical ratio between Negro and White averages = 3.12. Twenty-one percent of the Negroes equal or surpass the White Median.

Grace Arthur
Equated Group

	White	Negro
Number of Cases	49	49
Range of IQ Scores	$140 - 46 = 94$	$120 - 51 = 69$
Average IQ Score	89.02	76.98
Median IQ Score	89.43	75.86
Standard Deviation	18.15	13.25
Skewness	$-.99$	$-.23$

Range from 120 to 51 includes 94% of the Whites and 100% of the Negroes.

Critical ratio between White and Negro averages = 3.75. Fifteen percent of the Negroes equal or surpass the White Median.

and the Grace Arthur Scale 33 points; but the Negro ranges remain constant. The percentage of Negroes equalling or surpassing the White median is naturally somewhat increased in the case of the equated groups. On the Kuhlmann-Anderson tests the percentage is raised from 17 to 20, on the Binet scale from 17 to 21, and on the Grace Arthur Scale from 11 to 15.

Although the White and the Negro samples equated for social status still show statistically significant differences in I.Q. on each of the three intelligence tests, this fact cannot be considered proof of the superiority of

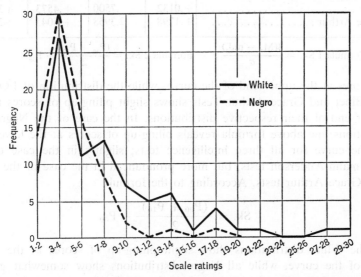

Figure 2. Comparison of 87 Whites and 72 Negroes on the Sims Socio-Economic Scale.

the White group, since the equation of the two groups is not entirely valid. The social status graph (Figure 2) clearly indicates the piling up of both White and Negro scores at the lower limit of the socio-economic scale. This automatically permits two children of different status to be matched, because the scale does not discriminate between individuals of low socio-economic status.

Before closing the discussion of Negro-White differences on the three intelligence tests, attention should be called to the skewness in the White and Negro distributions.

Table II gives the relative skewness of the White and Negro I.Q. distributions on the three intelligence tests, as measured by two formulas computed from different reference points in the distribution.

According to the formula $Sk. = \dfrac{3 \ (M. - md.)}{\sigma}$ the White distribution of I.Q.'s on the Kuhlmann-Anderson Group Tests shows slight piling-up

TABLE II
Relative Skewness of IQ Distributions on the Three Intelligence Tests

Formula*	White		Negro	
	1	2	1	2
Kuhlmann-Anderson (total)	−.0846	− .3059	+.0371	+ .4908
Kuhlmann-Anderson (sample) ...	−.1843	−1.0625	+.1602	+1.5905
Binet	+.0132	− .7500	+.4573	+3.7333
Grace Arthur	+.1298	−2.3958	+.5043	+2.5192

$$* \text{ Formula 1 Sk.} = \frac{3(\text{M.} - \text{md.})}{\sigma}; \quad \text{Formula 2 Sk.} = \frac{(P_{90} + P_{10})}{2} - P_{50}.$$

of scores at the upper end of the curve; while the distribution of I.Q.'s on the Binet and Grace Arthur Tests shows slight piling-up of scores at the lower end of their respective distributions. In the case of the Negro distributions, the above formula reveals piling-up of scores at the lower end of the curve for all three intelligence tests; slightly in the case of the Kuhlmann-Anderson tests, but more pronounced in the case of the Binet and Grace Arthur tests. According to the formula

$$\text{Sk.} = \frac{(P_{90} + P_{10})}{2} - P_{50}$$

all the White distributions show slight piling-up of scores at the upper end of the curve, while all Negro distributions show somewhat greater piling-up of scores at the lower ends of the distributions.

In view of the contradictory indications between the two formulas in regard to the skewness of two out of three of the distributions of White I.Q.'s, we can hardly say that the White I.Q.'s are skewed in either direction. On the other hand, both formulas agree in indicating that the Negro I.Q. scores are piled up at the lower end of the curve in the case of each of the three intelligence tests. This consistent positive skewness in the Negro distribution of I.Q.'s suggests "selective migration" as a possible explanation for the significant differences between the White and the Negro groups found in this investigation. The fact that Klineberg (9) found the school grades of Negro children who remained in New Orleans just as high as the school grades of Negro children who went North does not challenge the results of this study because his results concerning the mental ability of migrating and nonmigrating groups were based on an urban population while the results of this study are based on a rural population.

The fact that the White and the Negro distributions tend to be skewed in opposite directions makes it impossible to use the piling-up of scores at the lower end of the Sims Socio-Economic Scale (which is more pronounced in the case of the Whites) as an explanation of the piling-up of scores at the lower end of the Negro I.Q. distributions.

Besides the comparison of the White and the Negro groups on each of the three intelligence tests, the total White and Negro groups of 521 and 432 cases respectively were divided into 14 age groups between the limits of 6.0 and 12.9 years; and the average Kuhlmann-Anderson intelligence quotient was computed for each age level. This analysis was undertaken in order to see if there was a cumulative effect of environment on the I.Q.'s of either White or Negro children.

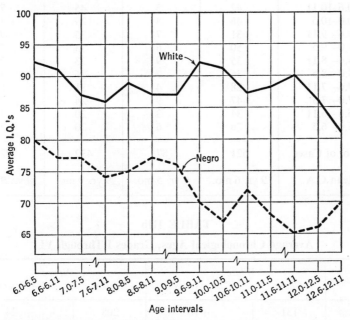

Figure 3. Comparison of the Average I.Q. at 14 age intervals of White and Negro children between the ages of 6 and 13 based on the Kuhlmann-Anderson I.Q. scores of 521 Whites and 432 Negroes.

The results (see Figure 3) show considerable fluctuation with a general lowering trend. The final White loss is 11 points; and the final Negro loss, 10 points. The loss of 10 points in I.Q. is not at all significant, since it is approximately the decline expected in I.Q.'s around 80. It is worth noting that the Negro decline is no greater than the White decline. This study does not support the results obtained by Murdock, Wells, Sunne, and Garth, all of which indicate an increasing difference between White and Negro scores with increase in chronological age. On the other hand, they are in agreement with the results obtained by H. E. Jones in the North, which show no general adverse cummulative effect of environment upon rural test performance.

TABLE IIIa
Age Distributions

Age groups	White Total group	White Sample group	Negro Total group	Negro Sample group
12.6–12.11	27	1	30	1
12.0–12.5	44	10	43	9
11.6–11.11	36	7	23	5
11.0–11.5	39	5	40	9
10.6–10.11	42	5	45	7
10.0–10.5	46	8	29	3
9.6– 9.11	31	7	35	9
9.0– 9.5	50	6	33	7
8.6– 8.11	35	9	23	2
8.0– 8.5	36	7	36	3
7.6– 7.11	28	4	31	5
7.0– 7.5	47	9	24	7
6.6– 6.11	34	3	20	3
6.0– 6.5	26	6	20	2
No. of Cases	521	87	432	72
Mean C.A.	9 yr. 6 mo.	9 yr. 5 mo.	9 yr. 9 mo.	9 yr. 9 mo.

TABLE IIIb
Average Chronological Ages, Grades I Through VI

Grade	White Cases	White C.A. excess	Negro Cases	Negro C.A. excess
1	131	+10	208	+ 24
2	91	+16	66	+ 30
3	92	+14	68	+ 27
4	77	+18	54	+ 23
5	94	+12	36	+ 16
6	48	+ 5	11	+ 6
	6 75		6 126	
	+12½ mo.		+ 21 mo.	

Table IIIa, gives the age distributions for the White and Negro total and selected samples. The average chronological age, and average mental age on the Kuhlmann-Anderson group tests, for each grade, I through VI, are given in tables IIIb, c. This analysis was made in order to reveal the relative retardation in school of the White and the Negro groups; and to determine the mental level of each grade for both groups.

TABLE IIIc
Average Mental Ages, Grades I Through VI

Grade	White		Negro	
	Cases	M.A. deficit	Cases	M.A. deficit
1	130	− 6	209	− 9
2	92	− 6	66	− 9
3	92	− 0	68	−11
4	78	+ 1	54	−18
5	94	− 4	36	−16
6	48	− 0	11	−15
	6	15	6	78
		− 2½ mo.		−13 mo.

The average retardation of the White group is about one year; the average retardation of the Negro group is almost two years. In spite of the fact that the children are over-age, the average mental age is 2½ months below normal for the White grades, and 13 months below for the Negro grades.

The Negro selected sample of 72 cases was also rated, by the experimenter, on a 5 point color scale; the findings indicated only four categories: light brown, brown, dark brown, and black. Since there were only two light brown, and two black cases, the Negro children were divided into only two groups, a light group of 23 cases, and a dark group of 49 cases. A comparison of the combined I.Q.'s on the three intelligence tests of the light and the dark Negroes yielded the following results:

Average of Scores on the Three Intelligence Tests

	Light group	Dark group
Number of Cases	23	49
Range of IQ Scores	102 − 63 = 39	122 − 46 = 76
Average of IQ Score	78.17	74.35
Median of IQ Score	76.00	73.00
Standard Deviation	9.61	14.59

Range from 105 to 61 includes 100% of the light group and 84% of the dark group.

Critical ratio between light and dark Negroes averages = 1.32. Forty-one percent of the dark Negroes equal or surpass the Median of the light Negroes.

The average I.Q. on the three intelligence tests for the light group is 78; and the average I.Q. for the dark group is 74. There are 90 chances out of 100 that a true difference exists between these two groups. Even this degree of reliability is remarkable in view of the fact that the range of the dark group completely envelops the range of the light group, with 41% of the dark group equalling or surpassing the median of the light group. It is also worth noting that the brightest Negro child is a member of the dark group.

Before closing the discussion of the Negro-White differences in I.Q. on the three intelligence tests, the subject of rapport should be mentioned. In the opinion of the experimenter rapport, on the whole, was excellent. The examiner cannot recall a single instance of emotional disturbance among the Negro children.

SUMMARY

The most important findings from the comparison of White and Negro groups on the three intelligence tests may be summed up as follows:

1. All three tests rate both Whites and Negroes below the average of the United States. These averages are probably lowered by the fact that very few, if any, of either the White or the Negro children are sent to feebleminded institutions, regardless of how defective they may be.

2. All three tests show significant differences between the White and the Negro groups, including the samples equated for social status. Owing to the inadequacy of the Sims scale, however, this equation cannot be considered entirely valid.

3. From 6 through 12 years of age, the Negroes show no greater decline in I.Q. than the Whites.

Comparison of the Three Intelligence Tests

In this chapter a statistical comparison will be made of the results from the administration of the three types of intelligence tests to the same group of children, the two racial groups being treated separately.

The statistical results from the comparison of the selected samples with the total groups from which they were chosen may be outlined as follows:

Kuhlmann-Anderson (total group)

vs.

Kuhlmann-Anderson (sample group)

	White	*Negro*
Range K.A. (t)	129 − 52 = 77	130 − 39 = 91
Range K.A. (s)	129 − 52 = 77	130 − 39 = 91
Average K.A. (t)	88.10	71.80
Average K.A. (s)	88.23	73.49
Critical ratio	.0714	.8642
Percent of (t) equal or surpass median of (s)	48%	47%

The above outline indicates that the selected samples of 87 Whites and 72 Negroes are quite representative of the total groups of 521 Whites and 432 Negroes. The ranges of the sample groups are identical with the ranges of the total groups, and 48% of the White total, and 47% of the Negro total equal or surpass the medians of their respective sample groups. There is less than 1 point difference between the average I.Q.'s of the sample and the total White group, and only 1.69 points difference between the average I.Q.'s of the sample and the total Negro groups. Apparently, both the White and the Negro selected samples chosen for individual tests on the Binet and the Grace Arthur tests are quite typical of the total White and Negro groups.

The Kuhlmann-Anderson and the Binet intelligence tests yield very similar results in the case of both Whites and Negroes, as can be seen in the following outline (see also Figures 4 and 5).

Kuhlmann-Anderson vs. Binet

	White	Negro
Range K.A.	$129 - 52 = 77$	$130 - 39 = 91$
Range B.	$130 - 51 = 79$	$127 - 50 = 77$
Average K.A.	88.23	73.49
Average B.	90.07	76.33
Critical ratio	.7515	1.1371
Percent of K.A. equal or surpass median of B.	48%	44%
* Correlation K.A. and B.	.84 ± .02	.86 ± .02

* The formula used to compute correlation was

$$r = \frac{\dfrac{\Sigma x'y'}{N} - c_x c_y}{\sigma_x \sigma_y}$$

The Binet average for the Whites is only 2 points higher than that of the Kuhlmann-Anderson tests; and in the case of the Negroes it is 3 points higher. The range of scores for the Whites is practically identical on the two tests; there is a total difference of only 2 points in I.Q. In the case of the Negroes, the Binet test shows a tendency to raise low I.Q. scores. The lowest Kuhlmann-Anderson score is 39 compared with 50 for Binet. The close resemblance between White Binet and Kuhlmann-Anderson scores is further exemplified by the fact that 48% of the Kuhlmann-Anderson scores equal or surpass the median on Binet. The correlation between the two tests is .84, ± .02. In the case of the Negroes the overlapping of the Binet and the Kuhlmann-Anderson tests is somewhat less; 44% of the Kuhlmann-Anderson scores are equal to or greater than the Binet median. The two tests, however, show a slightly closer agreement in rating the Negro children; the correlation is .86, ± .02, which is 2 points higher than the correlation between the two tests for the Whites.

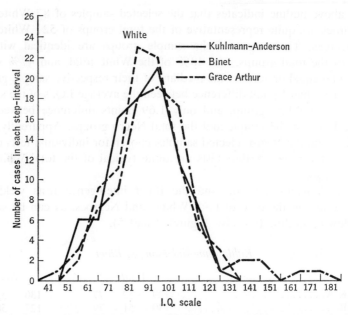

Figure 4. Comparison of I.Q.'s on the Kuhlmann-Anderson group test, the Binet individual test, and Grace Arthur performance scale. The curves are based on the scores obtained by the selected sample of 87 Whites.

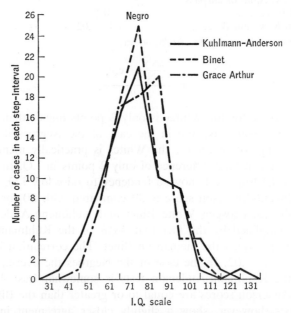

Figure 5. Comparison of I.Q.'s on the Kuhlmann-Anderson group test, the Binet individual test, and the Grace Arthur performance scale. The curves are based on the scores obtained by the selected sample of 72 Negroes.

The results on the Grace Arthur Performance Scale differ considerably from the results on the other two intelligence tests, as can be seen in the following outline of the statistical comparison of the Grace Arthur test with the Binet and Kuhlmann-Anderson tests (see also Figures 4 and 5):

Kuhlmann-Anderson vs. Grace Arthur

	White	Negro
Range K.A.	$129 - 52 = 77$	$130 - 39 = 91$
Range G.A.	$173 - 46 = 127$	$116 - 48 = 68$
Average K.A.	88.23	73.49
Average G.A.	94.21	77.10
Critical ratio	2.0159	1.4483
Percent of K.A. equal or surpass median of G.A.	41%	42%
Correlation K.A. and G.A.	$.65 \pm .04$	$.72 \pm .04$

Grace Arthur vs. Binet

	White	Negro
Range G.A.	$173 - 46 = 127$	$116 - 48 = 68$
Range B.	$130 - 51 = 79$	$127 - 50 = 77$
Average G.A.	94.21	77.10
Average B.	90.07	76.33
Critical ratio	1.4244	.3238
Percent of B. equal or surpass median of G.A.	39%	48%
Correlation G.A. and B.	$.63 \pm .04$	$.71 \pm .04$

The average White I.Q. on the Grace Arthur test is 94, that is, 6 points higher than the Kuhlmann-Anderson test and 4 points higher than the Binet average. There are 98 chances out of 100 that the difference between the results on the Kuhlmann-Anderson and the Grace Arthur Scale is greater than zero; and there are 92 chances out of 100 that the difference between the Binet and Grace Arthur tests is greater than zero. In the case of the Negro group, the differences between the Grace Arthur and the other two intelligence tests are less pronounced. The Grace Arthur average is 4 points higher than the Kuhlmann-Anderson and 1 point higher than the Binet average.

The chief result of the performance test, in the case of the Whites, is to extend the range, slightly at the lower end, and enormously in a few cases at the upper end. Its chief result in the case of the Negroes is to narrow the range, slightly at the lower end, and considerably at the upper end. The performance test when compared with the written and verbal tests increases the average I.Q. of the Whites more than the average I.Q. of the Negroes. In as much as the performance scale is generally considered to be less influenced by environmental factors than written and verbal tests, the Whites seem to benefit from the reduction of these factors more than the Negroes. The correlation between the performance and the group test is 65, ± .04 for the Whites, and 72, ± .04 for the Negroes; the correlation between the performance test and the individual test is 63, ± .04 for the Whites and 71, ± .04 for the Negroes. These correlations between the performance test and the written and verbal tests are considerably less than the correlation between the written and the verbal tests themselves, which was 84 in the case of the White group, and 86 in the case of the Negro group.

SUMMARY

The results from the comparison of the three intelligence tests may be summed up by saying that none of the three intelligence tests show statistically significant differences among themselves; however, there are 98 and 93 chances out of 100 that the respective White and Negro averages are lower on the Kuhlmann-Anderson than on the Grace Arthur tests.

*   *   *

[At this point the author gives a detailed (63-page) examination of the items and subtests on the three scales in an effort to find the locus of the differences manifested between the Negro and white groups and between both of these groups and the standardization samples. Her findings are summarized below.]

*   *   *

Summary and Conclusions

The purpose of this study was the localization of factors which are responsible for the subnormal intelligence quotients in the rural South, and which differentiate between the White and the Negro groups. The method employed was a statistical and qualitative analysis of scores on the "Kuhlmann-Anderson Group Tests," the "Binet Individual Test," the "Grace Arthur Performance Scale," and their component parts.

The group results of this study are in agreement with previous studies in this field. Rural populations are rated lower than urban populations on intelligence tests; and Negroes are related below Whites. . . . The earlier investigators tended to emphasize heredity, while the more recent investigators tend to emphasize environment, as the determining factor in this problem. At this point Tanser's study should be mentioned. This is an investigation of the intelligence quotients of White and Negro urban and rural children in Kent County, Ontario. Tanser's results differ from others in this field in that he finds rural Negroes rate higher than urban Negroes. In interpreting his results Tanser reverts to the opinion of the earlier investigators and places major emphasis on heredity to explain his Negro-White differences in intelligence quotients. In relation to his interpretation, attention should be called to the fact that the average intelligence quotient of his Negro group is within the lower limit of the normal range in I.Q. of 90-110; while the average intelligence quotient of the White group is slightly above the mean of the normal range. It is probably fair to say that although the schools are identical for Tanser's White and Negro groups, the environmental factor of the home has not yet been adequately controlled.

The present study differs from previous studies mainly in the method of analyzing data. It offers an approach to the problem of measuring the relative difficulty of subtests and items on three types of intelligence tests, in order to locate specific difficulties, and to determine whether the "new situation" or the "information" type of subtest is more difficult for the White and Negro rural children in the South.

The results of this study may be summarized as follows:

1. All three intelligence tests rate both the White and the Negro children in this investigation below the average of the United States. All three tests show significant differences between the White and the Negro groups.

2. In the attempt to explain these results, we turn first to the Sims Socio-Economic Scale. The findings here indicate the lowest social status yet reported on this scale for Whites and Negroes in the United States. The White and Negro distributions of socio-economic scores indicate that the White and Negro modes fall on the same interval in spite of the fact that the White range is almost twice that of the Negro range.

3. When a White and a Negro group were equated on the Sims Socio-Economic Scale, the difference between their average I.Q.'s was still statistically significant. This, however, cannot be considered proof of the innate inferiority of the Negro sample. One obvious difficulty is that the equation of the two groups was not entirely valid, due to the inadequacy of the Sims scale, which failed to discriminate between individuals at the lower range of the scale.

4. Although there is a considerable difference in socio-economic status between the White and Negro groups, it is not a sufficient explanation of the Negro-White difference in intelligence quotients, since the two groups resemble each other more closely in social status than in intelligence quotients. In seeking further explanation for the Negro-White differences, it becomes evident that all the Negro I.Q. distributions are positively skewed, *i.e.,* scores piled up at the lower end of the range, while the evidence of skewness in the White I.Q. distributions is contradictory. This consistent positive skewness in the Negro distributions suggests the possibility of "selective migration" as one of the factors responsible for the Negro-White difference in I.Q. This hypothesis does not force us to assume that the more intelligent Negroes migrate to the North, for they may find their way into Southern cities, owing to the difficulty of obtaining a livelihood from

agriculture in the rural South. The absence of skewness as evidence of "selective migration" in the White group may be due to the fact that the process is more gradual in their case, which would permit the curve to become normal at a lower range. This more gradual migration on the part of the Whites could be explained by the advantageous position they hold in the social order. On the other hand it may imply that there is no "selective migration" in the case of the White group. Or, in other words, that the subnormal I.Q.'s of the White group are not to be explained on the basis of the hereditary factor, but are the result of social factors alone.

5. When the results from the three intelligence tests on the same group of children are compared, no significant differences are obtained. The performance test did not give significantly higher ratings to Southern rural children.

6. The analysis of Kuhlmann-Anderson subtests reveals that the "new situation" type of test is just as difficult as other types of subtests. The analysis of Binet subtests fails to indicate that those tests which are more obviously influenced by specific environmental factors are more difficult than those less obviously influenced by such factors. And finally, the analysis of the Grace Arthur subtests reveals that the "speed" tests are relatively easier for both Whites and Negroes than the more discriminative "power" tests.

7. The analysis of items on the Kuhlmann-Anderson and Binet subtests discloses specific environmental handicaps and advantages; but fails to indicate that these specific environmental factors are responsible for the differences in difficulty between subtests. It is interesting to note that H. E. Jones also finds that the environmental handicap of rural children in the North manifests itself by the large number of failures on specific subtests, but is not a sufficient explanation for the subnormal I.Q.'s on the Binet Intelligence Test. In the present study, whether the differences in difficulty between subtests and between items be due to heredity or environmental factors, the consistently high correlations between the White and Negro groups indicate that some of the same factors are operative in both groups.

The fact that the "new situation" type of subtest is just as difficult as other types of subtests, and that the decline in I.Q. with the increasing age of the child is no greater for either the Whites or the Negroes than should be expected for I.Q.'s of this level, suggests that the hereditary factor is partly responsible for the low intelligence quotients of rural children in the South. On the other hand the experimenter wishes to emphasize the fact that the environmental factor should not be minimized. The 10 points deficiency in I.Q. of the Whites might be entirely accounted for on the basis of environmental factors, since many studies of individual cases show increases of at least 10 points when transferred from unfavorable to favorable environments. Although the Negro-White difference in average I.Q. may seem too great to be explained on the basis of environmental factors alone, we must not forget that the subtle depressing influence of a poor environment cannot be estimated by the localization of specific environmental handicaps in certain subtests; nor can it be measured by objective scales such as the "Sims Socio-Economic Score Card"; and yet this depressing influence of a poor environment is bound to have some detrimental effect on a child's performance on intelligence tests.

CONCLUSIONS

Since the White and Negro groups of this study resemble each other more closely in regard to their distributions of social status scores than in regard to their distributions of I.Q. scores, the investigator is inclined to believe that there is an innate difference between the particular White and Negro groups studied. However, the fact that all the Negro I.Q. distributions, including the sample of 432 cases, are positively skewed with the highest Negro score as high as the highest White score on both Kuhlmann-Anderson and Binet, suggests "selective migration" and possible racial equality. In any event the positive skewness of the Negro I.Q. distributions prevents this study from being used as evidence of the superiority of the White race to the Negro race.

The comparison of the three intelligence tests and the analysis of their subtests failed to show significant differences in favor of the "new situation" test. These results question the psychologists' attempt to avoid the environmental factor in intelligence tests by eliminating educational items and substituting the "new situation" type of test; and force the acceptance of either of two conclusions:

a. The "new situation" test is influenced by environmental factors, and hence does not increase the validity of intelligence tests, or

b. Children in the rural South are innately inferior in respect to intelligence.

Through the 1930's a running battle took place on the nature-nurture controversy. In 1940 it erupted in a series of violent articles in the various journals and in the Thirty-ninth Yearbook of the National Society for the Study of Education, Intelligence: Its Nature and Nurture. Unfortunately, many of the articles were too extensive to be reproduced here and permission could not be secured to publish the Yearbook articles. The following article, however, gives some of the intensive flavor of the dispute and an interesting example of the important phenomenon of regression in psychometrics. It emphasizes the need for controls and for a thorough understanding of the statistics of repeated measurements.

The Relative Potency of the Nursery School and the
Statistical Laboratory in Boosting the IQ*

FLORENCE L. GOODENOUGH

and KATHARINE M. MAURER

1940

In 1925 Woolley published an article purporting to show that attendance at the Merrill-Palmer Nursery School brought about very marked changes in the intelligence test scores of young children. These changes were not paralleled by the results of retests given to other children of comparable age who were on the waiting list. Although the study was based upon a relatively small number of cases, and such factors as differential acquaintance with the examiners or with materials and tasks similar to those used in the tests were not controlled, it, nevertheless, aroused much interest among those concerned with problems of mental growth. However, the results of later studies from other institutions yielded inconsistent results. A few seemed to lend more or less support to the Merrill-Palmer findings; others failed to show any measurable effect of nursery-school experience. Whether or not the differences could be attributed to the particular tests used for measurement—in some studies the 1916 Stanford-Binet was used, in others the 1922 Kuhlmann-Binet, and in still others the Merrill-Palmer Performance Scale—to special conditions of testing such as better rapport on the part of children who had attended nursery school or bias on the part of examiners who knew to which group the individual children belonged, or to differences in the educational regimes of the various schools could not be determined.

* Reprinted from *The Journal of Educational Psychology* (1940), pp. 541-549, by permission of Dr. Maurer and Warwick and York, Inc.

In 1932 Wellman published the first of a long series of articles from the Child Welfare Research Station of the State University of Iowa that have been appearing in both scientific and popular journals since that date. These articles deal with the effect of environmental changes upon child intelligence. The environmental factors considered are of three general types: School environment, home environment, and institutional environment. Under school environment are included the nursery school, the elementary school and the high school. Home environment has been studied chiefly in terms of the development of children placed in foster homes. Two kinds of institutional environment have been studied. The first, which consisted of residence in an orphanage at Davenport, Iowa, was said to be very non-stimulating in its effect upon child intelligence, while the second, residence in an institution for the feebleminded under certain described conditions, was judged to be stimulating in its effect.

In this paper, no attempt will be made to criticize these studies in detail. Such criticism has already appeared elsewhere. This study is merely a concrete illustration of the misleading conclusions that have resulted from a statistical practice that was begun in Wellman's 1932 study and which the Iowa authors continue to employ in practically all their investigations in spite of the fact that its mathematical indefensibility has been repeatedly pointed out. The procedure consists of classifying subjects on the basis of the intelligence quotients earned on the first test given and computing the mean change in intelligence quotient from initial to final testing for each of these groups separately. It is obvious that when this is done, statistical regression due to errors of measurement renders it mathematically certain that unless other factors are operating to obscure the results, the cases originally testing high will appear to lose and those originally testing low will appear to gain, since, owing to the fallibility of the measuring instrument, chance as well as true ability will play a part in determining the original grouping. When the chance errors are reassorted at the time of the second test, each group will "regress" toward its own true mean with the result that those initially at the upper extremes, whose position was determined in part by real ability and in part by good luck, will appear to lose while those who, for analogous reasons, were initially at the lower extreme will appear to gain. The amount of this regressive gain or loss will be the algebraic mean of the chance error for each group. Because the element of chance plays a much greater part in the mental test scores of young children than of older ones, the magnitude of the regressive shift at the early ages will be correspondingly large. If, moreover, as frequently happens in the case of young children, there is a general tendency toward better rapport at the time of the final than at the time of the initial test, with the result that the final mean of the entire group is shifted upward, the regressive "losses" of the upper group may be largely or wholly masked. Their IQ's will then show little change while the "gain" of the lower groups will be much increased, since the regressive shift is always toward the mean of the second measurement.

The Iowa claims for the effect of environmental stimulation rest to a very great extent upon the statistical fallacy just described. It is true that in some of their studies a small but measurable change in the general mean in addition to the large regressive shift has appeared. Unfortunately, however, particularly in the articles that have appeared in popular journals and newspapers and in the condensed accounts of their experiments that have been published in the scientific and educational journals, the figures quoted have not been those derived from the population as a whole, but the highly misleading figures obtained from one or the other extreme. If the article in question deals with the stimulating effect of a "good" environment, the "gains" of the initially low group are quoted; if it deals with the depressing effect of a "poor" environment, the losses at the upper levels are stressed.

The reason given by the Iowa authors for continuing to follow this practice is their belief that the factor of statistical regression is at least not the main explanation for the tendency of the children initially testing low to gain and those initially testing high to lose. It must be agreed that their explanation has a certain amount of surface plausibility. Briefly expressed, the theory is that the direction and extent of the gain or loss is determined, not by the absolute character of the environment but by the contrast between a new environment and that to which an individual child had previously been subjected. However, this hypothesis would carry more weight had the authors seen fit to ascertain how much of the observed change in IQ could fairly be attributed to regression alone. If the change proved to be greater than this amount, then and only then would it be necessary to evolve a further hypothesis in order to explain the residual. Although the statistical procedure for making this computation is well known, it has not thus far been used in any of the studies from the Iowa laboratory. The authors continue to quote the uncorrected figures from whichever end of the distribution fits the current line of discussion.

It has occurred to us that a re-computation of our own data on the effect of nursery-school training as recently published in the *Thirty-Ninth Yearbook of the National Society for the Study of Education* might serve as a concrete example of the fallacy involved.

Tables I and II reproduced from the *Yearbook* article show that after periods of one and two years' attendance at the University of Minnesota nursery school, the intelligence quotients of children on the Minnesota Preschool Test show, on the average, a measurable increase, but that a similar increase also occurs in children of comparable age and social status who have not attended nursery school when tested after a corresponding period of time. In both cases the change is best ascribed to the effect of practice in taking the test. Further examination of these tables will show that children of superior home background, as indicated by the occupational

TABLE I

Changes in Mean IQ on the Minnesota Preschool Test
after One Year of Nursery-school Training Compared
with Changes for Non-nursery School Children after a
Year's Interval

Occupational group		Nursery			Non-nursery		
		Age at test 1			Age at test 1		
		0–29	30–59	Total	0–29	30–59	Total
1	No. Cases	5	26	31	9	23	32
	Test 1	108.5	114.4	113.5	108.6	114.2	112.7
	Test 2	117.5	120.2	119.7	117.5	119.5	118.9
II, III	No. Cases	6	22	28	22	42	64
	Test 1	109.2	111.4	110.9	103.2	107.6	106.1
	Test 2	115.8	113.4	113.6	105.5	111.9	109.7
IV, V, VI	No. Cases	15	10	25	9	17	26
	Test 1	108.5	106.5	107.7	108.1	103.7	105.2
	Test 2	113.8	110.0	112.3	109.2	110.7	110.2
Total	No. Cases	26	58	84	40	82	122
	Test 1	108.8	111.9	110.9	105.5	108.4	107.6
	Test 2	115.0	115.7	115.5	109.3	113.8	112.2

TABLE II

Changes in Mean IQ on the Minnesota Preschool Test
after Two Years of Nursery-school Training Compared
with Changes in Non-nursery School Children after an
Interval of Two Years

Occupational group		Nursery	Non-nursery
I	No. Cases	15	9
	Test 1	110.8	114.2
	Test 3	118.5	124.2
II, III	No. Cases	19	15
	Test 1	108.0	107.5
	Test 3	114.9	112.5
IV, V, VI	No. Cases	17	5
	Test 1	106.0	118.5
	Test 3	112.5	112.5
Total........................	No. Cases	51	29
	Test 1	108.9	111.5
	Test 3	115.1	116.1

level of the fathers, make a slightly greater gain from initial test to retest than is true of those whose fathers belong to the lower occupational classes. The difference is small, but it is apparent both for the nursery-school group after either one or two years' attendance at nursery school and for the control group without nursery school training when tested after corresponding intervals of time.

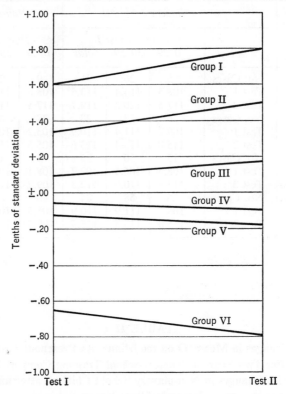

Figure 1. Changes in I.Q. from first to second test according to paternal occupation (expressed in tenths of a standard deviation from the mean of each distribution).

A similar pattern of differential change was observed in an earlier study by Goodenough in which the test used was the Kuhlmann-Binet (1922 Revision) and the retest was given after a mean interval of six weeks. The results are shown graphically in Figure 1.

In the report of the earlier study we considered a number of possible explanations for the differential type of change shown by the various socio-economic groups. The explanation favored at that time, as expressed in the following quotation, still seems to us the most plausible of any that we have been able to make.

"An additional factor to be considered is the comparative accuracy of the two tests. It is obvious that existent differences between groups will only be made apparent by means of a suitable measuring instrument, and that in so far as the results of the measurement are affected by chance, or by other factors unrelated to the general field of inquiry, both the means and standard deviations of the various subgroups will approach more closely to the general mean and standard deviation derived from the total distribution. If, therefore, factors which are unrelated to either variable enter into the results of one test more than the other, it is to be expected that, all other conditions being equal, that test which is less affected by adventitious factors will show the clearest separation between groups actually differing with regard to the trait in question. This is, of course, simply another way of saying that the correlation between two variables as obtained through the use of fallible measuring instruments can never, except by chance, be greater than that obtained through true measurement, and will ordinarily be appreciably lower. If an improvement in the measuring instrument used for one variable is brought about, either by an increase in reliability or in validity (with reference to the particular trait considered), the other variable remaining as before, an increase in the obtained correlation is to be expected. This increase in correlation involves a change in the slope of the regression line with a consequent increase in the absolute difference between the means of the positive and negative arrays. That such a difference in favor of the second of the two tests probably does exist in the case under consideration is indicated by three distinct sources of evidence: (a) The correlation between the ratings obtained for the first and second tests as compared to those on the second and third for fifty-six cases who were given a third test after an appreciably longer interval; (b) correlation between half-scales on each of the two tests corrected by the Spearman-Brown formula; and (c) the internal consistency of the separate items with the total, calculated by the method of biserial r. It will be shown that the second and third of these criteria show a distinct difference in favor of the second test, while the first shows no significant difference between the two in spite of the longer interval."

Table III, which is taken from the same study, shows the correlation between half-scales corrected for total length by means of the Spearman-Brown formula. These figures were derived from three hundred cases (fifty boys and fifty girls at each age) selected to constitute a representative sampling of the Minneapolis population. It will be noted that for each of the six groups considered, as well as for the total, the correlations are higher on the second test than on the first. This indicates that the second test yielded a more stable measure of child performance—or at least one that showed greater internal consistency—than the first. The explanation is probably to be found in better rapport at the time of the second examination with the consequent elimination of some of the adventitious factors not related to the purpose of the test.

TABLE III

Reliability of Total Scale as Determined by the Correlation between Half-scales Using the Spearman-Brown Formula

(Main Experimental Group)

	Age 2			Age 3			Age 4		
	Boys	Girls	Total	Boys	Girls	Total	Boys	Girls	Total
First test:									
r	.853	.836	.845	.899	.913	.910	.816	.865	.854
PE	.026	.027	.020	.018	.017	.012	.029	.024	.019
Second test:									
r	.886	.929	.911	.921	.921	.921	.861	.892	.883
PE	.020	.016	.012	.016	.016	.011	.025	.019	.014

Both the earlier study on the Kuhlmann-Binet and the later study reported in the *Thirty-Ninth Yearbook* agree, then, in showing a slightly greater "gain" in intelligence quotient for children who come from superior family backgrounds than for children of the lower classes. That this difference can be attributed largely or in part to a special kind of regressive phenomenon resulting from the greater accuracy of the I.Q.'s obtained at the time of the second testing seems apparent from the data presented. It is, of course, possible that a differential growth factor is also operative, but our data are insufficient to show whether or not this is the case. The point to be emphasized at present is that when cases are divided, not on the basis of initial IQ but according to some measured characteristic of the family background (which seems to us a preferable way of determining the contrast between home and school), those children for whom the contrast may be presumed to be greatest are the least affected by the change. Whether at school or at home, the children from the poorer homes gain less upon retest than those from better homes. Although the differences are small, they appear consistently in each of the three age groups studied in the earlier investigation, and after intervals of both one and two years in the later study.

The answer might, of course, lie in the peculiar character of the University of Minnesota nursery school. It is true that we make no claim to stimulating the intellectual growth of children. If, however, the Iowa theory that their results are not to be ascribed primarily to regression but to variations in contrast between the stimulating value of the different homes and that of the nursery school is to be accepted, it follows that subjecting our data to the same treatment as that used in the Iowa studies should not show a differential trend, since the "contrast effect" would not occur in the case of a school that does not influence mental growth either favorably or adversely. We have, therefore, reworked the data from the

Yearbook study according to the Iowa pattern wherein the cases are grouped not according to paternal occupation but according to initial IQ. The results of these computations are shown in Tables IV and V.

TABLE IV

Data from Table I Grouped According to Initial IQ

		Nursery				Non-nursery				Total	
IQ on first test	N	Mean IQ at test I	Mean IQ after interval of 1 year	Differ- ence between mean IQ's	N	Mean IQ at test I	Mean IQ after interval of 1 year	Differ- ence between mean IQ's	N	Mean IQ at test I	Mean IQ after interval of 1 year	Differ- ence between mean IQ's
Below 90......	8	85.50	101.38	+15.38	9	78.33	87.22	+8.89	17	81.70	93.88	+12.18
90–99.........	7	95.14	105.86	+10.72	26	96.46	104.23	+7.77	33	96.18	104.58	+8.40
100–109.......	18	104.06	114.72	+10.66	40	105.28	111.65	+6.37	58	104.90	112.60	+7.70
110–119.......	33	113.94	115.49	+1.55	27	114.30	115.93	+1.63	60	114.10	115.68	+1.58
120–129.......	13	124.08	122.62	−1.46	12	123.25	125.75	+2.50	25	123.68	124.12	+ .44
Above 130.....	5	136.40	127.40	−9.00	8	135.12	127.88	−7.24	13	135.62	127.69	−7.93
	84	......	......	......	122	......	......	......	206			

TABLE V

Data from Table II Grouped According to Initial IQ

		Nursery				Non-nursery				Total	
IQ on first test	N	Mean IQ at test I	Mean IQ after interval of 2 years	Differ- ence between mean IQ's	N	Mean IQ at test I	Mean IQ after interval of 2 years	Differ- ence between mean IQ's	N	Mean IQ at test I	Mean IQ after interval of 2 years	Differ- ence between mean IQ's
Under 100.....	9	89.67	105.33	+15.66	8	95.88	105.75	+9.87	17	92.59	105.53	+12.94
100–109.......	17	104.12	115.06	+10.94	8	104.75	114.62	+9.87	25	104.32	114.92	+10.60
110–119.......	20	114.40	116.30	+1.90	6	116.33	119.50	+3.17	26	115.85	117.04	+2.19
Over 120	5	126.80	125.60	−1.20	7	131.57	126.00	−5.57	12	129.58	125.83	−3.75
	51	......	......	......	29	......	......	......	80			

These tables show that when the fallacious statistical practices employed in the University of Iowa studies are duplicated, using for the purpose data that, when properly handled, show no effect of nursery-school training upon the intelligence quotient, results are obtained that do not differ materially from those reported from Iowa. Our conclusion is, therefore, that the Iowa statistical laboratory has played a far greater part in affecting the "intelligence" of children than has the Iowa nursery school, and that the differential pattern of gains and losses upon retest shown by children whose initial IQ's fell at the extremes of the distribution is a statistical rather than an educational phenomenon. A similar difference appears not only in the test results of children attending a nursery school that makes no claim to improve intelligence, but also in the records of children remaining in their own homes, provided that the same misuse of statistical methods occurs.

In this lucid monograph Woodworth, as a dispassionate observer, sets forth the logic and the findings of recent nature-nurture studies on twins and foster children. Only the section dealing with twins can be presented here. The emphasis on interaction of heredity and environment so long represented in Woodworth's writings is clearly evident here. The monograph is a gem of skillful appraisal which amply repays careful study and deserves emulation.

Heredity and Environment: Twins*

R. S. WOODWORTH

1941

Nothing is more certain, after a little consideration, than the statement that heredity and environment are coacting factors in the development of any living individual and that both are absolutely essential. If the individual's hereditary potencies could somehow be annulled he would immediately lose all physiological and mental characteristics and would remain simply a mass of dead matter. If he were somehow deprived of all environment, his hereditary potencies would have no scope for their activity and, once more, he would cease to live. To ask whether heredity or environment is more important to life is like asking whether fuel or oxygen is more necessary for making a fire. But when we ask whether the *differences* obtaining between human individuals or groups are due to their differing heredity or to differences in their present and previous environments, we have a genuine question and one of great social importance. In a broad sense both heredity and environment must be concerned in causing individuals to be different in ability and personality, but it is a real question whether to attach more importance to the one or the other and whether to look to eugenics or euthenics for aid in maintaining and improving the quality of the population.

* * *

The logic of twin studies. Scientific use of twins was one of Francis Galton's pioneer ventures (1875, 1883). Without having exact methods available for the diagnosis of identicals and same-sex fraternals, Galton was of course well aware that some twins were very much alike, while other pairs showed no more resemblance than other siblings. He sought by case

* Adapted from Heredity and Environment: A Critical Survey of Recently Published Material on Twins and Foster Children, *Social Science Research Council Bulletin*, No. 47 (1941). Reprinted by permission of R. S. Woodworth and the Social Science Research Council.

histories to determine whether the twins that were very much alike as young children grew to differ, and whether pairs showing a large initial difference became more alike as they grew up. Either effect might be laid to environment, but Galton could obtain very little evidence of either. Sometimes twins that were originally closely alike diverged because of illness affecting one of the pair, but otherwise they remained alike up into adult life. Twins originally quite different became more accentuated in their differences rather than more alike.

Galton's logic is perfectly clear in respect to identicals: if they are unlike or grow more unlike, the cause must be sought in the environment. With respect to twins originally much unlike, however, Galton's apparent assumption that they should grow more alike in the same home, i.e., that a common environment acting on differently endowed individuals should make them more alike, if it had any effect at all, is not self-evident. It was accepted by some of the earlier successors of Galton, but just the opposite assumption had seemed more reasonable to some investigators. In height and weight fraternal twins often grow more unlike as they approach maturity. If one has the genes for a tall man and the other for a short man, equal nutritive opportunity is not going to prevent this genetic difference from manifesting itself. Unlike individuals may be expected to respond differently to the same environment, and this is a reasonable expectation in regard to all kinds of ability and propensity. The observed divergence of fraternal twins can therefore be attributed to heredity. But it is also possible to attribute it to environment. The same home is not the same environment to children of very different characteristics. The same dinner table is not the same environment to the hearty eater and to one with a poor appetite; and the effective nutritive environment is evidently not what is set before you, but what you eat. Such considerations should lead to longitudinal studies of developing fraternal twins, but they indicate that not much capital can be made for either heredity or environment from the mere fact that fraternal twins tend to grow more unlike.

The "twin method" developed in Germany (Siemens, 1924; see Wilson, 1934) and much used there in the last two decades for the study of heredity and environment, consists in comparing the average resemblance of identicals with that of fraternals. The difference between identicals, due to environment alone, is compared with the difference between fraternals, due to heredity and environment. The difference between fraternals is greater in practically every trait that has been studied (Gottschaldt, 1939). Where it is very much greater, heredity is an important factor in causing individuals to differ, but where it is only a little greater, the environmental factor is the stronger. Mathematical formulas have been developed for estimating the relative importance of heredity and environment in respect to any given trait. These formulas have rested on the assumption that the environment is as similar for a pair of fraternals as for a pair of identicals. Probably the assumption is not far wrong in respect to the somatic characters that have usually been studied, since the social environment has little effect on these characters; and the method has yielded results that are apparently sound and sometimes quite important—as in regard to susceptibility to tuberculosis, etc. But intelligence and personality may well be much more dependent on the social environment, and there is evidence, to be presented shortly, that the social environment differs more for a pair of fraternals than it usually differs for a pair of identicals. The excess intra-pair difference of fraternals is therefore due to a complex of factors rather than to heredity alone; but with a suitable revision of its logic the "twin method" may still be of use in studies of intelligence and personality.

"Co-twin control" is the name given by Gesell & Thompson (1929) to a third method of utilizing twins. This method deals only with identicals and its logic is relatively plain and simple. Since identicals are alike in heredity, any difference that develops between them must be due to environment. (Exception must be made for certain asymmetries such as right and left handedness. As a single individual shows these asymmetries, it is not strange that a split embryo will sometimes develop them.) Co-twin control is applicable in various ways. To discover whether imitation plays any part in the child's assumption of the erect posture, one of a pair of identical babies might be prevented from seeing people in that posture until his twin was beginning to stand, the question being whether the isolated twin would stand on his own initiative. This particular experiment has perhaps not been tried but a variety of analogous experiments done in this country and in Russia have been fruitful enough to indicate that the method would be well worth using on a large scale. It was being used on a large scale in the USSR when some political interference put a stop to the project (Levit, 1935; Luria, 1936; Muller, 1935).

The study of identical twins reared apart belongs under this general head. If they develop differently, environmental factors are responsible, though usually it is not easy to discover the exact factors that have produced the difference in intelligence or personality. If separated identicals show greater intra-pair differences than unseparated, again environment is responsible, and again we cannot usually put our finger on the important differentiating factor in the social environment. The whole method could be tuned up by giving it a more experimental slant.

Social environment of identical and fraternal twins. Research on the effects of environment may well start with an attempt to discover factors that might probably cause a pair of twins to differ. From a rather external point of view twins, whether identical or fraternal, have the same environment. They live in the same home, probably attend the same school, and are exposed to the same neighborhood, community and cultural influences. So it was not unreasonable for the inventors of the "twin method" already discussed to assume that the environment was as much alike for fraternals as for identicals. Stocks (1930) was perhaps the first to question this assumption. As he says, it "may involve a fallacy in that many dizygotic twins are very different in general body build, healthiness, tastes and temperament so that they naturally tend to subject themselves, or be subjected, to differences in nurture to a greater degree than monozygotic twins who have usually the same needs, tastes and inclinations and are rarely seen apart during childhood." The inference is that the environment differs more for fraternals than for identicals.

In the same year Holmes pointed out the possibility "that fraternal twins by virtue of their differences soon get into different relations with their environment and come to experience very unlike reactions from their associates." That Stocks and Holmes were correct in suggesting that environment was more alike for identicals than for fraternals was demonstrated by P. T. Wilson (1934) by use of a questionnaire which was answered by 70 pairs of identicals, 69 of like-sex fraternals, and 55 of unlike-sex twins in California. To the question, how much they had been separated, identicals reported much less separation than fraternals; 43% of identicals as against 26% of like-sex fraternals had never been separated for more than a day. As to companions 76% of identicals as against 52% of like-sex fraternals reported having the same chums. Also identicals were more alike in dress and food preferences and in liking for games and studies. In practically every comparison a larger percent of identicals were alike. Wilson concludes that "in many respects the identical pairs lived under more similar conditions than the fraternals. This fact must be attributed ultimately to the influence of their heredity which led, or forced them to 'select' more similar environments."

This statement of Wilson deserves emphasis. Unless the environment is extremely limited and rigid the individual has some choice, and according to his native tendencies he will choose one or another *effective* environment within the range of the objective environment. Within the same home one child responds more to the father, another to the mother, one more to the indoor life and another to the outdoor, one more to the mechanical things about the place and the other more to the musical opportunities. Within the same home, then, two children may have very different effective environments, for the reason, at bottom, that they differ genetically. Quite possibly this is the most important fact in the whole problem of heredity versus environment.

The *interaction of heredity and environment* is at least one important consideration in the investigation of individual differences. Shuttleworth (1935) showed the necessity of taking account of interaction in any statistical approach to the problem. He had in mind particularly the fact that parents providing good heredity for their children will on the whole provide them also with good environment. To the degree that family heredity and family environment are positively correlated, the children of a community will differ more than can be accounted for by heredity and environment considered separately. It must be equally true that children in the same family develop differently because of the interaction of heredity and environment, rather than because of either factor alone or even because of the two factors taken separately. The children differ by heredity to start with, and because they differ in native capacities and propensities they are treated differently and respond differently to the opportunities offered by the environment.

We may accept the conclusion that the environment differs more for fraternals than for identicals. Another question is whether the environment is completely the same for identicals. Even in identical pairs that are very harmonious and always together, a sort of division of labor or differentiation of roles is often apparent, as von Bracken has shown (1936). One child is the Aussenvertreter, the "outside representative" or foreign minister of the pair. He answers when a question is addressed to the pair, he does most of the talking to a stranger, he opens the door for a visitor, accepts a present that is held out to the pair, and appears to have more interest than his twin in other people. . . . How can such a difference arise? Sometimes it is traceable to unequal size or vigor resulting from prenatal causes. Sometimes it may be imposed by the parents who are anxious to discover any distinguishing mark. But a differentiation of role may arise simply as a measure of economy and convenience. Less friction within the pair and more success in dealing with other people will result if it is understood who shall take the lead. The more harmonious the pair, the more we might expect some division of labor to occur. In many cases, observers report, the leadership of an identical pair is achieved not by a struggle for dominance but by mutual consent.

The important question for us is whether this differentiation of roles results in a divergence of abilities and personality traits. Slight indications of a corresponding differentiation of personality have been reported by von Bracken and his associates. In adolescence identical twins often select different occupations (Meumann, 1935; Bouterwek, 1936). A pair of girl identicals after finishing their schooling were taken into their father's business office, where one liked the work and the other not. The latter by mutual consent took over the family housekeeping which she liked. One twin showed business ability, the other housekeeping ability. The twins meanwhile remained closely attached to each other. Such a difference though manifesting itself first in early adult life may have been developed through childhood as a result of some less obvious differentiation of roles. But the conclusion is speculative in the absence of developmental studies of twins.

Such differentiation of roles as has been observed would probably cause identicals to differ in certain special abilities and personality traits, rather than in general intelligence or in temperament.

Prenatal and natal environment. Reference to this period of development may appear superfluous in a study concerned with heredity and the social environment. Life in utero is so sheltered, so we might suppose, that no differences between twins could possibly be produced by environmental factors operating before birth. But this supposition is far from correct. The unborn infant requires a large supply of suitable nourishment and of oxygen and can be injured by toxic substances from the mother. Twins are competitors for the maternal supply of nourishment and not infrequently one twin loses out in the competition and dies before birth or is underdeveloped. Identicals as well as fraternals are exposed to this danger. And before the child is "brought into the world" he has still to undergo the hazards of birth. He may suffer from a brain injury during difficult labor, or he may suffer from asphyxia, and the harm may be permanent. Twins are likely to be prematurely born, small and delicate and especially susceptible to birth injury. So it often happens that one of an identical pair is injured and permanently handicapped. Failure to take account of these possibilities may lead to serious error in the interpretation of twin data, and therefore it will not be amiss to consider a recent investigation that lays much emphasis on this type of environmental factor.

Rosanoff, Handy & Plesset (1937) were concerned primarily with the etiology of mental deficiency, so far as it could be revealed by a study of pairs of twins, one at least of each pair being mentally deficient. Their sampling method has already been indicated. In the public schools of California and in institutions for the feebleminded in several states they found 366 mentally deficient individuals known to have twin brothers or sisters. They located these brothers and sisters and determined their mental condition. In many cases the twin brother or sister was found to be feebleminded or to show some other abnormal condition such as epilepsy, birth paralysis or behavior difficulties. If the twin brother or sister was normal, the pair was said to be "discordant," otherwise "concordant." Out of 126 pairs of identicals there were 11 pairs in which one twin was feebleminded and the other normal; that gives 8.7% of discordant pairs. The normal twin serves as a control, proving that the defective one had the genes for normality and that the defect must have been due to some environmental factor. As the case histories indicated that the defect had existed from early childhood, the etiological factor probably belonged under the head of prenatal or natal environment.

In the same way the percent of discordant pairs was obtained for same-sex fraternals and for unlike-sex fraternals, and a figure for siblings was taken from another investigator (Humm, 1932). The approximate percents are presented in Table I.

Assuming as the authors think it safe to do from their case histories that postnatal factors play but a minor role in producing mental deficiency and that "the bulk of mental deficiency exists from birth," they compare the percents given in the table and ask the following questions.

TABLE I

Percent of Discordant Pairs
Normal Twins and Siblings of Mentally Deficient Individuals

Number of pairs	Relationship	Percent discordant
126	Identical twins	9
93	Same-sex fraternals	39
139	Unlike-sex fraternals	53
	Siblings	84

Of the unlike-sex pairs,
Both twins were abnormal in 47%
The male alone in   35%
The female alone in   17%

* Rosanoff, Handy & Plesset, 1937.

1. Why should there be any discordant pairs of identicals? Answer (as already given): Because of prenatal and natal factors.

2. Why should there be many more discordant pairs of same-sex fraternals than of identicals? Answer: Because the fraternals differ in heredity.

3. Why should discordance be more common in unlike-sex than in same-sex fraternals? And why should the male twin in such pairs be mentally deficient more often than the female? Answer: Probably because of some sex-linked factor in early development, the same, perhaps, that causes the excess of stillborn males.

4. Why should discordance be so much more common in singly born siblings than in fraternal twins? Answer: Because of prenatal and natal factors, the same factors that cause mental deficiency to be more common among twin-born than among singly-born children. Prematurity and underweight at birth, with resulting brain injury, are more common in twins.

From certain additional data the authors show that these conditions that favor birth injury are very common in the histories of mentally deficient individuals—about eight times as common, they estimate, as in the general population. All the evidence seems to them to point to the great importance of these prenatal and natal factors, and leads them to believe that "scarcely more than one-half of the cases of mental deficiency are of hereditary origin."

Since the investigation under review included no systematic study of the postnatal environment, social and educational, the authors quite possibly overestimated the importance of the prenatal and natal environment. Other studies (Strauss, 1939; Kephart, 1939) indicate that in children showing no sign of brain injury suitable education can produce an appreciable intellectual improvement. Even a small gain would take many individuals out of the class of feebleminded into the borderline group at least. But the authors last cited and many others admit the existence of a large group of mentally deficient individuals who are such because of prenatal and natal factors.

Rosanoff and his associates believe that birth injury is much more common than has been recognized. The injury may not be noticed at the time and yet may later give rise to some degree of mental deficiency. "Hereditary factors determine merely the potentially maximal intellectual development that may be obtained by a given individual." This full potentiality will not be realized except under favorable conditions. There must not be any prenatal condition leading to underdevelopment of the brain. There must be no cerebral injury during birth. In infancy and childhood there must be no serious head injury or disease affecting the brain. And on the positive side there must be such home, school and other environment as will properly stimulate intellectual development. "It is a question whether all these conditions are fulfilled for more than a limited minority of individuals in contemporary society."

The authors are thus led to formulate the concept of "relative mental deficiency." An individual may have normal or even superior intelligence and still be relatively deficient in that he has not realized his full genetic potentiality. When for example the authors found a pair of identical twins having intelligence quotients of 150 and 118, they argued that the one with IQ 118 was relatively deficient since his hereditary potentiality must have been the same as his twin's. The same argument would apply to any pair of identical twins showing a considerable difference in ability, and in such a case the possibility of birth injury in one twin needs to be excluded before the pair can be used in demonstrating the effects of social environment. In crucial cases a neurological examination or at least a good medical history would seem to be essential.

Physical and intellectual resemblance of twins. Of the numerous studies of twins reared together, which in general have yielded very similar results, we will take notice of one of the most complete and accurate, that of the University of Chicago investigators, Newman, Freeman and Holzinger (1937), respectively a geneticist, a psychologist and a statistician—a very desirable combination for such a study. They measured identical and fraternal twins reared together, and identical twins reared apart. A table showing the intra-pair differences and correlations for each of these three classes will be discussed at this point so far as concerns the twins who were reared together. For a much sharper statistical analysis than can be attempted here reference is made to the critical review by McNemar (1938) and the reply of Holzinger (1938).

From these differences and correlations (and from the whole distributions) the authors reach the conclusion that intelligence is more affected (differentiated) by the environment than are such physical characteristics as height and weight. In other words, the share of the environment in the

TABLE II
Differences Between Twins*

	Fraternals	Identicals reared together	Identicals reared apart
Stature	4.4 cm	1.7 cm	1.8 cm
Weight	10.0 lb	4.1 lb	9.9 lb
Binet IQ	9.9 points	5.9 points	8.2 points

Correlations Between Twins†

	Fraternals	Identicals reared together	Identicals reared apart
Stature	.645	.932	(.969)
Weight	.631	.917	(.886)
Binet IQ	.631	.881	(.767)

* Newman, Freeman, & Holzinger, 1937, pp. 72, 344.
† Ibid., pp. 97, 347.
Note. These correlations (except those in parentheses) have been corrected for age, and the last value in the table (.767) has been corrected for range, according to a suggestion made by McNemar (1938) and accepted by Holzinger (1938). Such correction is necessary because the separated identicals, taken as a group, were rather uniform in intelligence, their distribution giving an SD of 13.0 points as against 17.3 for the identicals reared together.

production of individual differences is greater in respect to intelligence than in respect to height and weight. The share of the environment is represented by the intra-pair difference of identicals (who are equal in heredity), while the difference between fraternals represents the combined effect of heredity and environment. The argument is that of the "twin method" already discussed and is subject to the same limitations. But for a moment let us consider the figures as they stand.

Consider first the table of differences. The fraternals always differ more than the identicals, but they differ 2.6 times as much (4.4/1.7) in stature and 2.4 times as much (10/4.1) in weight, as against only 1.7 times as much (9.9/5.9) in intelligence. Or, inverting these ratios, we say that the share of environment in producing the difference between fraternals is 39% in stature and 41% in weight, as against 60% in intelligence. On the face of the returns environment counts for much more in intelligence than in height and weight—as would indeed seem quite reasonable.

The argument breaks down, however, when we take account of the error of measurement which is relatively large in the case of the IQ. Retest of the same person within a week usually shows some shift of score up or down, averaging about 5 points of IQ. This amount is a fair estimate of the chance error of measurement affecting the obtained difference in IQ between two individuals. Identicals reared together, it will be seen, differ only a little more than this. Making allowance for this chance error we reach an estimate of 3.1 points net difference between identicals, and of 8.5 points net for fraternals. The fraternals then differ 2.7 times as much as the identicals; or the share of environment is $3.1/8.5 = 36\%$. There are chance errors of measurement in the physical traits, too, but they are quite small and allowance for them would not change the ratios very much. With allowance made for errors of measurement, then, the "share of environment" is approximately the same for intelligence as for the physical traits considered.

The same conclusion can be drawn from the table of correlations. When allowance is made for the error of observation the IQ correlations are raised to about .66 for fraternals and .93 for identicals. Thus the resemblance of fraternals was about the same in the three traits, the resemblance of identicals much higher but about equal in the three traits. The data afford no ground for making any distinction between the three traits, as concerns the shares of heredity and environment.

Having convinced ourselves (in considering the "twin method") that the environment differs more for fraternal than for identical twins, we cannot derive much information from a comparison of the results from the two classes of twins. From the results on identicals we can infer that environment can cause a certain amount of difference between individuals of the same heredity, and that the differentiating effects of environment are about equal in physical traits and in intelligence, when the identicals are reared together.

As to fraternals, we know that they differ more or less in heredity, and that their effective environments differ in (partial) conformity with their difference in heredity. Because of this combination of factors, fraternals differ more than identicals and they seem to differ about as much in intelligence as in physical traits. The interaction of heredity and environment in the case of fraternals leaves little chance for separating the two factors and assigning to each its share. There is really little point in comparing fraternals and identicals; there is more point in comparing fraternals with ordinary siblings, since the hereditary difference should average the same while the environment would on the whole be more alike for twins than for other siblings.

Identical twins reared apart. The first pair of separated identicals to be tested and carefully studied was that reported by H. J. Muller (1925). The principal series of such pairs was gathered with much labor over a period of years by the Chicago group, Newman, Freeman & Holzinger, and reported in their book on "Twins," 1937. They discovered, measured and tested 19 pairs of identicals who had been separated in infancy or early childhood and reared in different families and communities. Another pair has been added by Gardner & Newman (1940). And a British pair, reared apart up to the age of nearly ten years, has been studied by Saudek (1934). Diagnosis of monozygosity was carefully made in all these cases.

The following table presents certain data for each of the separated identicals. With regard to prenatal and natal environment, the case histories of the pairs numbered 1 and 8 suggest the possibility that the twin with lower IQ in each of these pairs got a poor start and perhaps suffered a slight but permanent handicap.

For the most part the environments in which the twins of the same pair were brought up did not differ extremely—not more than would be true of children brought up in the same community. In a few instances the difference was rather large. The greatest difference in education occurred in the case of two girls one of whom was reared in a good farming region and who went through college and became a school teacher, while her twin grew up largely in the backwoods and had only two years of regular schooling. This girl, however, obtained employment later in a large city and became a general assistant in a small printing office where she performed a variety of duties including typesetting and proofreading. On being tested her IQ came out at 92, while that of her college-educated twin sister was 116. This difference of 24 points in IQ was the largest found in any case.

Another pair of young women had been separated in infancy and one had been reared on a good farm and had gone to school only for the eight grades, while the other had lived in a small town, gone through high school, studied music and engaged in clerical work. The town girl's IQ as determined by the tests was 106 while the farm girl made only 89. In spite of this large difference in the tests the country girl gave the impression of being fully as intelligent, or competent, as her twin sister.

A pair of young men from Tennessee had been brought up, the one in a small town where he went through high school and engaged in business, the other back in the mountains with irregular schooling amounting to eight grades at the most. Tested at the age of 25, the mountain boy obtained an IQ of 77, the town boy of 96.

Identicals reared apart—treatment of data. There are two main ways of treating the data from separated identicals. The more obvious way is to compare them with identical twins reared together, as can be done either by comparing the mean difference between twins in the one class with the corresponding difference in the other class, or by comparing the correlation between the paired individuals in the two classes. Either method is essentially a study of intra-pair variance. The difference has to be taken without plus or minus sign, because in the identicals reared together there is no known differentiating factor to give either twin a distinctive place in the pair. Because the intra-pair difference is taken without sign, it needs to be corrected for the chance error of observation.

The other way of treating the data is to look for environmental factors that might differentiate the members of a separated pair and to determine

TABLE III
Some Data from Identical Twins Reared Apart*

| Case Number | Sex | Age at Separation | Age at Testing | Environmental Differences | | | IQ Difference |
				(1) in Years of Schooling	(2) in Estimated Educational Advantages	(3) in Estimated Social Advantages	
11	f	18 mo.	35	14	37	25	24
2	f	18 mo.	27	15	32	14	12
18	m	1 yr.	27	4	28	31	19
4	f	5 mo.	29	4	22	15	17
12	f	18 mo.	29	5	19	13	7
1	f	18 mo.	19	1	15	27	12
17	m	2 yr.	14	0	15	15	10
8	f	3 mo.	15	1	14	32	15
3	m	2 mo.	23	1	12	15	− 2
14	f	6 mo.	39	0	12	15	− 1
5	f	14 mo.	38	1	11	26	4
13	m	1 mo.	19	0	11	13	1
10	f	1 yr.	12	1	10	15	5
15	m	1 yr.	26	2	9	7	1
7	m	1 mo.	13	0	9	27	− 1
19	f	6 yr.	41	0	9	14	− 9
16	f	2 yr.	11	0	8	12	2
6	f	3 yr.	59	0	7	10	8
9	m	1 mo.	19	0	7	14	6
Muller	f	1 mo.	30	9	?	?	− 1
Gardner & Newman	f	1 mo.	19	0	2	?	− 3
Saudek	m	1 mo.	20	0	?	?	± 4

* (Newman, Freeman & Holzinger, 1937; Muller, 1925; Gardner & Newman, 1940; Saudek, 1934)

Note. The estimated differences in educational and social advantages are in "points" with a maximum possible of 50. From the case material each of five judges rated the environmental differences between every pair of twins on a scale of 10 points, and the figure given in the table is the sum of these five ratings. A minus sign before an IQ difference means that the twin who received the higher rating for educational advantages obtained the lower IQ.

whether a given factor has produced a significant difference between the favored and the disfavored twins taken as a group. For example, if it can be seen that one twin has received better educational advantages than the other, in each pair, we can determine whether there is a signficant difference in IQ in favor of the better educated twins. Here each difference has a sign, plus or minus, and the average difference (account being taken of the signs) does not need to be corrected for chance errors of observation. It is important to notice this distinction between the two methods of treatment. Suppose the mean difference between identicals to be 5 points IQ; this difference does not exceed the error of observation and therefore does not indicate any true difference. But suppose, in a sample of identicals reared apart, the better-educated twin averages 5 points higher in IQ than the other. This may be a significant difference (given an adequate sample), for the chance errors of observation would not favor either class of twins as against the other class.

Taken without regard to sign, the average IQ difference between separated identicals is 7.6 points. Correction for chance errors of observation would bring this difference down to 6 points net, a figure to be compared with the estimated net difference of 3 points between identicals reared together, and of 15 points or more between children paired at random from the same community. It is probable, then, that environment did make these separated twins differ in tested intelligence, though not to any such extent as obtains among the children of a community.

When the IQ differences are averaged with account taken of sign, the twin having the advantage in educational opportunities usually surpasses the other. On the average the IQ was 6.0 points higher for the better-educated twin. This difference is statistically reliable, being over 3 times its Standard Error. It seems safe to conclude that when one of a pair of identicals has been afforded better educational advantages than the other, the better-educated one will on the whole do better in the intelligence tests.

However, there were only 6 pairs differing very much in the amount of formal schooling received. These 6 show an average superiority of 13 points in IQ. The remaining pairs show only a small and unreliable IQ superiority for the better-educated twin (3 points on the average, and only 1 point when the two cases of possible prenatal handicap are omitted). It appears, then, that rather a large educational advantage is required to give any dependable superiority in tested intelligence.

Years of schooling are of course not an adequate measure of educational advantages. Newman and his colleagues endeavored to do a little better by going over the case histories of their 19 pairs and estimating the educational difference between the twins by aid of a rating scale. The ratings are given in our last table. There is a correlation of + .79 between the estimated educational difference and the obtained difference in IQ.

This substantial correlation depends largely but not wholly upon the few pairs whose education was very unequal.

The authors of this extensive study, when they express themselves separately and independently regarding the findings in respect to intelligence, differ somewhat in emphasis, but two of the three, at least, agree that rather large environmental inequality is needed to produce any reliable difference in intelligence.

Freeman (1937) says: The data indicate "that environment may affect all kind of traits, intellectual, temperamental, and social; that this influence is large enough to be of the greatest importance; and that human nature may be improved or debased to a degree which many have thought impossible."

Holzinger (1935) says: "Moderate environmental differences produce inappreciable effect upon twin characters . . . relatively great environmental differences must be present to produce noticeable effect upon traits such as here studied."

Newman (in Gardner & Newman, 1940), says: "Where environmental differences are rather large, fairly large differences result. Possibly, and even probably, we are dealing here with a matter of thresholds of influence and that, unless a certain threshold of difference is reached, the organisms do not respond differentially. . . . The geneticist of the group of authors must confess . . . that throughout the whole study of identical twins reared apart he was much more impressed with the very great intra-pair similarities of these twins, after they had been exposed to all sorts of environmental differences, than he was with their differences. . . . Nevertheless . . . fairly large environmental differences do modify physical, mental and temperamental traits and produce proportionately large differences even between hereditarily identical individuals."

Environment and personality. Newman, Freeman & Holzinger attempted to obtain some measures of temperament and personality but the available tests were not very good as is shown by the fact that these tests yielded no greater differences between fraternals than between identicals reared together. According to the tests, the identicals reared apart differed no more in personality than identicals reared together. Nor was there any measurable relationship between difference in social environment affecting the twins of a pair and amount of personality difference. The general impression of the investigators from personal contact with the separated identicals was to the effect that social attitudes were much dependent on the environment, while there was scarcely any effect on the temperament and deeper traits of personality (Newman, 1940, pp. 182, 193-196). In some cases there were personality differences corresponding to what one might expect from the known environmental differences. The college-educated schoolteacher had a polished manner, was careful of her personal appearance and sought to produce a favorable impression; while her twin, the little-educated assistant in the printing office, was "all business, without social charm or concern about how she impressed others." The farm girl was muscular, masculine and deliberate, while her city-bred twin was "far more excitable and responsive, almost neurotic." But the young man from the mountains who had engaged in a good deal of illegal activity appeared to be identical in personality traits with his twin, the steady, respected citizen of a small town. Both were rather individualistic and stubborn, but expressed these traits differently in conformity with their respective social backgrounds. In the German studies of criminals (Lange, 1930, 1937; Kranz, 1936, 1937) the "equivalence" of certain forms of illegal behavior with certain forms of legal behavior has been pointed out. They are equivalent in the sense that both identical twins may be behaving according to the same inherent tendency, though the form of the behavior is quite different from the social point of view.

Conclusions from the twin studies. If we return now to the results on the intelligence of identical twins reared apart, two conclusions seem probable even though the sample is still far too small to make either conclusion sure. In the first place, radical differences in education can create substantial differences in intelligence, so far as intelligence is measured by our tests. Differences in IQ as great as the standard deviation of the population have been found in several instances, corresponding to large differences in educational advantages. We can conclude that the educational environment, taken in a broad sense, had a marked effect on such intelligence as we are now able to measure.

In the second place, however, the differences between identical twins reared apart are remarkably small except in those cases where the contrast of educational advantages was very great. For the majority of the separated identicals the IQ difference was no greater than for identicals reared together. When individuals of identical heredity are subjected to environments differing about as much as those of the children in an ordinary community, such identical twins differ much less than the children of such a community. Therefore the differences found among the children of an ordinary community are not accounted for, except in small measure, by differences in homes and schooling. To repeat—if the differences in intelligence found among the children of a community were mostly due to differences in home and school environment, these differences would remain almost in full force even if the heredity of all the children were made identical. But when a trial is made of this hypothesis by placing identical twins in different families not too different in environment, the twins show only a small fraction of the difference found in the community at large.

This paper represents the effort to extend research on primary mental abilities to the level of children. It revealed clearly the emergence of a reconciliation between the work of the American and the British psychologists. As further writing in this volume will stress, "general intelligence" appeared to be creeping back into the analyses and a rapprochement was in order.

Primary Mental Abilities of Children*

THELMA GWINN THURSTONE

1941

For many years psychologists have been accustomed to the problems of special abilities and disabilities. These are, in fact, the principal concern of the school psychologists who deal with children who cannot read, have a blind spot for numbers, or do one thing remarkably well and other things poorly. It seems strange with all this experience in differential psychology that we have clung so long to the practice of summarizing a child's mental endowment by a single index, such as the mental age, the intelligence quotient, the percentile rank in general intelligence, and other single average measures. An average index of mental endowment should be useful for many educational purposes, but it should not be regarded as more than the average of several tests. Two children with the same mental age can be entirely different persons, as is well known. There is nothing wrong about using a mental age or an intelligence quotient if it is understood as an average of several tests. The error that is frequently made is interpreting it as measuring some basic functional unity when it is known to be nothing more than a composite of many functional unities.

The researches on the primary mental abilities which have been in progress for several years have had as their first purposes the identification and definition of the independent factors of mind. As the nature of the abilities became more clearly indicated by successive studies, a second purpose of a more practical nature has been involved in some of the studies. This purpose has been to prepare a set of tests of psychological significance and practicable adaptability to the school testing and guidance program. The series of studies will be summarized in this paper, the battery of tests soon to be available will be described, and some of the problems now being investigated will be discussed briefly.

* Reprinted from *Educational and Psychological Measurement*, 1 (1941), pp. 105-116, by permission of the author and publisher.

PREVIOUS STUDIES

The first study in this series involved the use of 56 psychological examinations that were given to a group of about 250 college students. That study revealed a number of primary abilities, some of which were clearly defined by the configuration of test vectors while others were indicated by the configuration but less clearly defined. All of these factors have been studied in subsequent test batteries in which each primary factor has been represented by new tests specially designed to feature the primary factors in the purest possible form. The object has been to construct tests in which there is a heavy saturation of a primary factor and in which other factors are minimized. This is the purification of tests by reducing their complexity.

These latter studies of the separate abilities were in each case made in the Chicago high schools. . . . In each series of tests, one factor was represented by a large number of tests, but all factors were well represented. In all of these studies the same primary abilities were identified as had been found in the experiment with college students. These studies led to the publication by the American Council on Education of an experimental battery of tests for the primary mental abilities, adaptable for use with students of high school or college age.

The identification of the same primary mental abilities among high school students as we had previously found among college students encouraged us to look for differentiation among the abilities of younger children. In the Chicago Public Schools, group mental tests are made of all 1B, 4B, and 8B children in the elementary schools and of 10B students in the high schools. The demand for a series of tests to be used in the guidance program for high school entrants and the advisability of not making too broad a leap in age led us to select an eighth-grade population for the next study.

THE EIGHTH-GRADE EXPERIMENT

In view of the purpose of investigating whether or not primary mental abilities could be isolated for children at the fourteen-year age level, the construction of the tests consisted essentially in the adaptation for the younger children of tests previously used with high school students. In some of the tests little or no alteration was necessary, while for other tests it was considered advisable to revise vocabulary and other aspects of the tests to suit the younger age level. A number of new tests were added to those selected from previous experimental batteries. Sixty tests constituted the final battery.

When the tests had been designed and printed, they were given in a trial form to children in grades 7A and 8A in several schools. Groups of from

50 to 100 children in these two grades were used for the purpose of standardizing procedures and, especially, for setting time limits.

*   *   *

Eleven hundred and fifty-four children participated in this study. The complete battery of 60 tests was given in 11 one-hour sessions to the children in the 8B grades in each of the 15 schools. The children enjoyed the tests and, with very few exceptions, the sustained interest and effort were quite evident. One thing which a psychologist might fear in such a long series of tests would be fluctuating movitation on the part of the students. Although the adjustment teachers administered the tests, every session was observed by a member of our staff, and we were highly gratified by the sustained interest and effort of the pupils.

In addition to the 60 tests we used three more variables: chronological age, mental age, and sex. The latter test data were available in school records. They were determined by the Kuhlmann-Anderson tests which had been given previously to the same children. Therefore, the battery to be analyzed factorially contained 63 variables.

The total population in this study consisted of 1,154 eighth-grade children. When all the records had been assembled, it was found that 710 of these subjects had complete records for all of the 63 variables. We decided to base our correlations on this population of complete records rather than to use the large population with varying numbers of cases for the correlation coefficients. For convenience of handling with the tabulating-machine methods, the raw scores were transmuted into single digit scores from which the Pearson product-moment correlation coefficients were computed. With 63 variables there were 1,935 Pearson correlation coefficients.

This table of intercorrelations was factored to 10 factors by the centroid method on the tabulating machines by means of punched cards. Successive rotations made by the method of extended vectors yielded an oblique factorial matrix which is a simple structure.

Inspection of the rotated factorial matrix showed seven of the factors previously indicated: Memory, Induction, Verbal Comprehension, Word Fluency, Number, Space, Perceptual Speed, and three less easily identifiable factors. One of these is another Verbal factor; one is involved in ability to solve pencil mazes; and one is present in the three dot-counting tests which were used.

We have computed the intercorrelations between the 10 primary factors. Our main interest centers on the seven primary factors that can be given interpretation and, especially, on the first six of these factors for which the interpretation is rather more definite. Among the high correlations we note that the Number factor is correlated with the two Verbal factors. The Word Fluency factor has high correlation with the Verbal Comprehension factor and with Induction. The Rote Memory factor seems to be independent of the other factors. These correlations are higher than the correlations between primary factors for adults.

Because of the psychological interest in the correlations of the primary mental abilities, we have made a separate analysis of the correlations for those factors which seem to have reasonably certain interpretation. If these six primary mental abilities are correlated because of some general intellective factor, then the rank of the correlation matrix should be one. Upon examination, this actually proves to be the case. A single factor accounts for most of the correlations between the primary factors.

The single factor loadings show that the inductive factor has the highest loading and the Rote Memory factor the lowest loading on the common general factor in the primary abilities. This general factor is what we have called a second-order general factor. It makes its appearance not as a separate factor, but as a factor inherent in the primaries and their correlations. If further studies of the primary mental abilities of children should reveal this general factor, it may sustain Spearman's contention that there exists a general intellective factor. Instead of depending on the averages or centroids of arbitrary test batteries for its determination, the present method should enable us to identify it uniquely.

We have not been able to find in these data a general factor that is distinct from the primary factors, but the second-order general factor should be of as much psychological interest as the more frequently postulated, independent general factor of Spearman. It would be our judgment that the second-order general factor found here is probably the general factor which Spearman has so long defended, but we cannot say whether he would accept the present findings as sustaining his contentions about the general factor. We have not found any occasion to debate the existence of a general intellective factor. The factorial methods we have been using are adequate for finding such a factor, either as a factor independent of the primaries or as a factor operating through correlated primaries. We have reported on primary mental abilities in adults, which seem to show only low positive correlations except for the two verbal factors. In the present study we have found higher correlations among the primary factors for eighth-grade children. It is now an interesting question to determine whether the correlations among primary abilities of still younger children will reveal, perhaps even more strongly, a second-order general factor.

INTERPRETATION OF FACTORS

The analysis of this battery of 60 tests revealed essentially the same set of primary factors which had been found in previous factorial studies. Six of the factors seemed to have sufficient stability for the several age levels that have been investigated to justify an extension of the tests for these factors into practical test work in the schools. In making this extension we have been obliged to consider carefully the difference between research on the nature of the primary factors and the construction of tests for practical use. Several of the primary factors are not yet sufficiently clear as regards psychological interpretation to justify an attempt to appraise them generally among school children. The primary factors that do seem to be clear enough for such purposes are the following: Verbal Comprehension V, Word Fluency W, Number N, Space S, Rote Memory M, and Induction or Reasoning R. The factors which in several studies are not yet sufficiently clear for general application are the Perceptual factor P and the Deductive factor D.

The Verbal factor V is found in tests involving verbal comprehension, for example, tests of vocabulary, opposites and synonyms, completion tests, and various reading comprehension tests.

The Word Fluency factor W is involved whenever the subject is asked to think of isolated words at a rapid rate. It is for this reason that we have called the factor a Word Fluency factor. It can be expected in such tests as anagrams, rhyming, and producing words with a given initial letter, prefix, or suffix.

The Space factor S is involved in any task in which the subject manipulates an object imaginally in two or three dimensions. The ability is involved in many mechanical tasks and in the understanding of mechanical drawings. Such material cannot be used conveniently in testing situations, so we have used a large number of tasks which are psychologically similar, such as Flags, Cards, and Figures.

The Number factor N is involved in the ability to do numerical calculations rapidly and accurately. It is not dependent upon the reasoning factors in problem-solving, but seems to be restricted to the simpler processes, such as addition and multiplication.

A Memory factor M has been clearly present in all test batteries. The tests for memory which are now being used depend upon the ability to memorize quickly. It is quite possible that the Memory factor will be broken down into more specific factors.

The Reasoning factor R is involved in tasks that require the subject to discover a rule or principle covering the material of the test. The Letter Series and Letter Grouping tests are good examples of the task. In all these experimental studies two separate Reasoning factors have been indicated. They are perhaps Induction and Deduction, but we have not succeeded in constructing pure tests of either factor. The tests which we are now using are more heavily saturated with the Inductive factor, but for the present we are simply calling the ability R, Reasoning.

In presenting for general use a differential psychological examination which appraises the mental endowment of children, it should not be assumed that there is anything final about six primary factors. No one knows

532   Studies in Individual Differences

how many primary mental abilities there may be. It is hoped that future factorial studies will reveal many other important primary abilities so that the mental profiles of students may eventually be adequate for appraising educational and vocational potentialities. In such a program the present studies are only a starting point in substituting for the description of mental endowment by a single intelligence index the description of mental endowment by a profile of fundamental traits.

THE FINAL TEST BATTERY

In adapting the tests for practical use in the schools for the appraisal of six primary mental abilities, we must recognize that the new test program has for its object the production of a profile for each child, as distinguished from the description of a child's mental endowment in terms of a single intelligence index. For many educational purposes it is still of value to appraise a child's mental endowment roughly by a single measure, but the composite nature of such single indices must be recognized.

The factorial matrix of the battery of sixty tests was inspected to find the three best tests for each of seven primary factors. In making the selection of tests for each primary factor we considered not only the factorial saturations of the tests, which are, of course, the most important consideration, but also the availability of parallel forms which may be needed in case the tests should come into general use. Ease of administration and ease in understanding of the instructions are also important considerations.

The three tests for each primary factor were printed in a separate booklet and the material was so arranged that the three tests for any factor could be given easily within a 40-minute school period. The main purpose of the larger test battery was to determine whether or not the primary factors could be found for eighth-grade children, but the purpose of the present shorter battery was to produce a practical, useful test battery and to check its factorial composition. The selected tests were edited and revised so that they could be used for either hand-scoring or machine-scoring. The Word Fluency tests constitute an exception in that none of the tests now known to be saturated with this factor seems to be suitable for machine-scoring.

In order to check the factorial analysis at the present age level, we arranged to give the selected list of 21 tests to a second population of eighth-grade children. The resulting data were factored independently of the larger battery of tests. There were 437 subjects in this population who took all of the 21 tests. This population was used for a new factor analysis. The results of this analysis clearly confirmed the previous study. The simple structure in the present battery is sharp, with only one primary factor conspicuously present in each test, so that the structure could be determined by inspection for clusters.

A battery of 17 tests has been assembled into a series of test booklets for use in the Chicago schools. An experimental edition of 25,000 copies has been printed, and the plan for securing norms on these tests includes their administration to 1,000 children at each half-year grade level from grade 5B through the senior year in high school. These records have been obtained during the school year 1940 to 1941. The use of such a wide age range in standardizing the test is at first thought, perhaps, rather strange. The effort was made in order to secure age norms throughout the entire range of abilities found among eighth-grade children since the tests are to become a part of the testing procedure for all 8B children in the Chicago schools. Separate age norms will be derived for each of the six primary abilities. If a single index of a student's mental ability is desired, it is recommended that the average of his six ability scores be used.

* * *

FURTHER PROBLEMS

One of our principal research interests at the present time is to determine whether primary abilities can be identified in children of kindergarten or first-grade age. A series of about 50 tests is well under way, and some of them are now being tried with young children. If we succeed in isolating primary abilities among these young children, our next step will be to prepare a practical battery of tests for that age. A subsequent problem will be to make experimental studies of paper-and-pencil tests for appraising the primary abilities of children in the intermediate grades, approximately at the fourth-grade level. We are fairly confident that such tests can be prepared for use in the intermediate grades.

It is a long way in the future, but it is interesting to speculate on the possibility of using the tests of the primary mental abilities as the tool with which to study fundamental psychological problems of mental growth and mental inheritance. Absolute scaling of the tests at the different age levels will make possible studies on the rates of development of the separate abilities at various age levels. Modifiability of the abilities will be another problem to which we shall later turn attention.

Although many studies of children suffering from environmental deprivation have been conducted, the study by Wheeler is of special interest because it takes its samples in the same geographical area at two different times a decade apart. The great changes which have taken place in the area are reflected clearly in the test scores of the children.

A Comparative Study of the Intelligence of East Tennessee Mountain Children*

LESTER R. WHEELER

1942

Certain trends in the investigations of the intelligence of rural and mountain children raise questions of vital importance to education. Does the deviation of these children from the normal distribution indicate that they are inherently inferior? Are they by training and experience made less capable of dealing with intelligence tests than children in other environments? To what extent do intelligence ratings vary as a result of improving environmental conditions? Is the decrease in IQ with an increase in chronological age due to defects in the process of maturation of intelligence, or to the increasing influence of poor cultural conditions?

Although investigators agree that variations do occur in the IQ, there is much controversy concerning the causes of these discrepancies. The *Thirty-ninth Yearbook* of the National Society for the Study of Education, sequential to the *Twenty-seventh Yearbook,* reviews the investigations and presents the nature-nurture discussion from various points of view. All the studies but one indicate that rural children make lower scores on intelligence tests than city children; the Scottish Council for Educational Research reports that no difference in intelligence is found between the rural and urban children of Scotland, and offers the explanation that, "nowhere has scholastic opportunity been more evenly equated than in Scotland—99.7 per cent of Scottish teachers are fully trained." Most investigators feel that environmental differences influence the lower ratings of rural children.

INTELLIGENCE OF MOUNTAIN CHILDREN

In 1930 we made a study of the intelligence of East Tennessee Mountain children. The Dearborn IA and IIC Intelligence Tests were given to eleven

* The Journal of Educational Psychology, 33 (1942), pp. 321-334. Reprinted by permission of the author and Warwick and York, Inc.

hundred forty-seven children in Grades I-VIII from twenty-one mountain schools, and the Illinois Intelligence Test was given to five hundred sixty-four of these cases in Grades III-VIII. The median IQ was 82 on the Dearborn and 78 on the Illinois Test. The IQ on the Dearborn Test was 95 at age six, and decreased to 74 at age sixteen. A marked school retarda-tion was evident, from one-and-a-half years in the first grade to over two years in the eighth grade. The conclusions reached were: (1) The results of both tests were materially affected by environmental factors, (2) the mountain children were not as far below normal intelligence as the tests indicated, and (3) with proper environmental changes the mountain children might test near a normal group. It was noted that,

The growing educational opportunities in the mountains are materially changing the isolated sections. The State is providing modern and adequate schools in the very heart of the mountains, and is sending well-trained teachers, many of whom are holding or working toward college degrees, into those schools to teach the mountain children. . . . Educational opportunities of the mountains have advanced with the improvement of roads, thus enabling consolidation of schools in a number of sections. As this is only a recent development, it will be interesting to note the influence of better schools on the results of later intelligence test data on the same groups of children.

Ten years have elapsed since this initial study was made, and we have retested the same mountain areas. The data for this second investigation were gathered during the Spring and Fall of 1940. Obviously we could not retest the same children, but we have repeated the same test on children in the same areas and largely from the same families; ninety-one per cent of the families represented in this study have been life-residents of the area, eight per cent have moved into the areas since 1930 from adjacent Appalachian Mountain sections, leaving only one per cent shifting into the mountains from undetermined areas. The overlapping of a majority of the family names in the two studies agrees with this general trend, and the data indicate that any major changes found in the results of the intelligence tests are due to other factors than population shift.

SOME ENVIRONMENTAL CHANGES IN THE MOUNTAIN AREA

During the past decade there have been many changes in the economic, social and cultural life of these mountain people. The State has completed an excellent road system which gives every community access to progressive areas outside of the mountains, and has developed transportation facilities for schools and industry. Our data show about sixty per cent of the families in one county and forty per cent in another had one or more members working in industrial plants. In 1930 neither State nor county provided transportation; in 1940, two thousand three hundred sixteen children were transported daily to and from school. This probably accounts for much of the seventeen per cent increase in enrollment in 1940, and for the thirty-two per cent higher average daily attendance. Basing the allotment of State money to county schools on the basis of average daily attendance now stimulates the teachers and community to keep the children in school. Hot lunches are served regularly in all the larger schools.

There has been a general shift from the one-room to larger schools, a re-organization made possible by improved roads. An improvement is also indicated in the types of school buildings. Many schools now have adequate playgrounds and fairly well equipped gymnasiums. A circulating library, maintained by the State and counties, makes available around fourteen thousand volumes for these schools, and free texbooks are furnished for the first three grades. While a decade ago the average training of the teachers was less than two years of college work, today it is about three years. A majority of the teachers are either college graduates or receiving training-in-service from accredited teacher-training colleges. New teachers employed are required to have four years of college training. Well-trained, progressive college graduates have displaced the politically appointed county superintendents of a decade ago. An excellent supervisory program is provided for the area with well-trained county supervisors and a State regional supervisor who assist in coördinating instruction. Schools have been improved by the innovation of a State rating system based on points for improved instruction, additional books and materials, provision for health facilities and general equipment.

During the past ten years the rapid growth of industry in the area enables the families to supplement its agricultural livelihood with ready cash through employment in the rayon, lumber, pottery and other industrial plants. Farming methods have materially changed; pasture lands now replace many of the corn fields on the rough mountain slopes, and stock raising and dairy farming is proving profitable. Small but modern frame houses located on or near the main highways have replaced many of the log cabins and small rough-board houses. There has been unusual development in the area, and the improvement in roads, schools, agriculture and the economic life of the communities has materially changed the general environment of these people.

In the 1930 investigation nine hundred forty-six children were tested from twenty-one different schools. In 1940 all the children in these schools, and an additional two thousand cases in nineteen other mountain schools, were tested in order to increase the statistical reliability of the study. Comparisons were made between the original and additional schools, and, when no significant differences were found between the distribution of intelligence in the two groups, the data were combined for subsequent treatment. Apparently any significant changes in IQ are not due to the additional cases. The median IQ for the original twenty-one schools is

87.6 ± .34, and for the additional schools, 87.2 ± .32. The administration and scoring of the tests was under the same supervision as in 1930.

The average mountain child is eight months younger for his grade than ten years ago, as shown in Table I and Fig. 1. The differences in chronological age range from three months in Grade I to fifteen months in Grade V. There is a consistent difference in favor of the 1940 group in each grade and a significant difference in most of the grades, substantiating other investigations which indicate that age-grade retardation decreases with improvement in instruction and general educational opportunities. There seems to be a tendency for the older children to leave the elementary school earlier than they did ten years ago, probably due to better opportunities for high-school attendance and industrial employment. . . .

INCREASE IN MENTAL AGE DURING LAST DECADE

Table I and Fig. 1 show a comparison of the median mental ages. An average mental age for all grades shows the 1940 group has gained about nine months over the 1930 group, or nearly one mental month a year for ten years. In other words, the average mountain child in 1940 is three-fourths of a year mentally superior for his grade than the average mountain child in 1930 was. The greatest differences between the two groups occur in the seventh and eighth grades, and the smallest in Grade III. Figure 1 shows that mental age increases fairly consistently from grade to grade, but falls below the chronological age level. The 1930 group was definitely older chronologically but younger mentally than the 1940 group; the difference between MA and CA of the 1940 group is about a third of that found ten years ago. There is still a tendency for the increments of mental growth to decrease with an increase in chronological age. During the first and second grades mental ages of the 1940 group lacks only four months of normality. This increases to eight months in Grade III, eleven months in Grade IV, and twelve months in Grades V-VIII. While the 1940 group is perfectly normal at ages six, seven and eight, the mental age falls below the chronological age in Grades I, II and III as a result of overageness and age-grade retardation. Beginning at age nine, the 1940 mental age falls from four months below normal to twenty-five months at fourteen years. The average difference between MA and normal CA is about a third as great as it was in 1930. These trends are shown also in the comparisons in Table III.

The distributions of IQ's for the 1930 and 1940 groups are shown in Table II. The median IQ for the 1930 group, 82 ± .40, has increased over ten points to 93 ± .25 in 1940. This gain is further shown by a study of the percentage of overlapping: Seventy-four per cent or about three-fourths of the 1930 cases are below the 1940 median. In 1930 the median IQ classified the children as a dull group, while in 1940 the group is within the normal classification. The wider range in 1940 is largely due to the increased number of cases.

Since 1930 there has been a noticeable IQ gain in all types of schools. In 1930 there was a greater tendency for the IQ to increase with the size of school. This trend was also shown in Baldwin's study, where Iowa farm children in one-room schools had a median IQ of 91.7, against 99.4 in the

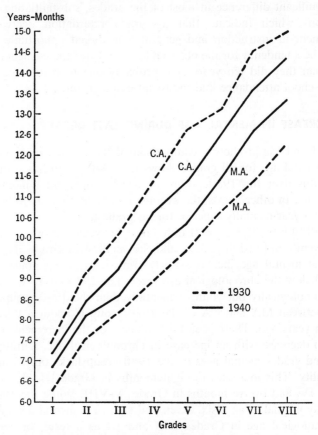

Figure 1. Comparison of chronological and mental ages of mountain children according to grade, 1930 and 1940 groups.

consolidated schools. The fact that there is less difference in the IQ among different types of schools in Tennessee mountain areas than in rural Iowa may indicate there is more uniformity of instruction and educational facilities in the mountain areas; perhaps the one-room schools are not so poor nor the larger schools as good as the consolidated schools in Iowa. Greater uniformity in instructional practices in 1940 may also be a factor in decreasing the differences among the various types of schools in the mountain area.

TABLE I

Comparison of Mental Ages of Mountain Children According to Grades and Chronological Ages

	Median CA	Median MA		Median MA
Grade I			Six-year-olds	
1930	7–5	6–3	1930.........	6–1
1940	7–2	6–10	1940.........	6–8
Difference	0–3	0–7	Difference.....	0–7
Grade II			Seven-year-olds	
1930	9–2	7–6	1930.........	6–10
1940	8–5	8–1	1940.........	7–6
Difference	0–9	0–7	Difference.....	0–8
Grade III			Eight-year-olds	
1930	10–2	8–2	1930.........	7–7
1940	9–3	8–7	1940.........	8–6
Difference	0–11	0–5	Difference.....	0–11
Grade IV			Nine-year-olds	
1930	11–4	8–11	1930.........	8–2
1940	10–7	9–8	1940.........	9–2
Difference	0–9	0–9	Difference.....	1–0
Grade V			Ten-year-olds	
1930	12–7	9–8	1930.........	8–10
1940	11–4	10–4	1940.........	9–7
Difference	1–3	0–8	Difference.....	0–9
Grade VI			Eleven-year-olds	
1930	13–1	10–7	1930.........	9–3
1940	12–5	11–5	1940.........	10–9
Difference	0–8	0–10	Difference.....	1–6
Grade VII			Twelve-year-olds	
1930	14–6	11–4	1930.........	10–2
1940	13–7	12–7	1940.........	11–3
Difference	0–11	1–3	Difference.....	1–1
Grade VIII			Thirteen-year-olds	
1930	15–0	12–3	1930.........	10–7
1940	14–4	13–4	1940.........	11–11
Difference	0–8	1–1	Difference.....	1–4
			Fourteen-year-olds	
			1930.........	10–11
			1940.........	12–4
			Difference.....	1–5
			Fifteen-year-olds	
			1930.........	11–4
			1940.........	12–7
			Difference.....	1–3
			Sixteen-year-olds	
			1930.........	12–2
			1940.........	13–3
			Difference.....	1–1

TABLE II
Comparison of IQ's of Mountain Children
According to Grades

	No. cases	Median IQ	PE	Q-1	Q-3	Q	Range
Grade I							
1930	115	84.10	1.14	74.91	94.42	9.76	45 to 115
1940	371	95.14	.57	86.08	103.73	8.83	50 to 165
Difference....	—	11.04	1.27				
Grade II							
1930	87	85.40	1.04	77.08	92.66	7.79	45 to 125
1940	282	95.66	.74	84.69	104.58	9.95	50 to 166
Difference....	—	10.26	1.27				
Grade III							
1930	103	83.96	1.27	72.92	93.54	10.32	45 to 150
1940	500	92.84	.64	80.67	103.62	11.48	35 to 160
Difference....	—	8.88	1.42				
Grade IV							
1930	172	81.50	1.18	69.30	94.17	12.44	45 to 135
1940	491	92.38	.71	79.83	104.83	12.50	45 to 160
Difference....	—	10.88	1.37				
Grade V							
1930	137	76.10	1.13	67.58	88.75	10.59	50 to 125
1940	465	91.36	.74	78.66	104.19	12.77	50 to 160
Difference....	—	15.26	1.35				
Grade VI							
1930	117	81.90	1.17	73.63	93.84	10.12	55 to 125
1940	458	92.41	.68	80.66	103.78	11.56	50 to 160'
Difference	—	10.51	1.35				
Grade VII							
1930	128	79.50	1.00	73.23	91.36	9.07	50 to 130
1940	360	92.63	.75	81.75	104.44	11.35	50 to 150
Difference....	—	13.13	1.25				
Grade VIII.....							
1930	87	84.80	1.13	73.25	90.14	8.45	55 to 120
1940	325	93.23	.76	82.78	104.80	11.01	40 to 150
Difference....	—	8.43	1.36				
All Grades							
1930	946	82.40	.40	72.70	92.62	9.96	45 to 150
1940	3252	92.22	.25	81.47	104.22	11.38	35 to 166
Difference....	—	10.82	.15				

TABLE III

Comparison of IQ's of Mountain Children According to CA

	No. cases	Median IQ	PE	Q-1	Q-3	Q	Range
Six-year-olds							
1930	33	94.68	2.03	89.06	107.75	9.34	75 to 115
1940	188	102.56	.64	95.34	109.38	7.02	75 to 165
Difference.......	—	7.88	2.12				
Seven-year-olds							
1930	62	90.90	1.38	81.25	98.61	8.68	55 to 125
1940	244	99.85	.66	91.38	107.77	8.19	65 to 160
Difference.......	—	8.95	1.54				
Eight-year-olds							
1930	60	88.88	1.09	82.33	95.90	6.78	40 to 110
1940	322	99.18	.70	90.50	110.71	10.10	60 to 160
Difference.......	—	10.30	1.29				
Nine-year-olds							
1930	94	86.38	1.79	79.95	95.22	7.72	60 to 145
1940	324	96.44	.74	85.73	107.07	10.67	55 to 160
Difference.......	—	10.06	1.93				
Ten-year-olds							
1930	99	84.25	1.64	74.29	94.75	10.23	50 to 125
1940	383	91.44	.73	81.33	104.04	11.36	45 to 160
Difference.......	—	7.19	1.79				
Eleven-year-olds							
1930	102	80.00	1.49	70.19	94.32	12.06	50 to 130
1940	358	93.87	.88	80.36	106.95	13.30	50 to 150
Difference.......	—	13.87	1.73				
Twelve-year-olds							
1930	107	81.41	1.06	74.25	91.88	8.81	50 to 135
1940	365	90.17	.80	75.67	100.13	12.23	35 to 150
Difference.......	—	8.76	1.33				
Thirteen-year-olds							
1930	109	77.61	1.22	66.56	86.97	10.21	45 to 120
1940	319	87.75	.87	75.30	100.04	12.37	50 to 145
Difference.......	—	10.14	1.48				
Fourteen-year-olds							
1930	125	74.72	1.09	63.39	82.80	9.71	45 to 115
1940	257	85.06	.75	74.05	93.33	9.64	50 to 125
Difference.......	—	10.34	1.32				
Fifteen-year-olds							
1930	61	73.44	1.39	65.56	82.93	8.71	59 to 95
1940	116	81.33	1.13	73.00	92.50	9.75	50 to 110
Difference.......	—	7.89	1.79				
Sixteen-year-olds							
1930	29	73.50	2.41	64.06	84.81	10.37	45 to 95
1940	34	80.00	2.08	68.12	87.50	9.69	40 to 110
Difference.......	—	6.50	3.18				

Table III shows the median IQ of the 1940 group is consistently higher at all ages. The differences are statistically significant at all ages except sixteen, where the limited number of cases tends to increase the PE's. Similar trends are seen in comparing the ranges of the two groups, and the first and third quartiles. Both groups show a decline in IQ with increasing chronological age.

OVER-AGENESS AND DECLINE IN IQ

The study of mountain children in 1930 showed a consistent decrease in IQ with increase in chronological age from 94.7 at age six to 73.5 at age sixteen, a decline of 1.9 points a year. The study in 1940 shows a similar decline from 102.6 at age six to 80 at age sixteen, an average of two points each year. The total decrease in IQ in 1930 was 21.3 points, and in 1940, 22.6 points. In 1930 the children were within the normal intelligence group at age six; the 1940 data definitely show that the children are normal at age six. Some investigators explain this decline in IQ and the low average intelligence of mountain children as due to a poor heredity, caused by inbreeding and the superior families leaving the mountains for better economic and educational opportunities in other sections. Others base their explanations on the theory that the mind develops with stimulation, maintaining that, since the rural environment is less stimulating, there occurs a general decline in the rate of mental growth as the children become older chronologically. It has also been suggested that the relative placement of the items of tests standardized on urban children does not adequately measure the development of the rural child, especially in the older age-levels.

Over-ageness and age-grade retardation among rural and mountain children has been observed by various investigators, and presents a serious problem in the rural schools of Tennessee. In order to study the influence of this factor on the decline of the IQ, in Table IV all children who were over-age one and two-or-more years were eliminated from each grade. In Grade I nearly half the children are over-age, and the retardation increases to seventy-three per cent in Grade VIII. For the normal-age groups the IQ remains normal at each grade level. The over-age group definitely lowers the total average for each grade. The effect of this age-grade retardation on the median IQ is shown in Table V. The retarded cases lower the IQ from four points at age seven and eight to 14.83 ± 1.53 points at age twelve. As over-ageness increases, and retardations accumulate from grade to grade, there occurs a corresponding decline in IQ, indicating that age-grade retardation causes the median IQ to decline with increasing chronological age. The IQ decreases with an increase in the amount of age-grade retardation.

The decline of the IQ with increase in chronological age is the same

TABLE IV

Showing the Effect of Over-ageness on the Distribution of IQ's

	Per cent of cases	Median IQ	Range
Grade I			
6-year-olds............................	51.3	102.56	75 to 165
7-year-olds............................	30.8	92.82	65 to 120
8 years and over.......................	17.9	90.04	50 to 115
All ages	100.0	95.14	50 to 165
Grade II			
7-year-olds............................	44.6	104.00	75 to 166
8-year-olds............................	30.2	94.00	60 to 150
9 years and over.......................	25.2	88.98	50 to 140
All ages	100.0	95.66	50 to 166
Grade III			
8-year-olds............................	40.5	103.28	75 to 160
9-year-olds............................	25.7	91.79	65 to 155
10 years and over......................	33.8	83.45	35 to 130
All ages	100.0	92.84	35 to 160
Grade IV			
9-year-olds............................	34.7	104.13	55 to 160
10-year-olds...........................	26.1	90.33	45 to 135
11 years and over......................	39.2	82.68	45 to 135
All ages	100.0	92.38	45 to 160
Grade V			
10-year-olds...........................	35.6	102.17	70 to 160
11-year-olds...........................	25.8	92.91	50 to 130
12 years and over......................	38.6	79.00	50 to 125
All ages	100.0	91.36	50 to 160
Grade VI			
11-year-olds...........................	32.8	103.44	60 to 160
12-year-olds...........................	31.3	93.09	65 to 130
13 years and over......................	35.0	80.70	50 to 120
All ages	100.0	92.41	50 to 160
Grade VII			
12-year-olds...........................	30.0	105.00	65 to 150
13-year-olds...........................	31.2	93.18	60 to 145
14 years and over......................	38.8	79.80	50 to 130
All ages	100.0	92.63	50 to 150
Grade VIII			
13-year-olds...........................	27.0	101.00	60 to 150
14-year-olds...........................	32.2	90.17	60 to 125
15 years and over......................	40.8	88.52	40 to 115
All ages	100.0	93.23	40 to 150

TABLE V

Showing the Effect of Retardation on the Decrease in IQ with Increasing CA

	No. cases	Median IQ	PE
Seven-year-olds			
1. Retarded cases eliminated	124	104.00	1.00
2. All cases	244	99.85	.66
3. Difference...........................	—	4.15	1.19
Eight-year-olds			
1. Retarded cases eliminated	178	103.28	.88
2. All cases	322	99.18	.70
3. Difference...........................	—	4.10	1.08
Nine-year-olds			
1. Retarded cases eliminated	148	104.13	.98
2. All cases	324	96.44	.74
3. Difference...........................	—	7.69	1.22
Ten-year-olds			
1. Retarded cases eliminated	146	102.17	1.30
2. All cases	383	91.44	.73
3. Difference...........................	—	10.73	1.49
Eleven-year-olds			
1. Retarded cases eliminated	128	103.44	1.21
2. All cases	358	93.87	.88
3. Difference...........................	—	9.57	1.49
Twelve-year-olds			
1. Retarded cases eliminated	94	105.00	1.31
2. All cases	365	90.17	.80
3. Difference...........................	—	14.83	1.53
Thirteen-year-olds			
1. Retarded cases eliminated	76	101.00	1.47
2. All cases	319	87.75	.87
3. Difference...........................	—	13.25	1.70

as it was a decade ago except that it is on a higher IQ level. Over a period of ten years the general level of intelligence of these mountain children has been raised ten IQ points. We have shown that although this investigation throws further light on the data and interpretations presented ten years ago, more research with other groups in other areas is needed before reaching any final conclusions as to the relative influence of nature and nurture on IQ changes. A check study should also be made to determine whether children in the general population score higher today on the Dearborn Tests than they did a decade ago. However, the general trends found in these mountain studies and in other investigations of rural children present a challenge for education: Large environmental changes appear to influence the IQ. In contrast to other social philosophies, our democratic ideals depend upon the opportunities each child has for developing his individual abilities.

SUMMARY

(1) There is a general agreement among investigators that urban children rate higher on intelligence tests than rural or mountain children.

(2) The majority of studies indicate a decrease in IQ with an increase in chronological age.

(3) There are diverse opinions concerning the factors which cause rural-urban differences and the decline in IQ.

(4) During the Spring and Fall of 1940, intelligence tests were given to three thousand two hundred fifty-two children in forty mountain schools of East Tennessee, and the results are compared with a similar study made ten years ago.

(5) During the decade there has been definite improvement in the economic, social and educational status of this mountain area.

(6) Today the average mountain child is about eight months younger chronologically and nine months older mentally for his grade than the average child of ten years ago.

(7) The difference between the chronological and mental age of the average mountain child is now about one-third as great as it was a decade ago.

(8) The 1940 group of mountain children is mentally superior to the 1930 group at all ages and all grades, as measured by the same tests.

(9) The average mountain child has gained ten points in IQ, or nearly one point a year during the past ten years.

(10) The average mountain child's IQ decreases about two points each year from age six to sixteen. This is about the same rate of decline as was found ten years ago.

(11) Over-ageness, or age-grade retardation, among mountain children appears to be the predominating cause of the decline in IQ with increase in chronological age.

(12) The results of this investigation gives further light on the findings of the 1930 study, and indicate that intelligence, as measured by these tests, may be improved with an improvement in educational and general environmental conditions.

The data from the Army intelligence tests of the First World War were revived in various fashions after twenty years and presented to "prove" or illustrate a writer's particular point of view. Alper and Boring, tiring of these partial analyses, made an attempt to focus attention of readers on complete sets of data. Their paper, though mildly written, is a reproof for investigators who become possessed with a zeal to convince readers of the correctness of their position at the expense of presenting all the facts.

Intelligence-test Scores of Northern and Southern White and Negro Recruits in 1918*

THELMA G. ALPER

EDWIN G. BORING

1944

Last spring the pamphlet of Benedict and Weltfish, *The Races of Mankind,* achieved national attention when the Committee on Military Affairs of the House of Representatives in Congress found it "unfit for U. S. soldiers" and got it withdrawn from general circulation in the Army. The statement in the pamphlet that especially aroused the ire of certain Congressmen was to the effect that the intelligence of Negro recruits in three selected northern states had been shown, in the First World War, to be higher than the intelligence of white recruits in three other selected southern states. The Committee on Military Affairs protested that Benedict and Weltfish had prejudiced their findings in favor of the Negro by selecting those particular states which would permit this conclusion.

Benedict and Weltfish had, of course, as had Klineberg before them, selected their states with a purpose. They wanted to show that score on an intelligence test is as much a function of geography as of skin color, that the differences in certain instances are due more to cultural advantages and disadvantages than to race, that the effects of geography and skin color on score may both be due to cultural influences, that for this reason being southern may be as great a disadvantage in attaining high scores on a test as being Negro. Most psychologists will agree with them in this matter, and few will assert that any unalterable racial differences in intelligence have ever been established, so great is the effect of culture upon intelligence test scores.

It seemed to us, since this issue has been raised about the recruits of

* *Journal of Abnormal and Social Psychology,* 39 (1944), pp. 471-474. Reprinted by permission of the authors and the American Psychological Association.

1918, that it would be interesting to present the total picture of the Army scores, as neither Klineberg nor Benedict and Weltfish have done, rounding out the account by the inclusion of the scores of the southern Negroes and the northern whites, by the addition of the scores on the Beta examination to those on the Alpha examination, and by then performing an analysis of variance in respect of geography and skin color.

Everyone knows that Negro recruits in both World Wars have scored much lower on intelligence tests than have white recruits, whenever the more obvious parameters besides skin color are kept constant. The data from the First World War showed that northern Negroes did much better on the tests than southern Negroes. Anastasi printed results for the Negro recruits on both the Alpha and Beta examinations, making it clear that Negroes in the North do better than Negroes in the South, but saying nothing about the comparison of the northern Negro with the southern white. Klineberg gave the results of the Alpha examination only for the whites of four southern states and the Negroes of four northern states, showing that the average score for the Negroes in each of these states was higher than the average for the whites in each of the southern states. Benedict and Weltfish repeated Klineberg's results, making them a little more striking by omitting the northern state in which the Negroes averaged lowest and the southern state in which the whites averaged highest. That was fair enough, since they wanted to show that the difference usually found can be reversed when extreme instances are selected. We chose for study in this note Klineberg's four states, since Klineberg's results have been so widely quoted. They are named in the legend of Table I.

TABLE I

Average Intelligence-Test Scores of 26,894 Northern and Southern White and Negro Recruits in the First World War

Entries are in terms of the Combined Scale, which combines the scores from the Alpha and Beta examination and gives figures not wholly unlike mental ages. Northern states: Illinois, New York, Ohio, Pennsylvania. Southern states: Arkansas, Georgia, Kentucky, Mississippi. SD: standard deviations of the distributions. N: number of cases.

			Skin color	
			Negro	White
Geography	*Southern*	Av.	9.8	12.7
		SD	1.82	2.41
		N	5425	3904
	Northern	Av.	12.0	14.1
		SD	2.41	2.60
		N	4455	13110

We have also combined the scores of the Beta examination with the scores of the Alpha examination by the method described by Carl R. Brown. This gives us scores in terms of his Combined Scale, with values that are not wholly unlike mental ages in their magnitudes. We thought that the inclusion of the Beta scores ought to give the Negroes some advantage that they did not have when Alpha scores were used alone. Beta was given to all men who scored low on Alpha, because they were either stupid or unable to read English. All illiterates, English speaking and non-English speaking, therefore, took Beta. Its instructions were given in pantomime and it required no reading. It was obviously not culture-free, for some of the more difficult items depended on a good deal of sophistication. Our results show that these Negroes were not advantaged by Beta, relative to the whites.

It ought to be said that the Army psychologists of 1919 were not ready to draw any conclusions at all about the relative intelligence of the recruits from different states. There were too many unknown factors operating in the selection of these samples. The psychologists printed the data for what they were worth and left interpretation to the future.

The primary results on the Alpha and Beta examinations for northern and southern white and Negro recruits in terms of Brown's Combined Score appear in Table I. They are what one might expect from what is already known. It was a disadvantage in the Army tests of 1918 for a white or a Negro to come from a southern state where education and economic opportunities are few instead of from a northern state where they are better, and also a disadvantage, whether northern or southern, to be Negro and not white. Thus the average score for the southern Negroes is lowest of the four because southern Negroes work against both these disadvantages, and the average score for the northern whites is, conversely, highest of all. Benedict and Weltfish might have avoided the criticism of selection of states

TABLE II
Analysis of Variance of the Data of Table I

"Interaction" is the additional variance due to the fact that the effect of skin color reenforces the effect of geography. Variance "within group" is the variance that still remains unexplained after the separate effects of skin color and geography and the effect of their mutual interaction have been analyzed out. The three F-values are so much more significant than 1 chance in 1,000 of their being random that they lie nowhere near the entries of the published tables.

Source of variance	Degrees of freedom	Sum of squares	Mean square	F
Total	26,893	203,776	—	—
Skin Color	1	32,812	32,812	5,697
Geography	1	17,010	17,010	2,953
Interaction	1	840	840	146
Within Group	26,890	153,114	5.76	—

TABLE III

**Numbers of Men Who Took the Alpha and Beta Examinations, and
the Totals, for the Data of Table I**

	Negro recruits			White recruits			Totals		
	Alpha	Beta	Total	Alpha	Beta	Total	Alpha	Beta	Total
Southern	1,456	3,969	5,425	2,817	1,087	3,904	4,273	5,056	9,329
Northern	2,538	1,917	4,455	10,306	2,804	13,110	12,844	4,721	17,565
Total	3,994	5,886	9,880	13,123	3,891	17,014	17,117	9,777	26,894

had they given all four of these averages instead of only two, for then they would have avoided the false implication that skin color made no difference in the states under consideration.

Tables III and IV show that very many more Negroes than whites took the Beta examination and that the number of men who took Beta in a sample is a rough prediction of how low the average score on the Combined Scale will be. That might, of course, be due to the fact that low intelligence sent many men to Beta, but certainly the Army psychologists of 1918 believed that the chief cause of being sent to Beta was illiteracy. In respect of the huge difference in these tables, Alpha might almost be considered as a literacy test.

TABLE IV

**Percentages of Recruits Taking the Beta Examination,
Derived from Table III**

	Negro	White	Total
Southern	73.2	27.8	54.2
Northern	43.0	21.4	26.9
Total	59.6	22.9	36.3

It is interesting to note in Table I that the average score on the Combined Scale for northern Negroes is not quite as high as it was for the southern whites. Since the direction of this difference reverses the direction for the Alpha scores as reported by Klineberg and by Benedict and Weltfish, it appears that the inclusion of the scores from the Beta examination, while they undoubtedly helped the Negroes, helped the whites more. Our only suggestion in explanation of this fact is that Beta is less culture-free than even we had supposed, that Beta is better adapted to whites than to Negroes. Thus the 23 per cent of the southern whites that took Beta raised the average score for southern whites more than the 43 per cent of northern Negroes raised the average score for northern Negroes. Of course, it is possible to say that Beta overcomes illiteracy more than stupidity, and that the proportion of Negroes who went to Beta because of stupidity was greater than the proportion of whites who went for stupidity, a conclusion fully consistent with the common prejudice about the low level of Negro intelligence. We should not, however, wish to draw this conclusion in view of the fact that cultural differences are known to have such a large effect on test scores.

In general, then, we think that Benedict and Weltfish were right about the importance of culture, or at least not demonstrably wrong; but we also think that they should have presented more complete data. They would have strengthened their case had they but shown clearly that skin color as well as geography did affect the test scores of the recruits in 1918, and had they then gone on, as they did, to argue that it is the Negro's educational disadvantages and not actually his color which handicaps him in these tests.

The Army General Classification Test was the "work horse" general-purpose test of the services in World War II, as the famous Army Alpha had been in World War I. It is important for the student to see here, as he will again later in Vernon's paper, the efficiency of a gross general-purpose instrument when applied to a heterogeneous adult population. Tables 6 and 7 offer a convincing demonstration of both the general utility of the test and of the effect of heterogeneity of sample on correlation coefficients obtained.

The Army General Classification Test*

STAFF, PERSONNEL RESEARCH SECTION

1945

I. *Introduction.* An important milestone in the history of psychometrics was established in World War I with the development of Group Examination Alpha. Not only was this the pioneer paper-and-pencil test of mental ability, but for more than twenty-five years, it has held a clear title to the honor of being the most widely administered test. This honor now passes to the Army General Classification Test whose upwards of nine million administrations leaves it no challenger to the title.

The Army General Classification Test (AGCT) is a test of "general learning ability." Developed by Army personnel technicians, it was completed before the first draftees arrived at reception centers in 1940 and has been given to every literate inductee since that time. During more than four years of use, four separate but comparable forms of the test were developed and released. AGCT-1a was released in October 1940, 1b in April 1941, and 1c and 1d in October 1941. The first two forms were discontinued (except for use of supplies on hand) with the release of forms 1c and 1d, and these latter were used continuously until replaced by a new type test battery, the Army General Classification Test-3, in April 1945.

AGCT-1 contains three types of items in spiral-omnibus form: vocabulary, arithmetic, and "block-counting." Forms 1a and 1b contain 150 test items and a separate practice booklet; 1c and 1d include 140 scored items and 10 practice items. All items are of the four-choice multiple choice variety, arranged for administration with a separate answer sheet to enable either hand or machine scoring. The time limit for all forms is 40 minutes, and the raw score is the number of "rights" minus one-third of the number of "wrongs."

* Reprinted from *The Psychological Bulletin,* 42 (1945), pp. 760-768, by permission of the Adjutant General's Office, U.S. Army, and the American Psychological Association.

II. *Development of AGCT-1a.* In the spring of 1940, a Personnel Testing Section was established under the War Plans and Training Officer of The Adjutant General's Office. With a small staff of two or three reserve officers on temporary tour-of-duty status, one civilian personnel technician (detailed from the Air Corps Technical School) and a few clerks, this section was assigned the task of developing a classification test for use with recruits reporting at receiving centers in the Army. The proposed test, to be used in the same manner as the Group Examination Alpha, was to be capable of reliably sorting new arrivals according to their "ability to learn quickly the duties of a soldier." In April of the same year, a Committee on Classification of Military Personnel Advisory to The Adjutant General's Office was established by the National Research Council. At the first meeting of this group, May 24, 1940, the proposed new test was discussed and the work so far accomplished was outlined. In a report to the committee at this meeting, Lt. Colonel (then Captain) M. W. Richardson enumerated the following specifications for the test:

1. The test includes both verbal and non-verbal items.
2. Assuming that modern warfare is rapidly becoming more technical, emphasis is placed upon items calling for spatial thinking and for quantitative reasoning.
3. It is planned to keep at a minimum items greatly influenced by amount of schooling and by cultural inequalities generally. To this end, the use of information items is not planned.
4. Insofar as possible, the time or speed element is to be minimized.
5. The general classification test is not intended to serve the purpose of trade tests.
6. It is specifically recognized that the test does not measure personality traits.
7. The test must appeal to the average officer and soldier as sensible.

At this time, approximately 5,000 test items had been constructed, including the following types: arithmetic reasoning, common sense, vocabulary, number series, synonyms and antonyms. In an effort to minimize the verbal character of the materials, work was being done with pictorial items (cubes, plane figures, etc.). In June an experimental test containing some of these materials was printed but proved to be too restricted in range of difficulty. Later a preliminary test composed of vocabulary, arithmetic, and block-counting items, in separate sections, was printed. And by August 1940, the first form of the Army General Classification Test (AGCT-1a) was ready for standardization. This form, like all subsequent editions, contained the same three kinds of items—vocabulary, arithmetic and block-counting—but was arranged in spiral-omnibus form.

III. *Standardization of AGCT-1a.* In World War I, the Group Examination Alpha was not administered on an Army-wide basis until the early part of 1918, by which time more than two million men had already been inducted and trained. The problem of standardization, therefore, was relatively simple. In 1940, it had been decided to provide a set of norms for easy interpretation of AGCT scores in such fashion that the average soldier would receive a score of 100 and the standard deviation of all scores would be 20. But in order to prepare this standard score scale in time for use with the earliest draftees, it was necessary to standardize the test for a population that had not yet been selected. In other words, it was necessary to compute a set of derived "Army Standard Scores" based on the universe of potential draftees. Since it was impossible to administer the test to a representative sample of the potential Army population, it was decided to administer it to a group of available men and to estimate the mean and standard deviation of the population from the statistics of the tested sample by means of a weighting technique. An optimal weighting procedure would require that the sample be stratified with respect to all variables whose joint effects would account for all of the test variance. Since it was impossible to infer all possible correlates, it was assumed that an adequate proportion of test variance would be accounted for by the three factors of age, education and area of residence.

The AGCT-1a was, therefore, administered to a sample composed of 3,790 Regular Army enlisted men and 606 CCC enrollees. After the selection of cases in the desired age brackets (20-29 years) and elimination of those with incomplete information regarding education and residence, the sample was reduced to 2,675. The computation of the Army Standard Score scale was then carried out in five steps:

1. Determination from census data of the proportion of the total potential Army population in each age group by education and by area of residence.
2. Determination of the same proportions for the sample tested.
3. Weighting each cell of the sample so that its characteristics with regard to the variables of age, education and residence were the same as those of the total population.
4. Determination of the estimated parameters of the potential population from the weighted raw score mean and standard deviation of the sample.
5. Computation of Army Standard Score equivalents for each AGCT raw score by linear transformation.

It is recognized that this method involves a number of assumptions which cannot be demonstrated to be in accord with the facts:

1. That the three variables considered account for a large proportion of the test variance.
2. That the distribution of scores within each cell of the sample is random with respect to the distribution of scores in the corresponding cell of the total potential population.
3. That there is no differential death rate for the various age groups (since the age distributions of the 1940 potential Army population were estimated from the 1930 census data).
4. That the actual Army population would be a random sample of the total potential Army population, i.e., that no bias would enter into the selection of those men in the total potential Army population who were to be drafted.

If these assumptions were justifiable, and if distribution of AGCT standard scores in the potential Army population were normal, then it might be
expected that the actual distribution of AGCT standard scores of inductees
would be normal and that the percentages in each of the five Army Grades
would be those listed in Table I (Expected Percentages). The obtained
grade distribution (last column, Table I) indicates that this expected

TABLE I
Expected and Obtained Distributions of Army Grades on AGCT-1a

Army grade	Limits in terms of standard deviation*	Limits in terms of army standard scores*	Expected percentages	Obtained percentages†
I	$+1\frac{1}{2}\sigma$ and above	130 and above	7	9.0
II	$+\frac{1}{2}\sigma-+1\frac{1}{2}\sigma$	110–129	24	36.4
III	$-\frac{1}{2}\sigma-+\frac{1}{2}\sigma$	90–109	38	29.0
IV	$-1\frac{1}{2}\sigma--\frac{1}{2}\sigma$	70– 89	24	17.0
V	Below $-1\frac{1}{2}\sigma$	Below 70	7	8.6

* On 15 July 1942 the lower limit of Grade IV was extended downward an additional half standard deviation from Army Standard Score of 70 to 60.

† Based on the population of 589,701 cases reported from November 1940 to
October 1941.

distribution was only approximated, and suggests that the assumptions involved in the standardization were not entirely warranted. In the first place,
it was not practicable to include race as a variable in the weighting procedure. Secondly, the actual Army population does not truly reflect the potential Army population due to the selective elimination of those with low
mentality and those with occupational and dependency deferments. There
are doubtless a number of other factors which account for the discrepancy
between the expected and obtained distributions.

IV. *Alternate Forms.* Following the release of the AGCT-1a, work
was started on the preparation of alternate forms. The first of these, form
1b, was authorized for use in April 1941. It contained the same three kinds
of items as form 1a: vocabulary, arithmetic and block-counting. The vocabulary items were presented in context, instead of in the "means the same as"
form of AGCT-1a. The block-counting items were the same as those in
the earlier form.

AGCT-1b was standardized on a population of 3,856 men who were also
given the 1a form. The raw score means and standard deviation for the
two forms, and the coefficient of correlation between forms were as follows:

	AGCT-1a	AGCT-1b
Mean	77.7	77.6
Standard Deviation	29.2	31.4
Correlation between forms	.954	
Number of Cases	3,856	

Standard score equivalents for each 1b raw score were computed from the combined regression equations of the correlational surface (i.e., linear transformation to a distribution having the same mean and standard deviation as the 1a standard score distribution for the population involved). This method was logical in assuming the error variance to be distributed equally between the two tests. And it resulted in an Army grade distribution for 1b which closely approximated that for 1a, which was desirable from the viewpoint of field use.

Forms 1c and 1d were prepared at the same time and were released in October 1941. Questions concerning modifications in content and format were considered, but were resolved in favor of the earlier forms. All items were newly constructed for each form except that the same block-counting items were used in both. The separate practice booklet was dropped, and the fore-exercise incorporated into the test booklet itself. The number of practice items was reduced to ten, and the number of test items to 140. The time limit remained the same.

Forms 1c and 1d were standardized at the same time on a population of 1,782 cases. This group was administered both new forms, in counterbalanced order, and scores on form 1a were obtained from the records. The means and standard deviations of the three forms are given in Table II. The

TABLE II
Means and Standard Deviations of the Various Forms of AGCT. Standardization of Forms 1c & 1d

Form	N	Mean*	Standard deviation*
1a	1782	104.37	23.41
1c	1782	59.72	26.90
1d	1782	59.05	26.27

* Values for 1a are expressed in Army standard scores, and those for 1c and 1d are in terms of raw scores.

two new forms are very well matched in difficulty, as judged by their means and standard deviations. No comparison between old and new forms is possible since the 1a values are given in terms of standard scores. In general, however, forms 1c and 1d are somewhat more difficult than 1a, and are more discriminating in the upper ranges of ability.

Standard score equivalents for the new forms were computed by a method which was intended to reduce some of the negative skewness of the earlier distributions, and at the same time, keep the meaning of the standard score scale for all forms essentially the same. This method involved the construction of an arbitrary criterion distribution for the population tested based on the combined values of all three forms, and the scaling of 1c and 1d raw scores against this new criterion distribution by the method of "equivalent percentiles." The resulting conversion table was used for both 1c and 1d. Using the same score limits for the five Army grades as with the previous editions, the two new forms placed 2–3% fewer men in grades I and II, and about the same percentage more men in the two lower grades. The distribution of 1c and 1d scores paralleled the theoretical normal distribution through the upper score ranges but deviated markedly below the mean. This marked discrepancy was mainly produced by the application of the test to illiterates or semi-illiterates who were completely unable to cope with it. Nearly a fifth of all the scores in the Grade V range are in the standard score interval of 40–44, and 27 per cent of them are below 50. When it is considered that the raw score equivalents of these intervals are,

Standard score interval	Raw scores
40–44	0, 1
45–49	2, 3

it is obvious that many men for whom the test is not appropriate are included in the distribution.

From the Army viewpoint, the excess of Grade V's was disturbing, since, rightly or wrongly, this grade has come to have a stereotyped meaning which often leads unit commanders to protest if allotted too many such men. As an expedient, therefore, the Grade V range was arbitrarily narrowed by extending the lower score limit of Grade IV an additional half standard deviation downward. This, of course, had no effect upon the distribution of scores but altered the grade distribution considerably. With these new score limits, the grade distribution became much more symmetrical, as shown in Table III. This table is based on more than 8 million cases tested in reception centers throughout the country prior to January 1945.

TABLE III

Grade Distribution of Men Processed Through Reception Centers 1940–1944

Army grade	Standard score limits	Percentage of total group
I	130 and above	6.0
II	110–129	26.5
III	90–109	30.5
IV	60–89	27.7
V	59 and below	9.3

Total number of cases.............. 8,293,879

V. *Reliability.* The reliabilities of each of the forms of AGCT have been computed a number of times and by various methods. Typical values of these reliability coefficients are presented in Table IV. These reliabilities are consistently high with the exception of the retest reliability of form 1a. There are several reasons for this: the interval between tests varied considerably; the conditions under which the tests were administered varied from test to retest; the population is highly selected (mean score of 118.6) and narrowly restricted in range (SD of 12.2). The correlations between forms are generally high, permitting them to be used interchangeably.

VI. *Relation to Other Variables.* Performance on AGCT is not related to age. The correlation, in a representative Army population, is .02 (Table V). There is some evidence, however, that with older and more

TABLE IV

Reliability Coefficients of the Various Forms of the Army General Classification Test

Form	Method	N		Mean	SD	Coefficient of reliability
1a	Kuder-Richardson #21	2,675		75.7*	24.5*	.94
	Odd-even, corrected	639		—	—	.97
	Retest (various intervals between tests)	501		118.6	12.2	.82
	Alternate forms	472	1a	87.7*	27.2*	.89
			1b	88.2*	24.4*	
1b	Kuder-Richardson #21	495		76.1*	31.7*	.97
	Alternate forms	3,856	1b	77.6*	31.4*	.92
			1a	77.7*	29.2*	
1c	Kuder-Richardson #21	1,782		59.7*	26.9*	.96
	Alternate forms (1–13 week interval)	593	1c	60.0*	27.3*	.90
			1a or b	104.4	23.9	
1d	Kuder-Richardson #21	1,782		59.1*	26.3*	.96
	Alternate forms	593	1d	59.6*	26.6*	.95
			1c	60.0*	27.3*	

* Values expressed in raw scores; all others in standard scores.

highly selected groups, the correlation is negative. With two groups of officers, for example, whose mean AGCT scores were 122.2 and 120.4 (SD's 12.5 and 11.9) and whose mean ages were 31.6 and 32.8, the correlations between AGCT and age were −.33 and −.20 respectively. This negative relationship is doubtless due in part, at least, to the fact that AGCT is administered as a time-limit test, and the speed element may be important despite original intentions.

As might be expected, the correlation between AGCT and education is rather high (Table V). With education expressed in terms of highest grade completed, the correlation is .73. When expressed in terms of number of years of education, the correlation is slightly lower; for some 20 different samples, the coefficients ranged from .16 to .66 with a median value of .60.

TABLE V
Correlation of AGCT with Age and Education

Variable	Form	N	Mean	SD	r
Age	1a	4330	70.4*	24.4*	.02
Education (highest grade completed)	1a	4330	70.4*	24.4*	.73
Education (number of years in school)	1c	500	104.1	21.5	.66
Education (number of years in school)	1c	461	116.9	14.5	.46
Education (number of years in school)	Uniden-tified	478	106.9	20.9	.66

* Values given in raw scores; all others in standard scores.

The relationship between the AGCT and some other well-known tests of mental ability (or intelligence) is shown in Table VI. Unfortunately, for the purpose of answering questions of comparability, most of these data are not wholly satisfactory. For the most part, the correlations listed are by-products of studies designed for other specific purposes. Most of the populations involved were consequently preselected on the basis of one or another of the two tests with a restriction in range on one or both variables.

This truncation is demonstrated by the AGCT means and standard deviations of the samples listed in the table. In three cases, the AGCT means are well above 100 and in four cases the standard deviations are less than 20.* Two of the populations cited approximate the AGCT distribution of the total Army, and in both of these cases the correlation is high. Evidently the AGCT, the Army Alpha, and the Otis test yield roughly comparable results over the range of ability represented in the Army.

TABLE VI
Correlations between AGCT and Various Other Tests of Mental Ability

Test	N	AGCT Means	SD's	r
Army Alpha (Well's Revision-long form)	434	115.4	12.3	.79
Army Alpha (Well's Revision-long form)	750	98.3	22.7	.90
Otis Higher Mental Ability Examination	1646	103.5	23.1	.83
ACE Psychological Examination	885	127.7	12.4	.65
ACE Psychological Examination	1371	114.1	16.3	.79
Army-Navy College Qualifying Test, C-3	251	108.6	14.5	.75

* Since these data are presented in terms of Army standard scores, the mean and standard deviation of a representative Army population would approximate 100 and 20 respectively.

VII. *Validity of the AGCT*. The major usefulness of the **AGCT** in the Army has stemmed from its value in selecting men for a large number of specialist training courses. Several hundred validity coefficients attest to its value in this connection. A sample of these validity coefficients is presented in Table VII. One or two points about the data presented there should be noted. In the first place, as is evidenced by the means and standard deviations listed, most of the populations were preselected on some variable correlated with AGCT (education, civilian occupation, etc.) or on AGCT itself. Secondly, in most instances the criterion employed is academic grades in the training course. Both of the points should be considered in drawing conclusions from the data contained in Table VII.

According to the table, the AGCT appears to be of value in predicting grades in a wide variety of training assignments. In the technical training courses (excluding the last three categories in the table) the correlations with grades range from .20 to .73. The lower figures are four courses in teletype maintenance (.20), photography (.24) and aircraft welding (.26); the higher values are for the theoretical phases of the plotter-teller course in aircraft warning (.73), and for grades in motor mechanics (.69), bombardier training (.62) and WAAC clerical training (.62). Comparisons are difficult, however, because of the factor of pre-selection. In each of the instances cited where low validity coefficients were obtained, the groups had been selected on several factors, including AGCT score. In some of the other groups, yielding higher coefficients, pre-selection was either not so rigorous (aircraft warning trainees) or was not exercised at all (motor mechanics).

In officer candidate schools, AGCT usually correlates with academic grades around .40, despite the rigid selection and restricted range of scores.* The correlation with leadership ratings, however, is low; consequently the biserial correlation against success or failure (grades plus leadership) is only .28. The test also correlates well with grades in English, mathematics and military topography for the first year at the U.S. Military Academy, but shows little relationship to grades in foreign language courses. As a predictor of grades in the Army Specialized Training Program, however, the AGCT comes off rather badly. This is partly accounted for by the selected character of the population of trainees;† and it is partly a function of the training program itself. Because the various courses and curricula were sharply accelerated, they leaned more heavily than is usual for college courses, perhaps, on a thorough background in high school subjects, and less heavily on abstract ability to learn. A special selection test involving English usage and mathematics of the type normally encountered in secondary school curricula yielded validity coefficients as high as .60-.70 for various AST courses.

* A score of 110 or better on AGCT is a prerequisite for officer training.
† An AGCT score of 115 or better was required of candidates for the AST Program.

TABLE VII

Validity Coefficients of the AGCT. Various Examples

Population	Criterion	N	Mean	SD	r
Administrative Clerical Trainees, AAF	Grades	2947	121.7	11.1	.40
Clerical Trainees, AAF	Grades (weighted)	123	125.9	9.9	.44
Clerical Trainees, Armored	Grades	119	125.3	8.3	.33
Clerical Trainees, WAAC	Grades	199	116.8	12.0	.62
Airplane Mechanic Trainees	Grades	99	104.8	10.6	.32
Airplane Mechanic Trainees	Grades	3081	118.1	10.7	.35
Motor Mechanic Trainees	Grades	318	88.3	24.4	.69
Tank Mechanic Trainees	Grades	237	116.6	11.3	.33
Aircraft Armorer Trainees	Grades	1907	117.3	10.9	.40
Aircraft Armorer Trainees	Ratings	449	112.7	12.1	.27
Aircraft Welding Trainees	Grades	583	114.8	10.3	.26
Bombsight Maintenance Trainees	Grades	195	129.1	10.5	.31
Sheet Metal Trainees, AAF	Grades	764	115.6	10.3	.27
Teletype Maintenance Trainees, AAF	Grades	487	123.5	12.1	.20
Radio Operator & Mechanic Trainees, AAF	Grades	1055	122.4	11.1	.32
Radio Operator & Mechanic Trainees, AAF	Code Rcg Speed, WPM	217	117.4	11.7	.24
Radio Operator Trainees, WAAC	Grades	152	116.2	11.7	.38
Radio Mechanic Trainees, AAF	Grades	419	108.0	13.0	.49
Gunnery Trainees, Armored	Grades	66	120.0	12.1	.50
Field Artillery Trainees, Instrument and Survey	Grades	68	102.7	6.5	.33
Motor Transport Trainees, WAAC	Grades	269	111.4	13.6	.31
Tank Driver Trainees	Ratings	330	87.7	19.5	.16
Truck Driver Trainees	Road Test Ratings	421	95.5	20.1	.13
Bombardier Trainees, AAF	Grades, Academic	40	111.5	18.6	.62
Aircraft Warning Trainees, Plotter-Teller	Grades, Theory	119	107.1	15.6	.73
Aircraft Warning Trainees, Plotter-Teller	Grades, Performance	119	107.1	15.6	.26
Intelligence Trainees, AAF	Grades, Academic	104	118.9	10.6	.51
Photography Trainees, AAF	Grades	431	123.0	11.9	.24
Cryptography Trainees, AAF	Grades, Phase 1	417	129.9	9.7	.31
Weather Observer Trainees, AAF	Grades	1042	130.2	12.5	.43
Officer Candidates, Infantry	Grades, Academic	103	123.0	10.8	.30
Officer Candidates, Ordnance	Grades, Academic	190	128.2	9.6	.41
Officer Candidates, Signal Corps	Grades, Academic	213	128.6	10.1	.36
Officer Candidates, Tank Destroyers	Grades, Academic	52	125.8	10.7	.44
Officer Candidates, Transportation Corps	Grades, Academic	314	126.4	9.8	.38
Officer Candidates, WAAC	Grades, Academic	787	128.4	11.3	.46
Officer Candidates, Infantry	Leadership Ratings	201	122.6	10.8	.12
Officer Candidates, Ordnance	Leadership Ratings	190	128.2	9.6	.09
Officer Candidates, 13 Arms and Services	Success vs. Failure	5186	128.7	10.0	.28*
AST Trainees, basic engineering	Grades, Inorganic Chemistry	222	126.6	7.8	.21
AST Trainees, basic engineering	Grades, Math. (Trig.)	222	126.6	7.8	.16
AST Trainees, personal psychology	Ranks in Statistics	132	134.2	10.4	.25
AST Trainees, personnel psychology	Ranks in Tests & Measurements	130	134.0	10.3	.29
West Point Cadets, 4th Class	Grades, English†	932	131.3	10.9	.40
West Point Cadets, 4th Class	Grades, Mathematics†	932	131.3	10.9	.43
West Point Cadets, 4th Class	Grades, Military Topography	932	131.3	10.9	.40
West Point Cadets, 4th Class	Grades, Tactics	932	131.3	10.9	.29
West Point Cadets, 4th Class	Grades, French†	167	130.2	11.0	.22
West Point Cadets, 4th Class	Grades, German†	164	132.4	10.9	.20
West Point Cadets, 4th Class	Grades, Spanish†	932	131.3	10.9	.19
West Point Cadets, 4th Class	Grades, Portuguese†	168	130.0	10.3	.12

* Biserial Correlation.

† First Term.

For four and a half years, the AGCT-1 was used, in one edition or another, throughout the Army at home and abroad. No exact count of the total number of administrations (both tests and retests) is obtainable. But it is certain that for all of that period, an average of more than four thousand persons were tested each day! In April 1945, the test was superseded, except for certain special purposes, by the Army General Classification Test-3a. While this new test is completely different from the earlier tests, (it is composed of four separately timed and separately scored subjects: Reading and Vocabulary, Arithmetic Computation, Arithmetic Reasoning and Pattern Analysis) the over-all score provides a measure practically identical to the older AGCT-1 score and thus permits continued use of this familiar and valuable index of general learning ability.

The following paper is an unusual use of the scientific
potential of opinion-polling organizations. The possibilities for
follow-up studies and various comparison studies are manifold.

Verbal Intelligence of the American Adult*

ROBERT L. THORNDIKE

and GEORGE H. GALLUP

1944

How intelligent are American adults? This is a question which interests us from two different angles. On the one hand, in a democracy we are always concerned to evaluate the competence of the public as a whole and of different fractions of the public. We would like to know the level of thinking that may be expected of voters in general and of particular groups of voters. On the other hand, we frequently need, both for research and for practical projects in adult intelligence testing, some yardstick by which we can evaluate the intelligence of a particular group. As compared with the general run of mankind, what is the intelligence level of convicts? Or of college students? Or of gifted children as they grow up? To answer these and many other questions, we need norms on a representative adult group to serve as a standard for comparison.

Our information about the intelligence of the general adult public is quite limited. This is, of course, due in large measure to the great difficulty of locating and testing a truly representative sample of adults. Only in institutions is it easily possible to get the coöperation of large groups of testees, and these institutional groups are not representative of the general population. The adults who are at hand for testing—in graduate schools on the one hand or in prisons or jails on the other—comprise limited and clearly atypical samples. Locating a group of adults who can be viewed with some assurance as being typical, and then getting their coöperation for purposes of testing has always been a difficult task. As a result, though adult tests are available, it is exceptional to find norms for representative adults provided for them.

The first and most imposing enterprise in testing representative adults was the testing of draftees in 1917. The scores for a large sample of those tested were analyzed and reported, and these scores have provided adult norms on the Army Alpha test. A translation of these results into Binet mental ages, giving approximately 13 years as the average mental age for the white draft group, aroused much heated debate during the years after

* Reprinted from *The Journal of General Psychology*, 30 (1941), pp. 75-85, by permission of the authors and publisher.

the war. The army results have the advantage of being based upon a large group selected to be a fair sample of the draft population. However, the draft testing cannot be guaranteed to be representative of the whole population. It may have been cut off at the lower end by the exclusion of defectives and illiterates and was very probably cut off at the upper end by the exclusion of married men, volunteers, and those in essential defense activities. Furthermore the group tested was all *young* adults and all men. The net picture may be a balanced one, but again it may not. There is, in addition, a speed element in the Army Alpha test, and this may introduce some question as to its appropriateness for groups of adults, especially the older groups.

Perhaps the most systematic attempt to get a representative adult sample, for purposes of test standardization, was that made by Wechsler in connection with the Wechsler-Bellevue Intelligence Scales. Wechsler selected his standardization group from a larger group tested in and around New York City in such a way that the proportions at different occupational levels corresponded to the proportions reported for the census. By selecting his sample in appropriate proportions from the different economic strata, Wechsler endeavored to get a truly representative cross-section group. In so far as the tested sample of New York residents is a fair sample of each occupational level for the country as a whole, this stratified sampling procedure should yield an adequate general sample. The chief limitation of Wechsler's material, for many practical purposes, is that it is based upon a time-consuming individual test. In many situations, time will not be available to use such an exhaustive individual test.

Other testing projects with adults which bear some relationship to our problem are studies of the age change in intelligence during maturity and senescence. In such studies as those of Miles and Miles and Jones and Conrad, the attempt has been to test a sample which is representative of the same population at each age level. An effort was made to avoid getting a different cut of the population at different ages, but there was no special interest in getting a nationally representative sample. The adults whom Jones and Conrad tested in a group of small New England communities or whom Miles got from religious and fraternal groups in California may or may not be representative of the country as a whole. That question was not primarily at issue.

The great bulk of the test standardization upon adults has clearly been upon selected groups. Most adult tests present norms for college students, and hundreds of investigations have been made upon intelligence in college groups. Similarly, there are a number of studies of workers in particular occupations. But the need for data on a general, representative, cross-section adult group still remains. It is at this need that the present study is directed.

PROCEDURE

The procedure in this investigation grows out of, and is based upon, the sampling and interviewing procedures of the public opinion polls. Any attempt to get an accurate estimate of public reaction to some idea whether it be *"Aid to Britain"* or *"Eat Crispy Kernels,"* depends upon approaching a representative sample of people and getting their coöperation to the extent of their giving a considered reply. The survey organizations have developed, on the one hand, plans of sampling which are designed to yield a group which is made up of the different elements of our public in the same proportions in which they occur in the total population being studied, and, on the other hand, techniques of approach to respondents which are successful in eliciting coöperative replies.

It seemed that these techniques might profitably be brought to bear on the problem of testing adult intelligence.

The test used in this study was incorporated as part of one of the regular weekly inquiries by the American Institute of Public Opinion. It was included in an inquiry sheet together with various questions calling for opinion on matters of current interest, and was presented as "some words which may be included in a quiz program." The respondents were approached in person by the interviewers. Of those interviewed, 3.7 per cent refused to respond to the test—about the same per cent that has been found for questions of opinion as presented by the interviewers.

The sample used in this study was the standard voting sample of the Institute. Cases were selected who were eligible to vote, and the proportions in the sample were planned to correspond to the characteristics of the voting population in the country at large. The voting population is a smaller group than the total adult population—about 60,000,000 as compared to 84,000,000. The conspicuous exclusions are Negroes in certain Southern states, aliens, mental defectives, occupants of certain institutions, people who are too indifferent to qualify themselves for voting by registering or paying whatever tax is required, and migratory adults who do not establish any permanent place of residence. In interpreting the results, these features of the sample must be remembered.

The cases in the voting sample are grouped according to the following factors: (*a*) Geographical distribution, both by states and by size of community. (*b*) Age. (*c*) Sex. (*d*) Economic level. (*e*) Voting behavior in the most recent presidential election.

The only one of these classifications which presents any possible ambiguity is that of economic level. In gathering a sample by economic level, the interviewers endeavor to get appropriate numbers in four categories: (*a*) receiving public aid, (*b*) poor, (*c*) average, (*d*) above average and wealthy. The proportions desired in each of the categories are based upon an analysis of occupations and incomes for the country as a whole. In classifying respondents, the interviewer gathers information of various sorts. This includes respondent's occupation, ownership of automobile, telephone in the home, location and character of home, weekly income reported for respondent's family, etc. The classification is a judgment based on these data. Our sample is described, in the table which follows, in terms of reported family income. In analyzing the results, the two lowest categories are thrown together, making three categories for analysis: below average, average, and above average.

The characteristics of the present sample in these regards are indicated in Table I.

TABLE I

Characteristics of Sample Tested

Geographical Distribution

New England (Me., N. H., Vt., Mass., Conn., R.I.)	8%
Middle Atlantic (N. Y., N. J., Pa., Del., Md., W. Va.)	27%
East Central (Mich., Ohio, Ill., Ind.)	23%
West Central (Mo., Ia., Wis., Minn., N. D., S. D., Kans., Nebr.)	15%
Southern (Va., N. C., S. C., Ga., Fla., Ala., Miss., La., Tex., Okla., Ark., Tenn., Ky.)	13%
Western (Mont., Ida., Utah, Colo., Wyo., N. M., Ariz., Nev., Calif., Or., Wash.)	14%

Age

21–29 years	21%
30–39 ,,	23%
40–49 ,,	24%
50–59 ,,	17%
60 years and over	15%

Weekly Income of Immediate Family

Under $15.00	21%
$15.00–19.99	14%
$20.00–29.99	21%
$30.00–39.99	15%
$40.00–60.00	17%
Over $60.00	12%

Vote in 1940 Presidential Election

Voted for Roosevelt	45%
Voted for Willkie	33%
Did not vote	22%

The sample was composed 58 per cent of men and 42 per cent of women. However, in all analyses, the scores of women and men were tabulated separately and given equal weight in the composite.

The type of test which could be used in this survey was sharply limited by the conditions under which the test was administered. The major problem was, of course, maintaining the coöperation and good-will of the testees. This required a test which was short, simple to administer, and sensible in the eyes of the testees. The purpose seemed best served by a short, steeply graded multiple-choice vocabulary test. The test actually used was a 20-word vocabulary test, made up of two words from each of 10 levels of the vocabulary section of the *I.E.R. Intelligence Scale CAVD*. Two parallel forms of the test were prepared. The standardization of this test has been described elsewhere.

All of the results from this study must be interpreted in the light of the test used. This is clearly a test of *verbal* intelligence. A vocabulary test may be criticized on the grounds that it depends heavily upon education and experience, though many test users have felt that the effects of formal schooling upon word knowledge are much less than would seem superficially to be the case. Certainly, a vocabulary test investigates the nature of *past* learnings and not the ability to make novel adaptations. Furthermore, this test is a power test, and places no premium on speed. Lorge has shown that the decline due to old age is less in the case of a power test such as we used than in a speed test, and various studies have shown vocabulary to be one of the abilities most resistant to the inroads of advancing years. We may argue at length as to the type of test which would give most nearly a "true" measure of adult intelligence. The fact remains that in this investigation we have used a test of verbal power.

As indicated above, the test was administered by the experienced interviewers who interview on the surveys of the American Institute of Public Opinion. The test was administered in the middle of the interview, and the specific form of the instructions was as follows:

Here are some words which may be included on a quiz program, depending upon how many people understand their meaning. We are trying to find out now how familiar these words are to people. Will you please look at this card (*hand card to respondent*) and give me the number of the word that seems to be closest to each word in capital letters.

The card handed to the respondent included instructions as follows:

Please look first at the word in capital letters on each line. Then look at the other words in smaller type on the same line and tell me which *one* of these words comes closest in meaning to the one in capital letters.

EXAMPLE

BEAST   1. afraid   2. words   3. large   4. animal   5. bird
The correct answer in this example is No. 4, since the word "animal" comes closer to "beast" than any of the other words.
Important: Do only one line at a time, and please take each line in order. Call off the word you are referring to first, and then the number of the word on the same line that you think comes closest to it.

All records were returned to the office of the Institute at Princeton, and were then submitted to statistical analysis.

RESULTS

The obtained distribution of test scores for the total population tested is presented in Table II. The entries in Table II are reported as percentages of those responding to the questionnaire, neglecting the 3.7 per cent of the complete sample of 2,974 individuals who refused to attempt the test. Re-

TABLE II

Distribution of Vocabulary Test Scores

Score	Form A	Form B	Both forms
20	0.5	0.4	0.5
19	1.5	1.4	1.5
18	1.8	3.0	2.4
17	2.8	5.4	4.1
16	5.1	7.2	6.1
15	6.4	8.1	7.2
14	7.8	8.5	8.1
13	7.9	8.0	8.0
12	9.7	7.5	8.5
11	8.7	7.9	8.3
10	9.5	7.7	8.6
9	7.6	5.4	6.6
8	7.4	7.2	7.3
7	6.4	6.5	6.4
6	5.0	4.9	4.9
5	3.9	3.3	3.6
4	2.1	3.0	2.5
3	1.4	1.2	1.3
2	0.8	1.2	1.0
1	0.5	0.4	0.5
0	3.2	1.8	2.5
Q_3	13.62	14.57	14.10
Median	10.75	11.48	11.08
Q_1	7.73	7.88	7.81
Mean	10.52	11.10	10.81

sults are presented separately for the two forms of the test, and for the total group. The median score on Form *A* is 10.75 words right. This has been found to correspond to a mental age on the Otis *Self-Administering Test of Mental Ability* of 16 years, 6 months. For Form *B* the median score is 11.46, corresponding to an Otis *MA* of 16 years, 2 months. The median Otis *MA* of those who took the test would therefore be estimated as above 16 years 4 months. The median score is very near that received by a class of high school students in a good residential New York City suburb in the first month of their junior year.

The individuals who refused to take the test present something of a problem to us. What scores shall we attribute to them? We would probably expect them to be somewhat below the group as a whole, but how much so? As a matter of actual fact, however, this is not such a serious problem, because of the small percentage of refusals. Suppose that we take an extreme position and assume that all the persons who refused the test would have fallen below the median of the group tested. In that case, the median for the total group would be lowered to 10.54 words or 16 years, 5 months *MA* for Form *A* and to 11.20 words or 16 years, 0 months for Form *B*. The true figure probably lies somewhere in the narrow range between these figures and those reported above, in which we counted just the group who actually took the test.

The lower quartiles for our group were 7.73 words on Form *A* and 7.88 words on Form *B*. These correspond to Otis *MA*'s of about 13 years 3 months and 13 years 9 months respectively. The upper quartiles fall at 13.62 words and 14.57 words for the two forms. We do not have conversion data to make it possible to interpret these in terms of mental ages, but we have data which make it possible to relate them to college freshman percentiles reported for the *American Council Psychological Examination*. They correspond to the 66th and the 68th percentile of the college freshman group respectively. The 50th percentile of college freshman has been found to correspond to scores of about 12.6 and 13.8 words on the two forms of our test and these scores are surpassed by 33 and 31 per cent of the adult group tested.

Various breakdowns of our data are available. The medians and quartile points for these fractions of the total group are presented in Table III. The scores from the two sub-tests are thrown together in reporting these results.

Sex differences in this test are small, but what difference there is favors the women. This is in accord with previous findings that women do better on verbal, less well on quantitative material than men.

Age differences for the test are almost nil until the group 50-59 years of age is reached, and it is only in the "over 60" group that any substantial drop in score is found. The drop from the 20's to the "over 60" group corresponds to a drop of 8 months in Otis *MA* (though drop on the timed Otis test over this age span has been reported to be much greater). In verbal power, then, there seems to be very little decline with age. The decline is probably somewhat larger than is shown in the table if we accept the hypothesis that refusals represent less than average ability, because the percentage of refusals increases from 1.5 in the 21-20-year group to 8.6 in the group 60 and over. The older individuals seem much less willing to expose their limitations on a test of this sort. However, even if we accept the extreme assumption and call all these refusals below average scores, the drop from the twenties to the "over 60" groups is only 1.40 words, corresponding to about 10 months of mental age.

TABLE III
Median and Quartile Vocabulary Scores for Fractions of Cross-Section Group

Fraction	N^*	Q_1	Med.	Q_3
Men	1738	7.64	10.87	13.91
Women	1236	7.99	11.27	14.30
21–29 years of age	615	8.18	11.34	14.33
30–39 ,, ,, ,,	680	8.15	11.31	14.21
40–49 ,, ,, ,,	684	7.64	11.24	14.03
50–59 ,, ,, ,,	483	7.72	10.90	13.98
Over 60 ,, ,, ,,	444	6.70	10.28	13.52
Family income under $20 weekly	1004	5.89	8.41	11.40
,, ,, $20–39.99 weekly	1041	8.61	11.27	13.96
,, ,, $40 and over weekly	831	10.68	13.56	15.77
New England & Middle Atlantic	1055	7.66	10.94	14.17
East Central	671	7.60	10.75	13.74
West Central	429	7.72	10.82	13.76
Southern	393	7.06	10.64	13.50
Rocky Mt. & Pacific Coast	426	9.26	12.30	15.42
1940 Roosevelt voter	1346	7.67	10.79	13.83
1940 Willkie voter	973	9.07	12.36	14.93
1940 non-voter	655	6.90	9.64	12.64

* N's for breakdowns differ, because some cases are unspecified.

The sub-groups which differ most conspicuously on this test are the three economic strata. The median score for those with family income under $20 a week, $20 to $39.99, and $40 and over are respectively 8.40, 11.3, and 13.6. Only about 25 per cent of the lowest income group come up to the median of the middle income group, and less than 30 per cent of the middle income group come up to the median of the upper income group. Slightly more than a tenth of the low-income group surpass the median of the high. These are the facts. The interpretation of them, of course, presents another problem. Our data provide no basis for determining what part of the observed differences is due to differences of education and opportunity. Nor can we infer to what other types of test this difference will extend. We can only say that there exist substantial differentials in verbal power between different economic groups.

Regional differences are in most cases small, though there is an appreciable difference favoring persons living in the Mountain and Pacific States. In interpreting the results for the Southern States, we must remember that this sample is limited to the *voting* population.

There is some difference in the average score depending upon the presidential vote cast in 1940. Willkie voters averaged somewhat higher than Roosevelt voters—a difference to be expected in the light of socio-economic differentials between the two constituencies. Of equal interest is the fact that those who voted for neither Willkie nor Roosevelt—meaning in almost every case that they did not vote at all—scored lower than the supporters of either candidate.

DISCUSSION AND SUMMARY

There are presented herewith data resulting from the administration of a brief verbal intelligence test to a representative sample of the American adult voting public. The test was a steeply graded, untimed, multiple-choice vocabulary test. The sample was the regular voting sample used by the American Institute of Public Opinion. Subject to such limitations as inhere in the test and the sample, the results provide norms for adult achievement in verbal intelligence. The median adult performance is found to correspond to an Otis *MA* of a little over 16 years. The results may be used as a basis for comparing special groups to the general public, or as a device for checking upon the representativeness of samples being studied for other purposes.

In discussing limitations, several must be born in mind. In the first place, our study is of the population eligible to vote. How much the results would be changed if adults not eligible to vote were included we cannot say, but it seems evident that the average score would be somewhat lowered.

The most plausible criticism of the sampling procedures used in the public opinion surveys is that they fail adequately to represent either the upper or lower extremes of the population in economic status and ac-complishment. One line of evidence from our data which would oppose this point of view is the enormous scatter of the scores in our group. One in 200 obtained a perfect score on the test—an achievement which has been found to be decidedly unusual among advanced graduate students. On the other extreme, 4 per cent either failed completely to score on the test or got only one or two words correct. This performance falls below that of even the slowest children tested in the seventh grade. It corresponds to the performance of children well down in the elementary school. Certainly, a very wide range of ability is represented in the sample.

Other possible limitations are found in the nature of the test. In the first place, it is very brief and affords only a rough grading of ability. For a group as variable as this adult sample, the reliability of the test is estimated as between .80 and .85, however, and this indicates a measure quite usable for rough screening purposes and group description.

More serious is the limitation of the test to a single type of verbal material. This seemed imperative under the conditions of testing. As a result, we must be extremely cautious in generalizing our results beyond the power vocabulary type of material. If the testing had included an element of speed, the older groups would almost certainly have compared less well with the younger groups and with school children. Again, age would probably have had more of a detrimental effect if the test material had consisted of some novel and unusual types of items, rather than the basic and familiar vocabulary material.

Because of the verbal character of the material, it may be deemed that it should not be used in inter-group comparisons where groups differ significantly in education or cultural opportunity. Such educational and cultural handicaps would be expected to affect the lower income groups, and perhaps in some measure the older groups. It is certainly true that the data from this test as they stand give no sure basis for judging *innate* or *biological* intellectual differences. It is to be hoped that future research will yield data on similar samples for other types of test materials.

The results of this investigation must be interpreted in the light of the foregoing qualifications with regard to sampling and test materials. If these are kept in mind, the data should be of broad value in interpreting and studying the abilities of adults in the United States and quite probably in other English speaking countries.

Garrett's presidential address in 1946 offers a startling contrast to the presidential address by Jastrow in 1901. The hypothesis of the progressive differentiation of intelligence is still the subject of some dispute, but the marked change in the methodologies, techniques, and available data utilized by Jastrow and Garrett make this address an interesting landmark in our picture of progress in the search for intelligence.

A Developmental Theory of Intelligence*

HENRY E. GARRETT

1946

I think we will all agree that anyone who uses the noun "intelligence" owes it to his audience to explain exactly what he means by the term. This I fully intend to do. But I shall approach my definition somewhat obliquely, perhaps, by first explaining what I do *not* intend to mean by "intelligence." I know that there is some risk involved in using the indirect method. The elementary textbooks which begin by telling the student what psychology is *not* are often left with rather meager and uninteresting fare when it finally becomes necessary to inform the student what psychology *is*. In the same way, my definition, after I have drawn up a negative bill of particulars, may sound astonishingly trite and simple. In spite of these obvious hazards I shall, nevertheless, follow the indirect approach as I believe it involves a risk worth taking.

At the outset, I think we must discard omnibus definitions which include a little of everything. To illustrate, as recently as 1943 a well-known author wrote that "intelligence is the ability to undertake activities that are characterized by (1) difficulty, (2) complexity, (3) abstractness, (4) economy, (5) adaptiveness, (6) social value, and (7) the emergence of originals and to maintain such activities under conditions that demand a concentration of energy and the resistance to emotional forces." This "definition," like the time-worn shot-gun prescription, can hardly fail to hit the trouble somewhere, but just *where* is not entirely clear. Omnibus definitions are in general too broad to be wrong and too vague to be useful. Again, I think we must avoid obvious and circular definitions. It is undoubtedly true that intelligence involves the ability to learn but our understanding is not greatly enhanced by saying so. Nor are we greatly helped by the oft-quoted cliché that intelligence is what the intelligence tests measure. The main and perhaps the *only* value in this smug (and I might almost say smirking) state-

* Reprinted from *The American Psychologist*, 1 (1946), pp. 372-378, by permission of the author and the American Psychological Association.

ment lies in the fact that it is "operational" in a loose sort of way. It is certainly not informative and was probably never intended to be.

With this long introduction over, I must now finally come to grips with the problem of formulating a positive definition. Omitting the qualification "general," intelligence as I shall use the term in this paper includes at least the abilities demanded in the solution of problems which require the comprehension and use of symbols. By symbols I mean words, numbers, diagrams, equations, formulas, which represent ideas and relationships ranging from the fairly simple to the very complex. For simplicity we may call the ability to deal with such stimuli *symbol or abstract intelligence*. This definition is essentially what Spearman meant by the eduction of relations and the eduction of correlates.

My own definition is by no means original nor is it particularly startling. Many years ago, Terman defined intelligence as the ability to carry on "abstract thinking." As early as 1920, Thorndike proposed that we recognize three levels of intelligence—the abstract, the social and the mechanical or motor. Thorndike's abstract level embraced essentially the activities which I have described above under symbol intelligence. It may be noted that Thorndike offered no proof for the existence of three kinds of intelligence:—adequate proof would, of course, be the demonstration of homogeneity among the measures on a given level, and of independence as between levels. Probably all that Thorndike really intended to do was to emphasize the fact that the biological notion of intelligence as adaptability to the environment is too broad to be useful and that, accordingly, it is more profitable to study individual differences in behavior within certain fairly well defined areas. Books, people, and machines constitute three sorts of things with respect to which it is important to measure a person's performance. These categories, to be sure, are not necessarily exclusive, nor do they run the gamut of human behavior. But they *are* important and they do cover a broad segment of life activities. Moreover, considerable experimental evidence for the existence of at least two levels (the abstract and the mechanical) can now be marshalled; and the social level might also be established if its constituents could be agreed upon and adequately measured.

At the risk of digression, it may be well to recall that the measurement of intelligent behavior began as a practical enterprise and that theory has in general followed rather than preceded application. Perhaps, had theory come first, we might have been saved much argument and many intelligence tests. The latter result would certainly have been a real contribution, but I am not so sure that the absence of controversy would have been a good thing. By actually measuring intelligence, however crudely, psychologists have been forced to set up theories in order to interpret what they have found. And eventually the impact of theoretical discussion has led to a better notion of what one is attempting to measure. Again, I would agree that intelligence is in reality an *adverb* and not a *noun*. It has been said that we do not learn by doing, but that learning *is* doing. And by the same token, an intelligent person does not possess "intelligence" but rather exhibits the capacity to act intelligently (make a high score) when faced by tasks demanding the use of symbols (words, diagrams, numbers, mazes) in their solution.

It is the thesis of this paper that intelligence, as I have defined it, changes in its organization with increasing maturity. In 1938 I proposed a differentiation hypothesis with respect to the growth of intelligence which I shall now present in greater detail. My hypothesis runs as follows: Abstract or symbol intelligence changes in its organization as age increases from a fairly unified and general ability to a loosely organized group of abilities or factors. If this hypothesis is true, the measurement of intelligence must perforce change in its methods and objectives with increase in age.

Over a period of ten years and more, we conducted at Columbia University a long range program designed to test out the differentiation hypothesis. Our work has dealt for the most part with children of school age, as symbol intelligence is obviously not readily measurable until the child can use language with some facility. In the remainder of this paper I shall cite our own and other relevant data in support of the differentiation hypothesis. I shall then try to present the implications of this formulation for mental measurement generally.

EVIDENCE FOR THE DIFFERENTIATION HYPOTHESIS

In a general way, our method has been (1) to analyze tables of intercorrelations for the presence of ability-clusters or factors, and (2) to study the changing relationship of such factors, i.e., their organization, with age. I shall first consider the results of four investigations carried out upon subjects differing fairly widely in age.

In a study of mental organization among school children, Schiller administered 12 tests to 189 third and fourth grade boys, averaging nine years of age. Four of these tests were classified as verbal, three as numerical, and five as spatial-non-language. Evidence for the existence of ability-clusters described, respectively, as verbal, numerical, and spatial, appeared clearly in the correlation tables. There was, however, considerable overlap as between categories. The average correlation between the verbal and number tests, for example, was .63; between the verbal and spatial tests, .33, and between the number and spatial tests, .41. When the 12 test vectors were rotated into a three dimensional space by the centroid method of factor analysis, there was a clear separation of the verbal, number, and spatial test groupings. Since the reference axes were oblique, the three primary factors were of necessity correlated. Vectors through the verbal and number test clusters were close together so that correlation of the verbal and number factors was quite high (.83). The correlations of the verbal and spatial factors, and of the number and spatial factors were much lower (.27 and .30, respectively). From these results it seemed clear that at the nine year level, verbal and numerical tests taken together constitute a homogeneous general factor which is fairly independent of the abilities employed in the spatial tests. The high correlation of verbal and number abilities for nine year old boys is in interesting contrast to the r of .26 between the verbal and number factors found by Schneck at the college level. Schneck's nine tests, five verbal and four numerical, were administered to 210 college men, 18 to 21 years old.

The same decrease in intercorrelation within a test battery as we go from children to adults is found in the work of Bryan and Anastasi. Bryan administered 11 tests of immediate memory to 100 five year old boys. The tests made use of pictures, objects, forms, colors, and blocks. All were given individually. For our purposes, the most significant finding is that these memory tests were as closely related to vocabulary (i.e., verbal ability) as they were to each other—indicating a considerable degree of homogeneity in the abilities utilized by these young children in dealing with symbols. In contrast, Anastasi's study of memory with adult subjects reports the correlation of the verbal factor with memory to be $-.085$; of the number factor with memory, .00. Anastasi administered four tests of memory, as well as two verbal and two number tests, to 140 college women, 16 to 28 years old. Anastasi also verified the low correlation for adults between verbal and number abilities found by Schneck, her correlation between these factors being .24.

These four studies agree in showing that for children, at least, skill in verbal and numerical tasks possess greater homogeneity than they do for adults. Other investigations have obtained essentially the same results. In Thorndike's CAVD, for example, the correlation of level V (vocabulary) and level A (arithmetic) for 126 fifth grade children was .52, while the correlation between level V (vocabulary) and level A (arithmetic) for 100 college students was .23. In the same two groups the correlations between levels C (completion) and A (arithmetic) were .64 and .23, respectively. I have verified these correlations among the parts of the Thorndike CAVD examination in a group of 313 college freshman women. The correlation of levels A and V in this adult group was .21, of levels C and A also .21. The Thurstones have carried out two extensive investigations of ability organization at different ages. In one study 60 tests involving words, numbers, spatial problems, diagrams, dot patterns, pictures, and mazes were administered to 1154 eighth grade children. By means of the centroid method of factor analysis, ten factors (later reduced to six primaries) were extracted from the correlational matrix. These factors were called, respectively, N (number), W (word fluency), V (verbal), S (spatial), M (memory) and I (induction or reasoning). Our present interest lies in the correlations found among the six primary factors. Some correlation was to be expected among these factors since oblique transformations were used in rotating the test vectors. From the table of interfactor correlations a general factor emerged, called by the Thurstones "a second-order general factor," and identified by them as probably equivalent to Spearman's "g." This general factor was most highly correlated with the verbal and word fluency factors (.715 and .615) suggesting that it is intrinsically "linguistic." In a further study on a smaller sample of 438 children in which 21 tests selected from the original 60 were employed, the same second-order general factor again strongly emerged. Its correlations with the verbal and word fluency factors (.676 and .686) offer confirmatory evidence as to its linguistic and abstract nature and substantiate the first finding. The highest r in the second study was that between the general factor and induction of reasoning (namely, .843), the tests of which category demand the ability to understand and manipulate verbal symbols.

In an earlier study of an older group, Thurstone administered 56 tests to 240 student volunteers, ranging in age from 16 to 25. The intercorrelations among the primary factors found in this study were quite negligible, the median of 72 r's being .03 and the largest r .24. It should be noted that the intercorrelations of these 56 tests gave almost the same factorial matrix whether the transformations were oblique or orthogonal. It thus appears that the primary factors extracted are essentially independent and that no second-order general factor was present. As stated above, in the study of eighth grade children transformations were oblique rather than orthogonal. While the use of oblique reference axes makes correlation among the primary abilities inevitable, the fact that oblique transformations gave the clearest result (closest approximation to simple structure) suggests that the second-order general factor is not an artifact introduced by the method.

To sum up, it seems clear that when we compare the extent of generality in tables of correlations obtained from subjects well separated in age, greater differentiation appears at the upper age levels. Criticism may be made of this finding on the grounds that the tests employed at successive age levels were not identical (though they involve the same materials) and that sampling differences may account for some or all of the difference found. Again, it may be argued that the use of oblique rather than orthogonal transformations allows the *method* rather than the data to determine the final result.

To meet these objections a second approach to the problem of changing mental organization with age can be made which will at least in part overcome these difficulties. This method is to compute intercorrelations of the same set of tests at successive age levels and note the change in correlations if such is present. Care must be exercised, of course, to have the subjects at different age levels comparable, and tests must have sufficient range to prevent skewness in the younger or older age groups.

Several comparative studies of this sort were included in our program. In 1935, Garrett, Bryan, and Perl administered ten carefully selected tests designed to measure memory, verbal, and number abilities, to groups of public school boys and girls at three age levels. In all, 646 children were examined, 225 at age 9, 196 at age 12, and 225 at age 15. Considerable effort was made to obtain comparable samples; precautions taken to this end are given in detail in the monograph. With one exception, the inter-correlations among the memory, verbal, and number tests showed a regular tendency to decrease with age from 9 to 12 and from 12 to 15. The average intercorrelation at ages 9, 12, and 15 were, for boys, .30, .21 and .18; for girls, .27, .30 and .10. A multiple factor analysis of the correlations at each age level—boys and girls kept separate—substantiated (as was to be expected) the correlational evidence. The proportion of variance accounted for by the first unrotated factory (roughly equivalent to "g") at ages, 9, 12 and 15 was, for boys, .31, .32 and .12; for girls, .31, .24, .19. This regular fall in the trend of relationship with age was verified by Asch who retested 161 of Schiller's subjects (originally tested at age 9) after a period of three years. From age 9 to 12 the average correlation for boys dropped from .56 to .41, for girls from .59 to .51; the correlation of the verbal and numerical tests dropped from .57 to .36 (boys) and from .64 to .49 (girls). Again we note a loss in generality with increasing maturity.

Two recent studies made upon different groups and with different tests substantiate further this general finding. In 1944 Clark administered the Chicago Tests of Primary Mental Abilities to 320 boys, roughly 100 each at ages 11, 13, and 15. Subjects were drawn from the public schools and were from the same social and economic levels. Scores in each of six primary factors, V, N, S, W, M, and R, when correlated at each age level, showed a regular tendency to drop with age. Average factor correlations (excluding M which was very unreliable) were as follows at ages 11, 13, and 15: N and the battery, .55, .44, and .43; V and the battery, .62, .55 and .49; S and the battery, .48, .47, and .35. These results confirm the existence of the second-order general factor found by the Thurstones, and show, moreover, that it gradually weakens with age. Reichard has in part verified Clark's findings, though the evidence from her work is not entirely clear. Reichard administered eight tests designed to measure verbal, numerical, and spatial abilities of 542 subjects, 280 girls and 262 boys, in public schools of suburban New York. Three age levels, 9, 12 and 15, were represented. Intercorrelations dropped sharply from age 12 to age 15 (.43 to .38 for the boys and .51 to .37 for the girls), but rose from age 9 to age 12—for both boys and girls. A reasonable explanation of this reversal seems to lie in the content of the tests which favored the nine year old group.

This group, too, was probably somewhat superior to average nine year olds in performance level.

From these various studies I believe we can predict a steady drop in correlation among tests involving verbal, numerical, and spatial concepts from about age 8 to age 18. With increasing age there appears to be a gradual breakdown of an amorphous general ability into a group of fairly distinct aptitudes. It seems highly probable that maturation has much to do with this differentiating process, but increasing experience and diverging interests must also contribute heavily.

It is difficult to test out the differentiation hypothesis with the preschool child and with the infant. Tests at these early ages are of necessity concerned with physiological fitness and with muscular development and co-ordination. Baby tests, as we know, show little relationship to language tests of the school years, and hence with symbol intelligence. In the new born infant behavior is at first of a very generalized character. Jensen writes "Stimulation of almost any group of receptors by almost any kind of stimulus will lead to a response in almost any part of the organism that is set to respond." As the baby grows older, specialization and localization of movements begin to appear. This sifting out process is repeated, apparently, in the differentiation of intellectual activities which we encounter later on during the school years.

IMPLICATION OF THE DIFFERENTIATION HYPOTHESIS FOR THEORY AND PRACTICE

Implications for Theory. The differentiation hypothesis has implications of a theoretical as well as of a practical nature. On the theoretical side, it seems to effect a rapprochement between the Spearman General Factor and the Group Factor theories. Over the elementary school years we find a functional generality among tests at the symbol level. Later on this general factor or *"g"* breaks down into the quasi-independent factors reported by many investigators.

It seems likely that the *"g"* factor which appears strongly at the elementary school level is, in large part, verbal or linguistic in nature. If the school child can read well, he can very probably do the rest of his school work well. Solving arithmetic problems is contingent upon ability to read and understand directions; hence a fifth grade child high in verbal facility may do as well in arithmetic as a child of much greater native aptitude for numbers. This notion is not entirely speculative. Thurstone found that in the seventh and eighth grades his second-order general factor entered with greatest weight into the reading and composition tests. Kelley reports the general factor to be stronger in power tests of reading and arithmetic for third than for seventh grade children. In the group of 126 fifth grade children mentioned above, the general factor in the CAVD had the following correlations with the four parts of the examination: with Completion, .90; with Arithmetic, .70; with Vocabulary, .86; and with Directions, .88. It is evident that the general factor at this age level is quite strong and is largely verbal. The "g" factor in CAVD for 313 freshman women had correlations of .70 with Completion, .45 with Arithmetic, .74 with Vocabulary, and .76 with Directions. Although still verbal, the general factor is considerably weaker at this age level and is much less highly related to arithmetic. The conclusion which I draw from these data is that the overall ability ("g") which looms large during the elementary school years becomes progressively less important at the high school and college level, where factor studies have shown it to be negligible or quite small.

It may be noted at this point that Thorndike's "quantity hypothesis" is not opposed to the differentiation hypothesis which I have suggested. Thorndike in 1927 advanced the view that the difference in intellectual performance between the very bright and the very stupid person is not qualitative (involving new sorts of mental processes) but is quantitative (demanding more of the same thing). According to this view, the very intelligent person, then, has access to more numerous rather than to new kinds of connections. As evidence for his theory, Thorndike showed that for fifth and eighth grade children the intercorrelations among (1) tests involving routine information, and (2) tests involving generalization and relation finding, are no higher than the cross-correlations between the two batteries. This finding he takes as evidence of a basic continuity in function from the simple to the more complex symbolic activities. According to the differentiation hypothesis, this continuity arises from the common general ability which runs through intellectual performances at the elementary school ages. With increasing maturity and with a more nearly common background of language facility, general ability dissolves into more specialized talents or group factors.

Implications for Practice. The differentiation hypothesis has definite practical implication for the interpretation of intelligence test scores over a wide age range. The best individual tests of abstract intelligence (e.g., the Stanford-Binet) are most useful over the age range from 6 to 15 years. To know that a boy of 10 has a Stanford-Binet MA of 12 and an IQ of 120 is to have valid and useful information. From his MA and IQ we can predict how well this boy will do in school and how well he might do (if not seriously handicapped in other ways) in occupations requiring the comprehension and use of symbols in the solution of problems. I do not think that at the elementary school level we should attempt, except very tentatively, to fractionate the IQ into, say, language ability, number ability, reasoning and the like. The test items which might reasonably be classified under each of these heads are too few to permit a definitive judgment as to specific abilities. This does not mean, of course, that for a given child one should not look for sharp deviations in performance upon significant items, or that one should not take note of the child's distinctive strengths and weaknesses in dealing with the test situations. But we should always remember that the total score on an individual intelligence test is a better measure of general ability than part scores on the same test can possibly be measures of more specific functions.

The group intelligence test is undoubtedly a useful means of classifying children according to degree of abstract intelligence. But I deplore the use of the IQ rather than the point score, say, to indicate performance on a group test—especially when the subjects are adults. The criteria which an intelligence test must meet in order to yield a numerically constant IQ have often been stated but may usefully be repeated here. These conditions are (1) regular and progressive increase in the SD's of the MA distributions with increasing age; (2) homogeneity of function throughout the scale; (3) absence of correlation between CA and IQ. With perhaps a few exceptions, group intelligence tests do not meet these conditions even approximately. The Stanford-Binet does; hence the IQ in my opinion should be restricted to this examination. Much of the controversy concerning changing IQ's, inconstancy of IQ, etc., grows out of confusion concerning what the term actually means, and when it can justifiably be used. A recent pronouncement to the effect that education raises the IQ was entirely fallacious because based upon changes in IQ's which were not IQ's at all but scores. No one would argue seriously that increased schooling does not in general lead to higher scores on *any* valid group test; but that such increases in score imply "true" increases in "intelligence" is certainly open to doubt.

At the high school and college levels, abstract intelligence breaks down, as we have seen, into a number of relatively independent factors. It would seem to be theoretically more defensible, therefore, and practically more useful, to measure verbal, numerical, perceptual or spatial ability, and perhaps other factors at these ages, than to give the subject a single over-all score. Perhaps some may wonder why, if this is true, total scores and not part scores were computed for the Army General Classification Test. I believe that the use of total scores for the AGCT was justified by reason of the wide range in schooling (and presumably in abstract intelligence) reported by the 8,000,000 or so men who took this test. In large samples, correlations among the three parts of the AGCT were quite high, indicating substantial homogeneity within this examination. This probably resulted from the fact that many soldiers were undoubtedly closer to the elementary school child than to the superior adult in the facility with which they handled abstract test material. Correlations among the three parts of the AGCT would almost certainly be lower if computed separately for high school and college graduates.

Factor scores have been shown to be useful predictors of college achievement in science, literature, and other fields. For highly selected students the part scores shown on the profile of such a test as the Graduate Record Examination are more useful in guidance than is a single omnibus score. In the case of adults tests designed to measure aptitude for special kinds of work are to be preferred to blanket measures of general ability. Profiles are useful as one means of presenting the structural patterns which part scores exhibit. Such typology is at first primarily utilitarian—a useful scheme of classification—though it is to be hoped that more fundamental relations may eventually be revealed.

The trial and error period in mental measurement is, I believe, drawing to a close. Much progress has been made over the war years in the construction and use of mental tests. I think we can anticipate a bright future for psychometrics, and by no means the smallest achievement will be an increase in the number of valid tests capable of measuring precisely defined aptitudes and traits.

The perennial question as to the relative brightness of males and females has not been neglected in the field of factorially distinguished tests. With the products of sophisticated test-development programs Hobson again put the question to the test and reaffirmed in part the classic pattern of sex differences.

Sex Differences in Primary Mental Abilities*

J. R. HOBSON

1947

Some knowledge about and common acceptance of variance in vocational and artistic talents among men antedated by a considerable period of time the formulation of the present generally accepted theories of individual differences in most human traits. The observation of "a square peg in a round hole" is older than any psychological laboratory. The phrenologist and the character analyst reached their zenith before the development of aptitude testing and the vocational guidance movement. Introspective man has always had a great curiosity as to "what he is good for."

While it is true that readily observable and measurable traits of physique, intelligence, and temperament do, at a comparatively early age, permit some guidance of a negative or elimination variety, it also appears that vocational aptitudes on the whole crystallize rather late in a child's school life. A generally accepted exception to this observation are those musical and artistic aptitudes based on sensory factors. The investigation of interests, while a standard and useful tool in guidance procedures, is of much greater reliability at college and adult levels than during high school years.

Since, in most public school systems, differentiation in educational offerings and vocational guidance per se begins at the Junior High School level, it has always appeared to the writer that reliable objective measures of clearly differentiated mental abilities at this level are a prerequisite to proper guidance. We may even go further and theorize that such primary mental abilities are the basic ingredients out of which aptitudes crystalize a little later. There is of course nothing novel or original in this hypothesis, the basis for which has been suggested by Kelley, Spearman, Thompson, and others. The application of factoral analysis to the measurement of adult intelligence by L. L. Thurstone in 1938 resulted in the reported isolation of such prime abilities. Further work by L. L. and T. G. Thurstone in cooperation with the Chicago Public Schools resulted in the publication in 1941 of

* Reprinted from the *Journal of Educational Research*, 41 (1947), pp. 126-132, by permission of the author and publisher.

the Chicago Tests of Primary Mental Abilities in which six primary factors are isolated in the cases of children between the ages of eleven and seventeen years. These six factors are described by the authors as follows:

The Number factor N is involved in the ability to do numerical calculations rapidly and accurately.

The Verbal factor V is found in tests involving verbal comprehension, for example, tests of vocabulary, opposites and synonyms, completion tests, and various reading comprehension tests.

The Space factor S is involved in any task in which the subject manipulates an object imaginally in space.

The Word Fluency factor W is involved whenever the subject is asked to think of isolated words at a rapid rate.

The Reasoning factor R is found in tasks that require the subject to discover a rule or principle involved in series or groups of letters.

A Rote Memory factor M has been clearly present in all test batteries. The tests for memory which are now being used depend upon the ability to memorize quickly.

TABLE I

**Showing Sex Differences in Primary Mental Abilities and
Kuhlmann-Anderson IQ of Ninth Grade Boys and Girls
in 1943**

Primary ability	Boys (222)		Girls (250)		Difference		
	M	σ	M	σ	Diff. M.	σ Diff.	C. R.
N	126.71	34.38	129.32	31.57	−2.61	3.06	− .85
V	89.43	20.09	91.38	17.32	−1.95	1.77	−1.10
S	83.38	30.62	68.97	30.34	14.41	2.79	5.16
W	68.41	16.62	75.17	17.56	−6.76	1.56	−4.33
R	53.94	14.58	61.72	15.00	−7.78	1.36	−5.72
M	13.11	5.22	15.67	4.98	−2.56	.47	−5.45
K-A IQ	110.64	16.10	113.21	15.29	−2.57	1.44	−1.78

While it is true that some severe though constructive criticisms have been directed at this series of tests by other test authors, it is also true that the basic validity of at least four of these factors has been admitted by these same critics. Furthermore, it may be observed that if the test consumer waits for instruments of universally admitted validity, perfect reliability, and undoubted applicability to a given situation he will never have the assistance of objective tests because no test ever measures up to these criteria. True validity, applicability, and general value must be determined in the crucible of use.

With the foregoing hypothesis in mind and against the background of the philosophy of test use expressed above, the 1941 edition of the Chicago Tests of Primary Mental Abilities consisting of seventeen sub-tests and purporting to measure the six primary abilities described above was administered to 222 boys and 250 girls in the ninth grade in Brookline High School in February, 1943. A tabular summary of the results is shown in Table I.

In January, 1944, the revised single-booklet edition of the same tests purportedly measuring the same primary factors but including only eleven of the original seventeen sub-tests was administered to 265 ninth-grade boys and 260 ninth-grade girls. These data are shown in Table II below.

TABLE II
Showing Sex Differences in Primary Mental Abilities
(Single-Booklet Edition) and Kuhlmann-Anderson IQ
of Ninth-Grade Boys and Girls in 1944

Primary ability	Boys (265)		Girls (260)		Difference		
	M	σ	M	σ	Diff. M.	σ Diff.	C. R.
N	71.56	21.67	74.23	20.08	−2.67	1.82	−1.47
V	67.60	15.09	65.56	14.14	2.04	1.28	1.60
S	42.11	21.33	32.73	21.47	9.38	1.88	4.99
W	55.38	14.21	61.02	15.84	−5.64	1.31	−4.31
R	29.65	7.88	32.98	8.85	−3.33	.74	−4.53
M	9.41	4.03	11.35	4.14	−1.94	.36	−5.39
K-A IQ	108.47	14.77	113.50	16.69	−5.03	1.37	−3.67

In order to move the administration of the Chicago Tests down to the eighth-grade level, the same single-booklet edition was also administered to all eighth-grade boys and girls in January, 1944 and annually in January since that time. These data for 1944, 1945, and 1946 are combined in Table III.

The results shown in tabular form above are quite striking and their interpretation is rather clearly defined. To begin with, the girls exceeded the boys in mean IQ as determined from the Kuhlmann-Anderson Tests in each of the three groups and by margins of undoubted significance in all but the 1943 ninth-grade group.

It is also evident that the girls exceeded the boys by markedly significant

TABLE III

Showing Sex Differences in Primary Mental Abilities (Single-Booklet Edition) and Kuhlmann-Anderson IQ of Eighth Grade Boys and Girls 1944, 1945, and 1946 Combined

Primary ability	Boys (720)		Girls (716)		Difference		
	M	σ	M	σ	Diff. M.	σ Diff.	C. R.
N	68.03	19.48	68.53	18.50	− .50	1.00	− .50
V	62.99	14.77	60.52	14.49	2.47	.79	3.14
S	40.58	20.07	31.45	18.89	9.13	1.03	8.86
W	51.54	14.50	55.73	14.72	−4.19	.77	−5.45
R	27.16	8.49	30.44	8.21	−3.28	.44	−7.45
M	9.79	3.64	10.92	3.88	−1.13	.20	−5.65
K-A IQ	111.31	13.93	114.46	13.20	−3.20	.70	−4.49

margins in the W, R, and M factors in every instance. It may be noted that in all three groups the degree of superiority of the girls as reflected in the C. R. was greater in the cases of the Primary Mental Abilities involved than it was in the case of Kuhlmann-Anderson IQ. In other words, the differences in the specific factors as measured by the Chicago Tests appear to be real and not due entirely to the generally higher level of academic intelligence displayed by the girls. On the other hand the medium chosen for the measurement of the R factor, particularly, seems to the writer to be a very narrow delineation of inductive reasoning and one which would by its very nature appeal more to and be easier for girls.

The most salient result disclosed by a perusal of the tabular data above is of course the margin by which the boys exceeded the girls in the S factor despite the significantly higher IQ of the girls. There is nothing in the nature of the spacial orientation tests to support any supposition that the tasks in them are closer to the previous experiences or interests of boys than of girls. The boys' superiority appears to be a real one of considerable magnitude. Because of the universally conceded importance of spacial orientation in such vocational fields as architecture, art, engineering, and mechanics, the marked inferiority of girls in this primary ability may help to explain why women as a group have not challenged men in these vocational areas to the same degree they have in others.

While the superiority of the boys in Verbal Comprehension assumes a significant magnitude only in the larger eighth-grade group, it may be interpreted as a real superiority because it is positive in the 1944 ninth-grade group as well as in the face of girls' significantly higher IQ's in both instances. There is no question but that the Kuhlmann-Anderson Intelligence Tests at the eighth- and ninth-grade levels involve considerable verbal comprehension. A more minute inspection of the 1943 ninth-grade results would be necessary to determine whether the inclusion of an additional sub-test of the V factor (1941 edition) may have tipped the scales slightly but not significantly in favor of the girls in this instance.

The slight superiority of the girls in the N factor in all three instances is offset in each case by their significantly higher IQ.

The point should be made in passing that the girls probably showed a higher mean IQ on the Kuhlmann-Anderson Tests because these tests are more heavily weighted with primary factors in which the girls are superior, namely, N, W, and R, than with V and S in which the boys are superior. In fact, an analysis of the Kuhlmann-Anderson Tests at these grade levels would, in the opinion of the writer, reveal that the S and M factors are not sampled at all as these factors are measured in the Chicago Tests.

In comparing the eighth and ninth-grade means on the single-booklet edition test results, it may be observed that the ninth-grade means are consistently and substantially higher than the eighth-grade means in the first five factors. This is not true in the case of M in which the ninth-grade boys' mean score was slightly lower than that of eighth-grade boys, while that of ninth-grade girls was only slightly but not significantly higher than that of eighth-grade girls.

While repeated measurements of the same individual would perhaps be necessary to establish the fact, the data in Tables II and III might lead to the conclusion that, whereas the first five Primary Abilities appear to increase in the cases of both boys and girls between the ages of thirteen years four months and fourteen years four months, which are the average ages represented in grades eight and nine respectively in January in Brookline, this does not appear to hold true for visually verbalized memory as measured in the single-booklet edition of the Chicago Tests. It should be noted that the age norms published in the manual or on the back of the Chicago Tests Booklets were obtained by administering the tests to different pupils at different age and grade levels. While the data in the manual are not specific as to the number of cases at each age level on which the norms are based, the writer feels that the data quoted in Tables II and III in consideration of the number of cases involved cast considerable doubt upon the increase in M between the ages represented.

Because of the observed significant sex differences in the Primary Mental Abilities as measured by the Chicago Tests, the tables of age norms in the Manual of Instructions in the 1941 edition and the profile of age scores on the back of the test booklet in the single-booklet edition of 1943 which make no differentiation for sex were felt to be of limited use for individual guidance purposes locally. Accordingly, from the beginning all individual ratings have been reported in terms of percentile standings in the year's group of the same sex. In an extreme instance the same raw score in the same primary ability means a difference of as much as eighteen points in percentile standing between boys and girls.

The following excerpt from a much broader account by Vernon is illustrative of the difference in emphasis between the British and American approaches to the description of the factors of intelligence. It is clear throughout this book that the initial conflict in views [for example, general intelligence vs. specific intelligences or primary factors] progressively modified on both sides of the Atlantic. The difference is now one of emphasis, preference, and utility. Vernon here makes the case for a hierarchical structure, different levels of which may be utilized depending on the psychologist's interests. The article begins with an account of testing in the British Services, the tests used and test construction techniques, and then turns to factor-analytic studies. The factor-analytic portion follows.

British Army and Navy Research on Intelligence*

P. E. VERNON

1947

Some sixty factor analyses were carried out, the mean number of tests being close to 11 and the mean size of population 300. The main uses were:

a) to study the abilities measured by the standard tests and their organisation in different populations;

b) to analyse the content of new tests in terms of factors defined by established ones;

c) to simplify questionnaires or rating scales on interests and personality traits by factorial item-analysis;

d) to explore unfamiliar abilities such as Radar operating, Anti-Aircraft work, athletic, scientific, etc., and in particular the structure of mechanical ability;

e) to analyse follow-up or validatory criteria, in order to show whether several sets of marks or assessments could reasonably be regarded as measuring a single general type of proficiency, or two or more relatively distinct types.

Burt's simple summation or Thurstone's centroid method was always applied as a first step, in order to indicate what statistically significant general and bipolar factors were present. But some form of general + group factor analysis was generally preferred to rotation of axes in eliminating negative loadings. The outstanding finding was the prominence of the general factor in representative adult populations. Although most if

* Taken from Research on Personnel Selection in the Royal Navy and the British Army, *American Psychologist*, 2 (1947), pp. 35-51, by permission of the author and the American Psychological Association.

TABLE I

Factorial Analysis of Group Tests in a Representative Army Population of 1,000 Recruits

	Unrotated simple summation analysis				Group factor analysis					Communalities		
	I	II	III	IV	g	k:m	ed.	v	n	Summation Est.	Summation Obt.	Group factor
1. Matrix	.77	+.23	+.10	−.16	.79	.17				.675	.682	.654
Dominoes (non-verbal g test)	.80	+.09	+.19	−.12	.87					.695	.697	.752
Group Test 70 Pt. I (ditto)	.74	+.16	+.03	−.08	.78	.13				.580	.577	.621
6. Squares	.63	+.35	−.00	+.01	.59	.44				.525	.523	.541
26. Assembly	.37	+.54	−.15	+.28	.24	.89				.515	.523	.850
4. Bennett	.69	+.33	−.17	+.07	.66	.31				.625	.617	.540
10. Verbal	.88	−.24	−.26	−.14	.79		.29	.45		.920	.919	.904
Dictation Test	.79	−.42	−.25	−.11	.62		.54	.48		.880	.876	.896
14. ATS Spelling	.81	−.32	−.20	−.11	.68		.41	.43		.800	.799	.818
11. Instructions	.89	−.06	+.11	−.15	.87		.23	.09		.820	.820	.819
9. Arith. Pt. I	.84	−.29	+.22	+.23	.72		.49		.39	.885	.889	.914
Arith. Pt. II	.86	−.16	+.12	+.13	.80		.38		.16	.800	.797	.815
13. ATS Arith.	.84	−.21	+.26	+.14	.77		.36		.32	.845	.840	.817
Variance per cent	52.5				52.5	8.7	8.4	6.9			73.5	76.5

not all Admiralty and War Office psychologists began their work with a somewhat dubious or suspicious attitude toward Spearman's views, the trend of our results pointed inescapably to a g + group factor theory as preferable to 'simple structure.' In seven typical analyses the g factor obtained 2½ times the variance of all other factors combined, and the most representative study, whose results appear in Table I, yielded a g covering 52.5 per cent of variance, spatial-mechanical group factor 8.7 per cent, educational and verbal group factors 15.3 per cent. It is noteworthy that American naval psychologists also, in factorising the test scores of a heterogeneous Navy population, concluded in favor of a general factor with a variance of over 30 per cent, and mechanical, spatial and educational group factors. But as soon as we took selected populations such as officers or mechanical trainees, correlations between some of the spatial-mechanical and verbal tests sunk to zero or slightly negative values; that is, the g which is common to these two main types of test tended to disappear, and independent factors akin to those which Thurstone obtains in selected college and high school populations provided a more satisfactory picture.

The second main finding was the ubiquity of the contrast between verbal, arithmetical and educational abilities on the one hand, and spatial, practical and mechanical abilities on the other hand. The same general pattern occurred among all types of male recruits, including African natives, and applied not merely to psychological tests but also to proficiency assessments. For example, ability at theory is set off from ability at Morse in naval, Army and ATS signallers and telegraphists; informational attainments contrast with typewriting and stenography among clerks, technical acquirements with personality qualities among officers, and so on. When suitable batteries of tests are analysed these "v:ed" and "k:m" types subdivide into innumerable more specialised group factors, although such subtypes do possess something in common over and above g. Thus in Table II the v:ed tests are best represented by a common educational factor and independent verbal and numerical sub-factors. A clerical group factor, and a subdivision of educational tests into primary vs. secondary school, or into rote vs. reasoning, types, were also often discovered. But in representative populations these sub-factors carried very low variance, whereas the v:ed factor was so prominent in all tests and jobs, that the vocational psychologist was generally able to make very successful predictions of performance in any kind of theory or bookwork training by means of mathematical and verbal tests.

In contrast the k:m pole is so heterogeneous and amorphous that it would seem to be not so much a positive practical ability as a complex of those abilities which are not linguistic and not usually affected by schooling. Not only mechanical-comprehension, mechanical-information and assembly tests, but spatial judgment tests, performance tests (e.g. Kohs Block), some non-verbal g tests (e.g. Matrix), physical tests and manual dexterity tests all have something in common, beyond g, but readily break down into largely independent sub-types. The practical group factors in proficiency assessments are also relatively independent, hence vocational predictions are much less accurate in this field. An experiment in which the same tests were applied to groups of recruits at different stages of training showed that the structure of mechanical ability alters markedly with training. The Bennett test, for example, appears to test mechanical comprehension in beginners, but to become an educational attainment test among highly trained artificers. In another study of 27 sets of marks objectively awarded to Electrical Mechanics during their six months workshop training, it was concluded that, while a general ability at all mechanical jobs does exist, distinct from g, it is of small variance, and group factors specific to the particular type of operation (fitting, turning, milling, etc.) are more prominent. Each test job, occupying the trainees several days, may be aptly compared to a single mathematical test item, in reliability and in overlapping with other jobs or items. Hence a very extensive sampling of jobs over months may be needed to yield a reliable criterion of mechanical ability.

Owing to restrictions in the application of specialised tests, little data was collected on factors other than g, v:ed and k:m. A prominent physical factor was, however, found among athletic performances, age and medical category (partially overlapping with k:m). Among nine sensory-motor tests for the selection of anti-aircraft personnel, specificity was so great that common factors only accounted for 12 per cent of variance, g for 4 per cent, and the sensory-motor factors showed no relation to job proficiency. Trials of manual dexterity tests among mechanics gave similar results. Two entirely different efficiency rating questionnaires, employed in the Army and the ATS, yielded closely parallel common factors which were identified as:

1) keenness, smartness, conformity to discipline
2) social qualities
3) stability and thoroughness
4) ability at the job.

An analysis of 39 items in a biographical questionnaire, applied to one thousand naval recruits, gave:

1) a general cultural level factor
2) tendency to fill in many or few items—an additional general factor
3) mechanical interests and experience group factor
4) athletic interests group factor
5) domestic interests group factor
6) social interests group factor.

Over half the variance, however, of the average item was found to consist of specificity and unreliability.

A defect of such analyses is that the correlations were usually tetrachorics. Recently Slater has developed a technique for factorisation of chi-squareds, which should be more accurate.

VALIDATION

It is the boast of British vocational psychologists that they know more about the validity of their tests or other selection techniques than do doctors or teachers or any of the innumerable organisations which conduct scholastic, professional or trade examinations. During four years in the Navy, for example, there were 76 follow-up investigations, covering over 31,000 recruits, in which some criterion of proficiency was correlated usually with six or more selection tests, often with other data such as source or mode of entry, age, education and civilian occupation, sometimes also with numerous items such as interests or leadership experience, taken from the recruits' biographical questionnaires. The median size of sample is 300. In all of these the tests were given, or other data collected, on entry and the recruits' success or failure traced later, usually at the end of training. Validatory trials of new tests are not included.

Researches in the Army, while equally numerous, were more scattered, so that a similar complete list is not available. Soon after the introduction of regular selection procedure, 2,500 recruits in representative jobs were followed up. Thereafter many investigations were made of jobs where specific information was needed, e.g. in order to establish appropriate test standards. In the main ATS follow-up, some 6,000 auxiliaries were studied in the 27 commonest jobs, the median size of sample being 106.

It is obviously impossible to summarise all these data. An account has been given elsewhere of the abnormal distributions and the correlation techniques applied to them, the unreliability of the criteria of efficiency, methods of dealing with squad or class variations, the effects of selectivity and the difficulties in using multiple correlation and correction for multivariate selectivity. The value of a single composite test score, namely T2, is well illustrated by Table II, which shows the 90th, 50th and 10th percentile scores for men employed in 36 representative naval branches. Clearly there is excellent differentiation between the more and less highly skilled jobs. Table III shows the 90th, 50th and 10th percentile raw validity coefficients for the most frequently used tests in all naval investigations, and Table IV the corresponding figures in ATS investigations corrected for selectivity (the uncorrected multiple r's in the two Services are almost identical in median and range).

The general level of validity of these group tests is higher than might have been anticipated from pre-war experience, though obviously too low for accurate selection in the absence of other information. The highest coefficients tend to occur with jobs involving lengthy training, including a fair amount of theoretical work, when the final assessment of proficiency is based on thorough examinations, and when there is no psychological selection scheme already in operation. Still higher ones would doubtless

TABLE II

Ninetieth, Fiftieth and Tenth Percentile T2 Scores of Men
Employed in Different Branches of the Navy

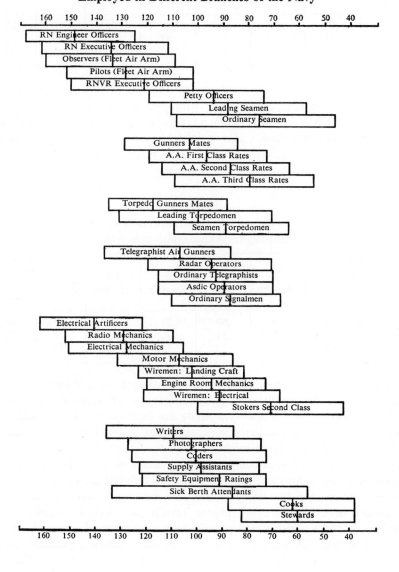

TABLE III
Raw Validity Coefficients of Standard Naval Selection Tests

Test ...	1 Matrix	3 Shipley	4 Bennett	5 Maths.	6 Squares	T2	Multiple r (uncorr.)
90%ile	.45	.49	.44	.57	.38	.57	.70
50%ile	.28	.30	.28	.35	.22	.40	.47
10%ile	.10	.11	.13	.17	.05	.20	.32

have been found had the Services made any use of objective attainment tests. The lowest coefficients occur with jobs where the work is highly specialised (such as Radio Mechanics), or where previous trade experience is of paramount importance, also in jobs (such as Seaman) where assessments of efficiency are based more on personality qualities, e.g. dependability, than on any definite skills or knowledge.

TABLE IV
Validity Coefficients of Standard ATS Selection Tests
Corrected for Multivariate Selectivity

Test ...	1 Matrix	4 Bennett	13 Arith.	6 Squares	11 Clerical	Multiple r Uncorr.	Corr.
90%ile	.65	.41	.69	.51	.66	.69	.84
50%ile	.49	.30	.51	.40	.56	.47	.65
10%ile	.27	.19	.26	.20	.35	.35	.30

Since almost all the samples followed up had been selected by psychological procedures, the results are inevitably distorted by selectivity. Moreover statistical corrections for such selectivity are inadequate, since it does not merely involve reductions in the variance of test scores. Often, for example, personnel selection officers might allocate to a certain branch men with low tests scores but with compensating qualities of keenness or relevant experience, and when these men did well they reduced the corrected correlations between the test and the criterion. In some branches, successive validatory investigations gave poorer results as selection became more efficient. Table V illustrates this trend in a new mechanics branch of the Navy. The first 300 men sent for training were almost unselected, since little was known about the job requirements, and the validity coefficients of all tests are remarkably high. Among the next 300, more information was available to the personnel selection officers; also the content of the training course altered. As the Training School got used to the better qual-

TABLE V

Correlations Between Tests and Proficiency Among 1,100 Mechanics

Test	First 300	Next 300	Next 500
1. Matrix	.623	.399	.255
3. Abstraction	.465	.568	.294
4. Bennett	.527	.352	.329
5a. Arithmetic	.553	.379	.164
5b. Mathematics	.638	.426	.369
6. Squares	.377	.282	.276
T2	.685	.532	.375

ity of well-selected trainees, the course was stiffened, and the validity co-efficients among the third group of 500 are quite low.

In general the most striking result of follow-up investigations was the uniformity of the relative validities of different tests in all jobs. The mechanical-spatial tests were relatively less useful than verbal-numerical ones in Clerical and Communications jobs, but they were just about as useful among officers, seamen and gunnery ratings as among mechanics. In some branches, all the tests might achieve high coefficients, in other branches all low, but almost always the Mathematics test obtained the highest relative validity, and the Spatial test the lowest. Often in fact the Mathematics test got better coefficients than T2—the sum of four tests. The Bennett Mechanical test gave useful predictions of practical efficiency, but was not outstandingly successful in mechanical branches, where the trainees possessed very diverse trade experience. Just the same was found in the Army with the Bennett and with the still more mechanical Assembly test. Although the Bennett is not generally appropriate for women yet, to-gether with a Meccano Assembly test, it actually showed greater differential value in the ATS than in the men's Services, presumably owing to the smaller influence among women of previous experience. The conclusion followed, then, that almost all branches wanted the same type of man, one with good education (especially in mathematics) as well as good intelli-gence. Thus selection became largely a matter of apportioning the available supplies of high quality men among the branches according to their needs; differentiation between jobs was based more on interests and interview judgments than on tests.

In the Army the Clerical or Instructions test (whose only difference from an ordinary clerical test battery is that all the operations have to be done in rapid rotation instead of in separate "slabs," hence its instructions are rather elaborate) vied with Arithmetic for top place in most branches, followed by the Verbal test and Bennett. Clerical was outstanding, for example, among drivers and in officer selection. In the ATS the same test did best, followed by Arithmetic and Spelling.

Several factors may be involved in this result. First we have seen that tests like Clerical and Arithmetic are more reliable than, and have as high g-content as, say, Matrix. Secondly most of the validatory criteria consisted of training results rather than assessments of operational efficiency, and tests with educational content might be expected to be the most successful in selecting men who could be trained rapidly. Numerous attempts were made to carry out operational follow-up, none entirely adequate. But the following experiments are worth citing.

A correlation of .624 between T2 and assessments of efficiency during fighting in Italy was obtained among 200 Royal Marine signallers, but the group tests were, in this instance, not applied until after the unit returned to Britain. . . .

For the four component tests the coefficients were all between .46 and .49. Thus Arithmetic appears to retain good predictive value, but the spatial test improves, when compared with an operational criterion.

Some seven thousand men in all Arms of the British Liberation Army were assessed for efficiency at the conclusion of hostilities in Germany, and the test scores which certain groups had obtained on recruitment were traced. Among 260 infantry, the Arithmetic test gave a correlation of .263, and all other tests smaller coefficients. While this figure is low it compares favorably with the correlation of .297 between the operational assessments and efficiency gradings given shortly before the invasion.

In the ATS over 600 trainees for Anti-Aircraft duties were followed up, and later some 1,300 were assessed for efficiency after serving two or more years. . . . Most of the tests, and multiple r, drop considerably in validity at the operational stage. But Spelling achieves a much higher coefficient, and the Clerical test is relatively more valid than at the training stage.

*   *   *

All the above evidence would seem to show, then, that the high validity of the v:ed tests is not primarily due to the use of training results as validatory criteria. A third consideration is that, as already mentioned, shortage of personnel, time and materials prohibited the use of specialised tests which might have had greater differential value. Actually many such tests were tried out and were found to add so little to the multiple r's obtained with the standard group tests alone, that they were not pursued. This occurred with the battery of sensory-motor tests for Anti-Aircraft personnel, with the old Morse Aptitude test for signallers, with Chleusebairgue's discrimination reaction time test for drivers, and others. The most useful supplementary tests, which did produce significant rises in multiple correlations, included No. 22 Reading Comprehension (naval officers, writers and stores assistants), No. 25d Doppler effect—a phonograph record based on Asdic sounds (Asdic operators), a scale and graph reading test (Radar operators), No. 8 Electrical Information (radio and electrical mechanics and wiremen), and occupational tests such as Nos. 29 and 31.

As none of these reasons appears adequate, the writer is inclined to attribute the success of such tests as Mathematics and Clerical first to the extreme heterogeneity of recruits in g and v:ed (as shown by factor analysis), and secondly to these tests involving certain personality qualities such as stability and persistence, in addition to cognitive abilities.

* * *

Predictions of population trends in intelligence have been freely made in the past but rarely substantiated with data. Near the close of World War II one psychologist thought to avail himself of a draft sample to evaluate such predictions. His rather surprising findings are neatly and briefly set forth in the following article.

Soldier Intelligence in World Wars I and II*

READ D. TUDDENHAM

1948

Cattell, Lentz, Maller and others, arguing from the observation that family size is inversely related to test performance, education and socio-economic level, have contended that the mean I.Q. of the population is declining at the rate of three or four points per generation. In contrast, data collected by the Personnel Research Section, AGO, during the closing months of World War II indicate at least for that fraction of the population selected for military service, that performance on a group test of the kind usually described as measuring "general learning ability" or "verbal intelligence" has markedly increased from World War I to World War II. The study here reported was a byproduct of another research and is not so unequivocal as one should like. Nevertheless it offers direct evidence on a problem hitherto attacked only indirectly, and suggests that the future may not be as black as the eugenicists would have us believe.

In the course of establishing the score equivalence between certain Army tests and several commercial ones, the Wells Revision (Form 5) of Army Alpha Examination was administered to a representative sample of the World War II draft. The population consisted of 768 white enlisted men selected on the basis of Army General Classification Test (AGCT) scores, as recorded on their qualification cards, to yield a distribution by Army Grade like that for all inductees entering during 1943. The distribution desired and that obtained are compared in Table I.

Since the correspondence was very close, the 768 men without further selection were administered the Wells Revision (Form 5) of Army Alpha Examination.

The correlation between Wells Alpha and AGCT was .90, indicating a very large degree of community in the functions measured. The AGCT yielded a mean Army Standard Score of 98.3 and a standard deviation of 22.7. The mean raw score on Wells Alpha was 101.2 and the standard

* Reprinted from the *American Psychologist*, 3 (1948), pp. 54-56, by permission of the author and the American Psychological Association.

TABLE I

Army grade	Army standard score	Inductees entering in 1943	Experimental sample
I	130 and above	6.4%	6.4%
II	110–129	28.6	28.8
III	90–109	31.1	30.7
IV	60– 89	28.5	28.8
V	below 60	5.4	5.3
		100.0%	100.0%

deviation was 46.0. Centile norms for the two tests are presented in Table II.

TABLE II

Centile Equivalents of Scores on AGCT and on Wells Alpha Examination, Form 5, for a Sample of 768 White Enlisted Men

Centile	AGCT standard score	Alpha raw score	Centile	AGCT standard score	Alpha raw score
99	145	194	50	100	104
95	132	175	45	97	97
90	126	160	40	94	90
85	122	150	35	91	82
80	118	143	30	87	74
75	115	136	25	83	66
70	112	130	20	78	58
65	109	122	15	73	50
60	106	116	10	67	38
55	103	110	5	59	23
			1	42	3

The comparison of the intelligence test performance of soldiers in World War I and World War II is complicated by the fact that for the purposes of the major study it was necessary to test the World War II group with the commercially available Wells Revision, Form 5 of the Alpha Examination instead of the original Alpha used in World War I. However, there is general agreement that the two versions yield very similar score distributions, especially in the upper quartile.

Bingham states: "The Wells Revision . . . . make(s) the examination more suitable for use in schools and industries while preserving the irreplaceable norms. Scores which fall in the upper quartile of the distribution are directly comparable with the original Alpha scores." The published norms on Wells Alpha for the "general adult population" agree closely with norms obtained on the original Alpha for literate white soldiers of World War I. Lorge has published data indicating that the Wells Alpha yields larger raw scores than does the original form, but that the difference is not greater than five percentile points.

TABLE III

A Comparison of Performance on Alpha Examinations of 48,102 White Enlisted Soldiers of World War I and a Representative Sample of 768 White Enlisted Soldiers of World War II

Centile	World War I original Alpha raw score	World War II Wells Alpha, form 5 raw score	Centile	World War I, original Alpha raw score	World War II, Wells Alpha, form 5 raw score
99	166	194	50	62	104
95	137	175	45	57	97
90	120	160	40	52	90
85	108	150	35	48	82
80	98	143	30	44	74
75	91	136	25	39	66
70	84	130	20	35	58
65	78	122	15	30	50
60	72	116	10	25	38
55	67	110	5	18	23
			1	8	3

If it is conceded that scores on the Wells revision correspond closely to scores on the original Alpha Examination, it is difficult to escape the conclusion that soldiers of World War II were markedly superior to their fathers in the functions measured by this test.

As may be seen in Table III, the differences between the two groups are very large throughout the range, and are as conspicuous above the seventy-fifth centile, where the equivalence of raw scores on Army Alpha and Wells Alpha is best established, as they are below this point. For the principal literate white sample of World War I reported in the *Memoirs,* the median raw score is 62. This is in close agreement with a median of 61 for Wells Alpha as cited in the published norms. However, a raw score of 62 reaches only the 22nd centile of the World War II distribution. Conversely, a raw score of 104, the median for the World War II group, falls at the 83rd centile of the World War I population. Such differences are, of course, highly significant.

No satisfactory answer can be given to the fundamental question of whether a similar difference exists between the national population of 1917–18 and 1940–45 from which the troops were drawn. Indeed, the members of the armed forces constitute by far the largest and most representative sample of the general population ever subjected to psychometric procedures. Considering the greater size of the Army in World War II, it seems likely that the draft population during the recent conflict was more nearly representative of the general population than was the case in World War I. However, the size and direction of selective differences between the armies and the populations from which they were drawn can only be guessed at.

Considering only the Army samples here reported, many factors can be adduced to account for the superiority of the World War II group. Only a few can be mentioned here.

1. For soldiers in World War I objective tests were wholly unfamiliar. Most soldiers in World War II had had considerable experience with them in schools, industry, etc. Previous practice on AGCT probably served to raise the Alpha scores of the men here reported. However, practice effects on AGCT produce an average gain of only about five points in taking a second form of the same test and would be even smaller in taking a different test, as in this instance. It seems unlikely that greater familiarity with objective tests can account for a very large part of the superiority of the World War II sample.

2. Numerous investigators have reported that as a nation we are increasing in height, in weight and in longevity. The indirect influence of improvements in public health and nutrition may have operated to increase test performance, though to an unknown degree.

3. The Army of World War II was definitely superior to that of World War I in amount of education. Since amount of schooling is correlated with test performance, it seems likely that educational differences contribute heavily to the superior test performance of the World War II group. In the present study, the number of years of education completed by each of the 768 enlisted men was recorded from his qualification card. The mean was 10.0 years; the S.D. was 3.0 years. The correlations between years of education and test score were .74 and .75 for AGCT and Wells Alpha, respectively. Comparable statistics for the principal literate white sample of World War I soldiers have been computed from the *Memoirs*. The correlation between Alpha and years of education completed was .63. The mean education was 8.0 years; the S.D. was 2.6 years. As a rough device for estimating the amount of difference in Alpha performance attributable to educational differences, the columns of Table 281 (*Memoirs*) were re-

weighted to conform to the distribution with respect to education of the World War II sample. Decile values were then computed from the re-weighted table, with the following results:

TABLE IV

Decile	World War I unweighted raw score	World War I weighted raw score	World War II raw score
90	120	144	160
80	98	125	143
70	84	110	130
60	72	97	116
50	62	85	104
40	52	73	90
30	44	61	74
20	35	49	58
10	25	34	38

Weighting of the World War I findings to make the population comparable in education to the World War II sample removes over half of the obtained difference in test scores between the two groups. If additional allowance is made for the progressive increase in the length of the school year and for improvements in school facilities and in the professional preparation of teachers, it is evident that the superior test performance of the World War II group *can* be accounted for largely in terms of education.

While the data presented in this study offer no proof, the writer is inclined to interpret them as indicating that the present population is superior in mental test performance to the population of a generation ago, and that a large proportion of this superiority is a consequence of more and better education for more people.

The *magnitude* of the improvement in test performance from World War I to World War II cannot be established on the basis of existing data, nor is it possible to estimate it very precisely even for Army populations. The major potential source of error in the present study is the use of two different measuring instruments, Army Alpha and Wells Alpha, in comparing the World War I and World War II groups; but a comparison which involved only Army Alpha would not eliminate difficulties of interpretation. Various items of the original version have grown obsolete and cannot be assumed to have remained constant in difficulty. Yet omitting such items, or replacing them with new material would alter the instrument and introduce, though perhaps in lesser degree, the same source of error which may be operative in the investigation reported here.

The findings of the present study, despite their limitations, cast doubts on Cattell's contention that the national I.Q. is dropping at a rapid rate. His references to I.Q. changes seem to imply a belief that the population is declining with respect to intelligence as measured by psychological tests. The present study indicates a change in the opposite direction, though one cannot rule out the possibility of a decline in the purely native component of intellectual performance were it possible to measure it. On one point the writer would be in complete agreement with Cattell,—viz., that changes in the population, as well as the obsolescence of test content, make it desirable that test norms be subjected to periodic revision.

In the following paper Anastasi takes a long, searching look at "traits" and reminds psychologists that "traits," after all, are observed behavioral unities which in themselves should be accounted for. She points out that many current findings suggest possible factors active in shaping traits and urges that research be pursued in these directions. The student should note with caution that hereditary sources of trait determination are conspicuously ignored (except for species differences) in the article. This omission is perhaps more than compensated for by the strong hereditary biases of many, if not most, factor analysts. In any event, the major point of the article must be dealt with by the science if we are to advance beyond simple description.

The Nature of Psychological "Traits"*

ANNE ANASTASI

1948

I do not propose to add another to the many definitions and classifications of traits which have appeared within the past decade. Rather is it my object to inquire into the sources of diversity among trait theories, in the belief that such an analysis will itself help to clarify the problem of traits and to point the way toward significant investigations.

SIMILARITIES AND DIFFERENCES AMONG EXISTING TRAIT THEORIES

First we may ask whether *any* common ground can be found in a survey of existing trait concepts. Reduced to its most elementary terms, a trait may be regarded as a category for the orderly description of the behavior of individuals. Even this simple statement, however, will undoubtedly meet with difficulties. Some may argue over the term 'category'; others will object to 'description'; a few may be alarmed by such a word as 'behavior'; some will resent the *s* in 'individuals'; while a number will give descriptions that are the reverse of orderly!

But if for the moment we keep our eyes firmly fixed upon similarities, even though these similarities may not be universal, we find that most trait theories are concerned with the *organization and interrelationships* of behavior, and are therefore derived from the observation of varied behavior manifestations of the individual. Trait concepts also refer, as a rule, to relatively *enduring* characteristics which thus have some predictive value. In general, they cover those characteristics which appreciably *differentiate* the

* Reprinted from *The Psychological Review*, 55 (1948), pp. 127-138, by permission of the author and the American Psychological Association.

individual from others. Thus if the observable similarities in a particular mode of response far exceed any individual differences therein, such a characteristic is not likely to be incorporated in current trait schemas. Finally, a *cultural frame of reference* is also evident, although not always explicit, in most trait classifications. It is those aspects of behavior which are significant within a particular culture or environmental setting that are usually identified and described as traits.

From this brief overview of the possible points of agreement among trait theories, we may turn to the less taxing search for their disagreements. The *number* of traits proposed varies from a single general factor to innumerable highly specific elements, with the majority of those psychologists who approach traits through the medium of factor analysis favoring a relatively small number of 'group factors' of an intermediate degree of generality. As to *stability,* traits are regarded by some as fixed and immutable throughout life, by others as undergoing a uniform and predetermined course of development with age, by still others as the constantly evolving resultant of the myriad influences which play upon the individual. Similarly, in the degree of *universality* of the proposed traits, theories vary from an implicit belief in a universal pattern of primary human traits, at one extreme, to the insistence that truly significant traits are unique to each individual, at the other. Attempts have also been made, at a highly speculative level, to identify traits with various *anatomical mechanisms,* such as neural patterns or genes. On the other hand, some writers have argued that such identifications are precluded by the very concept of traits as they envisage it. Similarly, traits have been endowed with *causal* properties by some psychologists, while others regard them as theoretical constructs or as points of reference in the classification of behavior.

DESCRIPTIVE APPROACH VERSUS A SEARCH FOR PRINCIPLES

It is our thesis that this diversity of trait concepts is the result of an underlying methodological limitation which has characterized not only trait studies but many other types of psychological investigations as well. The trait investigator has usually asked: *"What* is the organization of behavior?" or *"What* are the traits into which the individual's behavior repertory groups itself?" rather than asking, *"How* does behavior become organized?" and *"How* do psychological traits develop?" Much of the content of psychology —including trait theories—still consists of generalized factual descriptions rather than principles of behavior. It represents a cataloguing of responses within a specific (although not usually specified) setting, without reference to the conditions which bring about such responses. Within the typical textbook, for example, one finds an account of how the individual looks and acts—and possibly how he feels—when angry or afraid or elated; or a discussion of the stages through which the child passes in learning to climb stairs, pick up objects, or talk English; or a compilation of the drives which motivate behavior; or a listing of primary mental abilities.

Such content has been criticized by students of comparative culture as being 'community-centric.' It has been argued that textbooks of so-called general psychology are in large part textbooks of the 'psychology' of people in western Europe and America. A good portion of their content might in fact be characterized as the psychology of "American college students and urban school children." When emotional expressions, or stages of child development, for example, are checked in different cultures, the results are quite dissimilar to those reported in the typical text which purports to cover human behavior. The writings of many anthropologists and social psychologists furnish a rich source of illustrations of such behavior divergencies in different cultures.

The factuo-descriptive approach is at once too narrow and too broad. From the viewpoint of comparative culture, its findings have proved to be too narrow. The clinical psychologist, on the other hand, often complains that it is too broad for his purposes. This is the basis for the aversion to what has been inappropriately labeled the 'nomothetic' approach. By definition, a nomothetic approach is one which seeks fundamental laws and principles. The clinician objects to so-called nomothetic generalizations because they yield only crude approximations of the individual cases with which he must deal. But it is not against the *principles* of behavior that he is actually arguing. It is against the generalized—or perhaps unduly overgeneralized—factual descriptions that his criticism is in effect directed. The truly nomothetic principles of behavior apply equally to all individuals and will in fact explain the very uniqueness of each individual's behavior in terms of the unique combination of antecedent conditions.

It is no real solution to revert to the solitary contemplation of one individual. To do so is simply to substitute an individuo-centrism for the community-centrism of many current psychological generalizations. At best this would only yield information known to be applicable to a single subject, information whose usefulness would quietly expire with the demise of that privileged individual. But actually, if followed seriously and faithfully, such an individuo-centric method would not even furnish that much information. It is doubtful whether any understanding of such an individual could be achieved without previous familiarity with at least a few behavior principles which had been discovered under controlled conditions. It is as if a physician attempted to diagnose a case of cancer or appendicitis through a prolonged and sympathetic observation of his patient, but without benefit of any of the experimental findings of physiology, histology, chemistry, and other nomothetic disciplines.

To repeat, the factuo-descriptive approach yields approximate knowledge of relatively restricted groups of individuals. Such knowledge is neither sufficiently extensive—i.e., applicable outside the cultural setting in which it was obtained, nor sufficiently intensive—*i.e.,* completely and precisely applicable to any one individual. Principles of behavior, on the other hand, are at once universal and precisely applicable to each individual. It is only through a search for principles, therefore, and not through anti-scientific revolts and individuo-centric procedures, that we can transcend the limitations of the factuo-descriptive approach.

THE THEORETICAL IMPLICATIONS OF FACTUAL INCONSISTENCIES IN TRAIT RESEARCH

A survey of recent trait studies reveals various superficial inconsistencies, which we would expect to find because of the predominantly factuo-descriptive approach of such investigations. The diversity of trait concepts which have been proposed is closely paralleled by a diversity of factual material collected in descriptively oriented research.

'Intellectual' and 'emotional' traits. In the search for the *conditions* associated with this diversity of results, we first come upon a differentiation between studies concerned with 'abilities,' or *intellectual traits,* and those concerned with *emotional traits* or 'personality characteristics' in the popular sense. In studies on intellectual characteristics, the emphasis has generally been on 'common traits,' such as those discovered by factor analysis —traits which are common to large groups of people. Verbal, numerical, and spatial factors are among the now familiar 'traits' which have been identified in various factor pattern analyses. On the other hand, students of 'personality,' concerned primarily with the emotional and motivational aspects of behavior, have more often argued for 'individual traits,' rejecting common traits as unrealistic, artificial, and abstract. Some have maintained that they find it more useful to describe each individual in terms of his own peculiar behavior relationships, rather than to look for common patterns of relationship shared by many individuals. Factor pattern analyses of emotional and motivational characteristics have also yielded results which are less consistent and more difficult to interpret than in the case of intellectual characteristics.

Whether found by factor analysis, type studies, or genetic and biographical observation of a single individual, a trait is always essentially a pattern of relationship within the individual's behavior. The so-called 'common trait,' located by studying a group of persons rather than a single individual, is simply a generalized description of a pattern of behavior relationship which is shared by a group of individuals. Why, then, have such common traits found more support in studies of the intellectual aspects of behavior than in those dealing with its emotional and motivational aspects?

The reason is not difficult to find when we consider the greater *uniformity and standardization of experience* in the intellectual than in the emotional and motivational sphere. An obvious illustration of this fact is furnished by our system of formal education in which the standardized content of instruction is directed towards intellectual rather than emotional development. Furthermore, even if the schools were to institute a rigidly standardized curriculum of 'personality development' (a rather depressing thought!), we still would not find the uniformities of organization characteristic of intellectual development, since much of the individual's emotional development occurs through domestic or recreational activities. Not only educational courses, but also occupations and other traditional areas of activity within any one cultural setting tend to crystallize the individual's intellectual development into relatively uniform patterns. Such patterns become more clearly evident the longer the individual has been exposed to these common experiences. Those aspects of behavior in which the individual's activities are less standardized in our culture will exhibit a correspondingly more idiosyncratic organization into traits. A further reason for the greater standardization of intellectual responses is the relative degree to which these responses have been verbalized, as contrasted to emotional responses which are more largely unverbalized. It is also relevant to point out that the very distinction between intellectual and emotional aspects of behavior is itself culturally determined.

Nature of subjects. A second major source of diversity in trait research is associated with the type of subject under investigation. We may consider in this connection the categories of age, educational level, occupation, sex, cultural grouping, and species. *Age differences* in the pattern of trait organization have now been quite clearly established. Correlation studies on preschool children show a large general factor, frequently identified with 'intelligence,' with little or no specialization into group factors. Among school children, the weight of the general factor decreases with increasing age, and group factors of memory, verbal, numerical, spatial, and other aptitudes appear. The independence of these factors from each other tends to increase with age. Studies on college students have consistently shown prominent and relatively independent group factors, with only a negligible general factor. The latter, furthermore, is more closely identified with verbal ability among the older subjects. The increasing differentiation of ability and clearer emergence of specialized traits with age has been demonstrated both by the comparison of subjects of different age levels and by the more direct approach of re-testing the same children at successive ages.

Such a developmental approach to trait organization is a step toward the reconciliation of factual divergencies. No longer need we be disturbed by the fact that an investigator who obtains his data from fifth grade school children seems to support a general factor theory, such as Spearman's 'g,' whereas another investigator, testing college sophomores, 'proves' the presence of verbal, numerical, spatial, or other aptitudes which are almost completely uncorrelated with each other. Both are demonstrating the differentiation of traits with increasing age.

In discussions of age changes, however, there is often a tacit implication that maturational processes are involved, that the changes would occur regardless of what the individuals had been doing during those years. This is not a matter for assumption, but rather for investigation. Other group comparisons need to be made in the effort to clarify the source of the obtained age differences. Some of these comparisons have been made, but the available data are not so extensive as in the case of age differences. In fact, the information is often so meager as to do no more than point the way for a type of comparative investigation which should be pursued as thoroughly as has been done with age.

In this connection, we may consider next the influence of *educational level*. It should be noted that nearly all the trait studies showing differentiation with age have also included the variable of education, which increased concomitantly with age: the older groups of children were attending higher grades in school; the adolescents and adults were generally college students, not elementary school graduates.

Some highly suggestive data regarding the rôle of education are furnished by an analysis of the scores on the Army General Classification Test used in World War II. Within a sampling of 5000 men, carefully chosen so as to be representative of the entire army, with a mean age of 27 and mean education of 9½ grades, intercorrelations were computed among the scores on the verbal, numerical, and spatial sub-tests of the AGCT. The correlations proved to be decidedly higher than those found for similar tests among college students. But a more significant finding was the relative uniformity of such correlations among all tests, regardless of content. The correlation of the two numerical tests with each other, for example, was not much higher than the correlation between the numerical and verbal, the numerical and spatial, or the spatial and verbal tests.[1] Similarly, the three parts of a Mechanical Aptitude Test correlated about as highly with total and sub-test scores of the AGCT as they did with each other. These results were closely corroborated by correlations obtained on another sampling of 500 men who had taken different forms of the AGCT and Mechanical Aptitude Test.[2] Such findings suggest that among adult men in the army whose education was little better than elementary school graduation, test performance was relatively undifferentiated. In this respect, their trait structure thus re-

---

[1] AGCT–3, consisting of (1) reading and vocabulary, (2) arithmetic computation, (3) arithmetic reasoning, and (4) pattern analysis. Correlation between the two numerical tests was .90; correlations between verbal, numerical, and spatial ranged from .71 to .81. The three parts of the Mechanical Aptitude Test correlated .67, .78, and .71 with each other and correlated .77, .76, and .77, respectively, with total AGCT scores. Correlations of the four sub-tests of AGCT with the three sub-tests of the Mechanical Aptitude Test ranged from .65 to .72.

[2] AGCT–1, consisting of (1) vocabulary, (2) arithmetic, and (3) block counting. Intercorrelations of the three parts of the Mechanical Aptitude Test ranged from .60 to .78; correlations of these part scores with total AGCT scores ranged from .58 to .69.

sembled more closely that of elementary school children than that of the college students tested in the earlier studies on adults. Similarities of educational level seem therefore to be more influential than similarities of age in trait organization.

Further evidence of the relationship between education and trait organization is to be found in a factor analysis conducted with some of the standardization data of the Wechsler-Bellevue Intelligence Scale. The average intercorrelation of the ten sub-tests of this scale dropped consistently from .37 at age nine to .18 in the 25–29 year group. In the 35–44 year group, however, it rose to .31 and in the 50–59 year group it rose again to .43. Similar decreases and increases were found in the average contribution made by the first factor to all of the tests. Now, it is significant to note that the educational level of the two oldest groups was lower than that of the 25–29 year group. The latter had a range of education from one to four years of high school; the next older group from the sixth grade to one year of high school; and the oldest group from the fifth to the eighth grade. Thus we again find that among subjects of lower educational level, irrespective of age, abilities are less highly differentiated and the general factor is relatively conspicuous.

Occupation is a third category whose rôle in trait organization may be considered. The data assembled by the Employment Stabilization Research Institute of the University of Minnesota, for example, demonstrate clear-cut and consistent differences in the profile or pattern of test scores in various occupations. A further question, of more relevance to the present inquiry, concerns the intercorrelations of such scores within each occupational group. Very little direct information on such correlations is available to date. The interpretation of the findings is complicated, furthermore, by the fact that the occupational groups tested are not usually equated for such variables as age and education. Some suggestive data, however, can be found in the University of Minnesota studies to which reference has already been made. Three groups of unemployed men were given a battery including two or three tests in each of the following categories: intelligence, clerical aptitude, spatial aptitude, and manual dexterity. The three groups of men had previously been employed as clerks, skilled trades workers, and operatives in repetitive tasks, respectively. Intercorrelations among the tests were fairly similar in the three groups, the averages of all the intercorrelations being virtually identical in all three. A few specific differences can be found, however, which are of interest. Thus, the intercorrelations of the three manual dexterity tests were consistently higher among the operatives than among either of the other two groups. The dexterity tests also correlated consistently higher with tests of clerical aptitude and intelligence among the operatives than they did among clerks or skilled trades workers. On the other hand, the dexterity tests correlated lower with the spatial tests among the operatives and the skilled trades workers than they did among the clerks.

One could speculate regarding the implications of these group differences. For example, perceptual accuracy, closeness of attention, and motor speed may be important common factors in the operatives' performance on the clerical and intelligence tests, as well as on the dexterity tests. On the other hand, the performance of clerks and skilled trades workers on the clerical and intelligence tests may be much less dependent upon such functions and therefore less closely related to their performance on the dexterity tests. Among the clerks, manual dexterity may be largely a function of the amount of manual-mechanical experience they have had, a fact that would link their scores on the dexterity and spatial tests more closely than in the other groups.

It would also be interesting to determine the degree to which the general factor is associated with verbal ability in different occupational groups. Most of the studies conducted to date suggest an increasing identification of verbal ability with whatever general factor is found, as the individual advances in age. Remembering that the older subjects employed in factor analysis studies have generally been college students or college graduates, we may ask: Could not the heavy reliance of higher education upon verbal ability account for this relationship? If we carried out a factor analysis on manual workers, might not any general factor found in such a population be more closely identified with such characteristics as accuracy of observation, perceptual speed, attention control, and the like?

A fourth category for comparative investigation is that of *sex*. The differences in the traditional educational, vocational, and recreational activities of men and women are still sufficiently large to be reflected in sex differences in abilities. Sex differences in mean scores in verbal ability and memory in favor of the women and in numerical and spatial ability in favor of the men have been well established on representative samples in our culture. The interrelationships of abilities in the two sexes have not been as fully checked as their respective levels, although intercorrelations and factor pattern analyses on a few comparable samplings of the two sexes are available. There is some evidence to be found in such studies which suggests that the nature and organization of intellectual traits are not identical in men and women.

In an early English study on mechanical aptitude in school children, for example, the boys' scores on the various spatial tests correlated more highly with each other and less highly with estimates of 'general intelligence' than did the girls' scores. On this basis the investigator suggested that performance on spatial tests depends more largely upon special aptitude among boys, while among girls it is more largely influenced by those processes which are included under the rubric of 'general intelligence.' In a more recent study on 7-year-old English school childen, a factor pattern analysis revealed a spatial factor among the boys, but not among the girls. This author likewise concluded that some of the tests which involved a space factor for the boys were done by the girls "by means of their general intellectual facility."

Corroborative evidence is furnished by studies on American school children at the 9 and 12 year level. In these groups, the correlations of the spatial tests with verbal and numerical tests were higher among the girls than among the boys. In the same groups, the intercorrelations of verbal tests with each other tended to be higher among the girls, while the intercorrelations of numerical tests with each other were higher among the boys. The sex differences in intercorrelations were more clearly apparent in the 12-year-old than in the 9-year-old groups. Similarly, a factor pattern analysis of the performance of English secondary school boys and girls on a battery of verbal and numerical tests yielded factors which differed in number and location in the two sexes.

Studies on memory, conducted with school children of three age levels, from 9 to 15, as well as with college students yielded evidence which suggests that memory operates more nearly as an independent 'trait' among women than among men. Thus the intercorrelations of memory tests with each other tended to be higher among female subjects. At the same time, the community between memory and non-memory tests tended to be greater among male subjects.

Such data indicate the possibility that those groups which excel in performance within a given area, such as spatial or verbal aptitude, exhibit a more closely knit organization of performance within that area. Thus, in the studies cited, the women excelled in mean scores on the memory tests and also yielded higher intercorrelations among such tests than did the men. In mechanical aptitude, the boys excelled in score and also showed higher intercorrelations among the mechanical tests than did the girls. Furthermore, the correlations between spatial and non-spatial tests were lower among boys than among girls. Might this not suggest that the very conditions which make for good performance along certain lines tend also to crystallize and unify such performance into a clearly defined 'trait'?

A fifth category we may consider is that of *cultural groupings*. Relevant data are virtually non-existent in this area, the principal reason undoubtedly being the difficulty of devising a battery of tests applicable to widely diverse cultural groups. Although attempts have been made to devise tests which are relatively 'culture-free,' such tests do not offer sufficient variety and breadth of content to permit factor pattern analyses of the scope of those conducted within our culture. An analysis of the intercorrelations of scores on even the limited type of tests available would, however, be illuminating. It would be very surprising indeed if in cultures very unlike our own we should find the emergence with age of the verbal, numerical, spatial, and other familiar 'aptitudes' of our factor studies. To be sure, a certain degree of differentiation into relatively unified behavior 'traits' might occur with age within the initially amorphous and homogeneous pattern of behavior. But the nature of such traits and the degree of differentiation would probably be most unlike those found within our culture.

Turning to *species*, our sixth and last category, we may inquire what investigators on infrahuman animals have to offer to the concept of traits. A number of factor pattern analyses have been made, most of them on white rats, but their results have all but defied interpretation. In one study, for example, the intercorrelations of performance in nine tests were so low and insignificant that nothing could be concluded beyond extreme specificity of behavior. As for the rest, the interpretations of the 'factors' are highly speculative. Most of these factors were limited to a particular type of situation or learning problem. Some have been defined in terms of specific techniques which the animal may use in solving more than one problem, such as the principle of turning alternately right and left. One is impressed, furthermore, with the frequency with which factors related to the emotional aspects of behavior appear in conjunction with 'intellectual' factors and with greater prominence than the latter. Thus we find in the factor descriptions such terms as "a combination of intelligence and tameness," "wildness or panicky behavior," "wildness-timidity," and "self-confidence."

The difficulty of identifying factors in these infrahuman studies, as well as the intertwining of 'ability' factors and 'emotional' factors, is not surprising when we consider that white rats have not been subjected to formal education with standard sequences of courses in Elementary Maze-running 1–2, Problem-solving 5–6, or Advanced Seminar in String-pulling. Unlike the school children or college students of the human factor studies, white rats have not experienced that classic dichotomy between curricular and extra-curricular, between standardized intellectual development and unstandardized emotional development. It would seem that genetic studies of the *development* of factor patterns in animals living under controlled laboratory conditions might be the most fruitful contribution that infrahuman investigations could make to the concept of traits.

Experimental development of traits.   The comparison of trait organizations found among the different categories of subjects which we have considered points up the need for a more direct investigation of the mechanism by which traits develop—the way in which the specific experiential background of different individuals determines the organization of their behavior into more or less unitary and stable 'traits.' A preliminary, exploratory study of this question was conducted by the present writer about ten years ago. Though the interpolation of a relevant experience, the pattern of relationship among five tests was experimentally altered in a group of 200 sixth grade school children. The experience consisted of the acquisition of special techniques which would facilitate performance on three of the five tests employed, thereby introducing a new bond among these previously unrelated tests. An interesting parallel in an everyday life situation is furnished by a study on the organization of mathematical ability in English school children. Wide variations in the correlations among arithmetic, algebra, and geometry test scores were found in different school classes, and these variations were related to such conditions as whether or not these subjects were taught by the same teacher or whether the methods of teaching them emphasized similarities of techniques.

Also relevant are studies on the effect of practice upon factor patterns. Woodrow found, for example, that after prolonged practice, marked changes in the factor loadings of tests occurred. Nor were these changes a matter of greater reliance upon speed or upon general ability after practice, as might have been expected. Specific changes in the factor composition of most of the tests occurred in the course of practice, with no evidence for the increasing rôle of speed or general ability.

Such experimental approaches to the development of traits open a way for exploring the mechanism whereby the trait organizations found in the purely descriptive, 'cross-sectional' studies may have developed. The accumulated effects of education, occupation, and other everyday life activities upon behavior organization may be illuminated by a study of the condensed effects of short-range experimentally controlled experiences.

It has been argued that in such experiments what is changed is the *method of performing* the tasks set by the tests. Such an explanation is indeed plausible, but it should be invoked consistently. For example, when the test scores of subjects of different ages, occupations, or educational levels show diverse patterns of 'trait organization,' such differences too may be explicable in terms of different methods of work. Similarly, any uniformity in factor pattern among members of a given population may in part be the result of commonly acquired methods of work. Factor pattern analyses reveal only the organization of performance as it is found in a group of subjects, but do not indicate the etiology of such organization. If we grant that the 'traits' discovered by factor analysis are simply 'functional groupings' observable within the subject's behavior, then such traits cannot at the same time be conceived as underlying abilities which remain unaffected while the subject's methods of doing a task and his objectively observable behavior are profoundly altered. Even the common assumption that certain ultimate limits of performance are imposed by each individual's sensory, neural, and motor equipment must be modified in the light of the possible variety of work methods. Changing the method of work may in part overcome some of these physical limitations and thereby permit the individual to surpass his previously established 'capacity level.'

In summary, it has been the object of this paper to demonstrate that the diversity of trait concepts as well as the apparent factual inconsistencies in trait research result in large part from a predominantly factuo-descriptive approach. It is suggested that the greater consistency and ease of identification of traits in the intellectual as contrasted to the emotional aspects of behavior illustrate the greater cultural standardization of activities in the former category. The comparison of factor patterns among subjects differing in age, education, occupation, sex, cultural grouping, and species contributes towards an understanding of the conditions under which traits develop and presents a fruitful field for future research. A more direct approach is the experimental manipulation of behavior organization through the interpolation of relevant controlled activities. The problem of 'traits' is seen as but one illustration of the need for a more active search for the underlying behavior principles which unify the superficial divergencies of the descriptive approach.

As factor-analytic procedures became increasingly complex many psychologists came to regard the entire enterprise as a statistician's field which was abstruse, technical, mechanical, and far-removed from psychology itself. In this address Thurstone reaffirmed the essential psychological nature of the process and reviewed some of its current findings. Thurstone stressed the fact that for the psychologist factor analysis is a tool to be used with all the other techniques in the field to advance our understanding of psychological problems.

Psychological Implications of Factor Analysis*

L. L. THURSTONE

1948

Factor analysis originated in an epoch-making paper by Spearman in 1904. Spearman probably saw important implications in that paper but it seems doubtful whether he could have realized at that time the superstructure that was to be built on his first observations on what he called hierarchy. For a quarter of a century the journals were full of controversy about Spearman's single-factor theory of intelligence. His hypothesis and his uni-dimensional methods were extended to the n-dimensional case in 1930. In the last seventeen years, multiple-factor analysis has seen a very fast development so that even in this short period there have been published several thousand papers on multiple-factor theory and experimental results.

Our purpose here is to review some psychological implications of multiple-factor analysis and to make only incidental reference to the factorial methods as such. It is time that we take stock more frequently of how the factorial methods are affecting psychological concepts, and how these in turn affect the development of appropriate factorial methods. It should be emphasized that factor analysis is a scientific method that must be adjusted to each problem. It is not merely a statistical method, and it is not a routine that can be applied fruitfully to every correlation table in sight.

In the light of a good deal of experience with the factorial methods, we should be able to give students a few practical suggestions. In the Psychometric Laboratory at Chicago, we spend more time in designing the experimental tests for a factor study than on all of the computational work, including the correlations, the factoring, and the analysis of the structure. If we have several hypotheses about postulated factors, we design and invent new tests which may be crucially differentiating between the several hypotheses. This is entirely a psychological job with no computing. It calls

* Reprinted from the *American Psychologist*, 3 (1948), pp. 402-408, by permission of Dr. Thelma G. Thurstone and the American Psychological Association.

for as much psychological insight as we can gather among students and instructors. Frequently we find that we have guessed wrong, but occasionally the results are strikingly encouraging. I mention this aspect of factorial work in the hope of counteracting the rather general impression that factor analysis is all concerned with algebra and statistics. These should be our servants in the investigation of psychological ideas. If we have no psychological ideas, we are not likely to discover anything interesting because even if the factorial results are clear and clean, the interpretation must be as subjective as in any other scientific work.

Another hint for the student is that he usually tries to accomplish something too ambitious in his first factorial studies but that is also typical in the formulation of other thesis subjects. A factorial study is more likely to give convincing findings if it covers a restricted domain with only enough measures of known factorial composition to serve as a linkage between the factors that are already known and the factors that we hope to discover or isolate.

Most of the factorial studies that have been done so far have been concerned with the cognitive domain. Previous work had discovered a number of group factors such as the verbal, the numerical, and the visual. These were more clearly revealed by the more powerful multiple-factor methods. The further breakdown of the cognitive intellective functions into primary factors has revealed that the cognitive field represents a large number of functional unities or factors. We no longer speak of "the" verbal factor as if it were unitary. At least three verbal factors are known and several additional verbal factors are clearly indicated. One of these verbal factors has been denoted V and it represents facility in understanding verbal material. Another verbal factor has been denoted Word Fluency W and it represents facility in finding words to represent restricted context. A third verbal factor F represents ideational fluency with words. There is indication that a naming factor exists which is independent of the three that have been mentioned. In some forms of aphasia we seem to be dealing with patients who have one or more of these verbal factors intact while they are lacking in other verbal factors. Without understanding the differences between the several distinct verbal factors, one is at a loss to understand why the patient can do certain verbal tests while he fails on other verbal tests. This field should be experimentally investigated more intensively in the light of factorial results.

The ability to memorize has been found to be a primary factor that is independent of other cognitive functions. Incidental memory seems to be an ability that is distinct from the ability to memorize intentionally. There is good indication that auditory memory is not the same ability as visual memory.

One of the most important of the primary abilities is that of visualizing space which has been denoted the Space factor S. It is involved in all thinking about solid objects and flat objects in space.

The perceptual functions have been broken down into a number of distinct primary factors. Among the most interesting are those which represent facility in perceptual closure in which there are very large individual differences. Perceptual closure has been found in a battery of visual tests and also in a battery of twenty-eight auditory tests that were specially designed for factorial analysis. It is a curious circumstance that we do not yet know whether the closure factor in visual material is the same as the closure factor in auditory material. In order to solve that problem, it will be necessary to include both visual and auditory tests of closure in the same factorial analysis. It will then be interesting to ascertain whether perceptual closure is a primary factor that transcends the visual and auditory modalities. If so, then closure is a central factor that may be of considerable importance in the human intellect. On the other hand, it may be found that closure is represented by two or more factors that are specific for each modality. An extensive study of perceptual abilities has recently been carried out by Harold P. Bechtoldt.

It is not our purpose here to summarize all of the primary factors that have been identified but only to describe the general nature of these findings.

When we consider the increasing number of distinct functional unities into which the field of cognition is being divided, we find that it is necessary to revise very fundamentally our notions about general intelligence. Factorial results make it imperative that we describe each individual in terms of a profile of mental abilities instead of by a single index such as the I.Q.

With further progress in this field we shall have a profile for each person with a very large number of columns. It is our present belief that if we knew the twenty most important primary factors we should be able to undertake educational and vocational counseling with more confidence than at present. Even in the present state of knowledge with about ten of these factors identified, we certainly can do much better in appraising the intellective assets of a person than by the older methods by which each person was described in terms of a single I.Q.

Factorial work raises interesting questions about the general intellective factor of Spearman. According to his hypothesis, general intelligence is mediated by a central intellective factor which he denoted "g." This hypothesis has been the subject of much controversy in the last forty years. When the multiple-factor methods began to isolate quite a number of primary factors in the cognitive domain, it looked at first as if the Spearman single-factor hypothesis would have to be discarded but that does not seem to be necessary. It was found that the primary factors of cognition were positively correlated. For adults, most of these correlations are under $+ .30$. When the positive correlations between the primary factors are examined factorially, there appear second-order factors, and the most conspicuous of these second-order factors agrees well with Spearman's hypothesis. Here we have a clue to an interpretation that may unify the early work of Spearman and the later work with multiple-factor analysis. The interpretation that seems plausible at this time is that the primary factors represent different kinds of mental facilities such as several kinds of memory, several kinds of perceptual closure, several visualizing factors, and several verbal factors. These primary abilities may be regarded as media for the expression of intellect and people differ markedly in the effectiveness with which they can express themselves in these different media. The second-order factors may represent parameters that are more central in character and more universal in the sense that they are not determined by the efficiency of each modality or imagery type. The first-order primary factors may be regarded as separate organs, in a general sense, while the second-order or general factors represent parameters which influence the activities of the several organs or primary factors. The general factors may then be expected to have no particular locus whereas some of the primary factors may eventually be rather definitely localized.

This attempt to unify Spearman's work with the later multiple-factor work seems to be plausible in terms of the findings of recent factorial studies but it should not be taken very literally. We can make only a tentative sketch of the underlying order at this early stage of knowledge of the organization of human intellect. If Spearman's general intellective factor is the same as the second-order inductive factor, then we can now determine that general factor uniquely. That is something which Spearman was never able to do. I have spoken of second-order factors in the plural. The reason is that we seldom find a single second-order general factor which would be indicated by Spearman's original hypothesis. Such complications are to be expected with the development of any science and it should not be interpreted as a discredit to Spearman's early work on which all of us have built.

In introducing our speculation about the relation of Spearman's general intellective factor "g" to later multiple-factor studies, we have noted that the primary factors are positively correlated. This also introduces a conflict between our statistical habits and psychological judgment. Some students of factorial theory bring to this subject their statistical habits and they sometimes insist that factors must be uncorrelated in order to be meaningful and useful. This is a curious situation. We deal all the time with meaningful measures that are correlated such as height and weight, but when we turn to the mental abilities, we are told that we must force them to be uncorrelated. Scientific judgment dictates that we report the correlations between primary factors as they are actually found, irrespective of statistical convenience. The correlated abilities are represented in factor analysis by oblique reference axes. That is not so convenient as a coordinate system in which all of the axes are at right angles.

Psychological studies of aptitudes frequently refer to such categories as mechanical aptitude, artistic aptitude, and musical aptitude. We shall describe briefly a current study of mechanical aptitude as an illustration of the psychological aspects of factorial analysis. It is rather common to hear mechanical aptitude referred to as if it were a single entity but it is our hypothesis that mechanical aptitude is a complex of abilities rather than a single unitary trait. It also seems plausible that we are dealing here with a rather restricted number of abilities. It is our job now to try to discover how many important abilities are involved in the complex known as mechanical aptitude and what those abilities are. Further, we make the hypothesis that mechanical aptitude is mostly in the head. It is not uncommon to hear this type of talent described as if it were in the finger tips, even associated with a certain amount of stupidity and a willingness to get one's hands dirty. In fact, it is rather common in the public schools to send the verbally slow learners into technical schools with the idea that if a boy is sufficiently stupid, he may become a good machinist. This is one of the educational blunders of our generation. It is our hypothesis that when a mechanic inspects a piece of machinery that is misbehaving, and when he diagnoses what is wrong with it, he is using his head and only incidentally his hands. Musical talent is also a complex that is not confined to finger dexterity. The psychological problem in the current study is to discover, if possible, what cognitive primary functions are involved in mechanical aptitude. If we could solve that problem, we might make a contribution of importance to education as well as to industry.

In the current study of this problem, we have made some tentative hypotheses which are in turn represented by differentiating tests that were specially designed for the purpose. One hypothesis which will almost certainly be sustained, as it has been in previous studies of this problem, is that mechanical aptitude consists in some large part of the space factor S, namely, the ability to think about objects in two-dimensional and in three-dimensional space. There are tremendous individual differences in this ability to visualize space, and in an educated audience we could find a fairly large proportion of individuals who, although otherwise gifted, are very poor in this ability. The tests by which this factor has been identified all involve the visualizing of objects that are stationary. In dealing with mechanical problems, one must be able to think of objects in motion. Their relative motions have definite restrictions that are studied in a separate discipline known as kinematics. We might therefore add another psychological hypothesis, namely, that there exist one or more abilities that are revealed in the ability to think about solid objects in motion as distinguished from thinking about them when they stay still. Another hypothesis about this group of aptitudes is that the ability to remember visual form has some part in mechanical aptitude. Still another hypothesis is that the perception of fine detail is involved. Perhaps one of the most fruitful hypotheses is that mechanical aptitude involves non-verbal reasoning.

When a list of hypotheses has been assembled, the next step is to invent a set of experimental tests which shall be crucially differentiating among the hypotheses. When that has been done, the tests are prepared and tried out for suitable time limits and performance instructions. Then they are given to several hundred individuals who are known to differ widely in mechanical aptitude. There is no need to represent the general population. In fact, it is wasteful to assemble a group of experimental subjects so as to represent the general middle range. It is better to include extremes of all available types in the experimental group. It will generally be found that all this work requires more time than the computational work that follows.

Similar studies should be undertaken in the fields of artistic aptitude and of musical aptitude in the hope of determining the dimensionalities of these fields. It has been our experience that no domain is completely determined in a single factor study because every study raises more psychological problems than it answers, but this is the natural course of science.

When a factorial analysis has been completed, one is tempted to try to interpret all of the common variance in terms of common factors, but it usually happens that some of the factors are indeterminate while some of them are clear and easily interpreted. It should be pointed out that a factorial study can make a major scientific contribution to our understanding of mind, even if it does not attempt to identify all of the common factors clearly. An important contribution can be made even if only one new factor is isolated and psychologically described even if all of the rest of the variance remains an unknown muddle. Such results depend on the structure that happens to be found in the factorial battery that is assembled to represent a domain, and every factor study is in this sense a gamble.

The inheritance of mental abilities has been investigated on 150 pairs of identical and fraternal twins. They were given forty psychological tests, including both group tests and individual performance tests. It was found that the identical twins were more nearly alike than the fraternal twins. Their differences were especially marked in the visualizing factors. It was found that spelling ability was one of the most conspicuous in differentiating the identical from the fraternal twins. The ability to learn spelling seems to be quite independent of most other abilities and it should be investigated to determine its relations to the primary factors.

One of the most important implications of factorial work is the breakdown of the line of demarcation between intellect and temperament. It is becoming increasingly evident that these two domains are not so completely separated as they have frequently been assumed to be. For example, the primary factors that identify perceptual closure are certainly cognitive in character and yet they seem to be definitely related to temperamental characteristics as well. In this connection the recent work of Dr. John G. Lynn is of special interest. He gave some tests of primary mental abilities to psychiatric patients and he noted in particular those patients who were relatively much better gifted in the space factor than in the verbal factors. He noted also the opposite extreme, namely, those patients who were much better gifted in the verbal factors than in the space factor. He found interesting differences in the symptoms of these two groups of patients. For example, he found that among the patients who were much higher in the space factor than in the verbal factors, there were no hallucinations. This field calls for very intensive study so that we may know more definitely the relations between the emotional symptoms and the relative strengths of the cognitive primary factors. Other studies of normal subjects have shown indication of temperamental differences between those who excel in the visualizing factors and those who excel in the verbal factors.

Factorial work is customarily based on experimental populations of several hundred subjects and the primary factors are isolated, ordinarily, on populations of normal subjects. I should like to suggest a parallel form of experimentation that should give results consistent with the factorial experiments. It is well known that among feeble-minded subjects we find occasionally conspicuous cases in which one or more abilities remain intact and even of superior quality while the subject is otherwise so poorly endowed mentally that he must have institutional care. I believe that significant studies could be made of single subjects in order to clarify our understanding of the primary mental abilities. For example, a single patient might be found who excels on a few similar tests while he fails hopelessly on the rest of them. Now, the investigator should alter slightly the several tests which the patient can do in order to determine just what characteristics must be retained in order for the patient to be able to do the task and just what characteristics of the test are associated with his failures. The investigator would have to try a large number of slight variations in the tests in order to be able to draw a sort of psychological map, as it were, to show just what the patient can do and what it is that he fails to do. If it can be assumed that one or a few of the abilities are intact in the patient, then we might be able to determine from the successive performances of a single patient just what each primary factor involved. The results should then be verified factorially by a study of normal subjects. I am calling attention to this type of inquiry in order to show again the intimate relations between factorial experiments and psychological hypotheses. We must not regard factor analysis merely as a toy for the statisticians to play with. It is a scientific method that should be useful in testing hypotheses in experimental, clinical, and social psychology.

To emphasize this point in another way, we may consider the task of interpretation of factorial results. When I found some years ago that there were two verbal factors in the battery that had been analyzed factorially, I was curious to know what these two verbal factors were like psychologically. I played solitaire with these tests, and I introspected for each test to see what was going on in my own mind when I did the two kinds of tests which were to be differentiated. Then I found what should have been obvious at the start, namely, that one kind of verbal test required the subject to produce the words, sometimes without regard to their meaning, whereas the other kind of test required the subject to understand the words that were presented to him. These were the factors V and W which have since been verified in a number of factorial studies. Last summer, the ideational fluency factor F was differentiated in the same manner by Calvin W. Taylor. When a factorial study is under way we are always eager to complete the computational work so that we can begin the more interesting job of psychological interpretation, which is the goal of the factorial study.

It is my conviction that the domain of temperament can be clarified by factorial studies in a manner analogous to the studies by which the primary factors of cognition are being identified. Most of the tests of temperament are really not tests at all. They are only questionnaires in which the subject controls the answers completely. It would probably be very fruitful to explore the domain of temperament with experimental tests instead of questionnaires. Most psychologists would probably regard the early work of June Downey as obsolete and possibly as representing a false lead. It is my belief that she had the right idea to investigate temperament with experimental methods rather than with questionnaires. It would probably be fruitful to return to that lead but it would not be necessary to limit such inquiry to handwriting as the medium.

As a cross between cognition and temperament, it might be profitable to make a factorial experimental study of symbol association with response time recorded separately for each subject and for each symbol association. The several tests might consist of specified types of association to be made by the subject in response to the stimuli. The readiness with which the subject makes a specified kind of associational response would constitute his score in a test. A factorial study of the results might be very revealing, and it would not be surprising if the factors so determined would have intimate relations with both intellect and temperament.

Some of the implications of recent factorial work are of educational significance. A factorial study has been made with seventy psychological tests that were given to several hundred five-year old children. Since most children at that age cannot read, it was necessary to design all of the tests in pictorial form. The results of that study indicated essentially the same primary mental abilities that have been found among high school students and adults. The mental profiles of five-year old children show the same great variation as adults. The number factor in children of this age seems to be more inductive than in adults so that it can be called quantitative thinking. It seems to be possible to identify the space factor in children even at the age of three or four. For example, if a very young child shows interest in jigsaw puzzles, one can probably make the inference that he is a good visualizer. It certainly is evident that young children are capable of more complex reasoning than we ordinarily give them credit for. As adults, we are so accustomed to the verbal medium that we are likely to misjudge the reasoning powers of young children who have not yet developed adult vocabulary. The frequent early development of quantitative thinking at the kindergarten age makes one question the current practice of delaying instruction in arithmetic until a later age.

One of the important educational problems in the first few grades is that a certain proportion of children have difficulty in learning to read. In many cases this difficulty does not seem to be associated with low intelligence, but it seems to be more specific. Studies have been initiated in order to relate the mental profiles at the kindergarten age with subsequent performance in reading. There is a possibility that the methods of teaching reading should be adjusted to the mental profiles of the children. If it should be found that children of different mental profiles profit by different methods in teaching reading, then the same type of problem can be raised at all subsequent ages. It may be specially important to adjust the teaching methods at the early ages to the mental profiles of the children.

Since the primary mental abilities have been isolated as functionally distinct, even at the kindergarten age, one naturally raises the question of differential growth in the primary factors. It is still a question of fact whether children differ markedly in the rate of development of the different primary factors. If there are great individual differences in the primary mental abilities themselves, it would not be surprising to find that there are also individual differences in the rate of growth of the different factors. Besides the possible individual differences in rate of growth, we already know that some factors mature much sooner than others. Perceptual closure seems to mature at the age of nine or ten, so that there are no differences between nine-year olds and adults in mean performance. The verbal comprehension factor V probably matures more slowly than any of the others. The growth of verbal comprehension is difficult to appraise because the estimation of this factor is more influenced by schooling and experience than some of the other primary factors. Instead of worrying about the constancy of the I.Q. we shall probably find ourselves worrying about the relative constancy of the profile throughout the life span.

It is one of the most common questions about primary abilities whether they can be trained, and the answer is in the affirmative. On the other hand, if two boys differ markedly in one of the primary abilities and if they are given the same amount of training, it is to be expected that although both of them improve, their difference will be increased by training. Even though the more gifted profit more by training than the less gifted, it is of course generally agreed that training opportunities should be as nearly universal as possible. A full year's curriculum has been prepared for kindergarten children by which the primary abilities are trained in a large number of games that vary from day to day. It is not unlikely that similar training material for the primary abilities will be introduced for the later years in the school curriculum.

In educational and vocational guidance it has been the practice to find by trial and error those tests which are diagnostic for different curricula and for different occupations. With increasing knowledge of primary abilities it may be expected that job analyses will be made in terms of these abilities. When jobs are so described, the selection tests can be prepared rationally instead of by crudely empirical methods and we shall then predict with confidence that the selection tests will have validity for the jobs. The same reasoning applies to the more complex fields of vocations and professions. We shall then have rational vocational guidance instead of trial and error search for valid tests for each job.

Mental profiles have been determined for over half a million high school children in Chicago and it has been found that all possible combinations occur in the profiles. The records show many hundreds of interesting case histories. A boy who was a poor reader was considered to be a dunce by his teachers. His mental profile showed that he had the highest score on Space and Reasoning, and high scores in all other factors except the verbal factor V. His teachers changed their attitudes when they saw that his handicap was quite specific. An amusing case was a girl who talked herself out of a number of situations involving truancy and misbehavior by fantastic but plausible stories. When her lies were eventually discovered, it was also found that her mental profile was very low in all factors except one, namely, verbal fluency. If the profile had been seen earlier, her teachers would have been warned about the possibilities of such a strange profile. It requires often considerable insight of the examiner to relate the mental profile to the circumstances of each case, but there is no question but that the profile is more helpful than the I.Q. in the interpretation of educational and behavior problems.

We shall conclude with a few implications of factor analysis for social psychology. The complex of social attitudes on current political issues, both in domestic and international relations, could be investigated as to its principal dimensions. One of the writer's first papers in factorial theory was a crude attempt to isolate the blocs in a legislative body by the voting records of its members. That problem can be investigated by the so-called obverse factor methods in which correlations are determined between persons instead of between tests. An obverse factor analysis is now being made by James W. Degan of the voting records of the Supreme Court judges. The object is to ascertain by analytical methods whether the voting records show consistent factors among the judges that determine their votes. Such a finding would indicate the extent to which their votes are determined by legal reasoning and the extent to which their votes are determined by political philosophy or expediency. The study promises to be of some general interest.

The whole problem of race differences is reopened by the factorial results. Since the races differ physically, it seems plausible that they also differ in cognitive and temperamental traits. If this should be found to be the case, it would not necessarily imply that they differ markedly in intellectual level. It may be expected that they differ in average mental profiles both in the primary abilities and in temperamental profiles. If such differences are found, they may eventually be capitalized in the same way that individual differences within any population can be appraised as a national asset.

I have tried to review some of the implications of recent work on multiple-factor analysis with special reference to its contributions in psychology. The factorial methods have been applied in other sciences with some interesting findings but we are concerned here with the use of these methods in psychology. My final remark is that the factorial methods will be fruitful in the advancement of psychology only in so far as we use these methods in close relation to psychological ideas.

A curious finding which often perplexes educators is that gains in scholastic achievement over short periods frequently show little correlation with pupils' tested intelligence. In the following paper Tilton examines this question and suggests a method for better research.

Intelligence Test Scores as Indicative of Ability to Learn*

J. W. TILTON

1949

If one starts with the assumption that the most dependable measure of learning is secured by subtracting a measure of status before from one after the period of practice, study or instruction, he finds himself in an arresting situation with regard to the definition of intelligence as the ability to learn. This is so because measured changes in score tend to be negligibly correlated with intelligence-test scores. What then shall we say about the validity of the use of intelligence-test scores in schools, and elsewhere, as indices of the ability to learn? Must we conclude from this reported negligible correlation, in spite of a long period of use for that purpose, that intelligence-test scores are not indicative of the ability to learn? The position taken in this paper is not a categorical yes or no. The paper is not a full consideration of the topic. The emphasis in the paper is that the measures of learning which have provided the low correlation are not an adequate basis upon which to claim invalidation.

DEFINITION OF AN ADEQUATE CRITERION

What are the qualifications for measures of gain, if they are to constitute a criterion for the validation of intelligence-test scores as indices of the ability to learn?

First, the reliability of the measures of gain must be known, and should be as high as that for end-scores. This seems like a trite observation, but it seems to be needed. The tendency is to be satisfied with having used end-tests of acceptable reliability, and to let it go at that. To use reliable end-test scores is good, so far as it goes, but it is not enough. Even with the coefficient of reliability for the end-tests as high as .95, the reliability of the differences may be zero. The end-tests contribute only unreliability to the measures of differences. All you can say for reliable end-tests, is that the more reliable the end-tests, the less handicap there is to be overcome in the

* Reprinted from *Educational and Psychological Measurement*, 9 (1949), pp. 291-296, by permission of the author and publisher.

measurement of gains. How reliable the differences are depends chiefly upon what happens to change the pupils between testings. In other words, since reliability is the ratio of true variance to obtained variance, the reliability of gains is a positive function of the differentiation, which learning introduces, and a negative function of error in measurement.

The trouble in practice is that we do not wait for learning to introduce enough differentiation. We think we are doing well if we allow a whole school year to elapse between the initial and final tests. But even after a year, reliabilities of gains, for instance, on the parts of achievement-test batteries, are still low. Whatever the reliability is, it needs to be measured and reported. Without such information most measures of gain may be assumed to be very unreliable, and to show very low correlations with intelligence-test scores, or with any other independent measure, merely because of that unreliability.

But for the measures of gain to be sufficiently reliable, or at least of known reliability, is not enough. A second requirement must be set up. If the measures of learning are to be used as a criterion against which intelligence-test or other scores are to be validated as measures of the ability to learn, something must be required of the learning situation. It must provide an opportunity for each to learn according to his ability.

Data with regard to spelling, reported by Carroll, illustrate a situation in which such an opportunity does not exist. At the beginning of the year pupils were tested as to their ability to spell the words to be taught during the year. Had they been tested again at the end of the year, the brighter pupils could not have made the larger gains, assuming 100 per cent mastery, because they knew 81 per cent of the words at the beginning of the year whereas the duller pupils could spell only 40 per cent of them. The bright could gain only from 81 to 100 from the situation, while the dull could gain from 40 to 100.

Gains obtained under such circumstances, where there are clear limitations of opportunity, are obviously not suitable as criteria of the ability to learn. It is quite possible that such limits are often present in the school situation; limited offering, because of the tendency to organize content into years and semesters, limited instructional help because of the pressure upon teachers to get about 95 per cent of the class above the required standard. At any rate, not all measures of gain are suitable to serve as criteria, even if satisfactory so far as reliability is concerned. Intelligence-test or other scores may not be invalidated as indices of the ability to learn in situations in which the possibility of validation is curtailed.

In the third place, and finally, the possibility of validation must be uncurtailed not only in the teaching or learning situation, but also in the testing situation. It is not enough that each has the opportunity to learn according to his ability, he must also have an opportunity for the full amount of that learning to be reflected in the measure of gain.

Here again, as in the case of reliability, the tendency is to err by assuming that if it is a good test it will give good measures of gain. But if the test is a good initial test (ranging in difficulty from 0 to 100 through a central tendency of 50 per cent) it will not be a good final test and will yield poor measures of learning. If a good distribution of measures of learning is to be obtained, it will not come from a good initial test but only from a good test for measures of learning. It can be secured only after the use and repetition of a wastefully long test. It will be made, presumably, of items ranging from 0 to 100 through 50 per cent difficulty. Only in this case, the difficulty to be examined is not beginning difficulty nor end difficulty, but difficulty in learning. Item analysis for this purpose will not be based upon the per cent answering correctly, but upon the per cent learning to answer correctly. Such an examination of the measures of gain would not alone provide sufficient assurance of the adequacy of the measures, but it would reveal some of the grosser inadequacies.

These, then, are the qualifications for an adequate criterion against which intelligence or other scores may be compared, as indices of the ability to learn. For the measures of gain which have provided the published low correlations, the reliability has not been determined, it is not known to what extent the opportunity to learn was curtailed, and, if the opportunity to learn was adequate, it is not known whether the tests permitted good measures of the learning. If the validity of status scores, as indices of the ability to learn, is to be checked, data are needed, and they need to be chosen specifically for that purpose.

TWO ATTEMPTS TO SECURE AN ADEQUATE CRITERION

There were, in the writer's files, two sets of data which it was thought might yield satisfactory criterion-measures of learning. Both were in the social studies area, one at the seventh-grade level and one at the twelfth. The data to be reported here for the seventh grade are for a sample. The sample is composed of all cases with a full set of scores from 6 of the 9 control sections in an experiment. For the whole grade in the single junior high school, (N = 515), the mean Otis Group IQ was 100.0, the sigma was 22.2. For the sample (N = 134), the mean and sigma were 102.9 and 23.1. The sample is therefore fairly representative of the whole seventh grade. The data to be reported for the twelfth grade are for the full twelfth grade in one high school, N = 156.

The tests in the seventh grade were made for four experimental units of instruction. They were composed of 300 items, and covered eleven weeks of instruction. The twelfth-grade test was the *Columbia Research Bureau American History Test,* composed of 200 items. The period covered was one school year.

In each case most of the items were discarded. What was wanted, as stated above, was to be sure of differentiation as to learning with the least curtailment of opportunity. The choices were arbitrary. First, it was assumed that when fewer students answered an item correctly at the end of the period than at the beginning, the loss was a chance difference. Then all items were discarded unless the gain was larger than the largest loss. Second, it was assumed that if the abler students were being penalized in the full test, it was by the presence of items answered correctly at the beginning by a majority of the students. Arbitrarily, for the seventh grade, items were discarded which initially were answered correctly by more than 45 per cent. For the twelfth grade, for which a greater caution seemed advisable, all items were discarded if answered correctly by more than 25 per cent at the beginning of the year.

There remained for criterion tests of learning, 54 items for the seventh-grade sample, and 20 items for the twelfth grade. The 54 items ranged in learning difficulty from 7 to 83 per cent, averaging 34 per cent. The 20 items ranged from 18 to 58 per cent, with an average of 38 per cent. The reliability coefficients are .93 and .73.

THE USE OF CRITERION SCORES

How well should intelligence-test scores agree with criterion measures of learning? What "passing mark" may be set, above which validity may be said to have been established? It is easy enough to agree that if the correlation is zero, validity has not been established. But is it reasonable to require the correlation to approach unity? There are two reasons why that would be unreasonable. One is that the factors of interest and application are unaccounted for. The other is specialization of ability. It has not been assumed that intelligence-test scores are equally indicative of learning in all areas. A reasonable requirement is that the agreement between index and criterion should approximate that between the index and initial status in the area of the criterion learning.

This requirement is met in the seventh-grade sample and in the twelfth grade. The correlations for the seventh-grade Otis IQ are with initial .50 and with the learning criterion .49. For the twelfth-grade Terman Group IQ's, the correlations are with initial .43 and with the learning criterion .49.

DISCUSSION

As it turned out, in these two cases the construction of criterion measures with selected items was in a sense a wasted effort. The correlations of IQ with gains using all items were not reliably less than with the criterion measures. In other words, the gains on all items were proved to be good criterion measures, as they were—fairly reliable (.72 and .68), and obtained in a situation in which there was plenty of opportunity both to learn and to be measured. The criterion measures gave evidence of superiority only with respect to reliability, .93 for 54 items as compared with .72 for all 300 items, and .73 for 20 items, as compared with .68 for all of the 200 items.

CONCLUSION

It may be said that within the two sets of data described, intelligence-test scores predicted learning fairly well. But this paper has been presented, not so much for the weight of the evidence presented, as to serve as a stimulus to similar reports, a plea for better data than are available. In hundreds of experiments, intelligence-test scores have been used in equating groups. The correlation between these scores and gains should be reported, with measures (or good estimates) of the extent to which the gains are suitable criteria. If intelligence-test scores are to be discredited as indices of the ability to learn, it must be done with more concern for defensible criteria than has been given to the problem.

As the nature-nurture controversy cooled somewhat, it became apparent even to the fiercest advocates that both positions were partially correct. In the following paper both
genetic and environmental components are, we believe, clearly
evident. The original article, in addition to a more detailed
text, contains a complete appendix of the relevant data
gathered throughout the study. This commendable inclusion
makes possible a complete and detailed study of many aspects
of the data of interest to any subsequent investigator.

A Final Follow-up Study of One Hundred Adopted Children*

MARIE SKODAK

and HAROLD M. SKEELS

1949

A. HISTORICAL BACKGROUND

While there have been a substantial number of studies reporting the
intelligence status of foster children, repeated evaluations of the same children into adolescence or early adulthood have been rare. This report constitutes what will probably be a final chapter in a long range study in which
the same group of adopted children have had intelligence tests on four
occasions. Reports of the results of the first three examinations provoked
a great deal of discussion and many questions regarding the *IQ* and the
rôle of heredity in determining the eventual status of the children. The intensity of the debates over the relative functions of environment and
heredity has dissipated in the past decade as evidence from other studies
has shown that modifiability of intelligence is not an unusual phenomenon. . . .

The study originally began, not as a research, but as a service project.
This difference in orientation accounts for some of the gaps in information,
for the techniques selected and for the general planning, which might have
been done otherwise had the project been conceived primarily as research.
However, there is a practical question of whether the study could have been
accomplished at all had it been weighted down with all the scientific safeguards which the perspective of 15 years of study might have suggested.
Because of its simplicity and apparent inoccuousness, the study was accepted by lay people, parents, and children with a minimum of explanation.

* * *

Abridged from *The Journal of Genetic Psychology*, 75 (1949), pp. 85-125, by
permission of the authors and the publisher.

Parents interested in adoption would write directly to the state office, the institution, agency, or one of the field workers. The application blanks contained only the minimum information regarding the type of child desired, the family's financial and vocational status, and the names of at least three references. The field worker would then visit the home, interview the applicants, evaluate the physical and emotional resources and the possible future demands with regard to education and vocation. References were contacted by mail, phone, or visit. The degree of investigation varied. Families who were well known or who were manifestly capable were accepted with less scrutiny than families in more modest circumstances or where there were questions regarding the present or future adequacy of the home. It is not known what proportion of applicants were rejected, but in many cases families were dissuaded from completing an application if it seemed unlikely that a child would be placed with them.

On the whole the foster families were above the average of their communities in economic security and educational and cultural status. They were highly regarded by the town's business, professional, and religious leaders and usually had demonstrated a long-time interest in children through church or community activities.

The placement procedure in both organizations used as sources was essentially similar. In the state agency after the application was accepted the family was placed on the waiting list and their name was considered at the monthly staff meetings when assignments were made. At these case conferences, attended by the head of the Children's Division, the superintendent of the institution, the psychologists, and head nurse, the available babies and available homes were discussed. Factors in the assignment included religion, sex, age, color or complexion, physique, medical history, and report of the family background. Pre-placement psychological examinations were not available for the children in this study. In many instances the information about the child's family background was so meagre that it was of little or no value. The primary factors in matching were the stipulations of the foster parents regarding religion, sex, and hair color in that order.

This method of placement of children from relatively inferior socioeconomic backgrounds into substantial homes thus provided the setting for the study. Perusal of the child's social history as recorded in the institution and comparison with the field's agent's pre-placement evaluation of the adopting home was disheartening. It did not seem possible that children with such meager possibilities, as projected from the intellectual, academic, and occupational attainments of their parents, could measure up to the demands of cultured, educated parents. Yet careful examination of one child after another showed none of the retardation or misplacement which might have been anticipated. Following a preliminary survey of results it was decided that a follow-up study was imperative, and the coöperation of the foster parents was solicited and received.

B. DESCRIPTION OF THE SAMPLE

* * *

1. Subjects of This Study

The criteria for inclusion in this study were as follows: (*a*) The child was placed in an adoptive home under the age of six months. (*b*) The child had been given an intelligence test prior to November, 1936, and after one year's residence in the adoptive home. (*c*) Some information, though of variable amount and reliability, existed concerning the natural and the adoptive parents. (*d*) The child was white, of North European background (it so happened that no children of South European, Latin, or other social backgrounds met the other criteria either).

In this study all of the children were received for care as infants. The Iowa Soldiers' Orphan's Home, indentified as the public agency, was the placing agency in 76 per cent of the cases and the Iowa Children's Home Society, a state-wide, private, non-sectarian organization placed 21 per cent. The remaining three children were privately placed and were included because they were available and met the criteria set up for the other children.

It was earlier pointed out that 96.6 per cent of the 319 children committed to the two agencies under the age of six months between 1933–1937, were placed in adoptive homes. In only four cases was the child withheld from adoptive placement because of poor family history. The remaining seven had serious health problems. Since the majority of the children originally in the study had been placed during this period, and the remainder had been placed earlier during a time when the policies regarding family background had been even more lenient, it was concluded that the children in the study were representative of all those placed by these organizations.

During 1934–36, when the mental testing program was coördinated for the two agencies, and 1933–37 for the public agency alone, it was found that 90 per cent of the children placed under six months of age had been given at least one intelligence test. The mean *IQ* of this group was 119, slightly above the mean *IQ* of 116 achieved by the members of the follow-up group on the first examination during the same calendar years.

It was evident that the group of children who constituted the first sample were representative of the available children since there was no systematic withholding of numbers of children because of poor histories, nor was there a group with lower initial intelligence test scores who were excluded from the study.

In the first follow-up report, out of a total of 180 children who met the criteria of age at placement, race and date of examination, it was possible to retest 152 children during 1937–38. On the third examination 139 children were seen during 1940–41 and the fourth and final visit in 1946 resulted in the present sample of 100. The major factor in the reduction of the size of the sample has been time and expense. The families, all originally in Iowa, are now scattered over many states and Canada. To locate and visit the 100 children in the 10 weeks available for the study, it was necessary to drive over 12,000 miles even though accurate addresses were available and careful preliminary arrangements had been made with planned appointments acceptable for the parents and the child.

* * *

The comparisons between the continuous group of 100 and those who dropped out at the various retest points, are given in Table I.

These figures account for the original 180 children who met the qualifications for age at placement in an adoptive home and date of first examina-

TABLE I

	Test I	Test II	Test III
Continuous Group (N 100)	117	112	115
Dropped after 1940 (N 39)	113	107	110
Dropped after 1937 (N 15)	114	111	
Dropped after 1936 (N 26)	120		

tion. Systematic selection which would influence the character of the final group of 100 is not evident from the comparisons between the mean IQ's of the group at the various re-examination periods. The standard deviations for all means are large, ranging from 11.9 to 17.2, and none of the differences is statistically significant.

It may be concluded that this group of 100 children is probably representative of the total group placed by these agencies at comparable ages, and that conclusions based on the pattern of mental development of these children are probably applicable to others with similar experience and social backgrounds and placed under similar circumstances into comparable homes.

2. Test Techniques

The purpose throughout the study was to secure the most reliable and valid measure of the child's intellectual ability at the time of the examination. On first examination the children ranged from 11 months to six years in age with 78 per cent of the children between one and three years. Four children had been placed at a few days of age and were tested shortly before the expiration of the one-year observation period. The 1916 Stanford-Binet was suitable for use with the 19 per cent over three years of age and was occasionally used with younger children who were obviously accelerated in mental development. The Kuhlman Binet was routinely used with all children under three years, and occasionally as a clinical supplement with some children over three.

The re-examinations were begun in 1936 when the Revised Stanford-Binet was not generally available and the 1916 revision was consequently used. In this series of tests, although 17 per cent of the children were under 3–0 years of age, they were all over 2–6 and sufficiently accelerated to make the 1916 Stanford-Binet a usable test. Therefore, all test scores reported for the second examination were based on the 1916 revision.

When the third examination was scheduled in 1939–40, the question of "best test" was raised. From the standpoint of fatigue and future rapport, it seemed advisable to limit the number of tests given and the 1916 revision was again selected. Survey of the literature showed that between 5 and 11 years, the ages of these children at the third examination, the results of the 1916 and 1937 scales were most nearly identical. Not only had the 1916 test been used in the earlier examinations, but it also had been used in examinations of the mothers and a few of the fathers of the children. Direct comparisons of test scores were thus made possible without getting into the knotty problems of comparability of standardization of the different revisions. The problems of such a long-time research underscore the need for an intelligence test which results in comparable scores at all ages.

When the fourth and last examination was scheduled in 1946, the children were between 11 and 17 years of age. In view of the problems surrounding the 1916 revision at these ages, it was decided to impose on the good nature of the subjects and give both the 1916 revision and Form L of the 1937 revision. This set up a program involving approximately two hours, often a great deal more, if there was marked scatter on either or both tests. Since there are a number of overlapping items, these were given and scored simultaneously. The 1916 revision was completed first and the 1937, Form L, second. Whatever advantage of practice effect there might have been, was judged to be cancelled by fatigue. Every effort was made to keep the interest and effort of the examinees at an optimum level. No subject refused to take the tests after an appointment was made and only two were openly antagonistic in typical adolescent behavior. Even these were persuaded to cooperate and no greater compliment to the intrinsic interests of the tests can be made than to say that in spite of themselves even these reluctant subjects became interested and made scores consistent with their earlier test results and their current school placements.

*   *   *

C. MENTAL DEVELOPMENT OF THE CHILDREN

All of the children had been seen on four occasions and a few for various reasons had been given additional tests. In these cases the test given at an age nearest the mean age for the group was selected for use in the major comparisons. . . . The mean age at first examination was *2 years 2 months,* at second examination *4 years 3 months,* at third examination *7 years 0 months* and at fourth examination *13 years 6 months.*

The group included 60 girls and 40 boys. The range, median, and mean ages for both sexes were essentially the same.

Ages and results may be summarized for the 100 children as given in Table II.

TABLE II

Test	Age	Mean IQ	SD	Range	Median
I	2 yrs. 2 mo.	117	13.6	80–154	118
II	4 yrs. 3 mo.	112	13.8	85–149	111
III	7 yrs. 0 mo.	115	13.2	80–149	114
IV (1916)	13 yrs. 6 mo.	107	14.4	65–144	107
IV (1937)	13 yrs. 6 mo.	117	15.5	70–154	117

The mean *IQ* of this group of children has remained above the average for the general population throughout early childhood, school age, and into adolescence. It would be generally accepted that if major changes in intellectual functioning occur after this age, they probably result from psychiatric and emotional problems rather than from developmental abnormalities.

An interesting problem in test evaluation is posed by the results from the "simultaneous" administration of the 1916 and 1937 Stanford tests. Comparative studies of the 1916 and 1937 revisions support the general impression of clinicians that the 1937 revision tends to overrate the average or above average adolescent, while the 1916 revision tends to underrate him. This dilemma was frequently encountered in the examination of these children since differences of 15–20 points between the two tests were moderately frequent. Years of clinical and guidance experience with young people of these ages provided a background against which the quality of their responses, their school achievement and their general intellectual maturity as evaluated from an interview could be projected. The result was a feeling of dissatisfaction with both tests and a fervent wish that a more adequate instrument were available.

*   *   *

TABLE III

Changes in IQ Between Tests

	Between Test I and II Number	Between Test II and III Number	Between Test III and IV '16 Number	Between Test III and IV '37 Number
+36 to +40				
+26 to +35	1	4		
+16 to +25	7	7	1	1
+ 6 to +15	11	26	12	14
− 5 to + 5	34	42	30	32
− 6 to −15	25	17	30	34
−16 to −25	18	4	25	18
−26 to −35	3		2	1
−36 to −45				
−46 to −50	1			
Total	100	100	100	100

	Between Tests I and III Number	Between Tests I and IV '16 Number	Between Tests III and IV '37 Number
+36 to +40	2		
+26 to +35	2	2	2
+16 to +25	5	5	5
+ 6 to +15	21	12	14
− 5 to + 5	30	19	21
− 6 to −15	23	29	29
−16 to −25	13	16	14
−26 to −35	3	11	10
−36 to −45	1	6	5
−46 to −50			
Total	100	100	100

	Between Tests II and IV '16 Number	Between Tests II and IV '37 Number
+36 to +40		
+26 to +35		1
+16 to +25	8	8
+ 6 to +15	15	17
− 5 to + 5	22	26
− 6 to −15	31	31
−16 to −25	21	14
−26 to −35	3	3
−36 to −45		
−46 to −50	—	—
	100	100
Total		

Rather wide fluctuations in *IQ* between tests were found throughout the entire period. Table III summarizes the changes found. The general trend is toward losses when the first test is taken as the basis of comparison, as the mean *IQ* on succeeding tests would indicate. Since the total number of cases is 100, the percentages may be computed automatically and only the actual number of cases is given in the table.

These results, together with the correlations reported later, are consistent with findings from other studies, which show that *IQ* fluctuations of considerable magnitude are found among children who live with their own parents. The greater the time span between tests the greater the probability of wide difference between successive test scores. From a clinical standpoint this serves as an additional caution in the use of a single test score in long range prediction of intellectual attainment. Yet inspection of the raw data for individuals gives somewhat more assurance. By and large the children did not change their positions relative to the population as a whole as drastically as these figures might lead one to conclude. When marked changes occurred there were related factors which could usually be identified in the individual instances.

Correlations between successive tests may be summarized as given in Table IV.

TABLE IV

	Test II	Test III	Test IV '16	Test IV '37
Test I	.54 ± .05	.44 ± .06	.35 ± .06	.35 ± .06
Test II		.70 ± .03	.58 ± .05	.59 ± .04
Test III			.71 ± .03	.75 ± .03
Test IV '16				.92 ± .01

These correlations do not differ markedly from those reported in other studies where the retests are separated by similar time intervals. From the standpoint of prediction of individual status in terms of the child's future *IQ,* the early tests may be considered disappointing, yet this group is not unique in its variability or its fluctuation from one examination to the next.

Of special interest are seven children whose early mental development was average and who as adolescents are below 85 *IQ.* These cases include five children who occasioned concern from the beginning of the study. Three of them have been seen by psychiatrists at the initiative of the parents and are the only children in the group who have been referred for such help. No. 41G is a shy, diffident compulsive neurotic who is described as a meticulous housekeeper, who doesn't leave a task until it is complete in every detail. Characteristically she does poorly wherever there is a time limit and fails all tests at school though her homework is perfect and her individual reports to the teachers are good. She repeated the eighth grade, but in a medium sized high school she is a *B* student. It was felt that the 1916 Stanford-Binet *IQ* of 79 did not adequately represent her functional level. Nos. 82G and 76G are two of the disturbed children in the study. They have long histories of inexplicable erratic behavior similar to that seen in some post encephalitis cases. The tests have shown consistently wide scatter reflecting the difficulties in concentration, the short interest span, the erratic achievement of which teachers invariably complained to the parents. School progress has been based on other factors than achievement. As adolescents both have shown somewhat improved stability. In both cases it was felt that the test results adequately represented present functioning levels. Children 47G and 48G succeeded in making average scores as younger children, but the quality of their responses was consistently poor. These were the only children in this study whose legal adoption had been deferred a year since it was feared that their development might not prove to be normal in spite of an *IQ* of 100 on the Kuhlmann tests. Both have been unusually prone to severe accidents and illnesses including a skull fracture for 48G. They have been frail, thin children and on the basis of their physical health and interrupted schooling have attended special classes. It was felt that the tests adequately represented their present intellectual and academic ability. However, they have had splendid home training, are competent dancers and musicians, are socially poised, and thus give an impression of ability beyond the test scores.

Cases 81G and 23B are children in very simple home environments, where the intellectual stimulation is limited. In one home the father is dead, in the other extremely busy. Children of low average academic ability satisfy the aspiration levels of the parents. In neither case are the children encouraged to attain maturity or independence.

D. RELATIONSHIPS BETWEEN MENTAL DEVELOPMENT OF ADOPTED CHILDREN AND CHARACTERISTICS OF THEIR FOSTER PARENTS

1. Occupational Level

In the selection of foster homes all agencies give preference to families who not only have sufficient financial resources to assure adequate care for the child, but who show signs of culture, refinement, and intellectual and emotional understanding of the needs of children and the special problems of adoption.

The occupational level of foster families reflects this initial selection and has remained consistently well above the average for the general population.

In 1940 in the U. S. as a whole, 4.4 per cent of employed males were in professional occupations. In Iowa they constituted 3.7 per cent of the employed population while 14 per cent of the foster fathers were so employed. Although only 14 per cent of employed U. S. males are farm proprietors or managers, 29.5 per cent of Iowa men and 29 per cent of the foster fathers are so employed, thus farmers were adequately represented. In the U. S. approximately 17 per cent of men and in Iowa 19 per cent are unskilled laborers. None of the foster fathers, but 48 per cent of the natural fathers are so classified.

Further comparison between the figures for the foster parents, the general population, and the data for 73 true fathers for whom occupational information was available shows that the foster fathers are not only above the average of the population but are conspicuously above the mean for the true fathers. The latter are, in addition, well below the mean for the total population with an average equivalent to the status of an unskilled or very slightly skilled workman. The children whose natural parents, as a group, come from one extreme of the population were placed in foster homes representing the opposite extreme in occupational status.

Observation of the homes over the 13-year period showed that, although they were above the average in culture, resources, and financial security at the time the child was placed, they were, on the whole, even more prosperous at the end of the study. Only two fathers had been in military service, one as a professional man and one as a non-commissioned draftee. While some had benefited from high war wages, others on fixed incomes had been at a slight disadvantage. The general economic prosperity of 1945-47 was evident in most cases.

* * *

Relationships between the child's *IQ* and foster father's occupation are obscured because the personal qualities, the cultural opportunities and intellectual stimulation of the homes are not directly reflected by the occupational classification of the families. The opportunities of many of the farm (Class IV) and skilled trades (Class III) homes exceeded some of the teachers', physicians', and managerial homes (Classes I and II). The results, however, show persistent slight differences in favor of homes in the upper three categories. . . .

It can be concluded that, on the whole, children in homes in the higher occupational categories tend to have somewhat higher mean *IQ*'s at all ages. However, all the children, including those in homes of lesser occupational levels, are above the mean for the total population at all age levels where the number of cases is sufficient to warrant consideration.

2. Education

The average school attainment of the foster parents as recorded on the application record and verified in 1946 showed that mean and median attainment for the foster parents was high school graduation, with 15 per cent having completed college. According to the 1940 census figures the median education for native Iowans in a comparable age group (35-44 years of age in 1940) was 8.8 for males and 9.3 for females. In general, urban populations have an average of one more year of education than rural populations.

The educational status of the true parents is significantly below that of the foster parents and is below the average of a comparable age group for the state. The 1940 census showed that native Iowans 25-34 years of age had a mean education of 10.2 for the males and 11.0 for the females. While the information on the education of foster parents is reasonably accurate, there is evidence that the education of the natural mother has been over-stated by an average of one year.

These data again show that while the education of the foster parents is superior to the average for their age and region, the natural parents' education is below the average for their age and region.

Correlations between foster parent education and child *IQ* on successive tests are summarized in Table V.

Earlier reports on somewhat larger numbers of children showed a slight positive correlation between foster child *IQ* and foster parent education. In this array of correlations there is no discernible trend except a consistent lack of statistical relationship. Inspection of the original scatter diagrams confirms the lack of relationship. However, it should be pointed out that both the *IQ*'s and the educations represented here are confined to the upper

TABLE V

	Foster- mother education	Foster- father education
Child's Test I	−.03±.07	.05±.07
Child's Test II	+.04±.07	.03±.07
Child's Test III	.10±.07	.03±.07
Child's Test IV (1916)	.04±.07	.06±.07
Child's Test IV (1937)	.02±.07	.00±.07

segment of the total possible range. As long as the parents are highly selected, and the children as a group also have a limited range of *IQ*'s and are in the upper half of the total population, it is not likely that repetition of similar studies will produce any more significant correlations. Increasing the number of cases may extend the range and sharpen the focus on what little difference exists. These figures are lower than correlations generally reported in the literature for both foster child-foster parent and own-child-parent correlations. However, in other cases the range for both distributions has been wider.

The only conclusions which may be drawn from these data are that the foster parents are above the average of their age and regional group in education and that the children in these homes are above the average in mental development. The differences between these adoptive parents in amount of formal education completed are not reflected in differences in intelligence between the children.

E. RELATIONSHIPS BETWEEN MENTAL DEVELOPMENT OF ADOPTED CHILDREN AND CHARACTERISTICS OF THEIR TRUE PARENTS

1. Intelligence

Intelligence tests results were available for 63 of the true mothers. All were based on the 1916 Stanford-Binet except one Terman Group Test, two Otis, and one Wechsler-Bellevue. Since the scores on these tests were consistent with other evidence on the mental adequacy of the mothers, the scores were included. The tests were given by trained examiners, under ordinary testing conditions, usually after the mother had decided to release the baby for adoption. The release was not contingent on the mother's test score and examinations were not made when the mother was ill or obviously upset emotionally.

Table VI shows the distribution of the true-mother IQ's and child IQ's

TABLE VI

Comparison between Distribution of IQ's (1916 Stanford-Binet) of True Mothers and Their Children

IQ	Mothers		Children	
	No.	%	No.	%
130–134	—	—	2	3
125–129	1	1	6	10
120–124	—	—	6	10
115–119	—	—	7	11
110–114	2	3	6	10
105–109.	5	8	7	11
100–104	5	8	10	16
95– 99	6	10	8	13
90– 94	3	13	3	5
85– 89	7	11	3	5
80– 84	5	8	1	1
75– 79	8	13	1	1
70– 74	5	8	2	3
65– 69	5	8	1	1
60– 64	4	6	—	—
55– 59	—	—	—	—
50– 54	2	3	—	—
Number	63		63	
Mean	85.7		106	
Median	86.3		107	
Standard Deviation	15.75		15.10	

at a mean age of 13.6 based on the 1916 Stanford-Binet. This test was selected since it offered the maximum available degree of comparability for parent and child intelligence test scores. The mean *IQ* of these children on the 1937 revision is 10 points higher than on the 1916 revision. If a correction were to be made for the *IQ*'s of the mothers, as some investigators have suggested, the 1937 test scores of the children would be used, with the same relative difference between the two arrays of scores.

A difference of 20 points between the means of mothers and children is not only a statistically reliable difference (*CR* 9.2) but is also of considerable social consequence.

Previous analysis showed that there was no difference between the mean *IQ*'s of children whose mothers had been examined and those whose mothers' *IQ*'s were unknown. This was confirmed by examination of the present data.

Relationships between mother-child pairs, with regard to *IQ*, expressed in terms of correlation coefficients on 63 cases, are summarized in Table VII.

TABLE VII

Test I	.00 ± .09
Test II	.28 ± .08*
Test III	.35 + .07**
Test IV (1916)	.38 ± .07**
Test IV (1937)	.44 ± .07**

* Reliable at the 5 per cent level of confidence.
** Reliable at the 1 per cent level of confidence.

It is apparent that the above tabulation contains more questions than it answers and can be the source of considerable controversy. Certain conclusions can be drawn, however. Among these are the following: Test scores of children secured during the first two years of life bear no statistical relationship to the scores of their mothers, nor, it should be noted, do they show a very high relationship to their own later scores (*r* = .35). By seven years of age a substantial correlation with true mother's *IQ* is reached which remains of the same magnitude in adolescence provided the 1916 Stanford-Binet test is used with both children and mothers. The correlation is still further increased if the 1937 revision of the Binet is used.

Many reasons can and have been advanced for the low correlation between infant tests and later measures which will not be reviewed here. There is considerable evidence for the position that as a group these children received maximal stimulation in infancy with optimum security and affection following placement at an average of three months of age. The quality and amount of this stimulation during early childhood seemed to have little relation to the foster family's educational and cultural status.

The available data which can be statistically used—occupational classification and formal education—are not sufficiently sensitive to be useful in measuring these less tangible differences in child rearing practices. This point is important for the interpretation of the correlations between the child's *IQ* and his mother's *IQ* because it is possible to throw the weight of interpretation in the direction of either genetic or environmental determinants. If the former point of view is accepted, then the mother's mental level at the time of her examination is considered to reflect her fundamental genetic constitution, and ignores the effects of whatever environmental deprivations or advantages may have influenced her own mental development. Thus it would be assumed that the children of brighter mothers would in turn be brighter than the children of less capable mothers regardless of the type of foster home in which they were placed. The increasing correlation might be interpreted to support this point of view, since the occupational differences between foster parents are not large. It is, however, inconsistent with the evidence that the children's *IQ*'s substantially exceed those of their mothers and that none of them are mentally defective even though a number of the mothers were institutional residents. The rôle of the unknown fathers adds to the complication although the evidence indicates that the fathers resembled their unwed partners in mental level and education.

If the so-called environmental point of view is accepted, then the question is raised whether the increasing correlation between child and true mother *IQ* possibly reflects the tendency to place the children of brighter mothers in the more outstanding foster homes, and the influence of these homes becomes increasingly prominent as the child grows older.

The question regarding selective placement can be approached in at least two ways. The first is an inspection of the relationships between such characteristics of the true and foster families as education and occupation. Using these crude measures, correlations of .24 between true mother *IQ* and foster parent education and .27 between true mother and foster parent education

TABLE VIII

| | *Foster-father occupation* | | | | | |
	I	II	III	IV	V	VI
No. of foster fathers	14	17	27	29	2	5
Mean *IQ* of mothers of						
children in these homes	86	89	87	83	77	90
Number of cases	9	13	20	15	4	2
Mean education of mothers of						
children in these homes	10	10	10	8	8	8
Number of cases	12	16	28	25	9	2

were found in this sample. Comparisons between true mother characteristics and foster father occupation for the present sampling are summarized in Table VIII.

It is apparent from both types of analyses that while a trend existed, selective placement, as evaluated by these measures was not consistently practiced.

Another approach to this problem of relationship is to examine the data for two contrasting groups of children. Selected for this purpose were: (a) Those children whose mothers were known to be mentally defective, with other evidence supporting the known IQ of under 70 (N = 11). (b) Those children whose mothers were above average in intelligence as measured by tests. Since there were only three cases above 110 IQ, the next five, in the 105-109 IQ range, were also included (N = 8).

Comparisons between the two groups are shown in Table IX. It is evident from the table that there is a marked difference between the intelligence and education of the true mothers of children in Groups (a) and (b). On the basis of education and occupation the foster parents of both groups are essentially similar, with perhaps a slight advantage for Group (b). On the first examination both groups of children were above average. By seven years of age a marked difference in mental level between the two groups is observable which persists into adolescence and is reflected by both the 1916 and 1937 Stanford-Binet tests. While children in Group (a) show average mental development as a group, the children in (b) show superior mental development. A difference of 25 points in IQ has significance socially, educationally, and vocationally.

If reliance were to be placed on these data alone, the inference would be fairly clear. However, comparison of the actual situation in the homes leads to a different conclusion. As a group, the homes of Group (b) are superior to the homes of Group (a) on every count on which homes can be evaluated. The average income of Group (b) is easily double the average income of Group (a) families. Five of the eight had sent their children to private schools, nursery schools, or camps for more than one year, reflecting an intelligent interest in superior opportunities, financial stability, and social status. None of the families in Group (a) had been either interested or able to afford similar opportunities. All the children in Group (b) had had music, dancing, or art lessons, while only 5 of the 11 in Group (a) had such training. In the number of books, the extent of participation in church, civic, social, recreational, and cultural organizations, participation in Child Study and PTA groups, familiarity with and application of approved child rearing practices and attitudes, the number of toys, school equipment, typewriters, personal radios, the degree of freedom in spending allowances, deciding recreation, hours to be kept and other factors now believed to be essential for optimum social and emotional adjustment, the homes in Group (b) were definitely superior to the homes in Group (a). The one exception

TABLE IX

Comparisons between Children of Mothers of Inferior and of Above Average Intelligence

Case no.	True mother's IQ	True mother's educ.	Foster mid-par. educ.	Foster father occup.	Child's IQ Test I	Test II	Test III	Test IV	Test IV '37
Group A									
8B	64	8	16	I	126	125	114	96	106
10B	64	11	8	III	125	109	96	87	100
18B	65	8	9	VI	114	102	112	122	118
53G	63	8	13	III	127	121	119	101	111
54G	67	9	12	III	116	113	113	91	102
58G	54	8	13	III	117	114	119	98	113
60G	66	8	10	V	105	109	90	105	115
67G	65	6	12	IV	110	111	114	95	103
70G	63	1	10	II	110	113	107	101	118
76G	67	7	15	I	109	92	87	74	84
82G	53	3	12	IV	81	87	80	66	74
Mean	63	7	12	3.2	113	109	105	96	104
Median	64	8	12	III	114	111	96	96	106
Group B									
17B	128	12	12	III	120	128	148	127	145
22B	109	13	11	III	102	107	113	108	130
57G	109	13	16	III	99	126	139	132	130
61G	109	13	15	II	112	113	125	128	135
71G	113	12	19	II	128	112	114	114	122
72G	110	12	8	VI	116	92	105	103	104
73G	105	8	9	IV	125	111	129	110	131
87G	109	13	11	III	128	145	125	119	133
Mean	111	12	12.5	3.3	116	117	125	118	129
Median	109	12.5	11.5	III	117	112.5	125	117	130

was 72G. This was the home in which the foster mother had been hospitalized for mental illness. The foster father, well educated in a foreign country, is a railroad section supervisor. Finances are limited, intellectual interests are non-existent. For several years this girl has competently managed a household. It is possible to speculate that under more favorable circumstances she too, might have attained higher test scores.

The general conclusions which may be drawn indicate that while in this study an increasing correlation between child *IQ* and true mother *IQ* is observed with increasing age, it cannot be attributed to genetic determinants alone. A more sensitive measure of foster parental competence in child development is necessary before small sample techniques of comparisons and analyses of differences can be fruitful. The present measures of education and occupation do not evaluate the crucial differences between outstanding, average, or less effective homes. The fact remains that the children are considerably superior to their mothers in mental development. There is a socially important difference between a group of people whose average *IQ* is 107-117, depending on the test selected, and another group whose *IQ* is 87. Since the mean for the children is above the average for the population as a whole, it cannot be attributed to the phenomenon of regression alone.

2. Education

In addition to the intelligence test scores there was information on the education of 92 of the true mothers. Recognizing that it was an unreliable and questionably valid measure of ability, nevertheless, correlations between true mothers' education and child *IQ* were computed. Table X summarizes the results.

TABLE X

Test I	.04 ± .09
Test II	.31 ± .07*
Test III	.37 ± .06*
Test IV (1916)	.31 ± .06*
Test IV (1937)	.32 ± .06*

* Reliable at the 1 per cent level of confidence.

Here, too, there was an increase in correlations between the first and second tests, but the relationships then became stationary instead of showing a further increase with subsequent tests. Recalling the still lower correlations between child *IQ* and foster parent education, here again it is advisable to guard against an inclination to overvalue the significance of correlations of this size.

3. Occupation

Since both the true mothers and true fathers of the children originated primarily from the two lowest occupational classifications, attempts to identify a relationship between the mental development of the children and the occupational ranking of the parents were fruitless. The occupational status of the true fathers was occasionally considered in placement plans, but usually the information was not felt to be sufficiently reliable to influence the decision.

Goodenough, Terman and others have found that children living with their own parents in the two lower occupational categories have mean IQ's of approximately 95. In contrast, children living with their own parents in the professional and managerial occupations have a mean IQ of approximately 115. It is apparent that foster children in adoptive homes of all the occupational levels represented here compare favorably with own children in homes of the upper socio-economic level, rather than following the pattern found in the families from which they originated.

F. CONCLUSIONS

Perhaps the most important contribution this study can make to the planning of future research is to point out the inadequacies of easily available data, and the necessity of formulating more clearly the various criteria used in the selection and assessment of the foster homes and the children. It is clear that the objective data used here, education and occupation, do not represent the real basis for selection and are not closely related to the child's mental development. Judging from the trend of correlations between mother's and child's IQ's, one might conclude that a relationship exists which became increasingly apparent with age. This is complicated by the evidence of selective placement, yet without a parallel relationship between foster parent education and child IQ. This one set of figures must not be permitted to overshadow the more significant finding that the children are consistently and unmistakably superior to their natural parents and in fact, follow and improve upon the pattern of mental development found among own children in families like the foster families. What may be the salient features in the foster homes which have produced this development of the children, is only suggested in this study. It is inferred that maximum security, an environment rich in intellectual stimulation, a well balanced emotional relationship, intellectual agility on the part of the foster parents— all these and other factors contributed to the growth of the child. Unfortunately, there is still no scale for the measurement of these dynamic aspects of the foster home situation. The futility of arguments based on correlations involving measures of education and occupation applies to both sides of the discussion.

The conclusions which may be drawn from the material presented here suggest that:

1. The above average mental development of the children adopted in infancy has been maintained into early adolescence. There has been no large scale decline in *IQ* either for the group or for large segments of it, although certain children have shown either wide fluctuation or a steady decline or rise as compared with the first test results.

2. The educational or occupational data available for foster or natural parents in the typical social history record are not sufficient to predict the course of mental development of the children. Other factors, primarily emotional and personal, and probably located in the foster home, appear to have more significant influence in determining the mental growth of the children in this group.

3. The intellectual level of the children has remained consistently higher than would have been predicted from the intellectual, educational, or socioeconomic level of the true parents, and is equal to or surpasses the mental level of own children in environments similar to those which have been provided by the foster parents.

The implications for placing agencies justify a policy of early placement in adoptive homes offering emotional warmth and security in an above average educational and social setting.

In the following paper Wechsler addresses to a clinical audience a plea for an understanding and appreciation of the importance of factor-analytic findings. It is similar in many ways to Thurstone's 1948 address. The view that personality and intellectual factors belong in different domains is a persistent attitude of many psychologists in the United States and one that is only slowly breaking down under the pressure of recent research findings.

Cognitive, Conative and Non-intellective Intelligence*

DAVID WECHSLER

1950

It is always a good omen for science when different men in different places make independent discoveries or arrive at similar conclusions. In the last two decades psychologists in their efforts to define the nature of general intelligence seem to have arrived at the threshold of such a situation. In this paper I wish to present to you what appears to me to be the germ of the impending re-orientation: it is this, that general intelligence cannot be equated with intellectual ability however broadly defined, but must be regarded as a manifestation of the personality as a whole.

From an historical point of view, the first one to argue against the identification of general intelligence with intellectual ability was Henri Bergson. Already in his *"Donees Immediate de la Conscience"* and more emphatically in his *"Evolution Creatrice,"* he pointed out the insufficiencies of the human intellect or, what was for him the same, normative logic, in dealing effectively with man's total environment.

I shall not here restate Bergson's arguments nor his attempted solution of endowing the human mind with a new faculty, creative intuition, and its generating force, the "elan vital." I wish only to call your attention to the fact that in our attempts at measuring intelligence we have persisted in treating intelligence as if it consisted exclusively of intellectual elements or factors. What, in fact, are these intellectual elements which we have continued to use and to posit in appraising intelligence? They are abstract reasoning, verbal, spatial, numerical, and a few other specified factors, all of which in some particularized manner deal with man's cognitive ability. Shades of Bergson, are we confirming his claim that human intelligence, as the psychologist conceives it, can only deal with geometric and logical symbols?

Now, the remarkable thing is that while this is what we are saying in

* Reprinted from the *American Psychologist*, 5 (1950), pp. 78-83, by permission of the author and the American Psychological Association.

our tests of intelligence, most of us don't believe it. What is more important, it isn't true! Our contemporary definitions of intelligence assert as much: intelligence according to these is not only the ability to learn, to abstract, to profit from experience, but also to adjust and to achieve. Everyone with clinical experience knows that the latter involve other capacities besides eductive, verbal, numerical, spatial, and the other intellective factors that have been demonstrated. Yes, but what are they? The answer is: they are *not* intellective. They are capacities and traits dependent upon temperament and personality which are not restricted to logical and abstract perception; they are, in my opinion, factors of personality itself. It is this point of view, independently sensed or suggested, at times only tangentially, by a number of investigators including Goldstein, Alexander, Wechsler, and more recently by Halstead and Eysenck, which I presented six years ago for the first time under the term *"Non-intellective Factors of Intelligence."* I wish now to present to you more fully the evidence in its support and to justify what appears to be not only the need for a reorientation in our concept of general intelligence, but of a new psychometric that will, in fact, measure what is purported in our definition of intelligence.

Let me begin by restating the issue in terms of the actual psychometric problem. The crux of this problem, as we have already noted, is the discrepancy between what the clinical psychologist does and what he says he does in clinical practice. If we examine any of the current psychological tests of intelligence, we shall find them to consist of sample tasks measuring, by definition, a variety of mental abilities. One would imagine that any summary of the results obtained with such tests would be essentially a report of the degree to which an individual possesses these abilities and the manner in which they vary. However, it will be found that once a summative score is obtained from them, whether in terms of MA, IQ, or whatnot, the clinical psychologist proceeds to enlarge his summary to include not only specific psychologic interpretations but broad social and biological implications as well.

An IQ is thus used, not only to determine comparative mental endowment, capacity to learn, presence of special abilities and disabilities, and evaluation of degree of mental deficiency, but also as a basis for school placement, for vocational guidance, for psychiatric diagnosis, and for the prediction of adjustment potentials in a variety of situations from infancy to old age, including such areas as child adoption, juvenile delinquency, fitness for military service, college success, and old age counseling.

Assuming that intelligence tests may be used in all these situations, and within limits I believe they may, the question arises how this is possible under the concept that general intelligence is a matter of a single basic or even a combination of a number of intellectual abilities. It is this question which I shall try to answer this evening. But I must first call your attention to the fact you are all aware of, that this is not the usual criticism of intelligence tests. The historic and continued objection to intelligence tests is not that they measure too much, but that they do not measure enough, or at least, not well enough.

You are all acquainted with the arguments against intelligence tests, and I shall not repeat them; the damaging criticism pertains, not as is generally emphasized, to the question of reliability, but to one of basic validity. Even such studies as those of Wellman, Goldfarb and others, showing changes in IQ produced by a variety of social and environmental factors, though relevant, are not crucial. The crucial instances are those where individuals obtain identical IQs (say an IQ of 65) but, on overall appraisal, must nevertheless be rated differently, say, one as a defective and the other as not defective. Such instances are not necessarily common, but neither are they rare exceptions. Here is a situation which needs explaining and cannot be by-passed.

The first to attack this problem was E. L. Thorndike. His answer, as always characteristic of his approach, was straightforward and to the point. Our tests measure intelligence to be sure, he said, but there is not just one unique, but several different kinds of intelligence, namely, abstract, social and practical. The first is manifested by the individual's ability to work with symbols, the second by his ability to deal with people, and the third by his ability to manipulate objects. Thorndike, himself, seems to have been primarily interested in the first kind of intelligence and, having made the above trichotomy, and along with it the distinction between tests which measure breadth, as against those which measure altitude, left the working out of these concepts to others. But relatively little has been done to verify or refute the hypothesis.

In the 1920's Moss published a test of social intelligence which consisted essentially of items involving memory and recognition of names and faces, and a series of multiple-choice questions involving social situations, in which the correct answer seemed to have been based on the notion that "the customer is always right." Although Moss's test for a time had some vogue among business firms, clinical psychologists, as far as I have been able to discover, seldom if ever make use of it.

The other important effort at producing a test of social intelligence is Doll's Vineland Social Maturity Scale. This Scale, as you know, consists of a series of questions listing a variety of social acquisitions, that is, of approved and useful acts and achievements, which a child may be expected to have learned from infancy to adolescence. The Scale is hardly a test in the ordinary sense of the term, since it involves no test performance or response by the subject, and can be completed, as it usually is, by other persons. But it does correlate fairly well with other tests of intelligence and has been shown by Doll and others to correlate positively and significantly with a number of practical criteria of social adjustment.

Clinical psychologists appear to have accepted performance tests, almost from the start, as a measure of practical intelligence. Only they seem to have regarded practical intelligence, as measured by these tests, as a kind of special aptitude rather than as a kind of intelligence. For many years the situation in clinical practice was something like this: a child would be given routinely a Binet test. Then, if his Binet MA did not seem to do justice to him, he would be given a Pintner-Paterson or similar performance battery as a supplementary test. But the child's score on the performance test, except in instances of language handicaps, would seldom be integrated with, or serve to alter, his Binet intelligence rating. Instead, it would usually be used as evidence of a compensatory useful special ability. Thus, if a child attained an IQ of 85 on the Binet, and one of 110 on the Pintner-Paterson, the reporting psychologist would ordinarily give the rating as "dull normal" intelligence with good practical or manipulative ability. It was not until the publication of the Bellevue Scales that any consistent attempt was made to integrate performance and verbal tests into a single measure of intelligence. The Bellevue tests have had increasingly wider use, but I regret to report that their popularity seems to derive, not from the fact that they make possible a single global rating, but because they enable the examiner to obtain separate verbal and performance IQ's with one test.

The Aristotelian hierarchical white-collar concept of intelligence dies hard. This, in spite of the fact, that performance tests often can and do contain a larger amount of g than do the verbal tests. Thus, in his differential study of "*Abstract and Concrete Intelligence*," W. P. Alexander, after correcting for communality, specific factors, and chance errors of measurement, found the theoretical g loadings for verbal and practical ability to be .60 and .81, respectively. Alexander concludes that "a perfect performance battery would be a better measure of g than a perfect verbal battery."

This and other findings by Alexander bring me to what constitutes the most compelling evidence for the reorientation in our concept of intelligence mentioned at the onset of this paper. I refer to the findings contributed by factor analysis. Here two important names appear on the horizon: Carl Spearman and L. L. Thurstone. I believe that the answers which they have given to the problem of the nature of general intelligence are incorrect. But I am sure that without the inspiration and without the tools which they furnished us, the solution of the problem would be altogether impossible.

Such a statement before a gathering of clinical psychologists may be unorthodox, because to many, factor analysis is almost anathema. But I can assure you, on the authority of expert consultants, that the mathematics of factor analysis is quite elementary, and on the basis of my own experience with it, extremely practical; and, with due apologies to Freud, even "sexy." For with what, in effect, does factor analysis concern itself, but with the bedfellowship of psychometric tests. For, mind you, it embraces matrices, correlational to be sure, and then tells you what test stays close to what other tests when axes are rotated. Now that, I submit, is what clinical psychologists want to know: what test, what factor, or, if you will, what function or what trait goes with what other factor, or function, or trait. And when the findings are examined some very interesting and unsuspected relationships come to light. For example, some tests of intelligence, like some human beings, are extremely promiscuous. Thus, vocabulary, the paragon of verbal tests, correlates very frequently, and to a considerable measure, with Block Designs, the perfect example of a performance test. But to return to a more serious vein, the importance of factor analysis is, of course, that it enables us to discover what our tests measure and the extent to which they measure the things they purport.

What are the elements which factor analysis has shown our intelligence tests to measure? The first is abstract reasoning. This is Spearman's g or eduction. Spearman argued that g was the only independent factor, and while he hesitated to identify g with general intelligence, his actual applications are tantamount to it. In equating g with general intelligence Spearman was in error, not because the tetrad equation is incorrect but because, in point of fact, it is not satisfied as he claimed. Spearman's answer to this finding was that we cannot expect the tetrad equation to be satisfied by all the tests of general intelligence but only by "good" tests of intelligence, like analogies and mathematical reasoning which require eduction. But of course, if you select your tests, you can choose them so highly saturated with a single factor that the residuals vanish. This is all that the tetrad equation says, and it was the perceptive insight of Thurstone which recognized the tetrad equation for what it was, namely, a mathematically special case of a more general solution of the factorial problem. What was needed was a statistical analysis which would permit the emergence of other factors when present. By the use of his expanded technique, it has now been shown that intelligence tests, such as they are, contain not one but several independent factors. Some five or six have been definitely identified; they are, to repeat, induction, verbal, spatial, numerical, and one or two other factors. Notice, however, that these factors, like Spearman's eduction, are all cognitive.

At this point it is important to bear in mind what a factor stands for in factor analysis. Basically, it is an identifiable independent variable which accounts for a certain portion of the total test variance in a correlational matrix. The amount of variance it accounts for in any given test is called the test's factor loading. In a perfectly factorialized correlation matrix, the sum of the factorial loadings of the extracted factors should be 100 per cent, that is, account for the total test variance.

Now, it is a remarkable finding that when matrices of intelligence tests are factored, the amount of variance accounted for is seldom more than 60 per cent of the total, and, what is perhaps of equal significance, the greater the number of different tests included, the smaller, generally, the total per cent of variance accounted for; and this is seemingly independent of the number of factors extracted. In the case of our present intelligence test batteries, factors beyond the first 3 or 4 usually contribute so little to the already accounted-for variance that it is generally not profitable to extract them. It is the observation of this important finding that in the factorialization of batteries of intelligence tests, there always remained a considerable per cent of unaccounted-for variance, which began to arouse my interest some years ago. It seemed to hold the key to our problem.

If after successive attempts at factoring out all the components of intelligence, there always remained a large residue of these unknown elements, the obvious inference to be made was that our intelligence tests measured other things than those accounted for by the extracted factors. The second inference was that those other factors were numerous and occurred in relatively small amounts, because it was impossible to extract single additional factors which would account for any considerable portion of the residual variance. I assumed that the principal reason for this was that the test batteries usually factored did not include tests which contained sufficient amounts of these other factors, to enable some of the remaining tests to cluster about them. Provisionally I called these residual components the non-intellective factors of intelligence. But in terms of more recent findings, I believe they can be more justly designated as the personality components of general intelligence, which in fact they are.

The evidence for this conclusion comes from a number of sources. As early as 1913, Webb, in factoring a battery of tests, along with a number of ratings which attempted to appraise traits of character, was able to extract a factor "W." "W" in a broad sense seemed to relate to a moral and conative propensity, which he called conscientiousness or purposeful consistency. A few years later, in Spearman's own laboratory, Lankes and Wynn Jones demonstrated the existence of another non-intellective factor, "p", or perseveration, which characterized their subjects tendency to resist changes in set, and which Spearman related to his law of inertia. In 1921, W. M. Brown discussed character traits as factors in intelligence tests, and in 1933, R. B. Cattell reported correlations between tests of temperament and ratings in intelligence. But perhaps the most crucial findings are those of W. P. Alexander who, in an extensive factor analysis of a large series of verbal and performance tests, supplemented by tests of achievement and academic marks, showed that in addition to the now familiar g, V (verbal ability), and P (practical ability), a considerable portion of variance had to be ascribed to two other extracted factors, namely, X and Z. X was a factor which determined the individual's interests and "concerns," in Alexander's words, "temperament rather than ability"; while Z was "an aspect of temperament related to achievement," in the case of Alexander's subjects, to school achievement.

The factor loadings of X and Z varied greatly from test to test, but even some of Spearman's ostensibly pure tests of g contained some Z and nearly all the performance tests showed considerable X or Z loadings. As might be expected, these factors played an even greater role in academic or technical achievement. For success in science, for example, the X factor loading was .74, as against only .36 for g, and for English .48 as against .43 for the g loading. From these findings one might even infer that lack of intellectual ability, beyond a certain point, accounts for relatively little of school failures. Indeed Dorothea McCarthy recently offered the "hypothesis," and I quote, "that emotional insecurity . . . is the basic cause of most educational disabilities and learning failures, which are not due to mental defect."

What are we to make of these two findings? First, that factors other than intellectual contribute to achievement in areas where, as in the case of learning, intellectual factors have until recently been considered uniquely determinate, and, second, that these other factors have to do with functions and abilities hitherto considered traits of personality. Among those partially identified so far are factors relating primarily to the conative functions like drive, persistence, will, and perseveration, or in some instances, to aspects of temperament that pertain to interests and achievement. This, to be sure, is just the beginning, but one of the reasons that not much more has been done is that psychologists have continued to assume that personality has little to do with intelligence. To Thurstone as well as to Spearman, general intelligence seems to be first and foremost a cognitive function, by Spearman to be accounted for by a single pervasive factor, by Thurstone by a number of factors.

It is curious that the clinical psychologist, so little impressed by or, at least, so little conversant with factor analysis, has almost from the start dealt with intelligence test findings as if the personality components in intelligence were already an established fact. For what does psychological diagnosis on the basis of intelligence test findings consist of but inferring adjustive capacities of the subject as a personna? It appears that the clinician, like the character in Moliere's "*Malade Imaginaire*," has been speaking prose all his life without knowing it.

One might add that diagnosing personality and personality disorder, at the level it is being done, is not very difficult. Practically every good individual test of intelligence lends itself to such application to a greater or lesser degree, the Bellevue Scales and the new Children's Test of Intelligence perhaps a little more readily. This does not mean that they are tests of personality, but they do suggest that our intelligence tests contain elements which are essentially factors of the personality as a whole rather than of specific cognitive abilities. When the neurotic does poorly on the Digit Span Test, it is not because of defective memory, but generally because of a basic anxiety mobilized by the test, as by any other situation, in which he is seemingly on trial. Conversely, when a mental defective does relatively well on the Maze Test, it is generally not because he has better planning ability, but because he is less impulsive. Similarly, a large variety of traits and personality factors may be inferred from test performance—for example, energy level from a subject's performance on the Digit Symbol, asocial tendencies from general comprehension, masculinity-femininity from the picture completion test. These are only a few of the traits and diagnostic constellations with which every clinician who has done psychological diagnosis is familiar.

The point here is not that personality traits can be discovered in psychometric performance, or, what needs no special argument, that personality and abnormal conditions influence intelligence test findings, but that personality traits *enter into* the effectiveness of intelligent behavior, and, hence, into any global concept of intelligence itself. It is one thing if a child does poorly on an intelligence test because he is disinterested or upset and quite another if he is congenitively impulsive or emotionally unstable.

One would naturally suppose that if intelligence is a function of the personality as a whole, one should find significant positive or negative correlations with measures of personality itself. Such, indeed, are the findings, but the results are extremely hard to evaluate. This is in part due to the fact that the studies in this area have been done primarily with the intent of discovering the extent to which intelligence accounts for variance in personality. In an article which appeared in 1940, Irving Lorge reviews the studies published to that date on the general relationship between measures of intelligence and various measures or estimates of personality. The personality tests included most of the current and older inventories (Woodworth, Laird, Thurstone, Bernreuter, Allport, et al.), as well as the association experiment and the personality measures of Hartshorn, May, and Maller. Some 200 correlation coefficients were analyzed. The range of coefficients was from +.70 to −.49 with a median of +.04. Disregarding the signs, half of the ratios were between .00 and .15, and one quarter of them .30 and above. Lorge's general feeling about the findings is that the range is so "extraordinary that anybody can make any statement." Nevertheless, his conclusion is "that some correlation between intelligence and personality exists."

All this is rather meager fare, but the findings are perhaps as satisfactory as could be expected. Apart from the known unreliability of paper-and-pencil inventories, there is the more disturbing fact of their uncertain validity and relevance. At times they do not measure the traits claimed for them, at others they measure only small segments of the personality, although in different ways; and at still other times, traits which are purely nominal. The latter, for example, was shown by Flanagan to be the case with the Bernreuter Inventory dichotomies. In the original publication the test was scored for six different traits, which by factorialization were then reduced to two.

Flanagan's study is a good example of how factor analysis aids us in getting at basic components. Mere evidence of concomitant variation is not enough; in fact, it is often misleading. For example, defective hearing may have a measurable effect on both learning arithmetic and size of vocabulary, but, obviously, has no basic relation to either arithmetical reasoning or verbal ability. A variable to be basic and scientifically significant must be independent. In the case of man's cognitive functions, these independent variables, in so far as they are relevant to general intelligence, have been pretty well identified. It may be possible to add one or two to Thurstone's list, but not many more. Those of personality are yet to be discovered. We have some knowledge of what the factors to be measured are likely to be, some on the basis of researches like those of Webb, Alexander, Guilford, Cattell, and Eysenck, others on the basis of general observation and clinical experience. The latter have thus far gone unrecognized, not only because we have no tests for them but because clinicians, like their more academic colleagues, still think of intelligence as consisting primarily of cognitive abilities. Any bit of behavior that seems concerned with or related to instinct, impulse, or temperament is ipso facto considered as having no direct relation to general intelligence.

Such, for example, is curiosity. This was one of the traits which Terman in his studies of genius found most frequently among his gifted children. But he did not have, nor do we as yet have, any test of curiosity. No attempt has been made to extract curiosity as a factor of intelligence. We all know how important curiosity is for biologic adaptation as well as scientific achievement. It is, to quote McDougall, "at the basis of many of man's most splendid achievements, for rooted in it are his speculative and scientific tendencies," and ". . . in men in whom curiosity is innately strong, it may become the main source of intellectual energy and effort." But what is curiosity? "It is the impulse to approach and examine more closely the object which attracts it," that is an instinct, and according to McDougall, one of the basic instincts.

One need not be afraid or ashamed to acknowledge impulse, instinct and temperament as basic factors in general intelligence. It is indeed because I believe they are that I have brought before you the arguments and evidence presented. My main point has been that general intelligence cannot be equated with intellectual ability, but must be regarded as a manifestation of the personality as a whole. I have tried to show that factors other than intellectual enter into our concept of general intelligence, and that in everyday practice, we make use of them knowingly or not.

What is needed is that these factors be rigorously appraised. Factor analysis has been emphasized because, at present, it is the only method which enables us to demonstrate and discover independent variables. We already have some clues as to what the non-intellective but relevant factors of intelligence may be. What we now need are tests which not only identify but measure them. This in effect demands broadening our concept of general intelligence and calls for a revised psychometric to measure these added variables as sub-tests of all general intelligence scales.

To say that general intelligence can be social and practical, as well as abstract, was just a beginning. We had to know what basic components of the mind were responsible for making an individual effective in one rather than in another area.

To realize that general intelligence is the function of the personality as a whole and is determined by emotion and conative factors is also just a beginning. We now need to know what non-intellective factors are relevant and to what degree. This is the task which lies immediately before us.

Increased research activity during the last two decades has considerably advanced our knowledge concerning brain functions. The task of anchoring behavioral studies of brain functions to psychological dimensions has been very difficult. One approach is illustrated here in Dr. Halstead's paper. It is clear that our current knowledge is tentative and provisional, but it is also clear that marked progress is being made.

Biological Intelligence*

WARD C. HALSTEAD

1951

The contributions of Alfred Binet to the problem of intelligence are known chiefly through the standardized test associated with his name. Less well known is the fact that Binet early in his investigations found it necessary to distinguish between intellectual *activity* and intellectual *level:*

Who has not encountered persons who busy themselves with a host of questions, have a great deal of information, speak of everything with warmth and an inexhaustible supply of words, are fertile in views, hypotheses, distinctions, neologisms? Very often they deceive as to their true value. They are thought very intelligent, while in reality they possess only intellectual activity.

Binet also emphasized the significance of intelligence as a form of biological adaptation: "One must remember that the faculty of adapting oneself is the property of the intelligence and that the power of adaptation is the measure of it; it is evident that from this point of view any confusion between the activity and the level is impossible."

Binet thus approached intelligence from the point of view of the biologically oriented psychologist. He recognized both genotypic and phenotypic components. There is little question but that he assigned the intellectual level to the former. As to the scale which Binet produced for measuring intelligence, and its subsequent modification by Terman, I suspect that it is a better measure of intellectual activity than of intellectual level. This, of course, is not the outcome which Binet had hoped for but, as Hebb has convincingly demonstrated, the I.Q. may or may not be changed and may be normal for the scale with the major part of both frontal lobes (about 30 per cent of the cerebrum) absent.

Binet's reaction to this recent finding would, I am sure, have been to make better tests. His clinical insight was too keen to permit the easy inference—which unfortunately is being made rather commonly today—that the frontal brain has nothing to do with intelligence.

* Adapted from the *Journal of Personality,* 20 (1941), pp. 118-120, by permission of the author and the publisher.

Binet's distinction between intellectual level and intellectual activity has largely been overlooked or forgotten by contemporary students of the problem. I would like to state parenthetically that if all other reasons were lacking, which they are not, the continuing need for parameters other than performance to aid in specifying level of behavioral organization is sufficient to link the future destinies of psychology and basic biology. It seems that this need is also felt in the rapidly developing field of biochemistry where their appears to be a gross correlation at least between the demands in energy level and the corresponding levels of behavioral functions organized around particular areas of the brain.

During the last several years, while exploring the behavioral effects of surgical lesions in the frontal lobes of man and other animals, the writer has identified certain recurrent forms of behavior which have their maximal though not exclusive representation in the cortex of the frontal lobes. Since it appeared that the functions thus isolated bore directly upon the capacity for controlled adaptability of the individuals involved, a concept of biological intelligence was generated. The adjective *biological* was appended when it became apparent that the functions were relatively independent of cultural considerations and had a wide generality.

Components of biological intelligence. Four factors have thus far been identified as comprising biological intelligence. They have been designated neutrally as A, P, C, and D factors respectively. Collectively they constitute a neural Gestalt which can be selectively impaired or enhanced by certain classes of stress such as anoxia, drugs, hypnotic inhibition, trauma, and disease. They have now been scaled fairly satisfactorily in several hundred individuals, including males and females through the age range of 12 to 75, in various stages of health and disease. The functions involved appear to mature sometime between 12 and 14 years of age. That they are relatively free from cultural considerations is further attested by their determined presence in Eskimos, Orientals, Negroes, and Caucasians. The functions are scalable with present indicators at a high level of objectivity. In recent test runs they have been satisfactorily scaled remotely, i.e., without any sensory contact between interpreter and subject. Each of the factors is correlated positively but to a low degree (r's of the order of .39) with both verbal and performance psychometric I.Q. That they project into the domain of personality is strongly suggested by positive correlations of the order of .70 between some of them and specific components of the Rorschach test. What is the nature of these factors?

The A factor. Two components of the A factor have been identified in grouping behavior. Both are involved in grouping to a criterion. One yields rational outcome and to some extent involves conscious awareness. The other yields an irrational outcome without dependence upon awareness. Behavior of the first class can be demonstrated by means of the writer's Category Test. In this test groups of simple geometrical figures are presented serially to the subject in such a manner that he can infer recurrent principles of organization in the stimulus material. Information as to the quality of response for each given set of items is fed back differentially via the auditory system of the subject in the form of a chime registering correct responses and a buzzer registering incorrect responses. In a test situation where several principles of organization are made effective through the exposure of 200 or 300 sets of figures, the orderly transition from trial-and-error groping to formation of constructs of limited generality, to the generalization of concepts of high generality can be traced in a clear manner for the normal subject. In some fifteen years I have yet to find an individual from any walk of life with known damage to the cortex of his frontal lobes who has succeeded in making the orderly transition from constructs to concepts of wide generality. This test of organizational activity or abstraction, which healthy twelve- to fourteen-year-old children with average I.Q.'s can pass without difficulty, has proved sensitive throughout a wide range of conditions involving frontal brain injuries. It will not detect reliably primary brain lesions occurring elsewhere.

Perceptual difficulties cannot account for the failures since the subject is always able to describe the items in detail. Likewise, failure of brief memory seems to be ruled out by the performances on the last subtest, which is a recognition test. Our evidence suggests that the differences arise in direct proportion to the blindness of the task for the various subjects. At various times the normal subjects seem to ignore very obvious dimensions of the stimulus configurations. They usually begin the test by isolating some stimulus dimension which is sufficiently recurrent to produce temporary signs of successful performance. But when this initial cue proves to be but an incidental rather than a necessary element of the task, they may persist for several items in projecting their initial construct onto the materials before moving to generate a valid principle or concept. In this respect they appear to differ only quantitatively from the brain-injured individuals; yet this difference is all important. They do shift more readily to other aspects of the situation and hence discover the necessary and sufficient attributes among the ambient dimensions of the stimuli at a much earlier stage. Ordering of their behavior with reference to test stimuli is at once more conscious and insightful, involving active effort. But lest we consider these latter qualities characteristic of the normal individual, let us examine the second type of ordered behavior wherein the normal individual generalizes towards an irrational outcome as blindly as do our most severely brain-injured individuals.

Schematic faces and affective behavior. Some years ago Brunswik and Reiter undertook an interesting study of certain physiognomic stereotypes in normal individuals. They employed ten judges. Using the method of paired comparisons they asked their individuals to match up certain personality traits with schematic outlines of faces. Out of several hundred comparisons, they were able to isolate a dozen or more relatively strong schematic faces which were commonly associated with personality traits. It occurred to me to apply such materials to the study of human brain-injured individuals. Professor Brunswik kindly made available to me photographic negatives of his originals. From these I selected nine faces for the purposes of my study. Three of these faces had been found by Brunswik and Reiter and also by Samuels, working with Harvard students, to be strongly associated with such desirable personality traits as gaiety, good character, intelligence, beauty, youth, etc. Five of these faces, on the other hand, had been found to be strongly associated with such undesirable personality traits as sadness, ugliness, bad character, unintelligence, and old age. The other face was found to be psychophysically neutral, being chosen with equal frequency for desirable and undesirable traits. Over a period of several years we have had an opportunity to study the responses of several hundred individuals to the schematic faces presented to them by a modification of the method of limits.

The extent to which grouping behavior of the second type with reference to schematic faces occurs among our subjects is shown in Table I. Here the percentages of various subgroups who selected the schematic faces according to desirable (D) and undesirable (U) are shown for each

TABLE I

Percentage of Agreement in Projecting Personality Trait Names onto Schematic Faces According to Categories of Desirable (D) and Undesirable (U) Traits, in Normal-Control, Brain-Disease, and Mental-Illness Subjects*

Trait	Controls N = 102 D	U	Brain disease N = 158 D	U	Mental illness N = 103 D	U
Gay	86		86		90	
Sad		95		92		87
Beautiful	92		92		80	
Ugly		92		91		93
Good Character	83		77		80	
Bad Character		76		81		76
Intelligent	68		77		73	
Unintelligent		89		82		84
Likeable	86		86		84	
Unlikeable		86		85		84
Young	90		87		91	
Old		89		86		89
Energy & Determination	60		64		56	
Lacks Energy & Determination		86		86		85

* Chance expectancy: $D = 33.3\%$; $U = 55.6\%$

of fourteen traits. Thus 86 per cent of our controls chose one of the expected three faces as the most gay, whereas chance would have yielded but 33.3 per cent. On the other hand, 95 per cent of them chose one of the expected five faces as being the most sad, whereas chance would have yielded but 55.6 per cent. Note also that our brain-injured cases and our severely neurotic patients matched gaiety and sadness in a very similar way. In fact, if we look at the various pairs of personality traits shown in this table, we are impressed by the striking similarities rather than by the differences in the grouping behavior. In this type of behavior, our normal individuals are just as irrational as our brain-injured individuals or as our psychiatric patients. It is difficult to see that such ordering behavior is on other than a blind basis. It seems quite unlikely that the child is born with an a priori notion that the distance between the eyes, the height of the forehead, the length of the nose, or the location of the mouth, the four varying elements in this series of faces, are invariable indicators of gaiety, intelligence, etc.

We are not clear when this process begins, but we have found one instance in which a child of four years and ten months required but slight translation of the trait names to show this conformity or stereotype in thirteen of the fourteen judgments. This situation may not be fundamentally different from the irrational or blind learning that takes place when a newcomer begins to take on the dialect of the community or from the process of identification of the child with one or both of his parents.

It is this strong projective tendency to fix upon particular aspects which we noted to occur under the more restricted conditions of our Category Test. Herein lies a clue as to the nature of the type of abstraction or grouping behavior that yields an insightful grasp of principles. The organism works initially less directly with the external material than with its a priori expectancies. True categorization is achieved only when these expectancies have been put through a special set of operations in which a redistribution of affective loadings or valences takes place. The altered content must be rendered affectively equivalent. It is this type of work for which the organism is perhaps least prepared by its biological heritage. The task requires deliberation with denial of immediate gratifications. It requires that the organism be able to protect its state of deliberation in the face of mounting frustration. If the organism is to maintain deliberativeness in the face of mounting frustration, there must be an adequate reserve of power, cortical or intellectual, for, as much experimental work indicates, frustration per se does not add power to the task but rather is parasitic to it.

The P factor.   One of our indicators appears to measure something which we interpret as cerebral power. We call this the P factor. It is measured with the simple task of adjusting the speed of a flickering light until the flicker disappears. This point represents a dramatic change in consciousness for the subject. For once he reaches the rate at which the separate flashes run together or fuse for him, he cannot tell the unsteady light from a steady one. He has broken with physical reality. This rate is much higher in our normal individuals than in our frontal brain-injured patients. It is as if the mental engine were running in the brain-injured, but running on inadequate power. It fails at the first little hill. From our measurements with this test under a considerable range of physiological conditions, it seems clear that the test reflects an important aspect of cerebral metabolism and possibly that of the cerebral cortex itself. For the power factor may not be lowered by the operation known as prefrontal lobotomy, wherein the deep white matter of the frontal lobes is destroyed by leaving the overlying cortex intact. Whereas it is lowered when the cortex is removed as in frontal lobectomies.

Support for our notion that we are measuring some aspect of cerebral metabolism has been obtained by studying patients with various types of metabolic disorders. Our endocrinologist, Dr. Allen Kenyon, has made many such cases available to us prior to and after treatment with various hormones. In patients with hypothyroidism or myxedema, for example, remarkable increases in the power factor occur as these individuals are placed on thyroid medication. In some instances, this change appears to reflect quite accurately a general improvement in the clinical status of the individual. Not only does the power factor increase but the ability of these patients to make the required adaptations to our Category Test likewise is improved—frequently to normal limits. ACTH likewise produces an increase in the power factor in some individuals. Other hormones, such as some of the estrogens, have failed in our experience to produce these effects.

The A factor, or capacity for abstracting universals or rational concepts, seems to be a general property of the cerebral cortex in man that is maximized in the cortex of the prefrontal lobes. The cerebral power factor P also seems to be represented throughout the cortex but again is maximized in the cortex of the prefrontal lobes. These two factors are disturbed together in unilateral or bilateral lobectomies of the frontal lobes wherein the cortex is removed along with the white matter. Both factors may be spared in lobotomies, however, wherein the white matter is destroyed leaving the frontal cortex essentially intact. On the other hand, spontaneous mild atrophy of the frontal cortex in middle-aged persons may first impair the A factor and only later as the atrophy progresses come to impair the P factor. Such individuals represent the obverse of clinical depressions. There may be no flagging of intellectual drive and ambition in the face of mounting judgmental incapacity. The mild clinical depression, probably as a direct function of the substrate, is associated with an acute drop in the P factor with only a more gradual restriction of the degrees of freedom for the A factor. If we restate the above in terms of Binet's distinction between *level* and *activity,* it is apparent that an individual may have high level in P and low activity in A, or vice versa, and all intermediate ratios of A and P. The possibility that psychotherapy, for example, is effective by changing the A factor and P factor ratios to a more "optimal" balance is a matter for future research.

The D factor. There is a third factor in our conception of biological intelligence which must be taken into account. This is the avenue or modality through which intelligence is exteriorized in any given situation. Our clue to the neural significance of the directional or D factor arises in studies of the aphasias. It is well know that an agnosia for printed words may so deform biological intelligence on the perceptual side that the affected individual may be able to transact his affairs by telephone but cannot read his mail. Or, conversely, an individual may have an apraxia for producing written symbols, and although he cannot write a single word be able to demonstrate in our tests that he is of normal intelligence. In the early stages of any skill, the modality or avenue considerations may be the most important. You have to "get the feel" of a golf club before you can develop an intelligent game of golf. Some of the agnosias and apraxias seem to result from focal cortical lesions, according to Nielsen. The cortical representations of others are as yet unknown. But certainly an operational description of intelligence must include among its necessary and sufficient conditions provisions for our D factor.

The C factor. It is the fourth factor in biological intelligence which poses special difficulties in finding its neural correlates. The C factor, or organized experience of the individual, is the memory factor in intelligence. It serves as the stable framework of the "familiar" against which "new" experience is tested. A nervous system that cannot store its experience, that is, remember, is in trouble for the level of adaptation to new situations will necessarily be low. Trauma or disease of the brain, and excessive affect or emotion may disturb the memory component of intelligence. There is as yet no clue as to what these agents have in common. As to the physiology of learning, our ignorance is virtually complete. According to Hilgard: "It is a blot upon our scientific ingenuity that after so many years of search we know as little as we do about the physiological accompaniments of learning." I would put the matter even more strongly and say that the physiology and biochemistry of learning are the missing keys to further understanding of certain functions of the brain. In support of this view, Dr. Joseph Katz, a chemist, and I have recently published a theory of the memory trace designed to elicit help from the biochemist on this formidable problem. We have suggested that the genetic apparatus is a recapitulation or memory device which is more than formally analogous to individual memories arising from human experience. We have presented arguments for the view that individual memory begins with the laying down of a template protein molecule similar to a gene. Like the gene, this template molecule then organizes available neural proteins into protein lattices which register the particular memory trace. New instruments and techniques for exploring the ultramicroscopic structures of the neural elements of the brain have recently been introduced. We must await their verdict on the ultimate nature of memory.

Theoretical extensions. Such then is a skeletal view of biological intelligence. Some of the possible biosocial extensions of the model are being examined currently with the help of clinical methods on the one hand and factor analyses on the other. There remains the task of testing the model against such concepts in general psychology as perception, emotion, motivation, learning, and thinking and against such related concepts as growth, maturation, homeostasis, and integration in general biology. As the above tasks approach various stages of completion, the writer grows in optimism concerning biological intelligence as an operational concept with scientific generality.

The following paper is one of the few studies which deal longitudinally with the change in intelligence test scores for a migrant Negro population. The study is a model of its kind. It should be noted, however, that it does not deal directly with selective migration as such, but rather with length of residence in an environment presumably superior to the one which the migrants left. This study and the Gist and Clark study given earlier illustrate complementary methodologies aimed at different aspects of the total outcome of changing environments.

Negro Intelligence and Selective Migration*

EVERETT S. LEE

1951

Beginning about World War I and swelling to unprecedented proportions during and after World War II, the migration of southern Negroes to northern cities has effected a remarkably rapid redistribution of the Negro population of the United States. Are these migrants more intelligent than those who remained in the South? The Army intelligence tests of World War I showed a definite superiority of the northern over the southern Negro. Was this because of selective migration or can the superior showing of the northern Negro be laid to a more stimulating environment?

The most extensive attempt to answer this question is found in Otto Klineberg's *Negro Intelligence and Selective Migration*. There are two major parts of this work, the first of which is concerned with a direct comparison between the relative marks in the southern schools of Negro children who migrated to the North and those who remained in the South. The school records in Birmingham, Alabama; Nashville, Tennessee; and Charleston, South Carolina were examined and it was found that migrating children did not differ regularly or consistently from their non-migrating classmates in the matter of school marks.

The second method used by Klineberg was to give intelligence and performance tests to southern-born Negro children living in New York and then compare the groups with different lengths of residence in New York. On the Stanford-Binet and National Intelligence Tests the scores of the migrants increased fairly regularly with increasing length of residence in New York and tended, after several years, to approximate those of the New York-born. However, on the Otis Self-Administering Examination and on

* From Negro Intelligence and Selective Migration: A Philadelphia Test of the Klineberg Hypotheses, *American Sociological Review*, 16 (1951), pp. 227-233. Reprinted by permission of the author and publisher.

the different performance tests there was no clear pattern of improvement associated with length of residence in New York. From these results Klineberg concluded:

> There seems to the writer to be no reasonable doubt as to the conclusion of this study. As far as the results go, they show quite definitely that the superiority of the northern over the southern Negroes, and the tendency of northern Negroes to approximate the scores of the Whites, are due to factors in the environment, and not to selective migration.

A number of criticisms have been made of this study. Klineberg himself pointed out the inadequacy of school marks as a measure of intelligence and admitted that even though the migrant children from Birmingham, Nashville, and Charleston were not superior to their classmates, their parents, the originators of the northward migration, may very well have been. On the whole, more weight is accorded the second part of the study. Here, one of the major criticisms is that Klineberg's conclusions are based on comparisons made among different groups rather than upon successive tests of the same individuals. Presumably, these groups differed only as to length of residence in New York but it is possible that they may have differed in native ability as well. It has been conjectured that the earlier migrants were superior to the later ones and that there has been less selectivity for intelligence as northward migration increased, a not illogical supposition. Nevertheless, Klineberg's study remains by far the best of its kind.

As is too often the case in the social sciences, there has been no independent repetition of this study, perhaps partly because of the time and expense involved in testing large numbers of children. Fortunately in the Philadelphia public schools there has been a long-continuing and intensive program of intelligence testing, the results of which may be gathered from the cumulative record maintained for each pupil. Thus it is possible to set up in Philadelphia a study which somewhat parallels Klineberg's New York study. Like New York, Philadelphia is of special interest because of the large volume of recent Negro migration from the South.

Following Klineberg, an attempt was made to test the hypothesis that there is a significant improvement in the intelligence test scores of southern-born Negro children as the length of residence in Philadelphia increases. The following conditions were held essential to an adequate test of the hypothesis.

(1) *A repetition of tests on the same individual.* It has been mentioned that the Klineberg study has been criticized because its comparisons are between different groups rather than between successive tests of the same individuals. One of the advantages of the Philadelphia testing program is that the Philadelphia Tests of Verbal and Mental Ability constitute a well correlated series, the different tests of which are given at various times during the pupil's school career and therefore offer an opportunity to deter-

mine whether there is a trend in the "IQ's" of the same individuals over a range as great as nine years. This, of course, does not preclude the use of intergroup comparisons, but adds evidence beyond that obtainable from such comparisons alone.

(2) *Tests of specific abilities.* It is conceivable that an increase in score on a general intelligence test may be indicative of improvement in a single ability. For example, an improvement in verbal ability would, in itself, raise the total score on a general intelligence test, even though there was no improvement in other factors. The Chicago Tests of Primary Mental Abilities, used in the Philadelphia schools, break intelligence into six factors, allowing an opportunity to determine whether any improvement in general intelligence is associated with only one or two abilities. To this is added the Minnesota Paper Form Board Test, a test of spatial ability and one of the tests used by Klineberg.

(3) *A control group of non-migrants who do not differ from the southern-born in the matter of pre-school training.* Over a third of the Philadelphia-born children have had pre-school training and some psychologists maintain that this raises the "IQ" for at least the first few years thereafter. It follows, therefore, that kindergarten training alone might serve to differentiate the non-migrants from the southern-born children, since very few of the latter have had pre-school training.

For practical reasons it was necessary to select a few schools for intensive study rather than attempt to sample the entire school population. On the basis of available information these schools were chosen from localities which presented widely diverse socio-economic characteristics. Two of the schools were in the heart of the city, one was near the city line, and the others were distributed widely in the intermediate area. One of the schools was a vocational school and another was chosen because a high percentage of its students were the children of foreign-born parents. Two of the schools drew children almost entirely from low rent districts; for the others, the pupils came from areas of higher rents with considerable variation from school to school. A major criterion in the selection of schools was the percentage of Negro students, which varied from a low of 23 to a high of 92. All of the schools were either junior or senior high schools and all of the students considered had attained at least the ninth grade. Nine schools were included in the investigation. The criteria for selection were, of course, arbitrary and no claim can be made that their populations are truly representative of those of the Philadelphia public schools in general.

Within the schools the records of each Negro student who had come to Philadelphia from a state south of the District of Columbia and east of the Mississippi River were included. As a control group a 20 per cent sample of the Philadelphia-born Negro students was selected by taking the record of every fifth Philadelphia-born Negro whose name appeared in alphabetical listings of each class. The control group was designed to be a check against the possibility that an increase in the test scores of migrants on succeeding tests is only a general trend to be found among all students.

The Philadelphia-born students were divided into two groups, those who had attended kindergarten and those who had not. Migrants were divided into five classes, according to the grade in which they entered the Philadelphia school system, and roughly at two-year intervals. Time of entering the Philadelphia schools was taken as the best possible estimate of the time of arrival in Philadelphia even though, in some cases, several months may have elapsed between the time of migration and the time of entering school. Place of last residence before coming to Philadelphia was taken from the school transfer and time and place of birth from the school's record of the birth certificate.

FINDINGS

The mean scores and standard deviations of the Philadelphia Tests of Mental and Verbal Ability are shown in Table I. These tests form a series of group intelligence tests, somewhat similar to the Otis series, and are given to pupils in grades IA, 2B, 4B, 6B and 9A. They have been standardized on Philadelphia school children, and equal scores on different tests represent equal distances, in terms of standard deviations, from the mean scores of the groups upon which the tests were standardized. The 1A test relies on oral instructions and includes such performance items as drawing the circle, square, triangle, and diamond, but beginning with the 2B test the series becomes increasingly verbal.

All of the individuals included in Table I took every test in the Philadelphia series given after they entered the school system. Because they had missed one or more of these tests, 292 of the 1,234 migrants whose records were examined were excluded from this table along with 326 of the 962 Philadelphia-born. Twelve migrants who had attended kindergarten were also excluded in order not to affect the comparison between the migrants and the Philadelphia-born who had not attended kindergarten. This is, of course, a loss of material, but it has the advantage of making the comparison of the scores of the same individuals on succeeding tests of this series possible.

From Table I, it is immediately apparent that there is a steady improvement in test rating as each of the migrant groups increases its length of residence in Philadelphia. For each of the three groups of migrants entering before grade 5A there is a significant difference between the first rating obtained on the Philadelphia tests and the rating on the last, or 9B test. In other words, the improvement in mean test rating could have been due to chance less than five times in one hundred for each of these three groups of migrants. For the groups entering in grades 5A—6B we have only two

TABLE I
Mean "IQ's" on Philadelphia Tests of Mental and Verbal Ability

| Group | N | Grade in which test was taken: | | | | |
		1A	2B	4B	6B	9A
Philadelphia-born who attended kindergarten	212					
Mean		96.7	95.9	97.2	97.5	96.6
σ		14.3	14.8	15.0	13.9	14.2
Philadelphia-born who did not attend kindergarten	424					
Mean		92.1	93.4	94.7	94.0	93.7
σ		13.8	14.4	14.6	14.1	15.1
Southern-born entering Philadelphia school system in grades:						
1A	182					
Mean		86.5	89.3	91.8	93.3	92.8
σ		13.2	13.3	14.1	14.5	13.6
1B–2B	109					
Mean			86.7	88.6	90.9	90.5
σ			15.2	13.6	14.4	16.1
3A–4B	199					
Mean				86.3	87.2	89.4
σ				15.3	14.8	13.7
5A–6B	221					
Mean					88.2	90.2
σ					15.1	14.7
7A–9A	219					
Mean						87.4
σ						14.3

test scores and the difference is not statistically significant. The trend, however, is upward, there being a 2 point increase in mean score. Of far more importance than the tests of significance is the steady improvement of the test rating within each of the migrant groups.

Table I may be used to make intergroup comparisons as well. Reading upwards, instead of from left to right, a comparison can be made between groups with different lengths of attendance in the Philadelphia schools. With only one exception (the group of migrants entering in grades 5A—6B is slightly better than the group which entered in grades 3A—4B) there is a steady improvement in rating associated with early entrance in the Philadelphia school system. On each test where a comparison can be made there is a significant difference between the mean of the migrant group entering in grade 1A and the group which had last entered and was taking its first test of this series.

A still further series of tests can be made. The hypothesis can be set up that there is no significant difference between the scores of the southern-born group entering the school system in grade 1A and the Philadelphia-born who did not attend kindergarten. For tests 1A, 2B, and 4B the hypothesis must be rejected, but on tests 6B and 9A the conclusion is that the groups are samples of the same population. In other words, the difference between the two groups, which was quite large in grade 1A, has narrowed until by grade 6B the difference is no longer significant.

The Chicago Tests of Primary Mental Abilities afford an opportunity to determine whether the improvement noted on the Philadelphia tests of general intelligence can be attributed to improvement in one or two specific abilities. These results are given in Table II, where again there is a striking

TABLE II

Mean Scores on Chicago Tests of Primary Mental Abilities

Group	N	Number	Verbal	Spatial	Sub-Tests: Word Fluency	Reasoning	Memory
Philadelphia-born who attended kindergarten	105						
Mean		72.1	45.3	38.2	43.1	31.2	12.3
σ		23.8	20.1	24.6	15.1	13.2	3.8
Philadelphia-born who did not attend kindergarten	193						
Mean		67.3	40.2	34.2	42.4	29.2	12.0
σ		21.7	19.6	25.4	14.6	13.7	3.9
Southern-born entering system in grades:							
1A	83						
Mean		68.2	34.9	35.3	41.9	27.4	12.4
σ		25.3	21.3	23.7	15.1	14.5	4.1
1B–2B	61						
Mean		64.3	35.6	32.4	40.3	27.9	12.3
σ		24.6	22.2	22.9	13.8	15.1	4.6
3A–4B	74						
Mean		61.6	32.9	28.5	40.8	26.3	12.6
σ		26.1	20.7	21.3	15.4	14.4	5.1
5A–6B	87						
Mean		62.1	30.7	29.7	39.3	25.4	11.9
σ		24.3	21.6	24.5	14.2	15.1	4.2
7A–9A	77						
Mean		59.1	28.8	30.8	34.1	23.2	12.5
σ		25.6	20.8	25.1	15.9	15.6	4.4

association between the test score and the length of school attendance in Philadelphia. The one exception to the general pattern of improvement is the memory test, the scores of which seem to vary at random from group to group; indeed, the second highest mean score was registered by the group which had last come from the South. On all the other tests there is a significant difference between the means of the migrant group entering in grade 1A and the means of the migrant group entering in grades 7A to 9A. In three out of the six sub-tests, the migrant group entering in grade 1A surpasses the Philadelphia-born non-kindergarten group. Since there is an improvement in every category except that of memory, no single factor can be said to account for the over-all improvement in the intelligence test scores of the migrants.

In Table III are listed the scores on the Minnesota Paper Form Board Test. Contrary to the findings of the Klineberg study, where the results were not clear, there is a definite association between length of attendance in the Philadelphia schools and the scores on the test. The numbers of cases in this study are, however, considerably larger than those of the Klineberg study, which in some of his groups were as low as 23 or 25. This may explain the difference between these results and his.

TABLE III
Mean Scores on Minnesota Paper Form Board Test

Group	Mean score	Standard deviation	N
Philadelphia-born who attended kindergarten	33.1	14.3	244
Philadelphia-born who did not attend kindergarten	30.3	13.5	468
Southern-born entering system in grade:			
1A	28.8	16.0	209
1B–2B	26.6	13.9	133
3A–4B	23.4	15.4	226
5A–6B	24.8	13.7	249
7A–9A	20.6	14.5	252

There are still two major reservations that must be made before accepting the conclusions that there has been a general increase in the ability of the southern-born children to cope with intelligence tests. First, there is the factor of increasing familiarity with the tests and with the testing situation. These alone could account for a rise in the scores of the migrants. However, it would be expected, if this were an important factor, that there would be a similar rise in the scores of the two control groups of Philadelphia-born children. These persons, in general, would have even more familiarity with the tests and with the testing situation, but there is no upward trend in the scores of either of these groups.

Finally, it is conceivable that the persons who missed tests in the Philadelphia series were persons who had done badly on one test and thereafter stayed away from school on the day the tests were given. Or it may be that there is an inverse correlation between test scores and absences from school.

Either of these factors, if true, could operate in a way to affect intergroup comparisons, but could not explain away the rise in test ratings of the same individuals over a period of time. To make certain of the effect exercised by the exclusion of these records, however, the means and standard deviations of the Philadelphia series of tests were recomputed using both complete and incomplete records. Intergroup tests of significance were then made. While there were slight changes in the means, the general pattern was undisturbed and the difference between the means of different groups was judged significant or not significant, exactly as before.

CONCLUSION

Klineberg's hypothesis that there is an increase in the intelligence scores of southern Negro migrants to New York with increasing length of residence in New York is, in the main, substantiated by independent evidence in Philadelphia. There is a significant and continuous upward trend in the intelligence test ratings of southern-born Negro children as their length of residence in Philadelphia increases. This increase manifests itself not only on a general intelligence test but also on each of the sub-tests of the Chicago Tests of Primary Mental Abilities with the single exception of memory. The increase in general score cannot, therefore, be attributed to an increase in any one specific ability. Nor can the increase be laid to increasing familiarity with the tests or the testing situation, or to a general trend to be found among all students since there is no such increase in the scores of Philadelphia-born students. It can further be shown that the migrant children, who entered the first grade in Philadelphia are on the first three tests definitely inferior to the Philadelphia-born on the Philadelphia series of tests, but by the time they have reached the sixth grade there is no significant difference in their test ratings and those of the Philadelphia-born group, who, like them, had not attended kindergarten.

The following paper deals with an important and critical problem whose study is beset with serious methodological difficulties. In principle it may be argued that ex post facto studies such as this are incapable of interpretation. Properly speaking, unless the subjects are randomly assigned to the educational conditions (an unlikely possibility in Western society), it can always be maintained that the groups which received different amounts of schooling were in fact different in some important respects at the outset. "After the fact" matching on any number of variables cannot then establish comparability. Careful study of this paper and thinking through the issues involved will be a valuable experience for the student.

The Influence of Schooling Upon IQ*

TORSTEN HUSÉN

1951

The influence of schooling on the results of conventional intelligence tests is one of the most debated problems in educational psychology, and from a methodological point of view, one of the most difficult to answer. A very large number of relevant variables have to be dealt with, and, as a rule, only a few of these are under control. Moreover, the problem of sampling, and the regression effect further complicate the interpretation of the results obtained.

Because of the great difficulties that are frequently connected with the administrative side of research, when after a considerable lapse of time, a retest of extensive material has to be conducted, only a comparatively few investigations of this kind have been undertaken so far. . . . Most of these investigators have employed more or less selected groups. The most interesting of these investigations was carried out by LORGE. He employed the test results obtained in 1921—22 and in 1941 for 131 men. At the first testing, the subjects were in the 8th class of a primary school in New York City, where they were tested by means of two achievement tests. On the second occasion, they were given two ordinary group intelligence tests; one of these was Otis's group test. The original group consisted of 863 boys; but LORGE was able to show that the 131 who were available for testing after twenty years, were a representative sample of the original group in terms of the initial test scores. The material was divided into various class intervals in terms of the 1921 test. In each class, the mean score in Otis's

* Adapted from the original article in *Theoria*, 17 (1951), pp. 61-88. Reprinted by permission of the author and publisher.

group test was subsequently determined for the various levels of schooling. Especially great differences were observed between those who had received higher secondary education, and those who had only had elementary schooling, in spite of the fact, that to start with, they had all been on the same level. Of those who in the 1921 test, had a score of 89—98, the ones who had had 8—9 years of schooling, obtained a score of 38—39 in Otis's test, as against a score of 53—54 for those with 15 years or more of theoretical schooling. In several respects, however, LORGE's results rest on a somewhat insecure foundation. He deals with particularly small subgroups, where the mean differences are rarely statistically significant. The two tests that are compared with one another, are really quite different in character. As has already been stated, the first was definitely an achievement test (reading and arithmetic tests).

* * *

METHODOLOGICAL PROBLEMS

When it is desired to investigate the effect of theoretical schooling on the intelligence quotient, the latter being defined by conventional group tests, it should be endeavoured, from the outset, to obtain a clear idea as to the extent that the schooling variable can be studied separately. This is of the greatest importance for the interpretation of the interindividual differences or group differences that arise. The possibility of attaining the ideal conditions for investigation, as given below, vary from case to case, depending upon the comprehensiveness of the data available for the investigator.

1. The use of a control and an experimental group is highly desirable, not to say necessary. If it is desired to study the influence of schooling on ability, it is preferable to employ two groups that are equivalent to commence with. One of these groups does not display any variations with regard to theoretical schooling received (control group), while the other has continued, after primary school, to a varying extent, to receive schooling (experimental group).

2. Naturally, the equivalence ought primarily to refer to the test variable which defines the IQ; but if possible, it should also embrace such social variables as parents' income, socio-economic group, education, occupation, etc. The ideal would be to match at random each control individual with an experimental individual, so that both individuals who constitute a pair would be similar as to all relevant variables. This matching should take place *a priori,* because if it is done *a posteriori,* there is a risk of the factor which has caused an individual to become an experimental or a control individual, being correlated with the variable whose effect it is desired to study. If, like WELLMAN, we desire to study the effect of nursery school teaching on intellectual development, and if, with this purpose in mind, a number of children are tested both before and after they have received this teaching,

and should these test results be then compared with the corresponding results for a group of children who have not attended a nursery school, the differences obtained will be very difficult to interpret. It may very easily be the case, that more well-to-do parents who are better educated and more socially ambitious, send their children to a greater extent to the nursery schools. The superiority displayed by children who have had a preschool training, when compared with those who have not, may, to no small extent, depend on the stimulation that the home environment is able to give from an intellectual point of view. The experimental and control groups, matched *a priori,* constitute, as has already been pointed out, an ideal that is as a rule unattainable.

3. Generally, the experimental group is already given in the form that some subjects have begun, or are about to begin, a certain course of training. This does not prevent one, however, from trying to make the two groups equivalent with regard to those variables that can be controlled. But here one is met with the difficulty that is due to the limited scope of the material. If we have, let us say, a group of 400 individuals, and wish to control this with reference to age, parents' income, and the subjects' schooling, there is considerable risk of obtaining such small subgroups that large group differences are required in order for these to be statistically significant. A way out, which has been used in this investigation, is to attempt to control one variable at a time. If it is desired, as in our case, to determine the influence of schooling on IQ, and the experimental and control groups are not equivalent from a social point of view, it is possible to compare the mean effect that every variable has in itself, when excluding the influence of the other variables.

4. The question of sampling is of the greatest importance. In longitudinal studies, we often obtain a positive selection, because, that part of the material which is worst off intellectually and socially, is more difficult to control as regards public registration. If, for example, a follow-up is undertaken for 300 children, and after a number of years, only 125 of these can be traced, naturally these 125 should not be compared with the original data for the 300, but with the corresponding data for the 125 remaining subjects.

*   *   *

5. One of the most important factors in longitudinal studies, when the same group is tested either twice or several times is, the so-called regression effect, the influence of which, with regard to the effect of training of ability, was first pointed out by McNemar. The regression effect implies that individuals obtaining extreme scores tend, when retested, to regress towards the average. If we test a number of persons, and select all who have an IQ over 130, and then retest them with the same test, we shall find that the new mean is 5—10 units lower. In the same way, we should have obtained

a mean that was 5—10 units higher, if we had chosen subjects with an IQ under 70. The reason for this phenomenon is the insufficient measuring accuracy of the test, its lack of ideal reliability. Random errors influence the individual scores. The regression effect is reversible. If we select all the subjects who attain an IQ of over 130 at the second testing, we shall find that their mean for the first testing was 5—10 units lower.

One must bear in mind that the regression effect, under certain conditions, can act as a contributory factor with regard to the appearance of group differences. If two groups, which are drawn from two different populations, are compared, and the two »mother populations» differ as regards the variable that the group comparison is concerned with, then the regression effect takes place. We shall have occasion to return to this problem later in connection with the group comparisons that our investigation gives rise to.

A condition, under which the regression effect makes its influence felt, may now be mentioned. If we examine the influence that secondary schooling has on the IQ at various levels of ability, it will be found that it »raises» the IQ on lower levels, and »lowers» it on higher levels. The phenomenon has, at times, been erroneously interpreted (inter alia, in the Iowa investigations), as if schooling exerted a »leveling» effect. But, since the extreme test scores, as has already been pointed out, tend on retesting to regress towards the mean, the changes described above, may be expected to occur. As a rule, they are interrelated with systematic changes of other kinds.

6. The magnitude of the deviations that take place between two test applications on different occasions, with the same or comparable tests and with regard to the same subjects, depends on three factors, viz.:

    a) the length of the interval,
    b) the subject's age at the first testing,
    c) the reliability of the test.

* * *

7. If possible, the same test should be employed for both test and retest. In principle, this is possible when carrying out follow-up studies of children within a limited interval or of adults within any interval. But if, as in our case, the same persons are tested at respectively 10 and 20 years of age, scales with a different content must be employed (the test items will have to vary), this does not imply, however, that there need be a difference in the structure of the scales. Both the test scales employed in this case, happened to have the same structure in the following respects. They were both

    a) group test scales,
    b) segregated (divided) scales with 4 subtests,
    c) time-limited scales, and
    d) scales where 3 subtests were mainly verbal and 1 was a non-verbal test.

It was not possible to use a scale that had been administered in Malmö in 1938 at the induction of the conscripts, because, for one reason, the distribution of the scores obtained, would have been positively skewed without any possibilities of differentiation in the better half of the subjects tested, where the majority of those who have had secondary education are to be found.

In what follows, we shall give an account of an investigation on the influence of schooling upon changes in IQ. In 1938 the whole school population, 1,549 children, in the third grade of the primary schools in Malmö, a Swedish city with about 140,000 inhabitants, was given an intelligence group test. The mean age of the Ss was 9.65 years. Ten years later, in 1948, the male part of the population was retested at the induction into military service. Complete test data and social data from 1938 were available for 722 boys, born in 1928. On a later occasion we succeeded in identifying 95 p. c. of the original population. Complete test data and school records were available for 85 p. c. or 613 Ss. The identified group could be shown to be a representative sample of the whole population in terms of the initial test scores. At the first testing, teachers' ratings of general ability on a 5-point scale were available.

The 1938 test was given shortly before any differentiation in school training had started. The 1948 test was given, when the differentiation was practically finished. The Ss were grouped in five categories acording to the highest school grade completed:

primary school (7 grades) .... 431 Ss
junior secondary school without leaving certificate (7 to 10
   grades .... 28 »
junior secondary school with leaving certificate (9 or 10 grades) 73 »
senior secondary school without leaving certificate (11 to 13
   grades) .... 66 »
matriculation (12 or 13 grades) .... 15 »

Total 613 Ss

The 1938 intelligence test was a segregated scale with 4 subtests, antonyms, sentence completion, identical figures (nonverbal) and disarranged sentences. The 1948 test also consisted of four segregated subtests, synonyms, word meanings, number series, and matrices.

IQ-DIFFERENCES IN RELATION TO SCHOOLING

The raw scores obtained in 1938 and 1948 were converted into IQ scores. Subsequently, the difference between IQ 48 and IQ 38 was determined for each one of the subjects. A positive difference implies a relative raising of the intellectual ability, while a negative difference signifies a lowering of the same. . . .

The mean differences, given to the first place of decimals, are as follows:

primary school .... − 1.2 ± 0.6
junior secondary school without leaving certificate ...... + 2.1 ± 2.3
junior secondary school with leaving certificate .... + 3.0 ± 1.1
senior secondary school with matriculation .... + 7.2 ± 1.1
matriculation .... +11.0 ± 2.6

It appears that a distinct raising of IQ takes place, the higher the level of schooling that is attained. A significant deviation from 0, only takes place with regard to the three highest groups. As will be seen, the increase is not linear, but grows rapidly above the secondary school stage with leaving certificate.[1]

We then come to the principal question; whether the existing mean IQ differences may be attributed entirely or partly to the differences in schooling between the various groups. Since recruitment to secondary schooling is considerably greater from the higher social and income groups than from the lower, there is good reason to ask whether these social variables that are correlated with schooling have not, to a quite appreciable extent, affected the mean differences observed. As has been stated in fuller detail, in another connection, there is a mean increase of about 3 units in the IQ in the highest income groups. Of the four social groups, it is only group 1 that shows a significant mean increase of about 7.5 units. The most »pure» of the social variables is income. Since the latter does not at all give rise to mean differences of the same magnitude, as are due to schooling, it is justifiable to attribute to the latter, the principal role in producing the differences. The mean increase in IQ manifested by social group I, can be mainly attributed to the fact that about 80% of its members received secondary schooling (the majority, about 60%, received senior secondary schooling).

A conclusion which may be drawn as a result of the analysis of the connections of the different variables with the IQ differences is that schooling, at any rate as regards the three lower social groups, has incomparably the greatest significance for the systematic changes in IQ between 10 and 20 years of age.

One may well ask, why the increase in IQ is considerably greater in the senior secondary school and matriculation groups, than in the junior secondary school group. Three reasons for this may be discussed: 1) A certain selection of ability, as regards facility for intellectual training, has taken place on transition from junior secondary school to senior secondary

---

[1] When interpreting these deviations, it should be clearly borne in mind that they are dependent on the size of the groups. M is by definition 0 for the whole of the material, which causes the absolute maximum size of the deviations to be in inverse proportion to the size of the groups in question.

school. 2) A decrease due to the lack of training, which might appear in the junior secondary school group without leaving certificate, on account of the interval between completion of schooling and test administration. 3) A gain due to training in the senior secondary school group, because of more prolonged intellectual training.

Since our junior secondary school group with leaving certificate, only contains those subjects who left school on passing this examination, we do not know what the distribution of the IQ differences was like for *all* who passed this examination. In the transition from junior secondary school, to senior secondary school, the manifested ability (defined by school reports, test scores, etc.), as well as social factors are of importance. In a ten-year follow-up study of the Stockholm population of school children born in 1925, BOALT has succeeded in showing that the correlation between each of the factors, school report, social group and income group, and the transfer to the senior secondary school, is in the vicinity of + .50. In our material, there is no significant difference in terms of the 1938 test, between the group with the junior secondary school leaving certificate, on the one hand, and the two highest groups of schooling on the other. No selection of ability of any importance, seems to have taken place. It is difficult to determine whether those who are more susceptible to training have been selected in this way.

The second explanation of the big increase in IQ in the senior-secondary-school group, viz. loss due to lack of training as regards the junior-secondary-school group with leaving certificate, is more difficult to verify. VERNON, who has carried out investigations in connection with English material, of the development of various forms of achievements between the ages of 14 and 18, concludes: »It appears . . . that general intelligence improves after 14 among the more gifted members of the population who receive further schooling, though not among those who leave school . . .» Here, it is a question of a comparison between those who left school after finishing the primary school and those who continued their schooling until 18 years of age. In our case, there are two groups that have received further schooling, and one of these was tested about 3 years after leaving school, and the other while still attending school or shortly after leaving school. But practically speaking, all the members of the secondary school with leaving certificate, have vocations that afford opportunities for verbal and numerical training, and consequently the loss due to the lack of training after leaving school, must be much less than for those who take up purely manual work.

The third explanation: the gain due to training which is dependent on prolonged theoretical training, may hypothetically, be looked upon as the most important.

We can get the distribution of the IQ deviations irrespectively of their signs. The average deviation for the entire population extends to 8.71

units. The median is 7.0. About one-third of the deviations is under 5 units, and a quarter is over 11 units. A small number of very large deviations exist. Expressed in the form of a correlation coefficient, the connection between IQ 38 and IQ 48, is + .72. This result appears to agree, very largely, with the extremely few investigations that were previously conducted in this field. . . .

A median deviation of 7 units or a correlation of + .72 between the test results obtained at ten and twenty years of age implies, in our opinion, a closer connection between the two testings than could have been expected. The low age (= 9.65 years) at the first testing, the long interval and two different test scales, are conditions that might well have caused the connection to have a lower numerical value than was actually the case. . . .

The deviations between IQ 38 and IQ 48 depend a) on random errors of measurement, »insufficient split-half-reliability», b) on systematic changes in Ss, c) on random changes in the Ss, and d) on the fact that, to some extent, the tests measure different things, test specificities. It may prove of interest to compute the correlation that would have been obtained, had the two tests been perfectly reliable. In this case, in our view, the retest reliabilities should be used for that computation, and not the split-half reliabilities. The reason for this is, firstly, that the latter type of reliability coefficient is often spuriously increased in time-limited tests. If retest coefficients are chosen, then in addition to random errors there is the influence exerted by the inconstancy of the subjects during short intervals. So far as is known, no retest coefficient has been determined for the group test of 1938. Since the latter is relatively short (56 items as against 160 for the I-test 1948), and since the retest coefficients tend to be lower for children than for adults, there is probably little risk of underestimation, if it is assumed that the reliability was + .85 for the 1938 scale. Retest investigations with different intervals have been conducted with I-tests on adult populations. The lowest coefficient was + .91, and the highest + .95. Consequently, it may be expedient to choose the highest coefficient in order that no undue »over-correction» should take place with regard to the influence of the reliabilities on the correlation between the tests. If the values are now inserted in the formula for correction for »attenuation» we obtain a coefficient of + .80, which thus, indicates the probable correlation between the two tests when reliability is perfect. It would then appear that this coefficient's deviation from 1, is partly due to changes in the Ss, and partly to the fact that the tests measure somewhat different functions. The latter factor seems to have played quite an insignificant role. As has been pointed out previously, the tests are, to a great extent, of the same structure. We have ourselves found, that specifically verbal group tests, with quite different test types and applied to a normal population yield a retest coefficient of more than + .90.

It would appear then, that already at ten years of age, one can count on being able to apply group tests with relatively good predictive value, as regards the test scores at a considerably higher age.

To sum up, it may be said that, there is reason to suppose that theoretical schooling, subsequent to leaving the primary school, considerably increases the intellectual level, which is measured with group tests of a conventional type. On an average, the increase lies between 0 and 10 IQ units, according to the scope of the schooling. On an average, the increase amounts for all who have received some form of further schooling to 4.84 units. The senior secondary schooling, raises the level, on an average, by 7—10 units.

CHANGES IN IQ ON DIFFERENT LEVELS OF ABILITY

Changes in IQ With the Test as a Criterion of Ability

So far, we have mainly been occupied with the mean deviations in various groups of schooling between IQ 1938 and 1948. This mean, we have considered in its relationship to various external factors, such as theoretical schooling—and in another connection—social group, income group and the number of children. It is naturally of the greatest interest to determine these mean tendencies, but it is also of interest to investigate whether the systematic changes tend to be different on various levels of ability.

As has already been pointed out, it may be assumed that the IQ deviations between 1938 and 1948 are due to the following factors:

   a) insufficient reliability of the two group-tests,
   b) the systematic influence of certain environmental variables on the Ss,
   c) the random changes that have taken place in the meanwhile,
   d) the specificities of the two tests.

Our aim is to determine the systematic influence that certain environmental variables, in this case especially schooling, have exerted. In this connection, it is important to attempt to decide the part that random changes have played (points a and c). The correlation of + .72 between IQ 1938 and IQ 1948 deviates from 1, partly on account of random changes. But it has to be borne in mind, that the systematic changes contribute even more towards lowering the correlation, since they change the original rank order of the IQ scores. One way of determining the influence of various factors is, to employ the analysis of variance. The total variance on each occasion can be divided into a variance between the groups of schooling and a variance within these groups. Thus, it is possible to estimate how large a part of the total variance on the two occasions is due to variation of schooling.

In this connection we shall, in the first place, endeavour to ascertain what IQ changes took place at various levels of ability. We employ as criteria of ability: a) the group test 1938, and b) teachers' ratings 1938. Since neither of the tests is perfectly reliable, and moreover, to a certain extent, they measure different functions (no doubt they possess a quite important specificity towards one another), a considerable regression effect must be taken into account. We have already defined this phenomenon, and have also pointed out some concrete examples of its influence. If, as in this case, it is desired to measure the »real» systematic changes in intellectual levels of achievement that have taken place at different levels, it is necessary to determine the influence of the regression effect.

TERMAN and McNEMAR were faced with this problem when they conducted their follow-up investigation of the group of »geniuses» that TERMAN had tested in the early 20's. Children with an original IQ over 140 were chosen. At the retest that took place in 1940, it was found, according to the method of computation employed, that a mean regression had occurred of from 10.4 to 17—18 IQ units. This change could be ascribed to four different facts, 1) the insufficient reliability of the tests, 2) the specificities of the tests, 3) systematic changes caused by the environmental conditions and spontaneous growth, and 4) random changes in time. McNEMAR tried to determine the magnitude of the regression effect. For such a highly selected group, as the one in question, the effect was quite considerable and could be estimated to be about ½ σ.

The correlation between IQ 1938 and IQ 1948 is, as has been mentioned, + .72, and the correlation table shows the presence of distinct regression effects. If the regression equations are determined, and if for the various levels of IQ 1938, the corresponding probable values of IQ 1948 are estimated, an expression will be obtained for the regression effect, which is a result of both the random and systematic changes, without separating the latter. The equation for the determination of the probable scores (x) 1948 that correspond to various scores (y) 1938 is

$$x = 0.72 \ y + 28.$$

From this equation, we obtain the following series of values for x and y, which make it possible to determine the amount of regression on different levels:

TABLE I

IQ 1938 (x)	IQ 1948 (y)	Regression
70	78.4	+8.4
80	85.6	+5.6
90	92.8	+2.8
100	100	±0
110	107.2	−2.8
120	114.4	−5.6
130	121.6	−8.4

The Distribution of the Material on Different Levels of Ability According to the 1938 Test

On every Level of Ability, the Differentiation of the Schooling, and the Changes of IQ, are Reported. For every level of Ability, the Mean Values in the 1948 Test for those who Received Primary Schooling (M_p) or Secondary Schooling (M_s) are given, and also the Number of Persons in the Groups of Schooling, who in 1948 where in a Higher (h), the same (s) or a lower (l) IQ-Class in Comparison with 1938

IQ 1938	Primary school			Junior secondary school without leaving certif.		Junior secondary school with leaving certif.		Senior secondary school without leaving certif.		Matriculation		M_p (IQ)	M_s (IQ)	M_p-M_s (IQ)
	Absol. (n)	%*	h, s or l	%	h, s or l	%	h, s or l	%	h, s or l	%	h, s or l			
65– 74	29	97	14 / 13 / 1	3	1	—	—	—	—	—	—	76	(105)	(29)
75– 84	79	92	40 / 25 / 8	3	2 / 1	3	2	1	1	1	1	86	(101)	(15)
85– 94	123	90	43 / 45 / 25	4	4 / 1	2	2	4	4	—	—	92	101	9
95–104	125	75	26 / 31 / 37	5	4 / 2	10	9 / 3	7	9	3	4	98	104	6
105–114	145	55	5 / 30 / 44	8	2 / 5 / 4	18	13 / 9	17	17 / 7 / 1	2	3 / 1	101	115	14
115–124	92	42	1 / 11 / 27	3	1 / 2	27	15 / 9	22	5 / 12 / 3	6	3 / 2	108	118	10
125–134	20	25	1 / 4	5	1	30	4 / 2	35	3 / 4	5	1	(118)	125	(7)

* The percentage refers to the absolute number in each row.

Thus, a regression effect of about $\frac{1}{2} \sigma$ is obtained automatically on levels 2 σ from the mean for the whole population. The question is now, to what extent does this effect on various levels of ability depend on random errors of measurement, and how far is it due to systematic changes? In what follows, we shall attempt, with the aid of various approaches, to find an answer to this question.

In Table II, each row gives the frequency of schooling in each class of 10 units of the IQ 1938. Within each class, the various groups of schooling are kept separate. With regard to each individual, it is stated whether in IQ 1948, he was in a higher (h), lower (1) or in the same (s) class as in 1938. Finally, we have determined the mean difference within each class, between those who only received primary schooling and those who had attended secondary schools. This difference is shown in the column farthest to the right in the table. In view of the few individuals in the extreme groups, we have mainly to regard the interval 85–124. There appears to be a tendency for the difference to increase in this interval, between those who have received primary schooling and those who have received secondary schooling (see Table III).

TABLE III

IQ-class 1938	Mean IQ difference between primary school and secondary school	No. of all individuals in the class interval with	
		Junior secondary school	Senior secondary school
85– 94	9	6%	4%
95–104	6	14%	11%
105–114	14	26%	19%
115–124	10	30%	28%

In this connection, however, it should be borne in mind that, on account of the selective influence of the social factors, the original difference between those who received primary schooling and those who received secondary schooling, is somewhat less at lower levels of ability. The mean difference for all four IQ classes is between 9–10 units. We had ascertained previously that secondary schooling should raise the IQ, on an average, by 5 units. The increase observed here, is due to two facts: 1) We are here dealing with subjects, some of whom received primary schooling and others secondary schooling, who originally were members of the same class interval of 10 units. It is very likely that the members of a given IQ class, who had received secondary schooling, had, *from the outset,* a higher test mean than those who had only received primary schooling. 2) We are here comparing subjects who had received primary schooling with those who had had secondary schooling, and not each of these two groups with itself (IQ 1938 with IQ 1948).

As follows from the values given above, the difference, between the mean IQ-deviations of those who had only received primary schooling and those who had received secondary schooling, was about 7 units. Con-

TABLE IV

Frequency of Ascent or Descent into Another Class Interval between 1938 and 1948 in Various Groups of Schooling

(The figures in % of the respective groups of schooling in the class intervals in question. Investigated range of IQ 105–134.)

IQ position 1948 compared with 1938	Primary school (n = 123)	Junior secondary school with leaving certificate (n = 57)	Senior secondary school and matriculation (n = 62)
higher interval	5	18	44
same interval	34	56	43
lower interval	61	26	13

sequently, we have no grounds for rejecting the estimate of 5–7 units for the increase in IQ due to secondary schooling.

It is of special interest to study columns »h, s and 1» in Table II where it is shown if the IQ 1948 for the persons in question was higher, the same or lower than their IQ 1938. From the column representing the primary school groups, it will be seen that the regression effect is very marked in the extreme IQ intervals. Out of 28 subjects whose IQ in 1938 was in the interval 65–74, 14 had gone up to a higher interval, 13 had remained in the same interval, and only 1 had gone down to a lower interval. Out of 39 subjects with primary school, and belonging to the interval 115–124, 27 had gone down, 11 had remained in the same interval, and only 1 had gone up to a higher interval. When we examine the columns for secondary schooling, it is again confirmed that the effect of schooling counterbalances the regression effect. To what extent this occurs, is clearly shown in Table V.

TABLE V

IQ 1938 Interval	Number (in %) of S's who descended to a lower interval between 1938 and 1948	
	Primary school	Secondary school
95–104	25	—
105–114	56	14
115–124	70	26

In the interval 105–114, but 5 out of 79 (6%) of those who had only received primary schooling, ascended to a higher interval; while not less than 31 out of 66 (47%) of those who had received secondary schooling, did so.

Finally, we can compare the IQ-changes in the 105–134 range of the various groups of schooling; that is to say, in a section of the material that was above average in the 1938 test (Table IV). On account of the regression effect, a very large number of those who had only received primary schooling had descended to a lower interval. Among those who had received secondary schooling, the regression effect had been counterbalanced by the effect of training, with the result, that ascent into higher intervals takes place increasingly, proportionally to the grade of schooling.

By way of summary, the following may be stated: Dividing the material into various levels of ability in accordance with the 1938 test, it has been possible to study in greater detail the influence of schooling on these different levels. Thus, descent to a lower IQ-interval has taken place in 61% of those who had received primary schooling, in 26% of those who had had secondary schooling with leaving certificate, and in 13% of those who had received senior secondary schooling, all of whom had been above average in the 1938 test. It was possible to carry out a study of the interaction between the effect of schooling and the regression effect.

Teachers in the different classes were asked to classify the children in 5 groups with regard to their ability. The groups were as follows: B (gifted), M + (above average), M (average), M − (below average), and S (poor ability). Further, they were asked to indicate, which pupils in the class belonged, from the point of view of ability, to the 15% most or least gifted. Naturally, the two latter groups coincided, to a great extent, with the B and S groups. In Table VI, the IQ-differences have been given for the 15% most and least gifted pupils, according to the teachers' ratings. Furthermore, the differences have been given separately for those among the gifted pupils who only received primary schooling, and for those who received secondary schooling.

The mean IQ for the 15% most gifted pupils was in 1938 about 115. The regression effect according to the equation given above, should be 4.2. According to table 5, we see that the mean IQ-deviation for those among the 15% most gifted pupils who only had primary schooling, was −4.5, which corresponds with the calculated regression effect. Previously, by studying the influence of several important environmental variables upon IQ, we found that schooling has a considerably greater systematic effect on IQ than the other variables have. Those among the 15% most gifted pupils, who received some kind of further theoretical schooling, do not show any significant IQ-difference.

Here, schooling and regression effect have cancelled each other out. Practically all the members of the group have passed their lower certificate examination or have completed the main part of the curriculum for the

TABLE VI

IQ-Differences (IQ_{48}—IQ_{38}) for the 15% Most Gifted and the 15% Least Gifted Pupils, According to the Teachers' Ratings

	15% most gifted Primary school	Secondary school	15% least gifted (only primary school)
n..................	22	49	63
mean IQ difference ...	−4.54 ± 1.48	0.00 ± 1.15	0.32 ± 1.32
σ..................	6.96 ± 1.05	8.04 ± 0.81	10.48 ± 0.93

senior secondary school. On the basis of our findings here, we may state that, further schooling at least up to passing the lower certificate examination increases the IQ in conventional group tests by 4–5 units among the most gifted pupils. This agrees in principle with our previous findings.

In Table VI, we find that the mean IQ-deviation for the 15% least gifted pupils amounts to + 0.32 units. Their mean in the 1938 testing was about 85, i. e. their position was 1 σ below the total average. According to the regression equation, we have the right to expect a regression effect of + 4.2 units. The IQ-deviation of + 0.32 differs significantly from the calculated regression value. Since none of the 15% least gifted pupils received any further theoretical schooling, we have no means of judging what effect theoretical schooling has on this level. The most plausible explanation of the fact that the IQ-deviation is 4 units less than what could have been expected is, that those who are intellectually the least gifted, on account of lack of training or for similar reasons, have regressed by an average of about 4 units as compared with the rest of the material. This also agrees with the investigations that have been conducted to ascertain the development of achievement on different levels of ability for pupils in their teens. The best pupils retain their level, even if the effect of schooling is excluded, while those intellectually least gifted regress.

VERNON has been able to show the same results in his follow-up investigation of children between 14–20 years.

The changes that take place on the various levels of ability can be studied more closely. . . . Before we try to interpret the IQ-differences obtained, it may be appropriate to attempt to determine the amount of the regression effect on all 5 levels. The following values are then obtained:

TABLE VII

	Gifted	Above aver.	Aver.	Below aver.	Poorly gifted
Observed IQ_{38}	113.5	107.4	100.0	91.5	83.9
Probable IQ_{48}	109.7	105.3	100.0	93.9	88.4
Regression:	−3.8	−2.1	±0	+2.4	+4.5

As we have already seen, the *primary* school group displays the least relative systematic changes; above all, this group is not influenced by the marked systematic effect that secondary schooling exerts. Consequently, it should manifest the regression effect much more clearly. It should be borne in mind, that those who received only primary schooling, show the lowest mean IQ-deviation, since they constitute the majority, and $M_{diff.} = O$ for the whole population.

By comparing, the IQ-deviations on various levels of ability obtained for those who received only primary schooling, with the calculated regression effects, we obtain the following series:

TABLE VIII

	Gifted	Above aver.	Aver.	Below aver.	Poorly gifted
Observed average IQ-difference	−3.5	−3.3	−1.5	+0.4	+0.5
Calculated regression effect	−3.8	−2.1	±0	+2.4	+4.5
Deviation:	+0.3	−1.2	−1.5	−2.0	−4.0

It appears that the deviation increases the more, the farther the distance from the highest level of ability. The great deviation between the calculated regression effect and the observed IQ-deviation on the lowest level of ability, we previously ascribed to the relative decline on this level of ability, *inter alia,* depending on lack of training, which occurs when the subjects are in their teens. There does not appear to be any reason for rejecting this explanation.

The next step is an analysis of the effect of *secondary* schooling on various levels of ability. This analysis is made more difficult, to some extent, because the »secondary schooling» of this group varies on the different levels of ability, with regard to the proportion of pupils who had received junior secondary schooling with leaving certificate, to those who had had senior secondary schooling. As will be seen by referring to Table II the differences in frequency are not so great that we are unable to ignore them for the time being. By comparing IQ-differences with the calculated regression effects on various levels of ability, we obtain the series of values shown in Table IX.

The deviations in a positive direction that we were able to show between observed IQ-differences and the calculated regression effect, must be connected with the systematic influence in a direction conducive to achievement. The average effect of training, that secondary schooling seems to give on these levels of ability, appears to be about 6 IQ units. By means of the procedure we employed in Table I, we found that the IQ-difference for those

TABLE IX

	Gifted	Above aver.	Aver.	Below. aver.	Poorly gifted
Observed average IQ-difference	+0.9	+5.4	+6.6	—	—
Calculated regression effect	−3.8	−2.1	±0	—	—
Deviation:	+4.7	+7.5	+6.6	—	—

who had received junior secondary schooling with leaving certificate, was 3 units; and for those who had received senior secondary schooling, it was 7 units. If these two groups are taken together, we obtain a mean increase in IQ of 5 units on account of the additional secondary schooling.

To sum up, it may be stated that, schooling up to the stage of junior secondary school with leaving certificate, or higher, raises the IQ by 5–7 units. Those who do not receive any further theoretical schooling beyond the primary school stage, show on an average, a slight regression of 1–2 units; and the regression is greatest, about 4 units, on the lowest level of ability, whereas those who are on the highest level of ability, maintain a status quo.

The following brief paper represents an ingenious and unusual use of the personal correlates of intelligence. The reader
should note the extensive and thorough cross-validation
procedure applied here in the progressive refinement of the
scale. Such cross validation is mandatory in a study of this
kind.

A Nonintellectual Intelligence Test*

HARRISON G. GOUGH

1953

The title of this paper may be something of a misnomer, for it is not at
all certain that the testing instrument which is going to be presented is,
actually, a measure of intellect. Nevertheless, it does correlate significantly
with conventional tests of intelligence, and seems to reveal other properties
which suggest that something along the line of intellectual ability, or perhaps more precisely intellectual efficiency, is being appraised. The other
part of the title—the "nonintellectual" part—has not been the cause of
any misgivings, because, as will be seen shortly, the test instrument does
not call for any problem solving, reasoning, abstract thinking, or any of the
other mental functions which are traditionally regarded as the key factors
in defining and measuring intelligence.

The two immediate aims of this project were first, to determine whether
a criterion-specific set of personality inventory items could be assembled
which would correlate significantly with accepted measures of intellect, and
second, if this was successful, to determine whether the individual items
could be combined in a scale which would have anything approaching
practical significance and value.

The second objective is added, because, as we know for instance from
work on the Rorschach, a series of variables can easily be identified which
will correlate significantly with intellect, but which will seldom rise above
the level of $+ .20$ and $+ .25$ into a region of more dependable utility when
pooled in a composite.

PROCEDURES

The first step in the present project was to write a series of criterion-
specific inventory items, and also to select appropriate items from standard
sources. An example of a specially written item would be, "I get sort of

* From the *Journal of Consulting Psychology*, 17 (1953), pp. 242-246. Reprinted
by permission of the author and the American Psychological Association.

TABLE I
Item Statistics for Four Items from the *Ie* Scale

	Per cent saying "True"					
	Higher scores on intellectual ability measures Schools			Lower scores on intellectual ability measures Schools		
Item	School A (N 28)	School B and C (N 21)	School D (N 48)	School A (N 28)	School B and C (N 21)	School D (N 48)
1. It is more important that a father be kind than that he be successful.	79	95	92	71	76	69
2. Parents are much too easy on their children nowadays.	36	43	46	50	71	67
3. I am not afraid of picking up a disease or germs from door knobs.	86	81	85	79	67	67
4. Most people make friends because friends are likely to be useful to them.	21	19	29	46	71	77

annoyed with writers who go out of their way to use strange and unusual words," and of an item from a standard questionnaire, in this case the MMPI, "I gossip a little at times."

These items were then reproduced in a booklet and administered to the senior students in four Minnesota high schools. In each school, the responses of students in the upper 25 per cent of the range on a conventional intelligence test were compared with those of students in the lower quartile.

TABLE II
Summary Statistics for the First (76-Item) Intellectual Efficiency (*Ie*) Scale in the Original Samples

Sample	N	M	SD	r*
School A	135	52.44	8.51	.47
School B	35	51.34	9.20	.68
School C	66	51.41	9.41	.64
School D	205	51.93	9.51	.54

* Intercorrelations between the *Ie* scale and a conventional IQ test in each of the schools.

Table I provides an example of the way in which the analysis was conducted. Items which showed consistent and significant differences in all Hi-Lo comparisons were retained for the scale. Altogether, 76 items were identified which met this criterion.

These 76 items were scored on the original samples with the results indicated in Table II. The next step was to cross-validate this scale. Table III presents the results observed in six cross-validating samples. In the first five, only MMPI items were available, but the sixth sample took the full 76-item scale. All of the correlations are clearly significant, statistically, and all save one are high enough to be of some practical value. An interesting finding here was the degree to which the scale retained its validity when checked in the graduate student samples where one would encounter rather severe attenuation of the criterion measure.

TABLE III
Summary Statistics for the First Ie Scale in Six Cross-Validating Samples*

Sample	N	M	SD	r†
I. For the abbreviated (59-item) scale.				
1. St. Cloud ninth grade	82	38.09	7.46	.53
2. Minneapolis ninth grade	190	39.44	8.24	.36
3. St. Cloud twelfth grade, 1947	231	39.55	7.50	.52
4. St. Cloud twelfth grade, 1948	271	40.30	7.70	.47
5. University of California advanced graduate students	40	48.58	4.02	.42
II. For the full (76-item) scale.				
1. University of California first-year graduate students in psychology	30	63.20	5.12	.44

* The first five samples were scored only for the 59 items taken from the MMPI. The psychology sample took the full scale.

† For the two graduate student samples, the criterion test was the Miller Analogies Test, form g. For the other samples, conventional IQ measures were used.

The individual items were also checked in the two graduate student samples, and it was discovered that 24 of them were contributing only slightly, if at all, to the correlations with the criterion tests. It was decided, accordingly, to eliminate them and to reduce the scale to 52 items. This 52-item scale is the one which is currently being used, and it is also the version included in the California Psychological Inventory. These 52 items, and the scored responses, are listed below.

1. I have had very peculiar and strange experiences. (False) 2. It often seems that my life has no meaning. (False) 3. When someone does me a wrong, I feel I should pay him back if I can, just for the principle of the thing. (False) 4. Any job is all right with me, so long as it pays well. (False) 5. People often expect too much of me. (False) 6. I get sort of annoyed with writers who go out of their way to use strange and unusual words. (False) 7. Success is a matter of will power. (False)

8. When in a group of people I have trouble thinking of the right things to talk about. (False) 9. It is more important that a father be kind than that he be successful. (True) 10. I was a slow learner in school. (False) 11. I must admit I

have no great desire to learn new things. (False) 12. My skin seems to be unusually sensitive to touch. (False) 13. Parents are much too easy on their children nowadays. (False) 14. I read at least ten books a year. (True)

15. I have the wanderlust and am never happy unless I am roaming or traveling about. (False) 16. My parents have often disapproved of my friends. (False) 17. Teachers often expect too much work from the students. (False) 18. I am not afraid of picking up a disease or germs from door knobs. (True) 19. I am quite a fast reader. (True) 20. I have had more than my share of things to worry about. (False) 21. I feel like giving up quickly when things go wrong. (False)

22. In a group of people I would not be embarrassed to be called upon to start a discussion or give an opinion about something I know well. (True) 23. I like to read about history. (True) 24. In school I found it very hard to talk before the class. (False) 25. I dread the thought of an earthquake. (False) 26. I like science. (True) 27. I am bothered by people outside, on street cars, in stores, etc. watching me. (False) 28. I have never been in trouble because of my sex behavior. (True)

29. I often get feelings like crawling, burning, tingling, or "going to sleep" in different parts of my body. (False) 30. I seem to be about as capable and smart as most others around me. (True) 31. I like poetry. (True) 32. I am quite often not in on the gossip and talk of the group I belong to. (False) 33. A windstorm terrifies me. (False) 34. I enjoy a race or game better when I bet on it. (False) 35. Most people make friends because friends are likely to be useful to them. (False)

36. I have never seen a vision. (True) 37. The future seems hopeless to me. (False) 38. I have had no difficulty starting or holding my urine. (True) 39. I often feel as if the world was just passing me by. (False) 40. I get pretty discouraged with the law when a smart lawyer gets a criminal free. (True) 41. The only interesting part of the newspaper is the "funnies." (False) 42. I gossip a little at times. (True)

43. At times I have been so entertained by the cleverness of a crook that I have hoped he would get by with it. (True) 44. I have had attacks in which I could not control my movements or speech, but in which I knew what was going on around me. (False) 45. I have had no difficulty in starting or holding my bowel movement. (True) 46. I like to read about science. (True) 47. I do not read every editorial in the newspaper every day. (True) 48. If people had not had it in for me, I would have been much more successful. (False) 49. I daydream very little. (False)

50. I have often been frightened in the middle of the night. (False) 51. I work under a great deal of tension. (False) 52. I seldom worry about my health. (True)

A review of these items is quite interesting in highlighting some of the personological correlates of general intelligence. The best method of extracting the immediate implications of the items is simply to read the list carefully, but as an aid in forming rational groupings and clusters the following synopsis is provided:

1. Self-confidence and self-assurance, freedom from unsubstantiated fears and apprehensions.
2. Effective social technique and adjustment, sense of social acceptability without dependence on others; not suspicious, touchy, or overly sensitive.

3. Good physiological functioning, absence of minor, debilitating symptoms and complaints.

4. Liking, and respect, for intellectual pursuits; wide range of interests.

Three additional samples were then obtained in order to cross-validate the 52-item revised scale. Table IV presents the findings. The validity coefficients are about what they were with the first six cross-validating samples, so it appears that the shortening did not weaken the scale's effectiveness.

TABLE IV

Summary Statistics for the Revised (52-Item) *Ie* Scale in Three Cross-Validating Samples

Sample	N	M	SD	r*
1. Rock Island, Illinois, high school	461	33.90	7.07	.49
2. Wellsville, New York, high school	230	34.08	6.39	.50
3. University of California undergraduate psychology students	43	40.05	5.16	.42

* Intercorrelation between the Ie scale and a conventional measure of intelligence in each sample.

Final high school grade averages were also available for the Rock Island sample. For the females, the correlation between grades and tested IQ was .56, and between grades and the *Ie* scale .59. For males the correlation between grades and IQ was .51 and between grades and the *Ie* scale .31.

In order to provide an over-all picture of the summary statistics at this point, the means and standard deviations for each sample have been proportionately equated to the 52-item test version with the results indicated in Table V. In this table one can observe a consistent rise in mean scores from junior high school groups, through senior high school and college undergraduate levels, to a final culmination in the graduate student samples.

ADJECTIVE CHECK LIST

The last data to be presented on this scale have to do with the "social-stimulus values" of persons scoring high and low on it. Forty graduate students seen in an intensive 3-day assessment at the University of California Institute of Personality Assessment and Research were given the scale. Staff judges completed Gough Adjective Check Lists for each assessee, and then these observer-reports were composited. Adjectives differentiating sig-

TABLE V

Ie Scale Summary Statistics for all Samples*

Samples	N	M	SD	r	SE
I. Original samples					
1. Bemidji twelfth grade	135	35.87	5.82	.47	.09
2. Dawson twelfth grade	35	35.12	6.29	.68	.17
3. Redwood Falls twelfth grade	66	35.16	6.44	.64	.12
4. St. Cloud twelfth grade, 1949	205	35.52	6.50	.54	.07
II. Cross-validating samples					
1. St. Cloud ninth grade	82	31.80	6.52	.53	.11
2. Minneapolis ninth grade	190	34.74	7.26	.36	.07
3. Rock Island high school	461	33.90	7.07	.49	.05
4. St. Cloud twelfth grade, 1947	231	34.84	6.61	.52	.07
5. St. Cloud twelfth grade, 1948	271	35.50	6.78	.47	.06
6. Wellsville high school	230	34.08	6.39	.50	.07
7. University of California undergraduate psychology students	43	40.05	5.16	.42	.15
8. University of California first-year graduate students in psychology	30	43.23	3.50	.44	.19
9. University of California advanced graduate students	40	42.80	3.54	.42	.16

* Scores for samples not taking the final 52-item scale were proportionately corrected to equate them to this standard.

nificantly between the composite reports on the 10 highest and 10 lowest scores on the *Ie* scale are given below:

  1. Adjectives checked more frequently about higher scorers.

adaptable	kind
appreciative	logical
capable	obliging
clear-thinking	persistent
conscientious	planful
considerate	pleasant
cooperative	reasonable
dependable	realistic
energetic	reliable
enterprising	responsible
helpful	sincere
honest	stable
industrious	thorough
interests wide	

  2. Adjectives checked more frequently about lower scores.

aloof	impatient
cynical	individualistic
defensive	moody
deliberate	resentful

effeminate   sarcastic
headstrong   sharp-witted

The general trend of adjectives ascribed is quite clear. High scorers are described as capable, clear-thinking, dependable, logical, realistic, etc., and low scorers as cynical, headstrong, impatient, and resentful.

The adjective findings lend support to the notion that the *Ie* scale is measuring something like personal or intellectual efficiency, with their emphasis on characteristics such as industriousness, planfulness, reliability, and thoroughness.

SUMMARY

A study was made of the relationship between intellectual measures and a series of opinion, attitude, and self-description items, believed, on a priori and theoretical grounds, to covary with intellect. Fifty-two items were found to possess empirical validity. These items were assembled in a scale which yielded median validity coefficients of approximately .58 in four original samples, and of .47 in nine check samples.

Adjectival descriptions of subjects scoring high on the scale tended to stress factors of dependability, intellectual clarity, persistence, and planfulness. The decision was made to call the scale a measure of "intellectual efficiency" in order to reflect these properties.

This paper represents a novel combination of twin data and factor-analytic techniques. The reader should observe with caution that the writer assumes that environmental variables have exactly equal weight for identical and fraternal twins. The writer's intention to specify the locus of resemblance of twin pairs by analyzing the variance into its constituent factorial dimensions indicates how far the field has advanced since the earlier studies reported in this volume.

An Experimental Study of the Inheritance of Intelligence*

D. B. BLEWETT

1954

Although the development of factor analysis has led, at least operationally, to more precise description of the field of human cognition, controversy as to the nature of intelligence has not ended, although there has been a marked narrowing of the differences between extremes of view. On the one hand, the monarcheal, or single factor idea, has been superseded by Spearman's two factor theory which has in turn been extended to the consideration of group factors. On the other hand, the multifactorial approach has been narrowed and refined by Thurstonian Multiple Factor Analysis. The primary Mental Abilities described by this method were found to be intercorrelated giving rise to a second order factor which Thurstone has suggested, may be not unlike Spearman's "g". Despite this basic disagreement as to the nature of the variable under consideration, results obtained have led investigators to almost complete agreement that what they have measured as intelligence is largely genetically determined.

However, the problem of determining the effect of inheritance upon the several primary mental abilities has not been reported upon. These abilities would seem to offer the most clear-cut operational definition of intelligence available to date. This question of relative genetic determination of the various primary mental abilities can be encompassed in an experiment framed to yield information central to the problem of whether intelligence is a complex of genetically determined primary abilities which have in common only the correlated effects of environmental additions to their basic form: or whether, like Vernon's group factors v:ed and to a lesser extent k:m, they are the sum of an underlying "g" and a narrower "group" ability which is educable.

* Adapted from *The Journal of Mental Science*, 100 (1954), pp. 922-933. Reprinted by permission of the author and the publisher.

Thurstone found his ability measures to be intercorrelated, giving rise to a second order factor. If this second order factor is comparable to Spearman's "g", it would follow that intelligence could be regarded as a core of "g" upon which environmental influences impose a consistent though diverse pressure leading to the relative hyper-development of certain facets of ability.

Under these circumstances, second order factor score estimates should show a greater degree of genetic determination than any single ability score and we may investigate the following hypotheses.

Hypothesis I: The second order factor derived from primary mental abilities test scores is in large part determined by heredity, and such individual differences as appear with respect to it cannot be accounted for in terms of environmental influences.

Hypothesis II: The second order factor score will be determined by heredity to a greater degree than any of the primary mental ability scores which contribute to it.

The method of twin study used in this investigation is one that has been used in a very large number of previous studies. In this method, differences found between identical twins being due to environment alone, are compared with differences between fraternal twins which are due to heredity and environment combined. Thus, where a marked discrepancy in difference scores is found between groups (identical twins showing less difference than fraternal twins), the influence of heredity is predominant. Where there is little discrepancy in difference scores, inheritance does not function in a causative role.

The twin method was pioneered in the 1883 study by Galton. Galton found that twins who were very much alike as children did not tend to become less alike, nor did twins who were unlike as children tend to grow more alike through living together. From this he concluded that environmental effects produce little change in physical and mental make-up which must, therefore, be mainly inherited.

Thorndike used an interesting method in carrying out the first twin study to employ psychological tests of the modern sort. These were tests which, on *a priori* grounds, opposed tasks which would be little modified by educational background and learning, to those in which learning played a major part. Finding no closer similarity in the latter than in the former, he concluded that the observed similarities were due to inheritance.

By 1924, Merriman was able to use standardized tests such as the Stanford Binet Scale and the Army Beta. He found much greater similarity between like-sexed twins than between unlike-sexed twins; results which were later confirmed by Wingfield and Hirsch in similar studies.

Further studies have established that the level of correlation between intelligence test scores of identical twins is generally above .90, whereas correlations for fraternal pairs tend to be lower, ranging upwards from .50.

Although in the reported studies many tests of general intelligence have been used and their scores have been shown to be affected by inheritance, no presently published study has gone a step further and sought information regarding the degree of inheritance of general intelligence as defined by factor scores. Another unanswered problem arises in connection with the relative genetic determination of scores on the Primary Mental Abilities Test. These scores are intended by Thurstone to represent factor scores and have been used as such in this investigation.

This emphasis on the use of factor scores rather than individual test scores is considered essential in view of a criticism brought forth by Eysenck and Prell. It seems requisite to discuss this criticism which bears upon twin studies of intelligence. They state: "Unless we can analyse the total variance of a test into its constituent parts, and measure these parts separately, no scientifically tenable conclusion can be drawn from the data."

They draw this conclusion by pointing out that the total variance of a test comprises general factor variance, group and specific factor variance and error variance. Assuming that more or less equal proportions of the variance are due on the one hand to the general factor variance, and on the other hand to group and specific factor variance (error variance being disregarded), it follows that equally high inter-twin coefficients could result either if the general factor alone is completely determined by inheritance, if the group and specific factors alone are completely so determined, or if both are genetically determined to an intermediate degree.

By the use of factor scores and scores from the P.M.A. "factor" tests in this study, the above difficulty is avoided.

The sample was drawn from four Metropolitan Boroughs in South London. This was done with the co-operation of the London County Council, who wrote to Headmasters of all the L.C.C. Secondary Schools in the Boroughs of Camberwell, Southwark, Lambeth and Lewisham, requesting a report of any twins on their registers.

TABLE I

Age Distribution, Zygosity and Sex of the Experimental Group

	Number of cases			
	Female		Male	
Age in months	Identical	Fraternal	Identical	Fraternal
140–149................	1	1	1	0
150–159................	3	2	3	1
160–169................	4	4	3	8
170–179................	4	3	4	4
180–189................	1	3	2	0
Mean age	165.3	167.8	166.8	166.8
Standard deviation	11.8	11.1	12.1	6.7

In this way 102 pairs of twins were located. The parents of 87 of these pairs were contacted by letter requesting permission to test the twins at the Maudsley Hospital. Permission was granted by the parents in the case of 59 pairs, from which group 56 pairs were subsequently tested. Data concerning the age, sex and ovularity of this group are summarized in Table I.

*　　*　　*

The method of sampling through the schools has been criticized as being subject to selective error. The selective factor here leads to an over-estimation of the closeness of relationship between results obtained by fraternal twins. This comes about since the twins most likely to be overlooked by the teachers are those fraternal twins who are quite dissimilar in appearance and behaviour.

A rough check on the adequacy of the sampling can be made by comparing the number of binovular and uniovular twins reported. Census figures indicate that some 65 per cent. of all twins are of the same sex. Since all unlike sexed twins are binovular, it follows that 35 per cent. of twins are unlike sexed binovulars. Assuming equal distribution of sex among binovular twins, 35 per cent. of twins will be like-sexed binovulars. In our sample we dealt only with like-sexed twins, so that the expected ratio of referrals would be 35 fraternal twins to 30 identical twins. From this we can determine the probability of a statistically significant sampling error. Of the 102 cases referred, ovularity was not established in five cases. There remain 50 pairs of fraternal twins and 47 pairs of identical twins, that is 48 per cent. of those referred are identical and 52 per cent. are fraternal. The expected frequency would be 46 per cent. identical and 54 per cent. fraternal. The x^2 in this case is .16 and P greater than .50. The difference is clearly not significant.

*　　*　　*

One further source of error in twin studies is pointed out by Anastasi and Foley. This is the mis-diagnosis of pairs of fraternal twins who are extremely alike, as identical. This results in a dilution of the identical sample and tends to decrease the differences between intra-identical and intra-fraternal correlations. Here also the error, if present, would tend to work against the considerations lending support to the hypotheses.

The criteria used in this study to differentiate between identical and fraternal pairs of twins were the following:

1. Facial features.
2. General habitus.
3. Hair colour and distribution.
4. Iris pigmentation.
5. Shape of ears.

6. Teeth.
7. Standing height.
8. Weight.
9. Ability to taste Phenyl-thio-carbamide.
10. Blood groupings.
11. Fingerprints.

For criteria 1 to 6, a three-point rating scale of closeness of similarity such as that used by Eysenck and Prell was utilized. Criteria 7 and 8 were straightforward measures in inches and pounds. For the tasting test with phenyl-thio-carbamide the subject was handed two test tubes, one filled with water and the other with a 1 in 20,000 solution of P.T.C. He was asked to describe any difference in the taste of the two liquids. Blood grouping was done at the Lister Institute by Race and Sanger who have demonstrated how to estimate, on the basis of parental blood groupings, the probability that same sexed twins with the same blood groups are dizygotic. Fingerprint analysis was carried out by the Genetics Department of the Maudsley Hospital, using the complex Discriminant Function Score developed by Slater. Reports giving the probability of binovularity in each pair were returned.

Twin identification was carried on for criteria 1 to 6 by three judges who made independent assessments.

In the sample generally, there was little difficulty in distinguishing between fraternal and identical twins. The fraternal pairs, with one exception, were quite obviously unlike in appearance, and even in the much more difficult task of determining identicality, pronounced doubt was present in only one case. Thus on the basis of appearance alone only two cases offered serious difficulty in diagnosis. These two difficult pairs were readily classified on the basis of taste reactions to phenyl-thio-carbamide, blood groupings and fingerprints.

It is interesting to contrast this with the more objective measures provided by blood groupings and fingerprint analysis.

While all pairs identical in appearance had the same blood types, it was found that three pairs, classified by appearance, taste reaction to P.T.C. and fingerprints as fraternal also had homogeneous blood groupings. It transpired that this was a result of the marked similarity between the blood groups of the parents.

On the basis of fingerprint analysis Nixon reports a mis-classification of 13 per cent. of the identical pairs and 42 per cent. of the fraternal pairs and overlapping in 60.7 per cent. of the cases. He points out that the very low probability of obtaining so high a mis-classification of fraternal pairs using Slater's discriminant function, indicates that this particular sample of fraternal twins is atypically similar as regards fingerprints.

In summary, it seems that the best method of differentiating between identical and fraternal twins is to make use of several indices, for in cases in which one index fails there is most frequently unanimous agreement among the other measures.

The intelligence tests used were the Thurstone's Chicago tests for the Primary Mental Abilities for age 11–17, and the Nufferno Tests of Intellectual Level and Intellectual Speed. The twins were tested in pairs at the Maudsley Hospital and tests of intelligence were administered in the above order. In all cases the tests were administered in early afternoon.

The P.M.A. Tests are in such general usage that it would serve no purpose to describe them here. The directions given in the Revised Manual were followed in administration and Thurstone's scoring methods were used.

The Nufferno Tests are as yet unpublished and a brief discussion of their rationale and general form might be useful at this point. The tests are devised to take into account the generally neglected fact that in attempting any problem a person may derive a correct answer, a wrong answer, or no answer at all. Since most intelligence tests are scored in terms of correct answers returned in given period, they yield composite scores involving these three types of behaviour in amounts which vary between individuals. To assess intellectual speed properly, time spent in arriving at unscorable solutions (i.e., incorrectly answered or abandoned items) must not be taken into account. Accordingly, the Speed Test was so devised as to give scores involving only time spent in producing correct answers.

The test is made up of letter series items such as those used in the Reasoning test of the P.M.A. battery, found to be of equal difficulty, that is, items passed by the same percentage of standardizing groups. They are relatively easy having been passed by 80 per cent. of that group. Stress is laid on speed not only in the instruction when the subject is told to work as quickly as he can, but also when, at a signal given every twenty seconds, he circles the last item he has completed.

In scoring, intervals during which wrong answers have been returned are disregarded. The score is the average of the logarithm of the time in seconds taken to solve each item, this score being used because solution time was found to increase disproportionately to item difficulty, whereas the relationship between log time and item difficulty was found to be linear. The score so derived appears to be a unidimensional measure of intellectual speed, being independent of level (for at least the top 80 per cent. of the population) since the test items are of equal difficulty and being purified of the effects of time spent in obtaining unscorable answers.

The Power or Level test is made up of letter series problems in cyclical order of difficulty. The usual time limit is thirty minutes, the subject being told that he has ample time for the test and that the examination is to determine not how quickly he can work but rather, how difficult a problem he can solve. He is accordingly instructed to try as hard as possible to complete each item as he comes to it and to leave no problem undone until he is certain that he cannot answer it. In the present study the length of the battery limited the time available for the test to 20 minutes.

Speed does not affect the score to the degree that it does scores in most intelligence tests since a subject can obtain as high a score by completing only the first section of ten items as by attempting all of the fifty items in the five sections of the test. Beyond the first set of items the cycles attempted only increase the reliability of the estimate of intellectual level, as the score is the average number of items correctly completed in the sections attempted.

This score is regarded by Furneaux and by Eysenck as a composite one including, as well as a measure of intellectual level, an element of persistence, enhanced by the fact that time necessary to complete problems correctly increases markedly as item difficulty is increased. However, the test is no more at fault in this regard than other intelligence tests, and would appear to be a much better measure of level than any speeded test.

RESULTS

Age was found to correlate with the verbal fluency and total scores of the P.M.A., while bi-serial correlations were found between sex and the Furneaux level tests, the P.M.A. Number, Fluency, Space, and Reasoning Scales. Age and sex were therefore partialled out of the matrix. . . .

The correlations given in Table II are thus independent of age and sex.

TABLE II
Intercorrelations of the Intelligence Scores

	1	2	3	4	5	6	7
1. P.M.A. Verbal							
2. P.M.A. Number..	.411						
3. P.M.A. Space....	.396	.225					
4. P.M.A. Reason ..	.496	.425	.515				
5. P.M.A. Fluency ..	.583	.401	.225	.490			
6. P.M.A. Total	.741	.689	.617	.813	.734		
7. Furneaux Level ..	.348	.297	.490	.691	.286	.597	
8. Furneaux Speed ..	.369	.204	.232	.411	.352	.440	.269

These P.M.A. sub-tests (factor) and total scores were included, with the Nufferno Tests of Intellectual Level and Intellectual Speed in an inter-correlation matrix of 20 variables. Twelve of the variables in this matrix were measures of personality and are irrelevant to this discussion.

The total score included for the P.M.A. test was calculated according to the formula $V + S + 2N + 2R + W$ in keeping with the practice outlined by Thurstone in the Test Manual. The intercorrelations between the sub-test scores and this total score are spuriously high.

The total score was included to give a point of rotation for the intelligence factor. By such a procedure intelligence has been defined for this study as the Primary Mental Abilities total score as calculated in the above formula.

The Thurstone method of analysis was used and four factors were extracted.

The first centroid was clearly of a cognitive nature. It accounted for 20 per cent. of the variance. The loadings of the intelligence tests on this centroid were Verbal .752; Number .544; Space .514; Reasoning .704; Fluency .675; Total .902; Furneaux Level .583; and Furneaux Speed .486.

The second centroid which took up 6 per cent. of the variance appeared to be an autonomic factor loading on physiological measures.

The third factor accounting for 5 per cent. of the variance appeared to be a factor of general emotionality (neuroticism). No attempt was made to identify the fourth factor extracted, which accounted for some 3 per cent. of the variance and left insignificant residuals.

The first factor was rotated through the P.M.A. total score criterion. The positions of the remaining three factors were determined by rotating for simple structure. Six rotations were needed.

Factor scores were computed in accordance with Lubin and Summerfield's square root method.

To compute intelligence factor scores, all of the intelligence test scores were used except the total score which had been used as a criterion of rotation for the intelligence factor. The Beta weightings derived for the tests used were: Reasoning .313; Number .241; Verbal .208; Fluency .186; Space .177; Power .114; and Speed .001.

CONCLUSIONS

The first of the hypotheses is supported by the data to the extent that when the test scores are weighted in accordance with the second order loadings reported by the Thurstone's (1941), the intra-identical correlation for the weighted total score is .754, whereas that for the fraternal sample is .394 giving rise to an h^2 of .594. When the scores are weighted on the basis of the regression equation derived from the factor loadings of the present analysis, the total score so obtained, has an intra-identical correlation of .732 and an itra-fraternal correlation of .446 and an h^2 value of .549.

These h^2 values are lower than one would anticipate in the case of cognitive tests. However, as Eysenck and Prell point out, more reliance can be placed on the correlation coefficients than upon the h^2 statistic. According to Newman, Freeman and Holzinger, the distribution of h^2 is very probably not normal. For this reason, it is not possible to assess the significance of differences between values of h^2. This fact makes it difficult to assess the evidence regarding the second hypothesis.

The class intercorrelations and the h^2 values for the P.M.A. tests and for the total and factor scores are given in Table III.

The fact that the h^2 values for all the total scores are considerably lower than those for the Verbal, Reasoning and Fluency test scores may be interpreted as support for the view that these abilities are determined to a greater extent by heredity than is the general factor to which they give rise. These results would indicate that in the tests having higher h^2 values than the total scores, group or specific factor variance as well as that contributing to the general factor is determined by inheritance.

A case can, however, be presented for the contention that the total and factor scores are more determined by inheritance than are the sub-scores.

As has been stated, the significance of the difference between values of h^2 cannot be determined, so that the differences found cannot be considered conclusive invalidation of the hypothesis.

Further, it will be noted that there is a very close correspondence in the rank order between the size of the h^2 for each of the tests and the size of the loading which Thurstone found the tests to have on the second order factor of intelligence.

TABLE III

Factor Saturations, h^2 Values and Beta Weights for Intelligence Tests

	Rotated factor saturations	Thurstone's 2nd order factor saturations	Intra-identical correlation	Intra-fraternal correlation	h^2 value	Beta weights
Intelligence						
Factor Scores	—	—	.764	.443	.576	—
Verbal..........	.681	.715	.726	.145	.680	.208
Space..........	.573	.502	.630	.248	.508	.177
Number	.608	.399	.489	.449	.073	.241
Reason	.781	.630	.708	.188	.640	.313
Fluency.........	.630	.615	.734	.257	.642	.186
Total A*........	.971	—	.583	.369	.339	—
Total B†........	—	—	.754	.394	.594	—
Total C‡........	—	—	.732	.406	.549	—
Furneaux Speed..	.393	—	.134	.372	—	.001
Furneaux Level..	.614	—	.640	.309	.479	.114

* P.M.A. Total Score from formula $V+S+2N+2R+W$.
† P.M.A. Total Score calculated on the basis of the square of Thurstone's second order factor loadings.
‡ P.M.A. Total Score calculated on the basis of weights derived from the Experimental Group.

It would seem to follow from this that since the tests showing the highest degree of genetic determination are contributing most heavily to the factor scores, the factor scores themselves should show a more pronounced degree of genetic determination than the contributing sub-test scores. In other words, it would seem that a total score weighted on the basis of these second order factor loadings would have a very high probability of producing an h^2 value in excess of the h^2 for any of the contributing tests. That such was not the case in this study may be due to the unreliability of the h^2 statistic. Another possibility is that error producing unreliability is not equally distributed as between the fraternal and identical samples. In this connection, the greater reliability attendant upon the increased number of items comprising total scores as opposed to sub-scores does not appear to affect the identical and fraternal correlation coefficients equally. Whereas the intra-identical correlations are not much enhanced, intra-fraternal co-efficients are markedly increased.

In any case, aside from these considerations, it may be pointed out that the inter-identical correlations are higher for the weighted total scores than for any of the Primary Mental Abilities test scores. That this is not simply a reflection of increased reliability due to an increase in the number of test items is strongly suggested by the fact that intra-identical correlations for the total score calculated on the $V+S+2R+2N+W$ formula is lower than are the coefficients for four of the Primary Mental Abilities Tests.

However, although evidence can be cited in favour of the hypothesis, it cannot, in view of the obtained values of h^2, be considered to have been established and the conclusion must be drawn that hypothesis two has not been supported.

Certain of the findings merit further consideration. The fact that Verbal Comprehension and Word Fluency Tests are found to be determined by inheritance to a larger extent than the other tests, would seem to call into question Vernon's suggestion that the principal group factor in intelligence, v:ed, is a verbal factor which is developed by education. It is also contradictory to Thurstone's view: "The growth of Verbal Comprehension is difficult to appraise because the estimation of this factor is more influenced by schooling and experience than some of the other primary factors."

The findings of the present study indicate that the Number, and to a lesser extent, the Spatial Factor, would be more readily educable than verbal or reasoning ability. One might speculate on this basis that good General Arts students, relying as they do on facility with verbal material, are born; whereas the mathematicians, statisticians, engineers and so forth must toil to earn their skills. Herein, too, may lie the stimulus of the avoidance reaction which statistical courses frequently evoke in the devotees of Psyche.

The relationship of the Furneaux Speed Test to the other tests in the battery is interesting. The speed and level tests yielded intra-identical correlations of .134 and .640 respectively, and intra-fraternal correlations of .372 and .309. The h^2 value for the Level Test is .479 while that for the Speed Test would come out as a meaningless, negative value. This is apparently due to error. There is some restriction of variance in the scores of the identical sample on the speed test, but the F ratio between the variance for the identical and fraternal samples is not significant even at the ·10 level.

It appears that the speed test insofar as it is a measure of level for the age group tested does correlate with the tests of intelligence. However, when factor scores are calculated, it is found to contribute nothing toward the prediction of the weighted scores so that the factor scores are independent of speed.

The results indicate that very little, if any of the individual differences in speed, as measured by the test, are due to inheritance.

The 1932 and 1947 Scottish Mental Surveys present data of exciting importance. The excellence of the samples involved has rarely been matched in intelligence research with children. The surveys, however, have raised more questions than they have answered. The following paper treats a few aspects of the studies and points to some of the unexplained outcomes. The interested student will want to read The Trend of Scottish Intelligence (London, University of London Press, Ltd., 1949), for a more complete description of the studies and their findings.

Intelligence, Fertility and the Future*

JAMES MAXWELL

1954

PROCEDURE

In 1932 a group verbal intelligence test was administered to 87,498 Scottish eleven-year-old children; and in 1947 the same test was administered to the corresponding group of eleven-year-olds, numbering 70,805. Each group comprised over 90 per cent of the estimated population of eleven-year-olds. In 1932, a sample of 1000 children was given the Stanford-Binet test, and in 1947 a sample of 1215 children, selected by date of birth, was given the Terman-Merrill Binet Test.

The information obtained about the 1947 children was considerably more extensive than that for the 1932 group. For all the 1947 eleven-year-olds, the size of family, the child's position in the family, and various matters of educational interest were recorded. For a 10 per cent sample, the children born on the first three days of each month, the father's occupation, the degree of overcrowding in the home, the mother's age, the child's place of birth, and the child's height and weight were also recorded. It was from this sample that the 1215 individually tested children were drawn; and both the 10 per cent sample and the smaller sample appear to be a good representation of the total eleven-year-old population of the survey.

COMPARISON OF INTELLIGENCE TEST SCORES

On the group test of 76 items, the average score of the 1947 children was 2.3 points higher than that of the 1932 group of children, the standard deviation of test score being about 16 for both groups. After calibration

* Reprinted from Eugenics Quarterly, 1 (1954), pp. 244-247, by permission of Mr. J. Maxwell and the publisher.

of the two versions of the Binet test, no significant change in average I.Q. was found. The main finding of the two Scottish Surveys thus was, that over a period of fifteen years, there was no sign of a decline in the average measured intelligence of the eleven-year-old child population, and some suggestion of a rise. Explanations of the increase in average group test score in terms of environmental improvement and familiarity with tests are possible but are unproven, and such explanations would require to be established by some positive evidence before being accepted.

INTELLIGENCE AND FERTILITY

A definite negative correspondence between the average intelligence test scores of the children and the size of their sibship was established in the 1947 Survey. The correlation coefficients are $r = -0.28$ for the group test, and $r = -0.32$ for the Binet test. The relationship between test score and family size is not known for the 1932 group, but various contemporary investigations did reveal a similar negative correspondence, so it is not unreasonable to assume a corresponding negative relationship among the 1932 children, though its degree is unknown.

It has been suggested that the negative relationship between family size and average intelligence is a function of birth order, the later-born children in a family tending to be less intelligent than the earlier born. The data of the Scottish Survey do not allow of this hypothesis being fully examined, as the children are all from different families, and all families are not necessarily complete. The data as they stand, however, give some indication that the last-born children may be slightly more intelligent than the earlier-born children, and there is no sign whatever of a negative relationship between test score and birth order. Because of the method by which the survey children were selected, *i.e.,* all eleven-year-olds, it is impossible to make any more precise statement. On the other hand, the younger sibs of the 1215 individually tested children have also been individually tested on reaching the age of eleven. Here it is possible to compare children of different birth order within the same family. The results (as yet unpublished) show no clear correspondence between birth order and intelligence. It can safely be inferred from the Scottish results that a differential relationship between birth order and intelligence has no part in the negative correlation between intelligence and family size.

On the basis of this negative correlation between intelligence and family · size, predictions of a decline in the average level of intelligence have been made; but the decline expected between 1932 and 1947 does not seem to have occurred. This is one of the paradoxes of the Scottish results, and its resolution implies either a "masked" decline, or inadequacies inthe methods of predicting future trends from one set of results. The environmental influences said to be masking a real decline have been neither precisely identified nor clearly established as operating; the prediction of future trends is a question that deserves fuller consideration than can be given here.

INTELLIGENCE AND SOCIAL ENVIRONMENT

From the information recorded for the 10 per cent sample in the Scottish survey, it has been possible to make several sociological classifications. The major classification was in terms of the father's occupation. Nine such occupational (or social) classes were distinguished; a brief definition of each is given below, together with the average size of sibship and average group test score of the children in each class.

TABLE I

Occupational class	Family size	Test score
I Professional and large employers	2.6	51.8
II Small employers and self-employed	3.1	42.7
III Salaried employees	2.5	47.7
IV Non-manual wage earners	3.1	43.6
V Skilled manual wage earners	3.6	37.2
VI Semi-skilled manual wage earners	4.3	33.2
VII Unskilled manual wage earners	4.6	31.1
VIII Farmers	3.9	36.2
IX Agricultural workers	4.3	32.3
All	3.8	36.8

There is here a clear differential relationship between occupational class and family size, and between occupational class and test score. There is also an almost perfectly inverse correspondence of test score and family size between occupational classes. These relationships suggest that the negative correlation between fertility and intelligence may be a function of differences between social classes. But further analysis of the survey data showed quite clearly a negative correlation between family size and intelligence test score *within each occupational class;* and these negative correlations were only a little smaller than that obtained for the survey population as a whole.

Thus a third element, social class, must be added to the fertility-intelligence differential. Though the Scottish Survey data do not completely represent the whole adult population, as childless couples are omitted and large families over-represented, it is likely that the differences between social classes revealed in the survey are a fair enough indication of the pattern in the whole population. This differential relation between intelligence, social class and fertility complicates the prediction of future trends of intellectual level, introducing as it does two further unknowns.

The first unknown element is the stability of the observed differences in fertility and intelligence as between social classes. There are some indications that in Scotland the social class-fertility relationship is in a stage of transition from a fairly uniform distribution of largish families over the various social classes to a more uniform distribution of smaller families over the various social classes, and that this process of reducing family size is more advanced in those social groups containing the more intelligent parents and children. If this supposition is correct, then the expectation would be that the negative correlation between family size and intelligence would be reduced, and what is more important, the number of large families containing the less intelligent children would become less.

The other unknown is the trend of social mobility between classes, and its effects on the intelligence-fertility relationship. There are grounds for believing that the fertility of parents whose social level has changed is intermediate between that of the class they are in and their class of origin. In the Scottish Survey, of the 6 per cent of children with highest test scores, nearly one-third were children of skilled manual workers, about one-sixth were children of professional men and large employers, and about one-seventeenth were children of unskilled manual workers. These children are estimated to be able to attain a University standard of education, and some may move to a different social class. Some of the children may remain in the class of manual workers. On the other hand some of the less intelligent children from the professional class may also manage to remain in that class. Whether the differential fertility of social class or the differential fertility of intellectual level will prevail remains unknown, but any estimates of future trends in the population must take these possibly conflicting influences into account.

HEIGHT AND WEIGHT

The heights and weights of the children in the 10 per cent sample were recorded, as well as their intelligence test scores. The pattern of the relation of height and weight with family size, and with occupational class, resembles closely that of intelligence test score, though the correlation of height and weight with test score is only of the order of $r = + 0.20$ to $r = + 0.25$.

Since records for height in particular are more extensive than those for intelligence, it is tempting to construct a model, using height instead of intelligence, and to test prediction from the model. The correlation of height with family size is a little smaller than that of intelligence with family size, and the differential relationship of height with social class only a little less marked than that of intelligence. What, then, is happening to the average height of the population? During the years between 1932 and 1947 the average height of Scottish children increased; and records from certain parts of Scotland show that this increase has been in progress since 1910 and is still continuing. There is evidence that a differential relationship between height and social class existed in 1910, and indirect suggestions that the differential relationship with family size also existed, though this latter cannot be established independently of social class. Children at school in 1910 are likely to be parents of children measured in later years, so it seems reasonably certain that, age for age, the children are taller than their parents. Further, the average height of the adult population does not seem to have altered to any marked degree over this century, and no evidence of a decline has been adduced. It appears possible, therefore, for a stable level of height to exist in the context of a differential correspondence between height and fertility, and height and social class. Though the environmental influences affecting height may not be the same as those affecting test score, it is not easy to conceive of a situation where the relationship of two variables with fertility and social class are closely parallel, and yet where for one (intelligence test score) the relationship is accompanied by a decline and for the other it is not. The model for height does not, by analogy, suggest a decline in average intelligence.

MIGRATION

For the purpose of the Survey, Scotland was divided into four types of areas, the four cities, the large towns, the small towns, and the rest of the country, this last being called the Other Areas. The cities and the Other Areas each contains about 40 per cent of the total survey population. For each child in the 10 per cent sample, there was recorded the place of birth and of present residence, both in terms of the four types of area mentioned above. About 11 per cent of the children were migrants. Those migrants were found to be a superior group, intellectually, socially, and physically. Considering the cities and Other Areas only, the average test score of children migrating from the Other Areas to the cities is 7.1 points higher than that of the children migrating in the opposite direction. The average score of all children born in the cities, whether migrating or not, is 1.5 points higher than that of all children born in Other Areas. During the eleven years of the survey children's lives, 1936 to 1947, there appears to be a definite flow of intelligent children, in smaller families, to the cities, and a corresponding flow of less intelligent children in larger families to the Other Areas. Because of the miscellaneous kinds of districts defined as Other Areas it is not possible to make anything but very rough estimates of the results of this trend, but it does seem that if the loss of intelligent children from the Other Areas had continued for any time at the rate indicated by the 1947 Survey, the difference between the average test scores of children born in cities and born in Other Areas would be much larger than it is shown to be. The explanation may be in social terms, or it may be another apparent paradox, that the Other Areas are continuously losing a proportion of the more intelligent children to the cities and receiving a proportion of the less intelligent children, but that the average intelligence in each of the two areas appears to continue at very much the same relative level.

CONCLUSIONS

This paper has confined itself to a discussion of the results of the Scottish Mental Surveys only. The findings of the 1947 Survey on the relations of fertility, intelligence test score, social conditions and stature are in substantial agreement with the findings of other corresponding investigations and raise much the same questions. Comparisons of the intellectual level of a given population over a period of time show somewhat more conflicting results, and the non-committal conclusion that there is no evidence of a fall in average intelligence appears to be the most fitting one. The positive contribution of surveys such as the Scottish ones is to reveal the nature and extent of the problems rather than to find conclusive answers to them, and to provide a framework of reference for more limited but more intensive investigations. Such investigations could profitably be directed to the elaboration of more precise methods of handling sociological and genetic data, to the establishment in greater detail of the interaction of social and genetic factors in fertility and intelligence, and, as the Scottish Mental Survey is doing with the 1215 individually tested children, trying to ascertain the bearing of intelligence test score, family size and social conditions on the future lives of the children. The main need, however, is to establish a link between one generation and the next. Neither extensive surveys nor limited investigations are themselves alone sufficient; the two approaches are necessarily complementary to each other.

As longitudinal studies of the intelligence of children began to mature, it became clear that the early cross-sectional studies had been misleading. In the following paper Bayley reviewed the evidence, particularly from the Berkeley Growth Study and formulated a new growth curve for intelligence. Special attention should be given to her handling of problems which arise in longitudinal research relative to the adequacy and comparability of testing instruments at several ages.

On the Growth of Intelligence*

NANCY BAYLEY

1955

One of the primary objectives of the Berkeley Growth Study has been to study the processes of the development of intelligence as measured by tests. During the 25 years since the study was started, there has been continual change in psychologists' ideas and theories about intelligence. As a result, some of the changing theories and emphases are reflected in the series of reports that have been made on the growth of intelligence in these children. What is more, by their very nature these longitudinal studies have themselves contributed something to our knowledge of, and theories about, intellectual development and functioning.

I should like here to review the data from the Berkeley Growth Study, together with some related material, as they bear on our knowledge of the growth of intelligence.

THE CONCEPT OF THE CONSTANT IQ

In early studies the intelligence quotient was found to be very practical: it served as an easily understood index of a child's relative ability, an index by which he could be compared with other children the same age or in the same grade at school. It was found that as a rule the IQ changed very little when a child was retested a week or a month or a year or two later. This gave people great confidence in the IQ's "constancy." Furthermore, there are advantages in being able to classify a child and have him remain as classified. But this very stability of scores over certain short periods of the life span led to the assumption that intelligence is a basic entity which changes only by accretions and decrements in quantity with childhood growth, adult stability, and senescent decline. Of course this is an oversimplified extreme position, though it seems to have been (and still often

* Adapted from *The American Psychologist,* 10 (1955), pp. 805-818, by permission of the author and the American Psychological Association.

is) held by many people who have used "IQ Tests" in education and in practice. It is not, however, a position held for long by those who have been actively engaged in studying the nature of intelligence and its growth.

Another result of the concept of the constant IQ has been its extrapolation, both forward and backward from the school age child, to include all ages, from birth to senescence. If the IQ is constant, then we should be able to classify a child in infancy according to his intellectual potential. We can plan his education, we can make better foster home placements, we can put the feeble-minded into custodial care very young, and so on.

* * *

PREDICTION FROM SCORES IN INFANCY

At the outset we had accepted the findings based on school age children, and assumed that IQ's were constant at all ages. Consequently we were amazed at the precocity of some of the babies whose mothers seemed not very bright, and embarrassed at the poor records of other babies who, by the laws of inheritance, should have done better. But we soon found that our embarrassments and amazements were alleviated with time: a slow baby would forge ahead and redeem his inheritance, a precocious infant often seemed to rest on his laurels while the others caught up with him. We were not too surprised, therefore, when the statistical treatment of the test scores revealed that there was no relation between relative performance in the first few months of life and scores earned at the end of the first year.

When the report on the mental scores of the Berkeley Growth Study children during their first three years was published, it was met by many with scepticism. However, in spite of their failure to conform with established theory, these Berkeley children continued to develop in their own individual ways. . . . Furthermore, these irregularities in mental growth were found to occur in other than Berkeley children. Wherever careful statistics have been applied to comparisons of repeated test scores on infants and very young children the correlations between tests separated by a year or two are low. It is now well established that we cannot predict later intelligence from the scores on tests made in infancy. Scores may be altered by such conditions as emotional climate, cultural milieu, and environmental deprivation, on the one hand, and by developmental changes in the nature and composition of the behaviors tested, on the other. These latter factors are the primary concern in this paper.

As the Berkeley Growth Study children grew older we continued to record their progress by successive tests at frequent intervals. We have from time to time reported the results of these tests, along with efforts to find relationships between mental growth and other factors. When the children were 8 years old a study of the individual growth records showed that only a fifth of the group had maintained any stability in their relative status over the eight-year span. Even these few had unstable Standard Scores during the first two years.

This lack of stability in infant test scores has resulted in various efforts to supplement and to correct the infant tests to make them more predictive. It has been suggested that the scales are not composed of the right kind of test items. However, efforts to devise other, more adequate scales, invariably run into the hard fact that infants exhibit a very limited range of behaviors that can be observed and recorded. The various scales of infant intelligence have a remarkable similarity of content. At first there is little to note beyond evidences of sensory functioning in reacting to appropriate stimuli. One can observe that the one-month-old looks momentarily at a dangling ring, or at a rattle or other small object. Or one can vary the source of the sharp sound that will make him start or blink. A little later the responses are evidenced in motor coordinations: the six-month-old may pick up a one-inch cube or a teaspoon placed in easy reach. There are some early evidences of adaptation to the presented stimuli, of memory from a past experience: the seven-month-old, for example, looks "aware" that a fallen toy is no longer there, and when a little older he may turn to look for it on the floor. One can note the progression of vocalizations as they become more complex and then as they are used meaningfully. There is a developing ability to discriminate differences, to be aware of new situations, to recognize differences between members of the family and strangers, and so on.

The question is: Which, if any, among these is the forerunner of later intellectual functions? Which, if any, will predict the individual differences found in school age children?

One method of testing and selecting predictive items has been to use a later (or "terminal") measure of intelligence as the criterion. Scores earned by infants or very young children on individual test items have been correlated with their later IQ's. Those items showing the highest r's with the criterion have in some instances been combined into scales. Theoretically, if other items of similar nature are then devised and added, such a scale can be expanded into an adequate predictive test. This method has been tried on infant scales by L. D. Anderson and by Nelson and Richards. They compared successes on items under one year with retest criteria at ages 2 to 5 years. Maurer compared scores on items in tests given children at 3 to 5 years with their scores at 15 years as a criterion. More recently Hastings compared preschool test items with 14- to 18-year scores from our studies at the Institute of Child Welfare. In all of these studies some items have proved to be better predictors than others. Hastings selected items from the Guidance Study records and validated them on the Berkeley Growth Study (19 boys and 18 girls). His predictive items were good for the boys, but not for the girls in the validating sample. These boys had a wide range of ability, and thus an unusually large *SD* of scores. Their 2-year performance on a scale made up of good predictors correlated .67 with scores at 16-17 years. The same comparisons for the girls gave an *r* of .34. In general the predictions were better at the later preschool ages.

We have tried to find predictive items from the First Year Scale on the Berkeley Growth Study children. Several years ago, using the six children at each extreme of intelligence as measured at the 14 to 16 year tests, we went through the First Year Scale item by item, noting the age at which each of these 12 children first passed each item. We were able to select 31 items in which the six high-scoring teenagers had, as infants, been two months or more advanced over the six low-scorers. These items were an odd assortment, and there was no evident reason for their superiority over other items. Most of the items occur in the second half year, where there is a fair amount of range in scores. In the first few months very few items had a range of more than two months in age at first passing.

Recently we computed scores for the total Berkeley Growth Study sample on this 31-item scale for three ages: months 6, 9, and 12. The *r*'s of these new point scores with the mean of the intelligence sigma scores at ages 16, 17 and 18 years (for 45 cases) are .09 at six months, .32 at 9 months, and .30 at 12 months. We were unable to get significant correlations even though our sample was composed in large part of the cases on whom the items were selected, including all of the extreme cases that would determine a relationship.

So far, none of these efforts has been successful in devising an intelligence scale applicable to children under two years that will predict their later performance. The moderate successes of Maurer and of Hastings have been on items at the two-year level of difficulty or older. Even here the *r*'s are not high enough for accurate prediction on individual children. As far as I know, no one has used these items to set up and standardize an expanded scale. There does seem to be some coherence in the types of function tested by the predictive items. It is interesting to note, too, that those items which are good predictors are often not the items that best characterize a child's current stage of development. It has even been suggested that a scale should combine both types of items and then be scored in two ways—one score for evaluating present status and one for predicting future development.

These findings give little hope of ever being able to measure a stable and predictable intellectual factor in the very young. I am inclined to think that the major reason for this failure rests in the nature of intelligence itself. I see no reason why we should continue to think of intelligence as an integrated (or simple) entity or capacity which grows throughout childhood by steady accretions.

THE CHANGING ORGANIZATION OF INTELLECTUAL PROCESSES

Intelligence appears to me, rather, to be a dynamic succession of developing functions, with the more advanced and complex functions in the hierarchy depending on the prior maturing of earlier simpler ones (given, of course, normal conditions of care). The neonate who is precocious in the developing of the simpler abilities, such as auditory acuity or pupilary reflexes, has an advantage in the slightly more complex behaviors, such as (say) turning toward a sound, or fixating an object held before his eyes. But these more complex acts also involve other functions, such as neuromuscular coordinations, in which he may not be precocious. The bright one-month-old may be sufficiently slow in developing these later more complex functions so as to lose some or all of his earlier advantage. This is the kind of thing that does seem to happen. Scores on tests given a month apart are highly correlated, but the longer the time interval between these baby tests the lower the intertest correlation.

If intelligence is a complex of separately timed, developing functions, then to understand its nature we must try to analyze it into its component parts. One approach to this process has been by factor analysis. Of the two main theories resulting from factor analysis, our data would seem to fit better into some variation of a multiple-factor than a two-factor theory. Or perhaps they fit better a theory that is intermediate, somewhere between the two.

The program of the Berkeley Growth Study has not been carried on in such a way as to make factor analysis on this material practicable. For one thing, the number of cases is too small for the usual factorial procedures. Also, for such a purpose one might have chosen a different or a more extensive series of tests. (As it is, the children have tolerated an amazingly large amount of testing and measuring!)

Nevertheless, some of our findings should point the way to new areas where factorial or other kinds of analysis would be fruitful. I should like to know, for example, where to look for g in the infant scales. One might expect g to be that factor on which prediction could be based. If g is not present at first, then when and how does it appear? Or does g itself change as it grows more complex? How do factor loadings distribute themselves in infant scales? Does a heavily-loaded first factor show a characteristic developmental process of change?

Richards and Nelson using the Gesell items, at 6, 12, and 18 months, obtained two factors which they called "alertness" and "motor ability." They found age changes in communality of the tests that were in part due to restrictions in the type of items included in the scales at the older ages. This very fact reflects the relatively undifferentiated nature of behavior in the very young. It may be a mistake to try to call any infant behavior before

6 months more characteristically "mental" than, for example, motor. In spite of progressive selection of behaviors observed in intelligence tests, the evidence of a motor factor persists in the early ages of the Stanford-Binet, according to McNemar's factor analysis. These studies only scratch the surface of what needs to be done to gain real understanding of the nature of early mental processes.

If the word "intelligence" is best used as a broad general term that we apply to a great variety of mental functions, then we will want to investigate the nature of these functions, their interrelationships and the changes that take place in mental organization with growth. We should expect a given "factor" of intelligence to be more important at one stage of development than at another. As Garrett has shown, in a summary of factor analysis, there is evidence of increasing independence of mental factors as children grow older. Does this trend continue indefinitely? Or do some of these factors become functionally reintegrated as they mature? The studies of Thurstone and others can be most valuable in yielding information on this point. Let us hope they will be continued, over the entire life span, with careful attention to the problem of selecting items to test all relevant mental functions at all ages.

The very fact that the scores of mental growth in individual children tend to exhibit gradual shifts in relative status supports the theory that a changing organization of factors is in process. Something akin to g, or a high first-factor loading, must appear soon after the second or third year. The correlations of tests at these ages become positive with the later test scores. After 5 or 6 years children can be reliably classified into broad categories of normal, defective, and bright.[1]

PROBLEMS ENCOUNTERED IN CONSTRUCTING CURVES OF GROWTH IN INTELLIGENCE

The use of intelligence quotients, or standard scores, in studying growth changes in children is helpful in showing a child's shifts in status relative to the norms. But a child's progress, in relation to his own past, is better represented if we can use scores that measure increments or *amounts* of intelligence. Here we run into the problem of comparable units. Lacking absolute units for measuring intelligence, we must settle for some measure of greater or lesser difficulty, or degree of complexity of intellectual func-

---

[1] Since this paper was read, Hofstaetter has made a factor analysis using the 18-year consistency correlations of my data. He obtained three distinct factors: the first is predominant for the first two years, the second between 2 and 4 years, and the third accounts for almost the entire variance after 4 years. He names them: I, Sensory Motor Alertness, II, Persistence, and III, Manipulation of Symbols. This latter is most likely the general intellectual factor that most intelligence tests are designed to measure. These are, of course, global, or total-test characterizations, but they illustrate the complete break between the kinds of function measured in infants and in school-age children.

tioning. The first, and perhaps still most generally used unit of intelligence
is mental age. Such a unit tends to force the same value on a mental age
increment of (say) a month, whether it occurs at 6 months of age, at 6
years or 16 years. Thurstone, Thorndike, and others have tried by various
devices to set up units that approximate equality of difficulty at all levels
of complexity. This is done usually by comparing the overlapping distributions of scores earned by children of successively older ages. Such units
would vary with the test and with the normative sample. In any event, they
remain only approximations. When we accept and label them as such, however, they become useful in comparing age changes in ability.

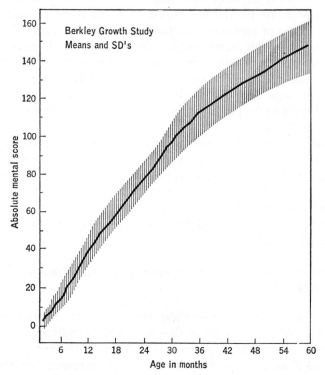

**Figure 1. Curve of intelligence, one month to 60 months, Berkeley Growth
Study, according to Thurstone's method of Absolute Scaling.**

Thurstone applied his method to the Berkeley Growth Study scores on
the California First Year and Preschool Scales for the first two years. We
later extended the scaling through five years, and obtained the curve shown
in Figure 1. This curve is positively accelerated for a few months, then
settles into a consistent rapid growth for almost a year, after which there
is a gradual slowing down in the rate, though growth continues to be fairly
rapid. The curve makes sense in the light of ordinary observations of

children's early development. It seems to be a useful approximation, even though one cannot claim absolute equivalence of difficulty of the units at different levels.

Problems of equating different scales. When the children grew older, and an extension of the scale was in order, we ran into another problem. We had to find new tests, adapted to the children's increased mental capacities. At the beginning of the study there had been no well-standardized infant and preschool scales, and we had found it necessary to develop our own. However, good standard tests were available for school age children. The 1916 revision of the Stanford-Binet was given at 6 years. Since that time we have consistently used standardized tests of intelligence, including the 1916, and both forms of the 1937 Stanford Revision of the Binet, the Terman-McNemar Group test, and the Wechsler-Bellevue Adult Intelligence Scale, Form I. But shifts in scales, with their different norms and units of increment, have complicated the problem of setting up a single continuous scale of mental growth units. This problem has not been solved, but I have approached it tentatively in several ways.

A few years ago, in presenting some data on mental growth for the first 18 years, I transposed the early scores into mental age equivalents. These scores, together with the Stanford-Binet mental ages, give us age units from birth to 17 years. The mean mental age curve of the Berkeley Growth Study children is shown in Figure 2. At 17 years, the latest available Stanford-Binet M.A. score for this group, the scores were continuing to increase. However, the rate of growth as expressed in M.A. units has diminished at the later ages. The standard deviations, shown in the lower part of Figure 2, do not increase at a constant rate but are relatively large around 10 to 12 years. Similar trends in variability may be found in other samples, and for other tests. This, I have argued, reflects a true state of increased variability in intelligence during early adolescence.

The curve of the mean mental ages is in many ways similar, for the same age intervals, to curves constructed by other investigators, using other units of mental growth. The general similarity holds whether the scores are based on longitudinal or cross-sectional samples.

Accordingly, I felt justified in using this longitudinal M.A. curve in conjunction with the Jones and Conrad curve based on cross-sectional data and standard score units, to construct a theoretical curve of the probable course of intelligence from birth to 60 years. It is similar to curves offered by Miles, Wechsler, and others. However, more recent data on the Berkeley Growth Study, together with data from other studies, raise questions concerning the representativeness of this curve.

The data on the Berkeley Growth Study do not stop at 17 years. The Wechsler-Bellevue Adult intelligence scale was given at 16, 18, and 21 years, and we are currently repeating the test at 25 years. A study of the growth of intelligence between 16 and 21 years, as measured by these tests,

is now in press. The scores were found to increase through 21 years. This was true for each category, at least to 18 years, and for the Efficiency Quotients based on the total test. It was even true of the IQ's. These trends are shown clearly in the curves of the means. . . . The total scores in Figure 3 are expressed as quotients: total IQ, and EQ, and Verbal and Performance EQ. (The EQ expresses the deviation of the weighted score from the norm for 20-24-year-olds). The gains occurred at all levels of ability within the group. All but one of the 33 subjects made some gain in total weighted score over the five-year period.

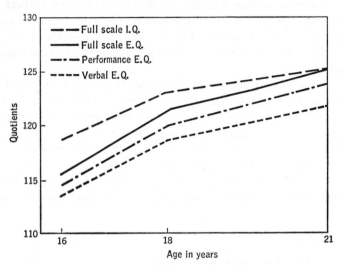

Figure 3. Age curves of Wechsler-Bellevue IQ's and EQ's, Berkeley Growth Study.

These data are in agreement with other investigators' findings on retests of the same individuals. Freeman and Flory, and Thorndike have found for different samples, and for different tests, that intelligence scores continue to increase at least to 21 years. Dearborn and Rothney have fitted the Harvard Growth Study data to a curve that, by extrapolation, indicates mental growth would continue to 30 years.

The general appearance of the Wechsler-Bellevue weighted score curve for the Berkeley Growth Study gives the impression that it could very well fit on as a continuation of the 17-year mental age curve. But to put the two curves into a single continuum would require transposing the scores into comparable units. This I have attempted to do, in the hope that it will give at least a rough approximation of the direction of mental growth.

The construction of the 16D Scale. The Berkeley Growth Study tests were scheduled so that alternating forms of the Stanford-Binet were given annually through 12 years and again at 14 and 17 years. The Terman-

McNemar Group test was given individually, Form C at 13 years and Form D at 15. The Wechsler-Bellevue was thus dovetailed in, having been given at years 16, 18, and 21. If we assume that the 16-year Wechsler-Bellevue scores earned by these subjects are equivalent in difficulty to a mental age at the 16-year point on their Stanford-Binet mental age curve, we can start at 16 years as a basis for equating the two sets of scores. At the adjacent ages the Stanford-Binet M.A.'s have standard deviations averaging 34 points, while the Wechsler-Bellevue *SD*'s were about 20 and the Terman-McNemar *SD*'s about 19 points.

With these data, starting with the Means and *SD*'s of the 16-year scores, we have constructed a method of transposing the scores from all tests into what may be called 16*D* Scores. That is, each child's scores at all ages are expressed in terms of the 16-year standard deviations from the mean score at 16 years.

To do this, a table of equivalents was made by extrapolating the Terman-McNemar scores and interpolating the Stanford-Binet scores, to obtain a 16-year mean, or assumed mean, score for this sample on all three tests. To get comparable standard deviations, for the three tests, the Stanford-Binet M.A. units were reduced by the fraction 20/34, and the Terman-McNemar units were increased by the fraction 20/19. Then, taking an arbitrary score of 140 to represent the 16-year mean, the three scales were related to this new 16*D* scale, point for point so that the 16-year mean

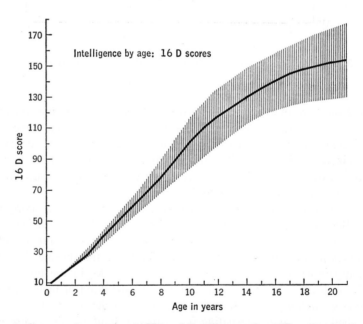

Figure 4. Curves of means and *SD*'s of Intelligence by 16*D* units, birth to 21 years, Berkeley Growth Study.

would equal 140, while plus and minus one *SD* at 16 years would equal 160 and 120 respectively. This scale can be extended in either direction. All scores for all ages are expressed as deviations from the 16-year level.

The resulting curve, based on the means and *SD*'s of the 16*D* scores, is shown in Figure 4. Whether or not it is a legitimate construct, it looks reasonable, and not too far from the probable trends of growth in intelligence. It would have been better to construct the curve on a more nearly average sample, but at least we may be justified in using the 16*D* scores to apply to the members of the Berkeley Growth Study, as one way of expressing their progress toward, and development beyond, their status at 16 years.

Sixteen years has no particular significance as a point of reference: it was chosen because it was the only age at which the three scales we had used could be approximately equated for this sample. It would have been more satisfying if we could have started at a terminal point, say, conception, or birth, or the age at which scores stop increasing. However, 16 years is one age that has been considered a terminal point, or at least the age beyond which the ratio IQ cannot be used without modification. The score of 140 at 16 years was chosen because, from this figure when the curve is extrapolated downward from the mean score obtained at month one, the curve approximates zero at conception.

THE VALUES AND LIMITATIONS OF STANDARD SCORES AND INCREMENT SCORES

Standard scores: Individual curves.   Let us consider some individual curves of intelligence scores earned by these subjects. In the past we have usually presented individual records in the form of Standard Scores or Sigma Scores for this group. Such scores are very useful for observing a child's changes in performance relative to others his age. We can see his ups and downs, and try to relate them to variable factors, environmental or other, that might have caused the changes. . . . We have found that the Standard Scores gave a truer picture of a child's relative status at successive ages, because there were age changes in variability of the IQ's. That is, the variability of the M.A. did not, as had been assumed, increase with age in such a way as to maintain a constant *SD* of 15 or 16 points in the MA/CA ratio. . . .

Intercorrelations.   In our comparisons with such things as emotional and environmental factors that could affect test scores, we have found the Standard Scores to be of value. For example, we have correlated the children's Standard Scores on intelligence at successive ages with the amount of schooling achieved by their parents. The age-changes in correlation (as expressed in *Z* scores) for this comparison are shown in Figure 5. The infants' scores at first are independent of parental status or negatively correlated, but after 18 months the r's become positive, and by 5 years are about .55. . . .

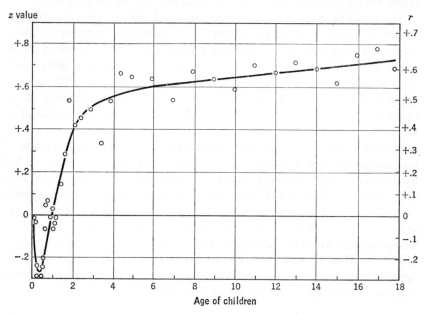

Figure 5. Correlations between children's intelligence scores and parents' education.

Standard scores have been used to correlate mental ability with emotional factors. For example the r's between children's standard scores and the amount of time they spent crying during the period of observation and measurement were at the zero level during the first year. Then, too, the repeated standard scores obtained for one child on intelligence, can be correlated with repeated scores on other variables, using the repeat observations on a single child as a population. For example, I obtained an "Optimal" score for each testing by combining 8 ratings that were indicative of the babies' responsiveness, or attitudes that might affect their performance on the tests. The r's between these Optimal scores and intelligence at any one age were close to .30. Twenty of the children had Optimal scores available for from 12 to 15 test ages each, for the age-span between 6 months and 3 years. Using the rank difference method of correlation, rho's were computed for each child between his mental standard scores and his corresponding Optimal scores. These rho's ranged from plus .77 to minus .33. For similarly-constructed "Attitude" scores, based on ratings made between 2 and 7 years of age, the individual children's rho's ranged from plus .76 to minus .46.

The wide range of correlations obtained corroborates the impression that observable emotional factors and attitudes (seen also in age curves of the different variables), rated at the time of the test, are to some extent related to the test scores, and evidently serve to help or to hinder the child's intellectual functioning. But other factors are also operative in determining a child's shifts in scores. These other factors may, in some cases, be so strong as to override the effects of emotional attitudes, resulting in negative correlations between mental performance and the child's observed responsiveness to the testing situation.

It becomes evident that the intellectual growth of any given child is a resultant of varied and complex factors. These will include his inherent capacities for growth, both in amount and in rate of progress. They will include the emotional climate in which he grows: whether he is encouraged or discouraged, whether his drive (or ego-involvement) is strong in intellectual thought processes, or is directed toward other aspects of his life-field. And they will include the material environment in which he grows: the opportunities for experience and for learning, and the extent to which these opportunities are continuously geared to his capacity to respond and to make use of them. Evidently all of these things are influential, in varying amounts for different individuals and for different stages in their growth. Many of these factors can be studied by observing concomitant variations in Standard Scores.

INDIVIDUAL DIFFERENCES IN GROWTH RATES

But Standard Scores, and other measures of relative status, have limited usefulness in the study of individual differences in rates of growth. Relative scores tend to make us forget that intellectual growth is a dynamic ongoing process, in which both averages and standard deviations in scores are related to the age of the subjects. It is worthwhile, therefore, to try to present individual curves of growth in units that will emphasize a child's change in relation to himself. Growth curves will enable us to observe a child's periods of fast and slow progress, his spurts and plateaus, and even regressions, in relation to his own past and future.

Such a growth curve has been shown in Figure 1, based on absolute scale units, for the first five years. . . . Study of the complete sample of individual curves reveals a great variety. There may be plateaus, periods of no growth, and occasionally actual decrements. There may be rapid forging ahead. Each child appears to develop at a rate that is unique for him.

By using the 16D scale we are now able to construct individual curves that extend for the entire period of the study. Figure 6 gives 16D curves for 5 boys. They cover the age span from one month to twenty-five years. Compared to the later years, the first five years seem very reduced in scope and the curves appear very homogeneous. If they are expanded to the same scale as the Thurstone curves, we find that for any given child both curves show the same periods of acceleration and retardation. The slopes of the Thurstone and the 16*D* curves are somewhat different, but the patterns of accelerations and retardations are generally similar in nature.

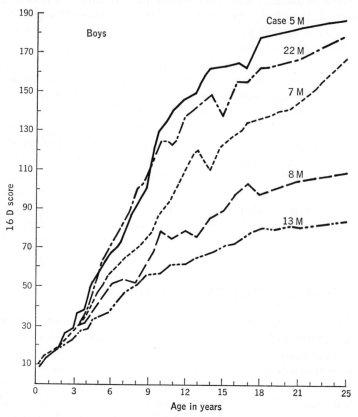

Figure 6. Individual curves of intelligence (16*D* units) for 5 boys, one month to 25 years, Berkeley Growth Study.

Although each child has his own individual pattern of progress, the patterns are not completely random. After the period of infancy there is a strong underlying consistency or constancy. Some children forge ahead and maintain relatively advanced positions after 5 or 6 years of age. Others grow slowly and lag behind. There is some shifting of position, but the changes are gradual over rather long intervals of time. Within such intervals we can expect to obtain fairly constant Standard Scores (IQ's).

It is notable that these five boys have all been tested at 25 years, and all five have continued to improve in their Wechsler-Bellevue scores. The continued growth occurs at all levels of ability. Case 13M, the slowest boy, has had increments in his Wechsler-Bellevue IQ's from 63 at 16 years to 78 at 25 years. This boy spent much of his childhood (ages 10 to 23 years) in an institution for the mentally retarded. When tested at 21 years he had never learned to read more than a few words. Now at 25 he reads, slowly to be sure, but he read aloud without error the Wechsler-Bellevue arithmetic problems.

*   *   *

Some of the dips in the individual curves are due to changes in the tests. For example, those who have trouble in reading make relatively low scores on the Terman-McNemar Group test. But often the irregularities cannot be attributed to changes in the tests used at different ages.

Slight irregularities may reflect temporary conditions of motivation, health, or emotional factors. The more constant shifts require other explanations. Though they may result from prolonged emotional or environmental influences, they may also express inherent tendencies to develop at given rates. I suspect that each child is a law unto himself: in some instances certain factors are more important, while in others different factors play the determining role.

TEMPORAL CHANGES IN ADULT INTELLIGENCE

The few 25-year scores so far available indicate that the intellectual processes measured by these tests have not yet reached a ceiling. Fourteen out of fifteen subjects tested show continued increments. If these are typical cases, what, then, may we venture to predict for the years ahead? The alternative explanation of practice effects from repeating the same test might be offered. But the intervals between repeats on the Wechsler-Bellevue are 2, 3, and 4 years. These are rather long times to remember much about the specific items. Nevertheless, there is probably some residual memory for, or vague familiarity with, the task and the type of solution found at the previous testings. At present we must assume that these factors account for part of the increment.

On the other hand, we have some recent evidence that some intellectual functions do continue to improve with age in adults. When the same individuals are retested after long intervals on the same test or on an alternate form of a test, the scores on the retests are significantly higher. These retests were carried out on superior adults, and their patterns of mental change may be different from those of less able persons.

In a recent study of the adult intelligence of the subjects of the Terman Study of Gifted Children, Bayley and Oden found that scores on the difficult Concept Mastery test increased on a second testing. For a population of over a thousand, composed of Gifted Study subjects and their spouses, comparisons were made between two tests that had been taken about 12 years apart. The increase in scores on the retest averaged about half a standard deviation. The subjects ranged in age from about 20 to about 50 years. When they were grouped into 5-year age intervals, the test-retest scores of all age groups increased.

Similar results have been reported by Owens who repeated the Army Alpha test at 50 years on 127 men who had first taken the test as 19-year-old freshmen at Iowa State College. Their scores improved by .55 *SD*'s over the 31-year interval. One can hardly claim practice effects after a lapse of 31 years. Even the 12-year interval of the Terman study is rather long for any such claim: also the Gifted Study subjects were retested on an alternate form, thus ruling out specific memories of items. Furthermore, there were control groups consisting of those who were tested only once, at either the 1940 or the 1951 testing. The differences in mean scores of these groups at the two testings are the same as for the twice-tested groups.

A SUGGESTED FIFTY-YEAR CURVE OF INTELLIGENCE

I have experimented with using the data from these two studies of adults to extend the 16*D* growth curve to 50 years. The subjects of the Berkeley Growth Study are, on the average, a somewhat superior group. Their 16-year Wechsler-Bellevue mean IQ is 117, and their 17-year Stanford Binet mean IQ is 129. A small group of 25-year-olds who have taken the Concept Mastery earned scores close to the average for the spouses of the Terman subjects at that age. We may assume, then, that this sample is rather similar to the Iowa State Freshmen and to the spouses of the Gifted Study subjects, in its general level of test performance. It has, therefore, seemed reasonable to join the data from the Berkeley Growth Study directly to the scores of either of the other studies, in extending the curve, as in Figure 7.

This joining of the curves has been done for the Iowa study simply by placing the 19-year initial point at 19 years on the 16*D* curve and the 50-year point at the equivalent on the 16*D* scale of an increase of .55 standard deviations.

For the Gifted Study spouses the process was a little more complicated, but it has yielded a series of intermediate points, giving some indication of the probable shape of the curve. To obtain these points, I plotted a series of *SD* increment curves, placing the successively older ages at points on the curves of the younger groups in such a way as to take into account the growth already attained at any new starting age.[2] From these series of overlapping curves, a smoothed curve was drawn, and equivalent 16*D* scores were read off at 5-year intervals.

---

[2] That is, the youngest group was tested at 20 years and again at 32, with a gain of .4 *SD*. The 25-year initial score of the next order group was then plotted at the 25-year point on the first curve (or at .19 *SD*) and their gain at 37 years was plotted as .33 *SD* above this point (or at .52 *SD*), and so on for successively older groups.

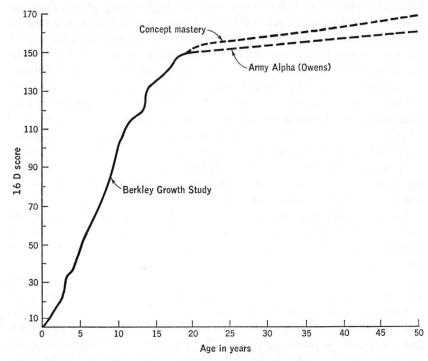

Figure 7. A proposed age curve of intelligence, birth to fifty years. Based on data from the Berkeley Growth Study, the Terman Gifted Study, and Owen's Iowa Study.

The resulting two-pronged curve for the 50-year span shows a more modest increment for the Alpha scores of the Iowa men. The Concept Mastery scores of Gifted Study spouses gain a full standard deviation, or about twice as much. Of course, since both of these curves are only approximations, neither may be more correct than the other. The differences are probably due, at least in part, to differences in the testing instrument. The Concept Mastery scale, for one thing, has far more top than the Alpha, and allows for much greater expansion upward.

We have here evidence that tested intelligence, as measured by verbal concepts and abstractions, continues to grow when populations composed primarily of superior adults are retested. Intelligence may also continue to increase in the less bright. Certainly, the less favored members of the Berkeley Growth Study are still improving their scores at 25 years. What is more, in several other studies there is evidence that this phenomenon is not confined to individuals tested at the University of California Institute of Child Welfare. Freeman and Flory, for example, divided the children in their study on the basis of scores at 12, 13, and 14, into low and high scorers. At the later ages, 16 and 17 years, the low-scoring group was continuing to improve at a faster rate than the high-scoring group. A recent study by Charles reports retest IQ's for 20 adults who had been diagnosed in childhood as feeble-minded. Their mean childhood Stanford-Binet, 1916, IQ was 58 and their mean adult Wechsler-Bellevue IQ was 81. Charles accounts for this difference in two ways: errors of diagnosis in childhood, and evidence from other studies that people who score low on the Binet test tend to make higher scores on the Wechsler. Similar explanations have been offered for similar findings in other studies. But a mean increase of 23 IQ points amounts to 1.5 SD's of either of the tests used. This is a rather large shift to be attributed to test differences in restriction of scores, to regression phenomena, or to errors in the original test. All 20 individuals improved on the retest. It seems to me quite possible that these people did continue to improve in their mental ability.

There are many gaps in our knowledge of the nature of intelligence, and many questions remain unanswered concerning age changes in mental organization. In the curve presented in Figure 7, there remains an unanswered discrepancy between the adult portion and data for these ages presented by earlier investigators, who have found decrements in scores with increasing age after about 21 years. In the earlier studies some types of functions held up better than others. Owens found that those abilities that had held up best on the cross-sectional samples were the same ones that increased the most on his retests. The real difference between the conflicting findings seems to lie in the longitudinal as opposed to the cross-sectional method of obtaining scores for successive ages. In the former we have a constant sample whose life experiences, age for age, will have been similar in pervasive environmental conditions, such as wars, technological advances, and methods of education.

If, after taking adequate account of practice effects, the increases still remain, then the next question is to inquire into the nature of the tests, and the extent to which they measure intellectual abilities. Do such tests as the Army Alpha and the Wechsler-Bellevue, for example, measure intelligence in adults? Or do they tend to reflect continued experience in an increasingly enriched environment? Do the younger generations have more opportunity to develop their intellectual capacities than did their parents, or even their older brothers and sisters? Or are we just measuring the effects of increasingly widespread informal education made possible by radio, television, and other modern means of communication?

If, regardless of the cause of the improved scores, they reflect actual degrees of competence outside of the testing situation, then these scores continue to have practical value. Another practical question is: What norms should be used in measuring deterioration resulting from brain injury, or from senescence? Perhaps it will be necessary to compare a present 50-year-old man's score with norms for, say, those who are 50 in 1954, rather than with 50-year norms for other decades.

What normal age changes should we expect in mental organization? The curve presented here is a composite. The forms of growth curves vary according to the functions measured. We should expect differences in the steepness of increment and decrement in growth curves of the different functions, and differences in the ages at highest efficiency. These differences have been found consistently in cross-sectional studies. The question raised here is whether more adequate studies, of the same individuals through time, will not show that the age of highest intellectual capacity is later than we thought, and that the decrements in abilities are, correspondingly, deferred.

This curve is offered as an alternative to previously published age-curves of intelligence. I should like to see it tested with further research that would refine, modify, and extend it into a more complete and accurate representation of intellectual changes over the entire life span.

Professor Cattell is one of the pioneers and most active workers in the field of systematic factorial research in personality. He has always maintained a high interest in general intelligence as an aspect of personality and has developed a culture-free intelligence test to measure one aspect of general intelligence. His long-term research on national intelligence and his concern with its measurement merit much further study by the student. In this paper, which is an appendix in his 1957 book, he presents his conception of two important "kinds" of general intelligence. The fruitfulness of his hypotheses in this regard are only beginning to be explored at the present time, but they propose an intriguing "solution" to some of the riddles posed by our current findings regarding intelligence.

Four terms in this appendix require interpretation. "L-data" refers to data collected from life-behavior situations. "Q-data" designates questionnaire data of the introspective, subject-report variety. "T-data" refers to objective test data which are not consciously self-evaluative. "U.I." indicates a Universal Index number by which Cattell refers to established factors.

Fluid and Crystallized Intelligence*

RAYMOND B. CATTELL

1957

General ability is so potent and ubiquitous a source trait that our correlation studies with personality variables have produced the pattern as an invariable accompaniment to the other dimensions, even when we were not seeking it. The pattern has recurred in L-, Q-, and T-data analyses, whenever the choice of variables has been comprehensive, i.e., made with due regard to the personality sphere concept.

In all three media the results agree in placing general ability, which is a second-order factor among Thurstone and Guilford's primary abilities, as a factor *of the same order as the personality primaries,* whence a possible conclusion is that the primary abilities are of one degree lower order than the primary personality source traits. This statement, however, can be only roughly true, for, until the relations of L-, Q-, and T-data factors are better known, the suspicion exists that T-data factors are partly of different order from the others.

Although the general ability factor, indexed here as U.I. I, is clearly recognizable, by its pattern and its very high loadings in analogies, series,

* Taken from Appendix 11, pp. 871-880 in R. B. Cattell, *Personality and Motivation Structure and Measurement* (New York, Harcourt, Brace & World, Inc., 1957), by permission of the author and Harcourt, Brace & World, Inc.

mathematical problems, etc., it is noteworthy that other "personality" factors also appear which have some substantial intellectual or perceptual ability content. If U.I. I were not so clearly "g" one might wonder if several Thurstone primaries might not be outcropping in personality. Thus Factor K, in L and Q data, has intellectual interests and skills attached, whereas in T data U.I. 16 shows speed of letter comparison, mazes, etc.; U.I. 19 has speed of gestalt closure, accuracy on Gottschaldt figures, etc.; U.I. 21 has the fluency measures and speed of judgment variables; and U.I. 26 has ability to state logical assumptions and poetic judgment. However, none of these show any striking resemblance to Guilford's intellectual factors, still less to Thurstone's primary abilities. Also, the second-order factors among the T-data personality factors do not group these factors as would be required by such identifications. Three of them—I, 16, and 19—come together with the right signs in Factor II, Ego Power; but the sense is of a far broader personality dimension than cognitive power alone. Further the content of the individual factors 16, 19, etc., is far more than intellectual power alone. So that, all in all, the best present interpretation is that these associated cognitive performances in primary personality factors are simply the natural expressions of temperament traits accounting for some of the variance in abilities.

Such overlap works in both directions, for it is also true that the factor among personality primaries which we now firmly recognize as "g," or the second-order general ability factor, in turn influences some purely "personality" manifestations, e.g., breadth of interest, conscientiousness (intelligent perception that "honesty is the best policy"?), memory, wit, and general information. The tendency of investigators in the field of ability to pack their matrices exclusively with ability variables (even in the excellent studies of Thurstone, Guilford, Carrol, Burt, Taylor, Vernon, and others) seemingly accounts both for their missing these loadings and also for their obtaining factors all at a lower order than ours. The undoubted influence of general ability upon some personality variables—even when they are defined in the strictest etymological sense of personality—invites a variety of hypotheses. Without space for illustration let it simply be said that the second-order L- and Q-data Factor IV, tying intelligence with dominance and radicalism, may express a *causal* role of intelligence, producing success and independence in most undertakings, and so reacting back upon personality formation. Second-order T-data Factor II is very similar and invites a similar explanation. But there are also personality-intelligence relations which require different types of hypothesis, namely, that the relation-perceiving power of intelligence *directly* aids certain personality developments, e.g., the growth of conscientiousness mentioned above. The reader will recognize that these examples support the general hypothesis that *direct influences* appear in the first-order factor and *trait feedback* in relations of factors in the second-order realm.

Our purpose in this Appendix is not only to confirm, by closer reasoning, the general relations of mental capacity within the personality realm, as above, but also to make the total position more clear by defining our conclusions regarding mental capacity itself. For, owing to a tremendous excess of social practice over research, the basic issues have become hopelessly neglected and obscured in most popular psychological discussions of "what intelligence tests measure." It is a *social* fact that the discovery of primary abilities caused a swing away from interest in general ability, but, except among those who misperceived what research was finding, the general ability concept has remained equally important and sound in *scientific* evaluation. The general and the primaries are two aspects of the same structure. Nevertheless, there has always been room for improvement of our knowledge of general ability *per se* and one of the most deplorable features of the past twenty years has been that basic research in this area has been virtually at a standstill. Still more unfortunate, this has coincided with a period in which innumerable test users have wanted "the latest thing" and have trimmed their sails to every light air of discussion of insubstantial theories. Consequently, as Anastasi well says, "Old and new categories, concepts and theoretical frameworks often become thoroughly scrambled in these discussions." Burt, in an article of classical completeness commenting on some recent shallow generalizations, observes that "few of the critics [of the general intelligence concept] show a clear or correct understanding of what the term really designates or of the reasons that have led to its introduction." Guilford, referring to a similar vagueness in intelligence test circles regarding what the unitary concept really implies says, "we have been too smug about the achievement [of intelligence testing], too content to rest on our laurels." It seems, indeed, at times as if intelligence test administrators were either uninterested or unable properly to grasp the concepts which researchers have discovered or mooted.

As stated earlier, to a first approximation the structure of abilities can be defined as a number of *primaries,* V, N, M, etc., among which general ability appears as one—the most important—of several as yet not well-defined *second-order* factors. Our concern is to examine this second-order factor, which has been called "general ability" or "general mental capacity." The only criticisms of "g" as a second-order factor which need serious regard are: (1) Vernon's argument that "g" is not uniquely determinable, but depends on the tests put into the matrix. (2) Guilford's objection that "g" is not general, since many "intellectual" tests can ultimately be found that do not positively correlate together, and "the simplest interpretation of a zero correlation between two tests of ability is that they have nothing in common." If there is nothing in common between even as few as two tests, there is no *universal* factor, hence no "g." (3) The criticism that the demarcation of "g" depends on the degree of obliqueness of the primaries, which constantly alters with the population or sample and thus introduces lack of uniqueness in a second sense. (4) The finding that there is *more* than one second-order factor among primaries.

The first and third are the most vital, for they strike at the very existence of "g" as a unique entity. The tetrad difference criterion was the original means of differentiating "g" from the mere sum of a pool of positively intercorrelating tests. If one rests the proof of "g" on its appearance as a first-order factor, as Vernon does, and at the same time has doubts about the legitimacy of the tetrad difference selection of tests, then "g" loses its claim to uniqueness. But the proper, most comprehensive basis for the uniqueness of "g" is its appearance as a second-order factor and one which, just like the primaries, must and can be *rotated to a unique simple structure position*. The exact determination of this position will require that more primaries be included in the analysis than any experiment has yet done, and these must include personality factors too, to create enough "hyperplane stuff."

Criticism number two is largely semantic. How universal is universal? Actually the label "general factor" has come to be applied, by careful users, even when *complete* universality cannot be claimed. It is understood that a general, i.e., nonspecific, factor will still never cover, for example, the whole personality sphere, and that the term is relative. It is impossible to decide whether "g" covers the whole "intellectual" area, if only because different pedants have different ideas about the use of the word "intellectual." However, in common dictionary use of abilities, *most* "abilities" have positive correlation with others, or, more precisely, are covered by the second-order factor labeled "g."

As to the third attack—again on uniqueness—the fact that in different populations we encounter varying obliqueness of primaries is nothing more than a special case of the general principle that all r's vary with sample and population! The important point is that the factor pattern should vary as one would expect it to vary when an identical source trait operates under changing statistical conditions. Thus, for example, "g" has larger total variance in child than adult populations and loads numerical ability less in a selected group of mathematics students than in the general population.

The last critical comment on the general ability concept, namely, that existing preliminary second-order factorings show not one, but three or four, second-order factors among primaries, is more significant and opens the door to a new theoretical development. However, our information on these factors is admittedly vague, and from this point on we are shaping hypotheses needing research.

Do they extend over all the forty to sixty factors which Guilford's work shows to be a likely total for the intellectual area? (Parenthetically, the writer would argue that the forty or so already found by Guilford will prove to contain many that are specifics rather than primaries, or, at least, factors of a lower order than the accepted level for primaries.) Our contingent conclusion is that (1) the second-orders run through most primaries, including Guilford and Thurstone's symbolic, thinking, evaluative, perceptual, adaptive, and memory areas. (2) Some of these second-orders are sufficiently different in pattern, especially when personality variables are brought in, and load *ability* primaries so moderately, that they are best considered second-order personality factors, and will, indeed, be found identical with the factors listed by us in Appendix 12 or with a general motivation factor. (3) Others, as Thurstone's monograph already indicates, are markedly cooperative. That is to say, two or three of them affect largely ability primaries only and affect them in much the same way.

As to the second point, it is almost certain, in accordance with McDougall's and Maxwell Garnett's original suggestions, and recent work by Furneaux in England on "intelligence as effort," that one of the second-order factors expresses the increment in all ability tests arising from sheer motivation to concentrate and work carefully (probably K in our L-data series). However, our special concern is with two other second-order factors, at present inadequately marked, which are true ability factors and which support the hypothesis of distinct "fluid" and "crystallized" *general ability* factors. The evidence of second-order factorings is that these two factors are so highly cooperative, i.e., so similar in most loadings, that the ordinary tetrad difference criterion, inherently loose, has failed to separate them, so that "g" has covered them both. It is likely to require considerable tactical skill in choice of variables, provision of discriminating hyperplane material, and contrasting of young and old populations, clearly to separate these two second-order factors. However, the hypothesis of two factors will be developed here on tentative and scattered evidence in such a way as to lead to a crucial experiment.

The theory of "fluid" and "crystallized" general ability was proposed in 1940 to account for a wide range of evidence (over and above the evidence just cited for two very similar second-order factors) suggesting two distinct, but very similar manifestations of general intelligence with the following characteristics:

Fluid Ability, "gf"	*Crystallized Ability, "gc"*
1. Measured by speeded tests, and a score expressing speed of solution.	Measured by untimed "power tests" (Thorndike), and specifically by freedom from error (Furneaux's second factor).
2. Reaches a maximum early (14 yrs?) and declines after about 20 years of age.	Reaches a maximum later (20 yrs?) and shows no age decline. Age of reaching plateau partly determined by school-leaving age.
3. Shows a less steep age increment over the growing years, in terms of sigma units (of individual difference) from the population at any one age	Shows a more steep age increment over the growing years, in terms of sigma units (of individual difference) from the population at any one age

level. Consequently the S.D. of the I.Q. is large—25 or more—but constant from culture to culture.

level. Consequently the S.D. of the I.Q. is smaller—16 to 19 points—but will vary with culture and period, because the age increment is a function of cultural pressure and school curricula.

4. Will fluctuate more from day to day with physiological influences, health, etc., being rooted more in efficiency of cerebral function.

Will show less diurnal fluctuation, and is unlikely to appear as a factor in P technique, because it consists of acquired habit systems, determined more by specific cerebral efficiencies and recencies of activation.

5. Shows itself best in novel or culture-free material.

Has highest loadings in acquired, complex, familiar, cultural activities and skills.

6. Largely innately determined, except for physiological influences.

Tends to have more of its variance contributed by cultural differences.

7. Effect of brain damage is to reduce performance over the whole factor without detectable differentials for different tests.

Some total loss, but also uneven loss of particular functions, e.g., verbal symbolism, mechanical skill, without comparable loss in others.

8. General factor saturation of tests in adults does not conspicuously decline.

General factor saturation reduced in adults, especially in heterogeneous populations of persons specializing in different fields.

9. Less clearly detectable primary ability structure—i.e., less variance contributed by "specifics."

Well-marked primary ability development.

10. More highly correlated with speed of learning in a new area.

Less highly correlated with speed of learning.

It is our contention that the empirical development of intelligence test devices to distinguish true intelligence deterioration in patients, from persisting high vocabulary, etc., e.g., the Shipley-Hartford test, is really directed to this theoretical distinction and might have progressed more cleanly and certainly under the guidance of the initial theory. In so far as the theory can be expressed in a few familiar words, it is that *fluid ability* ("gf") *is a general relation-perceiving capacity* which operates in all fields. It is measured, most saturatedly, by relation and correlate eduction of a complexity appropriate to the subjects, in any field where acquired skills are not differentiating; for it is independent of sensory content.

Crystallized ability ("gc"), on the other hand, must be measured on a basis of careful cultural sampling, for it is not independent of area and is simply a *sum of particular relation-perceiving skills acquired in specific fields*. The latter takes the form of a general factor less because of any existing *functional* unity of these powers than because they were acquired during growth under the influence of the unitary-growing "fluid ability." The analogy has been suggested for crystallized ability of the coral formation left after the live coral has receded. Thereafter, influences on parts cease to affect the whole, and greater unevenness can appear, through special interests, or atrophy and damage, than can be found in manifestations of fluid ability. The unity of fluid general ability should show in the fluctuations of short-term P-technique studies. Crystallized ability, on the other hand, has more historical than functional unity. The general model we propose would thus also agree with Ferguson's explanation of primary abilities as generalized learning effects within certain areas of symbolism, sensory content, or skill, which would account for the larger environmental variance supposed in (4) above for "gc" than for "gf," as we may symbolize respectively crystallized and fluid ability.

If Burt and Thorndike are correct in their inferences that the genetic influence in general ability has been underestimated, a reconciliation of their views with more environmentalist beliefs is possible by considering that the disputants are really talking of two different general abilities, namely, "gf" and "gc." Fluid general ability, by a further hypothesis, may be a direct quantitative function of the total number of cortical nerve cells, probably multiplied by some index of effectiveness of general cortical metabolism (illustrated, at their lower extremes, respectively in microcephalic and phenylpyruvic amentia). Physiologically, the basic work of Sherrington and Lashley and their co-workers suggest such a single product —a unitary relation-perceiving power—rather than a collection of localized influences.

The eight distinctions between fluid and crystallized ability drawn above, as well as further implications from the theoretical model, e.g., the P-technique difference, offer ample means for testing the theory (notably by first actually distinguishing two factors with the required patterns) and for constructing relatively pure tests of each whereby still further associates of "gc" and "gf" can be investigated. Indeed, it will be observed that if this theory is correct we should always apply, when a measure of *general* ability rather than primaries is required, *two* intelligence tests (separately for "gf" and "gc"). From their relations, predictions and conclusions much richer than those from a single test should be possible.

On the basis of this theory, and also for the practical purpose of constructing "fluid intelligence" tests (gf) that would be more free of accidental influence from cultural background, the present writer, with Sarason and Feingold, and following earlier leads by Line and Raven, set out to devise a series of Culture Free Intelligence Scales. For it will be observed that out of "gc" measures one can only hope at best to make a Culturally Equivalent Intelligence Test, i.e., one can set up a factor measure for journalists *equivalent* to one for engineers, or for Italians and Americans, but this will be accurate only for the typical member who has developed his abilities in the typical cultural areas so weighted.

Theoretically a culture-free intelligence test can be constructed by requiring relation and correlate eduction either on absolutely new content or on absolutely old (common) content. Thus one might use shapes and sounds never heard before, or world-wide, common, cultural content, such as sun, moon, stars, and parts of the human body, and their relations. If the latter principle is used, pictorial content must be restricted to this "greatest common denominator" of human experience, and, of course, no verbal

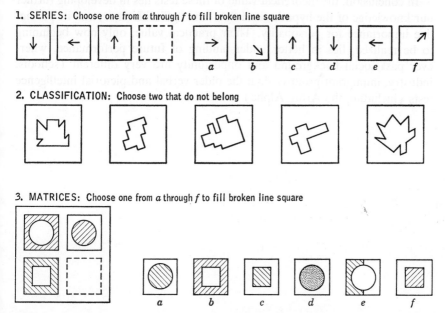

1. SERIES: Choose one from *a* through *f* to fill broken line square

2. CLASSIFICATION: Choose two that do not belong

3. MATRICES: Choose one from *a* through *f* to fill broken line square

Figure 1. Examples of Reasoning on Relation and Correlate Education in the culture-free intelligence test.

content or symbol peculiar to a culture could be used. The solution which we finally adopted in the published Culture Free Intelligence Tests asks for perceptual relations in *nonpictorial,* sensory impressions (visual—but auditory have also been tried) which are nevertheless part of universal sensory experience and abstraction ("perpetual intelligence tests"), as shown in Diagram 1.

Three scales have now been developed, extending from four years to the superior adult (graduate student selection) level. They have successfully met the two basic experimental checks: (a) proof that they measure intelligence by being at least as highly saturated as traditional tests in the general factor among primary abilities; (b) proof that they are far more free than older intelligence tests (except performance tests, which tend also to be relatively free of intelligence!) of cultural influence. This second proof has been established by showing with foreign immigrants, primitive people in process of urbanization (in Africa), etc., that there is less discrepancy of individual scores before and after acculturation than with traditional tests.

However, some cultural effect undoubtedly remains, unless the test is given with norms based on absence of a time limit, by reason of time demands' being more routine in some cultures than others. Consequently, brief training tests, to be thrown away, must properly be given in these circumstances to reduce what Vernon has aptly called the "test sophistication" increment.

In conclusion, the theoretical value of these tests lies in developing further our knowledge of the hypothesized "gc" and "gf" difference, and its predictive importance for personality. Their practical value, only now beginning to be realized, lies in better understanding of future performance, wherever past social background and opportunity are very different (schools, industry, immigrant groups) than the older verbal and pictorial intelligence tests (including the Army Alpha) can offer.

Asymmetrical mental development has long been of interest to psychologists. In addition to the fascinating puzzle posed by such cases in themselves, they have been important in demonstrating the relative independence of various aspects of high-level talents. The following case is included as representative of the many studies of this phenomenon.

Intellectual Defect and Musical Talent: A Case Report[*]

ANNE ANASTASI

and RAYMOND F. LEVEE

1959

That aptitudes may vary widely within the individual has been demonstrated through a diversity of research procedures. This well established fact underlies the current use of multiple aptitude batteries, the plotting of aptitude profiles, and other familiar testing practices. An extreme example of such intra-individual variability in aptitude level is provided by the so-called idiot savant. The latter term has been traditionally employed to designate a mental defective exhibiting one or more special talents which conspicuously exceed the general population norm. Although such cases are understandably rare, a number have been identified and a few intensively investigated.

* * *

The case described in the present paper is that of a high-grade, adult mental defective with exceptional musical talent, as well as superior rote memory of an apparently eidetic nature. The subject was observed and tested over a two-year period during which the junior author was employed as his tutor.

PERSONAL HISTORY

The subject (S) is the younger of two siblings in a family of very high socio-economic level with no history of mental deficiency or psychiatric disorder. Both parents and the sibling are college graduates. S was delivered by Caesarean section as a full-term baby. He is reported to have been a normal, healthy neonate, weighing 9 lbs., 2 oz. While in the hospital, he contracted epidemic encephalitis, which led to permanent brain damage. Between the age of 2½ and 27 years, he was examined by a succession of

* Reprinted with minor deletions from the *American Journal of Mental Deficiency*, 64 (1959), pp. 695-703, by permission of the authors and the editor.

eminent neurologists, psychiatrists, and psychologists, but the final conclusion was that the cerebral impairment could not be overcome. S walked by the age of 1½ years, but did not talk until his fifth year. It was observed that, before he could talk, S was able to hum tunes he heard on the radio or phonograph. To capitalize on this propensity, a speech therapist was engaged and S was eventually taught to talk through the medium of lyrics. To this date, a sing-song quality is discernible in his speech.

From an early age it was recognized that S's cerebral impairment necessitated special education. Nursery schools, camps, and day schools having been tried in turn and found to fail, private tutoring was finally utilized. Between the ages of 7 and 20, S was taught to read, write, and spell and was instructed in the rudiments of arithmetic, history, geography, English grammar, and composition. After a lapse of 18 years, formal tutoring was resumed, S's parents feeling that his interests had become too highly centered on music and that other pursuits should be encouraged. It was at that time that the junior author was engaged as tutor. Such tutoring involved short lessons in academic subjects and a good deal of time devoted to trips, concerts, sports, and other recreational activities. S's musical education began at the age of 7 and is still continuing under coaches, S having studied with internationally renowned teachers and concert pianists.

At the time of this study, S is a healthy, well-built 38-year-old man, 6 feet, 2 inches tall and weighing 195 pounds. He tends to be somewhat overweight and his body musculature is rather loose and flabby. S is sexually immature and incapable of reproduction. Two of his secondary sexual characteristics present a contrasting picture: although his beard is black and heavy, his voice has remained high-pitched and child-like. He manifests no sex interest and shows lack of appreciation of social sex distinctions in his dealings with other persons.

GENERAL BEHAVIOR

Except in his musical work, S is lethargic and lazy. His tennis, for example, can be characterized as "slow-motion playing." If a ball is hit at normal speed or is placed more than a foot away from him, he merely stands and watches it go past. Unless his clothes are laid out, he will wear the first thing that comes to hand. And it usually takes him 20–25 minutes to change clothing. If specific instructions are not given, he will not shower. Much as he likes music, he will not bestir himself to go to more than one concert a week.

S exhibits weak, shallow, and short-lived emotions. He evidences a certain fondness for his dogs, his mother, and his tutor. However, if the objects of his affection are absent for a day or two, S tends to forget them and gives no indication that he misses them. The only individuals he specifically dislikes are children, because they tend to disrupt schedules and routines. S has a deep-seated abhorrence of change of schedule, since new things apparently offer a challenge to his security. The rigidity of his routine is illustrated by the fact that if meals are not served at the regular hours, he becomes upset and will not eat. Once the tutor, ignorant of S's demands for strict adherence to schedule, arrived 15 minutes early. S, who was home alone, refused to open the door until the appointed time.

Relations between S and his father are somewhat strained, owing to the latter's disappointment that his sole male heir is unable to carry on the family name in business. Since this attitude on the part of the father is sometimes manifested in criticisms of S and in other expressions of displeasure, S avoids his father in every way possible. He will not speak to his father unless spoken to and he answers his father's questions in short, guarded, cryptic sentences. Only when frustrated in musical matters does S drop his guarded attitude toward his father. He will insist, for example, upon his right to practice or play regardless of inconvenience to his father or to anyone else. The music room he regards as his personal domain and he does not hesitate to ask his father to leave and close the door behind him. It should be added that interpersonal relations in the family as a whole appear to be lacking in emotional warmth.

As a rule, S is quite docile and polite. He has been well conditioned along lines of social expectancy with regard to manners and conduct. Except for his strange speaking voice, it would be difficult at a first meeting to recognize him as a mental defective. Once he becomes familiar and friendly, however, his defenses drop. He then reverts to childish behavior patterns that include making funny faces, talking to mirrors and other reflective surfaces, talking to himself, a peculiar and erratic dance routine, strange gesticulations, balancing objects on his head, laughing to himself, pacing the room, and kissing any inanimate object that happens to catch his eye. Occasionally, S displays excessive boorishness, pushing people out of his way in the street, belching, passing gas, licking his plate and utensils after a meal, and the like. Although readily recognizing the impropriety of these actions when his attention is directed to them, S appears to perform them inadvertently and automatically. He admits, however, that he sometimes uses such behavior as a goad for his father.

Ordinarily, his displeasure in persons, things, or places is expressed by withdrawal, S becoming childishly moody and uncommunicative. Whenever his musical pursuits are interfered with, however, S resorts to harsh words and aggressive actions such as pushing. On one occasion, for example, a musician with whom the subject was going to play happened to be unprepared to run through an ensemble. S berated the musician loudly and pushed him out of the music room.

S never reads anything voluntarily. Although he reads the newspaper, this is done only to avoid his father's chiding in case he cannot answer questions on current events. He will read stories required for his lessons if they do not exceed two or three pages a night and are not beyond fifth- or sixth-grade level in reading difficulty. The only stories he seems to enjoy are factual stories about great men in history or music, as well as animal stories. These he repeats verbatim during his lessons. Whenever there is a summary, he simply includes this in his report. He seems to have no conception of the function of a summary, but considers it foolish that the author has repeated himself. One of the most pronounced aberrant characteristics of the subject's behavior is his echolalia. S himself reports that he realizes he is repeating another's conversation, but does not always do so intentionally. At times it appears to be an automatic reaction.

SPECIAL TALENTS

S displays two outstanding talents, in the areas of memory and musical aptitude. His achievements in memory take two forms: (1) oral reproduction of a printed passage verbatim after one or two readings and (2) phenomenal recall of personal and historical events. As a demonstration of the former ability, S was asked on two separate occasions to read a selection from Carmer's *Cavalcade of American History* and to make an immediate oral report. The articles, dealing with Thomas Edison and George Washington, respectively, averaged 2½ pages each. After a single silent reading of the Washington article, S reproduced it perfectly. The Edison article he refused to repeat until he had been allowed a second reading. At that time, however, he gave another flawless verbatim report. Asked how he was able to perform such feats, S just laughed and said, "Anyone can do it." It should be noted that S was unable to grasp the significance of Washington's self-sacrifice or Edison's satisfaction in his business failure. Such concepts were too abstract for him to comprehend. Other evidence of S's reproductive memory will be presented in the following section on test results.

S's memory for isolated past events is equally conspicuous. Whenever members of his family are in doubt about a date, they ask him. He never seems to forget the time or place of family events. If asked about something that occurred a week or two previously—or even a few days earlier—however, he seems to be at a loss to remember either the details or the time. Yet when a month or two have elapsed he can give a full and accurate report of the circumstances and time. The junior author has verified this phenomenon on some five occasions by making a record of certain times and events and checking with S after lapses of two days and two weeks. Although S professed inability to recall at these times, he could remember after a month and seemed able to retain such data indefinitely thereafter. S remembers historical names, events, and dates without the time lapse required in his recall of personally observed events. He takes great pleasure in rattling off the dates of birth, marriage, death, and other important events in the lives of heroes from American history. Similarly, he has a large store of information about classical European composers. He can tell where they lived, when they were born and died, the titles of their compositions, when each composition was first published and played in public, etc.

With regard to S's musical performance, his instrument is the piano, which he plays by reading. He is reported to be an excellent sight reader, although there is evidence that he can also play by ear when the occasion arises. An impressive list of renowned musicians, who have either taught S or played with him in private recitals, agree that his musical ability is outstanding. At one time, S played the piano at rehearsals for a leading chamber music orchestra. He was well accepted by the professional musicians comprising that group. In fact, most of the members occasionally visit him and play his latest ensemble work with him.

In the course of his musical training, S has acquired a knowledge of musical theory. It is difficult, however, to ascertain the extent of his understanding of theory. Questions in this area are blocked by S with the reply, "It is too difficult for you to understand even if I explained it to you." His mother claims that he is quite advanced in theory. Regardless of whether or not S knows theory, however, it is evident that he never utilizes theoretical knowledge for either improvisation or composition.

S is a pure classicist, showing no liking for modern composers. His mother asserts that S has absolute pitch and hence cannot tolerate the discordant playing of current popular musicians. She maintains that this type of music is painful to his sensitive ears. S himself has never confirmed such a statement and in fact denies that such music bothers him. Nevertheless, he will not listen to anything but classical music played by experts. While listening to music, S habitually assumes a critical attitude toward the musical skill and technique of the artist. In his own performance, he is a perfectionist, apparently never playing for enjoyment only. He regards his playing as serious work, practice occupying the major part of his time. In winter, he practices at least nine hours a day, except on Sunday. Explaining that Sunday is his "day off," he devotes only six hours to practice on that day. During the summer months, when he occupies a house in the country, practice is reduced to six hours on every day of the week.

It is only when S is playing the piano that his face takes on a look of strength, concentration, interest, and emotion. Although he can converse somewhat intelligently on certain historical matters, on current events, and on classical music, in such conversations there always seem to be an indifference in his attitude and a tendency for his mind to wander. This is not true when he is playing. Even subtle musical nuances are captured through his mastery of expression with the piano.

TEST RESULTS

For the purposes of the present study, S was given the Stanford-Binet (Form L), the Wechsler Adult Intelligence Scale, and the Benton Visual Retention Test (Form C). On the Stanford-Binet, his IQ was 67. The mental age was 10 and the basal age 5 years. S's highest performance was attained in repeating six digits reversed, in which he scored at the Superior Adult I level. The only tests passed at the Average Adult level were Memory for sentences and Vocabulary. In Reading and report (X, 3) S gave an errorless reproduction after reading the paragraph in 20 seconds.

Although performing relatively well in tests requiring rote, concrete verbal responses, S showed a general disability in handling language at the more abstract, conceptual, and symbolic level. Thus he failed Similarities: Three things (XI, 6), Minkus completion (XII, 6), and Proverbs (AA, 5). In Verbal absurdities, he did not pass beyond the IX-year level. It is also noteworthy that, despite his remarkable facility in verbatim reproduction of long passages, S failed the Superior Adult II test on Repeating the thought of a passage. The rather abstract nature of this selection probably accounts for the failure. The subject was obviously disinterested in the material and made no effort to reproduce it. In his daily lessons, S likewise loses interest when given reading matter beyond the fifth- or sixth-grade level.

Memory for sentences, utilizing more concrete material, was passed at its highest level (AA, 7) as well as at all other levels except VIII, where S refused to try. Such refusal may be associated with the content of the particular sentences. The first deals with a boy and his father, a relationship evoking strong avoidance reactions in the subject. The second refers to a beautiful boat carved by a boy. It is interesting to note that S exhibits a strong aversion to all handicrafts. This dislike seems to have been augmented by a childhood camp experience, when repeated efforts were made to interest him in woodcraft despite vigorous resistance on his part.

That S is handicapped in reasoning is suggested by his complete lack of understanding of the Paper cutting (IX, 1), Plan of search (XIII, 1), Induction (XIV, 2), Ingenuity (XIV, 4), and Codes (AA, 2) tests. He likewise failed the tests of Finding reasons (X, 4) and Problem situation (XI, 5). Handicaps associated with brain damage are evident in his failure on Copying a bead chain from memory (VI, 2), Picture absurdities (VII, 1), Copying a diamond (VII, 3), and Memory for designs (IX, 3).

The subject's profile of scores on the Wechsler Adult Intelligence Scale is highly suggestive of organic brain damage. The score on each of the Verbal tests clearly exceeds that on any of the Performance tests. S's highest score, corresponding to a scaled score of 12, was achieved on Information, with Digit Span and Vocabulary tying for second place. By contrast, S's scaled score on Picture Arrangement was zero. On Block Design the scaled score was 1 and on Picture Completion and Object Assembly, 2. The Verbal IQ was 92, while Performance IQ was only 52. The Full Scale IQ of 73 is slightly higher than the Stanford-Binet IQ of 67 reported above. The latter discrepancy is in the direction usually found among mental defectives.

On the Benton Visual Retention Test (Form C), S failed to reproduce any of the ten designs without error. His "number correct" score was thus zero and his total "error" score was 26. In terms of the published norms for persons at S's age and IQ level, a "number correct" score of 1 or less and an "error" score of 12 or more may be considered to be a strong indication of cerebral pathology. Qualitatively, S's 26 errors were distributed as follows:

Omissions	5
Distortions	14
Perseverations	0
Rotations	3
Misplacements	3
Size errors	1

More than half of S's errors were distortions, including figure substitutions (such as square for oblique parallelogram and A for triangle) and gross errors in the reproduction of internal details. Next in frequency were omissions of both major and peripheral figures.

DISCUSSION

The special talents displayed by S are among those reported most commonly in published accounts of idiot savants. As suggested by previous writers, eidetic imagery may play an important part in some of the achievements of these individuals. This is certainly true with regard to feats of memory. It is also likely that eidetic imagery may be a special aid in the numerical calculations performed by certain idiot savants. Roberts has pointed out that the persistence of eidetic imagery beyond childhood among some mental defectives may be due to a reduction in competition from other visual images, as well as from other means of retention, such as language.

In connection with S's musical aptitude, which is the more highly developed of his two special talents, it is noteworthy that surveys of idiot savants give a prominent place to the arts—drawing, painting, sculpture, music, dance, dramatics, etc. The fact that investigations of the general population reveal especially low correlations between such artistic aptitudes and the abilities involved in intelligence tests and academic achievement is consistent with such findings. It is just in these relatively independent artistic aptitudes that extreme asymmetries of talent in individual cases would be expected. With regard to the unusually high level of S's musical talent in comparison with similar published cases, we must bear in mind the excellent training facilities made available to S as soon as his musical inclination was recognized.

Attempts to explain the etiology of the idiot savant have drawn upon a wide diversity of factors, from sensory deprivation and brain damage to parental personality and child-rearing practices. . . . Several of the proposed hypotheses fit the present case. Brain damage seems to be well established on the basis of both S's case history and his current test performance. Deficiency in abstraction, which constitutes the focal point in the hypothesis of Scheerer et al., is likewise fully demonstrated by S's test results.

The present subject's general behavior also shows many similarities to that of the autistic children first described by Kanner. Examples of such common characteristics include emotional shallowness, inability to relate to persons, resistance to change, desire to be alone, annoyance at interference, echolalia, and compulsive and ritualistic actions. A few of Kanner's cases showed special talents, principally in memory. Such talents seem to have been clearly related to over-exploitation by parents. An interesting point of resemblance with the present case is the prevalence of parents who were intellectually superior but conspicuously lacking in emotional warmth. On the other hand, two major differences between Kanner's cases and the present subject are that all of the former were children and, with one minor exception, presented no evidence of brain damage.

Sarason and Gladwin suggest that the sensory hyperactivity observed by Bergman and Escalona among a number of emotionally and intellectually disturbed children may also characterize idiot savants. This hypothesis, too, could apply to the present case. Unusual auditory sensitivity in childhood may have contributed to both the musical aptitude and the aberrant emotional behavior observed in S.

In conclusion, it seems apparent that no one hypothesis can account for all observed cases of idiot savants. Even the etiology of any one case, moreover, may involve the interaction of a multiplicity of factors. In the case of S, it is probable that deficiency in abstraction resulting from early brain damage, superior auditory sensitivity and other characteristics related to musical talent, and the emotional climate of the home were at least three independent factors interacting to produce the observed result.

SUMMARY

The case is reported of an adult male mental defective with exceptional musical talent and superior rote memory of an apparently eidetic nature. Socioeconomic and educational level of the family is very high. The subject appears to have incurred brain damage as a result of epidemic encephalitis contracted shortly after birth. Present performance on the Benton Visual

Retention Test, Stanford-Binet, and Wechsler Adult Intelligence Scale provides strong evidence of organicity. Stanford-Binet IQ is 67. WAIS IQ is 73, the Verbal IQ being 92 and the Performance IQ 52. Test results also show marked impairment in capacity for abstraction. The subject's general behavior and parental relations reveal many points of similarity with the cases of infantile autism described by Kanner. It is suggested that the etiology of the present case involves the interaction of at least three factors: deficiency in abstraction resulting from brain damage, auditory hypersensitivity, and emotional climate of the home.

Three Faces of Intellect*

J. P. GUILFORD

1959

My subject is in the area of human intelligence, in connection with which
the names of Terman and Stanford have become known the world over.
The Stanford Revision of the Binet intelligence scale has been the standard
against which all other instruments for the measurement of intelligence
have been compared. The term IQ or intelligence quotient has become a
household word in this country. . . .

It is my purpose to speak about the analysis of this thing called human
intelligence into its components. I do not believe that either Binet or Terman, if they were still with us, would object to the idea of a searching and
detailed study of intelligence, aimed toward a better understanding of its
nature. Preceding the development of his intelligence scale, Binet had
done much research on different kinds of thinking activities and apparently
recognized that intelligence has a number of aspects. It is to the lasting
credit of both Binet and Terman that they introduced such a great variety
of tasks into their intelligence scales.

* * *

Our knowledge of the components of human intelligence has come
about mostly within the last 25 years. The major sources of this information
in this country have been L. L. Thurstone and his associates, the wartime
research of psychologists in the United States Air Forces, and more recently the Aptitudes Project at the University of Southern California, now
in its tenth year of research on cognitive and thinking abilities. The results

* American Psychologist, 14 (1959), pp. 469-479. Reprinted with minor changes by
permission of the author and the American Psychological Association.

from the Aptitudes Project that have gained perhaps the most attention have pertained to creative-thinking abilities. These are mostly novel findings. But to me, the most significant outcome has been the development of a unified theory of human intellect, which organizes the known, unique or primary intellectual abilities into a single system called the "structure of intellect." It is to this system that I shall devote the major part of my remarks, with very brief mentions of some of the implications for the psychology of thinking and problem solving, for vocational testing, and for education.

The discovery of the components of intelligence has been by means of the experimental application of the method of factor analysis. It is not necessary for you to know anything about the theory or method of factor analysis in order to follow the discussion of the components. . . . I will say that each intellectual component or factor is a unique ability that is needed to do well in a certain class of tasks or tests. As a general principle we find that certain individuals do well in the tests of a certain class, but they may do poorly in the tests of another class. We conclude that a factor has certain properties from the features that the tests of a class have in common. I shall give you very soon a number of examples of tests, each representing a factor.

THE STRUCTURE OF INTELLECT

Although each factor is sufficiently distinct to be detected by factor analysis, in very recent years it has become apparent that the factors themselves can be classified because they resemble one another in certain ways. One basis of classification is according to the basic kind of process or operation performed. This kind of classification gives us five major groups of intellectual abilities: factors of cognition, memory, convergent thinking, divergent thinking, and evaluation.

Cognition means discovery or rediscovery or recognition. Memory means retention of what is cognized. Two kinds of productive-thinking operations generate new information from known information and remembered information. In divergent-thinking operations we think in different directions, sometimes searching, sometimes seeking variety. In convergent thinking the information leads to one right answer or to a recognized best or conventional answer. In evaluation we reach decisions as to goodness, correctness, suitability, or adequacy of what we know, what we remember, and what we produce in productive thinking.

A second way of classifying the intellectual factors is according to the kind of material or content involved. The factors known thus far involve three kinds of material or content: the content may be figural, symbolic, or semantic. Figural content is concrete material such as is perceived through the senses. It does not represent anything except itself. Visual material has properties such as size, form, color, location, or texture. Things we hear or feel provide other examples of figural material. Symbolic content is composed of letters, digits, and other conventional signs, usually organized in general systems, such as the alphabet or the number system. Semantic content is in the form of verbal meanings or ideas, for which no examples are necessary.

When a certain operation is applied to a certain kind of content, as many as six general kinds of products may be involved. There is enough evidence

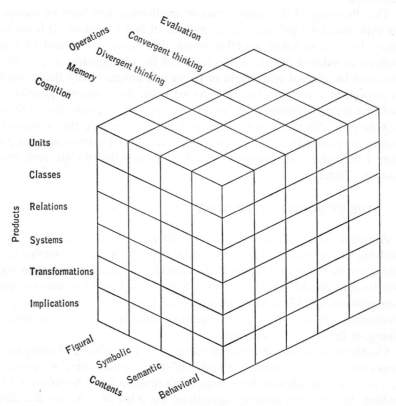

Figure 1. A cubical model representing the structure of intellect.

available to suggest that, regardless of the combinations of operations and content, the same six kinds of products may be found associated. The six kinds of products are: units, classes, relations, systems, transformations, and implications. So far as we have determined from factor analysis, these are the only fundamental kinds of products that we can know. As such, they may serve as basic classes into which one might fit all kinds of information psychologically.

The three kinds of classifications of the factors of intellect can be represented by means of a single solid model, shown in Figure 1. In this model, which we call the "structure of intellect," each dimension represents one of the modes of variation of the factors. Along one dimension are found the various kinds of operations, along a second one are the various kinds of products, and along the third are various kinds of content. Along the dimension of content a fourth category has been added, its kind of content being designated as "behavioral." This category has been added on a purely theoretical basis to represent the general area sometimes called "social intelligence." More will be said about this section of the model later.

In order to provide a better basis for understanding the model and a better basis for accepting it as a picture of human intellect, I shall do some exploring of it with you systematically, giving some examples of tests. Each cell in the model calls for a certain kind of ability that can be described in terms of operation, content, and product, for each cell is at the intersection of a unique combination of kinds of operation, content, and product. A test for that ability would have the same three properties. In our exploration of the model, we shall take one vertical layer at a time, beginning with the front face. The first layer provides us with a matrix of 18 cells (if we ignore the behavioral column for which there are as yet no known factors) each of which should contain a cognitive ability.

The Cognitive Abilities

We know at present the unique abilities that fit logically into 15 of the 18 cells for cognitive abilities. Each row presents a triad of similar abilities, having a single kind of product in common. The factors of the first row are concerned with the knowing of units. A good test of the ability to cognize figural units is the Street Gestalt Completion Test. In this test, the recognition of familiar pictured objects in silhouette form is made difficult for testing purposes by blocking out parts of those objects. There is another factor that is known to involve the perception of auditory figures—in the form of melodies, rhythms, and speech sounds—and still another factor involving kinesthetic forms. The presence of three factors in one cell (they are conceivably distinct abilities, although this has not been tested) suggests that more generally, in the figural column, at least, we should expect to find more than one ability. A fourth dimension pertaining to variations in sense modality may thus apply in connection with figural content. The model could be extended in this manner if the facts call for such an extension.

The ability to cognize symbolic units is measured by tests like the following:

Put vowels in the following blanks to make real words:

P__W__R
M__RV__L
C__RT__N

Rearrange the letters to make real words:

R A C I H

T V O E S

K L C C O

The first of these two tests is called Disemvoweled Words, and the second Scrambled Words.

The ability to cognize semantic units is the well-known factor of verbal comprehension, which is best measured by means of a vocabulary test, with items such as:

GRAVITY means _____

CIRCUS means _____

VIRTUE means _____

From the comparison of these two factors it is obvious that recognizing familiar words as letter structures and knowing what words mean depend upon quite different abilities.

For testing the abilities to know classes of units, we may present the following kinds of items, one with symbolic content and one with semantic content:

Which letter group does not belong?

XECM   PVAA   QXIN   VTRO

Which object does not belong?

clam   tree   oven   rose

A figural test is constructed in a completely parallel form, presenting in each item four figures, three of which have a property in common and the fourth lacking that property.

The three abilities to see relationships are also readily measured by a common kind of test, differing only in terms of content. The well-known analogies test is applicable, two items in symbolic and semantic form being:

JIRE   :   KIRE   :   :   FORA   :   KORE   KORA   LIRE   GORA   GIRE

poetry   :   prose   :   :   dance   :   music   walk   sing   talk   jump

Such tests usually involve more than the ability to cognize relations, but we are not concerned with this problem at this point.

The three factors for cognizing systems do not at present appear in tests so closely resembling one another as in the case of the examples just given. There is nevertheless an underlying common core of logical similarity. Ordinary space tests, such as Thurstone's Flags, Figures, and Cards or Part V (Spatial Orientation) of the Guilford-Zimmerman Aptitude Survey (GZAS), serve in the figural column. The system involved is an order or arrangement of objects in space. A system that uses symbolic elements is illustrated by the Letter Triangle Test, a sample item of which is:

$$\begin{array}{cccc} & \text{d} & \overline{} & \\ \text{b} & \text{e} & & \overline{} \\ \text{a} & \text{c} & \text{f} & ? \\ & & & \overline{} \end{array}$$

What letter belongs at the place of the question mark?

The ability to understand a semantic system has been known for some time as the factor called general reasoning. One of its most faithful indicators is a test composed of arithmetic-reasoning items. That the phase of understanding only is important for measuring this ability is shown by the fact that such a test works even if the examinee is not asked to give a complete solution; he need only show that he structures the problem properly. For example, an item from the test Necessary Arithmetical Operations simply asks what operations are needed to solve the problem:

A city lot 48 feet wide and 149 feet deep costs $79,432. What is the cost per square foot?

A. add and multiply
B. multiply and divide
C. subtract and divide
D. add and subtract
E. divide and add

Placing the factor of general reasoning in this cell of the structure of intellect gives us some new conceptions of its nature. It should be a broad ability to grasp all kinds of systems that are conceived in terms of verbal concepts, not restricted to the understanding of problems of an arithmetical type.

Transformations are changes of various kinds, including modifications in arrangement, organization, or meaning. In the figural column for the transformations row, we find the factor known as visualization. Common measuring instruments for this factor are the surface-development tests, and an example of a different kind is Part VI (Spatial Visualization) of the GZAS. A test of the ability to make transformations of meaning, for the factor in the semantic column, is called Similarities. The examinee is asked to state several ways in which two objects, such as an apple and an orange, are alike. Only by shifting the meanings of both is the examinee able to give many responses to such an item.

In the set of abilities having to do with the cognition of implications, we find that the individual goes beyond the information given, but not to the extent of what might be called drawing conclusions. We may say that he extrapolates. From the given information he expects or foresees certain consequences, for example. The two factors found in this row of the cognition matrix were first called "foresight" factors. Foresight in connection with figural material can be tested by means of paper-and-pencil mazes. Foresight in connection with ideas, those pertaining to events, for example, is indicated by a test such as Pertinent Questions:

In planning to open a new hamburger stand in a certain community, what four questions should be considered in deciding upon its location?

The more questions the examinee asks in response to a list of such problems, the more he evidently foresees contingencies.

The Memory Abilities

The area of memory abilities has been explored less than some of the other areas of operation, and only seven of the potential cells of the memory matrix have known factors in them. These cells are restricted to three rows: for units, relations, and systems. The first cell in the memory matrix is now occupied by two factors, parallel to two in the corresponding cognition matrix: visual memory and auditory memory. Memory for series of letters or numbers, as in memory span tests, conforms to the conception of memory for symbolic units. Memory for the ideas in a paragraph conforms to the conception of memory for semantic units.

The formation of associations between units, such as visual forms, syllables, and meaningful words, as in the method of paired associates, would seem to represent three abilities to remember relationships involving three kinds of content. We know of two such abilities, for the symbolic and semantic columns. The memory for known systems is represented by two abilities very recently discovered (Christal, 1958). Remembering the arrangement of objects in space is the nature of an ability in the figural column, and remembering a sequence of events is the nature of a corresponding ability in the semantic column. The differentiation between these two abilities implies that a person may be able to say where he saw an object on a page, but he might not be able to say on which of several pages he saw it after leafing through several pages that included the right one. Considering the blank rows in the memory matrix, we should expect to find abilities also to remember classes, transformations, and implications, as well as units, relations, and systems.

The Divergent-Thinking Abilities

The unique feature of divergent production is that a *variety* of responses is produced. The product is not completely determined by the given information. This is not to say that divergent thinking does not come into play in the total process of reaching a unique conclusion, for it comes into play wherever there is trial-and-error thinking.

The well-known ability of word fluency is tested by asking the examinee to list words satisfying a specified letter requirement, such as words beginning with the letter "s" or words ending in "-tion." This ability is now regarded as a facility in divergent production of symbolic units. The parallel semantic ability has been known as ideational fluency. A typical test item calls for listing objects that are round and edible. Winston Churchill must have possessed this ability to a high degree. Clement Attlee is reported to have said about him recently that, no matter what problem came up, Churchill always seemed to have about ten ideas. The trouble was, Attlee continued, he did not know which was the good one. The last comment implies some weakness in one or more of the evaluative abilities.

The divergent production of class ideas is believed to be the unique feature of a factor called "spontaneous flexibility." A typical test instructs the examinee to list all the uses he can think of for a common brick, and he is given eight minutes. If his responses are: build a house, build a barn, build a garage, build a school, build a church, build a chimney, build a walk, and build a barbecue, he would earn a fairly high score for ideational fluency but a very low score for spontaneous flexibility, because all these uses fall into the same class. If another person said: make a door stop, make a paper weight, throw it at a dog, make a bookcase, drown a cat, drive a nail, make a red powder, and use for baseball bases, he would also receive a high score for flexibility. He has gone frequently from one class to another.

A current study of unknown but predicted divergent-production abilities includes testing whether there are also figural and symbolic abilities to produce multiple classes. An experimental figural test presents a number of figures that can be classified in groups of three in various ways, each figure being usable in more than one class. An experimental symbolic test presents a few numbers that are also to be classified in multiple ways.

A unique ability involving relations is called "associational fluency." It calls for the production of a variety of things related in a specified way to a given thing. For example, the examinee is asked to list words meaning about the same as "good" or to list words meaning about the opposite of "hard." In these instances the response produced is to complete a relationship, and semantic content is involved. Some of our present experimental tests call for the production of varieties of relations, as such, and involve figural and symbolic content also. For example, given four small digits, in how many ways can they be related in order to produce a sum of eight?

One factor pertaining to the production of systems is known as expressional fluency. The rapid formation of phrases or sentences is the essence of certain tests of this factor. For example, given the initial letters:

W_____ c_____ e_____ n_____

with different sentences to be produced, the examinee might write "We can eat nuts" or "Whence came Eve Newton?" In interpreting the factor, we regard the sentence as a symbolic system. By analogy, a figural system would be some kind of organization of lines and other elements, and a semantic system would be in the form of a verbally stated problem or perhaps something as complex as a theory.

In the row of the divergent-production matrix devoted to transformations, we find some very interesting factors. The one called "adaptive flexibility" is now recognized as belonging in the figural column. A faithful test of it has been Match Problems. This is based upon the common game that uses squares, the sides of which are formed by match sticks. The examinee is told to take away a given number of matches to leave a stated number of squares with nothing left over. Nothing is said about the sizes of the squares to be left. If the examinee imposes upon himself the restriction that the squares that he leaves must be of the same size, he will fail in his

Item from the test Match Problems

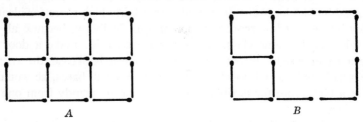

A   B

Take away four matches in *A,* leaving three squares and nothing more. Answer: *B.*

Figure 2. A sample item from the test Match Problems. The problem in this item is to take away four matches and leave three squares. The solution is given.

attempts to do items like that in Figure 2. Other odd kinds of solutions are introduced in other items, such as overlapping squares and squares within squares, and so on. In another variation of Match Problems the examinee is told to produce two or more solutions for each problem.

A factor that has been called "originality" is now recognized as adaptive flexibility with semantic material, where there must be a shifting of meanings. The examinee must produce the shifts or changes in meaning and so come up with novel, unusual, clever, or farfetched ideas. The Plot Titles Test presents a short story, the examinee being told to list as many appropriate titles as he can to head the story. One story is about a missionary who has been captured by cannibals in Africa. He is in the pot and about to be boiled when a princess of the tribe obtains a promise for his release if he will become her mate. He refuses and is boiled to death.

In scoring the test, we separate the responses into two categories, clever and nonclever. Examples of nonclever responses are: African Death, Defeat of a Princess, Eaten by Savages, The Princess, The African Missionary, In Darkest Africa, and Boiled by Savages. These titles are appropriate but commonplace. The number of such responses serves as a score for ideational fluency. Examples of clever responses are: Pot's Plot, Potluck Dinner, Stewed Parson, Goil or Boil, A Mate Worse Than Death, He Left a Dish for a Pot, Chaste in Haste, and A Hot Price for Freedom. The number of clever responses given by an examinee is his score for originality, or the divergent production of semantic transformations.

Another test of originality presents a very novel task so that any acceptable response is unusual for the individual. In the Symbol Production Test the examinee is to produce a simple symbol to stand for a noun or a verb in each short sentence, in other words to invent something like pictographic symbols. Still another test of originality asks for writing the "punch lines" for cartoons, a task that almost automatically challenges the examinee to be clever. Thus, quite a variety of tests offer approaches to the measurement of originality, including one or two others that I have not mentioned.

Abilities to produce a variety of implications are assessed by tests calling for elaboration of given information. A figural test of this type provides the examinee with a line or two, to which he is to add other lines to produce an object. The more lines he adds, the greater his score. A semantic test gives the examinee the outlines of a plan to which he is to respond by stating all the details he can think of to make the plan work. A new test we are trying out in the symbolic area presents two simple equations such as $B - C = D$ and $z = A + D$. The examinee is to make as many other equations as he can from this information.

The Convergent-Production Abilities

Of the 18 convergent-production abilities expected in the three content columns, 12 are now recognized. In the first row, pertaining to units, we have an ability to name figural properties (forms or colors) and an ability to name abstractions (classes, relations, and so on). It may be that the ability in common to the speed of naming forms and the speed of naming colors is not appropriately placed in the convergent-thinking matrix. One might expect that the thing to be produced in a test of the convergent production of figural units would be in the form of figures rather than words. A better test of such an ability might somehow specify the need for one particular object, the examinee to furnish the object.

A test for the convergent production of classes (Word Grouping) presents a list of 12 words that are to be classified in four, and only four, meaningful groups, no word to appear in more than one group. A parallel test (Figure Concepts Test) presents 20 pictured real objects that are to be grouped in meaningful classes of two or more each.

Convergent production having to do with relationships is represented by three known factors, all involving the "eduction of correlates," as Spearman called it. The given information includes one unit and a stated relation, the examinee to supply the other unit. Analogies tests that call for completion rather than a choice between alternative answers emphasize this kind of ability. With symbolic content such an item might read:

pots   stop   bard   drab   rats   ?

A semantic item that measures eduction of correlates is:

The absence of sound is _____.

Incidentally, the latter item is from a vocabulary-completion test, and its relation to the factor of ability to produce correlates indicates how, by change of form, a vocabulary test may indicate an ability other than that for which vocabulary tests are usually intended, namely, the factor of verbal comprehension.

Only one factor for convergent production of systems is known, and it is in the semantic column. It is measured by a class of tests that may be called ordering tests. The examinee may be presented with a number of events that ordinarily have a best or most logical order, the events being presented in scrambled order. The presentation may be pictorial, as in the Picture Arrangement Test, or verbal. The pictures may be taken from a cartoon strip. The verbally presented events may be in the form of the various steps needed to plant a new lawn. There are undoubtedly other kinds of systems than temporal order that could be utilized for testing abilities in this row of the convergent-production matrix.

In the way of producing transformations of a unique variety, we have three recognized factors, known as redefinition abilities. In each case, re-

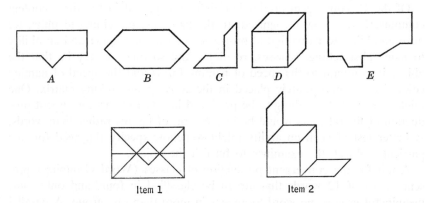

Figure 3. Sample items from a test Hidden Figures, based upon the Gottschaldt figures. Which of the simple figures is concealed within each of the more complex figures?

definition involves the changing of functions or uses of parts of one unit and giving them new functions or uses in some new unit. For testing the ability of figural redefinition, a task based upon the Gottschaldt figures is suitable. Figure 3 shows the kind of item for such a test. In recognizing the simpler figure within the structure of a more complex figure, certain lines must take on new roles.

In terms of symbolic material, the following sample items will illustrate how groups of letters in given words must be readapted to use in other words. In the test Camouflaged Words, each sentence contains the name of a sport or game:

> I did not know that he was ailing.
> To beat the Hun, tin goes a long way.

For the factor of semantic redefinition, the Gestalt Transformation Test may be used. A sample item reads:

From which object could you most likely make a needle?

> A. a cabbage
> B. a splice
> C. a steak
> D. a paper box
> E. a fish

The convergent production of implications means the drawing of fully determined conclusions from given information. The well-known factor of numerical facility belongs in the symbolic column. For the parallel ability in the figural column, we have a test known as Form Reasoning, in which rigorously defined operations with figures are used. For the parallel ability in the semantic column, the factor sometimes called "deduction" probably qualifies. Items of the following type are sometimes used.

> Charles is younger than Robert
> Charles is older than Frank
> Who is older: Robert or Frank?

Evaluative Abilities

The evaluative area has had the least investigation of all the operational categories. In fact, only one systematic analytical study has been devoted to this area. Only eight evaluative abilities are recognized as fitting into the evaluation matrix. But at least five rows have one or more factors each, and also three of the usual columns or content categories. In each case, evaluation involves reaching decisions as to the accuracy, goodness, suitability, or workability of information. In each row, for the particular kind of product of that row, some kind of criterion or standard of judgment is involved.

In the first row, for the evaluation of units, the important decision to be made pertains to the identity of a unit. Is this unit identical with that one? In the figural column we find the factor long known as "perceptual speed." Tests of this factor invariably call for decisions of identity, for example, Part IV (Perceptual Speed) of the GZAS or Thurstone's Identical Forms. I think it has been generally wrongly thought that the ability involved is that of cognition of visual forms. But we have seen that another factor is a more suitable candidate for this definition and for being in the very first cell of the cognitive matrix. It is parallel to this evaluative ability but does not require the judgment of identity as one of its properties.

In the symbolic column is an ability to judge identity of symbolic units, in the form of series of letters or numbers or of names of individuals.

Are members of the following pairs identical or not:
825170493_____825176493
dkeltvmpa_____dkeltvmpa
C. S. Meyerson_____C. E. Meyerson

Such items are common in tests of clerical aptitude.

There should be a parallel ability to decide whether two ideas are identical or different. Is the idea expressed in this sentence the same as the idea expressed in that one? Do these two proverbs express essentially the same idea? Such tests exist and will be used to test the hypothesis that such an ability can be demonstrated.

Figure 4. A sample item from the test Unusual Details. What two things are wrong with this picture?

No evaluative abilities pertaining to classes have as yet been recognized. The abilities having to do with evaluation where relations are concerned must meet the criterion of logical consistency. Syllogistic-type tests involving letter symbols indicate a different ability than the same type of test involving verbal statements. In the figural column we might expect that tests incorporating geometric reasoning or proof would indicate a parallel ability to sense the soundness of conclusions regarding figural relationships.

The evaluation of systems seems to be concerned with the internal consistency of those systems, so far as we can tell from the knowledge of one such factor. The factor has been called "experiential evaluation," and its representative test presents items like that in Figure 4 asking "What is wrong with this picture?" The things wrong are often internal inconsistencies.

A semantic ability for evaluating transformations is thought to be that known for some time as "judgment." In typical judgment tests, the examinee is asked to tell which of five solutions to a practical problem is most adequate or wise. The solutions frequently involve improvisations, in other words, adaptations of familiar objects to unusual uses. In this way the items present redefinitions to be evaluated.

A factor known first as "sensitivity to problems" has become recognized as an evaluative ability having to do with implications. One test of the factor, the Apparatus Test, asks for two needed improvements with respect to each of several common devices, such as the telephone or the toaster. The Social Institutions Test, a measure of the same factor, asks what things are wrong with each of several institutions, such as tipping or national elections. We may say that defects or deficiencies are implications of an evaluative kind. Another interpretation would be that seeing defects and deficiencies are evaluations of implications to the effect that the various aspects of something are all right.

SOME IMPLICATIONS OF THE STRUCTURE OF INTELLECT

For Psychological Theory

Although factor analysis as generally employed is best designed to investigate ways in which individuals differ from one another, in other words, to discover traits, the results also tell us much about how individuals are alike. Consequently, information regarding the factors and their interrelationships gives us understanding of functioning individuals. The five kinds of intellectual abilities in terms of operations may be said to represent five ways of functioning. The kinds of intellectual abilities distinguished acording to varieties of test content and the kinds of abilities distinguished according to varieties of products suggest a classification of basic forms of information or knowledge. The kind of organism suggested by this way of looking at intellect is that of an agency for dealing with information of various kinds in various ways. The concepts provided by the distinctions among the intellectual abilities and by their classifications may be very useful in our future investigations of learning, memory, problem solving, invention, and decision making, by whatever method we choose to approach those problems.

For Vocational Testing

With about 50 intellectual factors already known, we may say that there are at least 50 ways of being intelligent. It has been facetiously suggested that there seem to be a great many more ways of being stupid, unfortunately. The structure of intellect is a theoretical model that predicts as many as 120 distinct abilities, if every cell of the model contains a factor. Already we know that two cells contain two or more factors each, and there probably are actually other cells of this type. Since the model was first conceived, 12 factors predicted by it have found places in it. There is consequently hope of filling many of the other vacancies, and we may eventually end up with more than 120 abilities.

The major implication for the assessment of intelligence is that to know an individual's intellectual resources thoroughly we shall need a surprisingly large number of scores. It is expected that many of the factors are intercorrelated, so there is some possibility that by appropriate sampling we shall be able to cover the important abilities with a more limited number of tests. At any rate, a multiple-score approach to the assessment of intelligence is definitely indicated in connection with future vocational operations.

Considering the kinds of abilities classified as to content, we may speak roughly of four kinds of intelligence. The abilities involving the use of figural information may be regarded as "concrete" intelligence. The people who depend most upon these abilities deal with concrete things and their properties. Among these people are mechanics, operators of machines, engineers (in some aspects of their work), artists, and musicians.

In the abilities pertaining to symbolic and semantic content, we have two kinds of "abstract" intelligence. Symbolic abilities should be important in learning to recognize words, to spell, and to operate with numbers. Language and mathematics should depend very much upon them, except that in mathematics some aspects, such as geometry, have strong figural involvement. Semantic intelligence is important for understanding things in terms of verbal concepts and hence is important in all courses where the learning of facts and ideas is essential.

In the hypothesized behavioral column of the structure of intellect, which may be roughly described as "social" intelligence, we have some of the most interesting possibilities. Understanding the behavior of others and of ourselves is largely nonverbal in character. The theory suggests as many as 30 abilities in this area, some having to do with understanding, some with productive thinking about behavior, and some with the evaluation of behavior. The theory also suggests that information regarding behavior is also in the form of the six kinds of products that apply elsewhere in the structure of intellect, including units, relations, systems, and so on. The abilities in the area of social intelligence, whatever they prove to be, will possess considerable importance in connection with all those individuals who deal most with other people: teachers, law officials, social workers, therapists, politicians, statesmen, and leaders of other kinds.

For Education

The implications for education are numerous, and I have time just to mention a very few. The most fundamental implication is that we might well undergo transformations with respect to our conception of the learner and of the process of learning. Under the prevailing conception, the learner is a kind of stimulus-response device, much on the order of a vending machine. You put in a coin, and something comes out. The machine learns what reaction to put out when a certain coin is put in. If, instead, we think of the learner as an agent for dealing with information, where information is defined very broadly, we have something more analogous to an electronic computor. We feed a computor information; it stores that information; it uses that information for generating new information, either by way of divergent or convergent thinking; and it evaluates its own results. Advantages that a human learner has over a computor include the step of seeking and discovering new information from sources outside itself and the step of programing itself. Perhaps even these steps will be added to computors, if this has not already been done in some cases.

At any rate, this conception of the learner leads us to the idea that learning is discovery of information, not merely the formation of associations, particularly associations in the form of stimulus-response connections. I am aware of the fact that my proposal is rank heresy. But if we are to make significant progress in our understanding of human learning and particularly our understanding of the so-called higher mental processes of thinking, problem solving, and creative thinking, some drastic modifications are due in our theory.

The idea that education is a matter of training the mind or of training the intellect has been rather unpopular, wherever the prevailing psychological doctrines have been followed. In theory, at least, the emphasis has been upon the learning of rather specific habits or skills. If we take our cue from factor theory, however, we recognize that most learning probably has both specific and general aspects or components. The general aspects may be along the lines of the factors of intellect. This is not to say that the individual's status in each factor is entirely determined by learning. We do not know to what extent each factor is determined by heredity and to what extent by learning. The best position for educators to take is that possibly every intellectual factor can be developed in individuals at least to some extent by learning.

If education has the general objective of developing the intellects of students, it can be suggested that each intellectual factor provides a particular goal at which to aim. Defined by a certain combination of content, operation, and product, each goal ability then calls for certain kinds of practice in order to achieve improvement in it. This implies choice of curriculum and the choice or invention of teaching methods that will most likely accomplish the desired results.

Considering the very great variety of abilities revealed by the factorial exploration of intellect, we are in a better position to ask whether any general intellectual skills are now being neglected in education and whether appropriate balances are being observed. It is often observed these days that we have fallen down in the way of producing resourceful, creative graduates. How true this is, in comparison with other times, I do not know. Perhaps the deficit is noticed because the demands for inventiveness are so much greater at this time. At any rate, realization that the more conspicuously creative abilities appear to be concentrated in the divergent-thinking category, and also to some extent in the transformation category, we now ask whether we have been giving these skills appropriate exercise. It is probable that we need a better balance of training in the divergent-thinking area as compared with training in convergent thinking and in critical thinking or evaluation.

The structure of intellect as I have presented it to you may or may not stand the test of time. Even if the general form persists, there are likely to be some modifications. Possibly some different kind of model will be invented. Be that as it may, the fact of a multiplicity of intellectual abilities seems well established.

There are many individuals who long for the good old days of simplicity, when we got along with one unanalyzed intelligence. Simplicity certainly has its appeal. But human nature is exceedingly complex, and we may as well face that fact. The rapidly moving events of the world in which we live have forced upon us the need for knowing human intelligence thoroughly. Humanity's peaceful pursuit of happiness depends upon our control of nature and of our own behavior; and this, in turn, depends upon understanding ourselves, including our intellectual resources.

The following is an excerpt from pages 290-291 of a similar article by Guilford, The Structure of Intellect, Psychological Bulletin 53 (1956), pp. 267-293, reprinted by permission of the author and the American Psychological Association.

INTELLIGENCE AND INTELLIGENCE TESTS

A treatment of the factors of intellect would be incomplete without considering their implications for the concept of intelligence and for the present and future of intelligence testing. Is the concept of intelligence still useful? What is the nature of current intelligence tests in terms of factors? What should the future trends in intelligence testing be?

As to general terminology, the term "intellect" can be meaningfully defined as the system of thinking and memory factors, functions, or processes. The term "intelligence" has never been uniquely or satisfactorily defined. Factor analysis has fairly well demonstrated that it is not a unique, unitary phenomenon. A "general factor," found by whatever method, is not invariant from one analysis to another and hence fails to qualify as a unity, independent of research circumstances. The methods of multiple-factor analysis, which have been chiefly responsible for discovering the factors listed above, do not find a general psychological factor at the first-order level and they find no second-order factor that can properly lay claim to the title of "intelligence."

The term "intelligence" is useful, none the less. But it should be used in a semipopular, technological sense. It is convenient to have such a term, even though it is one of the many rather shifty concepts we have in applied psychology. It would be very desirable, for purposes of communication and understanding, to specify a number of intelligences—intelligence A, intelligence B, and so on. This could be done in terms of the combinations of certain intellectual factors and their weightings in the combinations.

We have such combinations now in connection with the intelligence tests and scales in common use. Let us consider what kind of combinations we have in two of the most used intelligence scales. A really good factor analysis of the Stanford Revision of the Binet scale would be rather difficult, and cannot be done satisfactorily without adding to the analyzed battery a liberal number of reference tests. This has never been done. The best analyses that we have were done by Jones, who found ten factors among 30 selected items. His resulting picture is not clear because among the 30 items were essentially alternate forms of tests (at different age levels) and no outside reference tests were used. A fully satisfactory analysis of the Stanford-Binet items would undoubtedly reveal more than ten factors present.

It should be noted that when so many factors are present, a composite score based upon all the items can measure each component only to a small degree, if they are nearly equally weighted in the composite. It can also be predicted that the factorial composition of the Binet IQ will be found to vary somewhat from one age level to another. This feature may contribute to a small extent to obtained changes in IQ where substantial age differences are involved.

As it actually happens, a Stanford-Binet IQ, or any IQ from a test whose components are predominantly verbal, is a total score heavily dominated by the *verbal-comprehension* factor. This leaves the other factors with little or no effective voice in the composite, even though they are represented in the scale. In nonverbal intelligence tests, there is likely to be less domination by any one factor, but the nature of the composite varies considerably from battery to battery.

Analyses of the components of the Wechsler-Bellevue scale have also been generally inadequate. The most adequate analysis has been done by Davis, who utilized a number of reference tests from outside the Wechsler battery. He found nine common factors, six of which are probably to be identified with factors in the intellectual list. Where standard tests of intelligence are widely used, it becomes increasingly important to attempt to write the specifications for their total scores as well as their part scores, so that obtained scores of individuals may be most meaningfully interpreted.

Intelligence tests will probably continue to be used for some time to come much as they are. In order to use them most wisely and to extract the greatest amount of information from their scores, the specification of such scores in terms of known factors is one important improvement that could be made. The other great step toward improvement in intelligence testing would be to emphasize more than at present some of the socially important factors that have to do with productive thinking. The knowledge of the factors of this kind and of the kinds of tests that measure them is largely available. Only by this kind of extension of intelligence testing can we do adequate justice to adult, human intellect.

Other extensions may also be very useful, for we are a long way from complete coverage of the intellectual factors in present tests. For differential prediction, and this includes the operation of vocational guidance, only single-factor scores will do complete justice in the description of individuals. As a necessary prelude to the use of factor measures for such purposes, we need innumerable validation studies in which factors play an important role.

Date Due

FEB 15			
7:30 Sun			
10/2/2 PM			
FEB 28 '73			
OCT 22 74			
JUL 0 9			
OC 20			
AG 28 04			
	PRINTED	IN U. S. A.	